READING GREEK VASES

Repetition and symmetry are the fundamental aesthetic principles underlying the shape and decoration of ancient Athenian vases. This book is the first comprehensive study of the role of repetition beyond its aesthetic value, as part of a code that conveys meaning to the viewer. Relying on the theoretical background provided by information theory and narratology, Ann Steiner uncovers the different kinds of meaning that painters created through the use of repetition. Using the reading of painted verbal inscriptions as a springboard, she demonstrates how repetition of imagery in multiple fields of a vase can create narration, paradigm, exploration of perceptual and ideological point of view, and parody. Steiner shows how the results of repetition on Archaic Athenian vases reiterate the activities of the elite *symposion* and the broader cultural values of elite Athenians. She provides an entirely new way to read ancient Athenian vases.

Ann Steiner is Shirley Watkins Steinman Professor of Classics, and Provost and Dean of the Faculty at Franklin & Marshall College. A scholar of Greek art, she is author of *Corpus Vasorum Antiquorum: Joslyn Art Museum* and *Joslyn Art Museum: Ancient Greek Pottery*. Her field experience includes work at ancient Torone, Corinth, and Poggio Colla where she has been Director of Research since 2002. She has received fellowships from the American Council of Learned Societies and the National Endowment for the Humanities, as well as the Lindback Award for Distinguished Teaching.

READING GREEK VASES

ANN STEINER

Franklin & Marshall College

CAMBRIDGE
UNIVERSITY PRESS

CAMBRIDGE UNIVERSITY PRESS
Cambridge, New York, Melbourne, Madrid, Cape Town, Singapore, São Paulo

Cambridge University Press
32 Avenue of the Americas, New York, NY 10013-2473, USA

www.cambridge.org
Information on this title: www.cambridge.org/9780521732352

First published 2007
First paperback edition 2009

Printed in the United States of America

A catalog record for this publication is available from the British Library.

Library of Congress Cataloging in Publication Data

Steiner, Ann, 1951–
Reading Greek vases / Ann Steiner.
p. cm.
Includes bibliographical references and index.
ISBN-13: 978-0-521-82522-1 (hardback)
ISBN-10: 0-521-82522-9 (hardback)
1. Vase-painting, Greek – Greece – Athens. 2. Repetition (Aesthetics). I. Title.
NK4645.S735 2007
738.3′820938 – dc22 2006009172

ISBN 978-0-521-82522-1 hardback
ISBN 978-0-521-73235-2 paperback

For Richard and Sarah

CONTENTS

LIST OF ILLUSTRATIONS

ACKNOWLEDGMENTS

This project has taken a long time, and there is likewise a very long list of people who have helped me complete it. The semantic meaning of repetition caught my attention as a compelling topic in the fall of 1988, when I participated in a seminar at Bryn Mawr College on theoretical approaches to the study of imagery on Athenian vases. This experience changed my perspective forever, and I am especially grateful to Gloria Ferrari for providing it. John Oakley kindly invited me to present a paper at a symposium in Athens in 1994 that became Chapter 2 of this monograph; this experience made me aware of broad international interest in my subject and was therefore a decisive moment as well. To Alan Shapiro I give special thanks for his encouragement to submit the manuscript to Cambridge. Jenifer Neils read sections of various drafts, and I have very much appreciated her enthusiastic support for the project. Penny Small was a great help to me in the early stages of my work.

My colleagues in the Department of Classics at Franklin & Marshall have helped in many ways, providing both moral support and concrete assistance. Michael Flower, Sam Houser, Zachary Biles, and Shawn O'Bryhim have my profound thanks. Alexis Castor has been a particular source of encouragement. I offer special thanks and appreciation to Judith Chien, our departmental coordinator, who undertook the massive task of organizing the photographs and permissions as well as writing the captions and photo lists. Her contribution amounted to months of work.

I have had substantial financial support from both Franklin & Marshall College and outside agencies. The American Council of Learned Societies granted me a senior fellowship during a sabbatical leave in 1994–1995, and the Franklin & Marshall faculty Committee on Grants gave me a great deal of support over the past ten years. The Samuel Kress Foundation provided a subvention for the cost of the ample illustrations.

The significant costs of photographs and permissions were largely covered by faculty development funds from Franklin & Marshall.

Most of the work of preparing the final manuscript took place while I was Associate Dean of the Faculty at Franklin & Marshall. Provost Bruce Pipes, now Emeritus, was incredibly tolerant of my distraction and my need for time to work on the project; had he been less so, it would not have happened. He has lived up to his promise to support faculty research programs as an institutional priority, and he has my profound thanks. I am grateful also to my assistant, Patty Hollister, who has pitched in graciously throughout the process. Kathy Elliehausen-Slobozien tirelessly wired money around the world to cover the costs of photos and permissions.

The research for this project was carried out at the libraries of Franklin & Marshall College, Bryn Mawr College, and the American School of Classical Studies at Athens. I am very grateful to the library staff at each place. Colleagues at the Beazley Archive, the British Museum, and the Louvre were extremely helpful during my research trips there.

There are two individuals who have left an indelible mark on this project. Guy Hedreen made careful comments on the original manuscript, and his insights caused me to rethink and to improve its organization. Sarah Peirce read and discussed with me every word of the final manuscript, and her contribution has been transformative. Both Sarah and Guy challenged my fuzzy thinking at every turn; I cannot convey the depth of my thanks to both of them. Their contributions are the latest acts of a lifetime of collegiality and stimulation. I apologize for those places where I remained stubborn and did not take their advice.

I am very grateful to Beatrice Rehl, Senior Editor for Arts and Classics at Cambridge, for her encouragement, her patience, and her consistent practical advice.

Finally, I wish to thank my family. My husband and daughter, Richard and Sarah Bidgood, gave me unflagging love and support that have sustained me through countless late nights and early mornings. They have sacrificed a lot to see this project through. I am indebted to my sister, Barbara Weiskopf, whose enthusiasm and pride have been unequivocal. I will never be able to tell our parents the extent of my gratitude to them, but I record it here nonetheless.

NOTES

To consult images of vases that are not illustrated in the figures here, readers may rely on the full references to Beazley (*ABV*, *ARV*^{2}, *Addenda*^{2}, *Para*) provided in the Endnotes. For unattributed vases, at least one reference to a published photo is provided.

Inscriptions on pottery are provided as close to their actual appearance as possible, with spelling uncorrected and letters upper-case. Spacing replicates the original as closely as possible. *Heta* appears as *h*. The following standard epigraphical symbols are used, after Immerwahr (1990):

ạ dot under letter: the letter, if taken by itself, is uncertain, usually incompletely preserved.

[ ] letters lost in original and restored.

.[.] dot outside bracket: an indeterminate trace of a letter. Dot inside bracket: a lost letter assumed to have stood in the original, if the number of lost letters is known.

[- -], [- - -] hyphens in bracket: an indeterminate number of letters lost.

⟨ ⟩ letters omitted in original and restored.

( ) letter misshapen or misunderstood by the writer of the inscription. Also endings supplied by editor.

{ } letters added in error in the original and to be deleted.

| line-break in the original.

ONE

READING BEYOND AESTHETICS

REPETITION AND THE INTERPRETATION OF IMAGERY

In 1977 Robertson published an Athenian pelike acquired a few years earlier by the Boston Museum of Fine Arts[1] [Figures 1.1 and 1.2]. He attributed it to an important painter, a very young Euthymides, in a style close to an experienced Euphronios.[2] These two artists were prominent members of a group of technical and stylistic innovators in late sixth-century Athens, and the appearance of a new vase from such distinguished origins is reason enough to pay close attention to it. The images and their mutual resonance make it even more compelling. On side A, two nude youths jump in midair, with fully frontal torsos, knees bent; arms are held out with elbows parallel to the shoulders, fists clenched at about waist level. Heads are turned sharply to the right. A third youth stands in profile to the left, wrapped in a *himation*, lifting the double pipes as he plays for his dancing companions. On side B a nearly identical youth also pipes, though here with his instrument nearly parallel to the ground. He, too, plays for two nude youths jumping in midair, with knees bent; they clench their fists. Legs are in profile. Two differences stand out: these youths show the viewer the left profiles of their faces and their backs, with arms nearly straight.

In combination the two compositions appear to be intentional reverses of one another. The painter acknowledges that one viewer of an actual performance would see the back view of dancers whose fronts were visible to a colleague directly opposite. The artist extrapolates from this imagined reality to suggest that the viewer of one side of the vase will likewise see the reverse of what his companion sees. Of course the pelike is not transparent, so the pairing of reversed images is playful, a mind game.

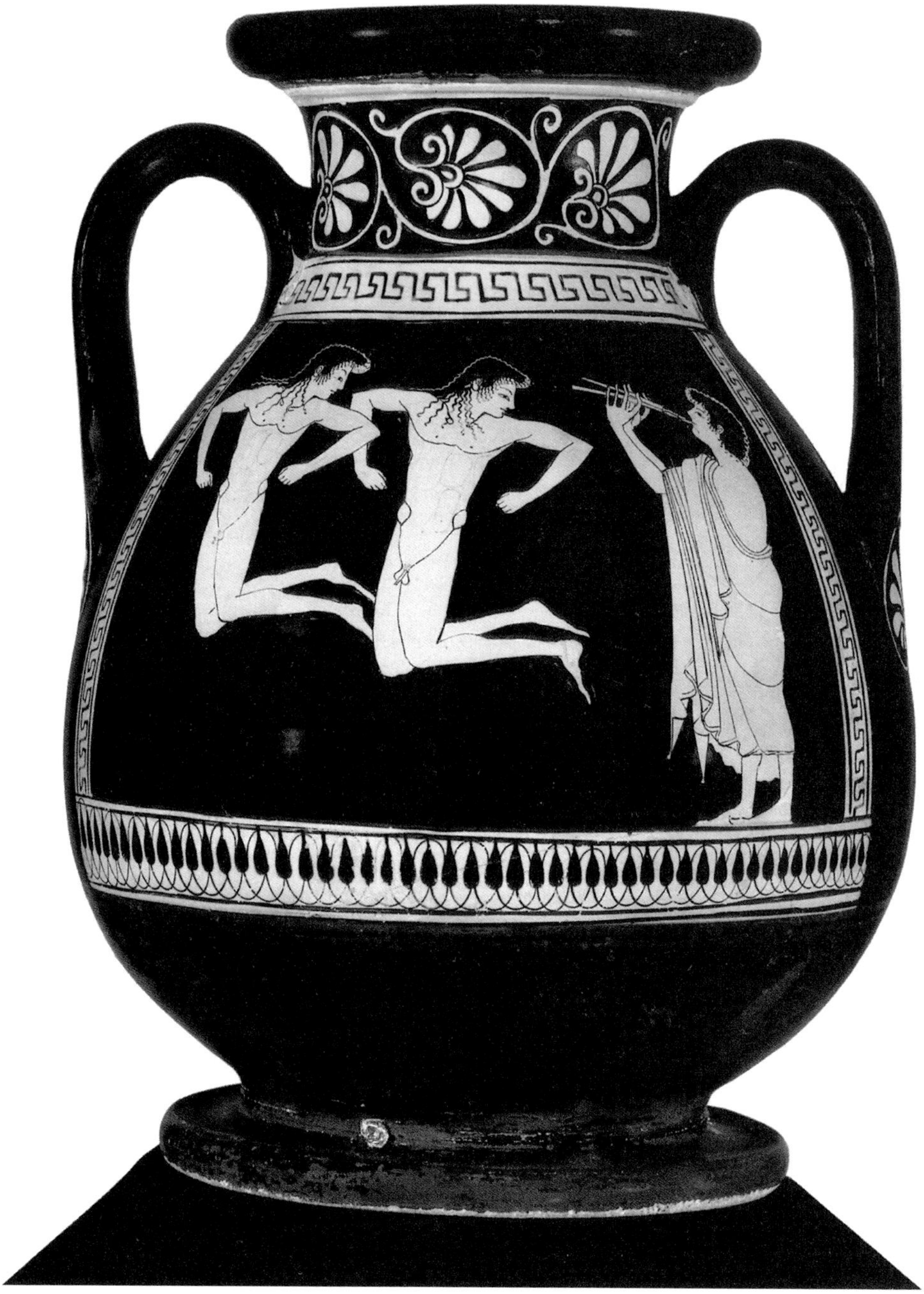

1.1. Red-figure pelike by Euthymides and Euphronios, ca. 510–500 B.C. Side A. Boston, Museum of Fine Arts 1973.88. (*Youths jumping*. Place of Manufacture: Greece, Attica, Athens. Height: 31.1 cm (12 1/4 in.); diameter (max.): 24.4 cm (9 5/8 in.) Robert J. Edwards Fund. Photograph © 2000. Museum of Fine Arts, Boston.)

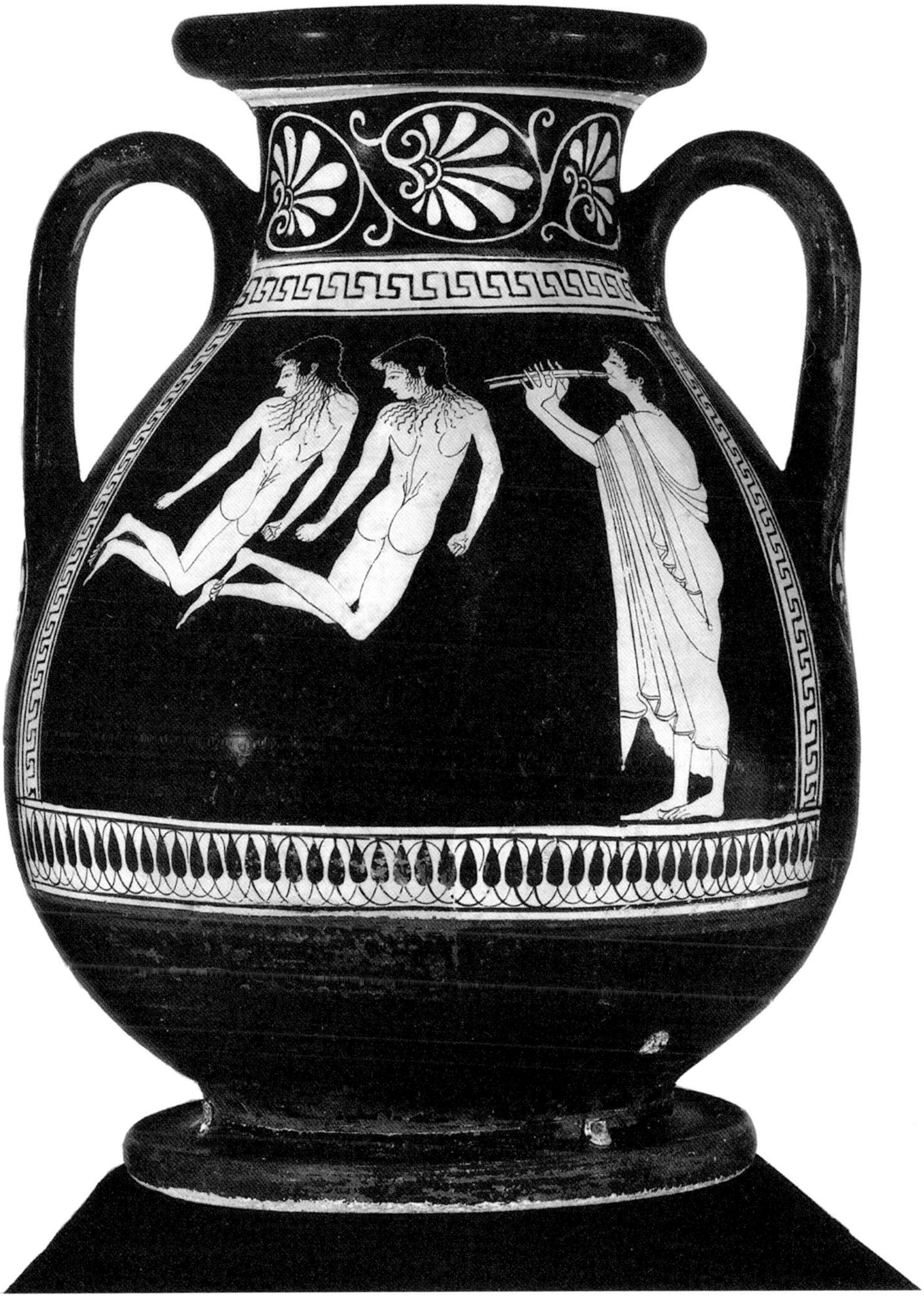

1.2. Red-figure pelike by Euthymides and Euphronios, ca. 510–500 B.C. Side B. Boston, Museum of Fine Arts 1973.88. (*Youths jumping*. Place of Manufacture: Greece, Attica, Athens. Height: 31.1 cm (12 1/4 in.); diameter (max.): 24.4 cm (9 5/8 in.) Robert J. Edwards Fund. Photograph © 2000. Museum of Fine Arts, Boston.)

This short interpretation requires us to believe that the painter of the pelike expected a viewer to take the two sides of the vessel into account in reacting to it. What evidence is there, other than a hunch played out in a plausible explanation, that this was his expectation? A look at the inscriptions provides corroboration.

On side A with the frontal jumpers are two proper names: AINEA<Σ>, "Aineas," in front of the piper and ΚΑΛ(Λ)ΙΠ(Π)ΙΔΕΣ, "Kallippides," above the heads of the right-hand jumper and the piper. Below the jumping figures is written ΛΕΑΓΡΟΣ ΚΑΛΟΣ, "Leagros is handsome." On the reverse, a third name is written retrograde, or left to right, in front of the piper, (Σ)ΜΙΚΥΘΙΟ(Ν), "Smikythion." Finally, also retrograde, is another statement that reads ΛΕΑΓΡΟΣΚΑΛΟΣΝΑΙΧΙ, "Leagros IS handsome, yes, indeed!"[3] located between the piper and the right-hand jumper, curving around his knees. Like the images, the *kalos* inscriptions are created in response to one another: one is a statement, "Leagros is handsome," and the other is a response, in agreement, "Leagros IS handsome, yes indeed!" The responsive relationship is made visual by the coupling of orthograde (statement, written left to right) and retrograde (response, written right to left), a verbal conjunction parallel to the combination of frontal and rear views of the jumping figures. The final affirmation, "yes, indeed!" derives its justification from its relationship to its companion statement on the other side of the vase. Although it is not absolutely clear which proper name labels what figure, there are a total of three names. If the figures on B are the same as the figures on A, the evidence from both sides provides the names of all three figures. In sum, the evidence from the inscriptions offers support for a hypothesis that the artist expected the viewer to take both sides of the pelike into account when assessing it. In fact, neglecting to take into account both sides of the vase diminishes the experience of it.

After a recognition that slight differences in the inscriptions matter, a return to the coupled images of the jumpers provokes a round of questions: Why are the arms of the B-side jumpers straight? Why are the pipes held lower by the musician on B? Are these significant deviations, suggesting a slightly different moment in the performance, corresponding to the length of time it takes for one person to utter a comment and another to respond to it, or are they accidental?

One way to describe the idiom adopted by the artist is "highly repetitive." Not only are there the identical aspects of figure and inscription already noted, but the framing ornament of each scene is repeated precisely on A and B, with palmettes on the neck, a trapezoid of simple meander on top and sides, and a ground line of upright lotus buds on the belly. It is the slight deviations from exact repetition in both inscriptions and image that demand attention and create engagement with the vase. There is a tremendous payoff for observing exactly what is repeated and what is not.

The present study starts from just this premise – noting repetition carefully yields a significant reward – so well supported by the Boston pelike. That Athenian vases are highly repetitive in shape and decorative scheme is obvious, but simply to acknowledge the existence of repetition and to note that it is fundamental to the aesthetics of Greek art is to overlook its interpretive value. Considering the conspicuousness of repetition on Athenian vases, it is very surprising that no one has undertaken a systematic study of its meaning. Virtually any discussion of the iconography of an Athenian vase must engage, either implicitly or explicitly, the issue of interpreting juxtaposed images, and when such images contain repetitions, this issue is particularly important.[4] It is a fundamental premise of this work that understanding repetition is crucial to knowing how Athenian pottery conveyed meaning to its audience. This view is informed by what is known about the uses and purposes of repetition in all forms of communication.

The special focus of this study is one category of ancient Greek pottery, black- and red-figure Athenian vases of the Archaic period. Most of the evidence discussed dates to about 600–480 B.C. This chronological period sees the first significant appearance of written inscriptions on vases, and analysis of repeated inscriptions is essential to understanding repeated imagery. Some evidence dates slightly earlier, some a bit later. Observable repetition in this category of vases exists on at least three levels:

1. Repetition of shapes together with repetition of schemes of decoration, including ornament and images themselves, resulting in classes or groups, called here "Types" of pottery.
2. Repetition in the imagery used to depict particular subjects, such as chariot-harnessing or Herakles fighting with the Nemean lion. Such repeated imagery, appearing on many examples, is commonly regarded as a visual "formula."
3. Repetitions in imagery on a single visual "text," a single vessel, either within a single field or in more than one field on a single vase.

To interpret better the meaning of the latter two types of repetition, and in particular the last, is the major goal here.

Because repetition is an indispensable agent in virtually all forms of communication, analysis of repetition has evolved in many fields. Particularly informing this investigation are the interconnected areas of information theory, social anthropology, structural linguistics, and narratology. The remainder of this chapter is devoted to a brief account of earlier discussions of the meaning of repetition in Greek art, including on Athenian vases, and to a survey of theoretical explanations of how repetition aids transmission of information in a variety of media. These explanations serve as our charter for understanding the meaning of repetition on Athenian vases.

EARLIER STUDIES

Bronze Age Art

Morgan, in her investigation of Aegean Bronze Age art, notes that repetition functions as a linking device: "repetitions of gesture, attribute, and clothing of people establish relations between scenes, acting as a means of identifying the characters and their situations," and she notes that the use of an unusual repeated gesture makes it likely that the same individuals are represented in two scenes.[5] Beyond merely linking scenes, the visual repetitions create associations that "are utilized as themes which evoke an idea in the mind of the spectator."[6]

Morgan explains, for example, how repetition helps to express the theme of hierarchies of power. She first describes the appearance of the lion in the context of a hunt on each side of a Mycenaean dagger.[7] She notes that the lion attacks its prey, the Mediterranean deer, on one side; on the other side, the lion is itself attacked by its adversary, the Mycenaean warrior. She believes that the reiteration is not to suggest sequence; rather, the effect of the repetition is to create a parallel between the strongest power in the animal world and man the hunter. Although she does not actually use the term "simile" or "syllogism," she assumes that the artist directs the observer to make a comparison: lion is like man as the dominant power in his respective domain; or lion is to deer as man is to lion.

In the Thera frescoes, Morgan sees repetition of even small details as crucial for creating coherence among different scenes. Her analysis, although stated briefly, is distinctive because its focus is so rare in scholarship on Greek art. She suggests that "repetitions of gesture, attribute, and clothing of people [the equivalent of lexical items as defined below] establish relations between scenes, acting as a means of identifying the characters and their situations." In one case, she cites the repetition of an unusual gesture as making it likely that the same men are represented in two different scenes.[8] Morgan's method of interpretation essentially relies on semiotics and narratology, theoretical approaches described in more detail below.

Marinatos analyzes art of the Aegean and Egypt to explore what she calls a "less well-explored 'rhetoric'";[9] and she names the phenomenon observed by Morgan a "pictorial simile": "A pictorial simile involves two dissimilar figures involved in a similar situation; the juxtaposition forces a comparison. Most common is the comparison between humans and animals. In such similes, the bravery or strength of the animal is compared to and thus transferred to the human."

Marinatos, like Morgan, discusses the inlaid daggers from Shaft Grave A at Mycenae. On these objects, human hunters are engraved on one side, lions on the other. At one point in her discussion, she relies on juxtaposition rather than visual repetition to make her point. Here because the scenes appear in the same position on opposite sides of the same dagger, she discusses the scenes as inviting comparison, and the human who hunts lions and the lion who hunts other prey are thereby implicitly equated with each other. At another point in her discussion, however, she does rely more on visual repetition as the basis for comparison: she points to the obvious similarities in the two compositions, as well as the repetition of vegetation motifs, to say that the similarities are reason enough to support the idea that the viewer will make a comparison, and that such a comparison was intended by the artist.[10]

Athenian Vases: Paradigm

Several scholars have discussed repetition in studies of post–Bronze Age art, and in particular of Athenian vases. Beazley noted the prevalence of repetition within this corpus. In lists of attributions, he often uses the phrase "the like," or the word "each," to indicate repetition of images on two fields of a single vase. Beazley was aware of repetition as a possible vehicle for connecting figures, especially divine or heroic figures and mortals: for example, in reference to a lekanis in Palermo, Beazley stated that "The quintet in the upper zone looks almost like a deheroized version of Paris, Hermes, and the Goddesses [in the lower zone]."[11] In the labeling of an amphora by the Princeton Painter, he said, "B, warriors leading women off (one would have said 'Recovery of Helen,' but the group is repeated)."[12] Beazley is, in these two cases, pointing out how an artist can, through repetition, vary the *expected* formula used to construct a scene, thereby both reminding the viewer of that formula and simultaneously eliminating it as the precise template for a particular iteration of the scene. Beazley observes a slightly different type of example on a plate fragment in Athens, "A youth leading three women to a youth . . . the judgment of Paris deheroized.' "[13] In the last case he acknowledges that artists might create scenes with the intention of reminding viewers of a familiar formula (that does not necessarily appear on the same vase) for depicting a particular mythological event. At the same time, the artist, by omitting some features from the repetition, makes it clear that he does not represent the mythological event itself. The result is the identification of a heroic paradigm for mortal activity.

Athenian Vases: Narration

Whereas Beazley's observation on repetition underscores the creation of paradigm, Froning discusses the role that repetition may play in early attempts to depict continuous narration.[14] She discusses an amphora in Geneva by the Princeton Painter, c. 540, depicting the birth of Athena twice in two slightly, but crucially, different scenes.[15] On one side, the goddess is emerging from Zeus' head; on the other she has been born and stands on his lap. Froning maintains that although one is accustomed to speak of such pairs of images as seen on the amphora as simple "varied repetitions," the combination of the two images on a single vase may well be for the purpose of representing two stages of a narrative. According to Froning, the artist extends the scene to two frames to stress the length of time the "actual" event takes.[16] In other words, the artist extends "discourse-time" in order to suggest the length of "story-time."[17]

In another example, Froning uses methods similar to those used by Morgan to connect images painted on two sides of a vase. A black-figure cup in the Vatican depicts two very similar sets of dice-players on each side; Froning points out, focusing on small details, that different figures are depicted in each case.[18] The players on the left differ with respect to details of dress and armor as well as hair length and facial hair; each right-hand player, although otherwise quite similar, has a different shield device. She concludes that the result is not a continuous narration of one story; rather two different sets of heroes are depicted on each side of the vase. However, Froning, unlike Beazley, does not propose that one purpose might be to create paradigm, that is, a situation where one sees that one set of figures is heroic or mythical and the other a mortal comparison to it.[19]

In Froning's example of the birth of Athena, the artist repeated the narrative center or "kernel" of a well-known story.[20] Scholars have also discussed repetitions that do not include the narrative kernel. Carpenter, for example, treats the phenomenon of repeated stock figures who observe scenes that are sometimes mythical narratives.[21] Carpenter characterizes these figures as representing types of upper-class Greeks and suggests that in some cases they are compositional fillers only and have no real meaning; they simply fill space.[22] Another view, explored here in Chapter 4, holds that the repetition of such figures is in fact meaningful, functioning in two different ways, both as signs serving to point out either similarities or differences between the scenes that they link and as indicating to whom the event is relevant and who ordains it as such.

EARLIER STUDIES IN HOMERIC EPIC

A recent current in literary analysis of ancient texts is informative because it also depends upon an understanding of repetition as producing meaning. In post–Milman Parry studies of Homer, many scholars in the twentieth century saw the frequent repetitions in epic diction as a meaningless artifact of oral composition. At least two studies present an alternative view, suggesting that repetition produces meaning as well, enhancing themes and aspects of character.[23] These examples are instructive.

Lowenstam acknowledges that there is so much repetition in Homer it is difficult "to determine when, if ever, repeated elements become significant for the literary interpretation of the poems."[24] He goes on to make the important point that "even if the use of a repeated detail can be ascribed to [composition by theme] we cannot preclude the possibility that the repetition also has literary significance."[25] Here he is speaking against the position that repetition in the epic is too familiar to the audience for any particular instance to have been significant to them.[26] Lowenstam begins by pointing out how integral repetition is to mythical paradigms, similes, and digressions, where repetition is essential for such features to have any meaning at all in the poems.

Admitting that noun–epithet combinations and themes are compositional building-blocks, Lowenstam explains that they are also vehicles to express the poet's meaning even when particular instances might seem like errors, where scholars hypothesize that a phrase difficult to make sense of must have been inserted for metrical convenience.[27] He shows how in repetition of themes such as "the quarrel," it is by comparison and contrast to other quarrels that the poet illuminates the main quarrel between Achilles and Agamemnon that drives the action in the poem. Lowenstam places repetition at the heart of how the audience understands what the poems are "about." He uses the "mechanics of repetition" to argue "... that the *Iliad* and the *Odyssey* are based on repeated antitheses," and that repetition simultaneously brings together analogous situations while highlighting their contrasting aspects.[28]

A second work on Homeric repetition, by Kahane, espouses a very similar view.[29] Like Lowenstam, Kahane maintains that there is meaning in repetition and, further, he attempts to understand how particular formal aspects of Homeric repetition express poetic themes.[30] His main purpose is "to expose diction which is capable of generating thematically significant ambiguities and shades of meaning."[31] At the heart of his argument is the idea that certain formal repetitions have semantic value. To provide a very simple and extreme example, Kahane points out that frequent repetition is an indication of a character's importance. For example, Achilles is mentioned by name 367 times and Bienor once. Put simply, repetition of Achilles' name reflects his greater importance in the poem.[32]

Through a very careful analysis, the author also reveals that repetition of certain words in particular metrical positions in the line has a role in conveying the poet's meaning. One detailed analysis focuses on localization of proper names in the nominative. Heroes such as Odysseus or Agamemnon tend to have their names at the end of a line. Telemachos, when his proper name is in the nominative, never has terminal positioning. This emphasizes to the audience that he is different from Odysseus; Kahane believes that the difference includes the message that he is less important, not the main hero of the story. He concludes that repetition of a very particular sort and variation from it enhance the message the poet constructs about the characters.[33]

Kahane is saying that repetition creates a means for the poet to define character, to construct how the character has similarities to and differences from other characters, through the use of a particular pattern. In a way the process is the verbal equivalent of the visual formula, conventional in most archaic and classical art, which places the victor on the left when a struggle is depicted.[34] This is a visual formula that carries meaning outside of the specific figures that "fill" the formula; to place a figure at the left makes that figure, whoever he or she is, the victor. On the rare occasions where the figure who is "supposed" to have won is placed on the right – in a famous example Achilles rather than Penthesileia is on the right – the artist introduces questions of how victory is defined.[35]

A NEW APPROACH

Many scholars, in pursuing the interpretation of either a certain image or a class of images, have suggested that repetition plays a role in constructing the meaning of a vase. Scholars likewise see verbal repetition not just as an artifact of composition, but as constructing meaning. The present study of repetition differs from these earlier studies because of its attempt to provide a theoretically grounded basis for such conclusions. Beginning with the recognition that repetition is an indispensable agent in virtually all communication, this discussion relies on the understanding of the purpose of repetition in the interconnected fields of information theory, social anthropology, structural linguistics, and narratology. What follow are brief summaries of the central ideas about repetition expressed in each of these fields.

Repetition and Information Theory

The principles of information theory can be applied to understand "any system in which a 'message' can be sent from one place to another."[36] Such systems are diverse, including ordinary language, visual images, and even genes. Understanding a few key concepts of information theory makes clear its applicability to this investigation of repetition.

Entropy

"Entropy" is for information theorists "disorder." A system of low entropy, with little disorder, produces a message; likewise, a system of high entropy has lots of disorder and instead of sending a message, it produces noise. A root beer float – scoops of vanilla ice cream in a glass of dark brown root beer – when first made, has relatively low entropy because it provides clear, unambiguous information and therefore "sends a message" about where the root beer and where the ice cream are. When the ice cream melts and the contents of the glass are stirred with a straw, the system has higher entropy, more noise, because the order has disappeared, providing less detail and therefore sending less information about the system as a whole. The system has become a unit of undifferentiated parts, a homogenized mixture of ice cream and root beer, and as such, it is harder to identify its components and harder to receive and understand the message of what it is.

Because disorder or high entropy and therefore noncommunication is the natural order of things, specialists in information theory have tried to identify mechanisms that separate messages from noise and order from disorder in a communications system. Repetition, or, in the language of information theory, "redundancy," is a fundamental and crucial ordering feature: "In nearly all forms of communication, more messages are sent than are strictly necessary to convey the information intended by the sender. Such additional messages diminish the unexpectedness, the surprise effect, of the information itself, making it more predictable. This extra ration of predictability is called redundancy, and it is one of the most important concepts in information theory. . . ."[37] As redundancy eliminates each alternative incorrect interpretation, clarity increases gradually.

A Language Code to Combat Entropy

Information theory maintains that written and visual messages are expressed through codes – languages – and the expression of such messages conforms to the rules of the code. Obviously, the code must be shared between sender and receiver. An example in English illustrates the way in which the rules of grammar enforce repetition and redundancy to reduce entropy or "noise" to get a message across:

In the statement, "There are three dogs," the word "three," in combination with the form of the verb and the absence of the indefinite article "a," reveals that the statement is in the plural, and the addition of "s" at the end of "dog" serves to confirm it. The redundant features make it less likely that "three" will be mistaken for a non-numerical (and nonsensical) adverb or adjective, such as "tree." To create an analogy from the visual arts: a vase displays a female figure wearing a helmet and aegis and holding a spear and a shield. The particular types of helmet, spear, and shield are by themselves probably enough to identify the figure as Athena and not, for example, an Amazon, but the addition of the aegis clinches it. In short, the tenets of information theory reveal that redundancy is of crucial importance in conveying messages in whatever code is being employed. Repetition is more than a formal aesthetic principle; it is an enabler of communication. Because repetition is so central to the code employed by Athenian painters, their system ought to reveal itself as low-entropy, low-noise, and high in effective message-delivery.

Cultural Codes to Combat Entropy

Social anthropologists have analyzed the function of repetition in cultural systems, and their understanding is derived ultimately from the principles of structural linguistics. The way Leach explains redundancy as a cultural phenomenon has a great deal in common with that of information theorists. The anecdote he uses to explain the purpose of redundancy treats the code of language at the level of content rather than at the level of form or "grammar," as in the "three dogs" example:[38]

> Now let us imagine the situation of an individual A who is trying to get a message to a friend B who is almost out of earshot, and let us suppose that communication is further hampered by various kinds of interference – noise from wind, passing cars, and so on. What will A do? If he is sensible he will not be satisfied with shouting his message just once; he will shout it several times, and give different wording to the message each time, supplementing his words with visual signals. At the receiving end B may very likely get the meaning of each of the individual messages slightly wrong, but when he puts them together, the redundancies and the mutual consistencies and inconsistencies will make it quite clear what is "really" being said.[39]

This principle of redundancy, therefore, maintains that myths with varying story lines can be rewordings of the same cultural message. Because Athenian vase-imagery is varied but still highly repetitive, we suspect that this is likewise a redundant system producing crucial cultural information. In fact, the huge multiplicity of differing scenes on Athenian vases sends a limited set of key messages. Many types of scenes, for example, convey a deep-seated cultural concern with status. Scenes as superficially diverse as athletic contests, military combat, and *symposion* are redundant versions of the same cultural message: elite status is maintained through winning in elite venues.

Repetition and Semiotics

Semiotics, itself integrated with structural linguistics both in origin and in application, gives us an explanation for why theoretical models developed for information theory can be applied to verbal and visual languages. Semiotics, simply defined as the science of signs, informs us that the visual imagery on Athenian vases is, in effect, a unified language with its own rules of grammar and syntax, where reality is encoded through visual symbols much as experience and objects are encoded through words in ordinary language. The works of Gombrich and Barthes are familiar and well-respected examples of art historical scholarship informed by semiotics.[40]

Semiotics teaches us that the images on an Athenian vase are more than straightforward one-to-one representations of reality: the language of the imagery is in fact a code. Images may represent one or more real events (sometimes even involving real people) in a sequence at the *syntagmatic* or denotative level.[41] Beyond this syntagmatic level is a set of connotative or *paradigmatic* associations aroused in the minds of the viewers of the images; the images individually and collectively belong to a wider set of contexts beyond that represented on a single vase. Our images of youths on the Boston pelike playing music and jumping in dance have more meaning than simply to record and describe a particular dance step; they reverberate with related images in the all-inclusive cultural code, the language in which the images are expressed. To understand all these connotations, we must look at a host of related images; for example, to know more about the meaning of the flute, we must look at other types of dancers who dance to flute music and other contexts where flute music is played. The repertory of images is thus interconnected. It is not a roster of all activities in which the purchasers of the vessels participate, but a selection of certain activities with a cumulative meaning that exceeds any one particular example for the ideal "intended audience."[42] The general handbook *City of Images* provides a very accessible demonstration through several case studies of the application of semiotics to imagery on Athenian vases.[43]

Repetition and Narratology

Defining the Text

Through the model provided by semiotics, the insights of narratologists, who concern themselves with how language codes convey narrative, can be applied to identify the meanings created by repetition. A narratologist begins with a text, a unit selected for analysis. That is, "text," as it is used in narratological studies, is whatever unit the investigator has identified as a coherent entity to study: this entity can be particular lines, paragraphs, chapters, or an entire work. For a narratologist, repetition creates one text out of many parts; its function is cohesive, to create logical connectedness.[44] As Bowditch puts it, "In order to understand the point of a story, listeners must understand that the linguistic utterance to which they are attending is indeed one text, and neither a series of unrelated sentences nor a sequence of different texts."[45] Repetition of syntax and/or lexical items creates cohesion, helping to achieve the status of "one text."

In this discussion, our texts are entire vases, including the images in two or more fields, subsidiary ornament, and the shape itself, all cohering into a single text; the vessel is then analogous to a verbal text composed of discrete units that cannot be expressed synchronously. Just as the reader or listener must progress through the written text, the viewer must progress through an assessment of the entire vase to get its total meaning. If we extrapolate from the kinds of repetitive devices used in language to create a unified text, we can see how these devices likewise serve to unite the decoration on a vase into a single visual text.

In attempting to understand why a text coheres, narratologists focus on, among other things, identification of repeated "lexical items" and repeated "syntax." The visual equivalent to a lexical item is, as defined by Bérard and used by Morgan, the "minimal formal unit" or the "smallest definable iconographic unit . . [,] the one which cannot have anything removed without disintegration of the recognizable form."[46] A lexical item can be as large as a garment, like the *himation* worn by each of the Boston flute players, an attribute like their double flutes, or a subunit of a figure, such as a mouth, but it cannot be an unrecognizable fragment, such as part of a line representing a drapery fold. Figures and objects are lexical items. "Syntax" refers to the way the lexical items are arranged, such as in a sentence at the most fundamental level in written texts. For this study, "syntax" includes both the compositional structure of individual fields of the vase and the decorative program of the vase as a whole.[47]

Defining and Identifying Narrative[48]

Narrative texts are distinct because they tell a story. Non-narrative prose texts include categories such as instruction manuals, lists of maxims, and cookbooks. Barthes, Prince, and Chatman have defined characteristics of narrative that are generally employed to distinguish it from other texts; much recent work on narrative in Athenian vase-painting relies on their work.[49] The publications of W. Steiner and Bal serve as models for the application of the fundamentals of narratology to visual story-telling.[50]

Definitions of narrative in general and characterizations of visual depictions of narrative in particular express the importance of repetition in conveying stories. Prince reminds us that narratives have temporal sequence, and the first and last major events of the sequence must be partial repetitions of each other; W. Steiner notes that when a specific figure appears twice in a visual text, the representation logically includes two distinct moments in time involving that figure, one of the necessary characteristics of narrative.[51]

A single scene in a framed panel on an Athenian vase only rarely depicts two separate events; instead, it can provide hints of more than one event through the inclusion of attributes or setting elements.[52] Sometimes the scene is limited to a single moment in a sequence of events, but a moment so clearly identifiable that it provokes recall of an entire story. Related scenes in two separate fields can be relatively simple to identify as "two . . . events . . . in a time sequence. . . ."[53]

Although scholars of Athenian vase-painting have developed a nuanced and complex taxonomy for the various ways that artists represent narrative in imagery, they do not agree unequivocally on a reliable way to determine whether certain scenes represent narratives.[54] Scholars understandably often use content to make distinctions between "scenes of myth" and "genre scenes."[55] Only myth scenes are generally useful in developing narrative taxonomies, because we know enough about the stories from written sources to analyze the various ways artists represent crucial actions, their sequence, and the outcome. However, there are many examples of scenes with no recognizable mythical content that still represent an event or action, a fundamental component of narrative. Stansbury-O'Donnell makes an argument for a more inclusive definition of narrative, distinguishing those that are more specific, which are often myth-stories, from those that lack specificity, which scholars often designate as "genre" and non-narrative. In his view, very few figural scenes depicting events on Athenian vases can be excluded unequivocally from the category of narrative depiction.[56] The aim in this study is to explore how repetition functions to link scenes of sequential events in examples that fit both broad and narrow definitions of narrative.[57]

DEFINITIONS AND OVERVIEW

To attempt to define repetition itself is important but challenging. Although there is a sliding scale of repetition, from "exact" to some point just short of "different," there is no objective criterion to establish the point where sufficient repetitions of lexical items or syntax are so lacking that two scenes on a single vase should not be viewed as a unified text. The conventions observed by Athenian vase-painters are so consistent, with such a respect for symmetry, that almost no examples of vases can be completely disqualified as texts. The seriousness with which this study takes repetition assumes there are virtually no examples of repetition in lexical items and/or syntax that are meaningless.

Throughout this discussion, the following definitions will obtain:

Repetition: A reproduction of something, determined through objective observation.

Verbatim repetition: A repetition in exactly the same words, or in exactly the same visual form, allowing for differences in individual style.

Duplication: A repetition identically copied from an original.

The difference between the last two rests in the intentionality implied in the second. A duplicate is intentional; a verbatim repetition may not be intentional.

Reduplicate: To repeat over and over again: to double in order to produce an inflectional or derivational form.

Redundancy: Repetition created to provide alternative functional channels in case of failure; repetition of parts or all of a message to circumvent possible transmission errors.

Use of this last term asserts a purpose for repetition but does not necessarily claim that the creator of the redundancy repeats with conscious intention.

Earlier scholars have noticed how important repetition is and have advanced explanations as to its purpose. None of these studies, however, has tapped into the theoretical material available to guide a study of repetition, to understand the development and parameters of its exploitation by Athenian vase-painters. They have left a lacuna that this study aims to fill.

This introductory chapter has reported briefly on many results of repetition. Repetition creates texts, and texts can convey further information including narratives and paradigm. There are many other results of repetition; for example, returning once more to the Boston pelike, we see that the pairing of the front and back views creates an opposition, front versus back, where one side of the vase is the direct opposite of the other. This result, antonymy, belongs to a set of collocative repetitive devices, words that regularly co-occur and are sometimes opposites, as is the case with antonyms such as "back" and "front."[58] This is but one example; there are many more purposes for repetition, and subsequent chapters will uncover them.

Chapter 2 is a consideration of the deployment of the uses of repetition by the careful and apparently intelligent painter Exekias. Discussion of Exekian repetitions provides examples to illustrate various theoretical explanations of the meaning of repetition that will reappear throughout this study. This chapter also includes a consideration of how his artistic solutions were inherited by his followers, to demonstrate how repetition becomes a standard part of the visual code. Chapter 3 moves to the other end of the spectrum, considering large numbers of nearly identical vases by anonymous painters. In these examples, repetition is analyzed for how it functions to create "Types" such as Horse-head amphoras, Komast-dancer cups, and *Glaux*-skyphoi. In addition, the impact of such highly repetitive Types on Athenian viewers when they are assessing the repetition on other vases that do not belong to a "Type" is discussed. Chapters 4 and 5 deal directly with the title of this monograph, laying out how writing on vases is essential to decoding the semantic value of repetition. Chapter 6 focuses on narration; a consideration of the uses of repetition in depicting narrative sheds light on an important tool painters use when they adapt stories to visual presentation. Alongside visual narration is the creation of paradigms through repetition. This is a very widespread and deeply embedded phenomenon on ancient Athenian vases, and Chapter 7 treats a broad spectrum of such examples. An important goal explored in Chapter 8 is to see how repetition works in creating visual versions of many of the same building-blocks of narrative employed by poets, such as characters and point of view. Chapter 9 assesses parody as a result of verbal and visual repetition. In Chapter 10, a summary application of the results achieved in the first nine chapters to six examples of red- and black-figure vases, selected for their illustrative value, is carried out. The final discussion in Chapter 11 asserts that an ideal use context for the many results of repetition is the elite Athenian all-male drinking party, *symposion*, and makes the case for how well the messages sent via repetition complement that setting and at the same time express wider cultural preoccupations. Each chapter, or, where appropriate, each section of a chapter, is arranged chronologically, so that ultimately a history of Athenian painters' use of repetition is retrievable.

TWO

THE MEANING(S) OF REPETITION: A PRIMER[1]

The purpose of this chapter is to provide an overview of the range of meanings repetition can create, each of which will be discussed in detail in Chapters 3–9. For each case, the theoretical basis for the identification of meaning is identified. The examples are all selected from the works of Exekias, and his body of work is suitable for several reasons. He is a careful and intelligent painter who pays attention to the smallest details. His *oeuvre* is very familiar, yet no scholar has specifically addressed his use of repetition. Likewise, the painter's chronology, style, iconographic inventiveness, and preferences in subject matter are well-discussed, but there has been no comprehensive study of his syntax, the way he arranges images on a vase.[2] Several scholars have already observed instances where it seems Exekias deliberately pairs subjects, either to continue a theme from one side of the vase to another or to create "thematic counterpoise."[3] These observations, however, have not focused on the identification of repetitions in images or compositions that might guide the viewer to take note of interconnections. This chapter treats those examples where there is at least one figure repeated in two different fields of a vase and where, according to the principles outlined in the previous chapter, there is good reason to posit that these repetitions create a foundation for interconnectedness in meaning. Following an analysis of Exekias' use of repetition, we turn to a few examples by his successors, the Andokides and Lysippides Painters. The analysis of their work provides a case study for how the use of repetition is carried on from master to pupil and becomes part of a widespread code, available to all painters to be implemented when useful and appropriate.

EXEKIAS

A short preliminary analysis, focusing on written inscriptions, builds confidence that Exekias thought about the effects of a careful conjunction of decoration on two sides of a vessel. Exekias was an inscriptional pioneer: he was responsible for painting one vessel and potting two more that preserve the earliest preserved *kalos* inscriptions.[4] On a plain lip cup, side A records the artist's signature: ΕΧΣΕΚΙΑΣΕΠΟΙΕΣΕΝ, or "Exekias made [it]"[5][Figure 2.1]. Corresponding to this on side B, in exactly the same spot, where a complementary painter's signature might be expected, is a nonsense inscription, ΕΝΕΟΙΝΟΙΟΙΕΝ, pronounced approximately as "en eh oin oi oi en" [Figure 2.2]. Immerwahr points out that the sound of the nonsense mocks the sound of the syllables in the word for wine, *oinos*.[6] It also approximates the sound of *epoiesen* – pronounced "ehp oi eh sen," – in its use of the epsilon augment, the "oi" diphthong followed by epsilon, and the final "en." The fact that the inscriptions are placed in the same spot on two sides of a single vase invites readers to compare them. A patron who reads the potter's signature on one side might well expect to find a painter's signature, another potter's signature, or even the patronymic on the other; he will be surprised that the writing yields only a garbled approximation of part of a signature.[7] The important point for this discussion is that the two sides of the vessel cohere via repeated placement and repeated sounds and that meaning is enhanced when the two sides are considered together. In addition to the cohesive value of repetition, it also creates parody. The nonsense mimics the sense. There is a full treatment of repetition as a generator of parody in Chapter 9.

Several examples preserve repeated imagery on two sides of a vessel. The clearest example of Exekias' pairing of scenes in order to continue a single subject from one side of the vase to another is his neck-amphora in Boston, where a harnessing scene extends over both sides of the vessel: the pole horses appear with the chariot on side A, and the trace horses are brought up on side B[8] [Figures 2.3, 2.4]. What unifies the two sides visually is the appearance of a nearly identical, standing, profile horse. This repeated figure, once noticed, invites the observer to begin a close comparison of the two sides. This inspection engages on several levels; the introduction of one frontal horse on B in contrast to the profile views of the remaining three on A and B is an exploration of perceptual point of view. The unity of the two sides is enhanced by the continuous frieze of animals at the bottom and the cock-fight motif on the shoulder. Looked at in isolation, each side strikes the viewer with the absence of what is missing, what ought to be there in comparison to typical depictions of harnessing scenes.[9] On side A, the trace horses ought to be there, whereas on side B, the chariot and pole-horses are missing. Each scene is a masterpiece of ellipsis.

Narratology identifies ellipsis as one of several important cohesive elements revealed through repetition. By its very nature, however, ellipsis is difficult to identify. An ellipsis is something left unsaid or not depicted that the listener or viewer has

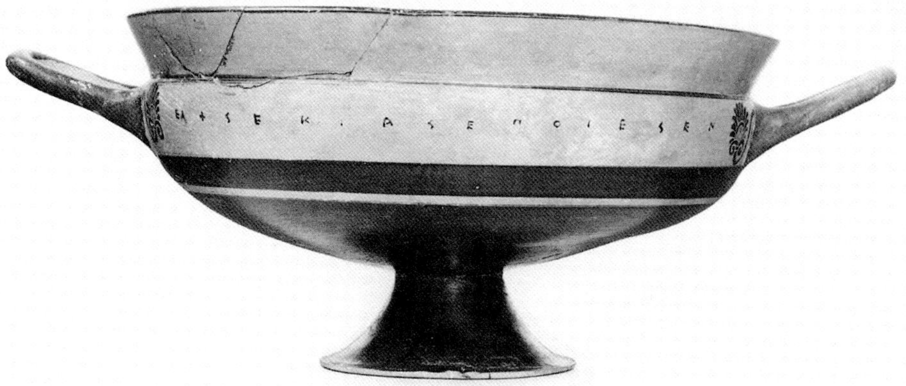

2.1. Little Master cup potted by Exekias, ca. 545–530 B.C. Side A. Athens, National Archaeological Museum 1104. (Photograph © National Archaeological Museum.)

to supply from his own knowledge or experience; there is discontinuity between the discourse, the telling of the tale, and the events of the tale itself.[10] In substitution, something is placed in that slot; in ellipsis, nothing is inserted.[11] Both only exist in the context of very close repetition. This sort of vase-syntax only works when a painter can count on his audience to know the visual language so well that individuals will realize what "ought" to be there in a conventional, formulaic image. The viewer finds what

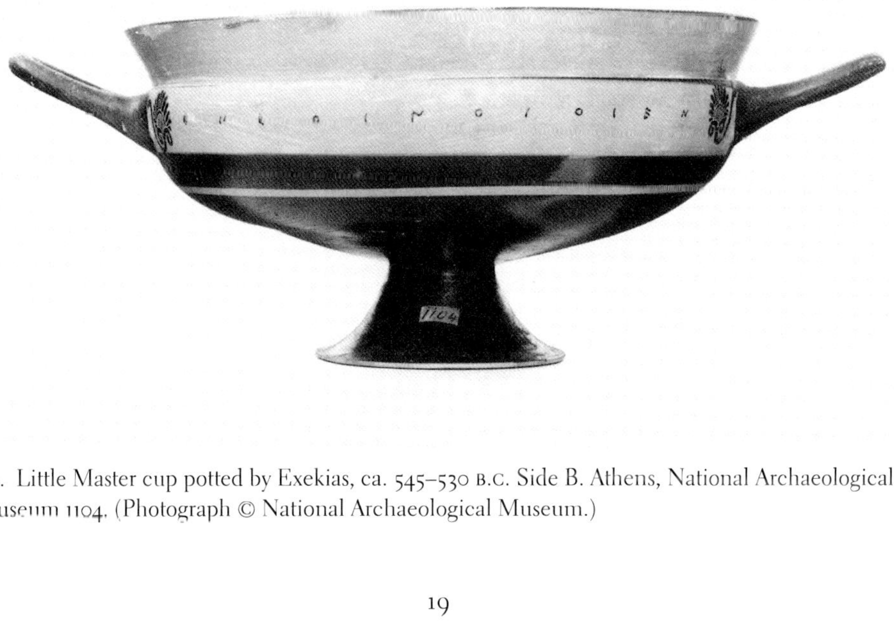

2.2. Little Master cup potted by Exekias, ca. 545–530 B.C. Side B. Athens, National Archaeological Museum 1104. (Photograph © National Archaeological Museum.)

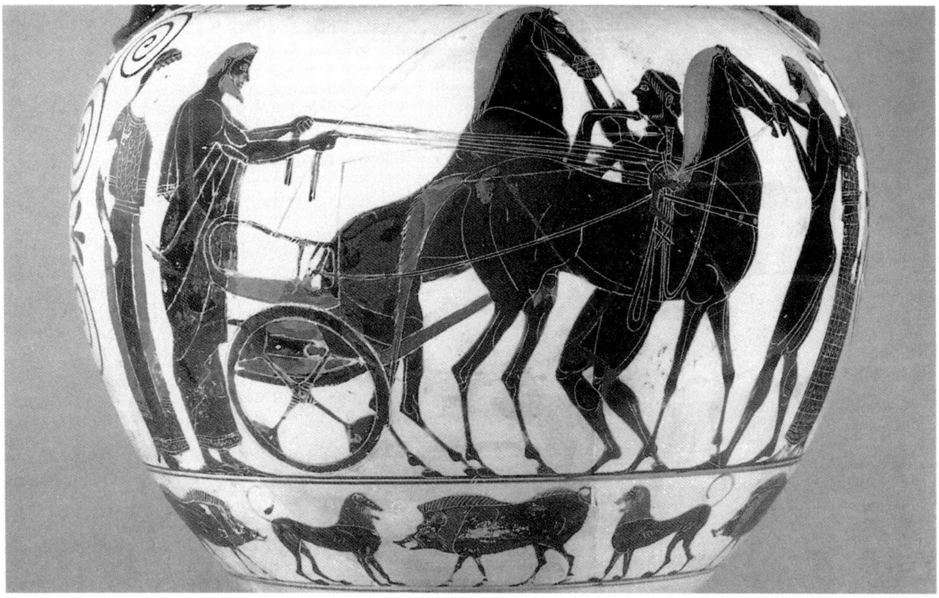

2.3. Black-figure neck-amphora by Exekias, ca. 545–530 B.C. Side A. Boston, Museum of Fine Arts 89.273. (*The harnessing of a chariot.* Findspot: Italy, Tarquinia. Place of Manufacture: Greece, Attica, Athens. Height: 52.5 cm (10 11/16 in.); diameter 37.3 cm (14 11/16 in.). Museum purchase with funds donated by contribution. Photograph © 1995. Museum of Fine Arts, Boston.)

is omitted on one side by looking at the other, and the recognition of the unity of the two images begins with a recognition of repetition.

The united scenes on this amphora open the door to a consideration of the role of repetition in expressing continuous narration visually. Froning, in an analysis of early representations of continuous narration, points out that when two consecutive phases of an activity, such as Herakles wrestling with the bull, appear on two sides of a vase, the result is to emphasize the extent of time over which the episode extends.[12] (Although Froning does not remark on this fact specifically, in her example the two sides are linked by near-repetitions of hero, animal, and the observing divinity, Athena.) However, in the example by Exekias, there are no identifiable mythical characters; it is a story, perhaps, or an excerpt from a story, but not an identifiable one. Here, the actions on the two sides appear to be simultaneous and hence there is no conjoining of sequential events as in continuous narration. Applying Froning's suggestion about emphasis on duration of time to the spatial dimension, we see that dividing the harnessing scenes into two fields here emphasizes extent of space: two actions directed toward the same goal take place in two separate spaces.

The painter's New York neck-amphora, with its enigmatic subject matter, employs both repeated syntax and repetition of images;[13] on each side there is a chariot with a woman driver and a man passenger. Other features differ: on side A, three black horses and one white horse pull the chariot, and a woman, a man playing the kithara, and a

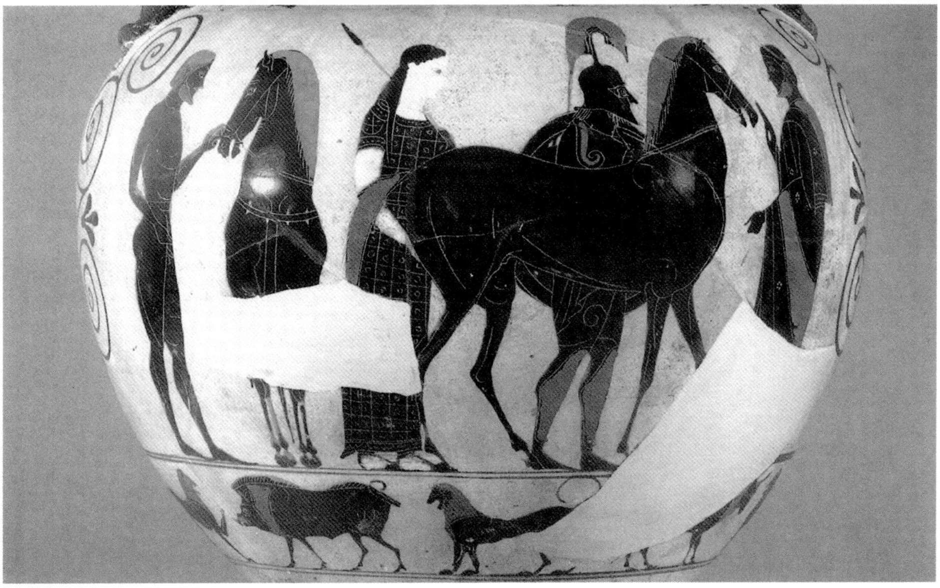

2.4. Black-figure neck-amphora by Exekias, ca. 545–530 B.C. Side B. Boston, Museum of Fine Arts 89.273. (*The harnessing of a chariot.* Findspot: Italy, Tarquinia. Place of Manufacture: Greece, Attica, Athens. Height: 52.5 cm (10 11/16 in.); diameter 37.3 cm (14 11/16 in.). Museum purchase with funds donated by contribution. Photograph © 1995. Museum of Fine Arts, Boston.)

child accompany the chariot-riders. On B, four black horses pull, and a woman and an older man attend. Clothing, including headgear, differs. Certainly this is not a single event repeated twice, because there are two distinct casts of characters, including two different teams of horses. When inspecting the vessel from the sides, that is, when looking at the area beneath the handles straight on, the viewer sees that the beginning of the group on A and the end of the group on B are both visible, because both compositions are strongly directional and open. Whatever the subject, these two chariots appear to be part of a single procession in the same way that the two sides of the Boston neck-amphora form part of a single harnessing. The repetitions are cohesive, unifying the two sides, suggesting a single event, and the appearance of a fight scene on the shoulder above each is another cohesive device, emphasizing unity.[14] Extrapolating again from Froning's interpretation of the purpose of repetition in conveying continuous narration over two sides of a vessel, here the spreading out of the procession over two sides of the vase tweaks two aspects of the subject, emphasizing its length and stately pace, its duration in space as well as time. To employ the nomenclature of the narratologists Genette and Chatman, the artist has lengthened discourse-time, the time it takes to tell the story, to convey something important about story-time, the real time occupied by the events in the story.[15]

Mythical narrative is conveyed through repetition on the Philadelphia amphora.[16] Most of the figures are labeled, identifying the Trojan War as the place, and the

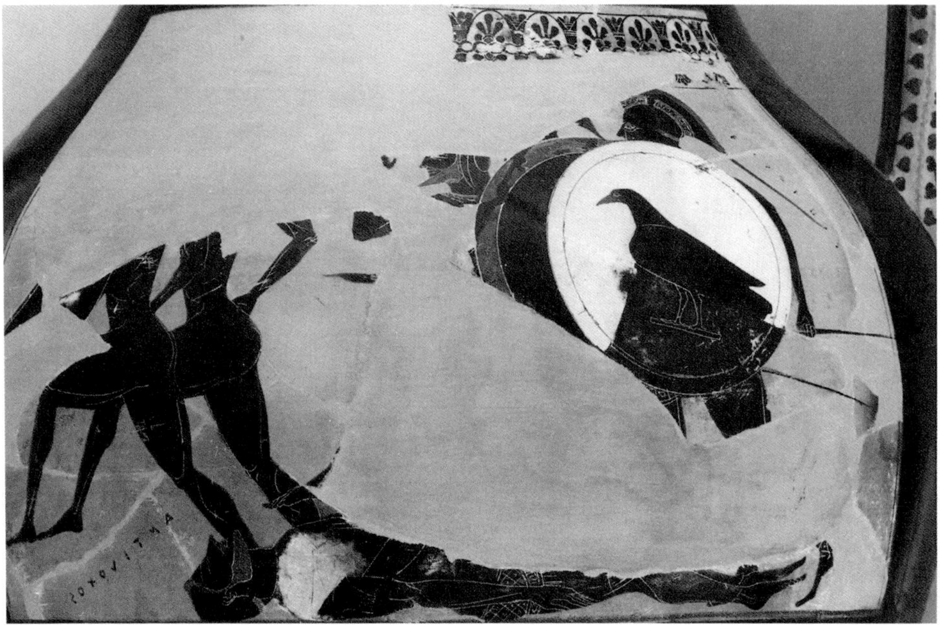

2.5. Black-figure amphora by Exekias, ca. 545–530 B.C. Side B, detail. Philadelphia, University Museum 3442. (Photograph © University of Pennsylvania Museum [neg. #MS 3442 B].)

deaths of Achilles and Antilochos as the stories. The two scenes display syntactical and compositional echoes while depicting two events that exist in a specific narrative sequence. On each side, there is an exposition of the aftermath of the death of a Greek hero, Antilochos on B and Achilles on A, clearly identified with inscriptions [Figures 2.5, 2.6]. Each side displays the supine corpse of one of the two Greek heroes and striding figures of colleagues who defend the corpse. In addition, there are running figures of blacks, usually identified as Ethiopians.

In creating his narration, the painter chose to use synonymy and ellipsis to engage the viewer in particular ways with the story. Synonymy in particular is created by "reiteration," the type of cohesive device involving not exact repetition but the substitution of a related item that has equivalence of meaning. In visual terms, the artist has set up the deaths of the two heroes as synonymous: each takes place on the battlefield at Troy, and in each case comrades defend the corpse. The third element that the two scenes share, the fleeing Ethiopians, is more puzzling and very interesting when considered within story time.[17] In the earlier scene, the death of Antilochos, Ethiopians are fleeing; this makes sense temporally – they are the followers of Memnon, who has apparently just killed Antilochos. Their presence creates awareness of an ellipsis – Memnon must have been there but he is no longer present – and the presence of his followers reminds the viewer of that fact. The deed is done, the perpetrator has fled, and his men follow and are pursued by the comrades of Antilochos. On the A side, the presence of the

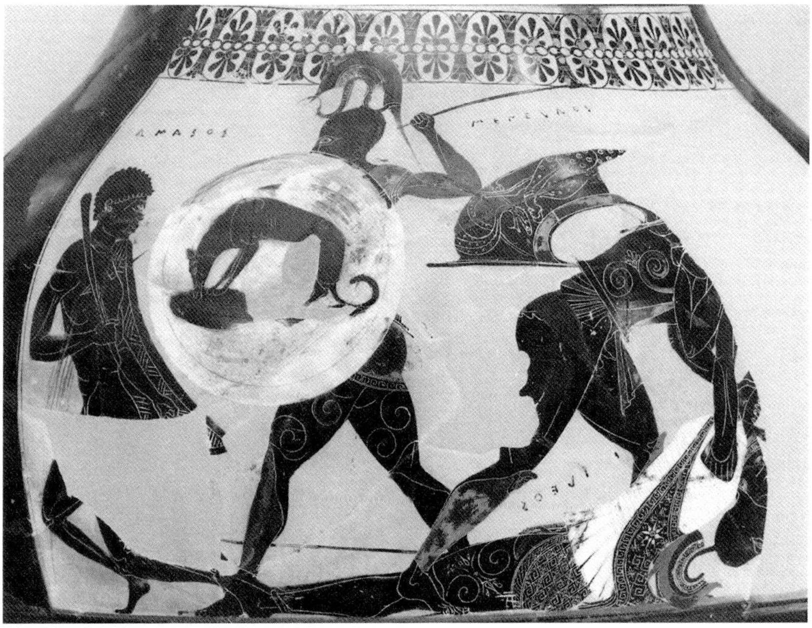

2.6. Black-figure amphora by Exekias, ca. 545–530 B.C. Side A, detail. Philadelphia, University Museum 3442. (Photograph © University of Pennsylvania Museum [neg. #MS 3442 A].)

Ethiopian is less easy to explain. The African man has been caught, and the flesh of his chest has been pierced by the spear of the Greek figure who is just beyond the corpse of Achilles. It is a surprise that an event which took place between the death of Antilochos and the death of Achilles – Achilles' murder of Memnon – is missing. Beazley pointed out that it is not likely that the followers of Memnon would still be on the battlefield by the time Achilles is killed: the Ethiopians ought to be long gone. The major difference between the retreating blacks on B and on A must be important: the single figure on A has been wounded; unlike his comrades on B, he will not escape. Memnon went on to fight after he killed Antilochos, and his retreating, unwounded companions on B would be available to accompany him; the wounding of the companion on A suggests the demise of Memnon and his entourage and serves to suggest that if Achilles is dead, Memnon must be also. Time is compressed, because the death of Antilochos and the death of Achilles appear to follow one after the other. The absence of Memnon on B and the absence of his death-scene, between the left-hand segment of the composition on A and the right-hand segment, is a double ellipsis. No matter how uncomfortable an observer is with such a truncated temporal tie between the deaths of Antilochos and Achilles, the artist has been careful to link the scenes by creating visual repetitions, joining the scenes and exposing them as equivalent and therefore synonymous.[18]

The repeated running Ethiopians in particular cause the observer to take a second look, because the retreat away from the center of each composition is unusual and startling syntax. The open composition, with the figures running out of the frame, further invites the viewer to consider the A side of the vessel in relation to the B side. Because the Ethiopians do not truly belong in the scene with the corpse of Achilles,[19] the very feature that departs from the syntactical norm to inspire a second look at the same time highlights a narrative sequence expanded through ellipsis. The difference between the two sets of similar figures – escape versus mortal wounding – is a temporal clue. The artist's manipulation of time through repetition-with-difference is impressive: he depicts two deaths and implies the third through an ellipsis, all in a unified location, Troy.[20] The single location is stressed by the unusual repetition: Ethiopians fought in only one place, and that place is Troy. Time, place, and sequence of events all are manipulated through repetition.

In addition to being synonymous, the two deaths depicted on the vase are causally linked according to one tradition. One interpretation of the *Aithiopis* maintains that Achilles returned to the fighting in order to avenge the death of his friend Antilochos at the hands of Memnon.[21] Thus the cause of Achilles' death on A is the death of Antilochos on B. Further discussion of the role of repetition in conveying causally linked visual narration will be taken up more generally in Chapter 6.

A similar example is to be found in the Type A cup in Munich.[22] Again, corpses, in this case one prone and one supine, together with attendant figures, invite comparison. Here, under the handles, are two very similar compositions with a wealth of repeated detail. Each corpse is surrounded by six men, three on each side. All of them wear high-crested Corinthian helmets, and three crests lined up, one behind the other in three of the four groups, asserting a strong connection between the two scenes. Still, the artist has taken special care to distinguish the figures on side A as different from those on side B.

There are no inscriptions on this cup to identify the fallen figures. Beazley attempts to connect side A with a specific mythological episode: "... in one picture the dead man, lying on his back, is already stripped; three warriors fight for the body on each side of the handle; one of them bends to take hold of it. This might possibly be the struggle for the body of Patroklos. At the other handle, the warrior, fallen prone, is still armed, but without spear, sword or shield."[23] Schefold – based on parallels with Exekias' krater in Athens – joins Beazley in identifying the nude warrior as Patroklos, and the one still clothed as Achilles.[24] If they are correct, here again is Exekias' use of cohesive repetition to yield narrative sequencing for the observer, because Patroklos dies before Achilles. The events are not merely in sequence; they are linked in terms of cause and effect.

The identifications of the dead warriors are speculative, but if they are correct, the scenes depicting them combine to create a narration of particular interest and sophistication. Because Patroklos' death indirectly causes the death of Achilles, the two scenes are not merely prior and subsequent; they are causally linked.[25] Moreover, the similarities between the two compositions urge the viewer to consider other similarities between the two deaths; one such similarity not referenced in the images is Apollo's role in engineering both. Each composition is itself symmetrical and closed. It is the repetition of figures and syntax that overcomes the formal independence of the two scenes, creating a single narration.[26]

On another belly amphora from Orvieto, the repetitions link a heroic scene and a mortal one, creating synonymy.[27] We see on each side a chariot with all four horses hitched; on each side, one horse is white. At the far right of the composition is a female figure with her arms down at her sides. In both cases a figure stands in the chariot. But the casts of characters are quite different: on side A the goddess Athena mounts the chariot, soon to be joined by Herakles, and on side B, a female figure hands over a corselet to a man standing in the middle of the composition. According to traditional interpretations, A is either Herakles' introduction to Olympus, where he will mount the chariot with Athena and go to Olympus with his divine escort, or the departure of goddess and hero to fight in the Gigantomachy.[28]

Beazley called the second scene "man in chariot."[29] The figures in the scene are lacking in heroic attributes, especially in comparison to their counterparts on A, where the artist has liberally included props for the identification of divinities and the hero Herakles. The difference in attributes signals a difference in the status of the participants. The presence of the chariot on side B, the side lacking in figures with divine attributes, brings up a persistent puzzler: does it alone make the scene heroic? Sinos suggests that the chariot makes clear a comparison between the departing mortal soldier and his divine counterpart, "uplifting the human activity by connecting it with a mythic paradigm."[30] By this logic, Exekias pairs these two scenes, using repeated figures to create synonymy, for the purpose of making the comparison between mortals and heroes vivid: to depart for war in a chariot makes one "like Herakles." Or more generally, "to depart for war is heroic." In any case, the repetitions in pose and syntax are certain indications that Exekias was once again inviting comparison.[31] In sum, this example displays another type of synonymy, that type of lexical cohesion and reiteration where there is substitution of a related item with equivalence of meaning rather than exact repetition. The repeated syntax points out a link between the scenes, exposing them as equivalent and therefore synonymous.[32] The inclusion of the chariot is redundant: it confirms, tells the viewer again, what the repetitions imply.

On the neck-amphora Berlin 1718 is another pair of synonymous situations, another comparison between mortal and heroic experience.[33] On side A is a scene identified by Beazley and many other scholars as Ajax with the body of Achilles and a grief-stricken Thetis [Figure 2.7]. The artist has paired this scene with one depicting the departure of a hoplite [Figure 2.8]. There are two striking repetitions: the white eagle as shield device, which is not repeated exactly, and the clothing of the women. The eagles, similar but not identical, establish a link between the "Ajax"-figure and the departing

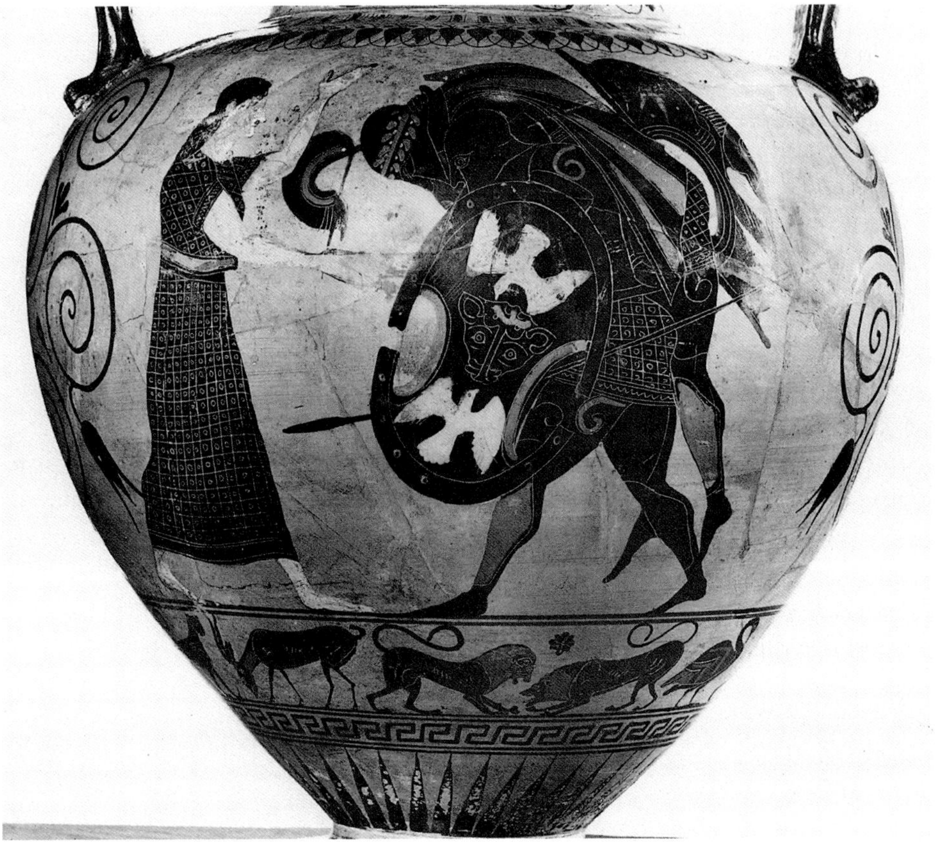

2.7. Black-figure amphora by Exekias, ca. 545–530 B.C. Side A. Berlin, Staatliche Museen 1718. (Photograph © Staatliche Museen zu Berlin, Antikensammlung [Neg.-Nr. 5588].)

warrior at the same time as the differences between them distinguish the two figures as different individuals. One important difference between the two sides is that the figures on the A side carry "Boeotian" shields, and the man on the B side carries a round shield. It is now commonplace for scholars to assert that the appearance of a Boeotian shield creates a heroic ambience in a scene, just as does the chariot in the preceding vase.[34] This difference, in contrast to the repetitions, must carry semantic significance. The repeated clothing links the women who bid the hoplite farewell and the grief-stricken female figure on the other side. An analysis of the links yields the following observations: to go to battle is heroic and elite; and departures resulted in casualities for heroic families, just as they do for elite mortal families.[35]

A very fragmentary belly amphora in Philadelphia preserves two scenes with many features in common.[36] On both sides is a grazing horse, at left. With each, holding the lead, is a male figure. On one side, he appears to be Greek, with a ram's-head cheek piece in his helmet and an eagle for a device on his round shield; on the other, he is a Scythian archer. Some decorative motifs appear on items of dress for both figures,

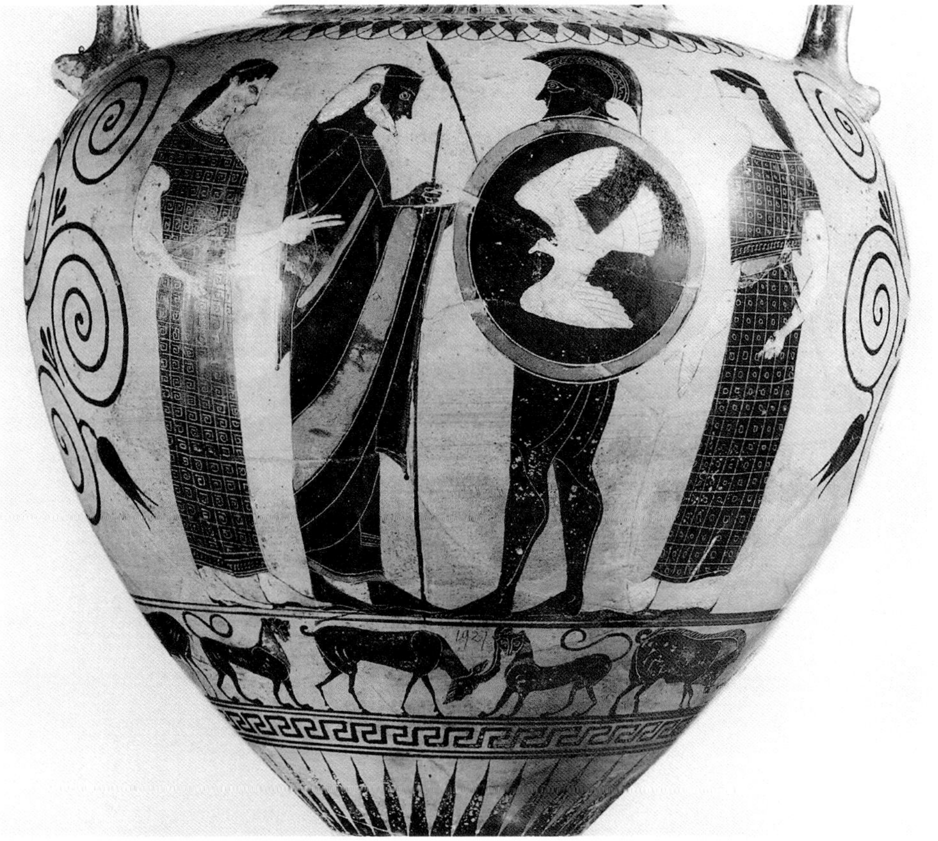

2.8. Black-figure amphora by Exekias, ca. 545–530 B.C. Side B, Berlin, Staatliche Museen1718. (Photograph © Staatliche Museen zu Berlin, Antikensammlung [Neg.-Nr. 5592].)

but are embedded in very different contexts: the spiral of the ram's horn on A's helmet reappears on the Scythian cap; the star pattern, one of several on the closely-packed embroidery of the Greek's tunic, reappears, enlarged, alternating with circles creating long vertical stripes on the Scythian's trousers.

The parallels in pose and composition, however, are striking. What point did the artist intend the observer to draw from the repetition? Analysis thus far suggests that Exekias employed repetitions not merely for compositional convenience, but also and indeed primarily for their semantic contributions. The viewer is invited to consider the similarities and differences between two types of men who fight and tend to their mounts: one is Greek, and one is not; the Scythian is normally the assistant of the Greek, and not his equal, yet here he is the precise syntactic equivalent.[37]

The Munich neck-amphora, where Beazley and many others see two renderings of Telemonian Ajax with the body of the dead Achilles, presents unusual challenges[38] [Figures 2.9, 2.10]. In strongly directional, open compositions, these are two close approximations of the A-side of the Berlin amphora discussed above. As with the

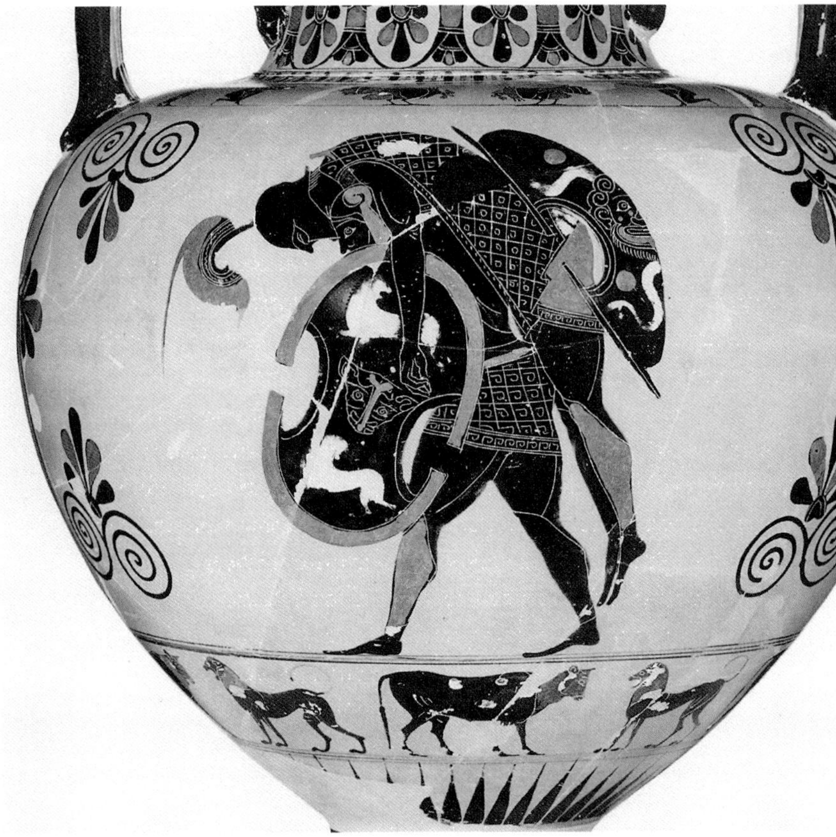

2.9. Black-figure neck-amphora by Exekias, ca. 545–530 B.C. Side A. Munich, Staatliche Antikensammlungen und Glyptothek 1470 (J. 1295). (Photograph © Staatliche Antikensammlungen und Glyptothek München [Neg.-Nr. KM 2908].)

Berlin example, Exekias provides no labels. However, the overwhelming impression is one of similarity, or homonymy, between the two scenes, and this piece merits our close attention, because it is closest in spirit to the bilingual vases discussed below.

Together with the similarities there are many variations in detail.[39] The differences include clothing, helmets, arm position of the corpse, and shield devices. In fact, the two "Ajax" figures have two different versions of a panther-head device, much as the hoplite and the "Ajax" figure have two different eagle devices on Berlin 1718, just discussed. In contrast, each "Achilles" figure is distinguished by a different device.[40] On the A side, Ajax stands more upright than on the B side, where he appears to slump under the weight of his companion. In these examples, it seems as though Exekias uses repetition to lead the viewer to conduct an inventory that will yield a recognition of difference; that recognition in turn leads the viewer to a main point. Experience therefore mandates taking the differences seriously.[41] The Exekian examples discussed up to this point suggest two separate events in sequence, that is, one figure taking off

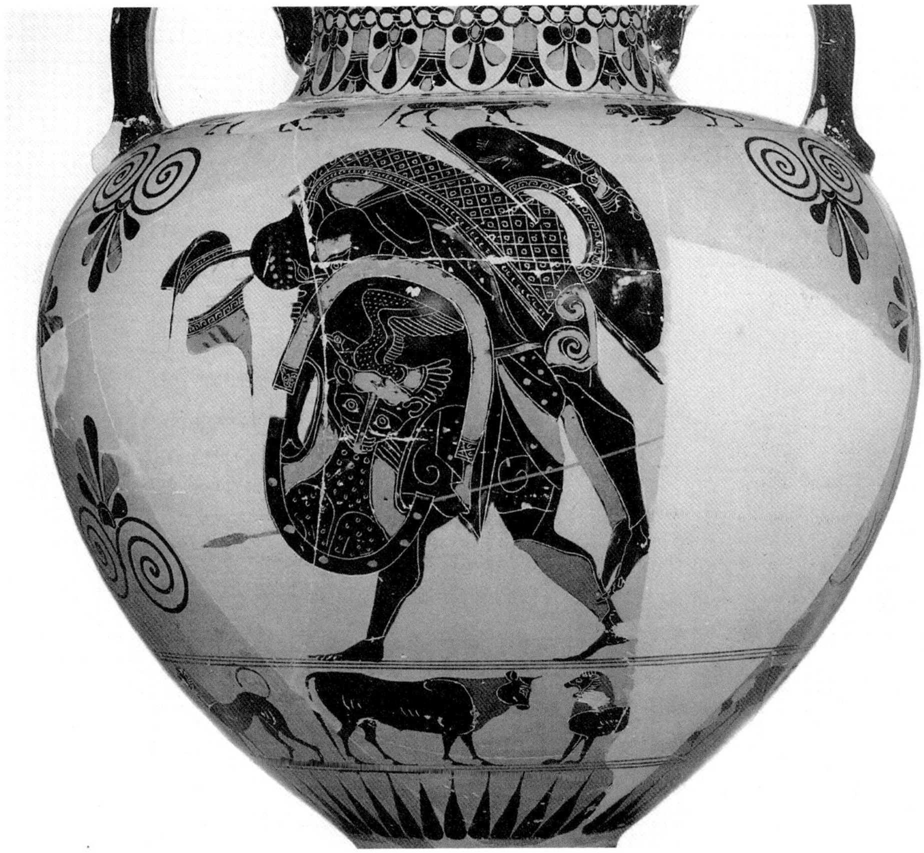

2.10. Black-figure neck-amphora by Exekias, ca. 545–530 B.C. Side B. Munich, Staatliche Antikensammlungen und Glyptothek 1470 (J. 1295). (Photograph © Staatliche Antikensammlungen und Glyptothek München [Neg.-Nr. KM 3637].)

two different corpses at two different times, or two figures who have something in common, as suggested by the common feature in the shield device, taking off two different corpses. However, the common view of the Munich amphora holds that the two subjects are the same.

Suppose for a moment, however, that Exekias does pair two slightly different renderings of a single subject. What would the purpose of that repetition be if the two scenes represent the same event? Many Athenian vases repeat an image in two fields, often so closely that the result is in effect an exact repetition. Not surprisingly, for example, scholars will disagree as to whether or not on a *Glaux*-skyphos, a type of vase where an owl is repeated on each side, the artist repeats one image or creates identical images of two different owls.[42] Such repetition surely unites the two images. However, narratologist Meike Bal makes the superficially surprising assertion that in verbal narratives there is no such thing as *exact* repetition: "Two events are never exactly the same. The first event of a series differs from the one that follows it, if only because it is the first and the other is not."[43] Is this true of texts – not only narratives – in general, and those expressed in images in particular? To consider the minting of coins, a process much more inherently capable of exact repetition than the various images painted on a vase by an individual, is instructive. The event is repetitive, and the creation "ought" to yield exact repetition. But the die wears down, producing a slightly different image with each strike, from the first issue on. Moreover, each user of coins sees the new coin for the first time only once; he views those that follow in light of that first view. Likewise, states Bal, verbal repetitions, even if they are precise, differ because one must be first, the others in a series following. The second, third, fourth, and so on differ from the first because they resonate with the previous accounts. A viewer cannot see both sides of an amphora or a cup or all three fields of a hydria simultaneously. If the amphora preserves two images, the viewer must see one first, and will interpret the one seen second in light of the first. The process creates a stereotypical image, and repetitions of stereotypical images and indeed plots create generic templates in light of which the audience hears or views individual examples.

We have now looked at every example in the *oeuvre* of Exekias where there is a repeated image in two different fields on a vase. A vase outside this category illustrates yet another aspect of Exekias' use of repetition. On an amphora in Orvieto, there are two scenes linked by a common protagonist, but *without* precise repetitions of either lexical items or syntax.[44] The two scenes are temporally and compositionally discrete. On side B of this amphora from Orvieto, Herakles is fetching Kerberos from Hades. The open composition depicts all figures standing or moving to right. On the other side, the gods on Olympus sit in two closed groups, one of which focuses on Herakles and Athena. Indeed, the artist almost seems to have deliberately avoided repetition; he has even divided up the attributes of the hero, so that each image is elliptical: in the scene in Hades, the standing hero wears his lion skin, with his short sword in its scabbard; on Olympus, he sits without lion skin and holds club and bow. The two representations of Herakles in comparison seem to manifest every possible difference, and this fact, together with the syntactical differences, results in a vivid example of echoing opposites: seated/standing; inaction/action; Hades/Olympus. The two scenes are otherwise for the most part lacking in the types of repetition in either imagery or syntax characteristic of the Exekian examples discussed thus far.[45] It is the character Herakles – and possibly Athena, too, if she is one of the partially preserved female figures on side B – and not the visual image or syntax that is repeated. The onlooker might not realize that this character is repeated until after figuring out what each scene is.

Other scholars have hypothesized about political motivations that may have caused Exekias to pair these two subjects, and such motivations might well have played some role in his selection of subject matter, but not necessarily in its precise manifestation.[46] Herakles was not simultaneously involved in life on Olympus and the fetching of Kerberos. Therefore, yet another result of the pairing is an exposition of the narrative sequence of the hero's life, in addition to the Hades versus Olympus opposition.[47] In fact, because the fetching of Kerberos is a cause of Herakles' apotheosis, an apparent combination of cyclical and continuous phased narration is depicted here.[48]

What is the justification for projecting a link between scenes here at all, when the lexical items used to express "Herakles" seem to be so deliberately different? Narratologists readily identify a type of repetition where the same narrative or character is repeated using different words, and this is its visual equivalent. Without repetition of lexical items, how does the viewer know that the two fields on this amphora form a single text? Of course, he cannot; this is a case where the artist links scenes by means of a repetition recognized intellectually rather than visually, especially when he expects that viewers will have developed a comparative habit, where they normally check all fields to see if they are linked. It is only the painter's expectation that viewers will compare fields that provides an explanation for why the missing elements on scene A are supplied by scene B. Those absent in A are present on B. Furthermore, these observations provide firmer ground to hypothesize that narration and even sociopolitical messages may have been among several of the painter's intentions. The difference between the argument here and that of other scholars is the insistence that it is justified to hypothesize links because the artist's *oeuvre* as a whole includes numerous examples where there are observable indisputable lexical and syntactical repetitions that create a single text out of images in separate fields.[49]

Thus far nine examples have been identified of the vases attributed to Exekias by Beazley that preserve repetition of lexical items and/or syntax; this is out of a total of twenty-two vessels that have more than one field preserved, eliminating fragments where both sides are not preserved, the plaques, the Panathenaic amphora, and the Orvieto amphora just discussed. Once again, this total excludes those examples where scholars have observed a reasonable thematic link between the two sides, but there is no visual repetition.[50] This is a high proportion of vases where repetition of the visual equivalent of lexical items plays a role in directing the viewer to an interpretation of the vase.

To summarize our survey thus far, we can conclude that Exekias accomplishes several results by repeating image and syntax. Repetition is crucial to his method of communication. He uses repetition as a hook to draw the viewer into a process of close comparison. These cohesive devices, in turn, communicate to the viewer a prominent message through such means as ellipsis, synonymy, and antonymy:

1. The event extends from one side of a vase to another, as in the harnessing scene, the least common type in the admittedly small corpus of surviving Exekian vases;
2. The story includes a sequence of events, such as events at Troy or events in the life of Herakles, that may be causally related; and

3. The composition invites comparison of beings at varying levels of existence: gods or heroes to other heroes or to mortals, mortals to Herakles, Ajax, or Achilles, mortals to one another.

We observe these same products of repetition widely dispersed among Archaic vase-painters. In the next section, we see a mechanism for how the use of repetition is transmitted from one artist to another by looking at its appearance in the workshop successors to Exekias.

THE FOLLOWERS OF EXEKIAS

There are examples of repetition by the successors to Exekias in several repertories in both black- and red-figure techniques. Because of their obvious incorporation of repetition, the bilingual vases attributed to the Andokides and Lysippides Painters will serve as the focus for this discussion. Indeed, most (though not all) scholars believe that the Lysippides and Andokides Painters spent time in the workshop of Exekias and were in fact his pupils, and most scholars see the influence of Exekias in the style, subject-matter, and compositional preferences of these painters.[51] Two additional questions are posed here: Did these successors acquire any of Exekias' particular brand of visual redundancy? And, perhaps of greater interest, were those habits influential in the creation of their bilingual vases?

Cohen has said "the Lysippides Painter stolidly depends upon Exekias, although he never understands the essence of his predecessor's achievements," and the following assessment supports her view.[52] The Lysippides Painter certainly did not explore the possibilities of redundancy to the extent that Exekias did, at least on the black-figure works scholars call uniquely his.[53] Of the works attributed to the Lysippides Painter, only two repeat an identifiable figure in two different fields, and this figure is Herakles. On the eye-cup London B 426, Herakles and Geryon appear on one side, and Herakles and the Amazons on the other.[54] The two scenes share many features: the hero strides right, wearing very similar lionskin, quiver, and scabbard, and using his sword in each case. Other figures in each field have both round and Boeotian shields. On another eye-cup, Munich 2080 (J.1028), Herakles and Apollo struggle for the tripod on one side and Herakles and the Lion fight on the other.[55] In the last, visual similarities between the two Herakles-figures are not stressed: the lion skin, while still worn by the lion on side B, is not stippled, though it is when Herakles wears it on side A. The hero carries his club on side A; it is absent from side B. This second Lysippidean example is very like Orvieto 2748 + 3048, where Exekias pairs two Herakles episodes on a single vase but uses ellipsis to create an antonymous link between the two renderings of the hero; like Exekias in the Orvieto example, the Lysippides Painter here links events that must be temporally sequential. In these examples, the repetition of the main figure,

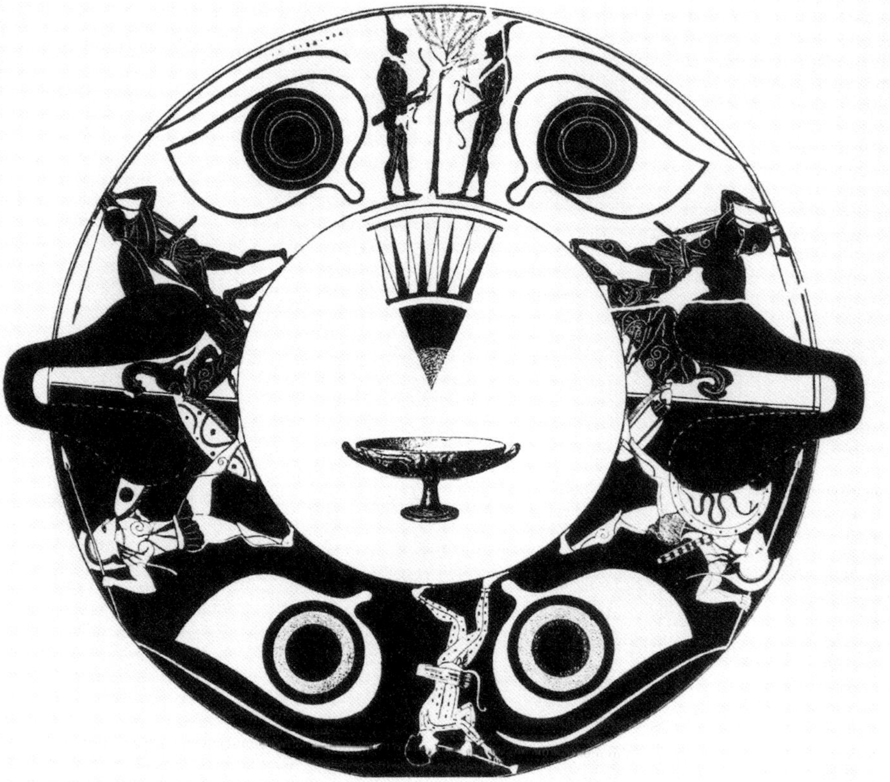

2.11. Bilingual cup by the Andokides/Lysippides Painters, ca. 530–515 B.C. Sides A and B and Interior. Palermo, Museo Nazionale V650. Drawing, *JdI*, 1889.

although low on specific repeated elements, is a cohesive device linking two situations in a time sequence. The unified text of the vessel is a short narration, but there are few visual clues to direct the viewer to recognize it. All of the narrative examples are of the cyclical type, rather than the continuous causally linked phased narration observed in some Exekian examples.[56]

The purely red-figure work attributed to the Andokides Painter yields a more complex picture.[57] Bothmer identifies Amazons on each side of the painter's amphora in the Louvre, in one case swimming and in the other arming for departure, and his suggestion is appealing.[58] Like some of Exekias' compositions discussed above, both scenes cause the viewer to do a double-take. The viewer registers surprise because the scenes are such unorthodox ones in which to find female figures. A turning figure at the far right of each scene is repeated, and their resemblance to one another serves to link the two sides of the vase. The repeated figures draw the viewer's attention to other shared elements, such as masculine behaviors and accoutrements: Figures arming and on horseback on side A and the Phrygian-type cap,[59] aryballos, and athleticism on side B. The meaning is fairly clear: the Amazons are first at "work" and then at play. Side B adds to the usual repertory of images of Amazons, extending their concerns from war alone to the hypothetical corollary for women who fight: women who take exercise as men. This is a more subtle use of redundancy than that employed by the Lysippides Painter, much more like the majority of Exekian examples.

Of the so-called bilingual vases by the Lysippides and Andokides Painters, four have subjects repeated on both major fields of the vase, and the repetition of subjects is expressed through repeated figures and compositions. Scholars assert that at least one reason for the pairing of red- and black-figure is a marketing ploy, to encourage the purchaser to compare the two techniques.[60] Based on the role of repetition in Exekian syntax, and because most scholars believe that the Lysippides and Andokides Painters spent time in the workshop of Exekias, there may be additional reasons, related to the exploration of the effects of repetition, for pairing the two techniques.[61] The following examination suggests that it is no accident that these particular bilingual vases appear as part of the legacy of Exekias.

The first example is the Palermo eye-cup, which, although it is much like his Munich cup, is the least Exekian of the bilingual vases under discussion here[62] [Figure 2.11]. The subject at each handle, depicted in closed composition, is combat: a pair fights over a fallen figure. There is also repetition in the figure type, but not in composition, between the eyes: a Scythian trumpeter in one case appears directly opposite two Scythian warriors in the other. Bow, quiver, and stippled costume are shared by figures on opposite sides of the cup, but the effect is very different because of the difference in technique. The two groups of handle figures are very like one another, with the exception of shield devices and elements of dress. The repetition of figure types and compositions is highlighted by the combining of techniques: in each case there are two black-figure warriors, one of whom is on the ground with a round red-figure shield, and one red-figure warrior. There is nothing about these triads that suggests specific identities. The crucial feature of fighting to strip or recover a corpse – suggesting one of several possible specific mythical identities – is lacking, unlike the images on the Munich cup and the Philadelphia amphora. Thus, an identification of two separate anonymous triads seems justified.

The red-figure shield held by the wounded black-figure warriors introduces a question: is the figure holding it the ally of the black-figure warrior or the red-figure one? In each case the figure falls from the black-figure group, yet his shield color is that of his adversary. With whom are the figures between the eyes allied, black- and red-figured Scythians, normally the assistants of warriors? How do these Scythians fit into a story? Do they unify time and/or place? Do they establish the setting as Troy, much as do the Ethiopians on Philadelphia 3224 [Figures 2.5, 2.6] and the Scythian in the fragmentary Exekian example in Philadelphia?[63] The casting of this superficially simple repetition into two different techniques in the particular way it is done here emphasizes questions of identity that are lacking in similar scenes wholly of one technique or another.[64]

Next is the Boston amphora with two renderings of heroes, identified as Achilles and Ajax, gaming[65] [Figures 2.12, 2.13]. The identifications are made by analogy to an inscribed Exekian masterpiece not discussed here.[66] Like the Munich neck-amphora with the two corpse-carrying images, this vase preserves two images that are close but not identical. The details that vary include clothing, shield types, and shield devices. Do the different shield devices signal different characters in each scene? Some scholars have proposed such a solution for very similar images, and in that case the relationship between the two images is either comparative or sequential.[67] However, setting the issue of identity aside, there is an obvious difference between the two sides, a temporal one. On one side, the two figures play without helmets, which rest behind them on top of their shields. The left figure has his fingers on the board, whereas the right figure has his pointed downward, about to touch a gaming piece. On the other side, both figures wear their helmets, and the "Ajax" figure makes a gesture with his right hand, which may indicate a score, "three." These differences are slight; however, they suggest two different moments of the narration: the black-figure, the middle of the contest, and the red-figure, a moment closer to its end. So in the same way that Exekias showed distinct events and allowed the viewer to place them in narrative sequence, the two sides of this amphora show two temporally distinct moments. The distinction is apparent through the drawing alone, but the difference in technique is a substantial help in highlighting the distinctive elements on each side. In this example, the repetition of figures encourages the viewer to see what elements are shared, while the change in technique emphasizes that there are differences as well.

A third example is the Munich amphora, where a figure reclines on each side of the vessel[68] [Figures 2.14, 2.15]. On the black-figure side, Herakles rests on a *kline* holding a kantharos. His attributes hang in the field. He is accompanied by three figures: Hermes, Athena, who gestures to the hero, and a wine boy, who stands at a dinos. The red-figure version on the other side shows many similarities, such as the reclining figure and Athena, but several differences as well: no Hermes, no wine boy, no dinos, and no attributes to identify the reclining figure. The vine is behind, in the background, instead of forming a canopy over Herakles. The clothing of the figures is different from that of their counterparts on the obverse. The positions of the cup and food on the table in front of the *kline* are reversed. Athena offers a flower to the reclining figure, who grasps his knee with his right hand, allowing his empty kantharos to tilt. Through the use of ellipsis, the absence of attributes for the reclining figure on the red-figure side startles the observer, expressly because the attributes do appear on the other side. The difference is so dramatic that some scholars have proposed that this might mean the figure on the red-figure side is not Herakles.[69] Considering the two scenes from the vantage point of an Exekian legacy yields another interpretation: there appears to be a temporal difference, on at least two levels. First, the black-figure

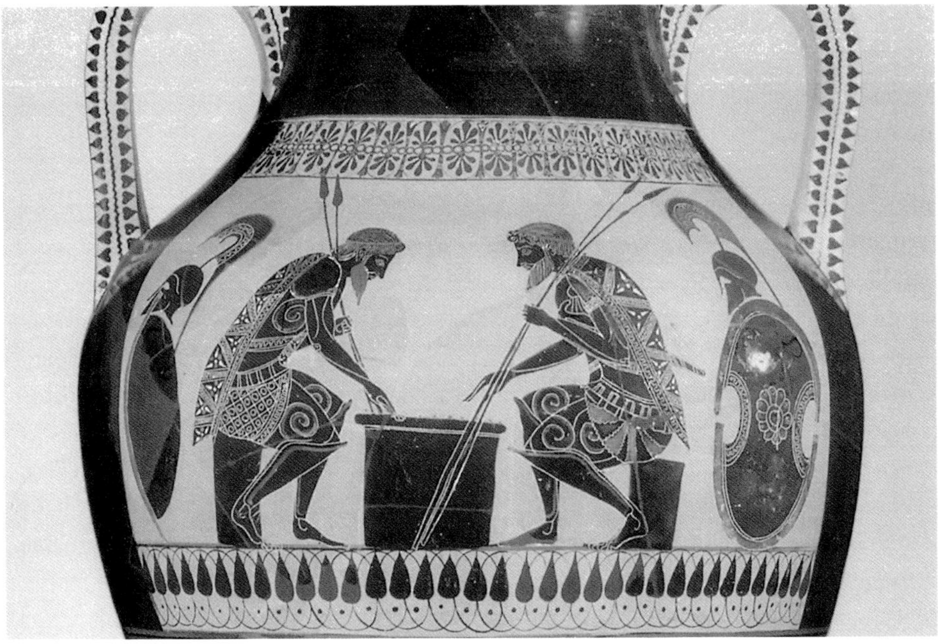

2.12. Bilingual amphora by the Andokides/Lysippides Painters, ca. 530–515 B.C. Side B. Boston, Museum of Fine Arts 01.8037. (*Achilles and Ajax*. Findspot: Italy, Umbria, near Orvieto. Place of Manufacture: Greece, Attica, Athens. Height: 55.5 cm (21 7/8 in.); diameter 34 cm (13 3/8 in.). Henry Lillie Pierce Fund. Photograph © Museum of Fine Arts, Boston.)

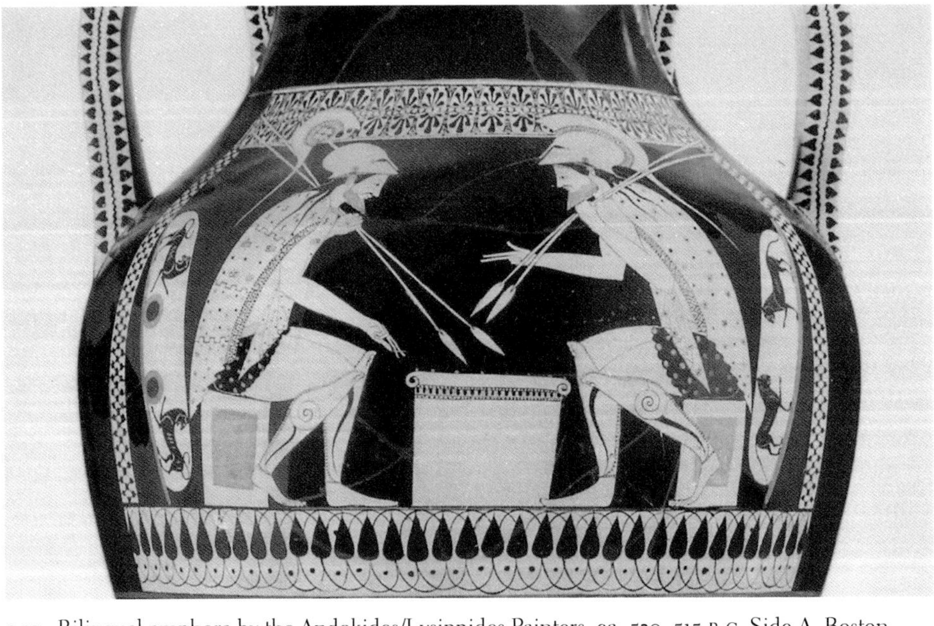

2.13. Bilingual amphora by the Andokides/Lysippides Painters, ca. 530–515 B.C. Side A. Boston, Museum of Fine Arts 01.8037. (*Achilles and Ajax*. Findspot: Italy, Umbria, near Orvieto. Place of Manufacture: Greece, Attica, Athens. Height: 55.5 cm (21 7/8 in.); diameter 34 cm (13 3/8 in.). Henry Lillie Pierce Fund. Photograph © Museum of Fine Arts, Boston.)

side shows a cup about to be filled and a crowd of figures, in contrast to an empty cup and a scene of intimacy. Second, the black-figure side evokes Herakles' past, through his attributes, and his passage to Olympus through the presence of Hermes, while the red-figure side points to Herakles' future, where weapons and divine escorts will not be necessary. For this discussion of redundancy, however, it is most important to note that the combination of two techniques helps to alert the viewer to differences in the face of a great deal of syntactic and lexical similarity. The contrast in technique casts the scenes as a discourse on likeness and dissimilarity, and this discourse imposes a comparative view of the two sides together.

The two sides of the Boston amphora depicting Herakles driving a bull to sacrifice show very few differences other than those in technique.[70] Not only is the subject unequivocally identical, but also the two images are so similar that they are favorite teaching tools, used to provide students with one-on-one comparisons between the elements of black- and red-figure techniques.[71] There is a profound difference in effect, but the difficulty in pinning down the differences leads to a crucial point in this discussion of redundancy, a discussion of the phenomenon of "exact repetition." This subject came up earlier, in the analysis of Exekias' Munich amphora, and it is crucial to investigate, because, outside of the repertories discussed here, it happens often.

Once again, narratologists provide insight. As pointed out above, Bal maintains that there is no such thing as "exact repetition" because only one telling of an event can be the first, and all other tellings must be subsequent and therefore different, if for no other reason than that they are not first.[72] The viewer who looks at the amphora cannot see both sides at once; the fact that one side is *not* first is highlighted by the difference in technique. In written narratives, exact repetition and slight variation have narrative function. One use is to express variations in perspective. If the narrator describes an event with language identical to the way a character describes it, the reader gets useful information about narrator, character, and event. A single event within the text may be described slightly differently by narrator and character. This phenomenon obtains with reception, too. A single event, told only once, may appear different to different readers. It is tempting to see such processes at work in this vase that appears to be a visual expression of this law: no two narrators will tell a traditional story the same way, no two listeners will hear it identically, and likewise no two viewers will see its representation in art in the same way. The closeness in the details of the two sides of this bilingual vase combined with the enormous difference in effect which each creates demonstrates that, despite manifold repetitions, this is not exact repetition. The ramifications of these observations as applied to the space in which this vessel and those like it were used, the locale of the *symposion*, where viewers see, hear, and speak from a variety of perspectives, will be taken up in our final chapter.

These four examples are among the most thoroughly and aggressively bilingual of all vases that preserve elements of both red- and black-figure techniques, and

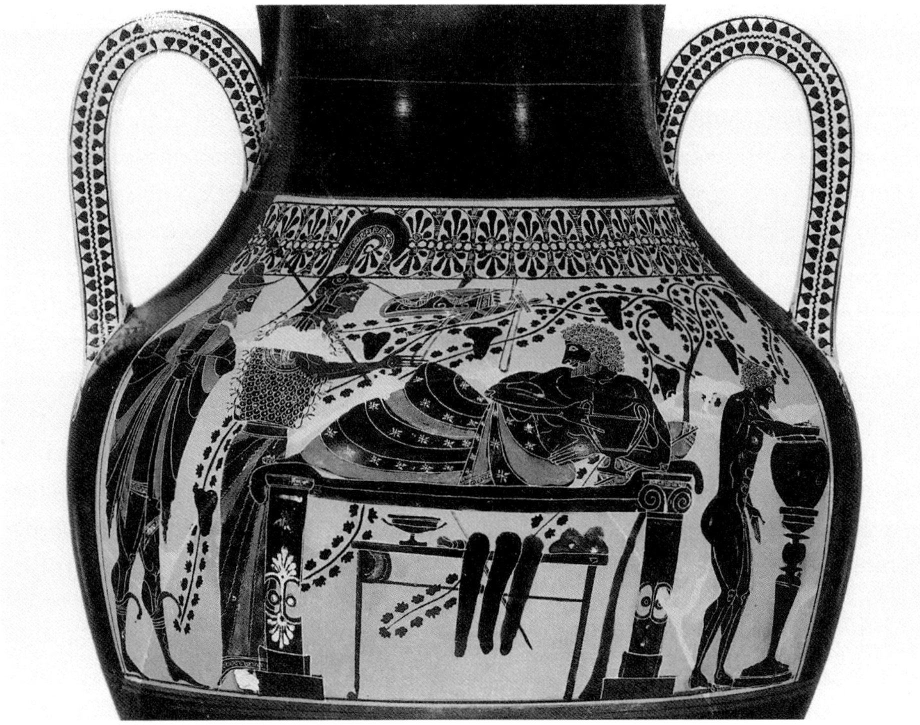

2.14. Bilingual amphora by the Adokides/Lysippides Painters, ca. 530–515 B.C. Side B. Munich, Staatliche Antikensammlungen und Glyptothek 2301. (Photograph © Staatliche Antikensammlungen und Glyptothek München.)

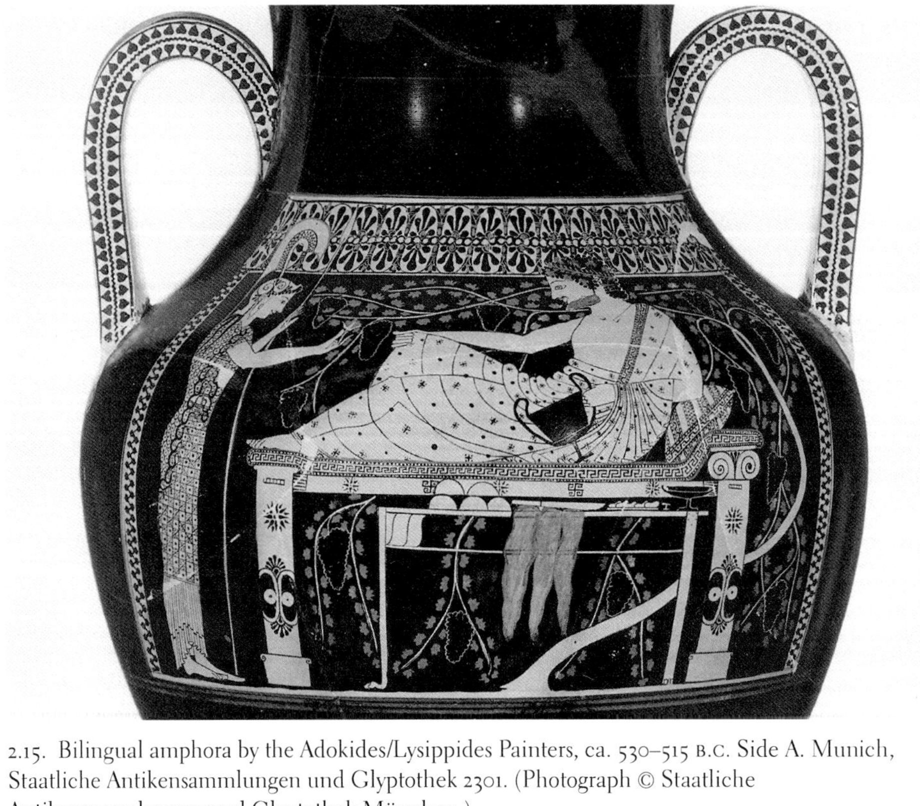

2.15. Bilingual amphora by the Adokides/Lysippides Painters, ca. 530–515 B.C. Side A. Munich, Staatliche Antikensammlungen und Glyptothek 2301. (Photograph © Staatliche Antikensammlungen und Glyptothek München.)

they claim special status owing to the fact that close repetition of imagery exists in conjunction with the combination of techniques. The spirit of their bilinguality grows from the mode of repetition specific to the Exekian repertory, inherited by these painters. Their combination of techniques heightens the viewer's analysis of redundant imagery, taking it a step beyond Exekias' already sophisticated use.

What conclusions does this look at repetition as used by a master and his pupils yield? Repetition of lexical items or figures and of syntax or composition and overall decorative program are options that artists can select to create unified continuous or cyclic narration, synonymous or antonymous paradigms, or exploration of point of view. These types of repetition direct the viewer, through cohesive devices, to a recognition of the thematic unity in the entire visual program of the vase. The repetition is essential to avoid transmission errors; without following through on the clues provided by the redundancy, the viewer will miss the overall message of the unified text of the vase. It may not be possible to retrieve all that these artists transmit through the use of repetition, but their purpose certainly goes beyond the merely aesthetic level. The use of repetition is an option that is not always employed thus its appearance suggests that an artist made a deliberate choice to use it. The way in which the artist uses repetition, like elements of style and iconography, may be part of what one artist teaches another.

THREE

REPETITION AND TYPES

The previous chapter surveyed different results an individual painter, Exekias, achieved through the use of varying types and degrees of repetition. For each of the effects achieved through repetition, we laid out the theoretical justification for seeing particular meanings. As a result, we have established a range of possible repetitive effects that will inform our wider investigation of Archaic Athenian vases. In this chapter, we start out from a very different perspective. We do not begin with an individual painter's use of repetition; instead, having surveyed the spectrum of vases themselves, we identify large groups of vases that stand out as nearly identical, by several painters. They are for the most part attributed to anonymous painters who are recognized not for the subtlety of their use of repetition but for their application of it in broad strokes. Consideration of the vases discussed in this chapter, all manifesting exact (or almost exact) repetition, allows us to initiate a wider investigation of repetition as it is conceived and developed by Athenian artists and as it would have conditioned the viewers of the vessels. The categories of vases discussed here preserve images that are identical or nearly so on each side of the vessel, and there are many examples of the same shape and decoration, substantial clusters of vases named here "Types."

BACKGROUND

We have already considered several vases that are closely allied in concept to Types. In the previous chapter, four vases stood out from the others because their decoration consisted of nearly exact repetition of the scenes on each side of the vase:[1] the A and B side scenes usually identified as Ajax with the body of Achilles on the black figure example by Exekias [Figures 2.9, 2.10] and three bilingual examples, Ajax and Achilles playing dice [Figures 2.12, 2.13], Herakles reclining alone [Figures 2.14, 2.15], and Herakles driving a bull to sacrifice, by the Andokides/Lysippides Painter. In each case two scenes differ in small details and, in the latter examples, in technique as well. Collectively these examples raised critical questions about the meaning of "exact repetition."

In addition to those examples where the entire iconographic program is repeated on each side of a vase are those examples that share a single defining repeated element. One such common repeated feature shared among the cups by Exekias and the Andokides/Lysippides Painters is the pair of eyes on each side [Figures 2.11, 3.7, 3.8]. The eyes are part of a consistent syntax that in each instance helps to unite the two sides of the vessel.[2] The conjunction of shape and decoration present in the eye-cups discussed in Chapter 2 is in fact very common in many other repertories, with examples numbering in the 100's.[3] Just as with the Exekian and Lysippidean/Andokidean example, the details of decoration, such as placement of additional figures, ornament, and interior decoration, vary among Type A eye-cups. All eye-cups are similar, but very few are identical. In this sense eye-cups may be said to form a genre as that term is used to identify categories of written texts, with shape and placement of eyes analogous to the rules of line-length, pattern of rhyme, and meter and the variable iconography similar to differing vocabulary in the individual poems. One difference between the eye-cups and these poetic genres is that the eyes themselves may carry meaning that goes beyond the level of consistent syntax.

Types

In the repertory of Attic vases, there are many other less ambitious and even more repetitive examples, where (1) the decoration consists of one composition or figure repeated on both sides of a vessel; and (2) most important, the same decorative scheme occurs not only on both sides of a single vase, but on many examples, all identical to one another. Using the nomenclature of Beazley, they are both "Class," unified by shape, and sometimes but not necessarily also "Group," unified by style.[4] Beazley did not name a category for vessels of the same shape with identical iconography on each side, for which this discussion uses the term "Type." Horse-head amphoras and *Glaux*-skyphoi are two such groups considered in this chapter. Instead of unique examples as created by Exekias and his followers, these are, like the majority of eye-cups, apparently mass-produced repetitive vessels and very numerous.[5] This discussion presents one end of a spectrum of degrees of repetition, a solid boundary from which individual examples employing partial repetition to convey a wide variety of results, as investigated in later chapters, diverge in various ways.

The very earliest Greek pottery includes examples of shape-plus-decoration "Types." Well-known are the Dark Age pendent-semicircle skyphoi, with consistent shape and decoration, documented throughout the eastern Mediterranean and, closest to Attica, at Lefkandi, whose craftsmen appear to have originated the Type.[6] Because

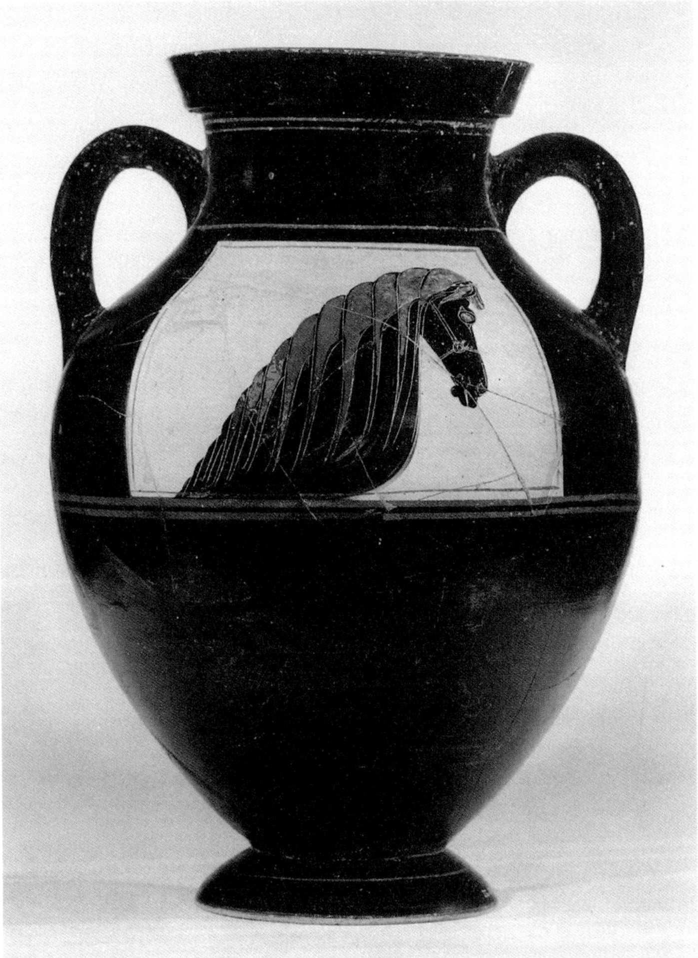

3.1. Horse-head amphora, ca. 600–580 B.C. Side A. New York, Metropolitan Museum of Art 26.60.45. (Photograph © Metropolitan Museum of Art, Fletcher Fund, 1926. All rights reserved, The Metropolitan Museum of Art.)

there is relatively little figural decoration, let alone mythical narrative, on pendant-semicircle skyphoi, these are not so striking as later examples. What follows is a discussion of three Types, briefly treated, to show that during the period considered in this monograph some Athenian ceramic artists were still engaged in the process of creating Types, using repetition in a particular way to do so.

HORSE-HEAD AMPHORAS

Horse-head amphoras are the earliest *archaic* Attic vessels to employ repeated figural decoration in a precise and consistent way in large numbers on identical shapes, and

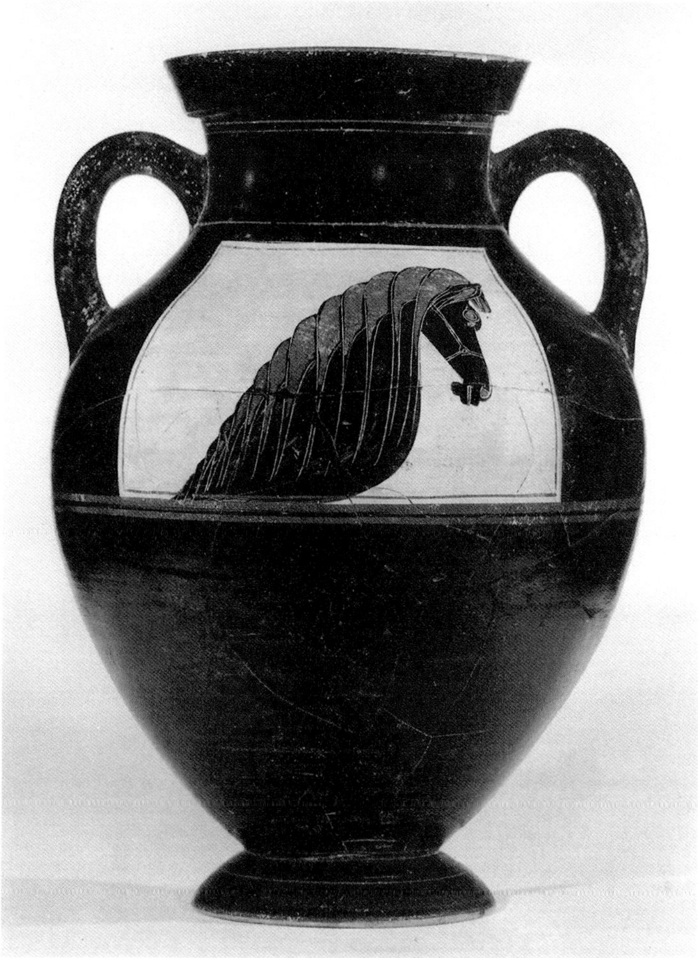

3.2. Horse-head amphora, ca. 600–580 B.C. Side B. New York, Metropolitan Museum of Art 26.60.45. (Photograph © Metropolitan Museum of Art, Fletcher Fund, 1926. All rights reserved, The Metropolitan Museum of Art.)

as such, they invite careful attention[7] [Figures 3.1, 3.2]. They stand out in contrast to many contemporaneous vases on which there are multiple decorative friezes or myriad examples where each side of a vessel presents a different subject. The vast majority have nearly identical horse protomes, facing right, on each side;[8] in general, even on shapes other than amphoras, horse protomes appear only rarely paired with other subjects.[9] Therefore within the first two decades of the sixth century, there is a class of vessels with consistent shape and consistent decoration that relies on repetition as the definitive characteristic to secure its identity. Ultimately, several different artists painted Horse-head amphoras. Whatever the function of the vessel, it is clear that repetition of imagery identically on each side is integral to its identification. It is not the repetition *per se* that is distinctive and novel, but the production of many examples of the same shape depicting the same repeated subject, creating a Type. To identify a member of this Type, the viewer must see a horse protome on each side and take note of the shape. He then identifies that individual vessel with the Type "Horse-head amphora." The two definitive characteristics are (1) the repetition of the horse protome (2) on this particular shape.

Where does the idea for the creation of this Type with strictly observed repetition originate?[10] Beazley believed that Horse-head amphoras were invented by the Gorgon Painter, and indeed they carry a decorative scheme that that painter and his associates used:[11] an animal, sometimes the same animal, in a panel on each side of an amphora. A related example, possibly by the Nettos Painter, a slightly earlier contemporary of the Gorgon Painter, preserves a siren on each side of a panel amphora, and this shape is almost a direct predecessor of the Horse-head Type shape.[12] On the Horse-head amphora Type, an eponymous horse protome appears in a panel on each side of the vessel in the same way that most of the Gorgon Painter's amphoras repeat an animal – not necessarily a protome and not necessarily the same animal – on each side. The important point here is that Athenian craftsmen created a Type by using existing formulas and intensifying the degree of repetition.

KOMAST-DANCER CUPS

Komast-dancer cups are a Type that begins slightly later than the Horse-head amphora Type, about 575 and extending to the mid-sixth century. Again, artists collect decorative and figural elements already existing in the artistic repertory and subject them to a rigid and repetitive syntax to create the Type.[13] In this case, however, the artists borrow from Corinth as well as relying on purely Attic traditions, so their deliberate manipulation of repetition is quite evident[14] [Figures 3.3, 3.4].

Komast-dancer cups form a coherent Type that can be defined as follows: a particular cup shape with a spreading conical foot, deep bowl, and offset lip is consistently decorated with a single subject – a *komos* consisting of two or three youths, men, and sometimes women – on each side of the vessel.[15] The komasts themselves are distinctive, in lively, exaggerated dancing poses and nude or lightly dressed, sometimes with padded buttocks. A palmette–lotus combination under the handles separates the two scenes. The interior is always painted black, and rosettes or a net-pattern adorn the set-off rim.[16]

The komast-dancer *figure* itself has a Corinthian origin and is abundantly paralleled on Middle Corinthian cups; however, in the Corinthian repertory, the dancers are depicted in a larger group, several appearing in a frieze, and are relegated to the upper of two friezes on the exterior of the cup. The dancers virtually never appear on both sides of a single cup, and the overall effect is very different. As Brijder states, "no known Middle Corinthian cups are decorated in the manner of Komast [-dancer] cups."[17]

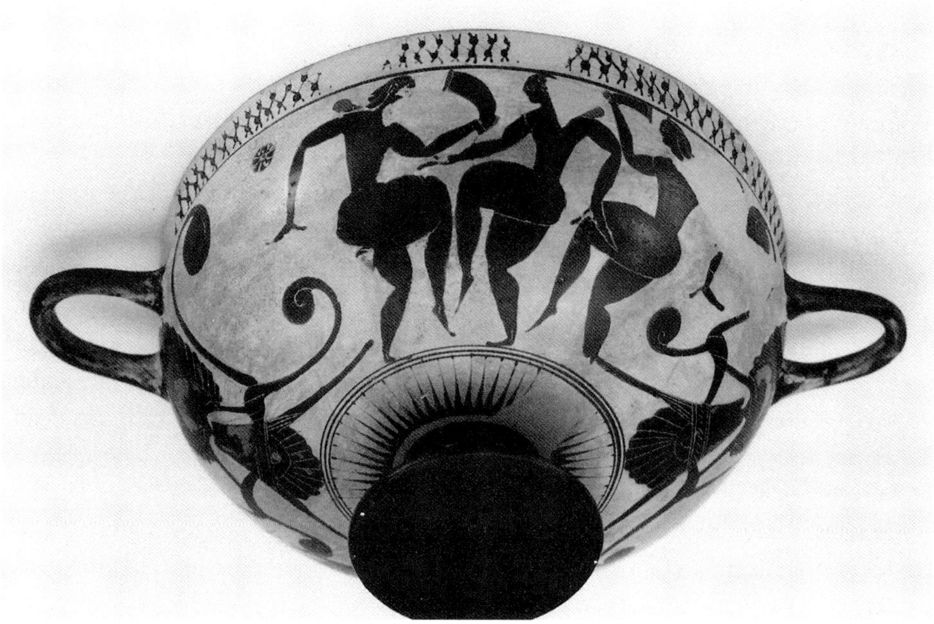

3.3. Komast-dancer cup by the Falmouth Painter, ca. 585–570 B.C. Side A. Omaha, Joslyn Art Museum 1951.885. (Photograph © Joslyn Art Museum, Omaha, Nebraska.)

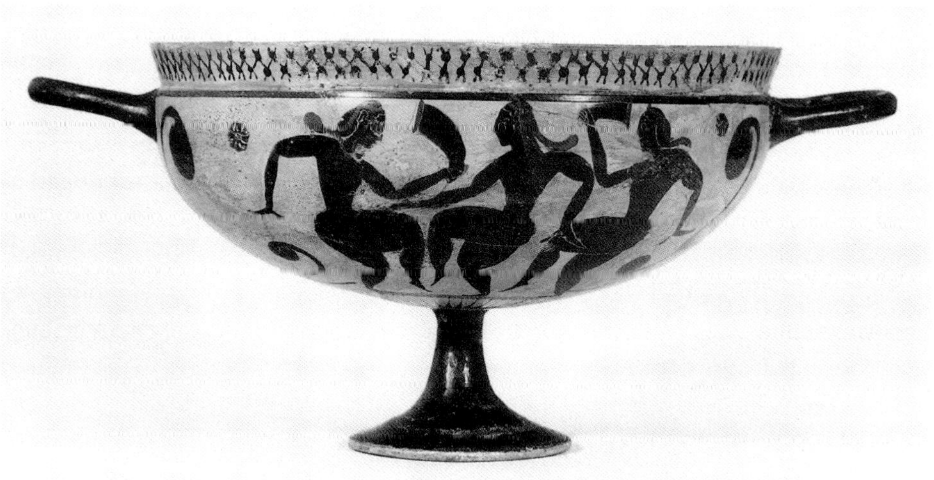

3.4. Komast-dancer cup by the Falmouth Painter, ca. 585–570 B.C. Side B. Omaha, Joslyn Art Museum 1951.885. (Photograph © Joslyn Art Museum, Omaha, Nebraska.)

The Athenian craftsmen extract the dancers from the Corinthian figural repertory and make them the decorative focus of the cups. For Attic painters of Komast-dancer cups, repetition of a subject on each side of a vessel was familiar, practiced by their predecessors such as the Gorgon Painter; Komast-cup artists' appropriation of the concept and consistent repetition of the komast figures resulted in the creation of another Type. As with the Horse-head amphora, the Komast-dancer cup Type is identifiable not only because the image on the vessel is repeated on each side, but also because the same repetitive decoration is repeated from vessel to vessel. Also, similarly to the Horse-head amphoras, komast iconography is relatively rare on shapes other than Komast cups. It is very unusual to find komast-dancers on shapes other than drinking vessels.[18]

A closer look at some examples of Komast-dancer cups reveals that the repetitions are not exact; that is, one side is not precisely identical to the other. They are therefore repetitive, but not so closely similar as the horse protomes on Horse-head amphoras. A common program keeps the gender and identity of dancers the same on each side, but the positions of one or more dancers differ: on one side, both feet may be on the ground, but on the other, one foot is off the ground and the leg is bent back at the knee.[19] Such examples suggest that the same dancers appear on each side, but at different moments of the dance, as though the two sets of images represent two different moments in a sequence of events. In other cases, much more rare, the casts of characters are not identical: for example, a youth may be replaced by an adult. On Vienna 3667, the figures on A and B are in identical poses, wear identical clothing, and have the same attributes.[20] On B, the right-hand figure is an adult male, whereas on A, he is a youth. The substitution may set up a collocative relationship of either synonymy or antonymy or a continuation of the subject; that is, there is one continuous dance shown at a single moment in time, with part on one side and another part on the other, interrupted by florals and handles. In any event, it is clear that, despite the small differences, a high degree of general repetition, in both "lexical" and "syntactical" terms, is crucial to the identification of the Type.

Komast-group painters also use exactly the same type of repetition to define a closely related Type, Komast-dancer skyphoi. This Type may even pre-date the cups slightly.[21] Some Komast-dancer skyphoi are identical iconographically to Komast-dancer cups, with komast dancers indistinguishable, varying from one another in exactly the same ways.[22] Like the cups, the Komast-dancer skyphoi appear to be one subject extended over two sides, emphasizing different elements of a spatially unified *komos* in each.

A look at other shapes by the painters of Komast-dancer skyphoi and cups convinces us that the painters regarded the Types as set off, separate, and special in terms of both the subject-matter and the degree of repetition they employ. On Komast-Group lekanides, column-kraters, and tripod-kothons, there are not generally komast-dancers. There is repetition of other subjects and motifs, but it is not so thorough or consistent as on the Komast-dancer cup and skyphos Types. The lekanis, which is the most cuplike of these three shapes, has continuous zones of animal frieze below, topped by zones where syntax is repeated but subject differs: for example, on a lekane from Rhodes, three pairs of animals flank a central element, with the only verbatim repetition a pair of sphinxes that frame a floral on one side and an arming scene on the other.[23] The upper zone is arranged to emphasize that the two sides are similar but not the same; through this syntax, the painter trains a spotlight on the arming scene, simply because it contrasts so sharply with its pendant, the floral ornament. The repetition of the composition but not the figures is primarily "syntactical" repetition rather than both "lexical and syntactical" repetition, as appears on the Komast-dancer Types.

The column-kraters by these same painters reveal still different conventions. As mentioned above, kraters do carry komast-dancers, but they are not repeated on both sides. A zone depicting an animal procession usually appears on column-kraters, below the main scene. The area below the handles is used by painters as a field to be decorated with figures, either animals, florals, or in two cases, komast-dancers; whatever the painter chooses to use here is always repeated under both handles. In the main field, broken into two sections by the handles and the motifs under the handles, subjects and motifs are not repeated. One example may preserve a subject that extends from one side of the vase to another, although there are few visual repetitions: figures on one side of the vase attack the Calydonian Boar on foot, with spears; figures on horseback, holding identical spears, appear on the other side.[24] Tripod-kothons do not appear to carry repetitions at all.[25]

This brief survey, then, indicates that the Komast-group painters repeat figures, compositions, and shape to identify two special groups of drinking vessels, Komast-dancer cups and Komast-dancer skyphoi. The Attic artist extracts a single figural type from the visual repertory of Corinthian counterparts, uses it in extremely repetitious ways to decorate a specific shape of vessel, and then creates many examples that are nearly identical. The process of the creation of this Type suggests that the Athenian artists had a particular sensitivity to the communicative power of repetition, because it is so thoroughly apparent in the Type: not only are two or three figures repeated on each side, but the two sides of the cup or skyphos are also repetitions of one another. The results of this case-study allow us to see the actual process of how *repetition of a consistent subject in consistent syntax on numerous examples of the same type of vessel establishes a Type or genre of vases.* Like eye-cups, these Types, the Komast-dancer skyphoi and cups, compare to a poetic form like the sonnet, but here the changes in vocabulary are even more slight, more like changes in accent.

GLAUX-SKYPHOI

The *Glaux*-skyphos is the final Type that we will consider here as a case-study.[26] With origins as early as 500 B.C. and most examples dating to the second and third quarters of the fifth century, the vessels are red-figure skyphoi of both Type A (two horizontal handles) and, more commonly, Type B (one horizontal, one vertical handle).[27] They

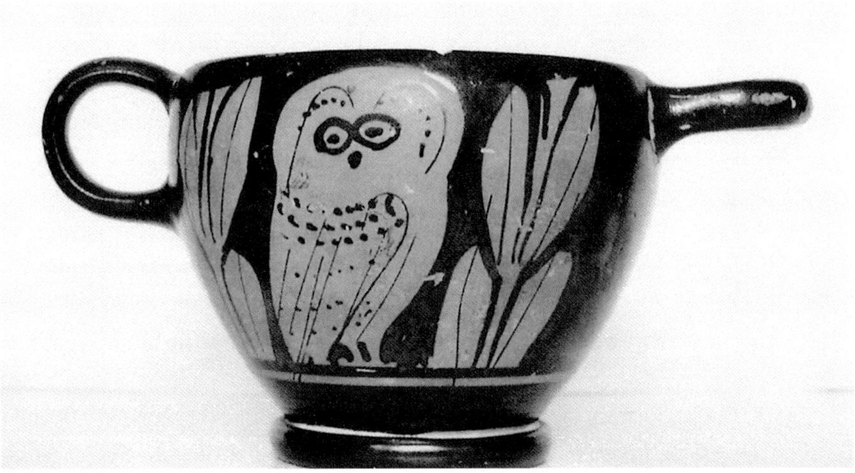

3.5. *Glaux*-skyphos, ca. 450 B.C. Side A. (Photograph © Collection of Jenifer Neils, Cleveland, Ohio.)

depict an owl and two olive sprays on each side[28] [Figures 3.5, 3.6]. Differences in style of rendering the owls and the vegetation allow us to divide the examples into six groups; what Johnson says in the case of two very similar groups applies to the Type as a whole: "The two groups are not only descriptively similar, but narrowly miss exact duplication."[29] A cluster of examples from the Athenian Agora preserves several vessels very close in size, with rims around 10 cm in diameter. There is also an Italian red-figure version of the Type, and many examples are found in Italian excavations. The *Glaux*-skyphos Type is much like the Horse-head amphora Type: the same single image is repeated on each side of a consistent vessel shape and size.[30]

The origin of the *Glaux*-skyphos Type is not as well understood as that of Horse-head amphoras or Komast-dancer cups. However, there is sufficient evidence to demonstrate that artists improvised and extrapolated from existing elements in the Athenian repertory to create a Type identifiable by its consistent repetitions. Johnson suggested that the first appearance of an owl like that appearing on *Glaux*-skyphoi is at about 500 B.C. on a red-figure cup painted in the manner of Epiktetos.[31] More recently, Kaeser has associated a black-figure Type B amphora in Munich with the earliest *Glaux*-skyphos.[32] The owl in a panel on each side of the amphora is, except for the black-figure technique, very like those on the skyphos series.

Whatever their individual uses and meanings, Types created by Athenian artists were adaptations of existing iconography and shapes. Repetition is key to the creation and identity of the Type. The subject on A is either identical or very similar in visual and formal terms to the subject on B, and while the very slight differences may be meaningful, these differences are of less compelling interest than those appearing on unique examples. When discussing unique examples of exact or nearly exact repetition in Chapter 2, we asked if the viewer actually sees the same thing twice when looking

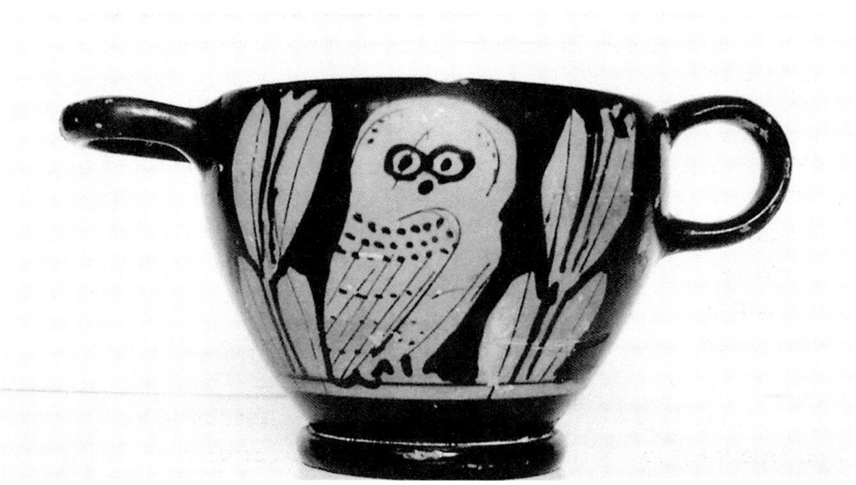

3.6. *Glaux*-skyphos, ca. 450 B.C. Side B. (Photograph © Collection of Jenifer Neils, Cleveland, Ohio.)

at the two sides of the vessel or if the image seen second is always different because it is not first.[33] Such questions are less relevant in processing the exact repetition of a Type, because the abundance of examples discourages the kind of close inspection that unique examples of highly repetitive syntax and iconography inspire. The repetitions on an individual example of any one single Horse-head amphora or *Glaux*-skyphos are therefore devalued in impact; instead, the repetitions allow the user to understand very quickly what the vessel means. The thoroughness of the repetitions creates a very directive message based on super-redundancy, helping to secure identity.[34] When a viewer recognizes a vessel that is a member of a Type, he has less motivation and less reward for looking carefully at subtle differences in images on the two sides of the vessel because he knows that the highly repetitive idiom is conventional and that the vessel belongs to a larger group. The group may have additional meanings related to function. For example, Scheibler, in her study of the Attic belly-amphora, points out that Horse-head amphoras have a standard height and capacity, suggesting to her that they were used as measuring-vessels and/or as prizes for games.[35] Her hypothesis brings out an interesting point: Types may have certain specific functions, limiting their use-contexts and thereby expanding into the realm of function the range of meanings that repetition creates.

As a final example, we return to eye-cups, which are especially interesting because they have characteristics of a Type, consisting of repeated iconography, but it is often combined with a number of other unique features. The shape of the cups and the eyes are the standard repetitive features of a Type, and they are fixed figural entities that allow its immediate recognition. Yet the other components of the decoration vary, sometimes in subtle and creative ways, as the examples by Exekias and the Andokides/Lysippides painters discussed in Chapter 2 demonstrate [Figure 2.11]. A

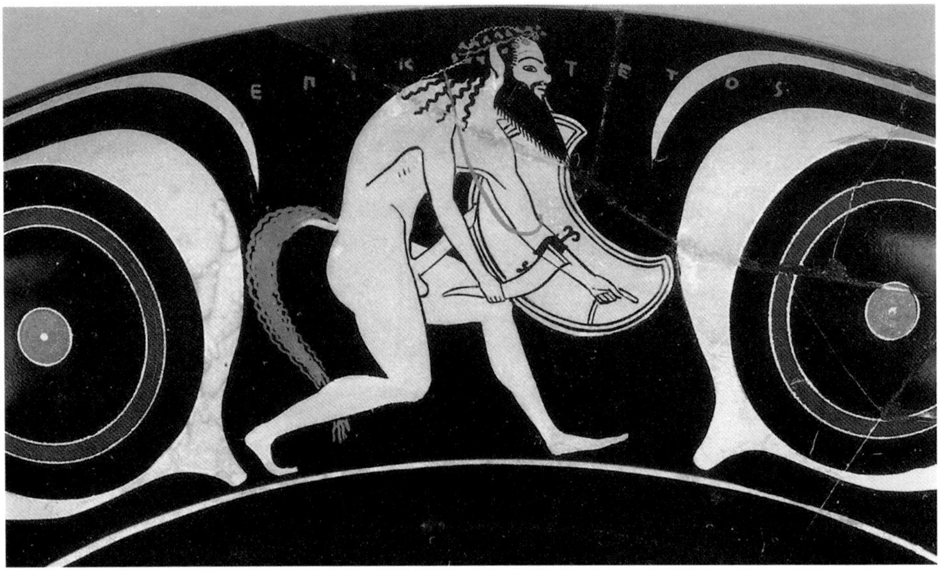

3.7. Red-figure eye-cup by Epiktetos, ca. 520–490 B.C. Side A. London, British Museum E 3 (814). (Photograph © Copyright The Trustees of The British Museum.)

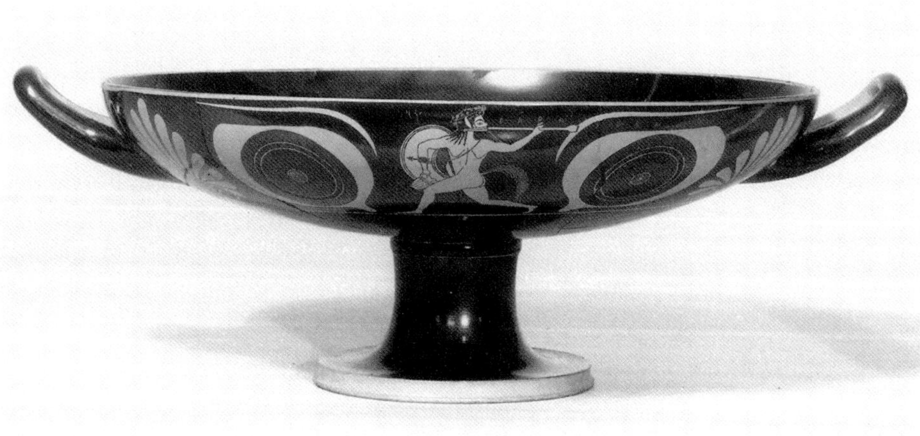

3.8. Red-figure eye-cup by Epiktetos, ca. 520–490 B.C. Side B. London, British Museum E 3 (814). (Photograph © Copyright The Trustees of The British Museum.)

Type A eye-cup by Epiktetos is another typical example of the Type[36] [Figures 3.7, 3.8]. Not only are the eyes repeated, but the artist's signature also appears divided at the top of the field between each pair of eyes. Lower down and still between the eyes on each side is an ithyphallic running satyr wearing an ivy wreath, holding a shield (*pelta* in one case and round shield in the other in the other) and a sympotic vessel (oinochoe and drinking horn). Both repeated syntax and the repetitions of figural detail and categories of attributes join two members of the Dionysiac roster into a single thematic unity. The disconnected figures wedged into the narrow space between eyes at a scale vastly different from the eyes, eyebrows, and framing palmettes could have the effect of disconnecting the two fields, of discouraging reading them as part of a single visual story, yet the opposite results. The two satyrs appear to be going to the same place to battle and to party. The means to this end is the exploitation of the repetitive features of a Type to achieve collocation. Again, eye-cups such as this one share characteristics of both full-fledged Types such as the Horse-head amphora, Komast-dancer cups and skyphoi, and *Glaux*-skyphoi and the unique examples of "exact" repetition, such as the amphoras by Exekias and the Andokides/Lysippides Painters. The latter, preserving nearly identical scenes on each side, gain meaning because they are *not* Types and do not exist as one of many identical examples. They will engage the viewer precisely because they are unique; because they are *not* part of a recognized Type, the viewer will be more apt to look carefully and assess similarity and difference.

The Types discussed in this chapter provide a benchmark for understanding the effect of repetition on Athenian vases. Repetition is at the core of their identity, whereas their membership in a large group of nearly identical vessels discourages close assessment of similarity and difference. To identify membership in the Type is the main point of the repetitions. In subsequent chapters, the material considered exists in varying relations to Types such as those discussed here. It is important to remember that to an ancient viewer, Types were commonplace. The vase with only some repetitive features shared between scenes calls attention to itself precisely because it is not a member of a Type and its repetitions are not known through other examples. Because the viewer cannot derive its meaning from that of the larger category, the Type, he is compelled to assess the unique or unusual example carefully.

FOUR

"READ ME": REPETITION AS METADISCOURSE

This chapter takes a slight digression from the focus on repeated imagery that guided Chapters 2 and 3. Here the topic shifts to a consideration of elements of metadiscourse, elements that guide the viewer to a specific interpretation of the vase, on Archaic Athenian vessels dating from about 550 to 470 B.C. Metadiscourse is mainly composed of written inscriptions, but includes also their semantic predecessors, images of repeated spectators. Written inscriptions form an unequivocally crucial body of evidence for this study overall because, as pointed out in the discussion of the Boston pelike in Chapter 1 and of Exekias' Athens cup in Chapter 2, they provide incontrovertible evidence that the viewer is expected to join two sides of a vessel in his assessment of it. Evidence of inscriptions whose meaning is completed through their complete or partial repetition in two or more fields on a vase rests at the very heart, therefore, of our justification for the belief that Athenian vases are texts to be read and that repetition is key to the meaning of such readings.

It is worthwhile at the outset to review one example of the inscriptional evidence we have considered thus far. The Boston pelike attributed by Robertson to Euthymides preserves inscriptions that both label participants and offer comments about a youth not apparently pictured on the vessel [Figures 1.1, 1.2]. The written sentence, "Leagros is handsome," with the response to it, "Leagros IS handsome, yes indeed!" together with the proper names that label the figures is not necessarily crucial to the story the images portray; because they add a level of specificity, the words have the effect of directing the viewer's reception of the vase in particular ways. They supply a prescribed reaction. Without them, the viewer might hypothesize the jumpers and flute player are any number of individuals or even no one in particular; he might not be fantasizing about Leagros at all, unless prompted by these comments. The fact that a statement appears on one side of the vase and the response to it is on the other motivates the viewer to combine the imagery on the two sides as well. Like all such writing on vases, the inscriptions narrow the interpretive boundaries; they provide additional extra-image data on how to interpret the entire text that is the vase.

Several vases considered in subsequent discussions of narration (Chapter 6) and paradigm (Chapter 7) preserve repetitions that include anonymous spectators, incongruous figures apparently unrelated to the main action at the center of the visual field yet clearly reacting to it. The hypothesis investigated here is that anonymous spectators, like inscriptions, exist to tell the viewer how to understand that action. In narratological terms, they are also metanarrative signs that greet the viewer, connect scenes, and ordain a particular interpretation.[1]

Data such as spectator-narratees and inscriptions are therefore components of metadiscourse, directive comments where another voice can be heard or seen along with the text itself. Metadiscourse instructs about how to interpret the text, presenting an ideal way in the view of the author/artist that excludes other ways.[2] In the example of the Boston pelike, the inscriptions tell the viewer to interpret the entire vase as a single entity and the musician and dancers in the context of particular individuals and elite pederasty.

This chapter is devoted to laying the groundwork for an exploration in Chapter 5 of how *repetition* of these components of written metadiscourse has an effect on the potency of its limiting and directing message. The analysis proceeds chronologically, beginning with the earliest nonverbal directives, "anonymous spectators," and ending with a discussion of the verbal commentary contained in the inscriptions on the vases and how it was "consumed" by the user. Chapter 5 deals with repeated inscriptions explicitly.

REPEATED SPECTATORS AS METADISCOURSE

In the second quarter of the sixth century, several striking new features, both subjects and compositions, appear in the work of one of the prominent artists who decorate Siana cups, the Heidelberg Painter. These new features are of compelling interest in this study, because they depend on repetition and appear to be closely focused on leading the viewer to construct meaning from these repetitions. "A centralized composition, in which the principal figures are flanked by onlookers is one of the chief features of exterior scenes [by the Heidelberg Painter]. Most commonly, the C-Painter and his companions [immediate predecessors of the Heidelberg Painter] arranged their scenes in a repetitive, frieze-like composition, comprising identical single figures or groups or a row of figures moving in one direction."[3]

The Heidelberg Painter also distinguishes himself because he paints different subjects from his immediate predecessors, the C-Painter and his colleagues. Very rarely does the Heidelberg Painter paint *symposia* and *komoi*; instead, he often depicts scenes of military and athletic activities. Several scholars have noted as well the Heidelberg Painter's immense interest in scenes depicting cult and/or myth, particularly those involving Herakles and Dionysos,[4] and they have tied it to widespread enthusiasm for these subjects that vase-painters reflect in the second quarter of the sixth century.[5] With this shift in interest concerning subject-matter comes, in the work of the Heidelberg Painter, his new compositional template for the exteriors of cups.

Although the C-painter and his companions occasionally depict onlookers who are not directly involved in the action, this formula is not a popular compositional scheme for them.[6] Moreover, the forerunners to the Heidelberg Painter only very rarely repeat scenes with onlookers in two fields of a single vase.[7] Because anonymous onlookers, the proliferation of mythical subjects, and repetition are all bound up for the first time in the repertory of the Heidelberg Painter, his repertory warrants close attention.[8]

In several examples by the Heidelberg Painter, repetition of the figures who watch a central scene on each side of the cup engenders syntactical equivalence that is collocative, either synonymous or antonymous.[9] In addition, there is often another another set of comparisons on these cups, unrelated to the repeated spectators, created by repetitions shared among figures involved in the main action on one or both sides and the tondo figure(s).

A cup in Taranto provides a good example[10] [Figures 4.1, 4.2]. Two bearded spectators holding spears watch scenes involving symposiasts, a flute-player, and dancing komast(s). They stand apart from the festivities, observing them. In one case a reclining symposiast plays the flutes, and two komasts dance. In the other, two symposiasts recline and observe, while one komast plays the flutes – making him directly analogous to the symposiast-musician on B – for his dancing companion; in each scene, different objects hang in the field. The spectators provide a consistent syntactical framework for the central scene, and in addition they are a common denominator for two different elements of or moments in a *symposion*. They have no particular obvious connection with the actors or the action.

There is a similar link created by the repetition of spectators in eleven cups by the Heidelberg Painter, most of which are discussed in this study as examples of paradigm-creation or the coupling of mythical *aition* and cult activity in Chapter 7. It is not always possible to be certain of the point the artist makes creating the links, but figuring out what the spectators mean, whom they represent, is crucially important to understanding how the artist expects the viewer to understand the scenes taken together.[11] Because the spectators are explicitly *not* marked as gods or heroes, Brijder is undoubtedly correct when he states that "these men, women, and youths, who are regularly distinguished by smart clothing and fillets, would represent upper-class Athenians."[12] Whether these elite Athenians populated the city in the mythical past or in the sixth-century present is not clear.[13] A careful tally of where such figures appear reveals that when they are not observing, they do not appear involved in other

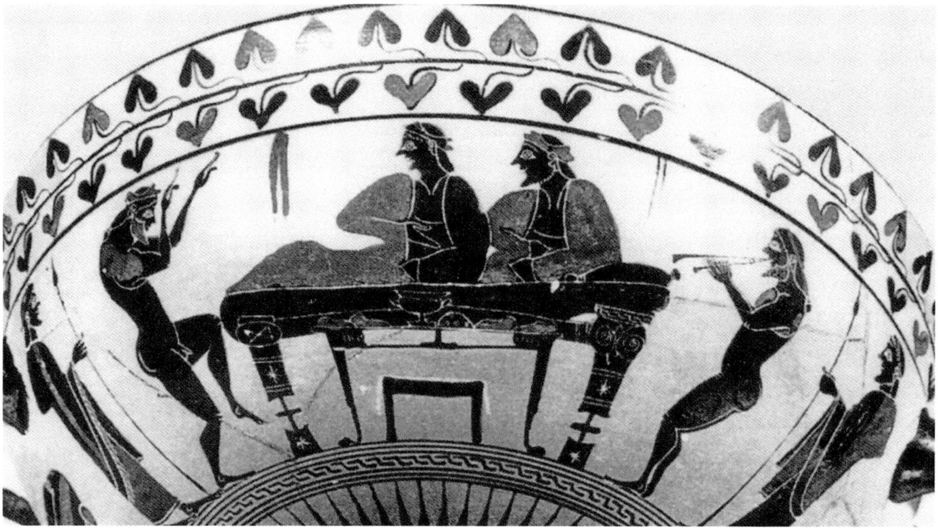

4.1. Siana cup by the Heidelberg Painter, ca. 565–555 B.C. Side A. Taranto, Museo archeologico nazionale 110339. (Photograph © Visual Resources Department, Bryn Mawr College, 2005.)

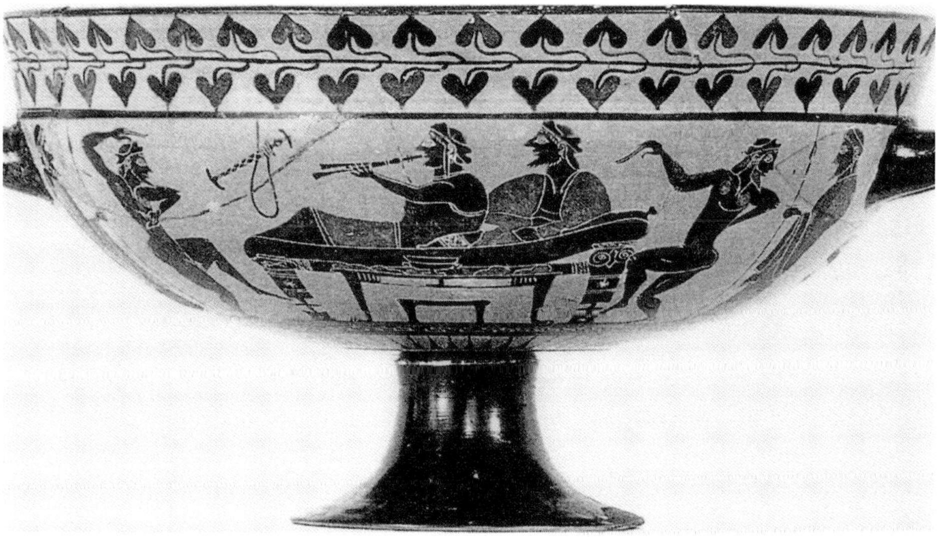

4.2. Siana cup by the Heidelberg Painter, ca. 565–555 B.C. Side B. Taranto, Museo archeologico nazionale 110339. (Photograph © Visual Resources Department, Bryn Mawr College, 2005.)

scenes in the Heidelberg painter's repertory. Modified slightly, with the addition of attributes, they become Dionysiac votaries. Minus their clothing under their fringed *himatia*, they become participants in symposia. They have a special relationship to gods and heroes, whose activities they observe at very close quarters. To dismiss them as "composition-fillers" begs the question, for the artist has selected these particular figures from many possibilities with which to fill the composition. Certainly they can qualify as "ideal" generic elite Athenians. Their rich clothing and elaborately coiffed hair, often bedecked with fillets, and even their attributes are identical to those we see on contemporaneous grave *stelai* and sculpture.[14]

How do these spectators influence the way the viewer of the vase perceives an individual scene? The painted spectators observe the event as it takes place, and to some extent, with their status proclaimed via clothing, gender, and gestures, they evaluate it positively.[15] Although we cannot always identify the scenes framed by the bystanders as particular narratives, we can still borrow insight and terminology from narratological studies to offer us a model for understanding their role. In the analysis of written texts, Labov describes *evaluation* of narrative as

> the means used by the narrator to indicate the point of the narrative, its *raison d'etre*: why it was told and what the narrator is getting at. There are many ways to tell the same story, to make very different points, or to make no point at all ... Every good narrator is continually warding off this question: when his narrative is over, it should be unthinkable for a bystander to say, "So what?"[16]

Alberti is writing on painted narration when he states, very similarly to Labov, that in an *istoria* (his term for a narrative), he likes

> to see someone who admonishes and points out to us what is happening there; or beckons with his hand to see; or menaces with an angry face and with flashing eyes, so that no one should come near; or shows some danger or marvelous thing there; or invites us to weep or laugh together with them. Thus whatever the painted persons do among themselves or with the beholder, all is pointed toward ornamenting or teaching the *istoria*.[17]

As evaluative devices like those described by Labov and Alberti, the spectators may serve as markers that reveal to whom a story is relevant. When we can be certain that the event shown is a narrative, we interpret such figures as narratees, figures depicted in the image who respond to the story or activity taking place.[18] We will use here the term "narratee" even when the text is not a narrative because the figure performs the same function for the non-narrative action, reacting to and evaluating whatever is depicted. Narratee and viewer of the vessel are not the same; the viewer is an actual living being who looks at or reads the text and evaluates it. The narratee and the viewer carry out parallel activities, one a construct of the artist within the image and the other totally independent of the author's creation and beyond his control. Depicted spectators at a mythical central event are narratees, and a living ancient Athenian, an Etruscan from Spina, and a modern scholar are all possible viewers.[19]

Wollheim has written a full analysis of the purpose and effect of the depicted narratee: "The function of the spectator in the picture is that he allows the spectator of the picture a distinctive access to the content of the picture."[20] An Athenian viewing a scene and identifying with the depicted spectator, the narratee, thereby gains a particular kind of access to the story or activity. The purpose for the inclusion of the spectator-narratees is almost didactic, then, meant to require special attention from the viewer to the scenes that the spectators frame. The spectator-narratees thus become markers for imagery that is prescriptive.

What does the *repetition* of spectator-narratees on two sides of a single cup convey? When the spectators are repeated, they guide the viewer to a further point, where the viewer must consider why the two subjects are linked subjects and how the point created through such linked images applies to or instructs about elite values and world view. If the anonymous bystanders, the spectator-narratees, are elites, whether of the mythical, ancient Athens or of the sixth century, the Heidelberg Painter's syntactical invention guarantees that the point made through the comparison of scenes is filtered through the social system, endorsed by the social types for whom the observing figures in the image have particular meaning, either as ancestors or as contemporaries. Although it is very difficult to find patterns in who watches what, there is no doubt that different image-topics are indeed valued differently: Brijder points out that some events are watched only by males, including athletic activities, arming, *komos*, *symposion*, and some mythological subjects; some are watched by a majority of females; but no events are watched by females alone.[21]

To achieve an even greater understanding of how spectator-narratees function in delivering a message, it is possible to equate them, repeated or not, with an additional category of narrative device, a kind of genre-indicator. Some types of narrative have formulaic introductions that alert the audience to the genre of text they are about to hear or read. "Once upon a time" tells the listener that the story to be told may not be based on fact, whereas "A reliable source tells us" suggests that the report ought to be believed.[22] In epic poetry, one familiar example is the invocation to the Muse which can open an epic poem. There is also a formulaic introduction of exempla and mythic paradigms; often the particles καὶ γάρ τε introduce such parallels, so that when the listener hears them, he knows to be prepared for that particular kind of information.[23] When in *Iliad* IX Phoinix brings up to Achilles the evidence to illuminate the present situation through the *litai*, it begins in this way. So, just as a listener to the *Iliad* would know that an exemplum was about to begin, a viewer of a cup with repeated spectators would know at first glance something about how the central scenes on a Siana cup ought to be processed.[24] The frequency and consistency with which framing spectator-narratees appear on these cups indicate that they are likewise formulaic. Do they introduce a particular type of message? Once again, the texts created on these cups are not always identifiable as narratives, but we can understand their function by borrowing a narratological concept: although anonymous elite Athenians do serve as narratees, at the same time they are participants in the action insofar as they are present at the scene. Their dual role, then, includes indicating to whom the message of the vase is relevant and from whom it is sent, and their appearance is a kind of opening statement to a particular audience. The narratee-spectators thus seem to fall easily into that category of metadiscourse called "metanarrative signs;" for our purposes, because we consider texts that are not always certainly identifiable as narratives, we will amend this term slightly to call the class "directives," understanding that such directives are elements of metadiscourse.[25]

To a limited degree, such spectators are also serving a "phatic" function, another feature of metadiscourse. Here we are using the term "phatic" in a way not strictly conforming to the usual understanding of that term among narratologists. Language that serves a "phatic" function is that which centers the communicative act on the *contact* between narrator and narratee.[26] Greetings are phatic elements in ordinary speech. If particular kinds of spectators identify certain topics as relevant to a particular group – upper class Athenians – they act first to establish contact with the proper receivers of the message, a phatic function, and then as both mirror and conduit. In addition to playing phatic and narratee roles, they can, when repeated, create collocative synonymy. In their narratee function, when such bystanders are repeated on each side of a vessel, they bring into comparison, as a central part of the communication event, the two topics they surround. The Heidelberg Painter has therefore invented a new type of composition that communicates several types of message. In these examples, scenes are not only linked and thereby potentially synonymous or antonymous; they are also explicitly earmarked as a relevant combination to a particular audience.

The pot-painter successors of the Heidelberg Painter each use this scheme as well.[27] An amphora in Paris by Lydos, whose career spans the period c. 560–540 B.C., preserves a multifaceted, subtle pairing[28] [Figures 4.3, 4.4]. An image of Herakles and the lion is coupled with a scene of homosexual courtship; repeated framing spectators create a context for comparison of central scenes. Adult males, with beards and hairstyles similar to Herakles' and draped in striped *himatia*, are at the far right of each scene. There is a nude youth on each side as well. The consistent frame unites the taming of the lion by an adult male with the conquest of the *eromenos* by the *erastes*. Moreover, a repeated gesture where two fingers and thumb are extended and raised, called *apagoreuein*, "to forbid," is used by one spectator-narratee on each side: a nude youth on A and a nude adult male on B. Although the connotations of this gesture are not entirely clear, it seems to convey a desire on the part of the user to stop aggression, to indicate that the user calls "time out."[29] The repetition of the gesture, as it links the images on the two sides of the vessel, emphasizes a fundamental similarity in observer-reactions

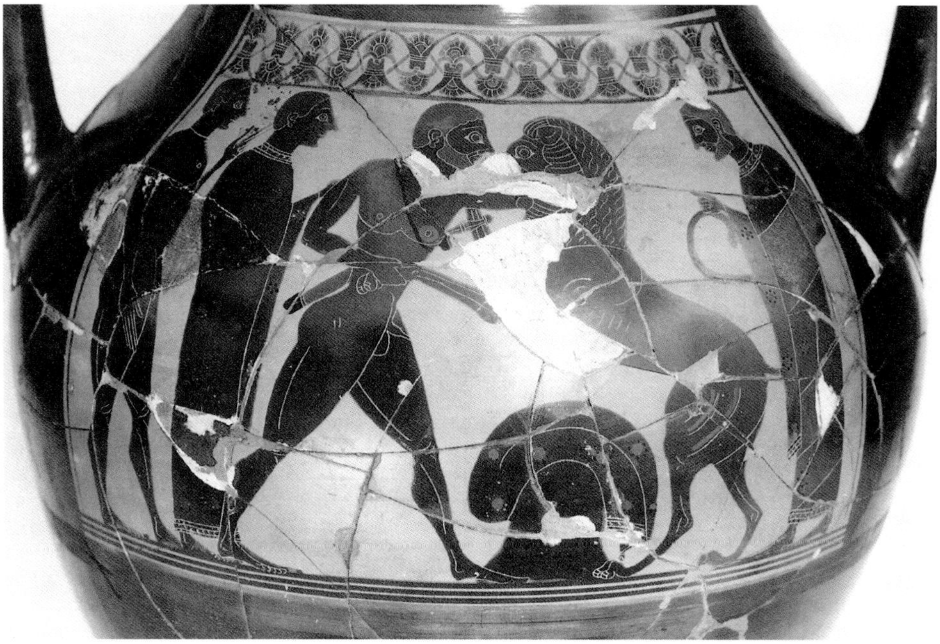

4.3. Black-figure amphora by Lydos, ca. 560–540 B.C. Side A. Paris, Bibliothèque nationale de France, Cabinet des Médailles 206. (Photograph © Bibliothèque nationale de France.)

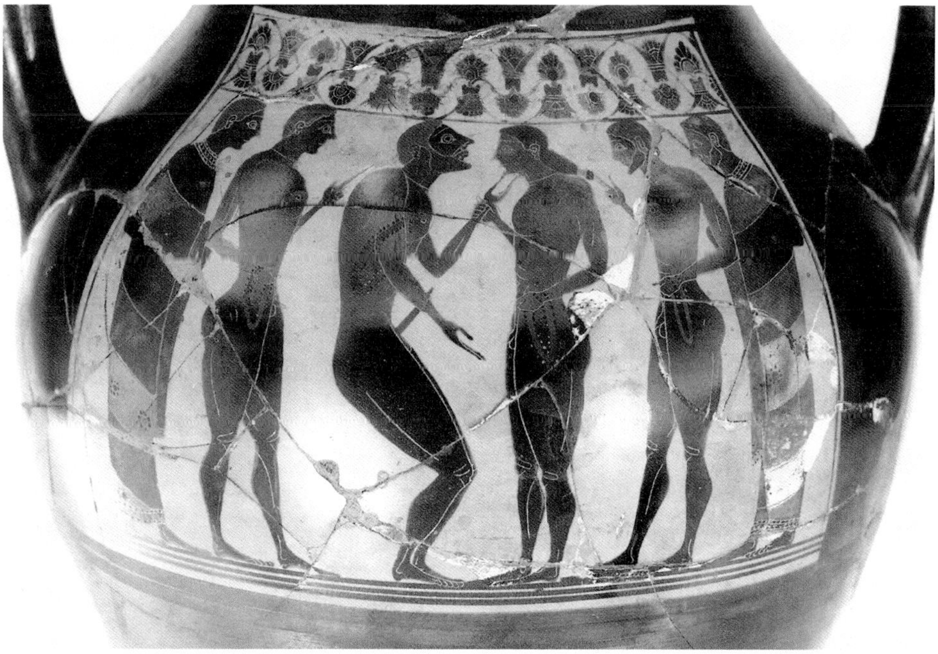

4.4. Black-figure amphora by Lydos, ca. 560–540 B.C. Side B. Paris, Bibliothèque nationale de France, Cabinet des Médailles 206. (Photograph © Bibliothèque nationale de France.)

to the subjugation of the lion and of the *eromenos*. That the couple sharing the gesture are a nude youth (A) and a nude adult male (B) mimicking the couple engaged in a seduction on the center of B suggests that the spectators are processing similarly the message sent by the central actions; their apparent processing of the paradigms is passed on then to their audience, thereby adding another directive.

To understand more about the nature of Lydos' directives, it is informative to explore the other contexts in which the spectators appear. Draped, bearded male figures with short hair like those on the Paris amphora also observe the following events on other amphoras painted by Lydos: boxing, running, wrestling, a man riding on horseback, and a seated old man.[30] These adult males rarely act, but in one case where they do, they are involved in nuptial activities.[31] Draped youths with short hair watch athletes, figures running, military fights, wrestlers, a centauromachy, and Theseus and the Minotaur.[32] Such youths never act; they only observe. Nude youths with short hair and draped youths with long hair are least common: they observe nothing other than homosexual courtship and Theseus' fight with the Minotaur, respectively. In summary, those spectators who do appear on other examples in the painter's repertory can be characterized as follows: they are observers of events and narratees to mythical stories that demonstrate male athletic, military, and social achievement; they are the audience for whom prowess is demonstrated and to whom it is relevant in the images.

The Amasis Painter, active from c. 560–530 B.C., also uses repeated spectators as links. The cup in New York showing the stable of Poseidon and the god's exhortation of troops at Troy serves as an example in Chapter 6 of a mythical narration that lets the viewer recognize both continuity and sequence while lengthening discourse-time[33] [Figures 4.5, 4.6]. The repeated spectators who help to alert the viewer to the fact that the two scenes are connected are narratees corresponding to the best-case viewers of this story: idealized men and youths who themselves would do well to remember the exhortation of Poseidon in battle, and for whom interaction with heroes and divinities is, in the world of images, an expected norm.[34]

Two examples from Group E, dating c. 560–540 B.C., clearly demonstrate affinity with these practices of their contemporaries, Lydos and the Amasis Painter. An amphora in Richmond links two mythical scenes via a repeated bystander, a narratee, who is characterized as military.[35] Male figures wearing high-crested helmets and greaves identifying them as elite warriors watch Herakles and the lion (B) and the birth of Athena (A), and they thereby connect the two events. Both of these strong mythical narratives are thus ordained as relevant to the elite male warrior, who, like lion-conquering Herakles, has Athena for his patron.

On a second Group E example in Munich, anonymous, incongruous spectator-narratees link a total of four scenes. Herakles and the lion appear twice, once

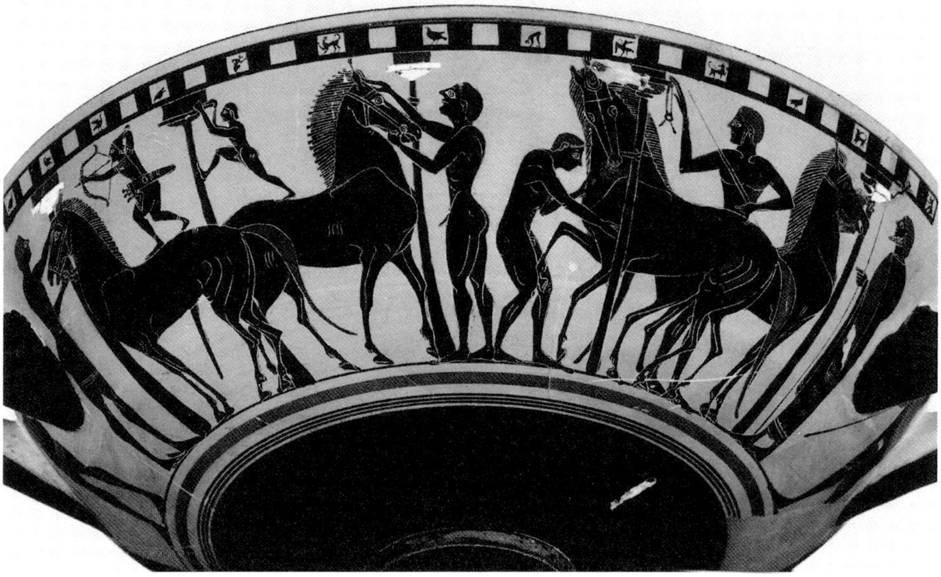

4.5. Black-figure cup by the Amasis Painter, ca. 550–530 B.C. Side A. New York, Metropolitan Museum of Art, Norbert Schimmel Collection 1989.281.62. (Photograph © The Metropolitan Museum of Art, Gift of Norbert Schimmel Trust, 1989. All rights reserved, The Metropolitan Museum of Art.)

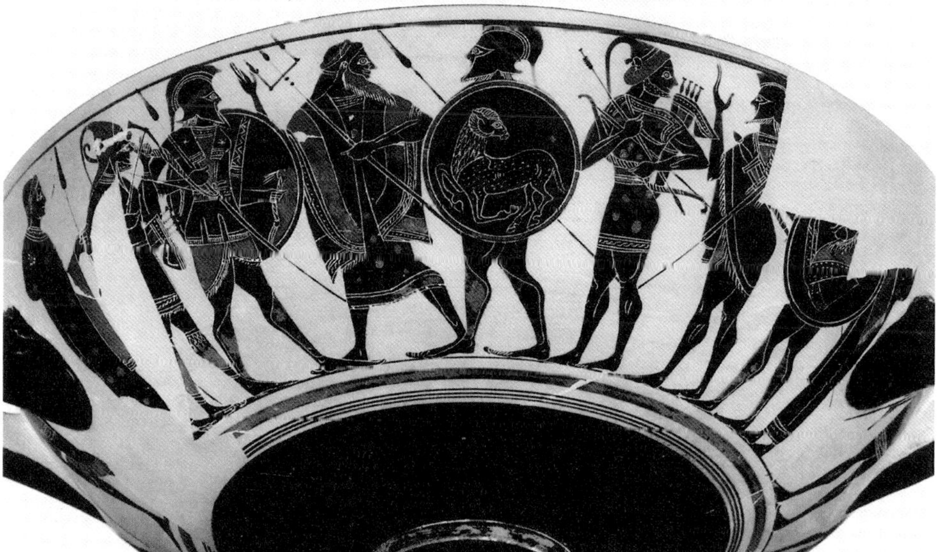

4.6. Black-figure cup by the Amasis Painter, ca. 550–530 B.C. Side B. New York, Metropolitan Museum of Art, Norbert Schimmel Collection 1989.281.62. (Photograph © The Metropolitan Museum of Art, Gift of Norbert Schimmel Trust, 1989. All rights reserved, The Metropolitan Museum of Art.)

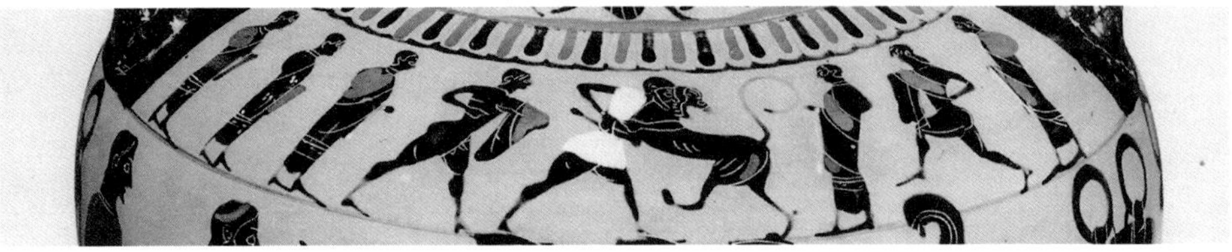

4.7. Black-figure neck-amphora by Group E, ca. 560–540 B.C. Side A, shoulder scene. Munich, Staatliche Antikensammlungen und Glyptothek 1471 (J. 476). (Photograph © Staatliche Antikensammlungen und Glyptothek München [Neg.-Nr. KM 3264].)

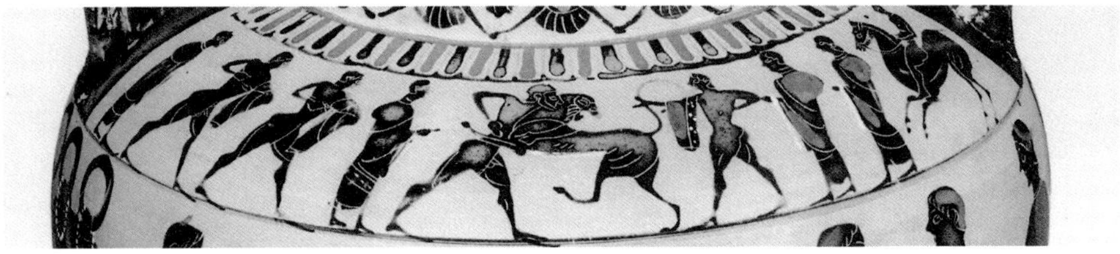

4.8. Black-figure neck-amphora by Group E, ca. 560–540 B.C. Side B, shoulder scene. Munich, Staatliche Antikensammlungen und Glyptothek 1471 (J. 476). (Photograph © Staatliche Antikensammlungen und Glyptothek München [Neg.-Nr. KM 3265].)

on each shoulder[36] [Figures 4.7, 4.8]. The main group itself varies only slightly in each rendering: on one side the lion-fighter wears a white tunic and grasps the lion's left paw with his right hand; on the other, the lion-fighter is nude and plunges a sword into the lion's chest. The spectators, eight in one case and seven in the other, are of four different male figural types, and all appear on each side, with the exception of a man on horseback who appears only on B. They are arranged in different order on each side. So, in the two shoulder panels, the artist has created a situation of difference in the face of much similarity. The artist gives the viewer an analysis of "lion-fighting," one version relying on brute strength alone and the other involving a weapon. The lion-fighters are carefully distinguished. Is a paradigm thus created, with one side depicting Herakles setting an example for his elite mortal analogue on the other? Paradigm-creation is often an ancillary result of the repetition of incongruous, anonymous spectator-narratees and is explored fully in Chapter 7.

The main scenes each preserve similarly posed runners, in one case a nude adult male and youth foot-racers, in the other a *hoplitodromos* [Figures 4.9, 4.10]. The similarities in the runners' poses heighten the contrast between the two events. Both groups are greeted or observed by examples of the same figural types appearing on the shoulders as narratees. Tripods separate the scenes. Clearly the repeated spectators link all four fields on this neck-amphora; there are links created between different types of runners, between all runners and two types of lion-fighter, one using a weapon and another using brute strength. Athletic prowess, military training, and heroic success are linked and, through the identical spectators, marked as significant for elite males.

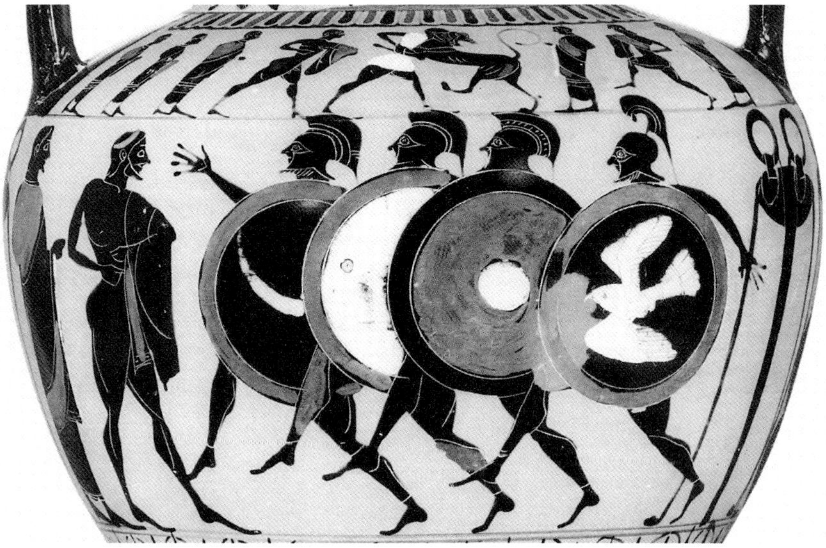

4.9. Black-figure neck amphora by Group E, ca. 560–540 B.C. Side A, main scene. Munich, Staatliche Antikensammlungen und Glyptothek 1471 (J. 476). (Photograph © Staatliche Antikensammlungen und Glyptothek München [Neg.-Nr. KM 3107].)

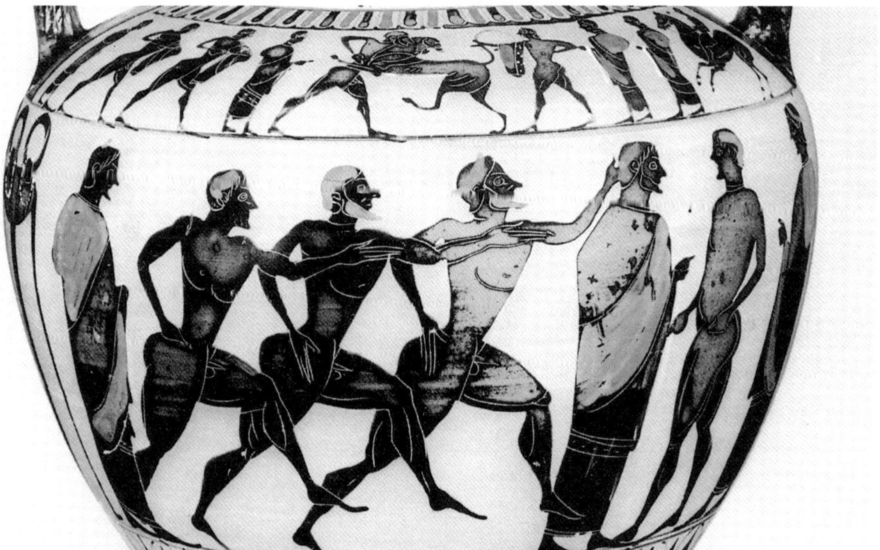

4.10. Black-figure neck-amphora by Group E, ca. 560–540 B.C. Side B, main scene. Munich, Staatliche Antikensammlungen und Glyptothek 1471 (J. 476). (Photograph © Staatliche Antikensammlungen und Glyptothek München [Neg.-Nr. KM 2454].)

WORDS AS METADISCOURSE

The silent bystanders discussed up to this point are not the only device used on vases to direct the audience in interpreting the image. As mentioned at the beginning of this chapter, inscriptions do much the same thing. For example, the inscriptions on the Boston pelike include a great deal of verbal repetition, helping not only to link the sides, but also to name the characters and embed the entire text in the ethos of pederasty and *symposion*. The placement, vocabulary, or both of written inscriptions are often repeated in multiple fields on a single vase, just as images are, so a consideration of repeated inscriptions is therefore integral to this study. This section provides background on inscriptions on Athenian vases, discussing their content, who wrote them, and how they were read. The review of the evidence here is a temporary diversion away from our primary focus on repeated elements, but is a necessary preliminary to the essential analysis of repeated inscriptions in Chapter 5.

The words on a vase are not independent texts; they are part of the total text that is the vase.[37] Their meaning is bound up in the format, the shape itself plus its conventional decorative program. Much is unknown. The precise relationship of some inscriptions to imagery and their role in the viewer's understanding of the vase are unclear. We do not know how often they were read, nor do we know who authored inscriptions. We can only guess at their impact on discourse in their use-setting.

Potentially, inscriptions have a major impact on the interpretation of the images they accompany because of their limiting and directive power. Although inscriptions do not accompany depictions of narratives exclusively, we can once again extrapolate from narratological models to say that inscriptions as a group fall into the category that has illuminated the analysis of spectator-narratees, that of "metanarrative signs," utterances that serve both to organize and to interpret images, called here "directives."[38] According to Prince,

> [Metanarrative signs] point out the set of norms and constraints according to which the text deploys itself and makes sense; they present a model for its decipherment; they put forward a program for its decoding. In other words, they partially show how a given text could be understood, how it wants to be understood . . . On the one hand, then, metanarrative signs help us understand a narrative in a certain way; on the other hand they force us to understand it in this way and not another.[39]

We interpreted the "anonymous spectators" of the Heidelberg Painter and his successors as "narratees," visual equivalents to metanarrative signs that evaluate a text. They may also perform a "phatic" function, to open and keep open the channels of communication between author or artist and reader or viewer. Indeed, written inscriptions can play these same roles. Some are more precisely phatic; for example, those inscriptions that express greetings serve to open a channel of communication as well as to convey particular content.[40] Labels, signatures, and even exclamations all limit and direct how the content of the images is to be perceived.

Background

Categories of Inscriptions

Vase-inscriptions communicate a wide range of information: signatures identifying who made and decorated vases, labels indicating whose image appears on the vase, captions that provide dialogue for figures pictured on the vase, greetings and invitations to the reader of the inscription, sometimes in conversational format, and the announcement that a particular figure, present or not, is handsome or beautiful. Some inscriptions may cross the boundaries of the categories just listed: a painter can be called "*kalos*"; dialogue can be construed as a greeting to the drinker, to the user of the vessel, or to the assembled company at an actual *symposion*; an artist's signature may emerge from the mouth of a komast [Figure 9.4]. In a few cases, this boundary-crossing creates parody. A good number of inscriptions appear to be barely literate or coherent.

Authorship

Who wrote inscriptions? There is consensus among scholars, on both technical and aesthetic grounds, that the placement and actual writing of painted and some carefully incised inscriptions must have been the responsibility of the painter, or at least of someone in his workshop. Kilmer has studied the inscriptions of the earliest painter who wrote extensively on black-figure vases, Sophilos, and he begins his discussion with the assumption that the artist himself wrote the inscriptions, a combination of name-labels, signature, and one caption, and that they reveal his level of literacy.[41] Similarly, Dover, in suggesting that inscriptions could be regarded as "a sequence of letters constituting a decorative motif," appears to regard inscriptions as part of the vase-painter's particular artistic practices.[42]

Dover therefore considers a range of possibilities when trying to explain who "really" authored *kalos* inscriptions, since it seems unlikely that the idea of designating someone as "*kalos*" would originate in the potter's quarter. Dover asks: "who composes the message and to whom does he wish to communicate it? One could imagine that the *erastes* commissioned a vessel which would include an acclamation of his own *eromenos*, thus declaring his passion to his guests at a *symposion* or that he commissioned it in order to give it to his *eromenos*."[43] Dover also suggests that certain inscriptions, including names of well-known persons, could have been selected at random for inclusion on the vessel by the artist: this "would be perfectly acceptable to the participants in an Athenian *symposion* even if they had little idea who exactly [X] was."[44] Dover also suggests that generic formulas like "the boy is beautiful" "[were] freely added to pictures by vase-painters . . . because an Athenian host would not want his guests to think that he was unsympathetic to the pursuit of boys."[45] Finally, he posits that in some instances the painter adapts the vernacular of elite pederasty to use [variations on *kalos*] in praise of his own work.[46] Dover allows for the content of inscriptions to originate with the artist in certain instances and from patron in others, and his view reflects the consensus of opinion. Whether tagged to particular individuals or "floating," *kalos* inscriptions situate the vessel in a particular environment, pederastic discourse in *symposion*, and thereby put the imagery that accompanies them in the same context. Although some of these inscriptions may have no direct relationship to imagery, they play a role in how that imagery is interpreted through the lens of elite pederasty. The *kalos* inscription is therefore a directive, whether originating with patron or artist, that guides and directs interpretation of the imagery on the vessel, narrowing its effect.

The Constructed Author-Artist

Although scholars have been concerned with identifying either artist or patron as author, a model derived from narratology and discussed in this section suggests we should not search for a distinct, living author for inscriptions. In the final product, a single entity *appears* to have "authored" the entire decorative program of the vase, inscriptional content and placement as well as images and ornament. In this model, the patron can supply some of the material while the artist and/or his workshop puts the whole into a final form that will appear to be coherent.

Narratologists observe that regardless of the ultimate source of an author's material, he appears in the created work not transparently as the man himself, but in the form of a "second self." The terms "style," "tone," and "technique" are variously used to name this second self, but each falls slightly short.[47] The sense of the artist and his attitudes we get when reading a work, the "constructed" version of the author, is called the "Implied Author" by some narratologists.[48] As Chatman points out, it is quite possible for a constructed author to be in fact composed of several real individuals: a Hollywood film will have a unified constructed author although it may have been created by several actual individuals. Likewise a folk ballad has a single constructed author but is in fact created over many years with the contributions of many people.[49] Ancient Greek epic is an obvious parallel as well. Similarly, we can see how, for an Athenian vase, the artist, on occasion the patron, and a strong tradition collaborate to create a single constructed author-artist who appears unified. When we read the inscription on the Boston pelike, the enthusiasm over Leagros's looks that helps to establish the lighthearted tone of the vessel is therefore best understood not as a direct communication from the artist or his patron about their personal feelings but is a projection of the constructed second self. Although the real artist might share the views of the constructed self apparent on the vase, we have no way to verify that view nor any reason to believe the artist holds it. That a single artist can have a number of constructed selves becomes clear when we compare different works by the same individual: the tone of Exekias' jocular, punning Athens cup [Figures 2.1, 2.2] is quite different from that of his Philadelphia amphora where heroic corpses lie on the battlefield [Figures 2.5, 2.6]. Euthymides' Boston pelike [Figures 1.1, 1.2] with its superficial tone contrasts with the epic formality of the Amazonomachy of the Morgantina krater [Figure 7.23].

These constructions are expressed through a consistent set of inscriptional categories with limited, repetitive content and the images they accompany are likewise limited and repetitive. The code through which the constructed author-artist is expressed in inscriptions appears to have been developed over decades from about 575 to 480 B.C., and certain consistent features appear, sometimes combined with innovation. In examples by painters who decorate the same type of vessel in the same workshop, such as the Little Masters (discussed in Chapter 5; see Figures 5.1–5.6) or the Pioneers, the constructed author-artists of several different real artists have very similar personalities.[50] In general, true diversity among the constructed author-artists who appear on Athenian vases is fairly limited. Originality takes shape through new and unexpected combinations, where an artist's signature or *kalos* inscription appears as performed song, for example.

The Intended Viewer

Like all texts, the repertory of inscriptions through which the constructed author-artist reveals himself anticipates a particular type of reader.[51] This ideal intended reader, called the Implied Reader by some narratologists, is recoverable by us through analysis of topics and vocabulary. The intended reader is literate, is willing to name the artist of a work, knows who youths such as Leagros are, what *kalos* means beyond simply "handsome," likes punning and verbal tricks, and identifies heroes and gods who appear in familiar stories. He may want to comment on what he sees. He likes to get the better of others by setting them up to look foolish, and may be the victim of others doing likewise to him. In short, the intended reader for Athenian vases with inscriptions appears to have an elite frame of reference most at home with elite conviviality as expressed in *symposion*. The case to support this claim is laid out fully in Chapter 11.

To construct the appropriate ethos, to be "good," the artist needs to project elite norms along with knowledge of how elites enculturate themselves and distinguish themselves from other groups. The result can have the appearance of the individual artist getting the better of the intended viewer, of artistic self-promotion or even self-deprecation. The living artist may appear to the modern viewer to "one-up" the elite user of the vessel in a person-to-person manner, but it is in fact the constructed author-artist who does so. The social code prizes making-fun highly, ultimately as a validation of existing social hierarchies. Thwarting of expectation, tricks, and games are likewise part of the elite code. The constructed author-artist has created the possibility of games permitting one-upsmanship because the intended reader requires it. In Chatman's terms, "no matter how indispensable to it [the narrative transaction] is in an ultimate practical sense," the persona of the Implied Author [constructed author-artist] is a careful construction, coded and fine-tuned to meet the expectations and the requirements of an Implied Reader [intended viewer].[52] In this case, when the text, the vase, is used in an Athenian *symposion*, the intended and real viewers are apparently extremely close together, almost one and the same, as is fully explored in Chapter 11.

The constructed author-artist provides mechanisms by which he informs the real viewer how to perform as the intended viewer. One such mechanism, discussed above, is the narratee-character, the anonymous spectator. When the narratee materializes as a character in the world of the text itself, perhaps identified through an inscription, he or she thereby makes even more explicit the desired audience stance from within the world of the text.[53] Iolaos and Athena, when they watch Herakles fight the Nemean lion, are spectator-narratees with proper names. Inscriptions that are part of the original decorative program of the vase are not clearly manifestations of the real author's opinions or of his power; rather they are part of his artful construction of an author-artist, what the community of craftsmen/artists know the constructed self must project in order to be successful in the opinion of their patrons.

Graffiti Inscriptions

Improvised inscriptions, *graffiti*, were most likely added after the vessel left the painter's domain, perhaps in the use-context of the vessel or in close anticipation of it. They create a disruption of the persona of the original constructed author-artist. A small group of such inscriptions cite "according to whose opinion" a particular thing is the case.[54] When we read that "so-and so is lewd to the one who wrote (this)," as an incised example, on a black-glaze vessel dating to about the mid-fifth century, ΣΟΣΙΑΣ ΚΑΤΑΠΥΓΟΝ | *h*ΟΣΦΗΣΙΝ*h*ΟΓΡΑΦΣΑΣ ["Sosias is a 'lewd fellow' (so) says the writer"], the very immediacy that the incision and careless script imply suggests that the real writer will be present with the individual who is the object of derision when the inscription is read in its intended context.[55] The "font" tells the audience that the inscription was not planned in advance – the reader will suspect that it was just added. The object of the jibe will have to guess who among the assembled company "really" holds the opinion.

READING THE INSCRIPTIONS

Who were the real readers of inscriptions, and if anyone did read them, did they read them silently or aloud? There is very little evidence to answer this question. Athenaeus, in listing types of sympotic vessels, includes a category called "lettered cup."[56] Two of his sources, the comic poets Alexis and Eubulus, date to the fourth century, and are late for this discussion. A third example is fifth century: a fragment of a satyr-play by Achaeus of Eretria (active just after 450 B.C.) portrays a satyr-character reading an inscribed skyphos. The vessel is animate; the satyr refers to the cup as calling him. The satyr then recites aloud the letters of Dionysos' name; he never puts the letters together into a single word but he apparently expects his audience to be able to do so through hearing rather than seeing.[57] Svenbro points out that the satyr is a parody of a successful reader: the satyr understands the vessel to have its own voice rather than one provided by himself, the reader. The satyr does not truly read the inscription, because he knows only the names of the letters and not how to understand the words composed of them.[58] The parodic context of this evidence, a satyr-play, makes it nearly impossible to apply it to understanding how a vase-inscription might be read in its actual use-context. The more general evidence for reading aloud versus silent reading in the archaic and classical periods, elusive as it is, can put reading vase-inscriptions into a hypothetical scenario at best.

Scholarly discourse on early reading has followed a polemic route. An article written by Balogh in 1927 made a case that reading out loud was the norm and silent reading was extremely rare in antiquity. Because there is so much evidence to the contrary, a succession of subsequent writers have argued against Balogh's view; most influential are articles by Knox and more recently Gavrilov and Burnyeat.[59] Simultaneously, discussions of the origins of literacy and a recognition that most early poetry, as well as early prose texts, was performed and perceived orally and aurally have appropriately raised sensitivity to the probable centrality of reading aloud.[60]

There is controversy about whether *scripta continua*, writing without breaks between words and little or no punctuation, is most easily read silently or aloud. The extant early texts written in *scripta continua* most like vase-inscriptions in their content and epigraphical style are on gravestones and dedications. Svenbro, in a thorough study of such inscriptions, has offered the very influential opinion that such inscriptions written in *scripta continua* are only comprehensible when sounded out aloud: he claims that because the individual words are not visually divided, the reader can make distinctions only when he makes the test audible.[61] Gavrilov has made precisely the opposite argument, relying on the results of research by psychologists who specialize in the acquisition and performance of reading, in the relationship between reading silently and orally, and in both reading speed and comprehension: "it is quite likely that the ability to read to oneself and to scan ahead may be all the more necessary for reading aloud from texts written in *scripta continua*."[62] A related viewpoint, stressing the difficulty of reading unpunctuated, undivided words, is Thomas' idea that early poetic and civic texts written in *scripta continua* were so user-unfriendly because their purpose was not so much to be read *per se* but rather to provide a mnemonic for "what people already knew or were going to learn by heart."[63] If that point of view is applied to the *scripta continua* on vases, it is not promising for the case that such writing was read aloud. Many inscriptions on vases are single words, however, so the issue of reading *scripta continua* is irrelevant in those cases.

The argument for reading aloud or silently ultimately arises from a study of the verbs used to describe the activities of reading. These verbs fall into two categories: a group that certainly implies that the act of reading involves speaking and hearing, ἐπιλέγεσθαι, "to speak," and ἀκούω, "to listen or hear"; and another group that certainly can include speaking and listening, but does not strictly require that interpretation: ἀναγιγνώσκω or "recognize," and ἀνανέμεσθαι, "distribute."

The earliest example preserved in a poetic text, c. 475 B.C., illuminates some of the difficulties: Pindar in *Olympian* 10, 1–3 asks the Muse to inspire him using the language of reading. He says, "read to me" (ἀνάγνωτέ μοι) "where it is written" (πόθι . . . γέγραπται) "in my mind" (φρενὸς ἐμᾶς). The poet embeds his obligation to compose an ode in the language of debt and repayment, and ordinarily an account-keeper would read aloud such an obligation to a debtor from a written record. Although many scholars believe the metaphor for how the Muse communicates with Pindar likewise relies on the idea of reading aloud, the example is not altogether clear.[64] The next cluster of preserved prose examples are Herodotean passages dating to about 425 B.C.; several are unequivocal evidence that reading is oral: ἐπιλέγω and λέγω, both forms of "to speak," signify a reading by the Ionians of a message from Themistokles carved in stone (VIII.22). Other written texts certainly identify hearing as crucial to reading: in Hdt I.124–5, ἔλεγε is "he read" a letter, and ἀκούσας is "having read." Gavrilov believes this is an epistolary metaphor for a conversation between friends;[65] Schenkeveld provides examples to prove that such an interpretation need not always be the case.[66] For purposes here, the language used to describe reading correspondence seems to be a special case and probably not immediately relevant to inscriptions on pottery.

Svenbro analyzes inscriptions on stone to demonstrate that early reading was embedded in orality. He makes the case that an epigram in honor of Mnesitheos from Euboea and dating 500–450 B.C. uses ἀνανέμεσθαι, "to distribute," to mean "to read" and that distribution necessarily means oral dissemination; he offers a new reconstruction of the text of the epigram to demonstrate that a second instance in the same epigram uses λέγω in its future form, ἐρεῖ, for the imperative "read."[67]

Fifth century texts from Aristophanes and Euripides demonstrate that silent reading of ordinary texts took place by the end of the fifth century;[68] and an important passage in Plato uses the verbs ἀκούω "to hear" and ἀναγιγνώσκω (*Phaedo* 97c) "to recognize" for the perception and acts of reading to describe slow, public reading but the verbs ὁράω "to see" and again ἀναγιγνώσκω (98c) "to recognize" to describe fast individual reading – even skimming – of the text.

There is no doubt that descriptions of the act of reading rely heavily on the language of orality, and that reading and comprehending reading had origins in audible discourse.[69] There is also much evidence to suggest that some reading was done silently. As Thomas indicates, there must have been texts and occasions appropriate for both silent and out-loud reading.[70] The only evidence contemporaneous with the sixth century vase-inscriptions is from dedicatory and commemorative inscriptions on monuments, and in content and construction they are not parallel to vase-inscriptions.

Boardman, in an effort to contradict the argument that vase-inscriptions were intended to be read aloud, has pointed out that images of readers on Athenian vases consistently show them with mouths closed. Contrastingly, artists depict singers, many with poetic texts emerging from their mouths, with mouths open.[71] A cup by Epiktetos presents an interesting combination of image and text that demonstrates how complicated the evidence actually is.[72] Side B of the cup shows a komast dancing while urinating into an oinochoe; he reaches toward a cup held by a companion who dips wine from a krater. From the dancing komast's closed mouth emerges not a song, but the painter's signature, ΕΠΙΚΤΕΤΟΣ | ΕΓΡΑ. .ΕΝ, "Epiktetos painted [it]" [Figure 9.4]. Surely a komast does not speak aloud with his mouth closed, yet the artist apparently means to indicate that he utters the signature. The intended viewer may also utter the words when he reads the inscription. The komast is then parallel to the user of the vessel – both use cups painted by Epiktetos and both state "Epiktetos painted it."[73]

Recently scholars influenced by Svenbro's contention that inscriptions on vases, like all early inscriptions (in his view), were read aloud have offered specific scenarios for how such reading aloud played out in *symposion*. These reconstructions originate in Svenbro's statement, "an inscription was a machine for producing *kleos* – 'acoustic renown.'"[74] In his view, vase-inscriptions induce repetition of their contents, which include names of living individuals, over and over in repeated uses of the vessel, by means of the reader's voice.

Snodgrass reconstructs a sympotic scenario replete with inscriptions as prompts for acoustic renown and other verbal interaction thus:

> Just as the numerous visual portrayals of symposiasts on these vessels would fit in smoothly with the real life enactment of very similar scenes, so the presence of writing would have its place in the atmosphere of convivial challenges, competitive recitation and singing, amorous discourse and table-games, which we know prevailed. A drinker would read out the inscriptions to his neighbors and thereby, especially in the caption – or portrait-*kalos* inscriptions – find himself involved in a sort of impromptu and involuntary exposition of the scenes to which they belonged. He would be identifying for the company the heroes portrayed in a legendary scene; or the boys or *hetairai* in a genre picture – with the faint possibility that the latter, at least, were physically present to hear the performance. He would likewise have to divulge the subjects of the detached *kalos* inscriptions without a picture, and perhaps to describe or more

> fully identify their subjects for the benefit of the uninitiated. He might even – though this is harder to imagine – read out the painters' and makers' signatures: a suggestion that seems slightly less far-fetched in the case of the drinking cups where the physical attributes of the vessel will have played some role in its user's performance at the game of *kottabos*. The likelihood that a participant at a *symposion* could bring his own cup with him, as was certainly sometimes the case, gives an added edge to this imaginary picture. The cup would then serve not only as a talking point at the party (with the added near-literal sense that an inscribed cup would be "talking" itself), but as a source of pride to its owner, who could repeatedly present its iconography and inscriptions to new audiences.[75]

N. Slater, writing simultaneously with Snodgrass and unaware of the latter's work, creates a very similar picture. Focusing on *kalos* inscriptions in particular, he casts them not as representations of speech, but as prompts for the creation and dissemination of a culture of fame. Therefore reading aloud is also intrinsic to his understanding of the function of inscriptions.[76]

This construct, that the inscription was read aloud to create sympotic conversation, becomes perplexing when we try to factor in those inscriptions that contain the pronoun "me." Who is this "me" sometimes referred to in vase-inscriptions? When the vase tells us "so-and-so made me" it is obvious that the reader who speaks those words aloud is speaking in the voice of the object. Svenbro, when discussing similar types of inscriptions in stone, suggests that the "I" (= me) serves to make the considered *object* inescapably present and thereby distances the *writer* from the "communication event."[77] Indeed there are numerous other ways in which the vase is personified, giving it an identity different from but parallel to the painter, potter, and inscription writer. It might have body parts, in either shape or decoration, like sexual organs or eyes. Lissarrague has written about the ways in which the vessel as a container for wine and the body of the symposiast as another container for wine exist in a metaphoric relationship that is often exploited by potter and painter in an interactive game for the purpose of exploring the "other."[78] The patron who says "So-and-so made me" makes himself like the vessel – filled with wine mixed with water. Nevertheless, there is a fundamental difference between those inscriptions where the vase refers to itself and those which, when read by the reader, could at least theoretically be his own: "Welcome!" "Have a drink!" "So-and-so is handsome!" even "So-and so painted THIS (!)" could all be sensible utterances of the reader. Moreover, there are examples where both types of inscriptions are mixed together on a single vessel.[79] This difference in "speaker" does not concern us here except except that it allows us to confirm that the purchaser and his guests operate in a system where an intended reader will in an *ideal* use context read whatever is written aloud (regardless of what he does in an actual situation), and may take on a variety of roles.[80]

This discussion concludes that the constructed author-artist expects the intended reader to read inscriptions. On some occasions a real reader probably read them aloud, possibly in the context of *symposion*. Inscriptions written in meter support this contention. For example, Exekias' signature on his Berlin amphora uses unusual orthography, leaving out a vowel, to create a perfectly designed signature that yields an iambic trimeter, ΕΧΣΕΚΙΑΣΕΓΡΑΦΣΕΚΑΠΟ[ ]ΕΣΕΕΜΕ, "Exekias painted and made me."[81] Many inscriptions certainly reflect and repeat typical sympotic conversation, may have been read aloud in context, and could serve as prompts for or transcripts of that conversation. The inscriptions often evoke *symposion*, bringing it into whatever space the vase occupies.

Vases are vehicles with a set of conventional controls or directives for how the traditional and social material they convey is interpreted. The images present one aspect of the interpretation of this material, and the observers of action, bystanders, serve as one category of metadiscourse. The addition of inscriptions helps further to limit and direct how the vase, together with its imagery, is interpreted. The written script, if spoken aloud, will not determine everything that is said about the images or the vase, but it may focus and narrow reaction to these images. A more complete analysis of how vases function in their use-context is taken up in Chapter 11; this discussion has now laid the groundwork for assessing the way in which *repeated* inscriptions coordinate with image and shape to create meaning. Some effects are lost if the writing is read silently, and many are enhanced if it is read aloud.

FIVE

READING WRITING[1]

This chapter looks at vases with repeated inscriptions, where either the placement is identical or content is repeated in two different fields. It builds on the conclusions reached in Chapter 4, which set out the case for seeing spectators and inscriptions as conventions with meaning beyond their face value, as devices having the potential to direct how the viewer should interpret the imagery on a vase. When these devices are repeated, their impact is increased, because they then both link and emphasize. The inscriptions on the Pioneer Boston pelike include repetitions with difference, helping to emphasize the same characteristic in the images[2] [Figures 1.1, 1.2]. Likewise, Exekias' cup in Athens that began the discussion in Chapter 2 preserves repeated sounds in letters placed identically on each side of the cup [Figures 2.1, 2.2]. The identical positions coupled with misspelling in the one case suggest that one inscription is a parody of the other.[3]

This discussion provides an overview of repeated inscriptions, identifying the categories into which they fall and discussing briefly some examples of each category. It investigates their relationship to repeated imagery to see how they reiterate, amplify, distort, undermine, ignore, or even replace its effect. Writing on vessels can communicate through where it is located on the vessel as well as through the content of the words. Repetition in inscriptional placement encourages the viewer to connect physically separated messages, and often meaning is completed or enhanced when they are read together. As established in Chapter 4, the meaning conveyed through the inscriptions is often metadiscursive, devoted to instruction on how to interpret the vase. Some inscriptions provide reactions to images in ways similar to depicted bystanders who serve as narratees; one goal of this chapter is to chart the evidence for such equivalence.

BACKGROUND

It is uncertain, as discussed in Chapter 4, whether or not ancient users read the inscriptions at all and if they did whether silently or audibly. Many of the examples discussed here support the belief that good constructed author-artists showed sensitivity to the sounds created by their writing. Some inscriptions use visual means – relating signature with imagery in particular ways – to suggest parallels between the utterance of artists' names and the reading or singing of poetry in *symposion*.[4] On the plain lip cup in Athens discussed in Chapter 2, Exekias clearly considered the effects of both orality and repetition[5] [Figures 2.1, 2.2]:

ΕΧΣΕΚΙΑΣΕΠΟΙΕΣΕΝ	eks ee key us ***eh**p **oi eh sen***
ΕΝΕΟΙΝΟΙΟΙΕΝ	en ***eh oi**n **oi oi en***.

Side A records the artist's signature, and complementing this on side B is a rhyming nonsense inscription playing on the word "*oinos*" "wine" and the closeness of its sound to "*epoiesen*," "made [it]".[6] Immerwahr names such examples, where the syllables remind the reader of a real word, "mock" inscriptions. Exekias is working here within a convention for repeated inscriptions established for Little Master cups, a convention similar to repeated images that create parody when they are very like one another but with crucial differences.[7] Imagine one person holding his cup up and reading "his" side: if read aloud, the artist's signature will sound coherent. His partner, reading the other inscription, will sound similar, but drunk.[8]

Inscriptions Continued from A to B

Little Master cups, created c. 550–525 B.C., are the earliest vessels to give prominence to writing in their decoration, and often, to get a complete message, the reader(s) must read both sides of a vessel.[9] Two good early examples relying on script are Little Master cups dating to the second quarter of the sixth century signed by Ergotimos and Kleitias, with A identifying the potter and B the painter:[10]

ΕΡΓΟΤ[ΙΜΟΣΜΕΠΟΙ]ΕΣΕΝ	"Ergotimos made me"
[ΚΛΕΙΤ]ΙΑΣΜΕΓΡΑΦΣΕΝ	"Kleitias painted me"

The reader must consult both sides to understand fully who collaborated to create the vessel and is encouraged to link the two inscriptions by the very similar appearance of each inscription and their identical placement on each side. Sentence structure and verbal syntax, in addition to the visual, is repeated: subject–direct object–verb. The direct object in both cases is elided. The reader finds difference in content in the face of great similarity of appearance, whereas the two inscriptions together very clearly create a coherent text. The content directs the viewer to analyze the vessel, to consider separately the two features of shape and decoration. The authors were confident that the user would be looking at both sides of the cups.

The general concept of distributing meaning over two sides of a vase is frequently paralleled in the visual testimony, as we have established. Examples discussed in Chapter 2 extend narrative by placing two episodes on different sides of the vase while including visual repetitions to induce the viewer to connect the two;[11] another example is provided by images on two sides combining to create an entire, integrated image, such as chariot harnessing[12] [Figures 2.3, 2.4; 2.5, 2.6]. Placing the artists' names in the main decorative zone is a strategy that promotes the creators of the vessel above its other features, not likewise highlighted by the artists. Visually similar to the examples by Ergotimos and Kleitias are two cups by Eucheiros where the inscription tells us on one side that Eucheiros made it and on the other that Eucheiros is the son of Ergotimos.[13] However, the painter has rearranged the expected order of things by separating the potter's name and the patronymic; side A gives what can suffice as the entire story, as on numerous other examples: so-and-so made (it). The addition of the patronymic in a separate visual field requires the reader to consult the other side in order to understand B at all.

ΕΥΧΕΡ⟨Ο⟩ΣΕΠΟΙ{Ο}ΕΣΕΝ	"Eucheiros made (it)"
*h*ΟΡΓΟΤΙΜΟ*h*ΥΙ*h*⟨Υ⟩Σ	"The son of Ergotimos"

The visual similarities between the inscriptions – they are identically placed on their respective sides of the vessel – link the two sides, and their meaning is exceptionally closely intertwined. The author expects the reader to hold the content of one inscription in his mind or in his ear as he or another person reads the other.

The bilingual painters continue a similar practice in the last quarter of the sixth century. Often, though not always, the two inscriptions will occupy the identical syntactical space, for example, along the top of the scene, just below the rim of a cup. Both Psiax and Epiktetos, on a variety of shapes, identify painter on one side and potter on the other.[14] Two cups by Epiktetos identify the painter on one exterior side and the potter in the interior tondo;[15] a variation on this scheme places the painter's name on one side, the verb on the other, and the potter's signature complete in the tondo.[16] Finally, there are vases where only one artist is identified, and the name appears on one side of the exterior and the verb on the other.[17] Without turning the vase around, it is impossible to get the total meaning. The practices are so widespread as to inspire absolute confidence that these bilingual artists took steps to direct viewers to take into account all fields of the vase. The Pioneers, around 510 B.C., also use this scheme, although much less often. On a rare example, Euphronios signs as painter on one side of the exterior of the foot and Chachrylion as potter on the other side.[18] The evidence of divided signatures suggests that craftsmen expected viewers to look at all fields of a vessel, put information together, and thereby achieve a greater total meaning. The metadiscursive directive to make the connection is most often the repetition of the placement of the inscription, identical on each side.

Inscriptions Continued from A to B with Added Words

Most examples combine divided signatures or their approximations with other kinds of verbal and visual repetitions; the effects are indeed intricate, communicating on several levels to engage the viewer with the vase. A good example is the extremely expressive and well-known Munich cup by Glaukytes and Archikles, c. 575 B.C. depicting scenes of Theseus and the Minotaur (A) and the Calydonian boar hunt (B) [Figures 5.1, 5.2]. It includes three types of text in addition to declaration of authorship: a conversational greeting, labeling of sphinxes (twice), and labeling of the figures that populate the mythical scenes.[19] Exact repetition is reserved for the two handle-areas, and the reader must connect the inscriptions to know the joint authorship of the cup:

ΓΛΑΥΚΥΤΕΣ|ΜΕΠΟΙΕΣΕΝ "Glaukytes made me"
ΑΡΧΙΚΛΕΣ|ΕΠΟΙΕΣΕΝ "Archikles made (it)"

The parallel compositions suggest equivalence of artistic contribution. As is common, the reader is required to put the inscriptions on the two sides together to get the entire message. In addition to the repetition of the verb, the labeling of the sphinxes and the greeting "XAIPE" are repeated at each handle, thereby adding two additional levels of discourse: the labels inform about the images, whereas the greeting reaches outside the discussion of authorship and story to embed the vessel in sympotic discourse. These greetings perform a phatic function, as discussed in Chapter 4, as anonymous bystanders or "spectator-narratees" on some vessels, establishing contact for the dissemination of messages the imagery sends. Greetings written on vases also serve this purpose in a very obvious way, informing the audience to be on alert for a message; when the greetings employ language typical of *symposion*, they further inform the reader about the nature of the message and the setting where the conversation is expected to take place. Greetings repeated on more than one field of a vessel connect fields, uniting all of them in sympotic ethos. Moreover, repeated comments create conversation, a template for an actual communication event consisting of greeting and response.

The similarity in the placement and orientation of the inscriptions engages the viewer to connect all of the inscriptions on one side. Labels are vertical and nonsensical on A, but horizontal with correctly spelled names on B. The inscriptional placement echoes the active poses (horizontal) of the boar hunters on B and likewise

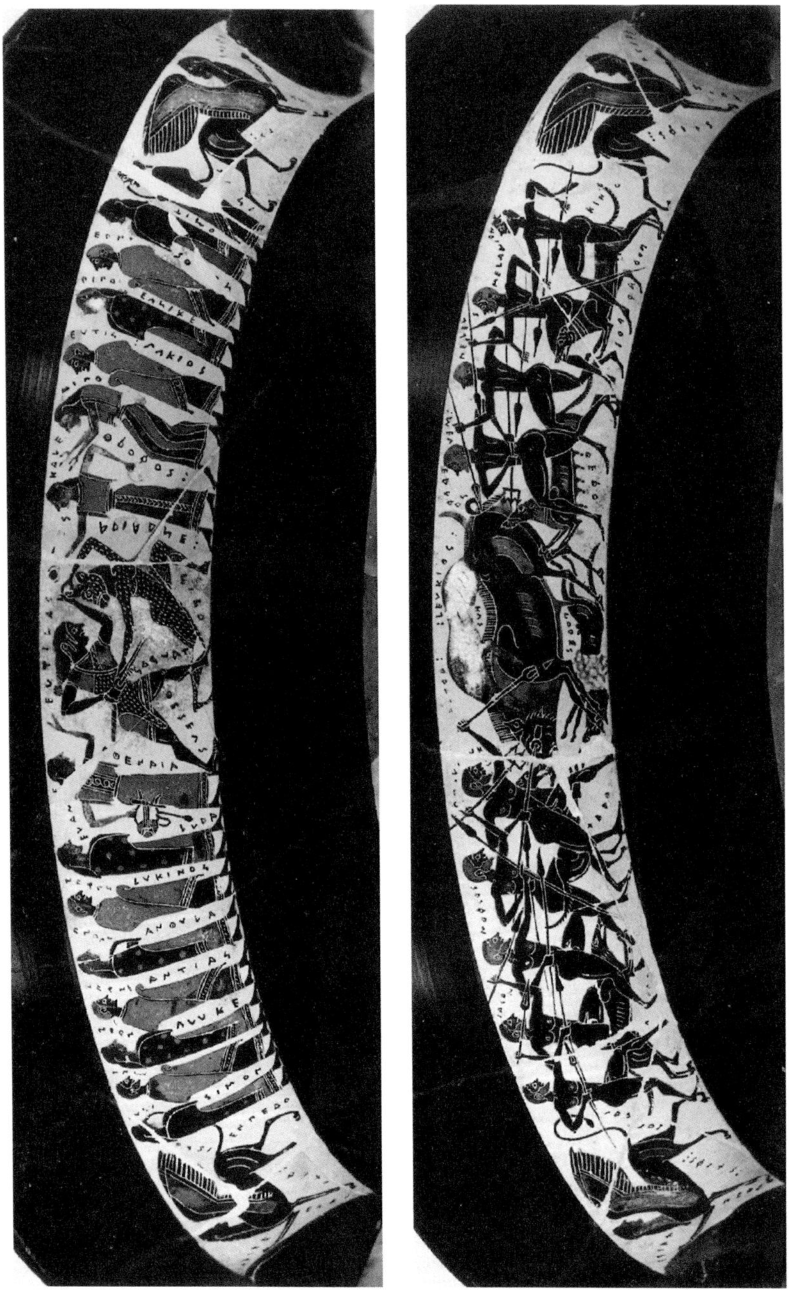

5.1

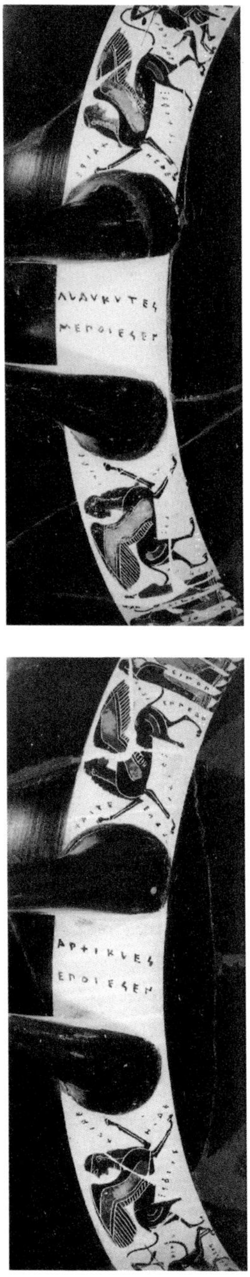

5.2

the static (vertical) poses of the Minotaur fight on A. The two scenes are in every respect quite distinct, essentially antonymous, as is appropriate for two distinct types of heroic adventure, the single fight versus the group hunt. The divided signature, however, creates a metadiscursive directive that works against the division created by the contrasting labels and compositions. Because the viewer must unite the inscriptions under the handles, he is in the process compelled to unite the A and B sides as well.

The cup in the British Museum signed by Phrynos employs conventions similar to those on the Archikles and Glaukytes cup, but in a novel and engaging way[20] [Figures 5.3, 5.4]. The inscription on B is a response to A, and the images on A are prior those on B, thus setting up a parallel dynamic. Side B depicts a seated Zeus receiving a striding Athena who drags Herakles to him by the arm; side A shows the birth of Athena. Although Athena's hairdo is similar on both sides, her *peplos* is different and she carries no shield on B; on side A, Zeus wears garments identical to his garments on B and sits on a throne identical to that on A, as Athena emerges from his head. In addition to the figures, the word XAIPE, "welcome," is repeated, and a drinking inscription appears on each side, centered identically under the figures:

A: ΦΡΥΝΟΣΕΠΟΙΕΣΕΝΧΑΙΡΕΜΕΝ	"Phrynos made (it); Welcome"
B: ΧΑΙΡΕΚΑΙΠΙΕΙΜΕΝΑΙΧΙ	"Welcome and drink me, yes indeed!"

The two parts of the conversation acknowledge one another – the NAIXI on B responds to the declaration on A in the same way the inscriptions connect on the Boston pelike that introduced this study.

On this cup, parallel texts, not apparently interacting, have been constructed – images on one level and words on the other. On the mythical level, we see two events that cannot be simultaneous linked by repetitions in the identities of two of the protagonists, as in Zeus' appearance and in Athena's; Athena's birth must be prior to her presentation of Herakles to Zeus. On the "conversational" level, the repeated word XAIPE, each time directly under Zeus, links two statements, thereby creating a sequence of statements, one later because it is a response to the other. The author, rewarding the reader for considering both sides of the cup together, cleverly integrates the artist's signature into the discourse. The author both establishes contact through

←

5.1. Black-figure cup by Archikles and Glaukytes, ca. 560–540 B.C. Sides A and B. Munich, Staatliche Antikensammlungen und Glyptothek 2243 (J. 333). (Photograph © Staatliche Antikensammlungen und Glyptothek München.)

5.2 Black-figure cup by Archikles and Glaukytes, ca. 560–540 B.C. Side A, under handle, and Side B, under handle. Munich, Staatliche Antikensammlungen und Glyptothek 2243 (J. 333). (Photograph © Staatliche Antikensammlungen und Glyptothek München.)

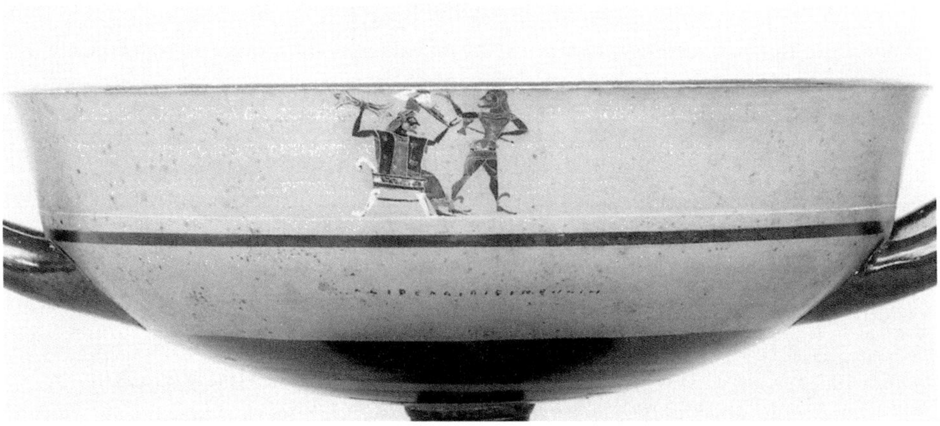

5.3. Black-figure cup by Phrynos, ca. 560–540 B.C. Side A. London, British Museum B 424. (Photograph © Copyright The Trustees of The British Museum.)

the phatic "welcome!" and attempts to script and to direct how the user(s) will interact with the cup. There is a sequence of inscription from A to B and a complementary sequence of images; this combination, as part of the viewing experience, plays games with temporal expectation.

Later artists also use a repeated greeting. At c. 530 B.C. Oltos' fragmentary Vienna amphora is one such example, preserving ΧΑΙΡΕ on each side along with labels naming divinities and the images of gods and goddesses.[21] The human reader of the "welcome" may appear to "speak" to or for the divinities, for if he reads aloud from left to right, he says "Athena . . . welcome!" The localization in the divine sphere of the conventional *sympotic* greeting ΧΑΙΡΕ on the vase further diminishes the distance between elites and divinities, who are depicted as using a common human greeting. The immediacy of the greeting also serves to minimize temporal differences between the human here-and-now and a time when humans and mortals intermingled.

Side A of the c. 530 B.C. multiauthored cup by Epiktetos, Paidikos, and an artist painting in the manner of the Euergides Painter preserves a greeting, ΠΡΟΣΑΓΟΡΕΥΟ.[22] This greeting is completed and given a subject, the name of one of the artists, ΠΑΙΔΙΚΟΣ, in the same position on B. Together the greeting is translated as follows: "I, Paidikos, greet you!" The surprise is the combination of signature and greeting, where it is the artist who articulates the phatic greeting. Two categories of sympotic discourse, signature and greeting, are blended. Indeed, a social challenge is also an effect: normally one would not expect the artist to be one of the individuals offering greetings at an elite *symposion*. The clue to combine the two sides is reiterated at the level of the image, where two perceptual points of view, with side A showing the front of the figures and side B the back, are joined and explored as is discussed in detail in Chapter 8.

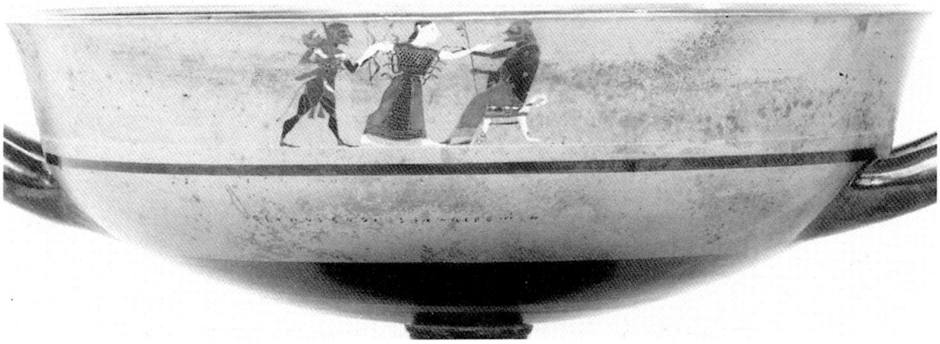

5.4. Black-figure cup by Phrynos, ca. 560–540 B.C. Side B. London, British Museum B 424. (Photograph © Copyright The Trustees of The British Museum.)

On a psykter by the Dikaios Painter, c. 510 B.C., in addition to labels for figures in a *komos*, a response to the greeting on A may appear on B:[23] on A, XAIPE is written twice, vertically between the figures; on B, XAPTA is written in the same place, in front of the figure at left. Is this an intensifier for the greeting on A? "Greetings!" "Truly, most certainly!" Two observers of the vase, looking at it simultaneously, perhaps reading aloud, could be prompted to a (scripted) conversation by these inscriptions, their unity conveyed by syntactical repetition.[24]

Repeated Inscriptions and Parody

On a cup c. 540 B.C. by the Epitimos Painter, a member of the Lydan circle, the inscriptions suggest parody.[25] We see here an important corollary to Exekias' cup in Athens discussed at the beginning of this chapter and in Chapter 2 [Figures 2.1, 2.2]. The images represent a mythical narrative, the fight between Athena and the giant Enkelados; the representation of narrative here is discussed at length in Chapter 6 [Figures 5.5, 5.6]. Underneath the outline "busts" of Athena and Enkelados, where only Enkelados' name is inscribed, the signature on one side, beneath Athena, is linked to a phatic greeting beneath the image of the giant:

ΕΠΙΤΙΜΟΣΕΠΟΙΕΣΕ[Ν]	"Epitimos made (it)"
ΧΑΙΡΕΚΑΙΠΙΕΙ Σ[Υ]	"Welcome and drink!"

The sound of the verb in the signature on A [eh *poi eh sen*] and that in the imperative together with the pronoun on B [*pee ay sou*] is similar, creating a redundant message that helps to establish a link between the images of the goddess on one side and her Giant adversary on the other. The artist plays on the repeated sounds in the two verbs, where each parodies the sound of the other. The similarity in sound

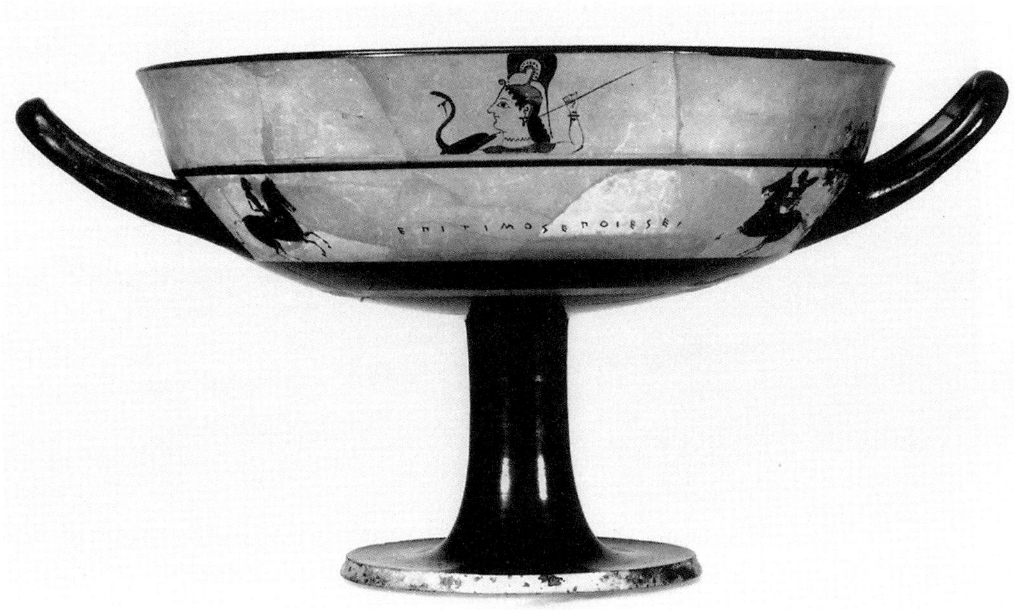

5.5. Black-figure cup by the Epitimos Painter, ca. 560–540 B.C. Side A. Copenhagen, National Museum of Denmark inv. no. 13966. (Photograph © Department of Classical and Near Eastern Antiquities, National Museum of Denmark.)

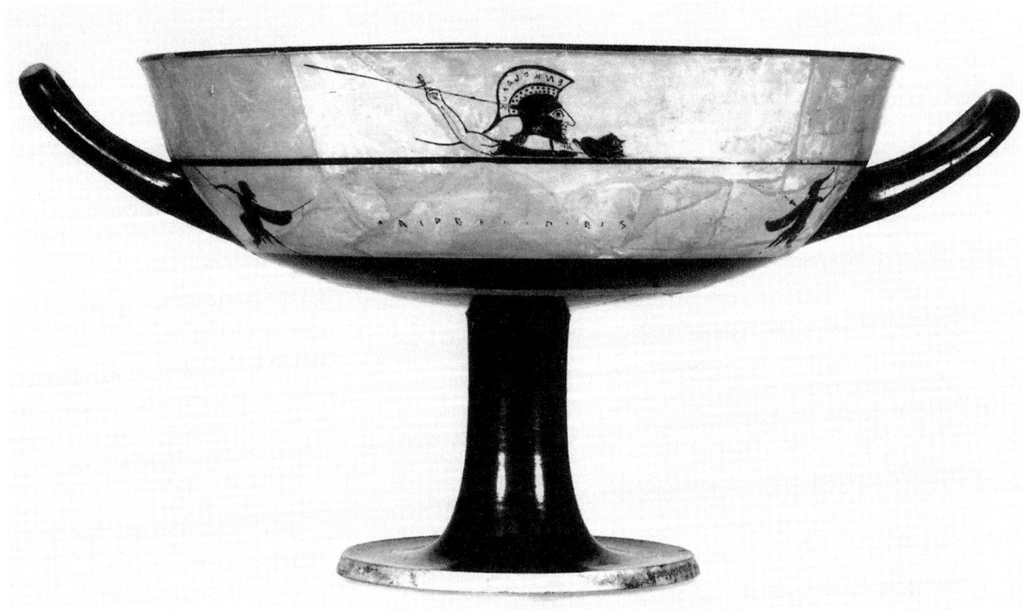

5.6. Black-figure cup by the Epitimos Painter, ca. 560–540 B.C. Side B. Copenhagen, National Museum of Denmark inv. no. 13966. (Photograph © Department of Classical and Near Eastern Antiquities, National Museum of Denmark.)

underscores and reflects the "close but not identical" relationship of the images as well as their interconnection. In his selection of what scripts to include, the author privileges convivial greeting, announcement of authorship, and identification of subject. Just as on the Phrynos cup [Figures 5.3, 5.4] and Paidikos' Naples cup, the craftsman's name is integrated into sympotic discourse.[26]

Similar to the last example is a c. 550 B.C. lip cup in Berkeley preserving Theseus fighting the Minotaur on each side.[27] The images are very similar to one another, and, like the images, the inscriptions vary only slightly, but significantly. The inscriptions do not complement the meaning of the images in an obvious way: under each image, nonsense syllables parody both "epoiesen" and "oinos" and seem to replace the "ΜΕ" ("me") that is often part of a signature with a "ΣΥ" ("you"):

ΕΠΟΙΥΕΠΟΙΥΕΠΟΙΥΝΣΥΝΕΣΥ *ep oi u e poi u e poi un su* ne su
ΣΥΕΠΟΙΥΕΠΟ[Ι]ΥΕΠΟΙΥΝΣΥ su *ep oi u e poi u e poi un su*

The inscriptions are located in the zone below the figures, in the area usually reserved for signatures. When reading them, the reader will do a double-take after his expectations, developed as he reads the first two syllables on A, are thwarted. The expectation that he will read the verb meaning "to make" is not fulfilled. Neither of the inscriptions is coherent, and each parodies comprehensible words, perhaps expected but not present on this particular example. A reader who spoke aloud would sound incoherent, even drunk; the inscription would trick him. Here potential one-upsmanship – the unsuspecting reader is the butt of the joke – is scripted and privileged in the text above either naming the images or identifying authorship of the cup.

Repeated *kalos*

The repertory of Exekias, beginning at about 540 B.C., serves as a benchmark in the history of the inscriptions-inventory because *kalos* declarations appear now for the first time, and they become numerous quickly. At this moment, the variety of inscription-types used by artists on vases is at its maximum. For example, the list of inscriptions on the Vatican amphora includes signature, vocalizations of the persons depicted (A), and labels naming the participants; the later two types are tied to the story itself, the narrative.[28] The *kalos* inscription that is repeated on each side, "Onetorides is handsome," is outside of story-time. In this case the *kalos* inscription is not syntactically or orthographically a verbatim repetition, as that on the B side is retrograde, spelled slightly differently and moved from far right (as on A) to a midpoint in the image. The orthograde-retrograde pairing will have no aural impact, but it contributes to the message sent visually. When uttered the two inscriptions sound almost identical. The visual combination of orthograde and retrograde establishes the *kalos* inscriptions as mirror images of each other, directing the viewer thus: "these two items respond to one another; connect them." The pairing of the inscriptions is analogous to the "transparent vase-effect" created by the combined front-and-back views of the images on the Boston pelike [Figures 1.1, 1.2].

In general, repeated *kalos* on more than one field of a vessel forms a series of links like those created by repeated *khaire* as employed by the Little Master and later artists. The *kalos* declarations are essentially metadiscursive directives, as that term is defined in Chapter 4, elements of metadiscourse serving to emphasize or maximize the effectiveness of channels of communication. Such declarations are similar to the endorsements created by the presence and gestures of repeated spectators: *kalos* statements, even when apparently unrelated to the depicted image, comment in the manner of a narratee, and when they are repeated, they join one scene to another. In addition, they link the total image program and the vase itself to pederastic discourse. Such repeated inscriptions can serve to catch the attention of the audience, to prepare them for the delivery of a second communication conveyed through the content of the images, and to suggest where that communication is applicable, the world of *kalos* youths.

The inscription identifying authorship of the images and an announcement that a flesh-and-blood Athenian individual is *kalos* are both *apparently* out of "story time" and in the present, as mentioned above. Yet when inscriptions are read, they are all read together, linked in a single moment. If Onetorides' name is spoken aloud, it is combined in a series with the names of Achilles and Ajax and with those of the family of the Dioskouroi. The result, then lays the groundwork for synonymy among the heroes and Onetorides, and oddly enough, the artist. This is an extension of the paradigmatic process outlined in Chapter 7 for images alone, a process much more like the linking of present celebrity with heroic prototype in epinician poetry, a phenomenon treated in detail in Chapter 11.

The work of Exekias, because it preserves some of the first *kalos* inscriptions, provides a baseline for investigation of repeated *kalos* inscriptions in the painters who follow him. In Exekias' *oeuvre* we see two interesting trends. First, there is a consciousness and implementation of earlier tradition, as outlined here on Little Master cups, where inscriptions respond to one another. Second, he shows an interest in thinking about the effects of reading all inscriptions, which may be from several different categories such as signature, *kalos* inscription, and label, together, in a series and therefore in one interpretive moment. He thereby directs interpretation of the entire text while at the same time making precise the meaning of particular images and referencing additional levels of discourse, including that of pederasty. For example, repeated *kalos* constructs around the images themselves an inclusive frame, restricting the context within which the viewer ought to consider the images. *Kalos* repeated on two sides of a vase directs the viewer to link the images on those sides, and at the same time the repetition casts the combined text into the pederastic "culture of fame," a key feature of *symposion*. When a proper name is attached to the adjective, the point is then further narrowed to a specific individual.

There are a number of formats artists use when implementing the connective potential of repeated *kalos*. Two cups by Oltos, dating to c. 510–500 B.C., provide vivid manifestations of one format, where identically placed orthograde and retrograde *kalos* inscriptions create a link between the two sides of the vessel.[29] In the best-preserved example, *kalos* appears once on each side, above the palmettes and below the rim in the handle zones; because only one inscription is retrograde, the two form a mirror-image diagonally across the rim of the cup, thereby linking one side of the cup to the other. On another example, *kalos* was apparently inscribed a total of three times, with two on the "B" side, again creating with one another a mirror image, because only one is retrograde. A third case preserves *kalos* under each handle, once retrograde and once not, and again twice on one side, just below the rim, with one instance retrograde and one not[30] [Figures 5.7–5.9]. In this last example *Memnon kalos* also appears in the tondo, thereby linking all fields of the vase through repeated *kalos* while at the same time focusing on a specific youth. A final example where inscriptions appear to mirror one another, this time in content, displays *kalos Memnon* on A and, with name and adjective inverted, *Simiades kalos* on B; the tondo repeats *kalos Memnon*, thereby linking three fields.[31] In other cases, the adjective is closely linked to a proper name, with name and adjective in consistent position, and the inscriptions link either two or three fields.[32]

Like painters' signatures, *kalos* inscriptions can be divided on two sides of a cup: on the Gorgos cup, ΚΡΑΤΕΣ, "Krates," appears on one side and ΚΑΛΟΣ "[is] handsome," on the other.[33] Much more numerous are those examples where *kalos* alone or a complete *kalos* inscription is repeated.[34] A few of these stand out because the repeated *kalos* inscriptions respond to one another as a result of their similar placement on each side of the vessel; the identical location of such inscriptions suggests one is a response to its mate. Twice Euphronios couples ΛΕΑΓΡΟΣ ΚΑΛΟΣ, "Leagros is handsome," with the same phrase retrograde on the opposite side of the vessel,[35] in one case placed in precisely the same spot on each side.[36] Of the most thoroughly interactive variety is the example with which Chapter 1 began, where two statements of ΛΕΑΓΡΟΣ ΚΑΛΟΣ appear, one conventionally orthograde and one retrograde, and ΝΑΙΧΙ is added to the retrograde statement. In tandem the two statements create a conversation.[37] As discussed above, the inversion in the inscriptions is directly paralleled in the imagery. We see the front and the back of both inscriptions and figures.

One example shows repeated *kalos* inscriptions with another group of linked inscriptions, repeated labels. On side B and the interior of a cup discussed fully in Chapter 7, the Triptolemos Painter repeats *h*Ο ΠΑΙΣ ΚΑΛΟΣ, "the youth is handsome." The image-program on A,B, and I joins mythical *aition* and mortal ritual; an "actual" Athenian, Euphiletos, is labeled on both interior and A[38] [Figures 7.30–7.32]. This repetition creates a second link across the lip of the cup; the metadiscursive directives serve to unite the total message of the vase in a frame of pederastic discourse.

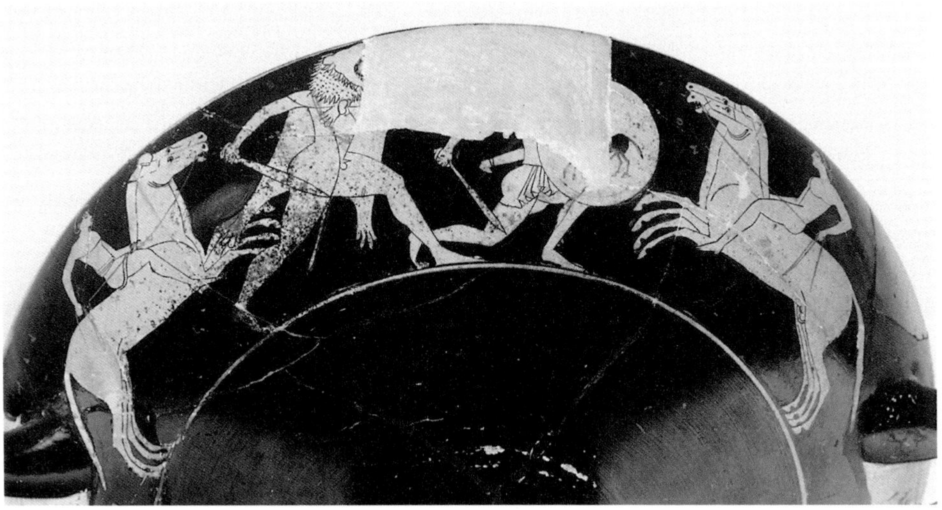

5.7. Red-figure cup by Oltos, ca. 525–500 B.C. Side A. Copenhagen, National Museum of Denmark inv. no. 3877. (Photograph © Department of Classical and Near Eastern Antiquities, National Museum of Denmark.)

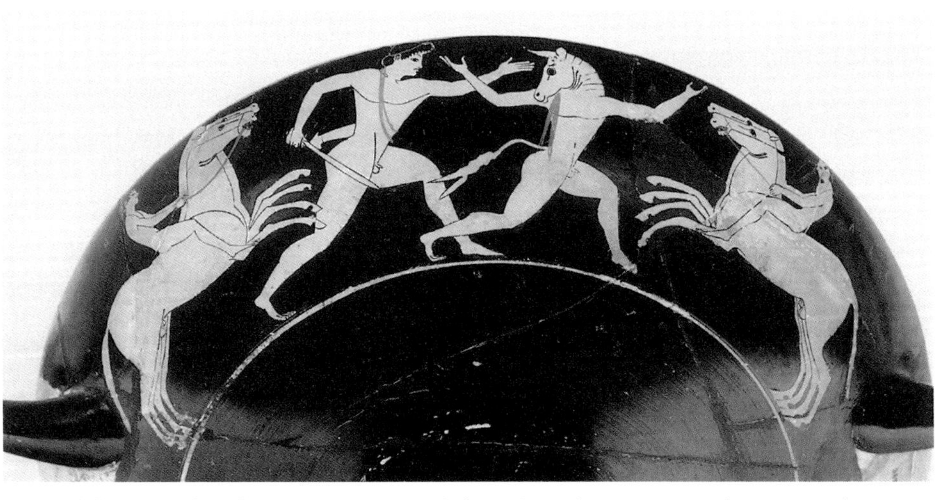

5.8. Red-figure cup by Oltos, ca. 525–500 B.C. Side B. Copenhagen, National Museum of Denmark inv. no. 3877. (Photograph © Department of Classical and Near Eastern Antiquities, National Museum, Copenhagen.)

One effect of the *kalos* repetitions is to focus the entire message of the vase, including shape, imagery, and script, on one important aspect of sympotic culture. Where there is crosswise linking and/or orthograde/retrograde pairing, there is evocation and perhaps prompting of actual sympotic discourse, where conversation goes back and forth across the *andron*. In subsequent chapters, we will see many examples where the effect of repeated imagery is in turn enhanced via the repeated inscriptions.

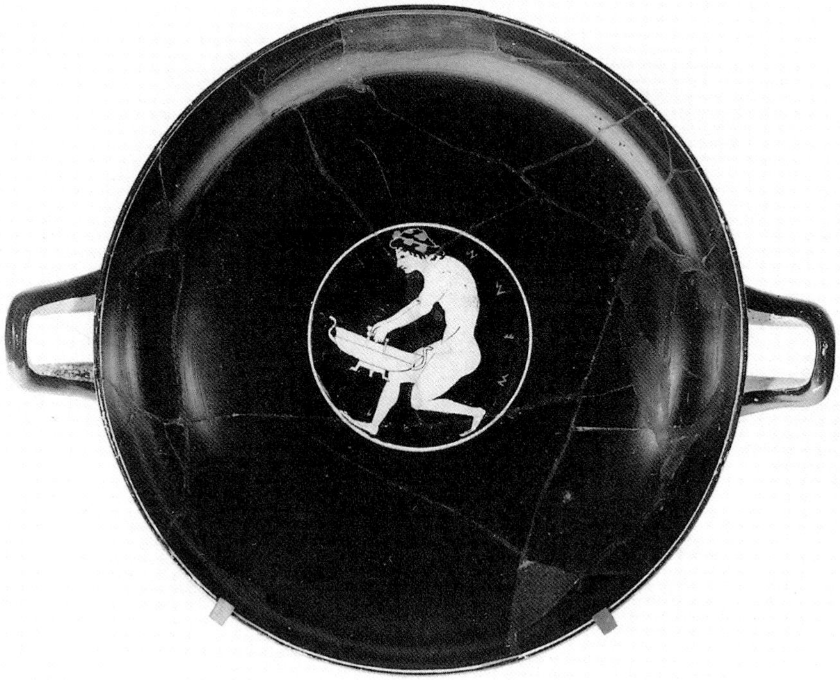

5.9. Red-figure cup by Oltos, ca. 525–500 B.C. Interior. Copenhagen, National Museum of Denmark inv. no. 3877. (Photograph © Department of Classical and Near Eastern Antiquities, National Museum, Copenhagen.)

Inscriptions Naming Spectator-Narratees

In Chapter 4 we established that "anonymous bystanders" in certain compositions create metadiscourse as narratees and that they also create metadiscourse by means of phatic functions.[39] These metadiscursive functions of spectators can be further enhanced by inscriptions, and the following examples provide various types of evidence that bystanders and inscriptions are intertwined in function. The cup by Oltos discussed above as an example preserving repeated *kalos* is illustrative.[40] On each side, identical repeated spectators appear on both sides of a heroic fight. On A, a single mounted rider (nude at right, wearing *chitoniskos*(?) at left) with an additional void horse frames at each side Herakles and Kyknos [Figure 5.7]; on B the same figures flank Theseus and the Minotaur [Figure 5.8]. The poses of each hero/monster pair at center are extremely similar, and overall these repetitions alone suggest that the two exploits are comparable. The beardless nude youths who observe on horseback have much in common with Theseus; they are not participants, but narratees. The inscriptions here specify: on A, Herakles is identified by an inscription, ΗΕΡΑΚΛΕΣ,"Herakles," retrograde, and a second inscription reads XION, "Chion." Beazley links XION with the word *kalos* that appears to the right of the right-hand youth, identifying the two words as a *kalos* inscription.[41] It is on B, however, that we see a striking situation: the spectators are not anonymous but appear to be named: ΔΙΧΙΣ (retrograde), "Dikhis," and ΓΛΕΝΟΣ, "Glenos."[42] Who are these youths? Their names are otherwise unattested, and therefore may not refer to mythical characters. Although vase-painters were quite adept at making up new (mythical) names for the (mythical) participants in myth scenes, in this case the figural repetition tends to discourage reading the youths on horses strictly as participants in the two different mythical stories. They appear instead as spectator-narratees to at least two different stories and therefore are not specific to either of them. The inscription on A reinforces what the repetitions suggest, that these narratees could be drawn from the "real" world of *kalos* boys, and that would make the labeled youths on B the status-equivalents of the youth named as *kalos* on A. The visual similarity between youth-spectators and Theseus helps to assimilate them to his status as both hero and youth. That the spectator narratees ride horses also reflects their elite status, shared with Athenian elites. They are certainly comparable to Athenian elites, and it is possible that they are even particular mortal individuals. Thus in the repertory of Oltos there is supporting evidence that our spectator-narratees, usually anonymous but here named, may stand for Athenian elites. They characterize the two heroic exploits as comparable and direct the paradigmatic fights very specifically to the appropriate audience.

Inscriptions Creating Comments as if Spectator-Narratee

Comments describing the action on vases also seem to limit reaction and narrow focus in diverse ways. Euthymides couples an observation with a parodic counterpart.[43] On side A of his amphora in Warsaw, c. 510 B.C., a youth, ΑΘΕΝΙΟΝ, "Athenion," holds a wine-amphora horizontally, and the wine is visible as it pours out [Figure 5.10]. A statement, a comment describing what he does, is located in three verticals, at left, between his legs, and again at right: ΕΝΧΕ (=ΕΓΧΕΙ)|*h*ΕΔ⟨ΥΝ⟩|ΟΙΝΟΝ, or "he pours sweet wine." On side B, the satyr blows one of his double pipes, and to his right, descending from a pipe held in his right hand, is a second inscription including a name and another description: ΒΡΙΚΟΝ, Brikon, and ΟΙΦΟΝ, Oiphon [Figure 5.11]. The latter, describing the satyr "Rascal" (Βρίκων), not only rhymes with ΟΙΝΟΝ ("oi-phon and oi-non") on A, but is apparently a first person masculine participle from the verb οἴφειν, which means "to mount" and is a euphemism for sexual congress.[44] The youth Athenion pours wine and the stayr Brikon "mounts;" the two sides of the vase are linked by the repeated sounds. Dover points out that this word, οἴφειν, appears in public *graffiti* as well as in the Gortyn laws, so it is not exactly vulgar, but it is certainly blunt. While the first inscription makes a real reader into an accurate spectator, the second reverberates as a clever parody of sound and substance. Moreover, the type of comment written on A, "Rascal mounting," is different from those considered up to this point. It appears to be the comment of a narrator who is explaining something to a narratee; in Chatman's analysis of the narrator, he describes an analogous phenomenon for written works, saying such comments sound like "bits from the narrator's half of a dialogue going on between the two."[45] In essence, the narratee is absent from the figural scene, but is supplied by implication, through the inscriptions. There must be someone to listen to the comment.

Another example pairs actual anonymous spectator-narratees on A with a *written* comment on B. On the Berlin Painter's Florence pelike coupling two deeds of Theseus, actual depicted spectators on A are paired with written comments on B.[46] Theseus appears very similarly on each side. He strides to right with left arm stretched out to grasp his opponent, and in each case he has short hair with a curly outline and sideburns. He is labeled on A in the center of the composition, and he is observed by spectators. It is theoretically possible to assign Athenian-youth identities to spectators in the story of Theseus and the Minotaur, but there are no such labels here. The figures become narratees: they react with gestures; there is no other commentary. On B, where there are no spectators, and the hero Theseus as he fights Skiron is not labeled, the comments ΝΥΓΕ or (Ε)ΥΓΕ (Immerwahr), "and now!" and ΚΑΛΛΙΣΤΟΣ, "most handsome!" appear at the top and at the left, filling the ellipsis created by the absence of spectators. The artist thus supplies a specific verbal reaction to be read by the viewer, who thereby becomes the surrogate narratee. The living symposiast who reads inscriptions on the B side of the vase creates a reaction to the hero. This reaction is analogous to that created by the depicted spectator-narratees who perform their typical metadiscursive function as spectator-narratees on the A side of the vase. The content of the supplied verbal reaction on B links, albeit hierarchically, the *kallistos*, "most handsome" Theseus to living youths who are also *kalos*.

Repeated Labels

Finally, the simplest type of repeated inscription is the repeated label, a name identifying a pictured figure. Some vases preserving repeated labels assure the viewer that he looks at the same figure in two fields. These labels can identify figures from myth, such as Achilles[47] or Theseus.[48] In one case involving Theseus, the label on A is combined with a greeting *to* Theseus on B, whereas the hero actually appears only on A.[49] Two examples by the Painter of the Birth of Athena name three divinities, some twice.[50] There are also cases where the repeated label appears to identify a contemporaneous Athenian, as with Euphiletos, mentioned above[51] [Figures 7.30–7.31]. Sosias may be labeled twice on Euthymides' Morgantina krater[52] [Figures 7.23, 7.24], and Phintias' well-known hydria in Munich appears to label Euthymides on the body and to mention him in a toast on the shoulder[53] [Figures 9.10, 9.11]. Euphronios may repeat the name "Teisis" on the Arezzo krater,[54] [Figures 10.9, 10.10]. The repetitions of labels serve both to link fields and to emphasize a particular character, at times drawing him into a context where he is not actually depicted.

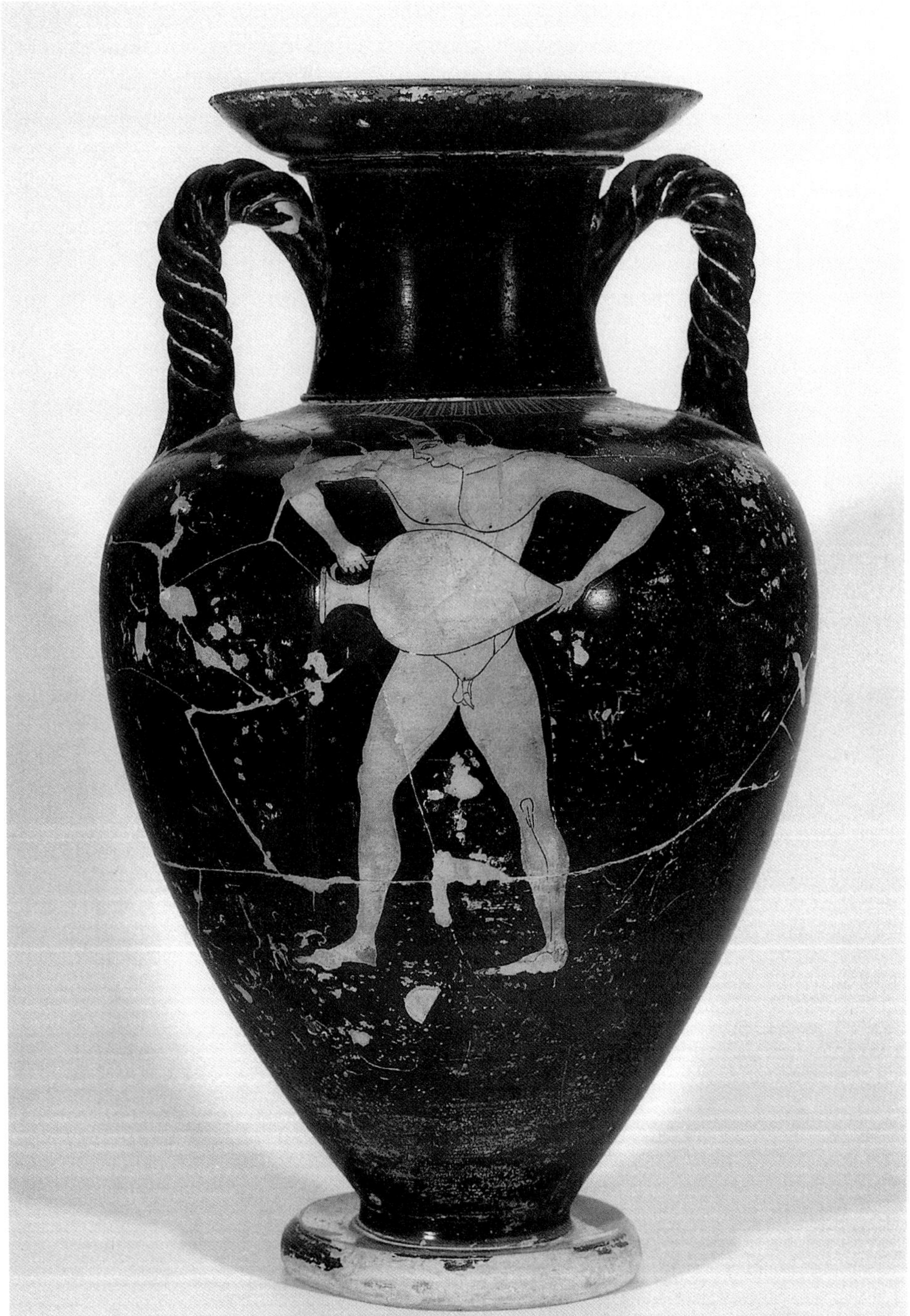

5.10. Red-figure neck-amphora by Euthymides, ca. 510–500 B.C. Side A. Warsaw, National Museum 142332. (Photograph © the National Museum in Warsaw.)

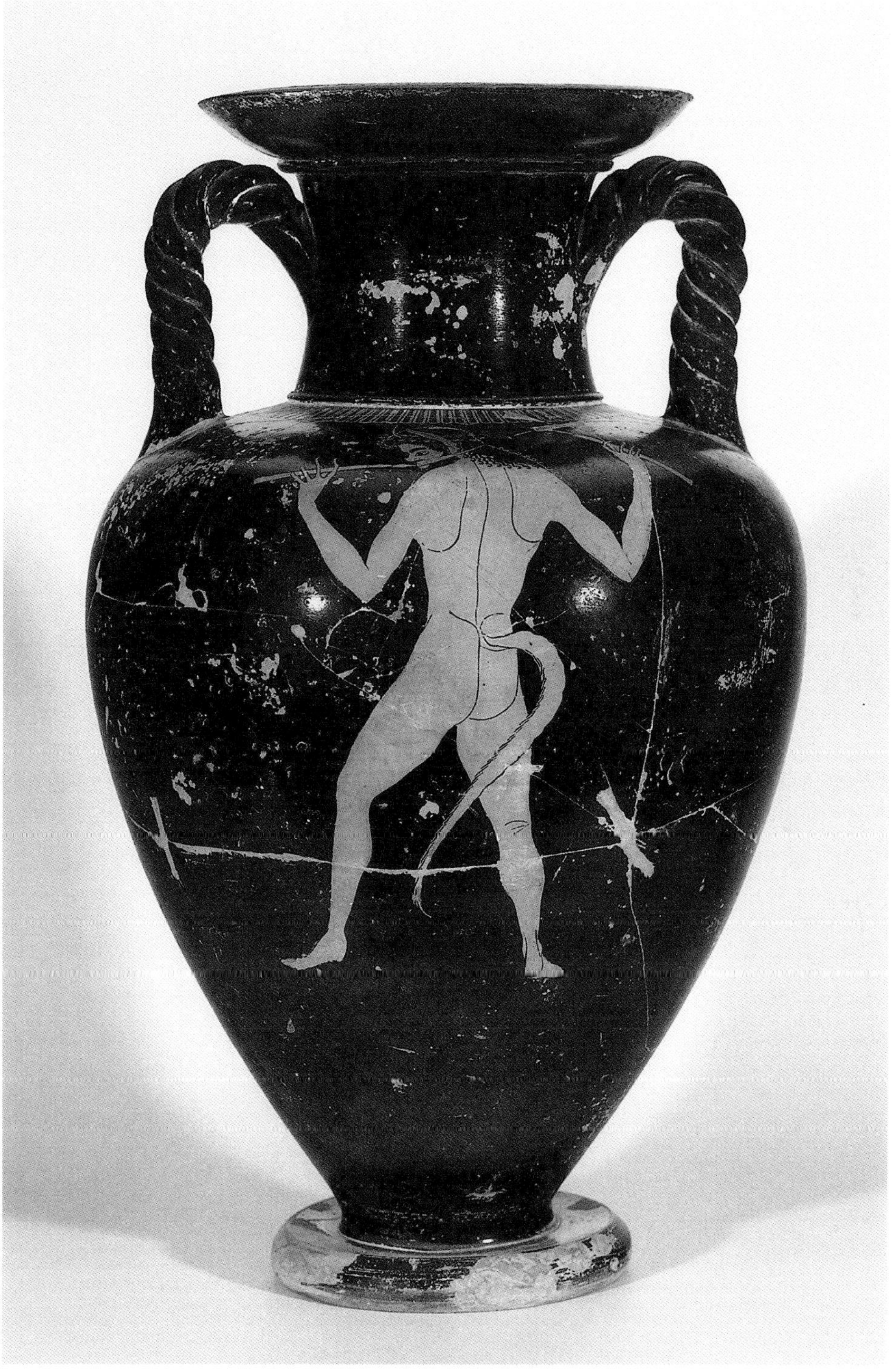

5.11. Red-figure neck-amphora by Euthymides, ca. 510–500 B.C. Side B. Warsaw, National Museum 142332. (Photograph © the National Museum in Warsaw.)

CONCLUSIONS

The conventions for repeated inscriptions from c. 580 B.C. to about 480 B.C. conform to the expectations developed in the analysis of imagery alone. Inscriptions that repeat words, sounds, and/or placement invite the viewer to take both sides of the vessel into consideration, and they create more levels of meaning when taken together than when taken singly. Information gained by following the cues provided via repetition is crucial to understanding the entire meaning of the vessel. Inscriptions function beyond the level of verbal or pictorial content, as directives, expressions, or signs, thereby opening channels of discourse and limiting and focusing how images are interpreted. It is clear that repeated inscriptions introduce more information and exert more control than either single inscriptions or even repeated images with no accompanying inscriptions. The selection of what is repeated is not random; the repeated element informs the reader what he ought to recognize as most important. The repetition itself is a directive, leading the viewer to privilege the repeated feature, whether signature, *kalos* declaration, or a particular character in his interpretation of the vessel.

Repeated inscriptions often demonstrate that artists expected the viewers to look at each side and field of a vessel and to connect the words found in each place. Conversations are constructed by means of repeated words and/or sounds; declarations are coupled with responses. Sometimes the inscribed words, with repeated sounds or entire phrases creating meaning in tandem, appear in conjunction with repetitions in imagery; this is some of our best evidence that the construction of meaning from repetition was intentional. Often, despite careful visual coordination between inscription and image, there is a disconnect between the meaning of the words and the imagery – the inscriptions tell us who made the vase or they supply us with greetings or drunken babbling, whereas the images create paradigm or narrative sequence. This disjunction ensures a more complex and more comprehensive role for the vessel in its use context. If that context is *symposion*, the possibilities for multiple levels of meaning are increased, as explored fully in Chapter 11. The repeated inscriptions overall are extremely prescriptive: as a category of metadiscourse directing the user to make connections, they focus and limit the ways that the observer interprets the vase. They buttress social competition and the testing and reaffirming of social hierarchies, for when read aloud they allow one person to make a fool of another. Yet the reading of inscriptions that include proper names sometimes appears to override social hierarchies by including artisans, elite youths, and divinities and heroes in the same conversation. Overall, the inclusion of repeated inscriptions by a painter leaves much less to chance – the written elements attempt to make certain that users consider the entire vessel to discern authorship of the vessel, converse over the vessel, make fun of one another, and know particular things about the images. The elements a painter chooses to repeat are thereby emphasized as important.

One particularly striking conclusion to result from the analysis of this evidence is the discovery of how written elements, repeated or not, can suggest and thereby replace depicted spectator-narratees. The elite patron, the intended viewer, when actually reading an inscription, expresses a message from the narrator, a creation of the constructed author-artist. The reader's identity is merged with that of the narratee.

INDEX OF ANCIENT SOURCES

SIX

REPETITION AND NARRATION

The analysis of repeated spectators and written texts in the last two chapters has focused on their metadiscursive properties. We turn now to a discussion focusing on the content of figural scenes. This chapter, the first of four to look in detail at figural scenes, considers the representation of narration and how repetition can play a role in storytelling. In chapter 1, we saw that Homeric scholars are investigating how repetition works not only as a compositional tool, but also as a way of creating levels of meaning in the narrative. We have seen that vase-painters, too, relied on repetition to tell stories in particular ways. The discussion in Chapter 2 brought out several examples where Exekias uses repetition to join scenes representing two phases of a narration and where the painter implicates several more phases through ellipsis. The Philadelphia amphora combining the removal of Antilochos' corpse with the removal of Achilles' [Figures 2.5, 2.6] and the combination of Herakles' fetching Kerberos with his apotheosis are two such examples.[1] In this chapter, the goal is to look at visual narration more deeply, to assess how repetition plays a crucial role in many prominent systems vase-painters use to tell stories.

STRATEGIES FOR VISUAL NARRATION

Athenian artists display their talent for depicting and creating narrative visually everywhere on their products. Scholars since the nineteenth century have been discussing the way Greek vase-painters convey narrative and the result is an elaborate taxonomy and somewhat confusing nomenclature that are themselves testimony to the diverse mechanisms artists use to tell stories. This discussion begins with a short review of the relevant parts of the taxonomy.[2] A comparison of several discussions, taking place over the past ten years, reveals the complex discourse that has emerged as scholars have translated terms coined in German into English and then struggled to refine descriptions of the many inventive ways Athenian painters depicted stories.[3] Terms to describe various types of visual narration, such as "unified," "progressive," "serial," and "episodic," have been created by scholars in the past twenty years, added to the older list developed in the nineteenth century, such as "continuous," or "cyclic." Each term attempts to describe a different strategy employed by artists to convey story lines. In this chapter, we explore how artists use repetition in their various strategies for depicting narrative. Although, as we have seen, many depictions of narrative in Athenian vase-painting show striking repetitions, repetition is not required for these artistic strategies. Rather, repetition is an optional tool an artist can use to underscore continuities in his story line. In this chapter, we explore how artists use repetition in their various conventions for depicting narrative.

Two types of narrative representation will not concern us, because they do not include repetition in two different fields as part of the discourse strategy. "Monoscenic" narration, called *Situationsbild* by Robert, employs one picture or scene representing one moment in time taking place in one space.[4] There are no repeated characters or multiple fields of images, by definition. This discourse-strategy works by using one scene to call the entire story to the viewer's mind rather than by issuing prompts from more than one moment in it. A "synoptic" composition will not ordinarily rely on repetition, either, because it includes no repeated characters and compresses several moments into one space by the use of characters, props, or setting elements that are proleptic and/or analeptic.[5] A third category is also limited to a single field but it can include repetition within that field. *Continuous narration*, as defined originally by Wickhoff,[6] depicts events take place over a period of time, but depicted one after the next in a single unified pictorial field. Characters may or may not be repeated. Scenes belonging to this category of narration are not common on Archaic Athenian vases, so they concern us only minimally here.

It is the use of repetition to connect two separate scenes, allowing different moments in the action to cohere into a single story, that is the focus of interest in this discussion. A prominent technique for narration where such strategies can be implemented is a subcategory of continuous narration, called cyclical narration. A cyclic strategy entails two or more distinct pictures involving the repetition of characters, more than one temporal moment, and more than one space where action takes place.[7] The events are not normally causally linked. A common subject suited to cyclical representation is the labors of a hero.[8]

Like cyclic narration, polyscenic narration shows events in more than one scene. However, these are chains of interdependent events rather than independent events simply linked by a hero, such as the cycle of the deeds of Theseus. Various subdivisions of polyscenic narration have been named serial, progressive, unified, and episodic.[9] Each of these subdivisions of polyscenic narration relies on at least two linked but separate pictorial units, and these units can themselves be linked through syntactical and iconographical repetitions, such as compositions, pose, clothing, and attributes. Each subtype of polyscenic narration enables a slightly different aspect of the narrative to be stressed. The most important of these are duration of time, extent of space, and cast of characters.

One subdivision of polyscenic narration is very important to identify. "Phased" narration refers to polyscenic narration[10] depicted in more than one field, repeated characters or not, different moments in time, and the same or different physical spaces *showing events in a specific sequence*. The Exekias example in Philadelphia[11] is a good example, where two sequential story-events or "phases" in the Trojan War tale, the death of Antilochos and the death of Achilles, are distinguished by their placement in distinct frames and are linked by repetitions [Figures 2.5, 2.6].[12] An extremely important variant of phased narration is the "causally linked" type, where the two or more scenes that are linked include scenes where the events in one seem to have caused those in the other. Again, the example by Exekias in Philadelphia [Figures 2.5, 2.6] preserves two phases of a narrative that are causally linked: as discussed in Chapter 2, the death of Achilles is indirectly caused by the death of Antilochos. One interpretation of the *Aithiopis* holds that Achilles returns to the fighting, where he is ultimately killed, to avenge the murder of Antilochos by Memnon. Antilochos' murder therefore indirectly causes Achilles'.

We must also deal with the category of generic story-telling. The categories of narration we have been discussing were developed to describe narratives that are mythical stories, and more rarely, historical stories where at least some of the events are well-known according to at least one version preserved in written texts. However, the broad treatment of conventions for depicting narrative here includes consideration of nonspecific, generic events. Although these are not proper narratives, they often join two events in a time sequence.[13] This discussion will include therefore a look at how repetition operates for "stories" that appear nonspecific or generic to us when they extend to more than one field on a vessel. The following discussion is organized by categories, and within each category chronologically.[14]

Unified Narration

We begin with that type of polyscenic narration called "unified," where one subject is extended over two fields of a vase. This technique of narration seems to be a typological predecessor of those polyscenic narrations, discussed here below, where two different actions are likewise joined. A good early example is by the Bellerophon Painter, dating to the end of the seventh century.[15] Bellerophon mounted on Pegasos appears on one side [Figure 6.1], and they chase the Chimaira, whose heads look back at the pursuers on the other [Figure 6.2]. The bodies of Pegasus and the Chimaira are strikingly parallel visually. By responding to the cue that repetition provides, the observer learns that the subject *continues* from one side to the other. The *story*, as defined by Chatman, is the subject matter of the tale; so here, it is the story of the hero Bellerophon meeting in combat the fantastic and terrifying beast, Chimaira, and ultimately defeating it. The *discourse*, that is, the telling of the tale, includes the lexical items, the figures themselves, the syntax or composition in which the artist embeds them, and even the vessel on which they appear.[16] As discussed in Chapter 3, vase painters for a variety of reasons depicted animals on both sides of a vase, in some cases creating "Types" such as Horse-head amphoras, with subjects not discernible as narratives to modern viewers. As a result, painters and viewers came to expect that a subject on A could be related in visual and formal terms to a subject on B. When the Bellerophon Painter painted this vase, his viewers were conditioned to see animals on one side and matching animals on the other; therefore when he painted the Chimaira on one side and Bellerphon on the other, he worked within the context of widespread expectation that the subject on A could be related to the subject on B. He reinforces the viewer's expectation by using the animal form as the element he repeats.[17]

A cup by a Little Master artist, the Epitimos Painter, dating to around the mid-sixth century, divides the combat between Athena and the Giant Enkelados over two sides of a cup[18] [Figures 5.5, 5.6] In Chapter 5 we established that the interconnected inscriptions combining signature, toast, and greeting are unrelated to the narration analyzed here. Immediately the viewer is drawn by the inscriptions to connect the two sides, even though the content of the inscriptions is unrelated to the images. When the viewer looks at first side A and then at side B, he sees only the heads of two combatants. Although Athena is identified by her attributes alone, for she wears her helmet and carries her shield and spear, the identification of Enkelados is redundant, made certain by an inscription on his helmet. The repetition of only parts of the body in each case – just the head, one raised arm, and a small portion of the shield of each divine figure – underscores that the two images form a pair. Further repetitions – spots below the helmet crest, and the high-relief shield devices whose facial expressions convey the aggressive interaction of the divinities – reinforce connections between the goddess and her opponent. What is repeated, the armor, weapons, and aggressive pose with arms raising spears aloft, indicates what is most significant about the story. The viewer must move from an apprehension of what is almost alike to recall a narrative in which these two characters are adversaries in order to understand the meaning of the pairing; the meaning further depends on the viewer's knowledge of the outcome, Athena's victory. The extension of a scene over two sides of a vessel, together with this particular type of visual parallel, is similar to the extension over two sides in the scene of Bellerophon and the Chimaira [Figures 6.2, 6.3]. In both cases, the observer supplies, after an initial recognition of visual similarity and through prior knowledge of the myth, the necessary information to connect the images to one another and to a story. Virtually no *context* is provided through the imagery alone.[19] The painter relies a great deal on the memory of the viewer – he does not show the fight; the viewer must remember it.

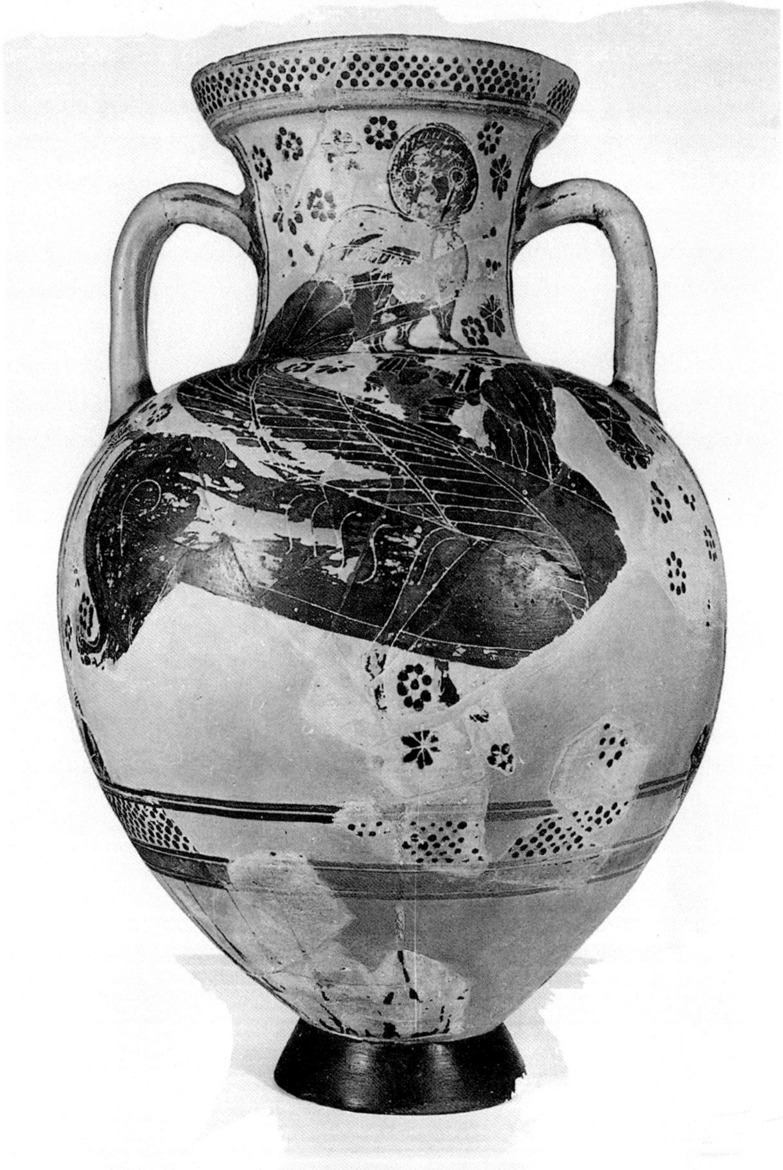

6.1. Black-figure amphora by the Bellerophon Painter, ca. 600–580 B.C. Side A. Athens, National Archaeological Museum 16389. (Photograph © National Archaeological Museum, Athens.)

The division of the action over two sides of a vessel accomplishes some things their placement on one side could not do so well. By choosing to extend the subject over two sides of the vessel the artist forces the viewer's perception into stages, allowing the artist to manipulate time. In each case, the fight cannot take place until the actors come closer together. The separation-induced delay, the creation of a unit of

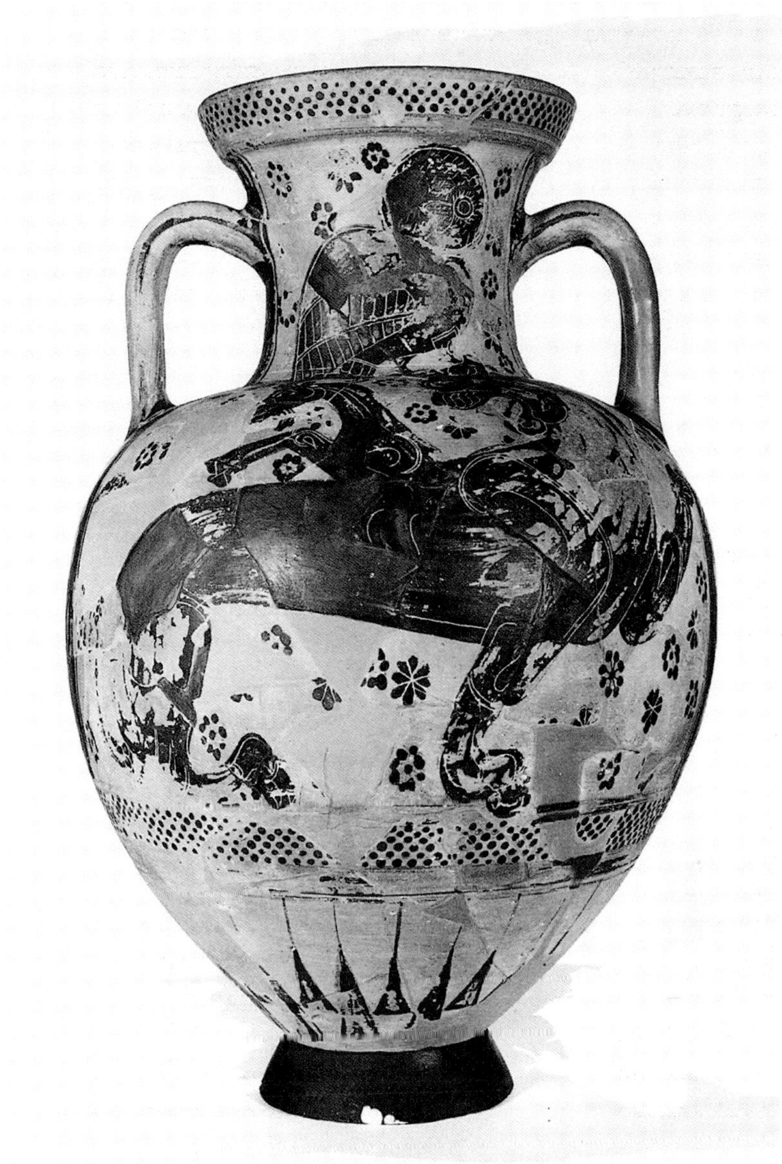

6.2. Black-figure amphora by the Bellerophon Painter, ca. 600–580 B.C. Side B. Athens, National Archaeological Museum 16389. (Photograph © National Archaeological Museum, Athens.)

time before the engagement begins, creates suspense – will another incident interfere with the expected outcome? Will Bellerophon trip and fall and the Chimaira escape? Will Athena let loose her spear too soon and the Giant overcome her? The viewer experiences this delay because the separation of participants on the vessel requires the viewer to turn it or move around it to apprehend the subject; it is as if the artist has drawn the viewer into story-time by manipulation of discourse-time.[20] In discourse that is by nature a summary, as defined by Genette, where the discourse-time, the time it takes to tell the story, or in this case to look at the vase, is clearly less than the amount of time the action of the story itself takes, the artist has managed to bring the relationship between story and discourse closer to a point where discourse-time and story-time are equal.[21] To categorize what the painter has done in terms of the components of plot, we can see that the artist has focused on satellites – not the major event or kernel, such as "Bellerophon kills Chimaira," or "Athena kills Giant," but a minor plot event, "Then Bellerophon chased the Chimaira, who looked back at his assailant in furious rage," or "Enkelados and the goddess raised their spears at just the same moment." Each case introduces suspense.

Pot painters such as Lydos also use repetition to create unified narration. A well-known column-krater displays the return of Hephaistos as a continuous scene, circling the entire vessel; its unity is clarified not only by the lack of interruption under the handles, but by the repetitions of figural poses from one side to the other.[22] A striking example of repetition is the figure with both arms raised to the left of center on each side, a silen on Side A and a nymph on B. Likewise, under each handle is a silen and nymph pair, where the silen looks back over his shoulder to see his sexually aggressive female companion. There is one moment of the event depicted, and repetitions help to convey this unity.

An example attributed to a member of Group E similarly links two actors in a story to extend a subject and thereby story-time, over two sides of the vase.[23] An unusually shaped neck-amphora displays in the main field a single wide-striding figure on each side, and the repetition in pose links them visually. The two figures are opponents in a single battle: Herakles on A prepares to shoot his arrow at Geryon on B. This is an identical compositional scheme with effects identical to those observed on the amphora showing Bellerophon and the Chimaira [Figures 6.1, 6.2] and appears also on the cup with Athena and Enkelados [Figures 5.5, 5.6]. Similarly, discourse-time is extended. Here, however, there are several additional repeated elements that serve to confirm the two sides are linked. Below each handle, between the two figures, is a flying siren. Around the neck, there is a single procession, interrupted by the handles. All the figures are identically posed and dressed; the appearance on each side is very similar; and the only difference is that we see one adult man on A, whereas the remaining figures on A and B are youths. Pipers lead both groups, and the pipers' clothing differs. There are many redundancies, additional repetitions to make sure the message is received.

In the late sixth century, examples of unified narration multiply.[24] Several expand narrative representation, extending discourse-time over two sides of a vessel, with varying results. Euphronios' Munich cup, if we read clues from repeated elements correctly, features a single story, the encounter between Herakles and Geryon, stretched over both sides of the exterior[25] [Figures 6.3, 6.4]. On side A, Herakles and Geryon are in

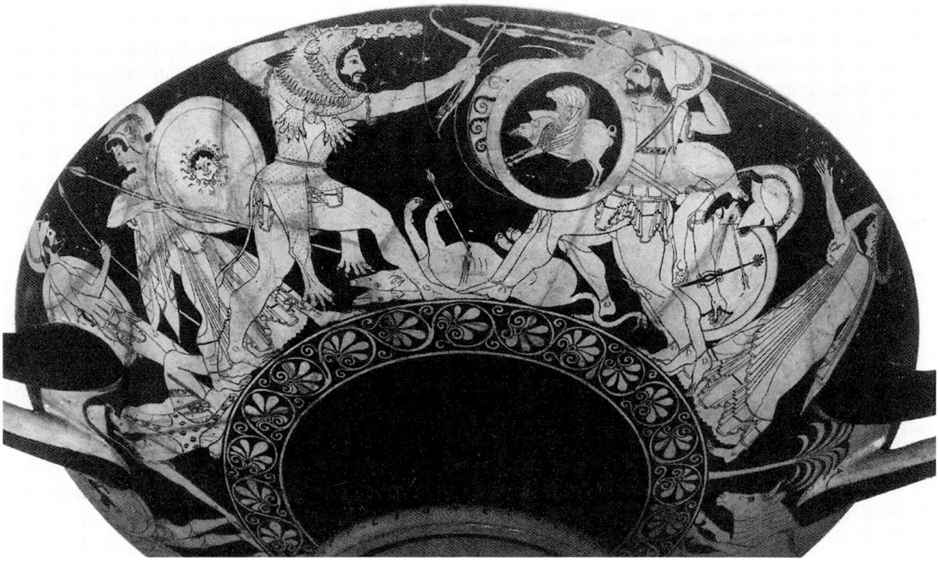

6.3. Red-figure cup by Euphronios, ca. 520–505 B.C. Side A. Munich, Staatliche Antikensammlungen und Glyptothek 2620 (J. 337). (Photograph © Staatliche Antikensammlungen und Glyptothek München.)

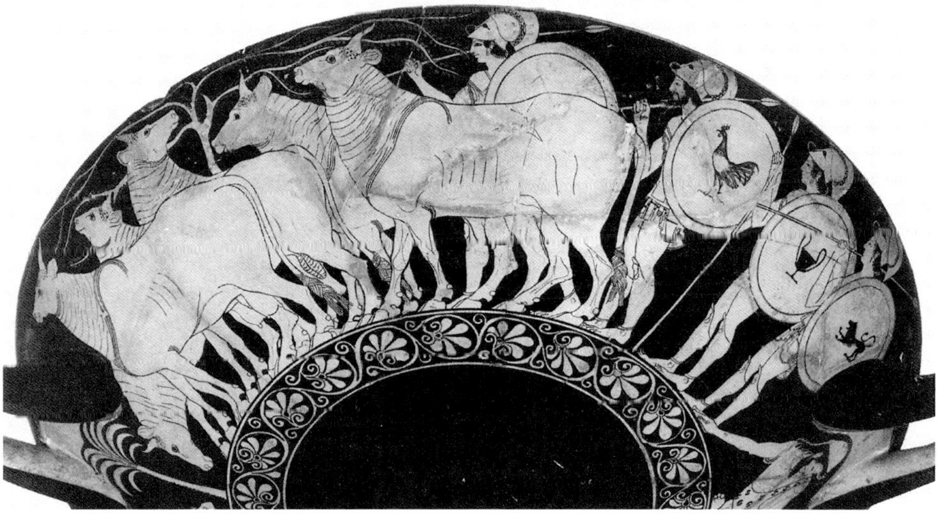

6.4. Red-figure cup by Euphronios, ca. 520–505 B.C. Side B. Munich, Staatliche Antikensammlungen und Glyptothek 2620 (J. 337). (Photograph © Staatliche Antikensammlungen und Glyptothek München.)

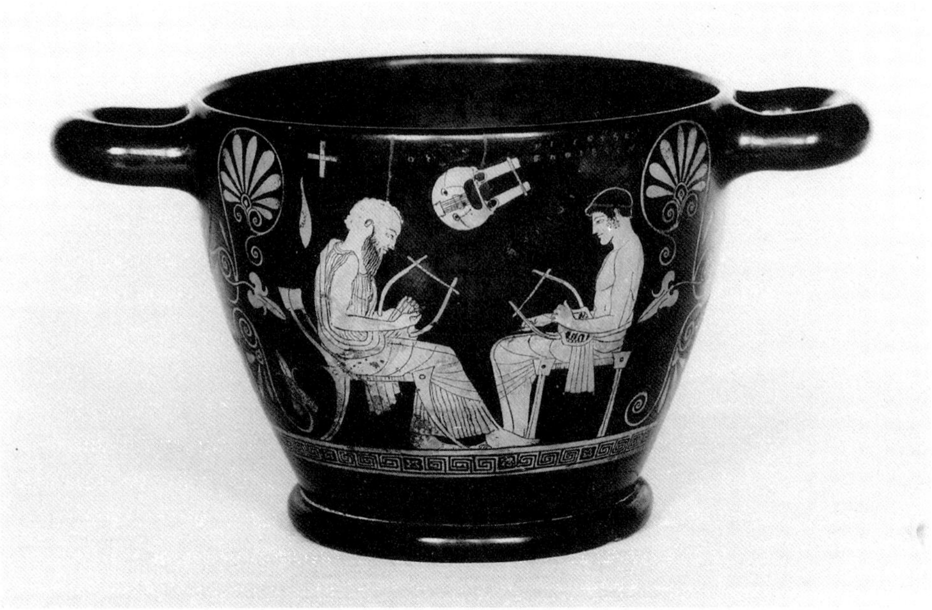

6.5. Skyphos by the Pistoxenos Painter, ca. 480–470 B.C. Side A. Schwerin, Staatliches Museum KG 708. (Photograph © Staatliches Museum Schwerin.)

combat. On B, armed men herd cattle. The strategy for narration is more complex here than on the earlier amphora by Group E that depicts Herakles on one side and Geryon on the other.[26] Indeed, Shapiro has identified the Munich cup as a unified narration, one showing two different but simultaneous settings and events.[27] Several repetitions in imagery between the A and B sides exist, although the compositions are quite different: side A is a combat, with hero and enemy meeting at center, whereas that on B is a procession with all figures moving left. The only mature male figure on B has numerous visual similarities both to the triple-bodied Geryon at right and to Iolaos, standing at the far left of the B-side scene. These are worth cataloging in some detail. Both the adult male on B and Geryon have beards, wear Corinthian helmet, tunic, cuirass, and greaves, and carry spears and round shields. Yet Geryon is quite literally three times the opponent a mortal would be; the many similarities between the monster and the "ordinary" adult also serve to showcase their fundamental difference. The adult male's *stance* and those of the youths who accompany him on B most closely conform to that of Iolaos on A, who also shares their clothing and attributes. We cannot see if the adult male on B *is* Iolaos, because the latter's shield device is hidden on Side A: we see Iolaos' right side but the left side of his double on B. The artists do not label any of the males who help to herd the cattle, so we do not know if they represent companions of Herakles who eventually help him to drive the stolen cattle back to Eurystheus in Mycenae. Shapiro suggests the figures on B are companions of Geryon who guard the cattle in one location

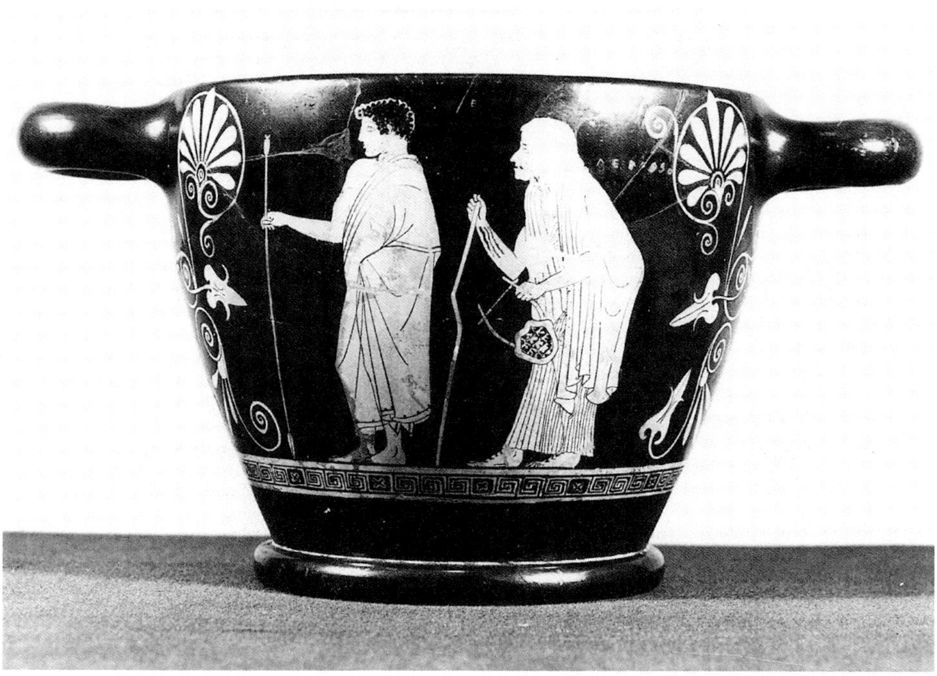

6.6. Skyphos by the Pistoxenos Painter, ca. 480–470 B.C. Side B. Schwerin, Staatliches Museum KG 708. (Photograph © Staatliches Museum Schwerin.)

on Erytheia, presumably trying to save them during the slaughter of Geryon and their herdsman in another spot on the island.[28] By looking at what differs in the two scenes, we can see that the trees stand out; if the palm tree under one handle locates the Geryon episode, the deciduous tree on B sets the cattle herding elsewhere.[29] Indeed, because the figures on B share so many visual similarities both with Iolaos and with Geryon, the viewer can link them easily either with Herakles' side or with that of his opponent. The result is the same as for the earlier examples: we see a stretching of discourse-time, the time it takes to tell the tale, but in this example the two simultaneous events are set in places much more widely separated from one another.

Our last example of a unified narration relies on repetitions that link a subject over two sides of the vase, and the repetitions that link the two compositions force the viewer to consider the (undepicted) next event in the story. The Pistoxenos Painter's skyphos in Schwerin, c. 470 B.C.[30] [Figures 6.5, 6.6], is, straightforwardly, a successor to the examples by the Bellerophon Painter [Figures 6.1, 6.2] and the Epitimos Painter [Figures 5.5, 5.6] just discussed; it is also a more sophisticated unified narration, displaying interior and exterior locations in very close proximity. The vase shows Linos (ΛΙ(Ν)ΟΣ) teaching a music lesson to Iphikles(A) (ΙΦΙΚΛΕ[Σ]) with Herakles (*h*EPAK [ΛΕΣ]) followed by a servant (B) (ΓΕΡΟΦΣΟ) about to arrive at the music master's studio. The story is depicted through a pendant display of similarity and difference. There are four elements that create a frame of syntactical similarity: these are identical vegetal tendrils of palmette and lotus surrounding the scenes, a simple, two-figure composition in each scene, a tortoise-shell lyre, held in the same place in the composition and at the same angle by Iphikles on A and Geropso on B, and the consistent placement, horizontal and in headline position at the top of each scene, of Linos' name on A and Herakles' on B. Contrasts include seated figures on (A) versus standing figures on B (B); old man with young man (A) versus young man with old woman(B); figures facing (A) versus figures in "procession" (B); and even smooth hair outline (Iphikles) versus curly hair outline (Herakles). The artist's signature appears only on A, ΠΙΣΤΟΧΣΕΝΟΣ| ΕΠΟΙΕΣΕΝ, "Pistoxenos made it." The tension created here anticipates what the educated viewer knows will be the difference in the lesson itself – in contrast to the serene scene of compliance we see on A, the student will attack and kill the teacher in his next lesson. Despite the fact that a single scene in two different locations extends over two sides of a skyphos, the repetitions that link the two compositions force the viewer to consider the (undepicted) next event in the story. An element crucial to this next event, the lyre murder weapon, also essential to the kernel of the tale, is stressed through repetition. Therefore repetition serves two functions. It links the two components of the unified narration, and it emphasizes what is important.

Cyclic Narration

Our analysis now turns to examples where events appearing on the two sides of a vessel cannot be simultaneous. The combination of just two labors of a hero on a single vessel is very common and does not give much scope for analysis. Discussion here therefore focuses first on two examples where three or more deeds are joined. A cup now attributed to Euphronios (formerly Oltos), dating to c. 510 B.C., apparently connects three deeds of Theseus, all discrete moments in the hero's life[31] [Figure 6.7]. The resulting combination is certainly a cyclic narration, with distinct pictures involving repeated characters, multiple temporal moments, and multiple settings. The representations are important to catalog in detail in order to demonstrate how the three scenes are connected and to show how repetition functions to link separate events in a cycle of deeds.

Repeated horses, shown in profile and stepping, provide visual links between sides A and B. Whereas on B the horse and riders frame a man and a woman, on A the horses are hitched to a chariot, and we see Theseus carrying Antiope – both labeled – as he steps into this chariot. More labels inform us that Phorbas and Perithoos, who stand behind the chariot, accompany the pair stepping into it. The composition on B shows a nude youth on horseback flanking each side of a confronting couple, a

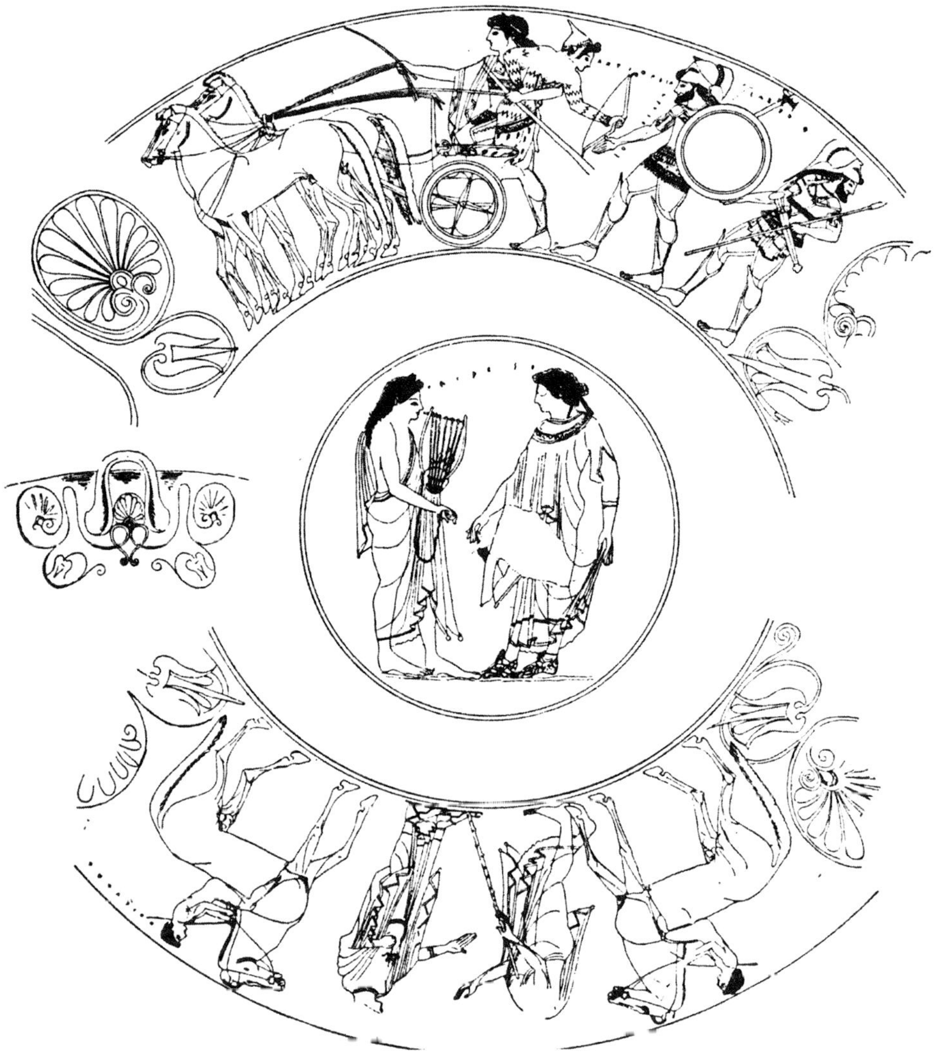

6.7. Red-figure cup by Euphronios, ca. 520–505 B.C. Sides A and B and Interior. London, British Museum E 41. Drawing, *Wiener Vorlegeblätter*, D.

male figure with a female, whose heads are not preserved. No inscriptions label any of the characters, but the potter, Chachrylion, is named in a horizontal inscription at the upper right. One interpretation of the vase, considered below, suggests that the horsemen flanking Theseus as he is about to seize Helen are an integral part of the narrative. Although the inscriptions do not repeat content from A side to B side, they share a common location and therefore act as a syntactical link: that naming Phorbas on A is in the same location, top horizontal, as the name of the potter Chachrylion on B. This link is formal, rather than one of content, but it suggests equivalence between sides A and B, supporting the conclusion that these are two deeds of Theseus.

The tondo shows a male figure holding a lyre confronting a richly dressed female, and the only inscription is a greeting, XAIPE ΣY, "Welcome!" Because the male figure carries a lyre, he can be identified as Theseus, for whom the lyre is a typical atribute; his female companion ought to be then either an anonymous rescued maiden (Beazley) or Ariadne (Neils).[32] This interior scene is linked to B via the repetition of imagery – the drapery, some of the attributes, and the general positions of the male and female figures. Specifically, the male figure in the tondo wears his *himation* in just the same way as does the figure on B, and "Helen" on B holds a blossom in her hand as does the maiden "Ariadne" in the tondo. Both women wear bracelets midway between wrist and elbow. Just as the blossoms are similar but not identical, the shoes worn by each female figure on B and I are alike but not the same.

The repetition on this cup helps to buttress Neils' theory that the three fields on the cup are linked and represent three exploits of Theseus, with the third his abduction of Helen observed helplessly by the mounted Dioskouroi on side B.[33] The hero is named on A; he is identified by an attribute, the lyre, in the tondo. Visual repetitions then link the tondo and side B. The very repetition of the sandals and flowers makes the difference significant – they are both Theseus' women, but they are different women.

If it is correct to see all three scenes on the cup as woman-related deeds of Theseus, this is an important example showing how repetition works as a link among three parts of a cycle. Euphronios shows us a selection of events that comprise parts of the story of the hero's life; they cannot be simultaneous because a single hero appears in all three, and they take place widely spaced over the hero's life, making the story the cup tells very like a phased narration. Another point established by repetition reinforces the conclusion that all of these scenes are on the same theme. All have to do with sexual conquest. The variations are in the mode of conquest: seduction, war, kidnapping. The tondo represents an event in Theseus' youth where he conquers through seduction, in contrast to violent encounters later in his life, the Amazon adventure (A) and the kidnapping of Helen (B). The artist uses a combination of repeated syntax and repeated images to weave the three women-stories together.

Theseus' declaration in the tondo, XAIPE ΣY sung to his lyre, brings the story of his seduction of Ariadne into the realm of *symposion*.[34] Although each of the exploits depicted on the cup involves Theseus' acquisition of or domination over a woman, his welcome to Ariadne and the fact that it is typical sympotic speech links the exploits to *symposion*, perhaps as topics for poetry or conversation and as aids to enculturation and paradigms for male behavior. A real reader of the inscription speaks Theseus' lines, taking on Theseus' identity. The hero's greeting to Ariadne is a typical sympotic greeting, and in becoming Theseus, the real reader also becomes the typical sympotic participant.

A poorly preserved cycle cup painted by Onesimos and potted by Euphronios dates to around 500 B.C. and depicts five deeds of Theseus.[35] It displays a more ambitious joining of events than in the previous example and is strikingly important, because it relies on both repeated inscriptions and repeated images to link episodes. Overall this is a cyclic narration, where the same character appears in separate frames, each with distinct story events, temporal moments, and settings. The repetitions here help the viewer sort out the relationship among three complex fields and two different types of narration, cyclic and continuous. The scenes show Theseus and Skiron on the left and Theseus and Prokrustes on the right in one field on A, and Theseus and Kerkyon at left and Theseus and the bull at right in one field on B; and on the interior, Theseus stands with Amphitrite and Athena. The major contrast to Euphronios' London cup is that two sequential events are depicted on each side of the cup. Thus in addition to the clustering of events in a cycle, we see what is technically *continuous* narration as defined above, within each field on A and B; in each, events take place over a period of time and are depicted in a temporal sequence in a single field. The repeated elements are not motivated by or crucial to plot; they consist of repeated inscriptions, setting elements, poses, and attributes. The exterior episodes are both separated and linked by recurring trees. In each case, a tree with a chlamys hanging from it roughly divides each field in two. Another set of trees, with sword and chlamys hanging from them, borders each side at the left. Each of Theseus' anthropomorphic adversaries has identical shaggy hair and beard. All of the struggles employ wrestling moves. Complete evidence for inscriptions is lost because the cup is not well-preserved, but Theseus' name appears to have been inscribed in both exterior fields as well as in the tondo, supplying verbal repetition. The image in the tondo is quite different, both in time and in place, from those on the exterior, clearly marking out the task of fetching the rings from Amphitrite as different from the struggles with the Bull, Skiron, Prokrustes, and Kerkyon.[36] In the interior, Theseus' long hair is down, he wears a *chitoniskos*, and his task involves no athletic prowess, but in fact requires the help of others.

This cup is of particular importance because it demonstrates, in the exterior fields, that even when the common habit of one scene per field is violated, the artist continues to rely on the rules of repetition as they have been developed to engage the viewer to link interconnected events as either similar or different. He feels free to use apparently arbitrarily selected features, unconnected to specific plot motivations, as signals for linkage. Euphronios' London cup is an important predecessor, where three scenes including Theseus, each in its own field, are apparently linked by means of repeated decorative syntax, words, figure-types, and attributes[37] [Figure 6.7]. Onesimos' Louvre cup is indeed a bold change from the Euphronion predecessor.[38]

Cyclic narration continues in the early fifth century. On the Berlin Painter's pelike in Florence, side A depicts Theseus battling the Minotaur, whereas B shows the hero with Skiron.[39] As with the Euphronios cup considered above, there are many repetitions serving to link the two units of the cycle. According to later literary sources, the two events can be placed in a rough narrative sequence. That is, Theseus

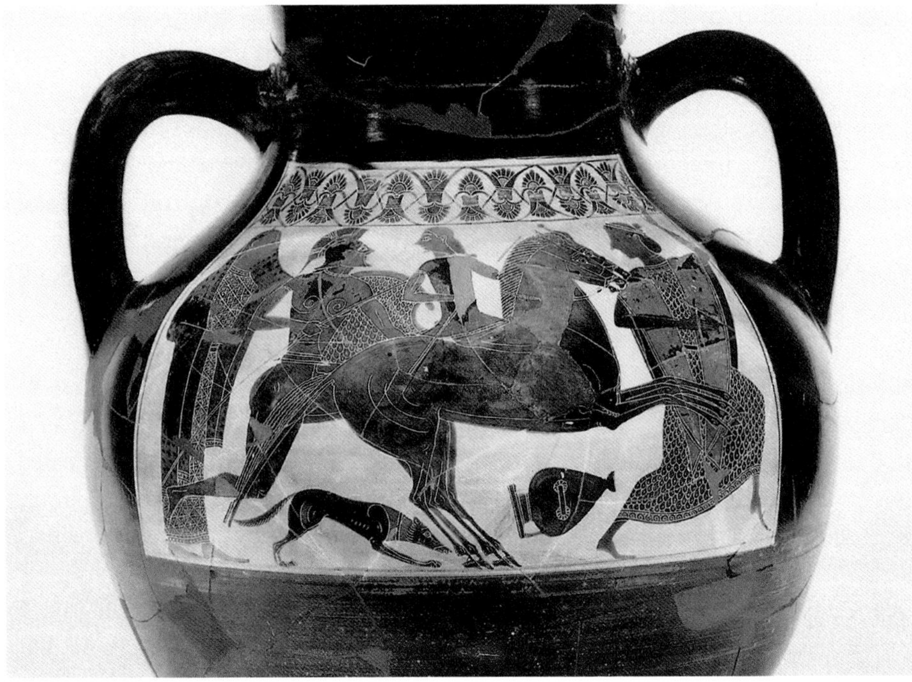

6.8. Black-figure amphora by Lydos, ca. 560–540 B.C. Side A. Berlin, Antikensammlung, Staatliche Museen zu Berlin 1685. (Photograph © Bildarchiv Preussischer Kulturbesitz / Art Resource, NY.)

had to reach Athens to be in a position to save the Athenian youths and maidens by slaying the Minotaur, so the Skiron adventure must be prior to the Minotaur fight. In each case, the hero strides to the right, grabbing his victim. Each victim falls as well, while leaning over to the right: the positions of the Minotaur's and Skiron's left hands are almost identical.

The inscriptions establish a third temporal zone, the present. As discussed in Chapter 5, a label identifying the hero, [Θ]ΕΣΕΥΣ, "Theseus," appears only on Side A, in the center of the composition. The artist supplies a reaction to the images from an undepicted spectator-narratee with the comments ΝΥΓΕ or (Ε)ΥΓΕ (Immerwahr) "and now!" and ΚΑΛΛΙΣΤΟΣ, "most handsome!" appearing at the top and at the left on B. The real reader of the inscription becomes the narratee, the observer within the story, for the events. The vocabulary of the reactions, especially the superlative of *kalos*, links the story to *symposion* and Theseus to youths admired as *kalos*. The inscriptions act as metadiscursive directives, indicating the ideal venue for dissemination of the stories and bringing the heroic story into the present situation, the *symposion*. Three moments in total are thereby collected together in this example, two through the combination of Skiron first and Minotaur second, and to these are added a third, *symposion*, in the present.

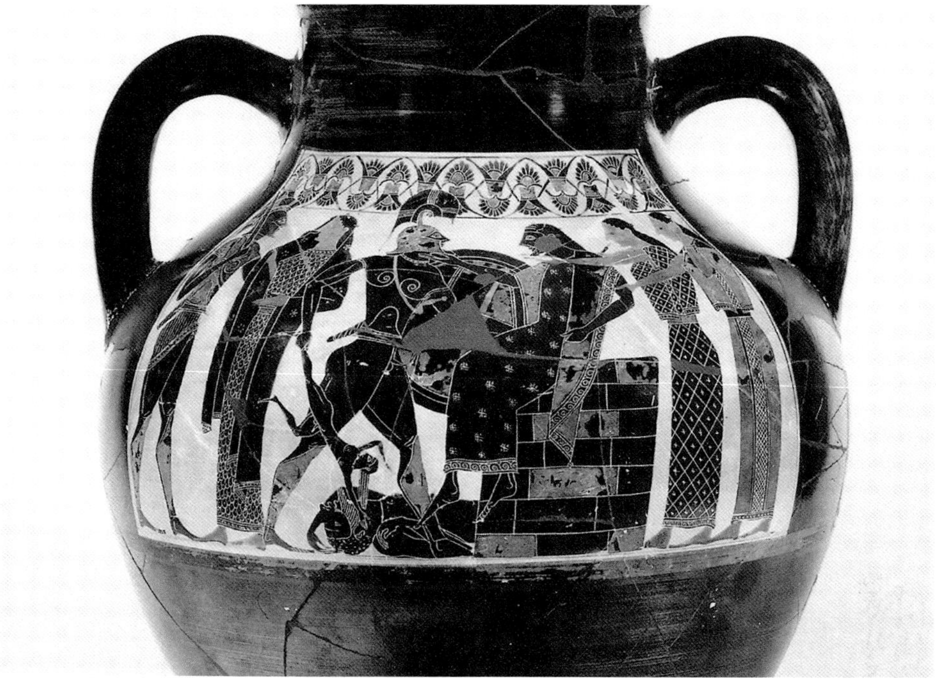

6.9. Black-figure amphora by Lydos, ca. 560–540 B.C. Side B. Berlin, Antikensammlung, Staatliche Museen zu Berlin 1685. (Photograph © Bildarchiv Preussischer Kulturbesitz / Art Resource, NY.)

Phased and Causally Linked Phased Narration

Lydos' amphora in Berlin is an excellent example to begin discussion of how both phased, causally linked narration and possibly even *continuous* narration are constructed through repetition at about the middle of the sixth century[40] [Figures 6.8, 6.9]. The scene on A shows an armed warrior in pursuit of a youth on horseback, framed by female figures. By conventional means – the presence of an overturned hydria, a running female figure at right, and a warrior's pursuit of a youth on horseback – we identify the scene on side A as the ambush of Troilos by Achilles [Figure 6.8]. A female figure at left stands holding her mantle forward, and some scholars identify her as the hero's mother, Thetis.[41] The fleeing female figure at far right is presumably Polyxena. Side B shows an Ilioupersis, featuring the death of Priam and a lifeless Astyanax, and at left is a second, distinct scene, a Recovery of Helen [Figure 6.9].

There are several repetitions in the renderings of characters and props or setting elements on the two sides. The figure of a woman holding out her mantle occupies the left part of each composition. She faces left on B and right on A. At the center of both scenes is a striding male figure, wearing a Corinthian helmet and a breastplate crossed diagonally with a baldric, who holds a circular shield so that the interior is visible. The repeated figures link the two sides, the scenes which comprise major plot events, or kernels, that are connected and clearly sequential: Achilles kidnaps Troilus long before his son kills Priam and Astyanax or Menelaus recovers Helen.[42] The artist instructs the viewer by means of repetition to link the two fields and then requires them to assess events in terms of priority. In addition to the creation of temporal linkage, the thematic links connect plot events as well: Achilles will kill one young Trojan boy. His son Neoptolemos kills another and will in turn kill the father of his own father's victim.[43] The two murdering characters, the father and son pair, are represented with a significant degree of visual repetition.[44] The evidence from Lydos' Berlin amphora therefore reveals that as early as mid-sixth century artists used repetition to indicate that different temporal phases of narratives, all causally linked, cohere. If Achilles had not kidnapped Troilos, Menelaus could not have reclaimed Helen, because the kidnapping of Troilos was a necessary condition for the fall of Troy.[45] This example has obvious similarities to the slightly later amphora by Exekias' amphora in Philadelphia, where he connects two sequential, causally related deaths at Troy, those of Achilles and Antilochos.[46]

The conflation of the Ilioupersis and the Recovery of Helen in a single panel on side B is itself a topic of interest because it is very like what scholars define as continuous narration, where events taking place over a period of time are shown one after the next in a single pictorial field.[47] The juxtaposition is similar to the joining of two deeds of Theseus in single frames on Onesimos' cup discussed above, where the Skiron and Procrustes examples are united on A and Kerykeion and the Bull are combined on B. The Death of Priam and the Recovery of Helen are both parts of the Ilioupersis, but they are not necessarily linked to one another in time or place.[48] If the events are indeed sequential, the panel does display continuous narration. This example by Lydos would therefore be a landmark in its use of repetition to depict both causally linked phased narration and continuous narration.

An amphora in Kassel by a member of Group E combines the Ransom of Hector and a "fight."[49] However, the artist extends discourse-time over two sides of the vessel, and he may couple two causally linked episodes in a narrative as well [Figures 6.10, 6.11]. There are no labels to verify absolutely that these stories are mythical. Many repetitions exist between the two sides. A prominent horizontal at the bottom of each scene is created by an outstretched corpse, supine on A and prone on B. The corpse on B, in the midst of battle, still wears a Corinthian helmet, and his round shield, in profile, rests on his buttocks; on A, in the ransom scene, a round shield, also in profile, is propped against the border of the pictorial frame, and a Corinthian helmet lies on a footstool at the corpse's belly. Note that the reclining Achilles' Boeotian shield hangs in the field and his (?) Corinthian helmet rests on a table at the head of the *kline*.[50] Identifying the numerous repetitions in corpse, helmets, and shields encourages the viewer to ask if the scene on B is not another Trojan War event, the fight over the corpse of Patroklos, which takes place prior to the death of Hector. If so, repetition of figures and attributes here links main plot scenes or kernels that are temporally discrete and

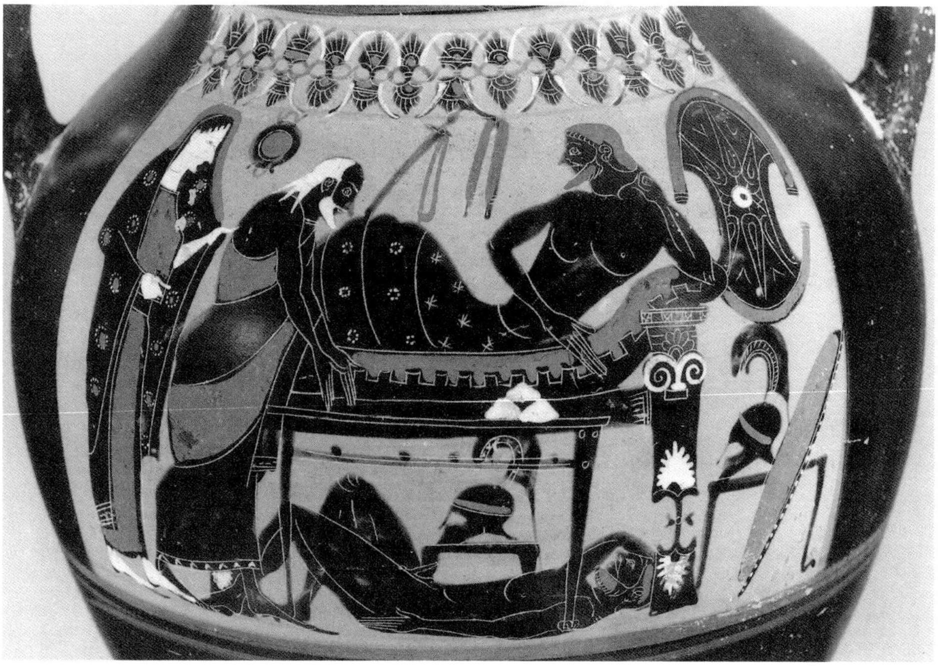

6.10. Black-figure amphora by Group E, ca. 560–540 B.C. Side A. Kassel, Staatliche Museen, Antikensammlung T. 674. (Photograph © Staatliche Museen Kassel [Neg. Nr. A3615].)

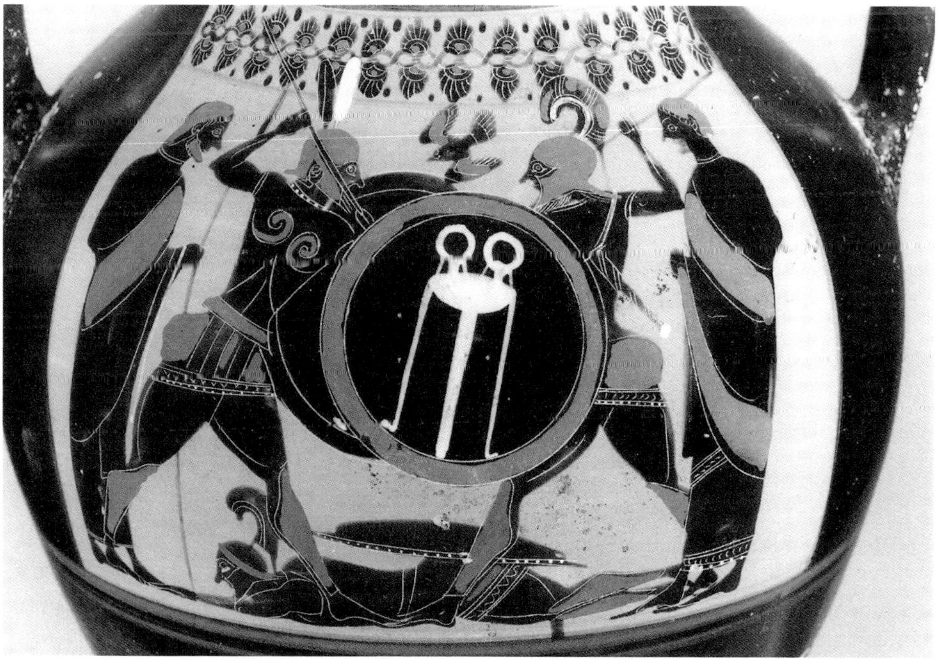

6.11. Black-figure amphora by Group E, ca. 560–540 B.C. Side B. Kassel, Staatliche Museen, Antikensammlung T. 674. (Photograph © Staatliche Museen Kassel [Neg. Nr. A3617].)

also connected in terms of cause and effect: Hector is made visually equivalent to the man he killed, Patroklos, and Achilles killed Hector to avenge Patroklos' slaughter. If the identification of the two topics depicted on the vase, the fight over Patroklos' corpse and the ransom of Hector, is correct, this is another early landmark example, the same sort of temporal sequencing as noted in the Berlin example by Lydos, where the Ambush of Troilos, the death of Priam, and the Recovery of Helen are linked[51] [Figures 6.8, 6.9].

Understanding how repetition links parts of a narration can help determine the likelihood that other ambiguous scenes may be linked components of a single story. A second example by the Amasis Painter, already introduced in Chapter 4, is instructive[52] [Figures 4.5, 4.6]. On a Type A cup on side A is a stable scene, where grooms ready horses for harnessing; side B shows a figure, identified by many scholars as Poseidon, holding a trident and exhorting a group of armed men. Repetitions to link the two sides are minimal: anonymous male spectators, apparently spectator-narratees, at the far right (A) and left (B) wear identical clothes, but one is a youth and one is an adult. Some scholars interpret the two sides in combination as two moments in the story of Poseidon disguised as Kalchas exhorting the Greek troops (*Iliad* 13, 45).[53] For them, side A shows the preparation for the god's departure in his chariot, a satellite event, and B shows him at Troy exhorting the troops, a main plot event. The narrative is therefore presented elliptically, since several intervening events are omitted. The fact of the ellipsis is obscured on the cup by the presence of full-height figures – both walking left – placed under the handles, giving the impression of immediate connection between the two sides.

Simon suggests an alternate reading: the stable depicted on A is not Poseidon's but Ares'.[54] Her interpretation obviously makes impossible an understanding of the two sides as linked segments of a single story. This discussion has now identified several examples where events presented in two different fields widely separated in time are linked: the deaths of Antilochos and Achilles; the Ambush of Troilos and the Death of Priam; and possibly the Death of Patroklos and the Ransom of Hector. Thus, working outward from these examples, here, too, repetition provides an answer. On the Amasis Painter's cup, both the repeated spectators framing each scene and the figures walking under each handle further link the scenes, despite the apparent time lag between the harnessing of Poseidon's horses and his presence among the Greeks.[55] The existence of these repetitions makes it necessary to suppose that the events on A and B of the Amasean cup are indeed connected and in fact sequential, linking preparation for the god's travel to Troy with his presence in the battle. Because there is other contemporaneous evidence on vase-paintings for linking of two events in a mythical narrative, it is reasonable to conclude that the two images are connected to achieve an extension of discourse-time.[56]

A cup by Epiktetos preserves images of events linked via visual repetitions that are components of a familiar narrative[57] [Figures 6.12–6.14]. In addition to repeated images,

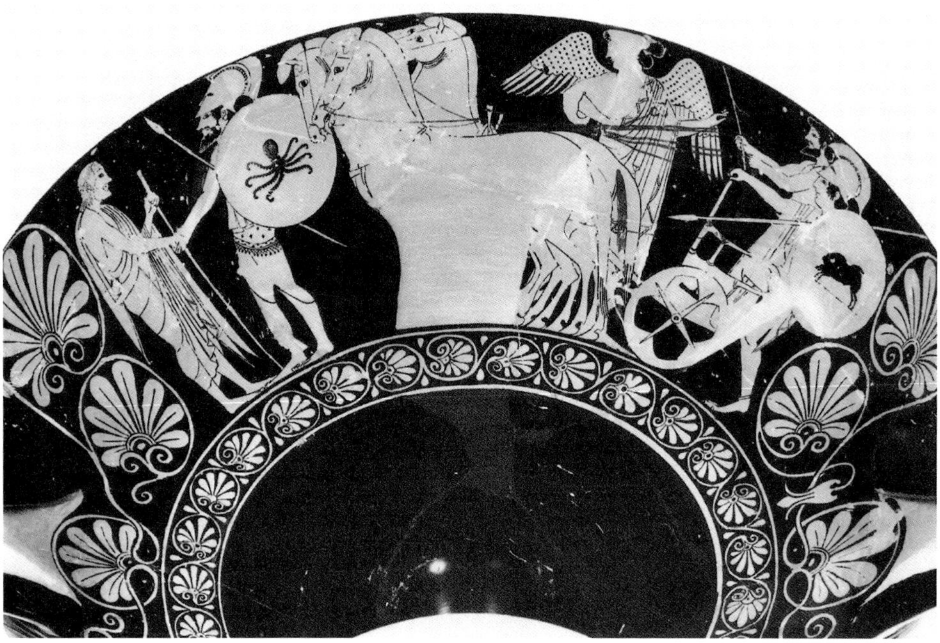

6.12. Red-figure cup by Epiktetos, ca. 520–490 B.C. Side A. Berlin, Antikensammlung, Staatliche Museen zu Berlin 2264. (Photograph © Bildarchiv Preussischer Kulturbesitz / Art Resource, NY.)

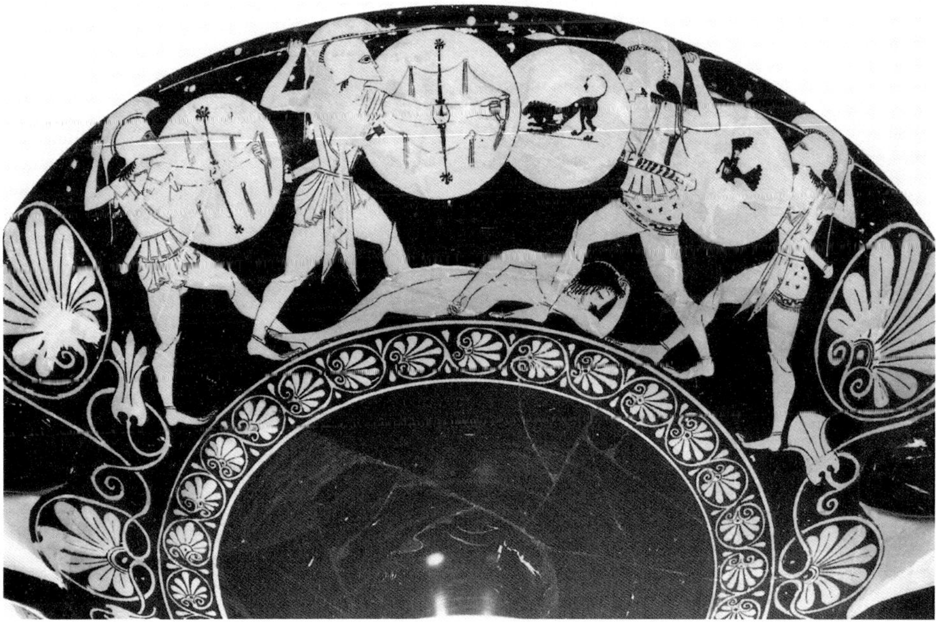

6.13. Red-figure cup by Epiktetos, ca. 520–490 B.C. Side B. Berlin, Antikensammlung, Staatliche Museen zu Berlin 2264. (Photograph © Bildarchiv Preussischer Kulturbesitz / Art Resource, NY.)

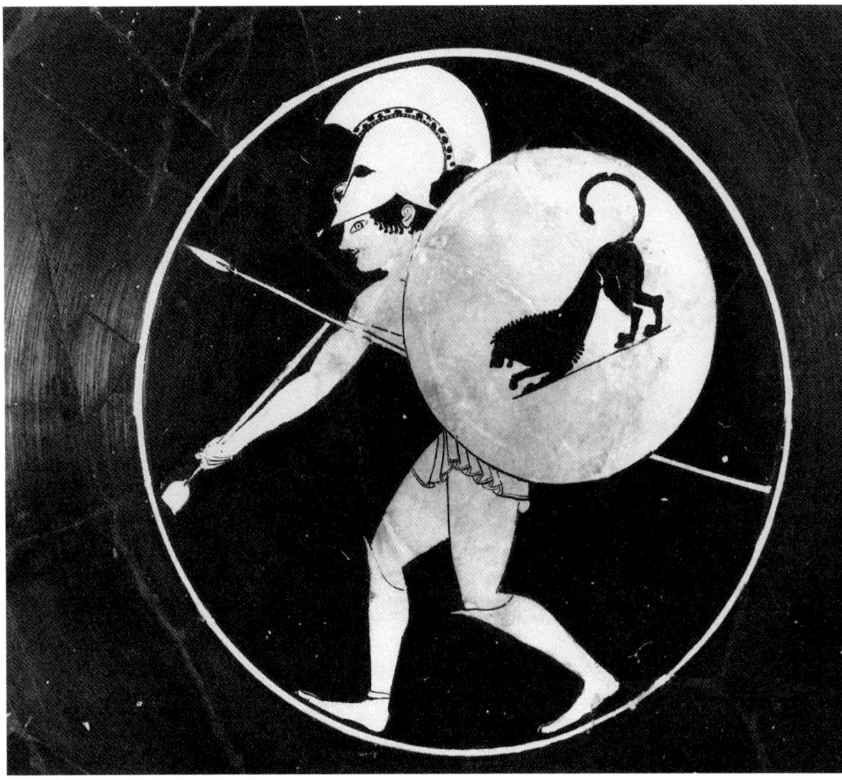

6.14. Red-figure cup by Epiktetos, ca. 520–490 B.C. Interior. Berlin, Antikensammlung, Staatliche Museen zu Berlin 2264. (Photograph © Bildarchiv Preussischer Kulturbesitz / Art Resource, NY.)

repeated *placement* – but not *content* – of inscriptions helps to create a unified text. There is again a definite order to two of the events that are linked. The cup is wholly devoted to epic military topics. Side B shows figures (Aias, Aineas, Hippasos, and Diomedes – all labeled) fighting over the body of Patroklos (also labeled). Side A seems to show the departure of Achilles to reenter the battle; Phoinix, Antilichos, Iris, Achilles, and Nestor are labeled. Linking the two exterior fields are repeated male figures carrying spears and wearing Corinthian helmets, round shields, and greaves. The unlabeled military trumpeter in the tondo is dressed identically to the exterior warriors, and his shield device matches precisely that of Aineas on the exterior. He is clearly associated with the theme of the story, albeit in a moment not identifiable to us. Signatures of both potter and painter accompany his image.

The inscriptions tell us that the scenes on the cup represent a single story. The figures named all belong to the story of the death of Patroklos and its aftermath. Further, the *placement* of some of the inscriptions, horizontally at the upper right of each composition, adds another syntactical repetition, beyond the content of the story itself. This repetition simultaneously links and distinguishes. The specificity of the inscriptions allows us to link the visually interconnected images with a single story: the death of Patroklos, its reporting to Achilles, and Achilles' reaction to it. Thus, once again, we have an exposition of scenes in temporal sequence. Unlike the three clustered, "cyclic" adventures of Theseus on the Euphronios cup in London, with Antiope, Helen, and Ariadne, these events are causally linked. Although Epiktetos separates each event into a different field, the net effect here is very similar to that achieved by Lydos on his Berlin amphora discussed above, where three causally linked Trojan events, the ambush of Troilos, the death of Priam, and the recovery of Helen, appear in two fields.[58]

The well-known Sarpedon krater by Euphronios in New York, dating to the last decades of the sixth century, preserves many repetitions in imagery[59] [Figures 6.15, 6.16]. Following the clues provided via repeated elements offers confirmation for one interpretation scholars have advanced for the vase, that the arming figures on side B are connected to the scene of the dying of Sarpedon on A. The actions of the figures on B may well be the result of the event depicted on A.

The youths arming on side B don the helmets, round shields, baldric and scabbard, greaves and spears of Leodamas and Hippolytos, the adult male Trojan warriors who flank the central scene on A. The youths share beardlessness, downy sideburns, and, in one case, almost complete nudity, with the dying Sarpedon, but they are putting on what has been stripped off his corpse. The adult male figure at the far right of A, Hippolytos, is almost a verbatim repetition of Axippos, the adult who accompanies the arming youths at the far right on B. The visual clues create links between the male figures on one side and the male figures on the other.[60]

The inscriptions on the krater cover three topics: identity of the figures, identity of potter and painter, and the announcement that a young man, Leagros, is *kalos*. The repetitions in both placement and content of the names help to reinforce the fact that figures on the two sides are comparable.[61] The shared "ἱππ" or "horse" root of the names ΑΧΣΙΠΠΟΣ(B), "Axippos," and *h*ΙΠΠΟΛΥΤΟΣ(A), "Hippolytos," underscores the similarity in appearance of the two far-right figures in each composition: The "ἱππ" root is repeated again in *h*ΙΠΠ⟨Α?⟩ΣΟΣ, "Hippasos," the name of the figure who bends over in the center on B, and Hippasos' name is placed vertically, like the name "Hippolytus" on A. These clues create a link between Hippasos and Hippolytos, and this link supports the identification of the arming figures on B as like those on A.[62] If these arming figures are in fact allies of Sarpedon, could they be reinforcements called to battle after Sarpedon's death, analogous to those men roused by Glaukos after the death of Sarpedon (*Iliad* 16.591) in *Iliad* 16.625? If so, the repetition may link two scenes in temporal sequence where the events on A bring about those on B.[63]

Reverting to a more typical formula for linking events where there is a common protagonist is the Berlin Painter's volute-krater in London, dating to around 500 B.C.[64] The two scenes are linked only through the reappearance of Achilles and are not

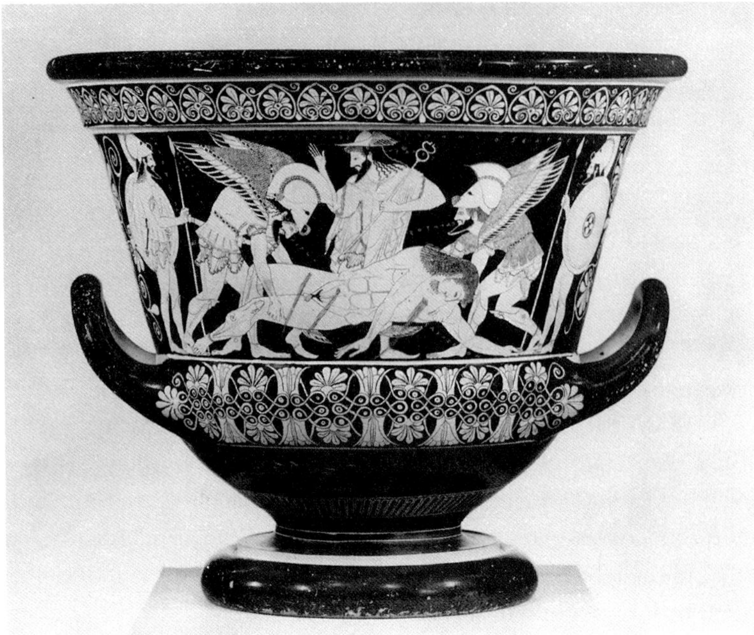

6.15. Red-figure krater by Euphronios, ca. 520–505 B.C. Side A. New York, Metropolitan Museum of Art 1972.11.10. (Photograph © The Metropolitan Museum of Art. All rights reserved, The Metropolitan Museum of Art.)

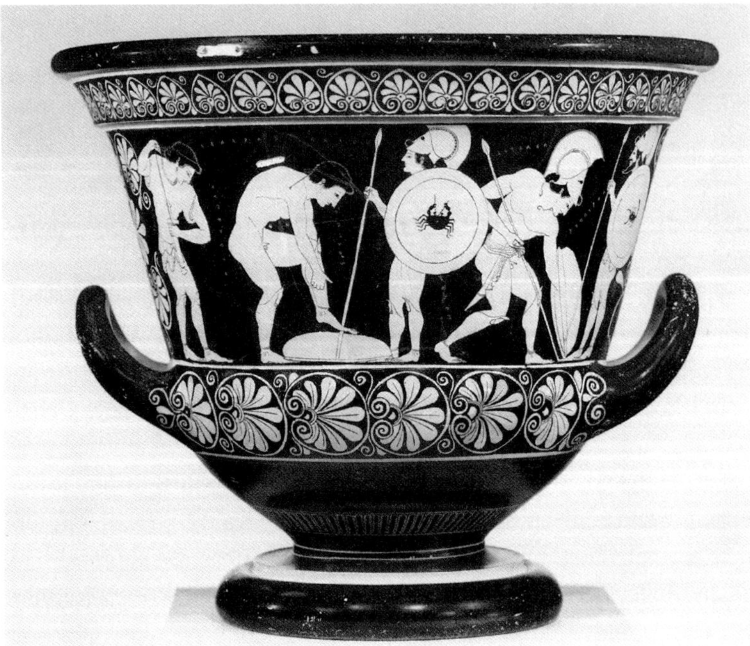

6.16. Red-figure krater by Euphronios, ca. 520–505 B.C. Side B. New York, Metropolitan Museum of Art 1972.11.10. (Photograph © The Metropolitan Museum of Art. All rights reserved, The Metropolitan Museum of Art.)

causally linked events: B does not happen because of A. In this regard, the mode of narrative representation is most like cyclic narration, where the hero is repeated in different adventures. The painter represents Achilles fighting on each side, with Memnon on A and with Hector on B [Figures 6.17, 6.18]. The figures on the left of each composition are nearly identical, and the inscriptions identifying Thetis and Athena are likewise placed almost identically. Each of the heroes is in a striding pose and has outstretched arms. Achilles' name and that of his adversary follow a similar diagonal line in each case, although placement is lower in one case and higher in the other. The figures at far right – Eos on A and Apollo on B – stride in different directions, but their names are placed in precisely the same spot. These inscriptions are labels, and they are forming a parallel text for the narratives conveyed in the images. Along with the attributes of some characters, the inscriptions help to make otherwise generic fights specific, and they generate comparison through repetition. The labels inform us that the images depict two different events involving Achilles; otherwise we would not know. Overall the decorative program and use of repetition here are very like the amphora by Psiax in Copenhagen discussed in Chapter 10 [Figures 10.1, 10.2], where inscriptions identify two nearly identical, otherwise generic departure-scenes as specific mythological events.[65] Here, though, the events have a particular temporal sequence, so the repetitions link events that have a particular relationship in time: Hector dies before Memnon.

A final example is a fitting one with which to end the discussion of mythical narration, as it is often cited in discussions of story-telling in imagery. What is new in the present analysis is the emphasis on the visual repetitions that unify the several parts of the story. Douris' kylix in Vienna, dating to about 480 B.C., preserves associated scenes that represent three causally linked stages of a single story: the dispute over the arms of Achilles[66] [Figures 6.19–6.21]. As a single vessel linking Trojan-related events, this cup has some notable precedents in the repertories of Lydos, Exekias, and Oltos,[67] but Douris relies on new categories of repeated images to link the three scenes, and his result is therefore significantly different. Whereas the earlier painters relied on repeated inscriptions, figural image-types, their attributes, or even props to connect different events and even to suggest a common location, Douris adds the motivating element for plot, the armor itself, to the roster of repeated elements.

Csapo and Miller have pointed out recently how this cup combines scenes "governed by linear and causal sequence rather than merely the presence of a single hero."[68] Indeed, the artist uses visual repetition of *both* figures and props that are crucial to the unfolding narrative to link the scenes: the artist also follows the comfortable system of repeating a central character in each scene – here, Odysseus – developed by earlier artists in collections of the deeds of Theseus, the labors of Herakles, or even two Trojan fights of Achilles. In each of the three scenes on the Vienna cup, there is an adult male with beard, short hair, and fillet and wearing a *himation*, who can be identified

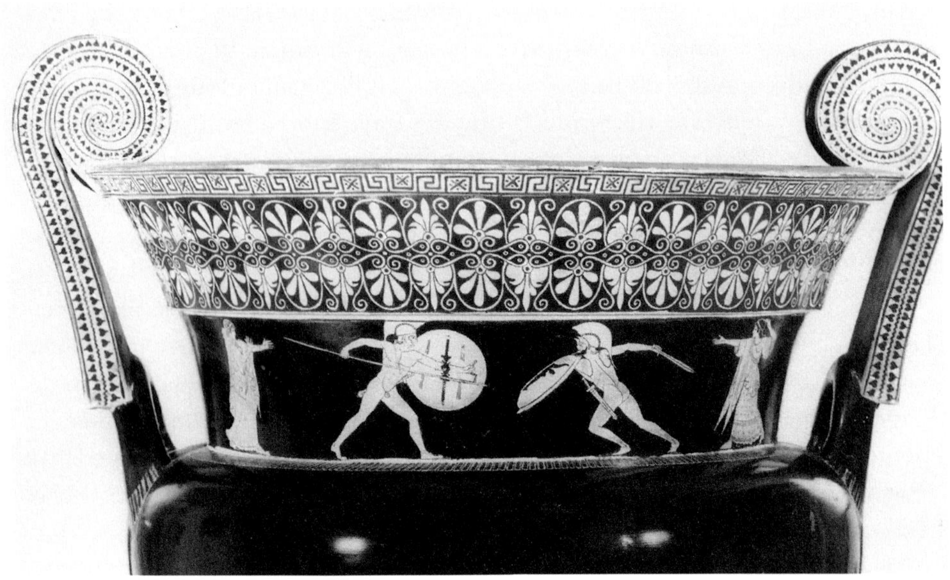

6.17. Red-figure volute-krater by the Berlin Painter, ca. 500–480 B.C. Side A. London, The British Museum E 468. (Photograph © Copyright The Trustees of the British Museum.)

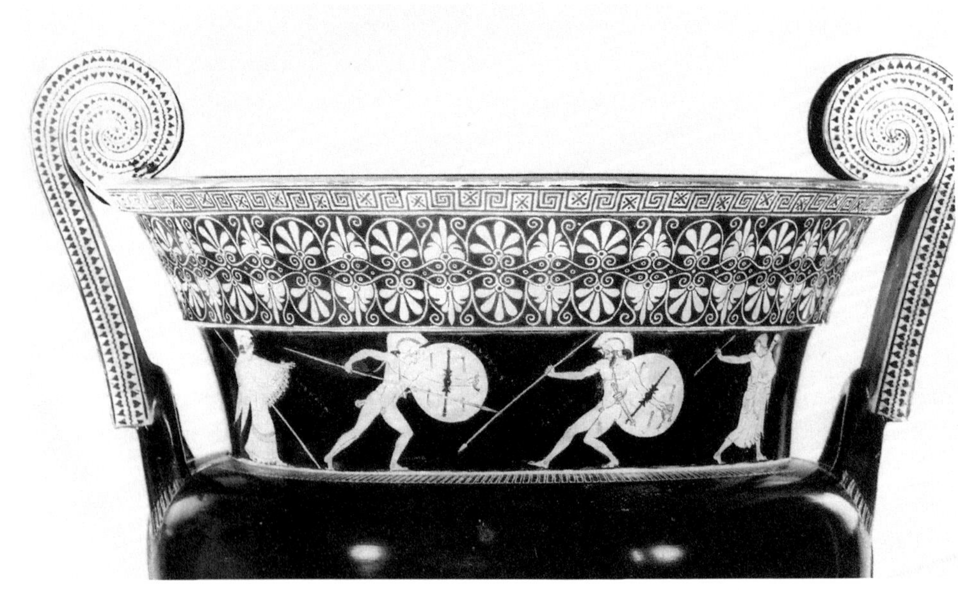

6.18. Red-figure volute-krater by the Berlin Painter, ca. 500–480 B.C. Side B. London, The British Museum E 468. (Photograph © Copyright The Trustees of the British Museum.)

as Odysseus. Further linking the scenes is a helmet in the center of each composition, in each case facing in the same direction, at the top of the pile of armor on A, on Athena's head (here, obviously not the helmet of Achilles)[69] on B, and being handed to Neoptolemos by Odysseus in the tondo. Finally, the arrangement of the armor in the tondo, as though it is being worn but with its wearer only evoked and not present, is all the more striking because of the contrast to the vital, living figure in exactly the same spot in the exterior scenes. The greaves and the shield appear in only one other place, and that is in the heap at the center of A. In a masterful use of ellipsis, Douris has evoked the dead warrior twice in differing ways. This cup relies on repetitions for its coherence, but it is truly redundant as well: there is excessive repetition to insure that the message is delivered.

The inscriptions are not directly related to the narrative, but they are placed similarly on the exterior and thereby also draw the two sides together: '*h*ΟΠΑΙΣΚΑΛΟΣ, "the youth is handsome," stretches along the top of A, and [Χ]ΑΙ[ΡΕΣΤΡΑ]ΤΟΣΚΑΛΟΣ, "Chairestratos is handsome," along the top of B. Further distinguishing the interior scene – the last in the sequence of events and the last to be seen by a drinker when handed a full cup – is the absence of a *kalos* inscription. Instead, the painter's signature follows the outline of the tondo, and the potter's signature is located on the exterior of the foot.[70] In sum, the artist adds to established conventions – the repetition of individual characters, props, attributes and inscriptions – a new category of repetition, the repetition of plot-motivating objects, to create a phased narration with maximum extension of discourse time to include three different pictorial fields. This important result is an extension of habits of repetition that are by this point over 100 years old. Note how the repetition of the plot-crucial armor parallels the linking device used by the Pistoxenos Painter in his nearly contemporary depiction of Herakles and Linos on the Schwerin skyphos discussed above, where the murder weapon, the lyre, is the primary figural repetition linking the two fields of the skyphos [Figures 6.5, 6.6].

Linked Generic Events

The same principles that link identifiably mythical narratives serve to join less specific events. A special model of a type A amphora in Würzburg by the Amasis Painter includes careful repetitions that connect sequential events, not necessarily causally linked except in the most general sense.[71] On A, satyrs make wine, and on B, they pour it for Dionysos, drink it, and dance. A *kantharos* appears in the ground on A; Dionysos extends it for filling on B. Striking is a repeated figure of an ithyphallic satyr who plays the double pipes, second from left on A and at far left on B. Three of the four satyrs on B have spotted skin and all five on A do. There are clear links here, both in characters and in props, and they direct the viewer to a recognition of sequence: the satyrs must make the wine before the god can drink it. The unity of the two sides is emphasized by the frieze of dancing nymphs and satyrs (interrupted by a seated Dionysos on A) above each panel. The overall context of similarity is complemented by the differences: the containers for wine making and mixing are lacking in the main scene on B, whereas, with the exception of the god's kantharos which appears in both places, only containers for serving and drinking wine appear on A.

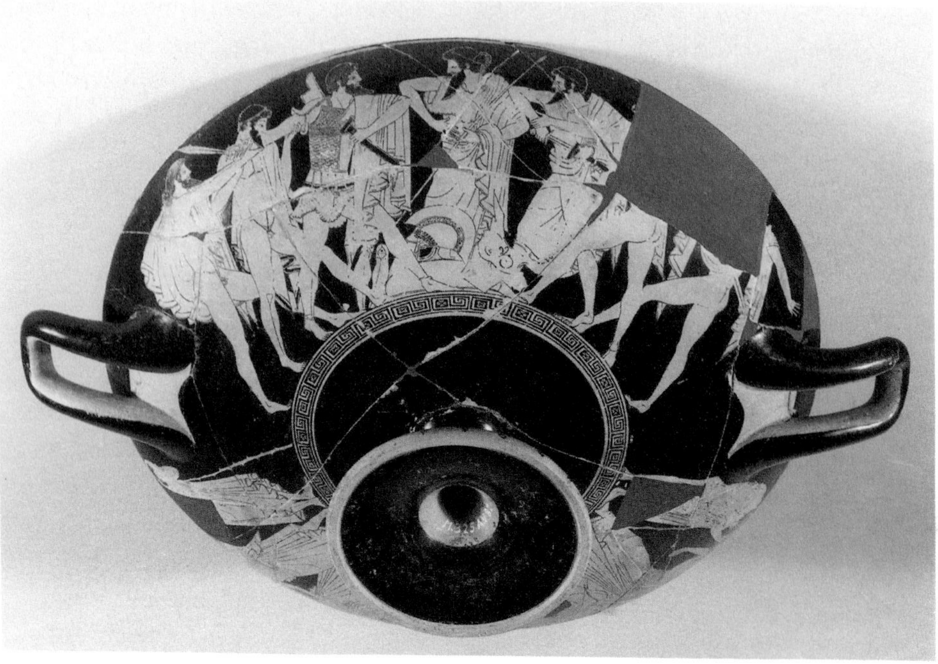

6.19. Red-figure cup by Douris, ca. 480–470 B.C. Side A. Vienna, Kunsthistorisches Museum 3695. (Photograph © Universität Wien, Institut für Klassische Archäologie, Archäologische Sammlung.)

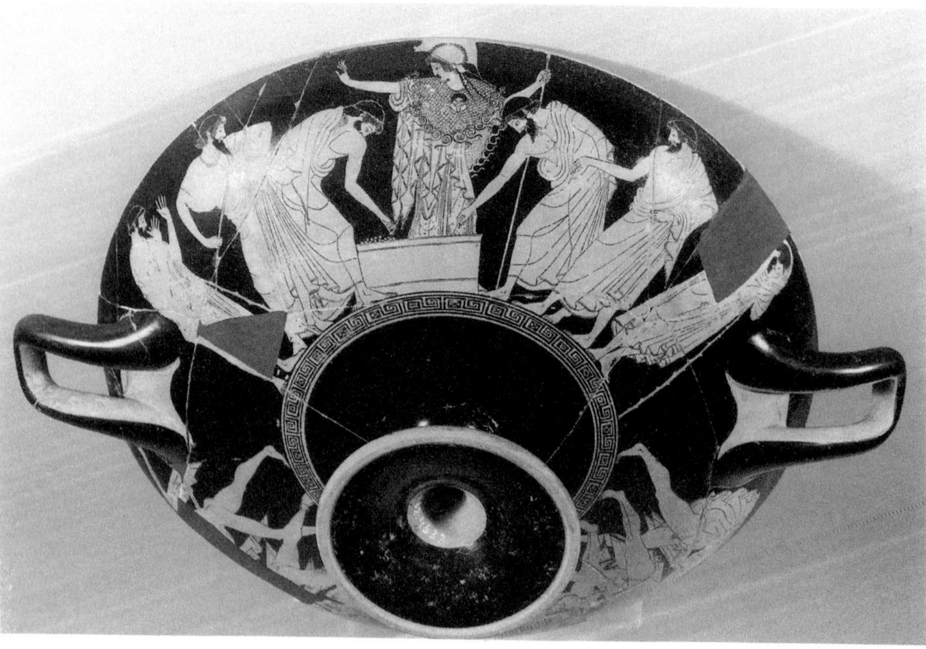

6.20. Red-figure cup by Douris, ca. 480–470 B.C. Side B. Vienna, Kunsthistorisches Museum 3695. (Photograph © Universität Wien, Institut für Klassische Archäologie, Archäologische Sammlung.)

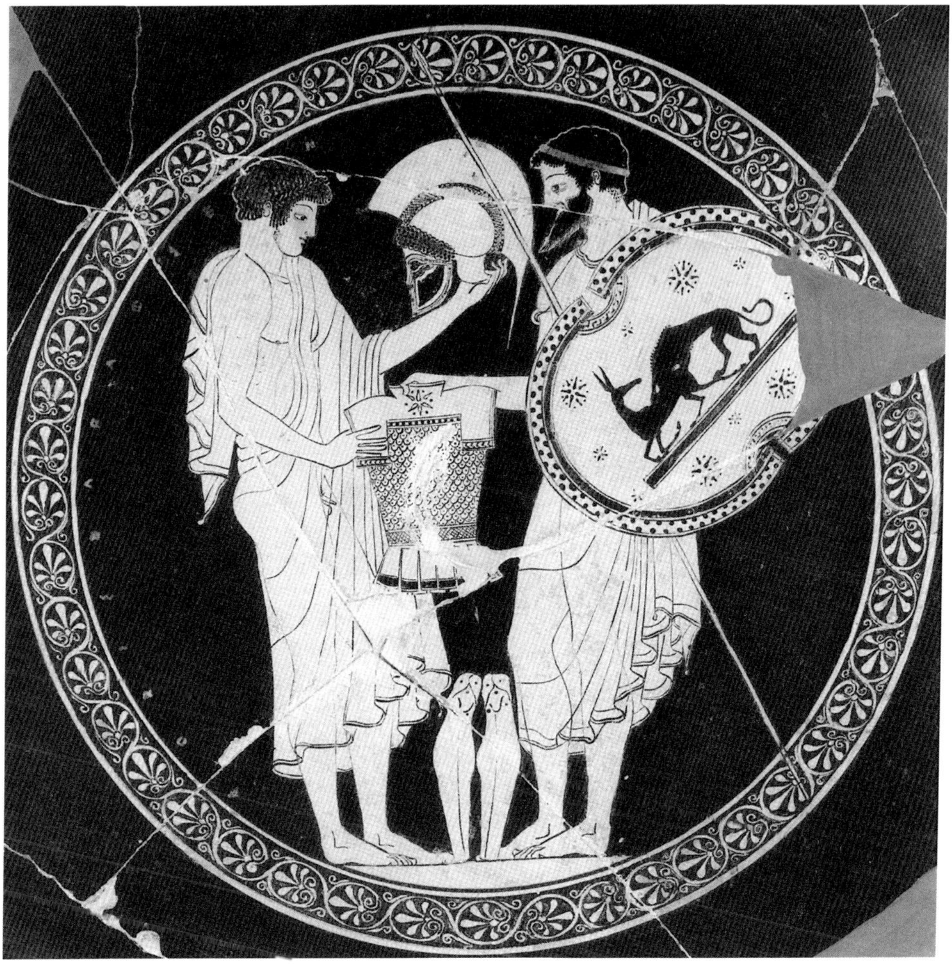

6.21. Red-figure cup by Douris, ca. 480–470 B.C. Interior. Vienna, Kunsthistorisches Museum 3695. (Photograph © Universität Wien, Institut für Klassische Archäologie, Archäologische Sammlung.)

In most cases there is no compelling reason to categorize such examples as the Würzburg amphora as proper narratives, but they are of interest in this study because they use clearly analogous types of repetition to link sequential events and to create coherent, unified texts. On a Siana cup in Athens, two depictions of groups of two men fighting on the A and B repeat poses and pairings, but all shield devices are different, suggesting that the men fighting on A are not the same men who fight on B.[72] Different people are occupying different space. An example in Berlin is similar. There is a *symposion* scene on one side, with four symposiasts reclining, and on the other side, in addition to three symposiasts nearly identical to those on side B, there are three standing men flanking the central reclining figure.[73] Thus part of the composition is repeated, but to the repeated composition on B is an added element that distinguishes A from B, the group of three standing men. Likewise, Siana cups in Hamburg and

Copenhagen depict a boar hunt with two hunters on horseback surrounding a boar on one side and additional hunters on horseback on the other.[74] Each of these examples relies on the handles of the cups, rather than reserved panels, to distinguish the two fields. In each case, there may be two sequential moments in a single story: "first these six hoplites battled, then another six followed suit"; "the *symposion* was in full swing and then a group of three men arrived and surrounded X"; "first the men rode on horseback to the boar's lair and then they attacked it." However, there is no discernible clue for the viewer to determine which event is first. Another good possibility is to see the scenes as generic analogies to Shapiro's unified narration, with two or more separate scenes depicting one moment in time in at least two different physical places and without repeated characters.[75] For these generic examples, it is pointless to try to identify a kernel (or main plot element) or a satellite event that is extended, but the artist has potentially lengthened discourse-time by the extension of his subject over two sides of the vessels.

Some other combinations of generic scenes are more clearly examples of phased events, where we see at least one notable candidate for a kernel, a major plot event from which the action can branch off onto more than one direction.[76] Side B of a Siana cup in New Zealand depicts youths on horseback, apparently racing.[77] Side A displays a nude youth riding, accompanied by another nude youth and three draped youths, with a wreath hanging in the field. Brijder, in identifying the subject on A, queries: return from the horse-race? If his suggested interpretation is accurate, the two sides are sequential: they are the horse race and its aftermath. The horse race could be a kernel, or main plot event, because it can have several results; the result coupled with it here is "and one youth won the race." The repetition of the nude youth on horseback, a character in the story, links the two sides, whereas the accompanying differences distinguish the two compositions. The comparison places two events in temporal sequence, representing a story where the episodes are causally linked. "The youth is awarded the wreath as a result of having won the race."

A panathenaic-shaped amphora by Lydos in Florence presents sequence in a similar way: on one side is a victorious charioteer, shown with short hair and a beard.[78] On the other, an identical short-haired, bearded figure appears with Athena, and the fillet he carries in his left hand identifies him as a victorious athlete. Thus the two sides, linked by repetition of the athlete, show the race and the victory ceremony that follows it. This example presumably depicts mortal activity rather than a strictly heroic or mythical event. Nevertheless the presence of Athena, whether the goddess herself or a statue, elevates the status of the mortal figure.

Civic Ritual and *Aition*

There are other categories of images where sequential events are linked but the subject itself does not qualify as narrative. Civic and religious rituals, where events are acted out rather than told, are two of these.[79] A well-known cup by the Painter of the Burgon Sianas is an example that appears to link two sequential actions, very likely parts of a civic ritual honoring Demeter, through repetition.[80] One side depicts dancers at an altar with flames; a nude youth tags along as the last performer, behind the women [Figure 6.22]. In his hand, he holds something round. The B side depicts agriculture. Many scholars identify the male pushing the plough as Bouzyges, the mythical first individual to use oxen for ploughing and the first to carry out one of the annual sacred ploughings in Attica. Both ploughman and sower are nude youths, and the figure who moves left, sowing seeds (?), is very similar to the male dancer on A [Figure 6.23]. In Ashmole's words: "this is perhaps the boy who has played a part already, though he looks a little older and of stouter build."[81] Indeed, his nudity and his youthfulness link him to the figure on the reverse, and his posture is particularly close to that of the boy dancer. Also noted by Ashmole, the two figures are shown in the same pose from different perspectives – we see the figure who dances from the back and the figure who sows from the front – thus establishing unity. In addition, the seeds the B-side sower holds look very much like the round object held by the boy on A. The visual repetition of this figure and the round object signifying seeds supports the view of those scholars who see the two images on this vessel as composing a single text depicting a Demeter festival. The repetition also links two ritual events which have a particular temporal relationship: the dancers prepare the ground before the plowman and the sower go to work.[82] Dancers soften the ground as they propitiate the deity at the altar, so that the seeds will grow. Despite the fact that it does not depict a mythical narrative, this cup is significant for this study. It joins two specific events through repetition of a single figural type, with the linked events associated thematically and in a particular time relationship. The text thereby created, composed of two significant actions, reproduces the activities of Demeter's ritual, depicted in two separate scenes.

In the *oeuvre* of Onesimos is an early fifth century cup in the Louvre closely allied in spirit to the last example, with an image program of civic rather than religious ritual. The Louvre cup includes repeated visual and verbal links and also joins fields by means of two provocative suggestions of acclaim in public space.[83] [Figures 6.24–6.26]. The subject is not apparently a religious ritual, but a civic one. All three fields on this cup depict similarly dressed youths on horseback; and Cahn has interpreted the exterior scenes as reflecting the final preparations for the *dokimasia* on one side and the arrival of the *hippeis* on the other.[84] If he is correct, this cup is an important document in the evolution of the depiction of two specific sequential, interrelated, but nonmythical events. Side A shows a youth in a fur cap using a long rein to lead a horse which he intends to mount, and a groom behind the horse holds his spears and a crop. Otherwise all figures on the cup are mounted, wearing fancy boots and chlamydes. Doric columns on both sides A and B provide background for these figures; it is the repetition of the setting elements that is particularly important to note, because it

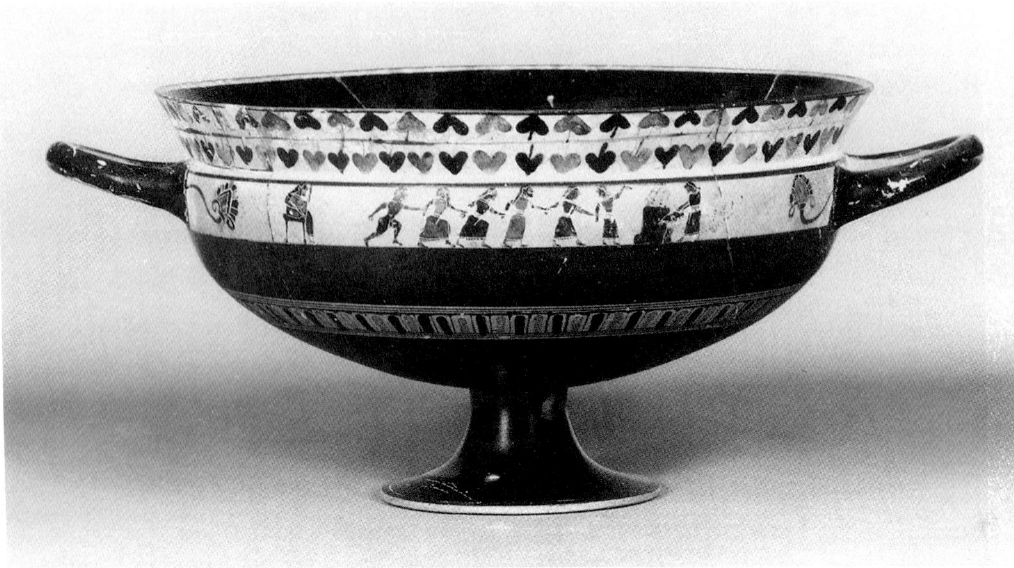

6.22. Black-figure cup by the Painter of Burgon Sianas, ca. 565–555 B.C. Side A. London, The British Museum 1906.12–15.1. (Photograph © Copyright The Trustees of the British Museum.)

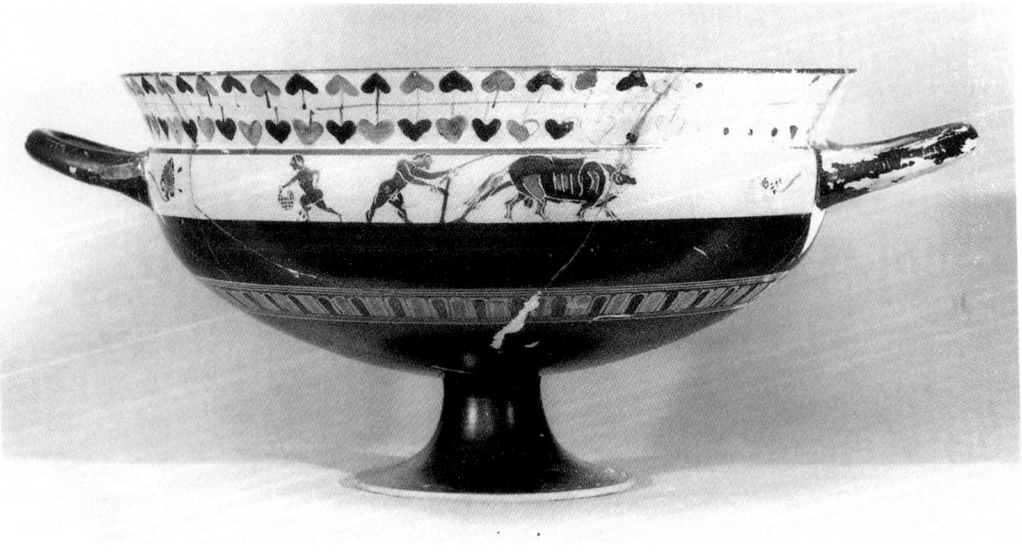

6.23. Black-figure cup by the Painter of Burgon Sianas, ca. 565–555 B.C. Side B. London, The British Museum 1906.12–15.1. (Photograph © Copyright The Trustees of the British Museum.)

stresses the significance of location, public space in the Athenian Agora, in the story. The use of repeated setting elements to connect events is relatively new at this point; it appears on Onesimos' cycle cup, just discussed, showing five deeds of Theseus, and later in the Kleophrades' Painter's Philadelphia stamnos [Figures 10.7, 10.8], where

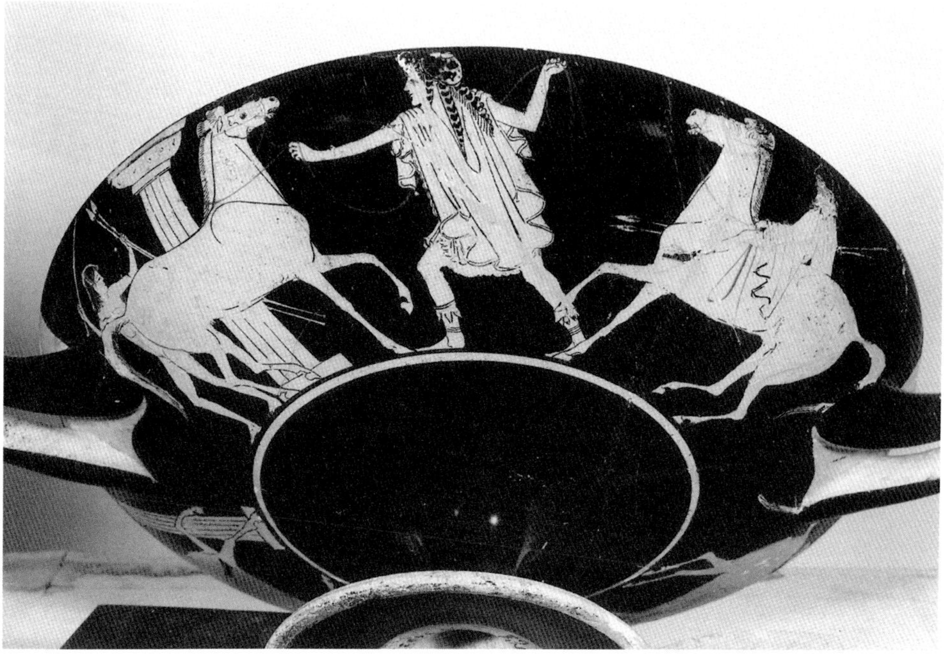

6.24. Red-figure cup by Onesimos, ca. 510–490 B.C. Side A. Paris, Musée du Louvre G 105. (Photograph courtesy of the Musée du Louvre, Dist. RMN / © Les frères Chuzeville.)

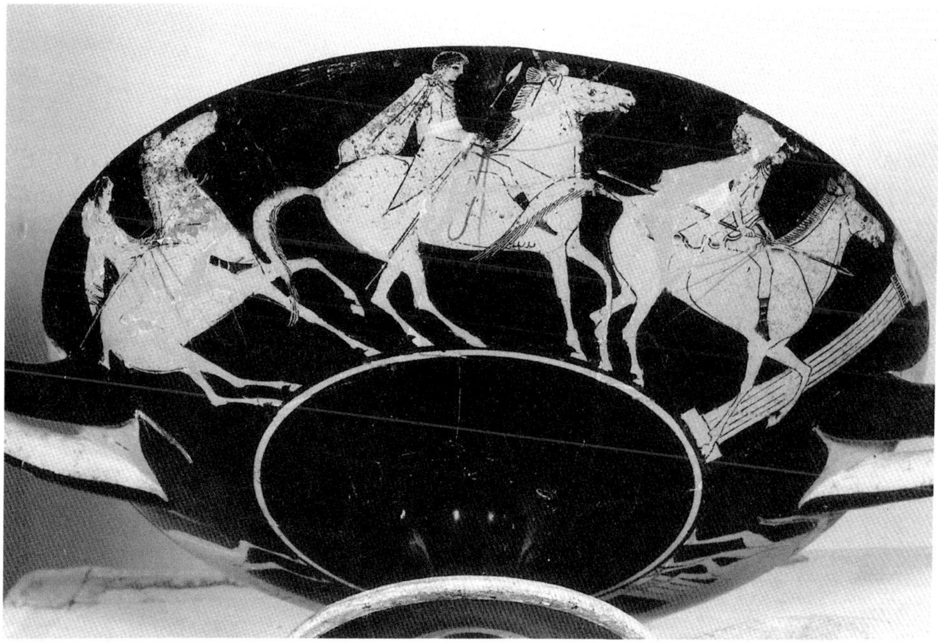

6.25. Red-figure cup by Onesimos, ca. 510–490 B.C. Side B. Paris, Musée du Louvre G 105. (Photograph courtesy of the Musée du Louvre, Dist. RMN / © Les frères Chuzeville.)

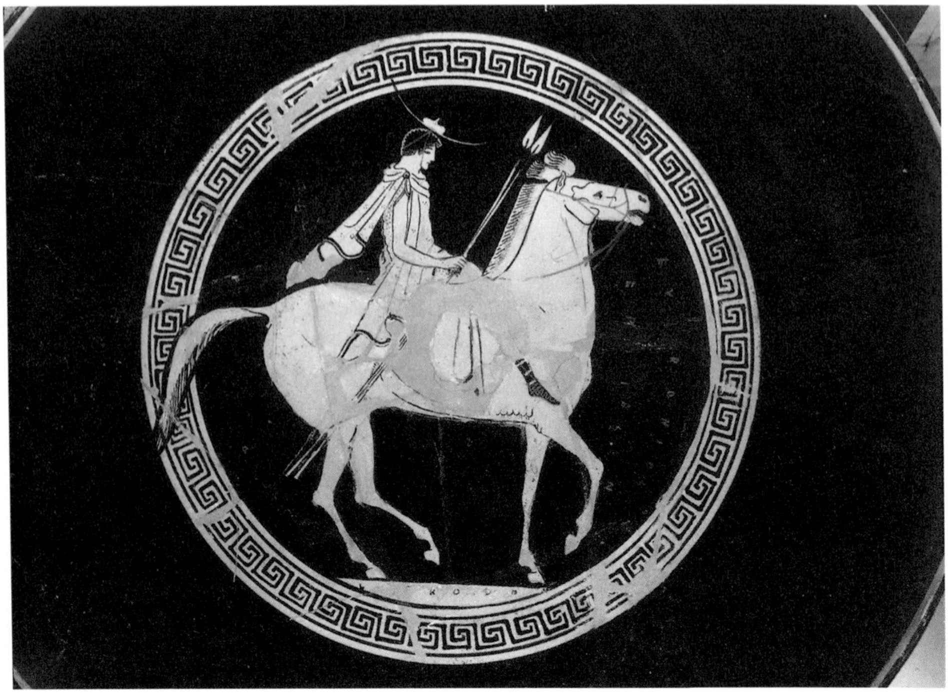

6.26. Red-figure cup by Onesimos, ca. 510–490 B.C. Interior. Paris, Musée du Louvre G 105. (Photograph courtesy of the Musée du Louvre, Dist. RMN / © Les frères Chuzeville.)

deciduous trees mark the "outside" locations of two heroic fights.[85] In the latter case, the repetition of the different types of trees marks the separate events as having *distinct* "outside" locations; here the repetition of the columns would mark the *same* outside civic location.

The tondo figure, who closely resembles all three figures on B except for his petasos, is accompanied by the signature ΕΥ[Φ]ΡΟΝΙΟΣ ΕΠΟΙΕΣΕΝ, "Euphronios made (it)," a declaration, ΚΑΛΟΣ ΕΡΟΘΕΜΙΣ, "Erothemis is handsome," and in the exergue, Λ[Υ]ΚΟΣ, "Lykos." The potter's signature complements the painter's signature on B, ΟΝΕΣΙΜΟΣ ΕΠΟΙΕΣΕΝ, "Onesimos made (it):" The *kalos* inscription is repeated on A, as is the name *Lykos*, ΛΥΚΟΣ, but on the echinus of the Doric capital rather than in the exergue. These repetitions interweave all three fields of the cup, creating an inclusive frame relying on conventions used by earlier cup-painters and discussed in Chapter 5.[86]

The two *Lykos* inscriptions are unusual in placement. *Lykos* is a well-documented *kalos* name and one favored by Onesimos,[87] but here the adjective "*kalos*" does not occur. In the interior scene, the inscribed name appears in the exergue, and it creates the visual effect of an equestrian statue with an inscribed base.[88] This is not to say the image is intended to be of a statue, but simply that it *recalls* an equestrian statue.

There is evidence from Athens for equestrian statues serving a variety of functions. From the Athenian Akropolis are archaic bases for equestrian statues, four of which are offered by equestrian victors; from Attica are equestrian grave markers; and from various places in Athens and Attica are equestrian reliefs that were probably votive.[89] At least one scholar suggests that the votive offerings may have been dedicated in thanks for a successful *dokimasia*.[90] Thus the placement of the inscription in the exergue may evoke another projected *public* venue for the articulation of Lykos' name, an honorific statue, perhaps specifically his recently completed *dokimasia*, if Cahn is correct in the assessment of the exterior scenes.

The inscription on A, *Lykos*, written on the echinus of a Doric capital, evokes another kind of public display, where *kalos* and similar inscriptions appear as graffiti in public spaces.[91] Typically these inscriptions are found in highly visible locations that are on architecture in places where ephebes congregate, observed by admirers.[92] In the Athenian Agora, we have a documented example, dating perhaps a quarter century after the cup by Onesimos: on a block reused in the euthynteria of the Stoa Poikile, excavators found *kalos* written as *graffiti*. These were apparently inscribed when the block had been taken already from its original location and was waiting to be reused in the Stoa Poikile.[93] The repetition of the name *Lykos* on Onesimos' cup, then, not only links two different phases of a civic ritual, already connected through repeated imagery; it also references two types of public discourse, inscriptions on statues and *graffiti* on public buildings. The cup itself, then, connects the youth Lykos and the private context of its use with prominence in the public arena.[94]

CONCLUSIONS

This survey has established that repetition links fields to accomplish story-telling. All categories of narrative depiction that can utilize more than one field on a vase, including unified, cyclic, and phased causally linked narration, do in cases like those discussed here use repetition to link scenes. In addition, the selection of what is repeated can serve to emphasize certain components of the tale, such as a particular character or a crucial action in the plot. By mid-sixth century, there are sophisticated examples by Lydos and members of Group E of phased, causally linked heroic narratives with scenes joined through repetition. The most complex and sophisticated type of phased narration, where a plot-motivating prop is a linking repetition, appears in the middle of the first half of the fifth century. Otherwise, all of the types appear ubiquitously from mid-sixth century through the first quarter of the fifth. In the early decades of the sixth century, many examples of linked generic events may tell anonymous stories but are not obviously full-fledged narratives. These examples continue into the fifth century. Scenes of civic and religious ritual, which are composed of linked events but are not narratives, rely on repetition in similar ways.

Extending stories into multiple fields on a vessel employing any available narrative strageties inevitably increases discourse-time and therefore compels a viewer to spend more time with a story and with the vase. Repetitions invite the viewer to read two or more fields together, reducing the likelihood that the total meaning will be lost.

SEVEN

REPETITION AND PARADIGM

The last chapter has shown that artists are adept at using repetition to enhance a variety of ways of connecting events and telling stories on vases. Paradigms, comparisons between a present situation or individual and (usually) a mythical precedent, frequently embedded in these stories, likewise rely on repetition. For example, the amphora Orvieto 2745 by Exekias discussed in Chapter 2 identifies a mythical paradigm for mortal activity by means of repetition: the painter brings a mortal fighter and Herakles into comparison by repeating the striking features of a chariot and a white horse. In Chapter 4, a lengthy analysis of repeated, anonymous, and often incongruous spectator-narratees demonstrated how a compositional template can highlight similarity between two sides of a cup; some instances create a paradigmatic relationship between a heroic or divine figure or episode and a mortal one. The goal of this chapter is to take a full look at the history and range of how artists make comparisons to create what is essentially a visual simile. For example, "The Athenian elite male is like Herakles" is the paradigmatic message sent by the Orvieto amphora. Such similes establish paradigms that are essential tools of Greek enculturation and education, and paradigms and their cultural applications are well-discussed in a vast scholarly literature.[1] This investigation begins with a short discussion of what previous scholars have said about paradigm in Athenian vase-painting, but Chapter 11 treats the phenomenon of paradigm in poetry, on vases, and in Greek *paideia* more generally.

SCHOLARLY DISCUSSIONS OF PARADIGM

Stansbury-O'Donnell tackles "paradigmatic extension," where repetitions in imagery link the contents in one field on a vase to another, in his broad treatment of narrative in Athenian art, and he devotes a substantial discussion of it to examples on Archaic vases.[2] His examples include those where there is repetition of syntax, including the use of generic visual formulas to create "an equivalence between two or more narrative images."[3] He points out how similar compositions and repetition of figures can unite two separate images of myths that share a common message. Specific vases cited by Stansbury-O'Donnell preserve repetitions in the poses of figures and in the compositions in different fields, linking heroic battles to one another and anonymous, mortal battles to heroic.[4] The present discussion expands the categories of subjects drawn into paradigmatic relationship to include more than myth narratives and to broaden the base of evidence that the creation of paradigm, establishing a mythical exemplum for mortal status or activity, is one consistent result of visual repetition.

Other scholars have made similar cases. Webster is thoroughly convinced of the centrality of paradigm to the selection of scenes that appear on many Athenian vases.[5] Webster sets out a theory that many Athenian vases were created as special commissions ordered by patron from painter. He postulates that certain mythical scenes are intentionally combined with particular scenes of human activity, presumably by order of the individual commissioning the vase, because they serve as a mythical paradigm for the human activity. In explaining his theory, he states that patrons appear to combine myths that were relevant either (1) to an ordinary human scene on another part of the vase or (2) to the present situation of the owner of the vase; he labels such a scene of myth a "mythological paradigm."[6] He lists both examples where contemporary parallels are explicitly expressed and those where a mythological comparison is shown, and the contemporary reference is left to the observer to discover.

Webster identifies more than twenty examples of this use of mythical paradigm. Some include visual repetition (tripod held by Herakles, tripod held by athlete), but most do not. Topics integrated into paradigmatic relationships include heroic athletic encounters compared to human; human athletes contrasted to heroes known in events preserved in the literary tradition; divine and heroic marriages compared to mortal; heroic military prowess or departure for battle as compared to mortal; women compared to heroines or female divinities. One example where Webster sees a subject as paradigmatic for the user of the vessel and not necessarily in relation to another image is his explanation of the popularity of Herakles. He explains the tremendous frequency of the hero's image in vases by Herakles' general paradigmatic value.[7]

Interestingly, Webster's framework is almost purely intellectual and not at all visual. If he thinks that the artist provides specific visual clues for linking paradigm to corollary, he mentions such clues only in passing and does not incorporate them into his explanation of how the artist expects the viewer to apprehend the paradigmatic relationship.[8]

He does offer the comment that "the boundary between myth and reality may have been clearer to the purchaser than it is to us"; and presumably here he refers at least in part to a visual boundary.[9]

Overall, Webster attributes a large role in paradigm-creation to the patron, the person who orders the vase, and he speculates on the way that poetry influences the selection of subjects: "poets such as Steisichorus, Simonides, Aeschylus, Pindar, Sophokles, and Euripides provide the ambiance which decides how the patron chooses his mythological paradigms and determines his personal choice."[10] Clearly Webster sees the setting of *symposion* as the one in which these paradigmatic vessels function.

Scheibler also sees the desire to set up paradigmatic relationships as influential in the selection of imagery.[11] Scheibler's scheme is somewhat different from Webster's; however, like Webster's, it does not rely on identifying visual repetitions to reveal paradigmatic relationships. Instead, Scheibler identifies a type of scene, where observing *kouroi* representing, in her opinion, model sixth-century Athenian youths, are learning about warrior-like behavior and other activities of primary importance to their socialization into the *polis* and its expected behaviors. Although Scheibler does not use this language, she treats the *kouroi* as elements of metadiscourse, as discussed in Chapter 4. They watch persons, mythical and not, engaged in military or other activities that are particularly relevant to them and their expected behaviors; in other words, they observe paradigmatic mortal or mythical behavior to learn how to act when they are adults.[12]

The concept of paradigm informs Sinos' interpretation of the appearance of chariots in sixth-century departure scenes as instrumental in setting up exempla. She repeats a long-standing query asked of departure scenes that include chariots: what is a hoplite doing in a chariot, when chariots apparently were not used by them either for getting to battle or for fighting once they were there? Her answer rests in the notion of paradigm: " . . . the chariot connects the hoplite soldier to the heroes of epic, suggesting a heroic ideal that inspired and exalted hoplite warriors even though their warfare was different in kind from Homer's. The ancient battlefield was certainly a place where men seemed to have left the mundane world and entered a heroic one, rising to the level represented to the Greeks by Homer's poetic account of heroic achievement. The chariot in these scenes effects this comparison between the hoplite soldier and his epic counterpart, uplifting the human activity by connecting it with a mythic paradigm."[13] More recently, scholars have contended that chariots were in fact still used in archaic warfare.[14] In this case, the depiction of men in military contexts with chariots would reflect a present reality, at the same time creating a link between mortal elites and heroic predecessors.[15]

This brief survey of scholarly work on paradigm makes clear that several different scholars, pursuing different types of inquiries, have proposed the existence of paradigmatic relationships among images on vases and how their appearance on vessels used in *symposion* is particularly appropriate.[16] The goal here is to demonstrate exactly how visual repetition plays a role in establishing paradigmatic relationships. In addition, we will identify related categories of images, including scenes connecting ritual and *aition* and scenes where mortals appear to intermingle with heroes and divinities.

Narratological insights into synonomy provide a way to understand how artists achieve paradigm. Synonymy, as defined in Chapter 2, is lexical cohesion and reiteration that relies not on exact repetition but on substitution of a related item with equivalence of meaning. The synonymy is created through repeated syntax (composition) and/or repeated content.[17] The author often thus connects a topic to something outside the story, and in so doing, programs reception of the topic or story in a particular way.

PARADIGM ON VASES

Early instances of synonymy exist in close relation to examples of exact repetition such as those discussed in Chapter 3 as Types or genres of vessels. The Gorgon Painter, from whose workshop the Horse-head amphoras emerge, repeats exactly a floral on each side of an amphora in the Louvre; however, because the floral is between lions on one side and sphinxes on the other, the result is a compositional parallel that creates the possibility of both synonymy and antonymy, like and unlike.[18] The possibility of antonymy is important, because paradigm can be both positive and negative, exhortation or admonition.[19]

A majority of the vases attributed to Sophilos are decorated with continuous animal friezes. Among the minority with panels and with separate fields on two sides there are examples with syntactical repetition.[20] An amphora in Paris juxtaposes two siren-and-sphinx pairs.[21] Each pair is posed antithetically and has very similar faces and wings. The sphinxes have heads turned back to the left and right respectively whereas the sirens face one another. The separating devices differ, too: a rosette between sphinxes and a panther between sirens. The effect is to stress both what sphinxes and sirens have in common – wings and female heads – and how they differ.[22]

Although the earliest examples of synonymy do not instruct in an obvious way, the Siana cups that follow preserve synonymous imagery that can be paradigmatic. In three typical works, mortals are linked to divinities and heroes in a way that provides examples of desired abilities, behavior, and even status. An early Siana cup in the circle of the C-Painter provides an example by identifying Athena as a paradigmatic warrior for hoplites.[23] The interior depicts a fully armed Athena, running [Figure 7.3]. The exteriors display fully armed hoplites, also running, with many visual parallels between the Athena in the center and the male combatants on the exterior friezes:

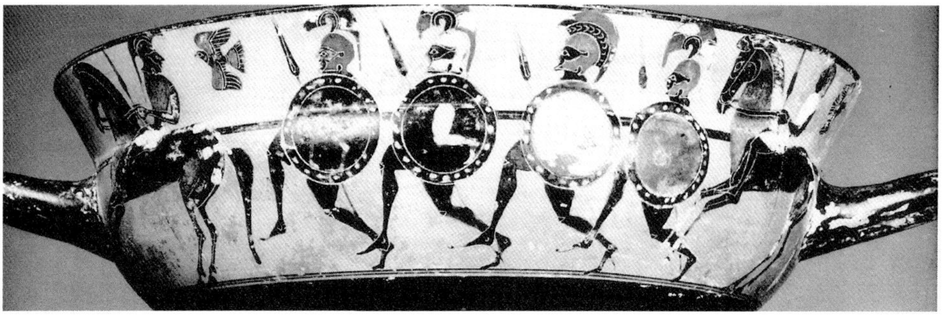

7.1. Black-figure cup from the workshop of the C-Painter, ca. 565 B.C. Side A. Copenhagen, National Museum of Denmark 3259. (Photograph © Department of Classical and Near Eastern Antiquities, National Museum, Copenhagen.)

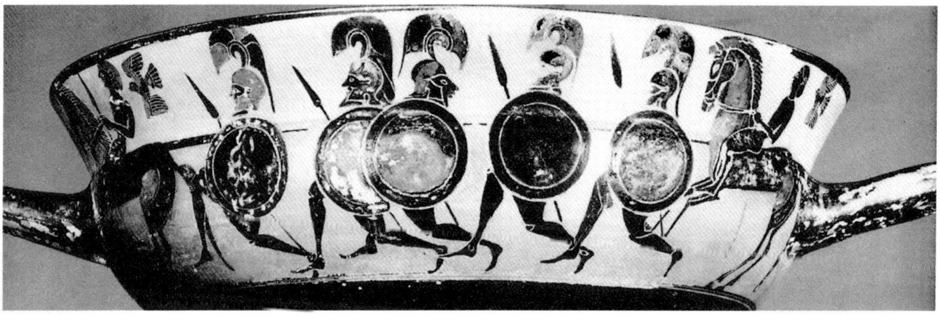

7.2. Black-figure cup from the workshop of the C-Painter, ca. 565 B.C. Side B. Copenhagen, National Museum of Denmark 3259. (Photograph © Department of Classical and Near Eastern Antiquities, National Museum, Copenhagen.)

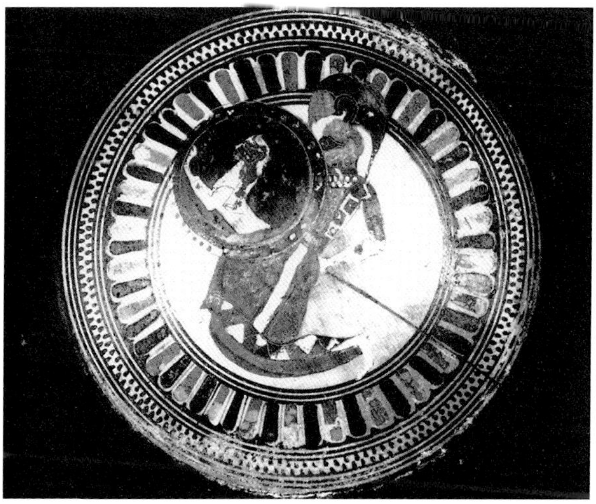

7.3. Black-figure cup from the workshop of the C-Painter, ca. 565 B.C. Interior. Copenhagen, National Museum of Denmark 3259. (Photograph © Department of Classical and Near Eastern Antiquities, National Museum, Copenhagen.)

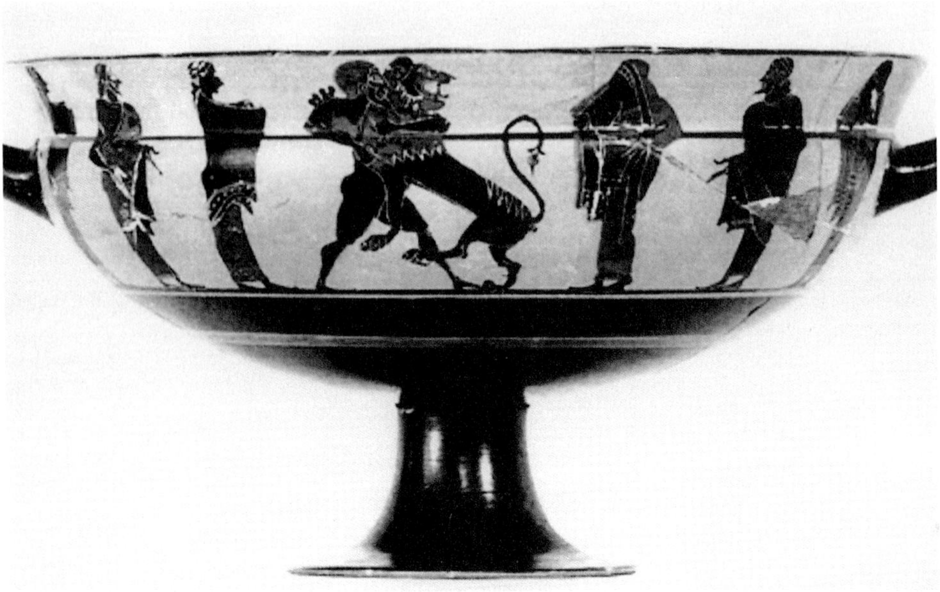

7.4. Black-figure cup by the Heidelberg Painter, ca. 565–555 B.C. Side B. Taranto, Museo archeologico nazionale I. G. 4342. (Photograph © Visual Resources Department, Bryn Mawr College, 2005.)

helmets, round shield, spear and running pose all are identical [Figures 7.1, 7.2]. There are many differences, to be sure, and the goddess' peplos and her unique shield device [Figure 7.3] are the most obvious; clearly mortals and divinity differ. The goddess appears closer to the point of attacking her adversaries than are the hoplites theirs, as her shield is raised and her spear is held horizontally rather than vertically. The similarities suggest parallels between the military prowess of goddess and mortals, and confers her imprimatur on their goals. The parallels provide both exhortation and description: "men, fight like Athena" and "she fights with you."[24]

A Siana cup in Taranto by the Heidelberg Painter preserving two scenes of a man fighting a lion provides a good example of a heroic-to-mortal parallel achieved through a similar type of partial repetition.[25] In the tondo, a bearded lion-fighter holds a knobby club, which ought to identify him securely as Herakles [Figure 7.5]. On the exterior, a similar figure, who is nude and bearded with short hair, uses an identical hold on a lion; however, he is minus the club and wrestles with a lion in the midst of spectators[26] [Figure 7.4]. Why is the identifying attribute absent on the exterior, making it unlikely that the figure depicted is Herakles? The absence of the club is especially striking in relation to its presence on the interior [Figure 7.5]; likewise, the presence of spectator-narratees contrasts sharply with the absence of witnesses to the interior fight. One result of the repetition-with-difference is to encourage the application of

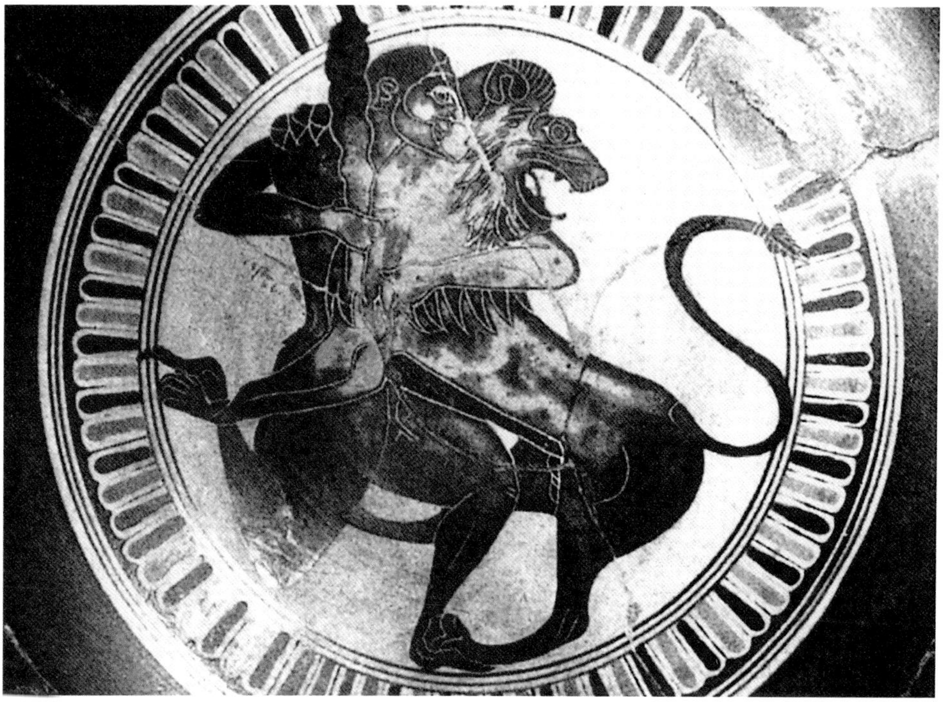

7.5. Black-figure cup by the Heidelberg Painter, ca. 565–555 B.C. Interior. Taranto, Museo archeologico nazionale I. G. 4342. (Photograph © Visual Resources Department, Bryn Mawr College, 2005.)

the heroic exemplum in the tondo to general mortal behavioral norms, not limited to (no doubt) imaginary lion-fighting.[27] The purpose and identity of the anonymous spectators, who endorse the transfer of heroic qualities and abilities to a fellow member of the elite on the exterior, are important considerations discussed fully in Chapter 4.[28]

A Siana cup in Berlin by the Heidelberg Painter preserves a slightly different way of comparing hero and mortal.[29] Pairs of warriors fight on each side of the cup, and the interior image appears to be closely linked with the exterior figures [Figures 7.6–7.8]. In the tondo, Herakles, wearing his lionskin, chases an Amazon to attack her; instead of carrying his usual attributes, club, sword, and bow, he carries a spear as do the warriors on the exterior [Figure 7.8]. The presence of a weapon that is unusual for Herakles catches the viewer's attention, and at the same time it makes the exterior warriors' mode of fighting like that of the hero. In addition, the Amazon carries a round shield instead of a *pelta*, and this difference, along with her high-crested helmet and tunic, relates her to the fighters on the exterior. There are therefore many variations from usual iconography that enable links between the heroic tondo fight and those on the exterior. The chariot in exterior side B also helps to unite hoplite battle and heroic prototype.[30]

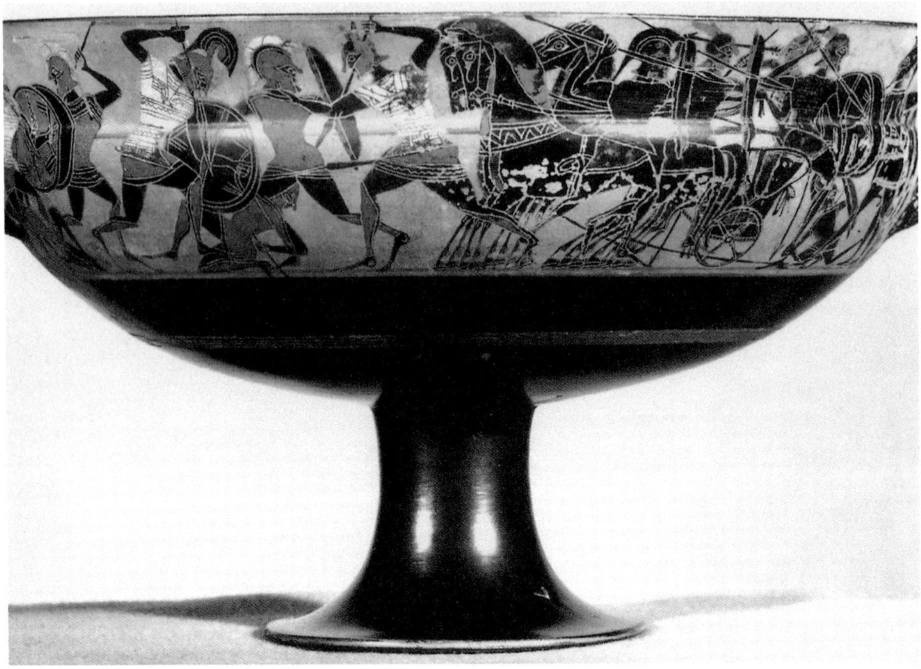

7.6. Black-figure cup by the Heidelberg Painter, ca. 565–555 B.C. Side A. Berlin, Staatliche Museen, Antikensammlung 3402. (Photograph © Bildarchiv Preussischer Kulturbesitz/Art Resource, NY.)

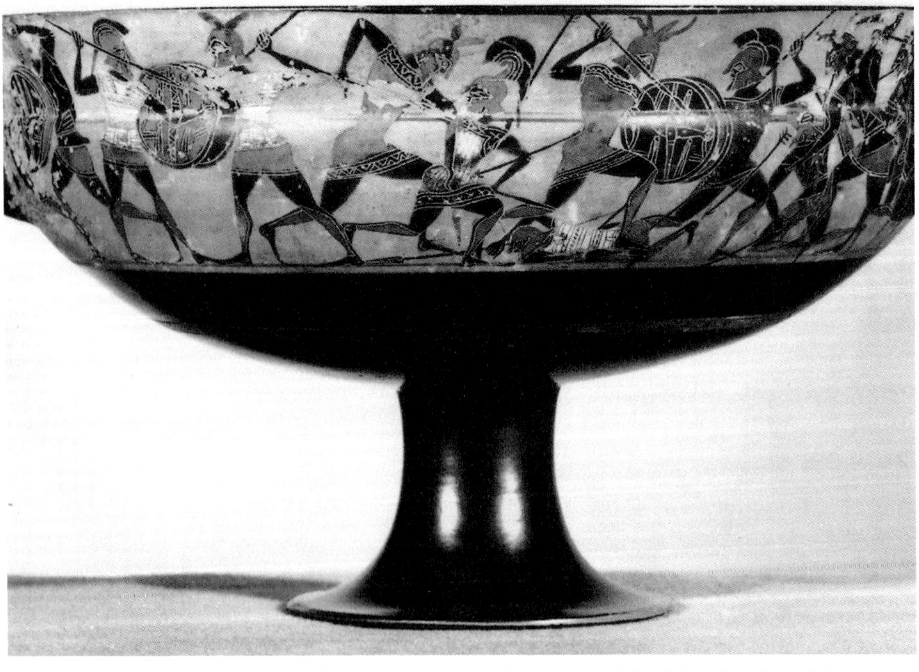

7.7. Black-figure cup by the Heidelberg Painter, ca. 565–555 B.C. Side B. Berlin, Staatliche Museen, Antikensammlung 3402. (Photograph © Bildarchiv Preussischer Kulturbesitz/Art Resource, NY.)

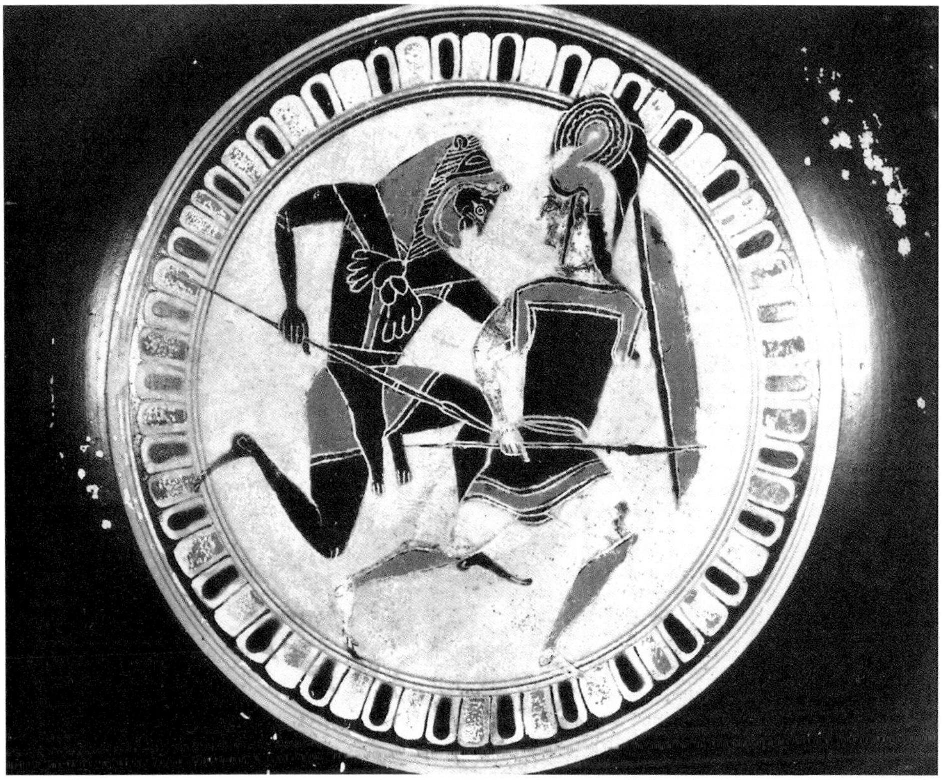

7.8. Black-figure cup by the Heidelberg Painter, ca. 565–555 B.C. Interior. Berlin, Staatliche Museen, Antikensammlung 3402. (Photograph © Bildarchiv Preussischer Kulturbesitz/Art Resource, NY.)

Paradigms for Bride-Selection

A group of scenes appear to cite specific mythical paradigms for both the selection of a bride and what might be termed "maintenance of marital bonds." Herakles and Deianaira, the Judgment of Paris, and Menelaos and Helen all serve as exempla. A cup by Lydos in Taranto is a typical example of the use of incongruous repeated spectator-narratees to link scenes, as discussed at length in Chapter 4.[31] A scene bears all the hallmarks of Herakles fighting the centaur Nessos with Deinaira: the nude Herakles-figure has short hair and a beard, and holds a knobby club as he approaches the centaur armed with stones [Figure 7.9]. Deinaira stands at the right and holds her *himation* in a "bridal" gesture. There are three incongruous spectators dressed in *himatia*, a seated male figure at both the far right and the far left of the scene and a standing male figure to the immediate left of Herakles. The reverse of the cup repeats this scene with a few crucial exceptions: the positions of the centaur's arm are reversed, the attacker is a youth wearing a pointed cap, and he is armed with a smooth baton rather than Herakles' knobby club [Figure 7.10]. The spectators are repeated verbatim.

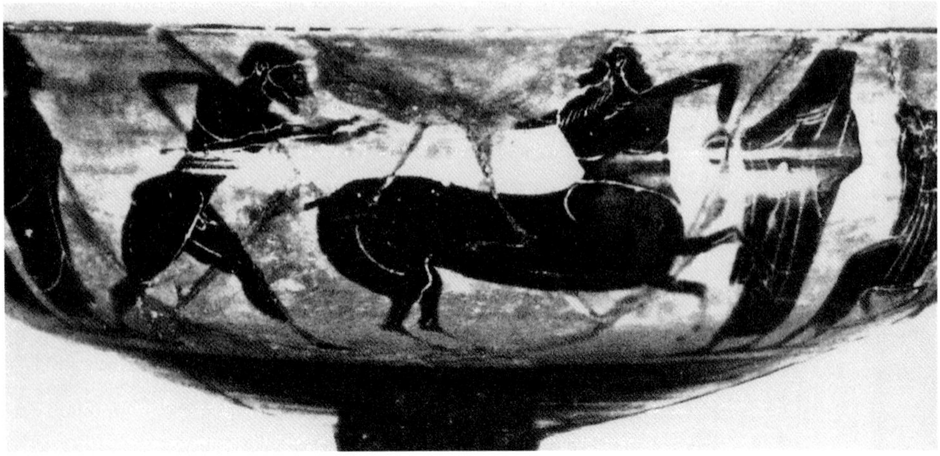

7.9. Black-figure cup by Lydos, ca. 560–540 B.C. Side A. Taranto, Museo archeologico nazionale I. G. 4363. (Photograph © Visual Resources Department, Bryn Mawr College, 2005.)

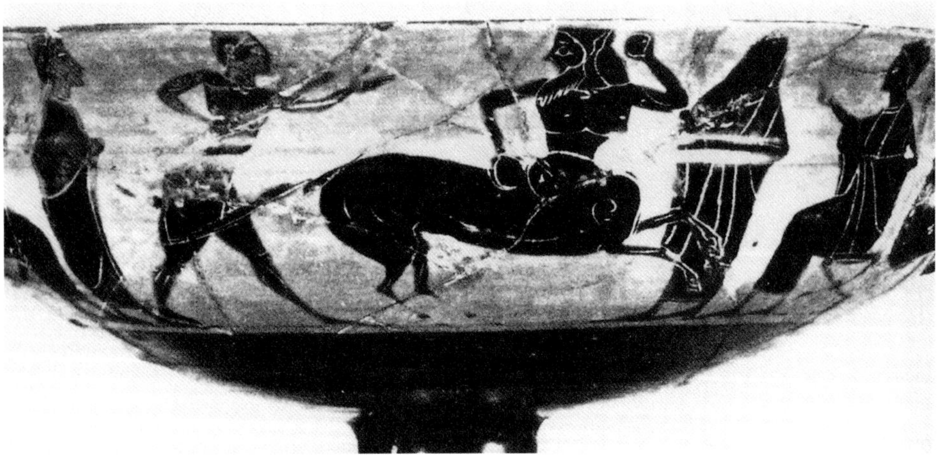

7.10. Black-figure cup by Lydos, ca. 560–540 B.C. Side B. Taranto, Museo archeologico nazionale I. G. 4363. (Photograph © Visual Resources Department, Bryn Mawr College, 2005.)

The artist has been careful to distinguish the youth from Herakles; his generic qualities associate him with elite youths. The different position of the centaurs' arms simply reinforces that the two scenes have differences. The repeated spectators not only create identical compositional frames linking central scenes, but also indicate the relevant audience for the paradigm. In sum, the two scenes cite a heroic prototype for elite bride-acquisition.

An amphora in Taranto displays a more complex version of the same type of paradigmatic relationship.[32] In nearly identical compositions, Theseus and the Minotaur on side A are matched with Herakles and the centaur on side B. Youths with long hair watch Theseus, himself a youth with long hair. These idealized youths are thereby likened to Theseus, a hero who succeeds in a fight with an opponent who is only partly human and very deadly. On the obverse, spectator-narratees are similar but not identical to those on side B: they are adult males with short hair and beards like the hero whom *they* observe. A syntactical parallel is created by the placement of a female figures at the middle of each composition, conventionally identified as Ariadne for Theseus and as Deianaira for Herakles. Deianaira is depicted making a nuptial gesture, with mantle held out from her face: this reminds the viewer that a display of Herakles' superior strength, a demonstration of willingness and ability to fight, will yield a bride. Theseus, too, fights for a girl: although she is not depicted here as a bride, Ariadne is a female "won" by Theseus. Theseus shows his youthful peers one way to acquire a bride, whereas Herakles shows adult males another way to accomplish the same goal. The repetitions thus link the two sides as synonymous hero-adventures and, further, as paradigmatic for two different groups of males in Athenian society. The repeated syntax links not only central scenes, but the two age-grades of males. The points made by the complete text of the vase are created by the visual links.

Additional pieces by or very near Lydos, dating from c. 560–540 B.C. form an interesting cluster of examples relating to this same theme, bride-acquisition, but focusing on the Judgment of Paris. Examples include an ovoid neck-amphora in Florence;[33] a column-krater in London;[34] a column-krater in Polygiros by the Painter of Louvre F 6;[35] and a lekanis lid in Palermo.[36] In assessing these examples, it is important to recognize that Lydos is demonstrably an innovator in conceiving how the fields of a vase frame scenes. In Chapter 6 we saw how he served as an important example of an early painter to depict two discrete episodes of a narrative in a single field, combining a "Recovery of Helen" with the Death of Priam on one side of the vase, and adding a temporally prior scene, the Ambush of Troilos, linked through repetitions, on the reverse [Figures 6.8, 6.9]. It is this last characteristic, the apparent fusing of two different episodes in a single panel, that allows us to be confident that the same artist may have joined a paradigmatic mythical exemplum with a mortal analogy in a single panel.

The two major panels on the Florence amphora show a Judgment of Paris scene that is accompanied by an anonymous couple on one side and on the other, a couple reclining on a *kline*, probably Dionysos and Ariadne [Figures 7.11, 7.12]. There are links between figures on the two sides: the beard and hairstyle of the Dionysos-figure are similar to those of the male figures in the Judgment scene, and the hairstyle of the Ariadne-figure is identical to those of the side-A female figures. These links between sides, however, are less prominent than those between two apparently separate groups, the Judgment and the mortal couple in the scene on side A. In the Judgment group, Paris flees at far right and Hermes chases him in a standard formula for depicting the scene.[37] Hermes is identified by *petasos*, *kerykeion*, and *chlamys*, and the goddesses are without attributes and are therefore identified by context.[38] The additional couple, however, is anomalous. The female member of the couple has clothing identical to that of the first and third of the three goddesses. Worn penguin-style, it includes a red

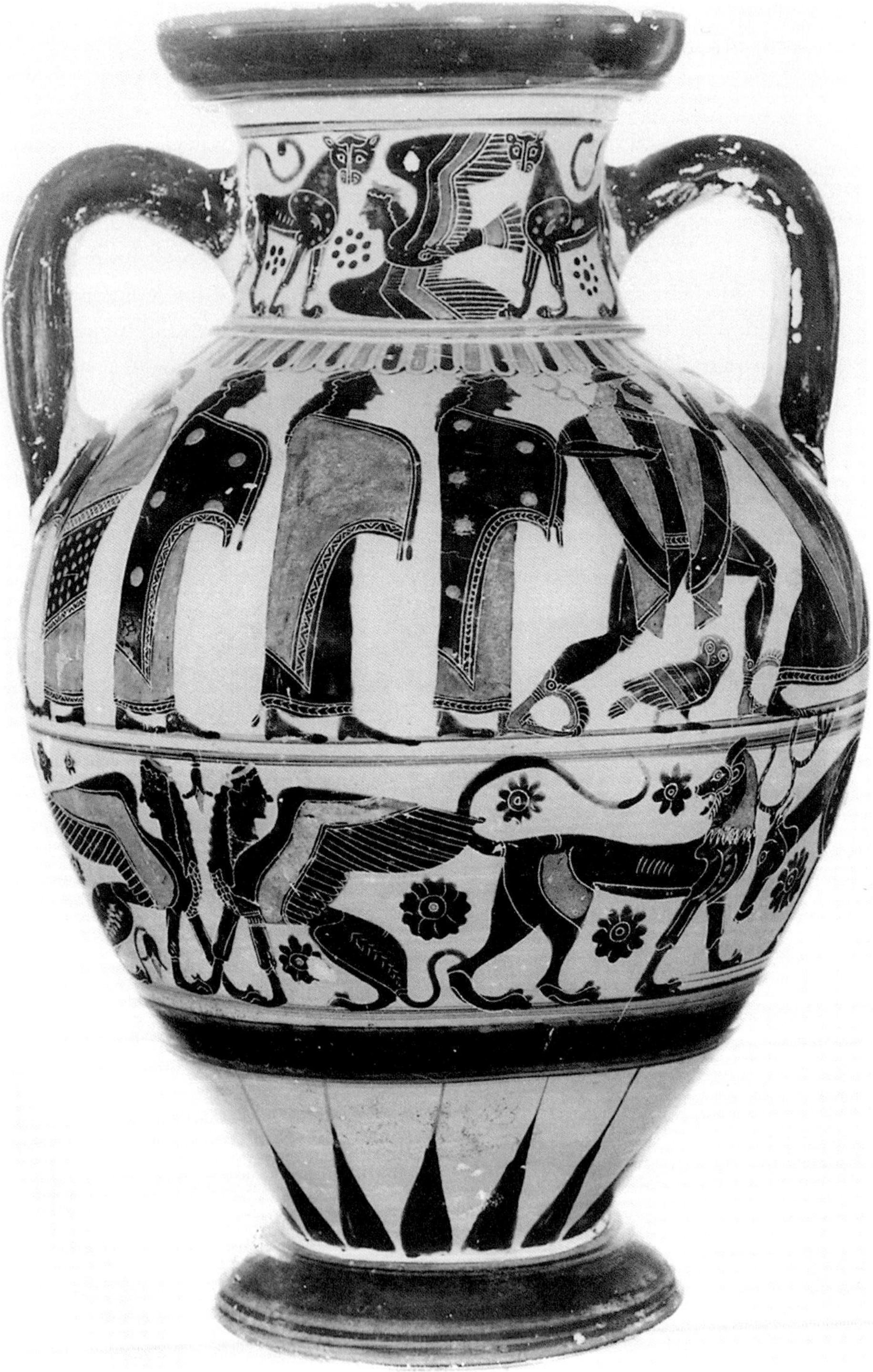

7.11(a). Black-figure amphora by Lydos, ca. 560–540 B.C. Sides A and B. Florence, Museo Archeologico Etrusco 70995. (Photograph © Soprintendenza Archeologica per la Toscana – Firenze.)

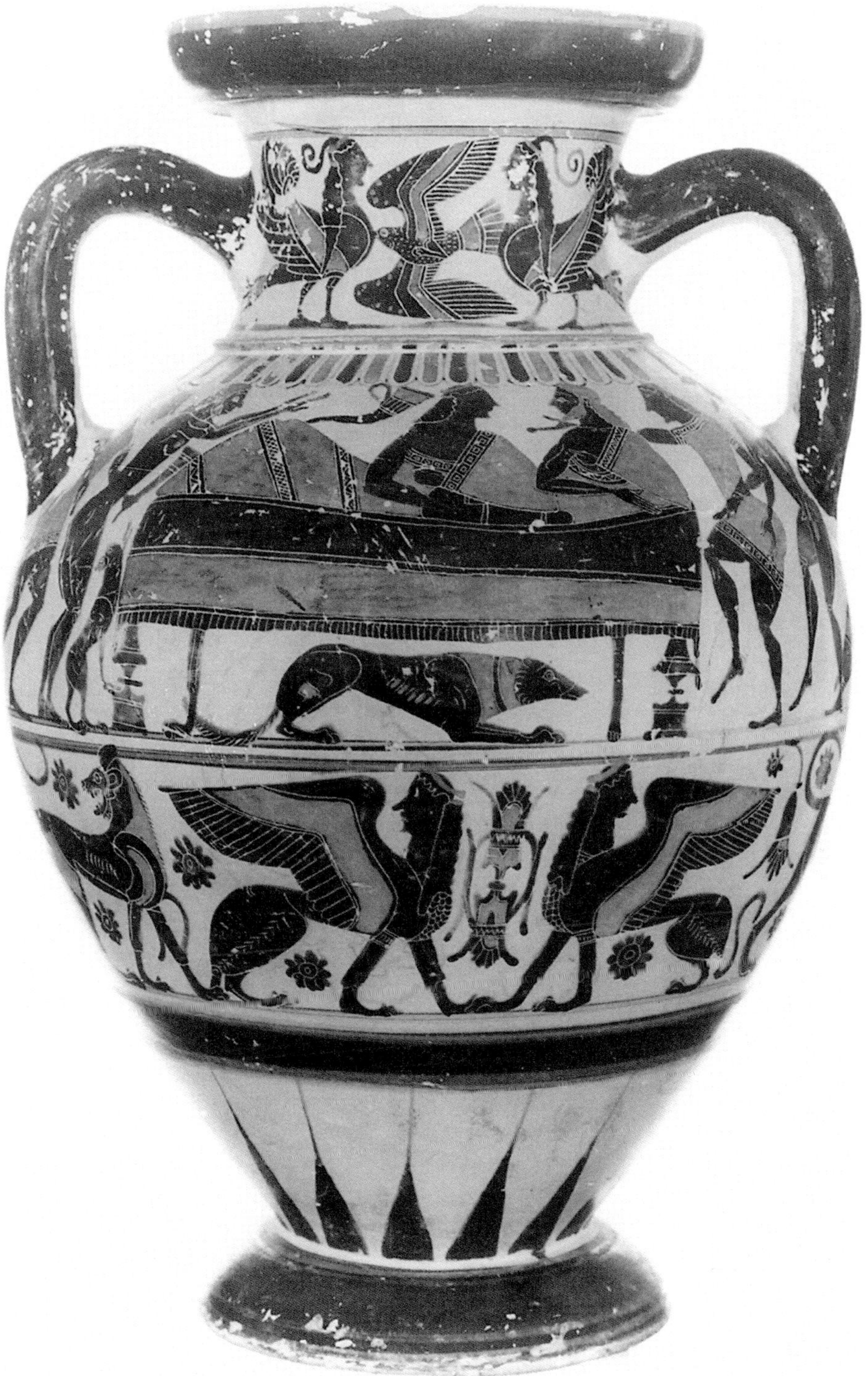

7.11(b) *(continued)*.

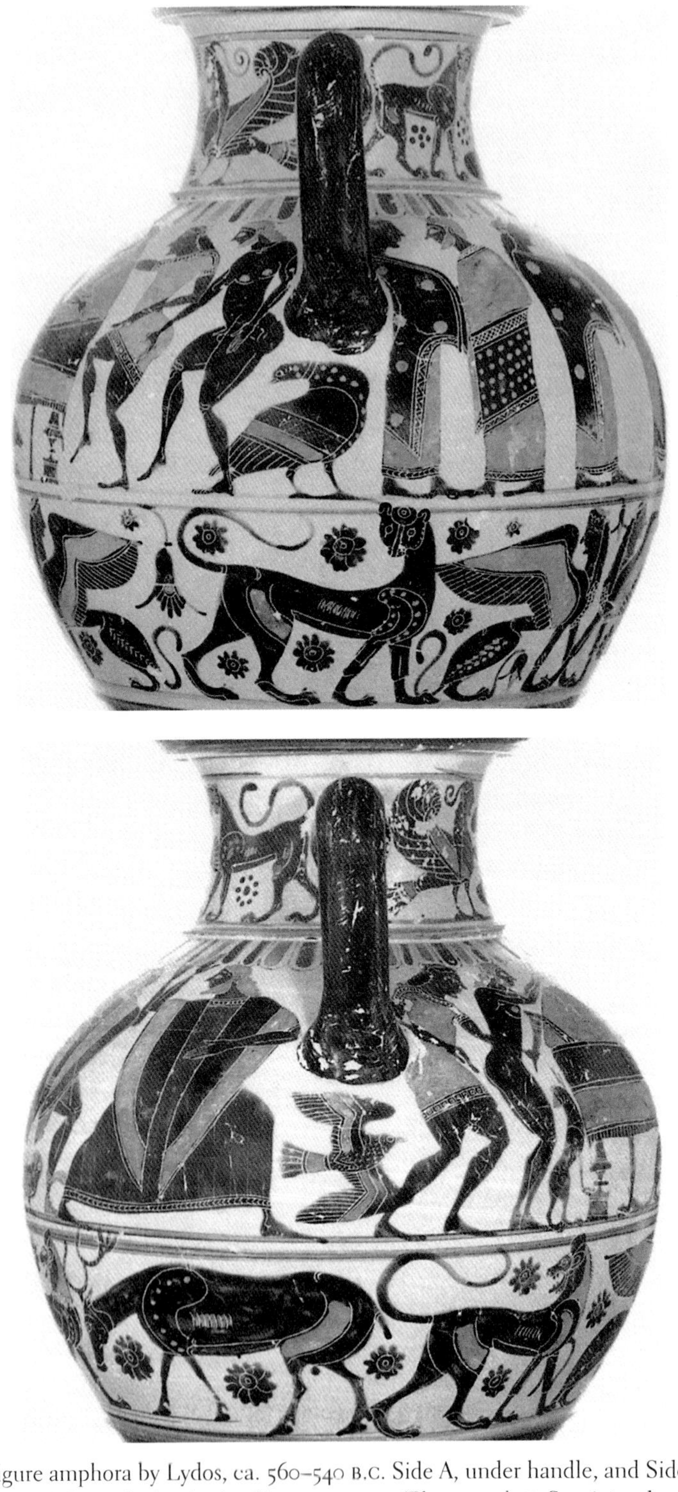

7.12. Black-figure amphora by Lydos, ca. 560–540 B.C. Side A, under handle, and Side B, under handle. Florence, Museo Archeologico Etrusco 70995. (Photograph © Soprintendenza Archeologica per la Toscana – Firenze.)

peplos with decorated border covered by a mantle embroidered with flowers and another decorative border. This repetition links the woman to the goddesses. The male figure who accompanies her has a beard and long hair like Hermes and Paris, but his clothing is ordered and composed, with *himation* tightly wrapped, rather than hanging loose to enable running like Paris' or short and loose as Hermes'. As a further distinction, although the anonymous male figure wears the same articles of clothing as Paris, *chiton* covered by *himation* display different patterns.

The combination of like and unlike plus the anomalous presence of the extra couple invites us to ask if the panel preserves a mythical example of bride selection plus an elite equivalent. Shapiro has pointed out how rare it is, outside of the examples considered here, to find extra figures in Judgment of Paris scenes; Lydos' scene is therefore very unusual because it includes the extra figures.[39] The similarities link the process of bride-selection to a divine and heroic prototype; the differences make that prototype appear ridiculous, with bridegroom dashing off and adult supervisor in close pursuit.

The scene on the B side of the amphora, as suggested above, provides additional similarities and contrasts. The divine couple on A, Dionysos and Ariadne, recline on a *kline*, looking intently at one another, with two dancing figures, a satyr with a nymph, at each end. The visual links, beard for Dionysos and hairstyle for Ariadne, connect this couple with both the Judgment scene and the anonymous couple on A; Dionysos and his wife can serve as another paradigm for mortal bride and groom. In aggregate there are a sympotic Dionysos and Ariadne, nymph- and satyr-couples dancing (side B), Paris selecting a wife, and an anonymous couple meeting (side A); the visual links on this amphora create an elaborate paradigmatic text joining mythical and elite couples. The unusual characteristic of the example is the coupling of paradigm and mortal analogy in a single panel on side A.

This same compositional strategy is apparent in at least two column kraters, one by Lydos and the other by the Painter of Louvre F 6. At the right in the main field of the Lydan London column-krater [Figures 7.13, 7.14] is the Judgment of Paris, including a fleeing Paris, a dog, Hermes – identified by *kerykeion*, *petasos*, and *chlamys* – and three goddesses. The goddesses are poorly preserved, but it is apparent that they wear rich clothing and have few, if any, attributes; their context identifies them, especially through their number together with the figures of Hermes and Paris. Difficult to identify is a trio at the far left of the scene. A female figure, also in rich clothing, stands holding her mantle in exactly the same manner as the goddesses at right; the males who stand on either side of her are bearded, as are Hermes and Paris, and their clothing with its embroidered floral patterns associates them with both the goddesses and Paris at the right. As Beazley puts it: "To the left of the major group, Lydos has added a minor group, a woman between two men. They are hard to name . . . "[40] The semantic function of the men, regardless of any specific identity as father, husband, or uncle, who surround the woman making the bridal gesture is to establish marriage as a concern of the elite male. The second column-krater, attributed by Tiverios to the Painter of

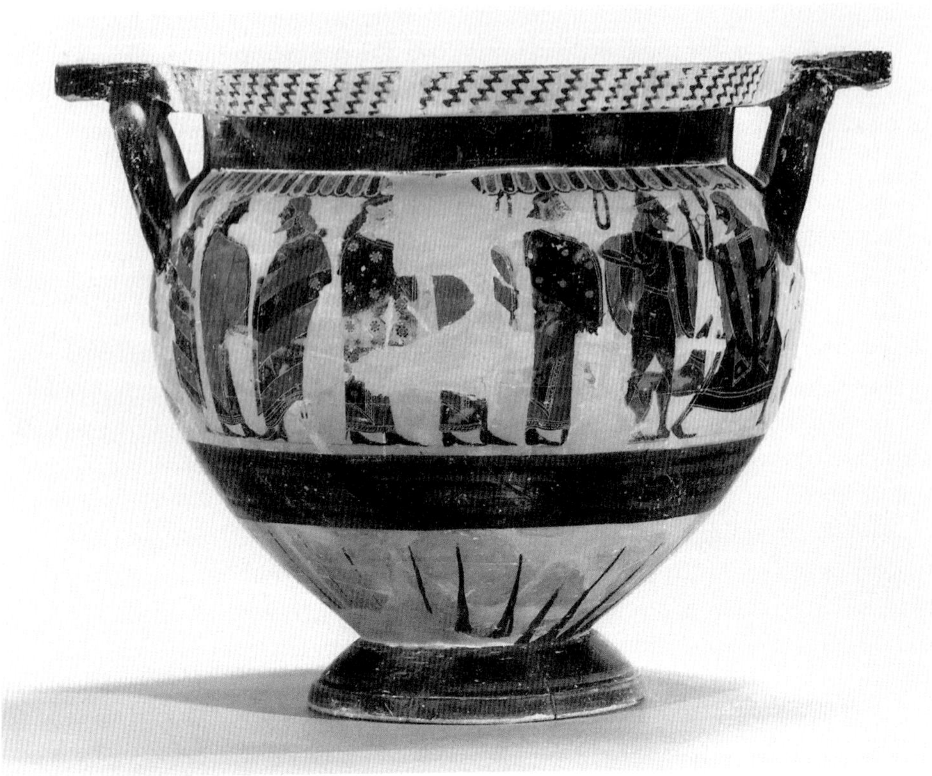

7.13. Black-figure column-krater by Lydos, ca. 560–540 B.C. Side A. London, The British Museum 1948.10–15.1. (Photograph © Copyright The Trustees of the British Museum.)

Louvre F 6, has an almost identical main scene.[41] These examples, then, appear to join the mythical paradigm with a mortal example just as does the Florence amphora.

A fourth piece, a lekanis lid painted by a member of Lydos' circle, is also connected to the group of three examples just discussed.[42] Repetition links a Judgment of Paris scene to a number of apparently nonmythical excerpts from and variations on it. The lid has two concentric zones of figural decoration, and each zone is further divided into multiple smaller fields of one or more human figures. Serving as borders between these smaller fields are lions and sphinxes in heraldic poses. In the innermost zone of the lid, there is one field containing a "complete" Judgment-like entourage, with three women led by a male figure to a second male figure. Beazley noted the similarity between this composition and more clearly identified renderings of the Judgment of Paris on other vases: "the quintet in the upper[=inner] zone looks almost like a deheroized version of Paris, Hermes, and the Goddesses."[43] What the deheroization amounts to is an absence of attributes for Hermes, since he is the only one of the core five figures who normally make up the Judgment scenes with specific attributes. In the remainder of the inner zone as well as in the outer zone of the lekanis lid, there are at least six other frames containing groups (and in one case a single figure) of male and female

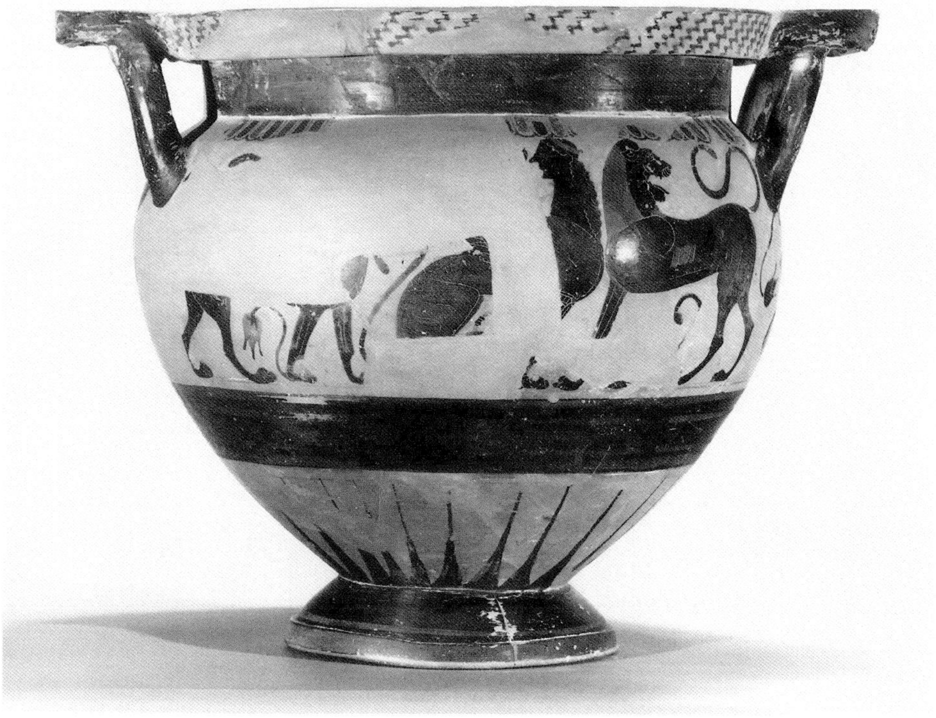

7.14. Black-figure column-krater by Lydos, ca. 560–540 B.C. Side B. London, The British Museum 1948.10–15.1. (Photograph © Copyright The Trustees of the British Museum.)

figures confronting one another, very similar to those in the complete Judgment-like scene in the inner zone. There is also on the outer zone of the lid another Judgment of Paris scene which is divided by groups of animals into two segments. The three goddesses are led by Hermes in one segment; Paris, running, and another female figure (Beazley suggests Iris) are in another. Lydos' associate has, in the decoration of the lid overall, created a context of multiple synonymy where mortal mate-selection (the couples) is linked to a heroic exemplum (the Judgment of Paris), and that exemplum is made more susceptible to paradigmatic analogy by its lack of identifying attributes.[44] Beazley points out the similarities among the "extra" couples and trios in the smaller framed scenes on the lid and the "side-scenes" on the London and Florence pieces by Lydos.[45] Apparently, this model of paradigm-creation, with exemplum and mortals in the same scene, enjoyed some degree of popularity within the Lydan workshop.

In sum, Lydos and painters near him apply the principles of visual redundancy to link figures both between and within scenes in a variety of ways to establish paradigms.[46] The Lydan group examples, creating paradigms within single scenes, stand out against the backdrop of more typical texts, where paradigms are created between scenes.

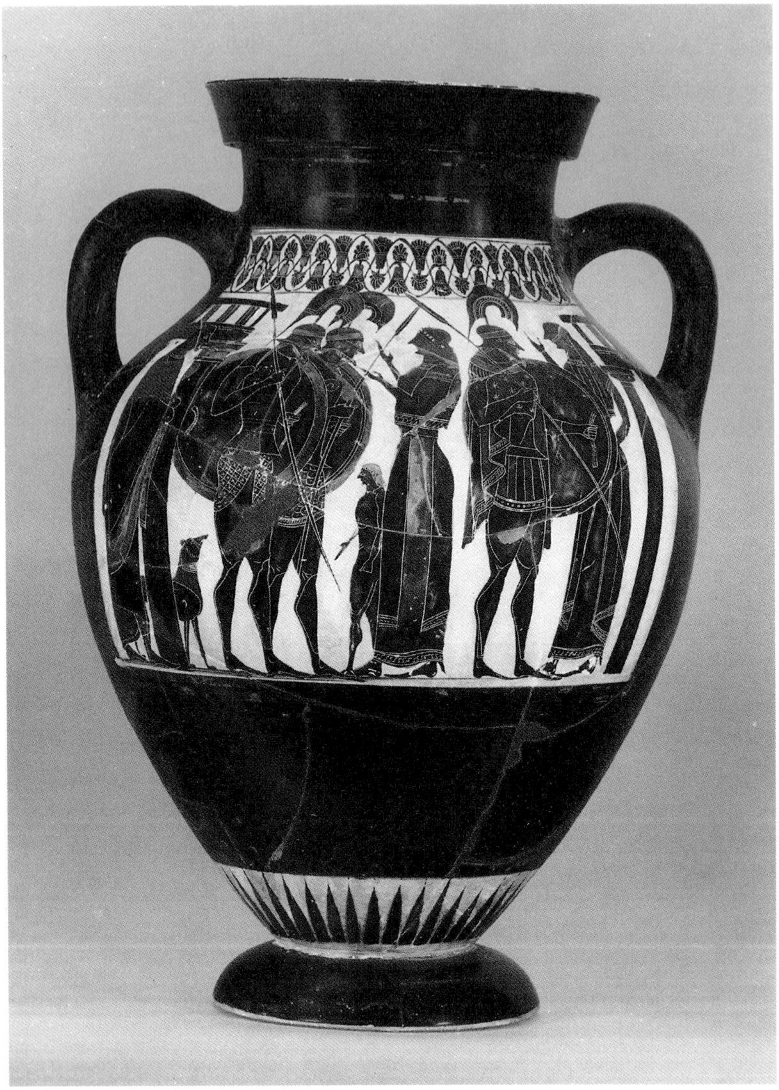

7.15. Black-figure amphora by Group E, ca. 560–540 B.C. Side A. Würzburg University, Martin von Wagner Museum 247. (Photograph © Martin von Wagner Museum der Universität Würzburg. Photo: K. Oehrlein.)

However, when Lydos paints topics other than the Judgment of Paris, his syntax is more typical of contemporary trends seen in other workshops, where repeated spectator-narratees serve as metadiscursive directives to link a mythical scene with a mortal one in order to establish heroic paradigms for elite Athenians.[47]

Other Heroic Paradigms

In the repertory of Group E are some further examples of clear paradigm-citation. These examples include repeated spectators, but in compositions that are more

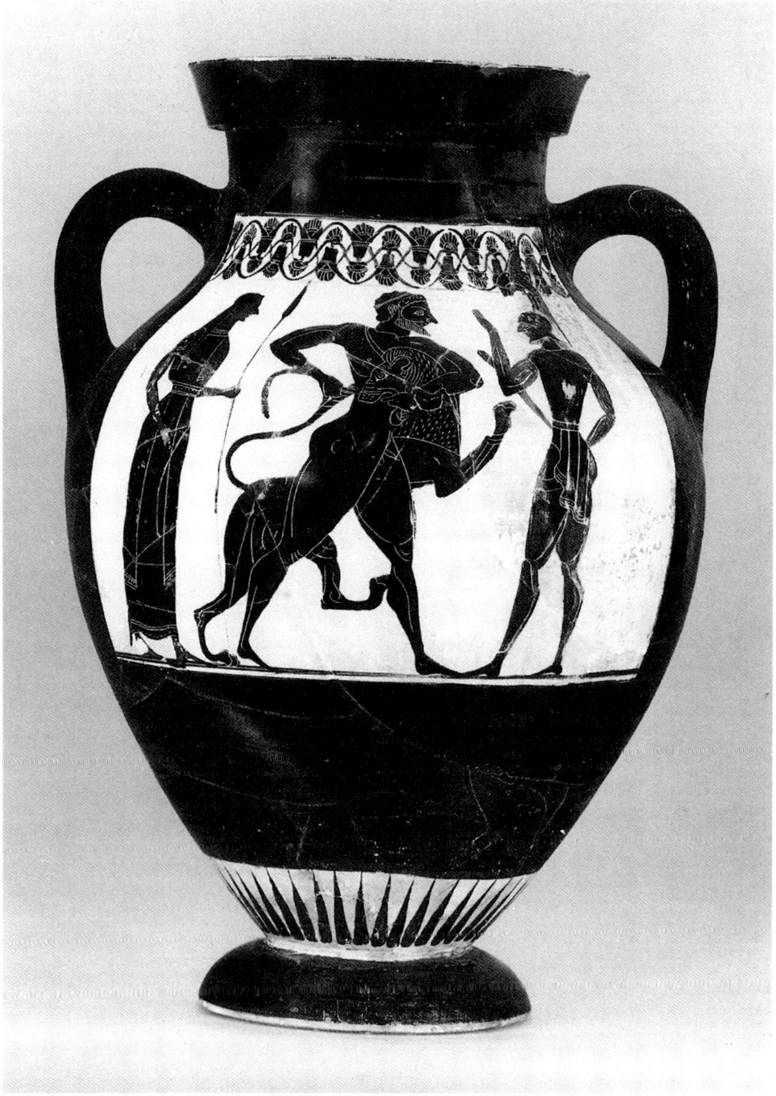

7.16. Black-figure amphora by Group E, ca. 560–540 B.C. Side B. Würzburg University, Martin von Wagner Museum 247. (Photograph © Martin von Wagner Museum der Universität Würzburg. Photo: K. Oehrlein.)

complex than those discussed in Chapter 4, where discussion focused on anonymous, incongruous spectator-narratees lined up on either side of a mythical, athletic, or military scene. Here the spectators explicitly share features with the main actors in the activities or narratives represented. On an amphora in Würzburg that depicts the most popular subject for this group of artists – Herakles and the lion – there are repetitions that create links between male and female spectators of the lion fight and to onlookers of departing hoplites, integrating images on A and B[48] [Figures 7.15, 7.16]. The soldiers who depart on A wear helmets and greaves identical to that of the "Iolaos" figure

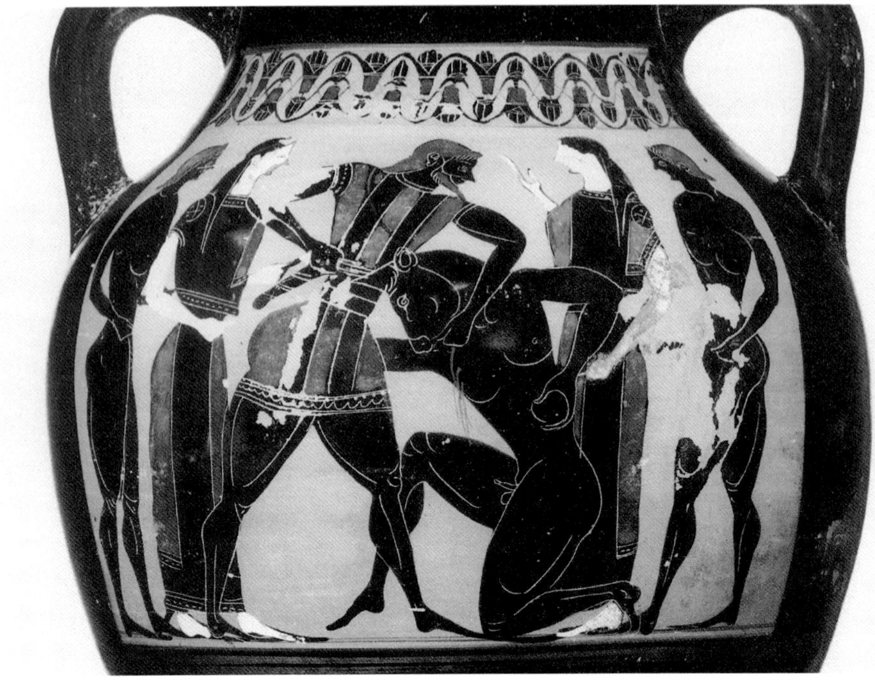

7.17. Black-figure amphora by Group E, ca. 560–540 B.C. Side A. Munich, Staatliche Antikensammlungen und Glyptothek 1397 (J. 1079). (Photograph © Staatliche Antikensammlungen und Glyptothek München.)

watching the lion fight on B, so they are very like the hero's assistant. This particular Iolaos figure is unusual within the Group E corpus in the degree to which he is armed: the most common assistant to the lion-fighter is nude.[49] These special similarities both draw hoplite and hero-assistant into synonymy and heighten the contrast between the spear, held by the departing warriors, and the baton, held by the Iolaos figure. Note also that the Iolaos figure's position, taking a step with one arm upright and one held down at his side, is identical to that of the female figure who is his counterpart on A, drawing the viewer further into a comparison of the two scenes. The female figures who bid the side A soldiers farewell are dressed identically to the "Athena" figure on B. The spear Athena holds is just like that of the departing soldiers on A. The net effect is a blurring of lines between the lion-fight, clearly a heroic scene, and the departure scene, one that could be mortal and present-day.[50] The departing warriors and their well-wishers are imbued with heroic qualities through the integration of their characteristics with those of the figures in the paradigmatic fight. This example shows, then, that even when painting their most frequently depicted subject, some Group E artists may be interested in creating links that draw the heroic and the contemporaneous into synonymy, with the status lines between the two deliberately blurred.

A second, very similar example in Munich makes such a point more clearly.[51] The basic pattern for the composition is the commonly used template where

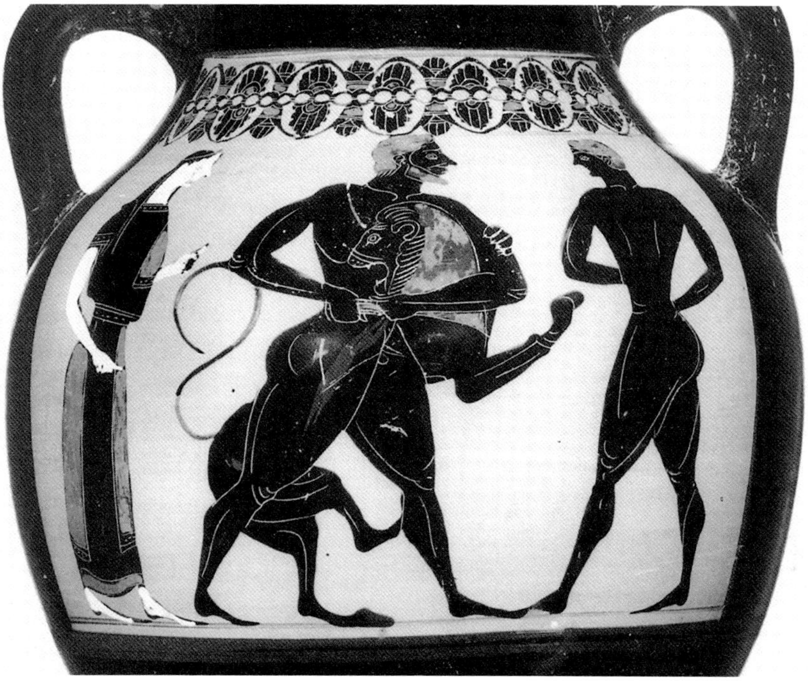

7.18. Black-figure amphora by Group E, ca. 560–540 B.C. Side B. Munich, Staatliche Antikensammlungen und Glyptothek 1397 (J. 1079). (Photograph © Staatliche Antikensammlungen und Glyptothek München.)

spectator-narratees are repeated on each side. For each story, there are identifiable myth-figures who typically observe the hero-fights, Athenian youths and maidens for Theseus and the Minotaur and Athena and Iolaos for Herakles [Figures 7.17, 7.18]. The two spectator-narratee groups on the A and B sides of this example have much in common: the nude youths who watch Theseus slay the Minotaur on A are very similar to a nude figure who observes Herakles' fight with the lion on B. Likewise, the female figures who watch the Minotaur-fight are identical, both in dress and pose, to the one female figure who watches Herakles. Interestingly, both heroes appear altered from their usual appearance. They have beards – unusual for Theseus but not for Herakles – and use swords – very common for Theseus and much less so for Herakles. Through this blending of attributes, the two scenes have more in common and come closer to synonymy. Theseus and Herakles are therefore alike. In addition, their similarities slightly alter their paradigmatic relationship for the observing elite Athenian youths and maidens. The heroes are not their peers, but adult males whose behaviors serve as examples to which they will aspire or which they will at least hold up as admirable, in the case of the female figures, as they mature.[52]

An example in Copenhagen makes a link between military and athletic victory explicit.[53] Here the linking device is strikingly inventive. On A, a fallen warrior, attacked by another warrior from a chariot, lies behind his ineffective shield decorated with a prominent tripod. His victory comes from *kleos* achieved through his death in battle. The fight-from-chariot suggests the heroic sphere. On side B a nude male figure crouches under a "real" tripod, about to lift it, and he is surrounded by more nude males wearing garlands and carrying wreaths. The tripod is rendered equivalent in two contexts; it is a symbol of victory, both for heroes as a device on a shield that will be taken as booty, and for elites in athletic competition. Again, the connection between present and past victories, elites and heroes, is made explicit.

The Louvre amphora signed by Exekias as potter is a landmark among Group E examples because it includes inscriptions otherwise very rare for this group of painters.[54] It is remarkable for the degree to which it informs us of the subject: inscriptions identify Herakles, the felled Eurytion, and Geryon. The inscription naming the (absent) Stesias as *kalos* is one of the earliest *kalos* inscriptions preserved on Attic pottery. On B, the figure in the chariot is identified as ΑΝΧΙΠ⟨Π⟩ΟΣ, "Anchippos," and all four horses are named. As is typical of the works *painted* by Exekias, the repetitions yield an unexpected result: the figure in the chariot and Geryon are drawn into synonymy.[55] Both the monster and the man wear high-crested Corinthian helmets and carry round shields. Anchippos, apparently a generic member of the elite but not known to us as a specific individual, is, as a fighter, comparable to Herakles' formidable opponent rather than to the hero himself.[56] The specificity that the inscriptions supply creates certainly about the mythical scene depicted and to whom it is compared, and this inscribed example thereby constitutes a landmark moment in the development of the depiction of paradigm.

Psiax suggests a specific heroic paradigm for an apparently elite male who remains unnamed on his hydria in Würzburg. Visual repetitions consist of horses who appear in shoulder, belly, and predella [Figures 7.19, 7.20]. The painter identifies the main scene as heroic, naming Adrastos as one of the figures in the chariot and the Greek Parthenopaos (inappropriately) as the Scythian archer who walks in front of it.[57] These labels specify the topic in the main scene as the Seven against Thebes and the subject as Adrastos' departure for the conflict. Because the heroes' names appear in the main scene and the figure hunting deer on horseback in the predella is not named, the hunter is made distinct from the heroes at the same time he is linked via the repetition of horses in each field. In addition, the anonymous hunters in the predella use spears like those carried by the figures in the chariot above. The absence of inscriptions in the predella creates an ellipsis, provoking the viewer-reader to wonder who precisely the unnamed figure is. Building on the visual repetitions, the viewer can conclude that the unnamed figure, a generic elite male who fights on horseback, is closely connected to the chariot-driving heroes of the Theban saga but that he is not one of them. By means of the connection between hero and mortal hunter, the character of the elite Athenian male is fleshed out as he is depicted in his characteristic activity and is demonstrably "like" heroes.

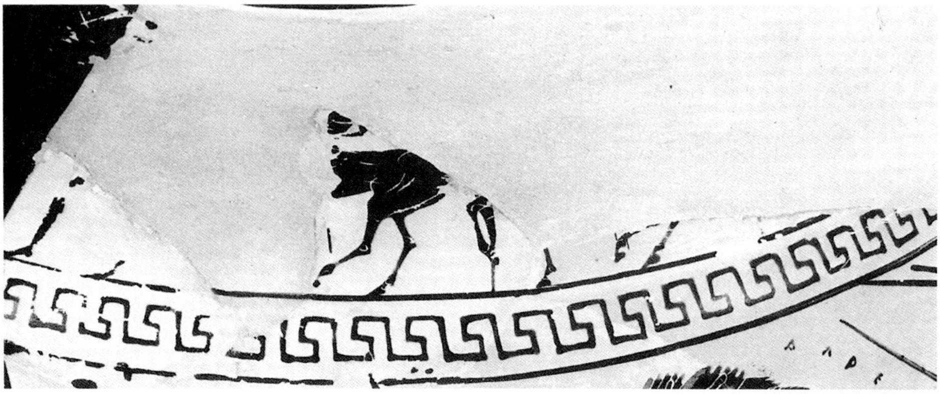

7.19. Black-figure hydria by Psiax, ca. 530–515 B.C. Shoulder detail. Würzburg University, Martin von Wagner Museum 319. (Photograph © Martin von Wagner Museum der Universität Würzburg. Photo: K. Oehrlein.)

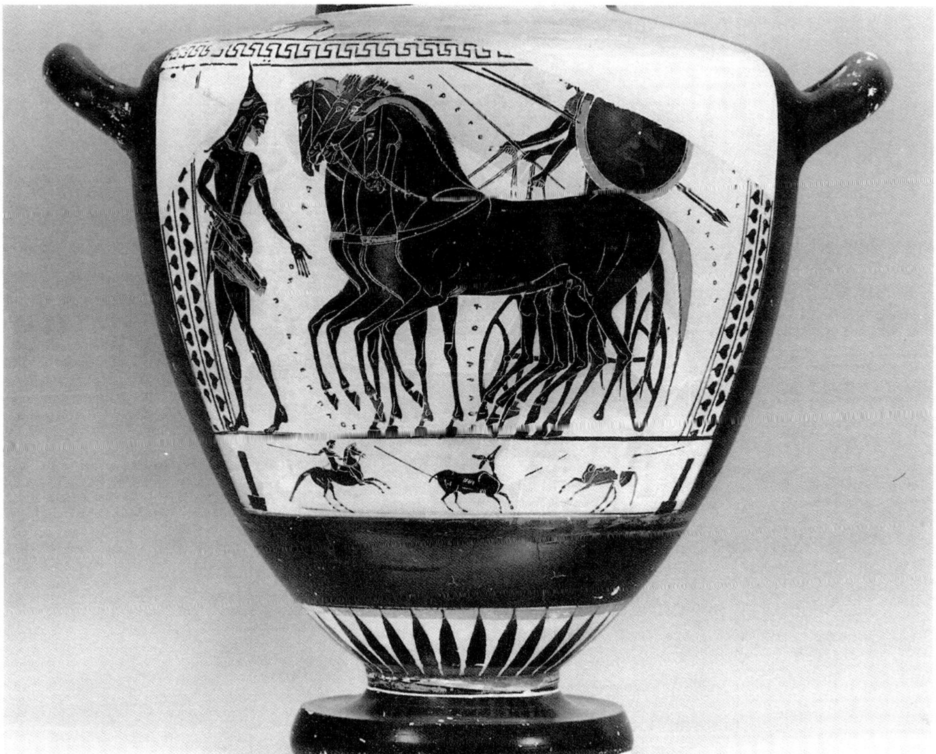

7.20. Black-figure hydria by Psiax, ca. 530–515 B.C. Main scene. Würzburg University, Martin von Wagner Museum 319. (Photograph © Martin von Wagner Museum der Universität Würzburg. Photo: K. Oehrlein.)

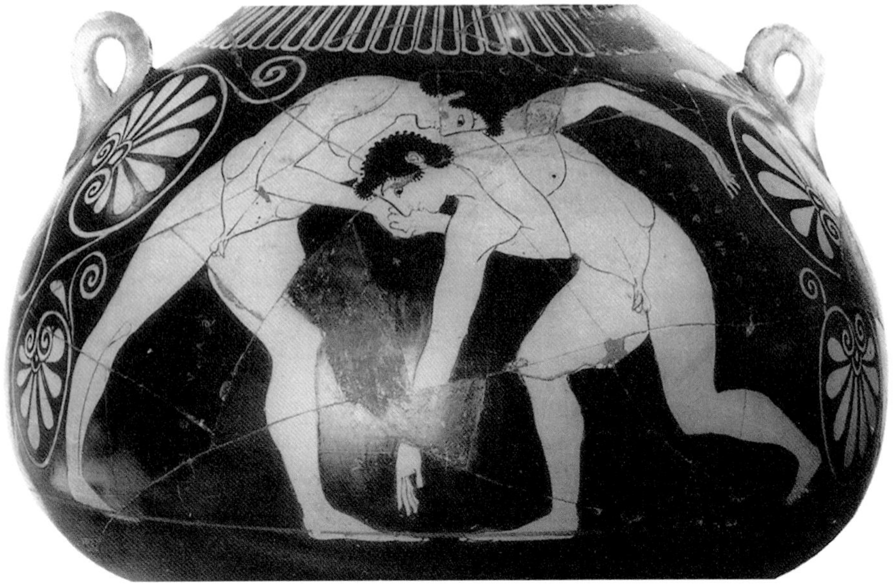

7.21. Red-figure psykter by Euthymides, ca. 510–500 B.C. Side A, Turin, Museo di Antichità 4123. (Photograph © Ministero per i Beni e le Attività Culturali [Soprintendenza per i Beni Archeologici del Piemonte].

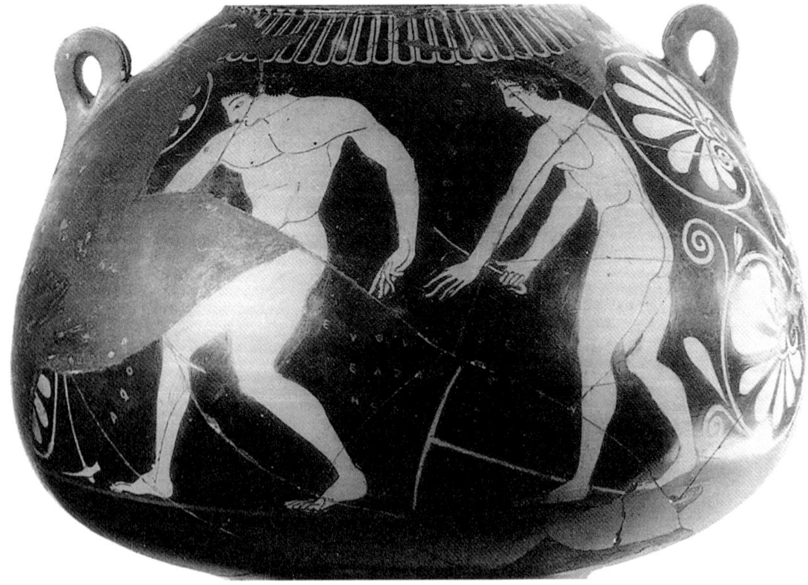

7.22. Red-figure psykter by Euthymides, ca. 510–500 B.C. Side B. Turin, Museo di Antichità 4123. (Photograph © Ministero per i Beni e le Attività Culturali [Soprintendenza per i Beni Archeologici del Piemonte].

With inscriptions come other paradigmatic examples that are very specific, targeting historically attested individuals. One striking example is Euthymides' psykter in Turin, where repetitions in inscriptions and imagery link sides.[58] Theseus (ΘΕΣΕΥΣ) on side A wrestles with ΚΛ[ΥΜΕΝ]ΟΣ, "Klymenos,"[59] [Figure 7.21]. The painter signs each side with an unusually complete signature, including patronymic. The mortal athlete Phayllos (ΦΑΥΛ⟨Λ⟩ΟΣ) on B and a companion are using picks to prepare the ground for athletic activity [Figure 7.22]; they are nude youths with body-types, musculature, and hairstyles identical to those of Theseus and his wresting opponent on side A. The youthful hero is an athletic paradigm for the mortal Phayllos.[60]

Negative Paradigm

Another example sets up a relationship of synonymy between a mortal athlete and a divinity. On his Louvre amphora, Phintias appears to make these extremely general paradigmatic connections through repetition of the *placement* of inscriptions and through repeated ΧΑΙΡΕ, ΚΑΙΡΕ, ΧΑ(Ι)ΡΕ (A) and ΧΑΙ(Ρ)Ε (B), "Welcome".[61] Athletes train on B and Tityos kidnaps Leto in the presence of Artemis on A. There are noteworthy similarities in the appearance of the figures on each side: all figures on the two scenes wear wreaths, and the wreaths of the central youth on B and that of Apollo on A are identical. The male figures on A are nude, while three of the four on B are as well. The adult man named Sosias (ΣΟΣΙΑΣ), at the far right of the field on B, is almost identical to Tityos on A.[62] In addition to the greetings, there are written labels identifying every figure but Tityos. Those on A are elite Athenian youths with two adults, and the figures are named Sotinos, Chares, Demostratos, and, as already mentioned, Sosias. Another elite Athenian, Sostratos, is referenced through a probable *kalos* inscription. The fact that Tityos is not labeled is very striking, and the void creates an ellipsis, about which Osborne has made the following observation: "By refusing to declare openly that this bearded man [Tityos] belongs to a separate world of myth [through an inscription], the artist prompts the connection of this man with the ordinary Greeks on the other side."[63] Cairns interprets the two scenes as interconnected, identifying Tityos, the rapist, as a negative paradigm for the elite, decorous, and self-controlled *erastes* on B.[64] Further emphasizing the nature of Tityos' crime is the particular way that Artemis' name is miswritten, ⟨ΑΡΤΕ⟩ΜΙΔΟΣ.[65] According to Immerwhar, the *mu* is miswritten so that the word resembles *aidos* or "modesty." Tityos' behavior is the opposite of *aidos*; he gives in to his lust, while the adult males hold back, simply admiring their youthful *eromenoi*. Cairns also points out how both the imperative greeting *khaire* and the *kalos* declaration place the vase and the paradigm in the context of *symposion*.[66]

Mortals as Paradigms

Not every paradigmatic example creates a comparison linking or contrasting mortals with heroes. Just as anonymous adult males can serve as paradigms for youths, so too can specific mortals. On a second example depicting the mortal athlete Phayllos, Euthymides links him not with Theseus as in the example treated above, but with a mortal youth[67] [Figures 9.9, 9.10]. A youth arming is made analogous to the vaunted Phayllos, here a discus-thrower identified by inscription. A simple three-figure composition appears on each side and includes a youth at center. The figures at the outsides of each scene adopt poses, including arm positions, similar to those of their direct opposites on the reverse side of the vase. The purely visual repetitions serve to link two sorts of activities of elite youths – athletics and the military. Vertical, similarly placed inscriptions identify all the figures on both sides, and all are apparently mortals. At least four of the names seem to be descriptive: ΠΕΝΤΑΘΛ[Ο]Σ, "Pentathlos," the figure to the left of Phayllos,[68] and ΟΡΣΙΜΕΝΕΣ, "Orsimenes," to his right on B and ΕΥΘΥΒΟΛ[Ο]Σ, "Euthybolos," and ΘΟΡΥΚΙΟΝ, "Thorikion" himself on A.[69]

Mythical Paradigm for Mortals, Pederasty, and *Symposion*

Several examples where paradigms are established have additional features linking imagery to pederasty and sometimes *symposion*. Some such examples include generalized praise for a figure serving as a paradigm for a youth, such as for Theseus as he wrestles on Euthymides' psykter discussed above [Figures 7.21, 7.22]. This vase, with its positive appraisal of Theseus, "well done, yes indeed!" records an evaluation, expressing admiration for a youth performing well. Other examples add *kalos* to scenes having no apparent direct connection to youths, interjecting the discourse of pederasty into apparently unrelated paradigmatic imagery[70] [Figures 7.19, 7.20].

A cup by Oltos discussed in Chapter 5 [Figures 5.7–5.9] depicts youths who are unusual examples of spectator-narratees[71]; they stand out because they are mounted on horseback, and two of them are labeled with unfamiliar names, Dixis and Glenos, which can be made-up names for either mythical figures or fictional Athenian elites. Theseus, who fights the Minotaur on B, shares his nudity, short hair, and beardlessness with the spectator-narratees and with the tondo figure, a youth carrying a brazier. Theseus therefore appears to be paradigmatic for both spectator-narratees and for the tondo youth. An inscription in the tondo, "*Memnon kalos*," connects the groups linked in the paradigmatic relationship to *symposion* and its pederastic ethos.

On a cup by Epiktetos, Theseus and the Minotaur are paradigmatic for youths celebrating a *komos* around a krater[72] [Figures 9.3–9.6]. In this example paradigm seems to blend with parody, as discussed in Chapter 9. The five youths on B, engaged in making music, dancing, playing games with vases (including using an oinochoe as a urinal!), and filling a kylix from a krater are like Theseus; both youths and Theseus wear wreaths, although Theseus' is of a slightly different style. The youths' dancing postures on B are slightly subdued versions of Theseus' intentional stride to thrust his sword into the Minotaur. The repetition of the verb ΕΓΡΑΦΣΕΝ "... painted it," on both sides A and B (ΕΠΙΚΤΕΤΟΣ ΕΓΡΑ[..]ΕΝ) acts as a link at the level of metadiscourse, directing the viewer to see what else the two sides have in common. The remaining imagery on the cup provides further detail on the ideal context for the synonymy between youths and Theseus to be played out: in the tondo, a bearded male symposiast reclines, singing, as he plays the *barbiton*. An inscription ΙΠΠΑΡ[ΧΟΣ] ΚΑΛΟ⟨Σ⟩, "Hipparchos is handsome," spills out into the field as if it conveys a song. If the inscription is read in *symposion*, Hipparchos' name can share space with actual *sympotic* song, whose topic might well be the Minotaur-contest and the parallels between elite youths and Theseus.[73] To put it another way, the symposiast's singing repertoire might include two kinds of songs, narrative songs about paradigmatic legendary heroes and erotic songs about boys and the symposium. The two probably intersect, just as they do on the imagery on the cup.

In two instances, there are suggestions of links between symposiasts/komasts and heroes fighting against the Amazons, and the Amazonomachy is thereby identified as paradigmatic for adult male symposiasts. The more secure of these is Euthymides' krater in Morgantina, where both a symposiast and a Greek warrior appear to be labeled ΣΟΣΙΑ⟨Σ⟩, restored by Immerwahr as "Sosias"[74] [Figures 7.23, 7.24]. There are visual repetitions linking the two relevant fields. The poses of the reclining symposiasts on side B echo those of two fallen Amazons on A;[75] the inscriptions on A may identify three participants in the Amazonomachy: ΑΝΔΡΟΜΑΧΕ, "Andromache," *h*ΕΡΑΚΛ[ΕΣ], "Herakles," ΣΟΣΙΑ⟨Σ⟩ "Sosias." A fourth inscription, ΧΑΣΛ, "Khasa," is called nonsense by Immerwahr.[76] On B, at least two of the inscriptions appear to prompt and to record sympotic dialogue: ΧΑ[Ι]ΡΕ and ΧΑΙΡΕ "welcome" appear between the first and second men at left and horizontally above the second figure from left.[77] To the right of these men, a musician plays a lyre and behind his head appears a second ΣΟΣΙΑ⟨Σ⟩ "Sosias." Finally, there is a fragmentary . . . ΙΟΣ. Neils has suggested that the lyre-player on B sings the song of the Amazonomachy depicted on A, and that both the song about and the depiction of the Amazonomachy include a Sosias. The location of ΣΟΣΙΑ⟨Σ⟩ on B would otherwise suggest a label. We can thus conclude that either the lyre-player sings of Sosias, invoking him here, *or* the figure to the right of the lyre-player (or the lyre-player himself) *is* Sosias.[78] In either case, a mortal participates in a heroic battle on A, and the repetition of his name on the B side of the vase links him to the *symposion* on B. A sympotic participant is thereby linked to and is like the heroic companions of Herakles in the Amazonomachy.[79] If the name Sosias refers to the potter Sosias as several scholars believe, the paradigm may be a joke. Other such jocular examples are discussed in Chapter 9.

In general, the joining through repeated features of a scene of *symposion* or *komos* with one of a mythical episode that could form a part of a sympotic entertainment has predecessors in the repertories of both Euphronios and Epiktetos.[80] The subject-matter for sympotic entertainment is often paideutic, selected for its suitability for providing examples of behavior to emulate and to avoid. Overall the roster of topics that lend

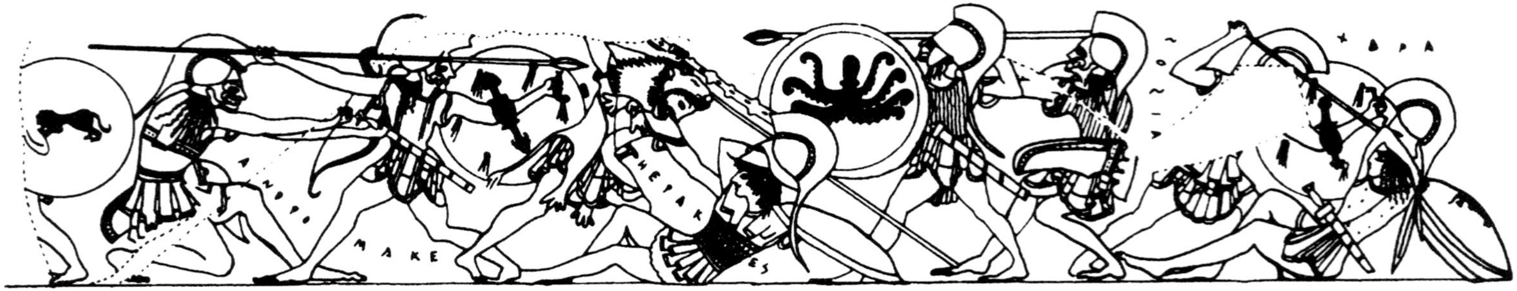

7.23. Red-figure volute-krater by Euthymides, ca. 510–500 B.C. Side A. Morgantina (Serra Orlando) 58.2382. (Photograph © Research Photographs, Department of Art and Archaeology, Princeton University.)

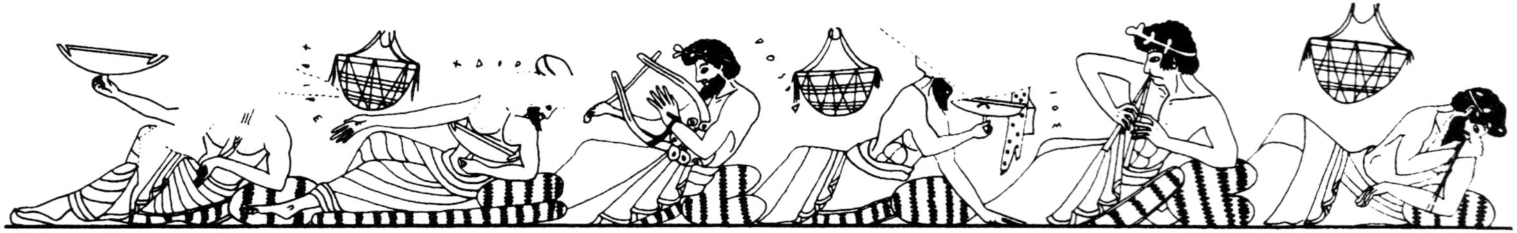

7.24. Red-figure volute-krater by Euthymides, ca. 510–500 B.C. Side B. Morgantina (Serra Orlando) 58.2382. (Photograph © Research Photographs, Department of Art and Archaeology, Princeton University.)

themselves to paradigm-creation appears to be quite short and the list of exemplary heroes, deeds, and activities is quite limited. The two most common groups, deeds of Herakles and Theseus, have obvious paradigmatic value for Athenian elites, and this relationship is frequently exploited.[81]

RELATED COMPARISONS

Comparisons created to engender paradigmatic relationships bring mortals closer to heroes and divinities, and in several examples we have considered, mortals are depicted as actually present, watching heroic or divine activity. There are in addition two other categories of related repetitive scenes also suggesting closeness between mortals and heroes or divinities. One type integrates figures with divine attributes with other figures who lack them, suggesting a kind of equivalence; a second group appears to couple a mythical *aition* with mortal behaviors, often apparently ritual. Both types share the underlying assumption that two groups have enough in common for the mythical events to serve as exempla for mortals.

Myth and Ritual

A black figure cup in New York displays two sides that are nearly identical[82] [Figures 7.25–7.27]. In both cases, a male figure wearing an ivy wreath and holding a drinking horn stands between two youths. The central triad on each side is flanked by two pairs of adult male spectators. A close inspection reveals that the central figures are not identical: the figure on the B side, unlike that on A, has long locks of hair that hang down on his chest and a white shawl is draped over his shoulder. It appears that the artist has been careful to distinguish the two figures from one another.[83] Although the iconography suggests a Dionysiac context, calling both figures "Dionysos" is problematic. The central figure without long locks on A is very like the spectator-narratees at the borders of A and B; he is also very like the two confronting figures in the tondo [Figure 7.27]. The repetition of the spectator-narratee figures in the tondo in fact unites all three fields. It appears there is a comparison on the A and B sides of the cup between myth and ritual, the *aition* for a ritual involving figures nearly identical to those who react it on the opposite side. The figures with the god in B would represent the first votaries of Dionysos engaged in a mythical event which the ritual on A reenacts. There is no discernible difference between those surrounding the mortal acting as Dionysos and those in the originating myth. The tondo figures likewise replicate the spectator-narratees on each side of the exterior. The resemblance is an important comment on the status of the participants in the ritual. The original myth is essentially a paradigm for the ritual reenactment; the ritual and the *aition* differ only through physical presence of the god in the latter. Otherwise elites are equivalent to those who were present in the initiating moment, a powerful comment on their status as they perceive it.

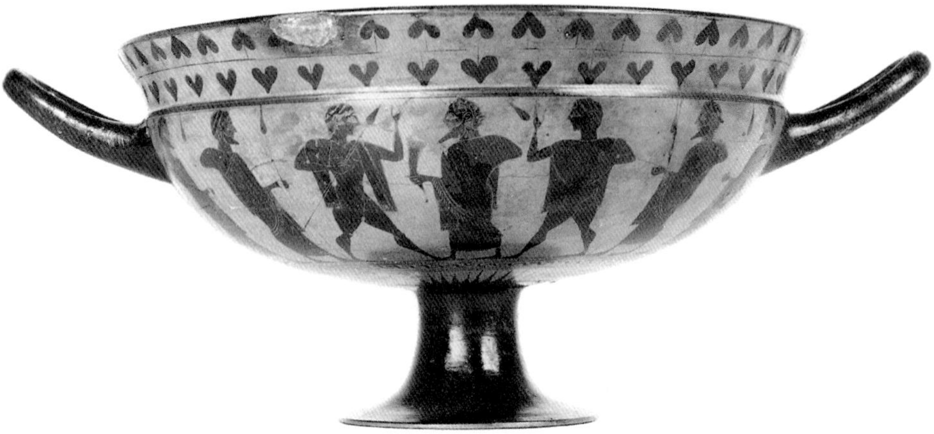

7.25. Black-figure cup attributed to the Heidelberg Painter. Attica, Greece, 565–555 B.C. Side A. Earthenware. 13.6 × 32.5 × 26 cm (5 3/8 × 12 13/16 × 10 1/4 in.) New York, Cooper-Hewitt Collection, National Design Museum, Smithsonian Institution. Gift of Anonymous Donor, 1921-1-1. (Photograph © Cooper-Hewitt, National Design Museum, Smithsonian Institution.)

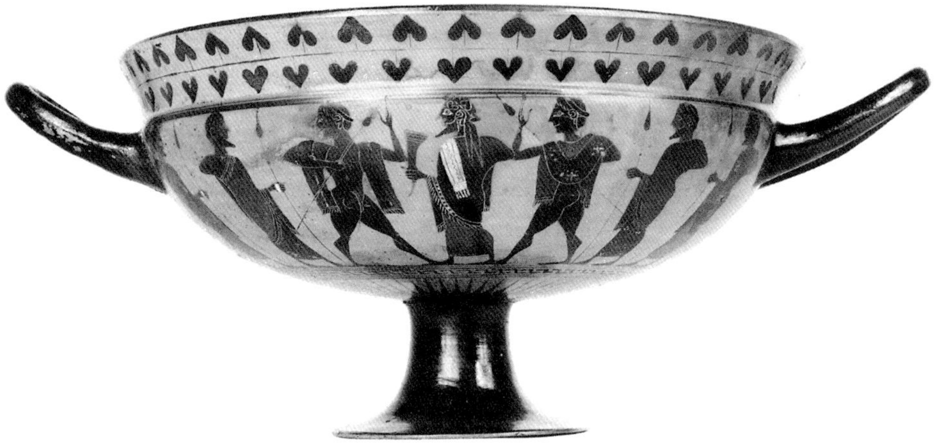

7.26. Black-figure cup attributed to the Heidelberg Painter. Attica, Greece, 565–555 B.C. Side B. Earthenware. 13.6 × 32.5 × 26 cm (5 3/8 × 12 13/16 × 10 1/4 in.) New York, Cooper-Hewitt Collection, National Design Museum, Smithsonian Institution. Gift of Anonymous Donor, 1921-1-1. (Photograph © Cooper-Hewitt, National Design Museum, Smithsonian Institution.)

The amphora by the Amasis Painter in Basel is an extremely clear example both of the interweaving of divine and mortal and of temporal sequence[84] [Figures 7.28, 7.29]. Dionysos is posed and dressed almost identically on A and B: he walks right holding out a kantharos in his right hand. He is framed by nymphs and satyrs on side A and by figures who appear to be mortals on side B. A nymph who dances with a satyr on A is posed very similarly to her apparently mortal counterpart in the composition on B. She holds an oinochoe, as does the satyr at center on A. In temporal terms, A

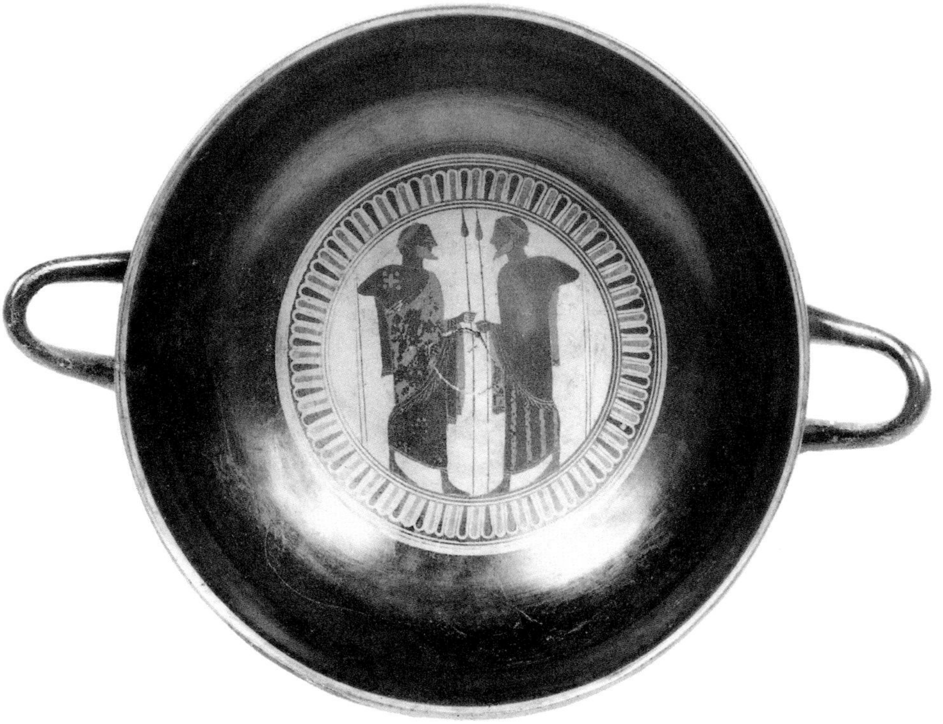

7.27. Black-figure cup attributed to the Heidelberg Painter. Attica, Greece, 565–555 B.C. Interior. Earthenware. 13.6 × 32.5 × 26 cm (5 3/8 × 12 13/16 × 10 1/4 in.) New York, Cooper-Hewitt Collection, National Design Museum, Smithsonian Institution. Gift of Anonymous Donor, 1921-1-1. (Photograph © Cooper-Hewitt, National Design Museum, Smithsonian Institution.)

shows the god in the context of winemaking and celebrating satyrs and one nymph; B shows wine-consumption only and the god with a *komos* of mortal youths and dancing women. Whereas the representation of the god is identical on each side, the youths and maidens on B are only "like" the satyrs and nymphs on A. The satyrs are nude, plump, with very long penises; the youths are also nude, but slimmer, and have small penises. The female figures are more alike: they share ivy wreaths in their hair and skirt-patterns in two instances. Although the repetitions certainly reveal sequence, from wine-preparation to consumption, they point to paradigm as well.[85] Side B appears to be a depiction of a mortal analogue to the mythical *aition* depicted on A. The repetitive effect here used is antonymous – satyrs are not youths and nymphs may not be girls, but the god is at the center in both spheres. Here, then, we have also a clear marker of elevated elite status as a consequence of the substantial list of commonalities. Youths and maidens are like satyrs and nymphs; the repetition of Dionysos as participant in story and as object of worship is clear and precise.

Oltos' cup in Florence focuses on the followers of Dionysos and mortal analogues.[86] The mortal context appears to be *symposion*, but the mythical referent is

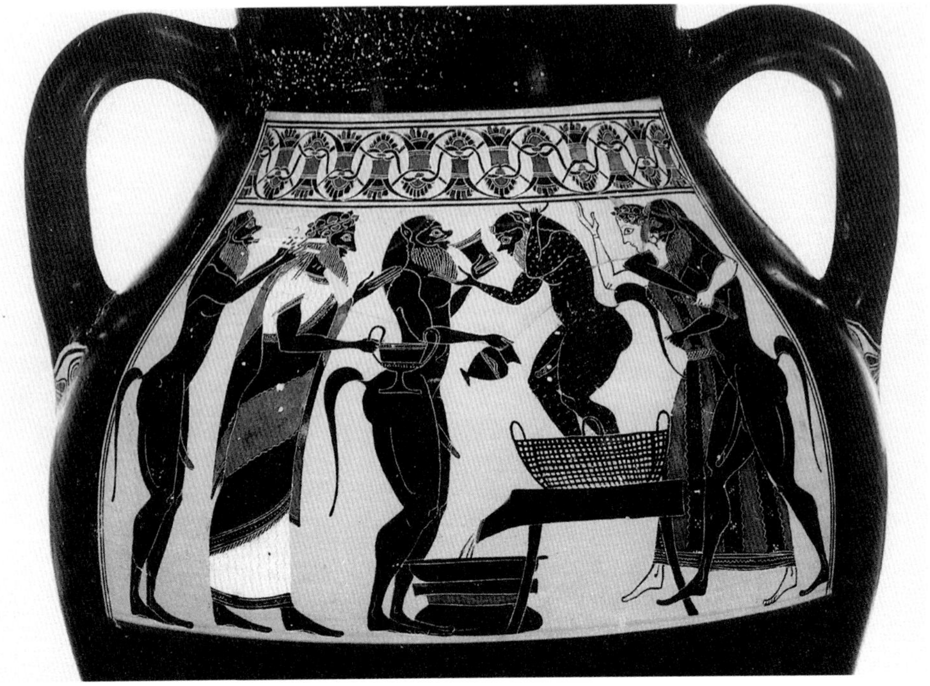

7.28. Black-figure amphora by the Amasis Painter, ca. 550–530 B.C. Side A. Basel, Antikenmuseum und Sammlung Ludwig KA 420. (Photograph © Antikenmuseum Basel und Sammlung Ludwig, Inv. KA 420. Photo: Claire Niggli.)

the followers of Dionysos, satyrs and nymphs, who play a part in cult. The compositions at the center of sides A and B differ: the youth holding a skyphos on A is replaced with a donkey on B, but the dancing satyr and nymph who flank the donkey on B adopt poses that closely echo those of the outermost komasts on A, linking the mythical with the mortal. Reiterating the link is the inscription of *kalos* and ΧΙΛ[ΟΝ] "Chil[on]," and ΧΙΛΟΣ, "Chilos," on A and B, respectively.[87] Because the name of the youth together with this label are typical language for the mortal *symposion*, their reappearance on the side with the mythical komasts brings the mythical and the mortal event together on a verbal as well as a visual level. The repeated writing amplifies the visual redundancy.

Epiktetos' earliest vase, a calyx krater in the Villa Giulia, in a similar way links Dionysiac revel with a mortal *komos*, suggesting a divine paradigm for mortal *komos*[88] The Dionysiac figures on A dance with bent knees, and one nymph carries an oinochoe with which she pours liquid into a vessel, now lost, held by Dionysos. One of the four komasts on B, whose dancing-positions are more dramatically exaggerated than those on A, also carries an oinochoe, held between his legs as he dances. There are no specific parallels between dancers on A and B; the repeated oinochoe is the primary visual link. The signatures, like those on the work of the painter's older bilingual colleagues, are incised, and they appear horizontally in the field, above the komasts on side B for

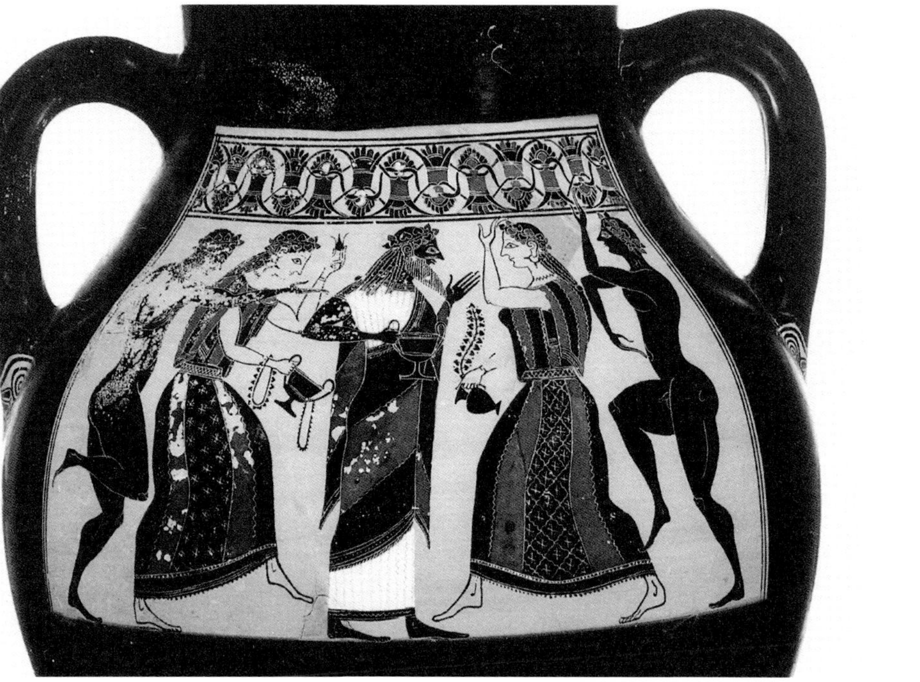

7.29. Black-figure amphora by the Amasis Painter, ca. 550–530 B.C. Side B. Basel, Antikenmuseum und Sammlung Ludwig KA 420. (Photograph © Antikenmuseum Basel und Sammlung Ludwig, Inv. KA 420. Photo: Claire Niggli.)

the painter and on the foot of the vessel on A for the potter. Just as the viewer must put together the inscriptions, factoring in their different locations, to understand fully the authorship of the vessel, he must consult both sides of the vase to understand the interconnection between mortal *komos* and Dionysiac revel.

The subtle example by Euthymides in Warsaw already discussed in Chapter 5 for its unusual parodic repeated inscriptions provokes a second look on the part of the viewer in its blending of satyr and *komast*, the mythical *aition* and its mortal analogue, linked[89] [Figures 4.10, 4.11]. The images of nude males, a youth on B and a satyr on A, appear frontally and from the rear, respectively. Because the figures adopt similar stances, the viewer must look carefully to realize that he sees the front and back of two distinct individuals. In this fashion, the images themselves prompt a double-take; it is as though the artist wants to encourage the viewer to believe the two images are front and back of a single figure and then to discover there are in fact two. The implication is that the *aition* and the mortal equivalent are very close but not the same, and the impression created by the repetition is of simultaneous conjunction rather than of temporal distinction.

The inscriptions include vertically arranged labels and statements on either side of each figure. On B, the youth holds a wine-amphora horizontally, and the wine is visible as it pours out. The three-part inscription describes what he does, i.e., "he pours sweet wine," and it names this figure ΑΘΕΝΙΟΝ, "Athenion."[90] On side A, the satyr blows one of his double pipes. A word, ΟΙΦΩΝ, modifying the name the of the satyr on B is obscene (οἴφειν is "to mount"). It also parodies the word "OINON" in the inscription on A.[91] The result is a clever inversion: the satyr provides the mythical prototype for the mortal *komast*, yet he imitates, crudely, mortal speech. The temporal implications for linking *aition* and mortal equivalent are complex; one ought to have preceded the other substiantially, yet they appear to be interconnected in the present. If the ancient viewer perceived the mythical prototype as just that – a prior event that the mortal reenacted – then temporal phases and possibly cause and effect are combined in the two images. Even if the ancient viewer sees the satyric *komos* as ongoing, eternal, and perpetual and not necessarily prior, the links between the two images create synonymy.[92]

A final example where a divinity and the mortals honoring him are linked in *aition* and ritual is the Triptolemos Painter's cup in the Louvre depicting Dionysos and Oinopoion.[93] The latter are decisively identified through attributes including kantharos, ivy wreath, and vine for the god at the center of the tondo [Figure 7.32]. Presumed by most scholars to represent an early dithyrambic chorus, the paired adult-youth couples dancing in procession appear analogous, because of similar clothing, hair, and wreaths, to Dionysos and his son. There is a ritual procession of male couples, either two youths or a youth and an adult male on side A of the exterior and on the interior around the tondo [Figures 7.30, 7.32]. All figures are labeled. The side A procession is linked to that in the interior very conspicuously by means of the repetition of the figure of the flute player and at least one of the participants, ΕΥΦΙΛΕΤΟΣ, "Euphiletos," whose name is repeated behind the first pair on the exterior and between the fourth and fifth pairs on the interior. Unnamed spectators to the event, both youths and adults, appear on side B of the exterior [Figure 7.31]. Tondo and exterior scene with spectators share the inscription *h*Ο ΠΑΙΣ ΚΑΛΟΣ, "the youth is handsome." The effect of the repeated *kalos* inscription is to link the *kalos* status of the god's son with the youths who watch and dance.

The mythical pair in the tondo [Figure 7.32] share several features with their reenactors of the *aition*, but their clothing, hair, and wreaths are more elaborate; whereas the god and his son wear their embroidered himatia wrapped around the waist and over a shoulder, the figures who process are completely muffled in plain garments. The god wears a *chiton* and an ivy wreath, whereas the men and youths do not reveal *chitons* under *himatia* and in their hair they wear simple fillets. Once again, there is an ambiguous temporal situation made doubly so through the repetition of figures and one inscription on interior and exterior. If myth time and mortal time are before and after, *aition* begetting ritual, then there are phased events, one prior to the other. If myth time and ritual time coalesce, then temporality is unified, requiring our careful consideration of how the results of repetition reflect perceptions of status.

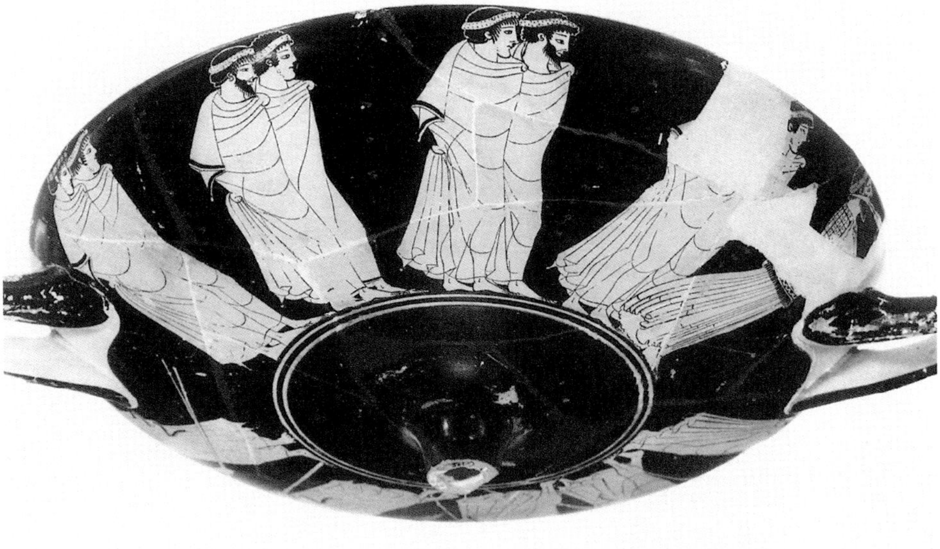

7.30. Red-figure cup by the Triptolemos Painter, ca. 480–470 B.C. Side A. Paris, Musée du Louvre G 138. (Photograph courtesy of the Musée du Louvre, Dist. RMN / © Christian Larrieu.)

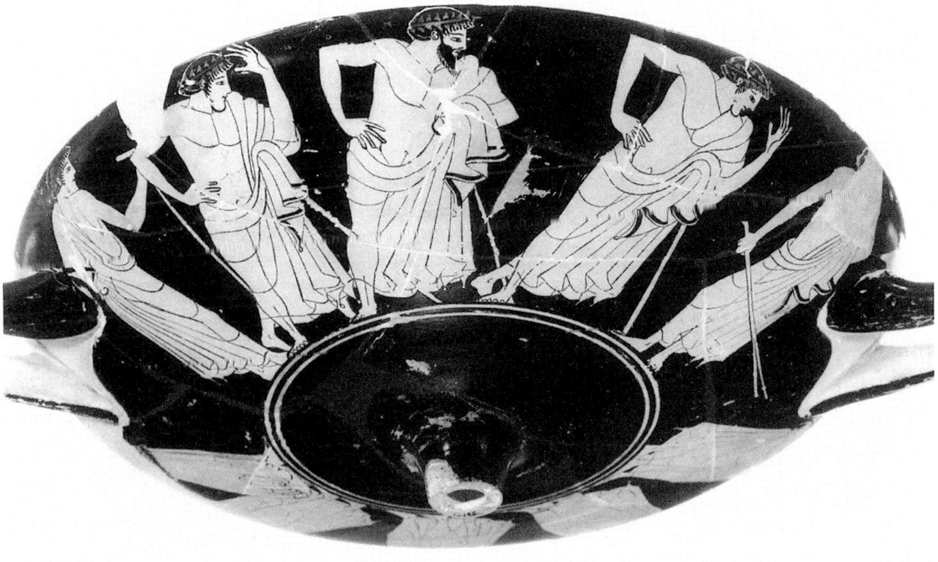

7.31. Red-figure cup by the Triptolemos Painter, ca. 480–470 B.C. Side B. Paris, Musée du Louvre G 138. (Photograph courtesy of the Musée du Louvre, Dist. RMN / © Christian Larrieu.)

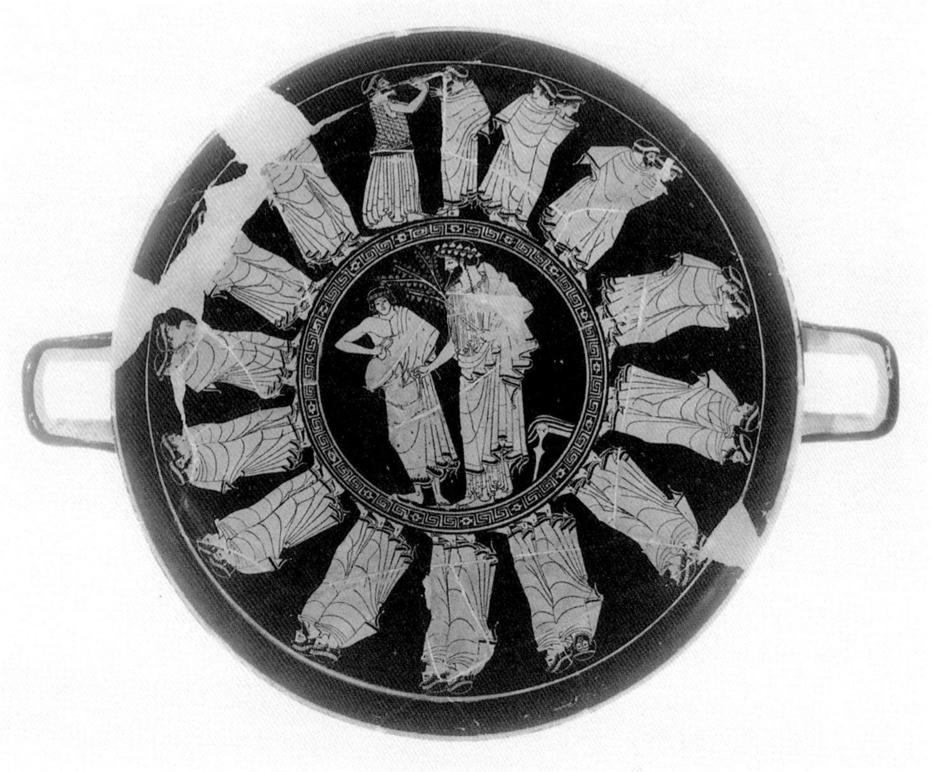

7.32. Red-figure cup by the Triptolemos Painter, ca. 480–470 B.C. Interior. Paris, Musée du Louvre G 138. (Photograph courtesy of the Musée du Louvre, Dist. RMN / © Christian Larrieu.)

Supporting the latter view is the double appearance of the *kalos* inscription, in the field with the divinities and again on the exterior among the spectators. Embedded in the ritual/*aition* relationship are paradigmatic links – the elite youths are like Oinopion, the adults like Dionysos.

Mortals and Divinities Intermingling

Having explored examples where repetition links ritual and mythic *aition* to identify paradigmatic events for mortal activity, we consider a group of vessels where the two categories, mythic and mortal, are not clearly separated from one another in different parts of a composition or in different fields of the vase. In this group of vases appear scenes where figures who are not marked as heroes or divinities are intermingled with those who are; these compositions are linked by means of repetition with others that are very similar. Because several examples by the Amasis Painter exhibiting this sort of intermingling have confounded scholars, our discussion makes a special point of considering his work. Looking at the examples by the Amasis Painter from the point of view of the results of repetition discussed in this chapter – the construction of paradigms both for general social values and for ritual – creates a basis for a claim that the Painter's work also accomplishes the creation of paradigm, but through a means that is distinct from that used by most other painters.

A predecessor to the Amasis Painter provides a starting point. A repeated single figure weaves together the exterior scenes on a Siana cup in Istanbul, a divine assembly on B and a mortal one on A.[94] The side B scene on Olympus shows Hermes, Athena, and Dionysos confronting a seated Zeus, all figures identified by attributes and pose. A "penguin-woman," distinctive in this context through her absence of attributes, is about to wreathe Zeus from behind. Poseidon holding his trident and standing behind Zeus' throne is followed by another wreath-holding "penguin-woman." The "penguin-women" are echoed precisely by two identical females on side A. One stands about to wreathe an adult male figure, who in turn faces an identical "penguin-woman" minus the wreath. Next, a crown-holding "penguin-woman" faces a male. Finally, a pair consisting of an adult male and a "penguin-woman" face one another. Each of the males has hair, beard, and clothing like those of the divinities on side B and each holds a spear identical to Athena's. The exact repetition of the "penguin-women" in particular links divine and mortal contexts. The effect is to invest the linking of apparently mortal men and women with a divine aura, and the mortal couples are elevated by the accompanying figures, the "penguin-woman," who on B share space with divinities. If a particular ritual is referenced, it is not clear which one.

Several well known examples by the Amasis Painter display similar interminglings. As Bothmer has stated, "The sphere of the gods . . . is often treated as an extension of daily life."[95] By this he means that mortals appear in scenes where divinities predominate, and there is no apparent specific mythical narrative depicted. Two amphoras, however, display compositions otherwise used to convey myth narratives. On an amphora in Berlin, a single repeated spectator is joined with several other repetitive features;[96] [Figures 7.33, 7.34] on side A, Hermes and Athena lead Herakles to an adult male figure who ought to be Zeus, but who has none of the god's usual attributes. Herakles, without lion skin, carries bow and club. These figures are accompanied by two dogs and a youth at far right who holds a spear and wears a fancy spotted mantle, almost a *nebris;* this youth appears to observe an introduction scene, one that is typical except for the lack of attributes identifying the Zeus figure. Side B [Figure 7.34] repeats Hermes, dressed differently, two dogs, positioned differently; the bow, this time together with an arrow, appears again in the hands of two youths. The framing youths here correspond to the youth at far right on side A; this repetition is one visual link that equates the central actions on the two sides. Holding a bow makes the youths like Herakles, and the youths are escorted by Hermes as are Athena and Herakles on the obverse. The lack of definitive attributes for most of the divine group and especially the absence of a lionskin for Herakles once again blurs the distinction between elites and divinities and heroes. We do not have here a clear visual "simile" as we saw earlier on

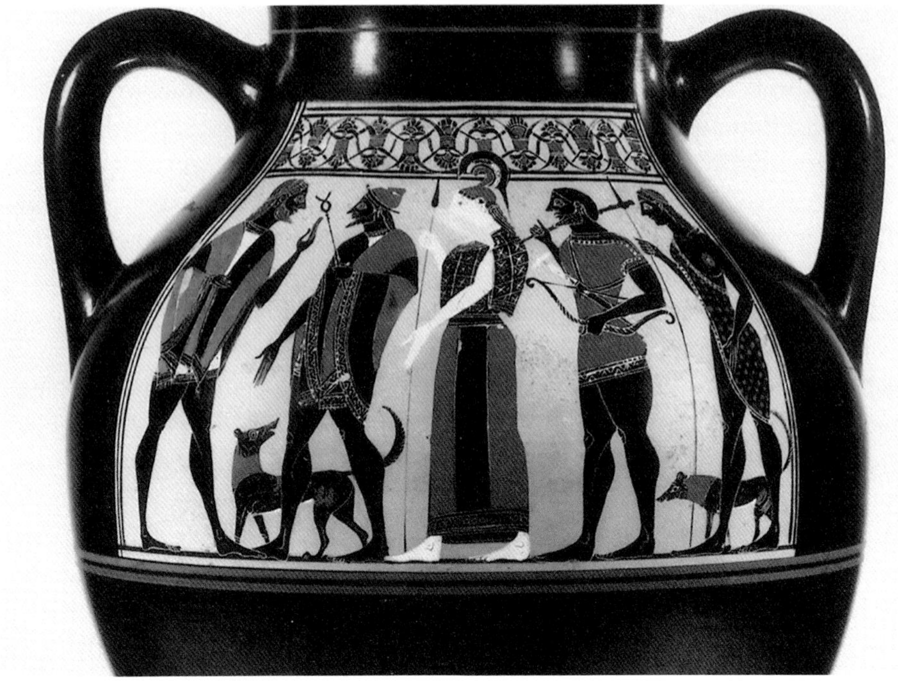

7.33. Black-figure amphora by the Amasis Painter, ca. 550–530 B.C. Side A. Berlin, Antikensammlung, Staatliche Museen zu Berlin 1688. (Photograph © Bildarchiv Preussischer Kulturbesitz / Art Resource, NY.)

the Siana cup in Taranto by the Heidelberg Painter [Figures 7.3, 7.4], where a mortal lion-fight is distinct from but like Herakles' lion-fight, depicted in another field. On the amphora in Würzburg by Group E, an elite hoplite is very like Iolaos [Figures 7.15–7.16], but separated from him in a different field of the vase. Instead, we have here a comparison where distinctions between the comparable elements are muted. This toning-down itself lessens further the distance between divinity or hero and elite. The message is reinforced by the presence of the repeated spectator-narratees in the Amasis Painter amphora, who not only link the scenes but also direct the status-message to its appropriate audience.[97]

Another panel-amphora in Basel presents different interpretive challenges because several figures are very like divinities but are curiously low on identifying attributes.[98] Side A depicts nude youths with expectant gestures and spears framing a trio: a woman with a spear, possibly Athena(?), stands between an armed warrior and a nude man holding spear and shield. Side B repeats the framing youths (only one here holds a spear), but substitutes a divine triad at center composed of a seated Zeus (?) holding a scepter but otherwise "un-Zeus-like," facing Hermes (?), who wears a *petasos* but carries a spear, and an adult male also carrying a spear coming up from behind. Both scenes are distinctive because they involve figures who are "almost-but-not-quite

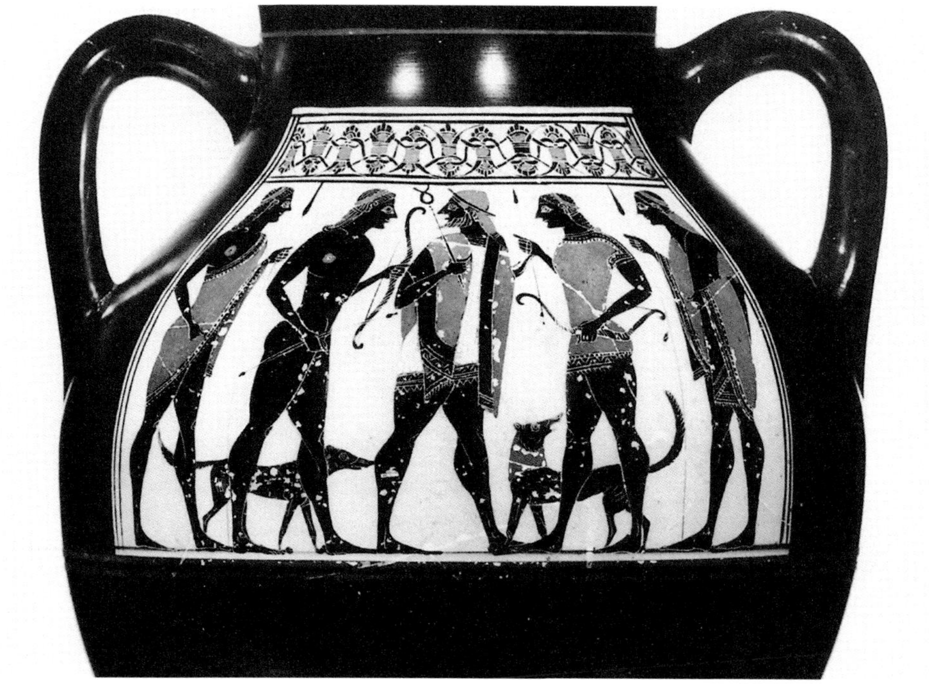

7.34. Black-figure amphora by the Amasis Painter, ca. 550–530 B.C. Side B. Berlin, Antikensammlung, Staatliche Museen zu Berlin 1688. (Photograph © Bildarchiv Preussischer Kulturbesitz / Art Resource, NY.)

Athena or Zeus" together with elite males, both youths and adults, who hold the same spears as Hermes and "Athena." The outermost youths on each scene are spectator-narratees, as defined in Chapter 4. Their common features with the nude adult male who acts in the central triad on A suggests an affinity that crosses a boundary, directly integrating the youth with the central scene. The relatively small number of definitive attributes of the divinities diminishes the differences between the two groups. The effect of the two scenes in tandem is to blur the boundary between elite mortal and divinity, to suggest that there is very little difference between the elite mortal adults, the divinity, and the elite youths who observe their elders interact with Zeus and with "Athena."

On an example employing a composition familiar from the repertory of myth narratives, two youths on side B frame a generalized "Recovery of Helen" scene[99] [Figure 7.35]. The Helen figure stands at center, with "Menelaos" to the left and another armed male figure at right. The nude youths at the edges of the scene hold identical spears in exactly the same way as the Greek warrior who accompanies "Menelaos." The youth at the far left holds in addition an aryballos, an attribute that resonates with associations of the gymnasium and pederastic love-gifts. On side A, all of the figures appear to be engaged in a wine-related event. Four youths, identical in hairstyles and

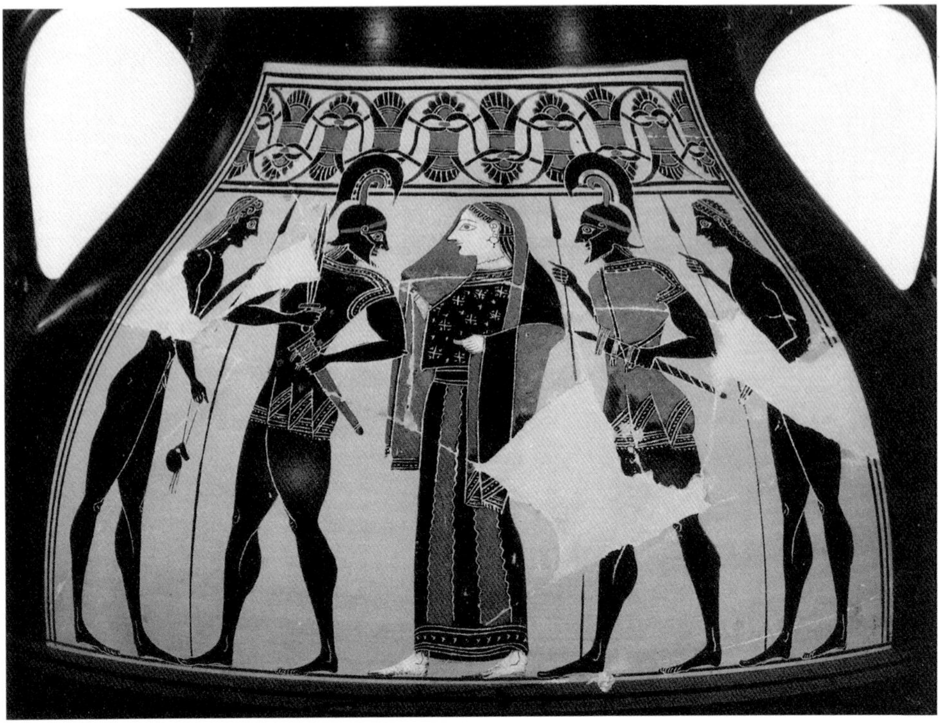

7.35. Black-figure amphora by the Amasis Painter, ca. 550–530 B.C. Side B. Munich, Staatliche Antikensammlungen und Glyptothek 1383 (J. 75). (Photograph © Staatliche Antikensammlungen und Glyptothek München. Photograph: C. H. Krüger-Moessner.)

nudity to those on B, frame a walking Dionysos on side A [Figure 7.36]. The two youths at the borders of the scene carry wineskins in place of the spear (and aryballos) held by the youths on B; the youth who faces Dionysos pours wine from an oinochoe into the god's kantharos, and he holds an ivy branch as does the god himself.[100] Only one youth holds no attributes, and he gestures expansively, standing behind the god. The youth facing the god corresponds in appearance to the iconography of Oinopion.

The repetition of the framing figures bestows an equivalence on the two central scenes; as a result both, on one level, focus on aspects of "coming of age," that is, initiation through a Dionysiac ritual (A) and introduction of adult male – military and marital – behavior (B). The differences in attributes carried by the youths on the two sides emphasize two different aspects of the social experience of Athenian youths: their initiation into adult religious roles in the polis – the wineskin and ivy – and their adoption of male roles in relation to women, war, and the gymnasium – the spears and aryballos.

Both sides of an amphora in Bloomington feature very similar compositions, a figure identifiable as Dionysos in the middle of two dogs, and four other figures.[101] The two scenes, especially those on side B, are in fact very like the two scenes on the cup

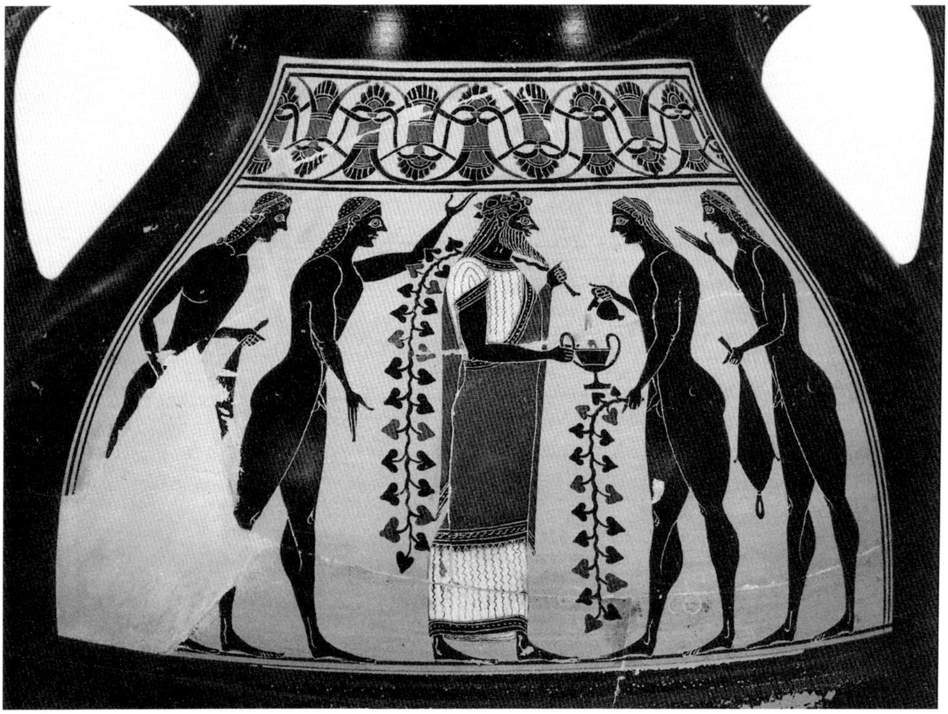

7.36. Black-figure amphora by the Amasis Painter, ca. 550–530 B.C. Side A. Munich, Staatliche Antikensammlungen und Glyptothek 1383 (J. 75). (Photograph © Staatliche Antikensammlungen und Glyptothek München. Photograph: C. H. Krüger-Moessner.)

in New York discussed above as a possible instance of myth *aition* and ritual[102] [Figures 7.25, 7.26]. However, there the god appears different in each scene, distinguished by the long locks of hair on one of the figures. In this case, the god is identical except for different stripes on his richly decorated clothing, but there are slight differences in the figures who surround Dionysos. Side A features dogs in excited poses – Bothmer refers to them as "snarling" – with a complement of four spectators: at left, two long-haired youths wearing *chlamydes* and holding spears and at right a man wearing a pointed cloth cap and *chlamys* with a youth who wears a *himation* and holds a spear. It is as if a very dressed-down Hermes is introducing a youth to the god. Side B preserves Dionysos in differently decorated garb, calmer dogs, and the following replacements of the right-hand figures: long-haired youths wearing *chlamydes* and carrying spears, identical to those at left and at left in the main scene on side A. The substitutions and change in tone are striking in the face of such a great amount of similarity; one interpretation is to see a mythical *aition* where four youths come upon the god, combined with an image of an initiation ritual based on this *aition*, where a youth is introduced to the divinity. Indeed, Scheibler believes the Amasis Painter's amphoras that preserve images including Dionysos and youths represent initiation-scenes.[103] The scenes make a point about the god's relevance to two subtly different casts of characters on two different occasions. The repetitions intensify the importance of the bystanders' attention to Dionysos and expand upon the nature of the occasions on which they share common ground with the divinity.[104]

These examples by the Amasis Painter appear to be closely tied to those examples where a mythical paradigm is cited as well as to those where the mythical *aition* for a ritual is coupled with the ritual itself. The myth figures are more generalized and the elite observers interact more directly with the divine than in the majority of examples by other painters treated in this chapter. In each case, repeated figures and/or repeated syntax links scenes to make a fuller and more coherent, if still ambiguous, point.

When mortals and divinities interact in repeated imagery, sometimes the event acts to create a paradigm, an *aition* for mortal activity. It is through performance of the ritual that the mortal becomes like the divinity or like those who once, in earlier times, interacted with the gods: it is this worldview that we see represented in the imagery. In many instances, the mythical *aition* is distinct from the human reenactment, appearing in a separate field of the vessel. In other examples, mortals, heroes, and divinities appear together, suggesting an imaginary time and place where the separation felt in the historical present does not obtain. Informing the world view that creates both paradigm and *aition* is a profound sense of similarity between elites, heroes, and divine. The world of the gods and heroes is directly applicable to that of Athenian elites in their construction of social values, social hierarchies, and the rituals that maintain both.

EIGHT

REPETITION, CHARACTER, AND PERSPECTIVE

The Boston pelike considered at the start of this study spotlights front and back images of dancers jumping [Figures 1.1, 1.2]. In combination the images provide two different visual perspectives on the youths. Likewise, the repertory of Exekias includes an example where similar but not identical figures are paired and shown from different visual perspectives: the Boston neck-amphora discussed in Chapter 2 shows two horses on A in profile and two more on B, one in profile as on A and another frontally [Figures 2.3, 2.4]. They are not the same horses, but in combination the scenes show "horse" from two different points of view. Examples joining different conceptual perspectives in representations of myth-narratives exist as well; one explanation for the close repetitions on the bilingual amphoras displaying Achilles and Ajax gaming, Herakles driving a bull to sacrifice, or Herakles resting on a *kline* by the Andokides/Lysippides Painters [Figures 2.12–2.15] is that the redundancies explore two points of view of a pair of ideal viewers of the vessel. That two "intended readers" can be different and have different reactions while seeing the same story told in images is made vivid by the radical change in color scheme between red- and black-figure.

In the same way that painters couple two points of view or otherwise highlight difference in perspective, they also sometimes pair two different traits or typical activities of a character. For example, the bilingual amphora in Munich showing Herakles reclining on a *kline* reveals two contrasting components of the hero's repertory of traits [Figures 2.14–2.15]. In black-figure, his weapons are visible above him in the field, emphasizing his track record as a fighter; in red-figure, they are absent and Athena extends a flower to him, highlighting the hero's special relationship with his sponsoring deity. The difference in technique emphasizes the different portraits of the hero. It is possible to see either "side" of the hero, and different situations will bring out the different qualities; to know the character more fully, the viewer must combine the two characterizations of the hero in the two different scenes in the vase.

Generic characters can represent particular social roles, and "elite youth," "adult male," or "*hetaira*" often figure in imagery. Articulating a range of behaviors typical of the holders of such roles is analogous to explication of different traits or facets of a hero or divinity.[1] Exposing facets of a character or a social role or differing points of view is dependent upon manipulation of ellipsis: there must be features left out of one image and provided in another, and at the same time there must be repetition of enough features to join the fields together.

Exploring point of view and aspects of character requires recognition that characters and events have multiple facets: Athena is both a leader in battle and a beauty contestant, just as her physical form has profile, frontal, and rear views. A good story will present at least one facet of Athena through her actions in it, but this facet will not contradict the other facets of the goddess depicted elsewhere. Two viewers may see this facet in two entirely different ways, both visually and ideologically. Athenian artists use repetition to explore both point of view and characters, and we will review at the outset how narratology and structural linguistics define these features.

POINT OF VIEW

Chatman, in analyzing narratives, divides point of view into two large categories, active and passive states:[2] *Active states* (from the point of view of the individual undergoing the experience) include *perceptual* point of view, through someone's own eyes. Active perception reveals how the onlooker sees what is told or seen: "He saw the goddess' back, but his companion opposite saw her front." Another kind of active state is *conceptual* point of view, revealing a given thing through someone's own world view or ideology: "From his perspective, as a follower of Aphrodite, Athena's celibacy was incomprehensible." *Passive states* can also be described as *transferred interest*, a situation seen through someone else's vantage point: "Croesus did not know it, but his misinterpretation of the oracle was fatal."

Athenian artists display consistent interest in perceptual point of view as construed from the vantage point of the viewers of the vase, from the front, from the back, obliquely. The images also explore conceptual or ideological points of view, exploring divinities, heroes, social roles, and activities of the elite Athenian. A combination of all points of view, both perceptual and conceptual, makes understanding the totality possible.

CHARACTER

Stories feature characters who act in particular ways as the plot unfolds. For most critics, beginning with Aristotle, a character's traits are determined and revealed by plot, by what he does.[3] Herakles kills a lion, so his primary character trait in that story is "lion-slayer."[4] Another component of Aristotle's definition of character recognizes that characters are made up of a composite of their actions in a large number of plots; a well-constructed character in any one plot will not display traits that are at odds with traits displayed elsewhere.[5] The recognition that a character has many diverse facets seems to be depicted in narration of myths on vases through pairings united by repetition.[6]

EVIDENCE ON VASES

The analysis below surveys a range of diverse examples where artists analyze character traits by clustering several in one text and exhibit analysis of point of view in much the same way. Topics include specific characters such as divinities, the social experiences of elites such as courtship and *symposion*, and a number of different social roles. Although we start with earlier examples, beginning at about 575 B.C., and progress to some dating in the early fifth century, there appears to be no real development or progression over time. The phenomena observed here are all-pervasive and thoroughly embedded in vase-painting evidence from the early archaic period onward.

A cup in London provides a partial character analysis of the divinity "Athena" in two separate narratives. A figure of Athena appears in two different fields, and the artist is careful to make them very similar [Figure 8.1].[7] In the interior Ajax and Cassandra are at the statue of Athena, and, on side B, Athena conducts Herakles to Olympus in the company of others [Figures 8.2, 8.3]. Both depictions of Athena show her almost identically, with the same shield device and same helmet. Yet there are also differences: in the introduction scene, Athena wears her aegis and she does not hold a spear, the spear is present in the tondo but no aegis is visible. Through this embellishment and ellipsis, the painter makes it a point to emphasize that the figures are extremely similar yet not quite the same. In fact, he successfully makes a distinction between cult statue and actual goddess, breaking down the character of the goddess into two essential components. In one instance the goddess helps her protégé; in the other she does not protect her priestess.

On a Siana cup in Athens dating to the second quarter of the sixth century is an early example of an analysis of the social role "elite youth."[8] Two repeated features among all three scenes on the cup stand out, a youth and a wreath. Each scene places the figure of the youth in a slightly different context. In the tondo the youth runs, wearing a short *chiton* and a mantle, carries the wreath, and is accompanied by a pantheress. On side A, several youths, dressed similarly but not identically to the

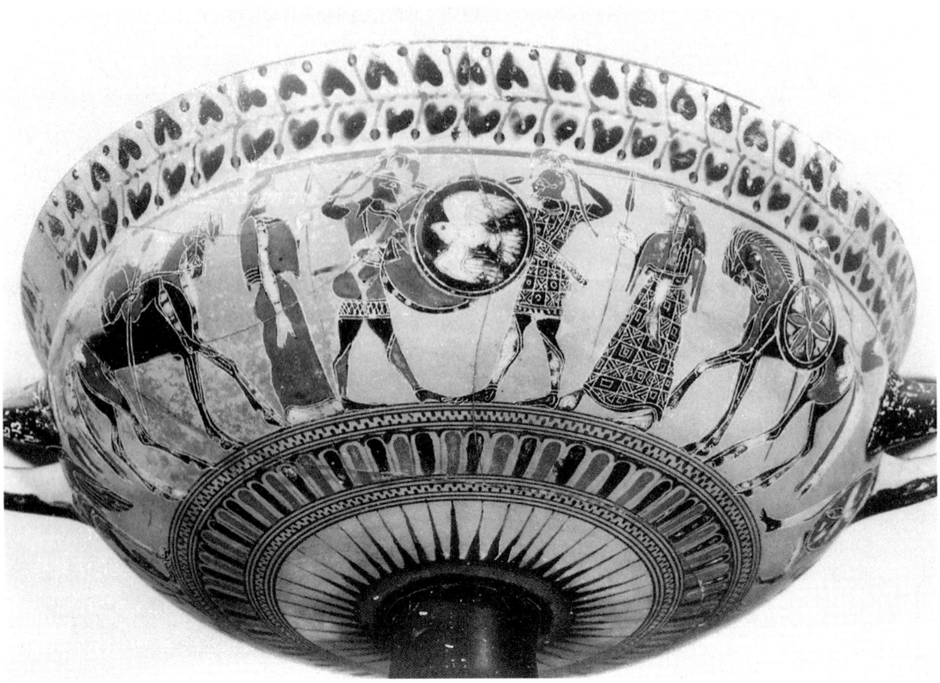

8.1. Black-figure cup by the Cassandra Painter, ca. 565 B.C. Side A. London, British Museum B 379. (Photograph © Copyright The Trustees of The British Museum.)

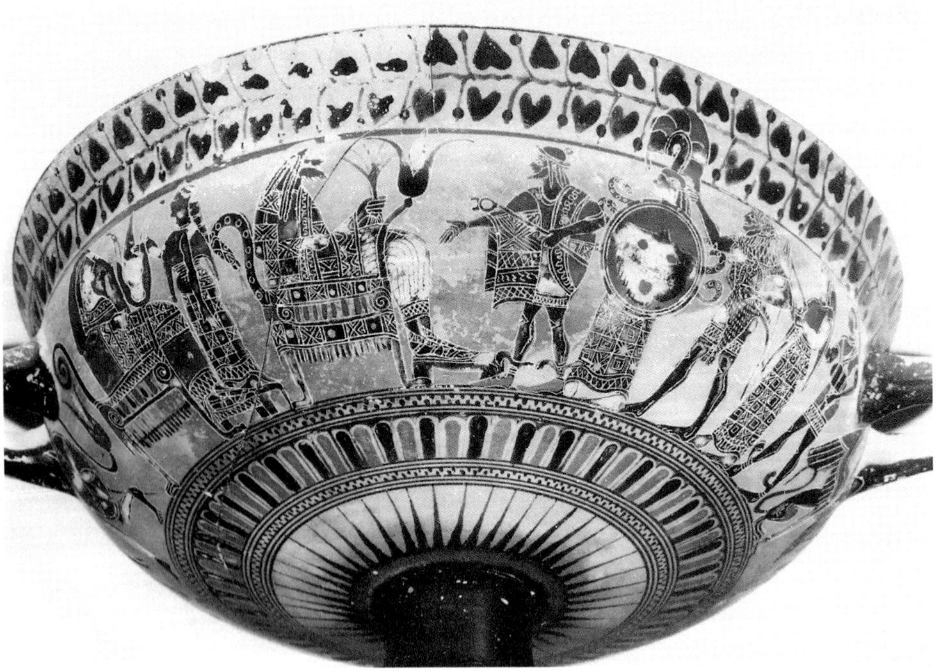

8.2. Black-figure cup by the Cassandra Painter, ca. 565 B.C. Side B. London, British Museum B 379. (Photograph © Copyright The Trustees of The British Museum.)

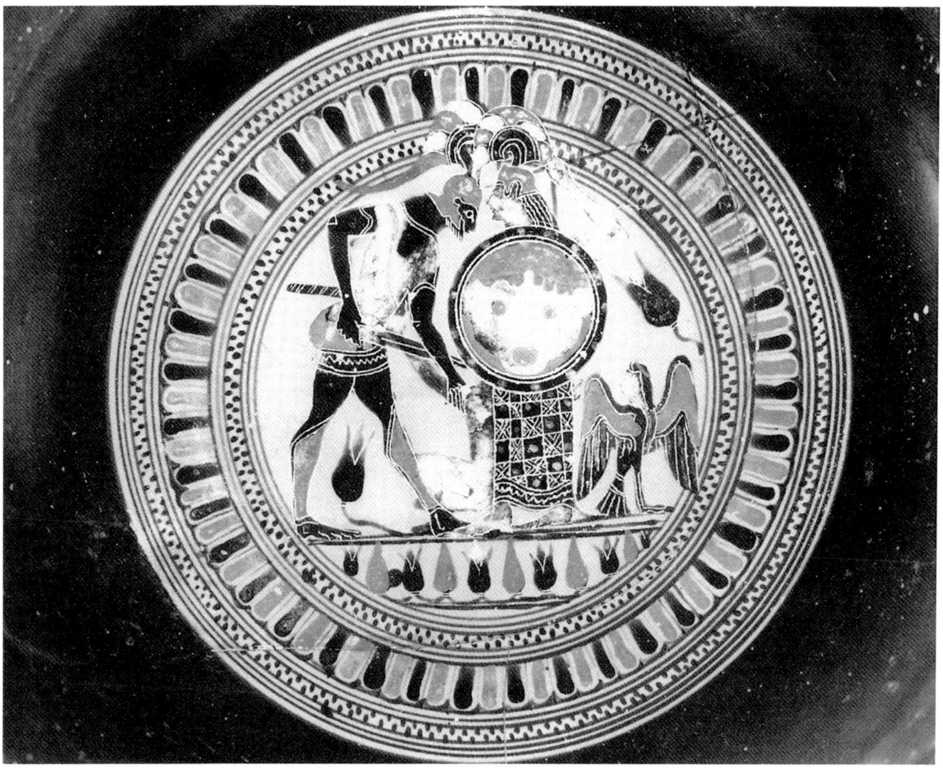

8.3. Black-figure cup by the Cassandra Painter, ca. 565 B.C. Interior. London, British Museum B 379. (Photograph © Copyright The Trustees of The British Museum.)

tondo figure, interact with adult males in a courting context. The youths are about to receive wreaths like the one held in the hand of the tondo figure. On side B a single youth, wearing a long chiton and himation like the adult males in the scene, sits at the head of a *symposiast's* couch. Another adult male approaches, holding a wreath, and a second wreath hangs in the field. There is no obvious myth narrative here, although the interior scene is apparently temporally subsequent to those on the exterior. The three scenes in combination identify a set of experiences of "elite youth;" in the tondo, the youth has received the wreath that is merely offered in the exterior scenes. In sum, status as *eromenos* is defined: the three scenes provide an array of amorous experiences of the generic elite youth. In this case, the repetitions are a cohesive device serving to create a single "text" about the experience of a youth selected as the recipient of pederastic courtship overtures.

An example in Cambridge explicates part of the elite adult experience of courtship.[9] Draped adult male figures and youths holding spears stand on either side of a seated adult male figure on side B [Figure 8.5]. On A, the same figures stand on either side of a triad. This threesome consists of Hermes, an adult male, whose fringed himation and lowered head are similar to the clothing and posture of the seated figure on B, and a female figure who in her left hand holds both a wreath and her mantle in the "bridal" gesture [Figure 8.4]. Hermes appears to be introducing the male and female figures to one another. The wreath and clothing of this female figure are identical to those of a woman in the tondo, who likewise holds a wreath but has her mantle off her head. Confronting this female figure in the tondo is a male figure dressed identically to both spectators on A and B and the "groom" on B, but with Dionysiac attributes, wreath and drinking horn, in addition [Figure 8.6]. Brijder identifies this scene as "Dionysos and Ariadne," yet it displays links with the exterior scenes, where the only divinity clearly marked is Hermes. In combination, a mythical paradigm appears to illuminate one of the facets of courtship and mate-selection. First, the man appears alone; then he is escorted by his colleagues and Hermes to a divinely sanctioned introduction to his bride. Finally, the links between tondo and exterior suggest a comparison, a synonymy, between the divine marriage of Dionysos and Ariadne and this mortal couple; the divine marriage is cited as paradigmatic for the elite mortal. At the very least, the cup is a single, unified text "about" marriage and gender relationships from the perspective of its protagonist, an elite male.

A mastoid cup in the Louvre by the Amasis Painter presents two scenes of figures handling sympotic equipment linked by several repetitions[10] [Figures 8.7, 8.8]. There is a high degree of equivalence, expressed through composition, pose, and attributes in these images. In each case a female figure stands at the center of the composition, and she transfers an object to a male figure who approaches from the right. Likewise in each case, a nude male figure stands behind her to the left. An ivy branch carried by the male figure at left on A is held instead by the woman on B. She holds a wreath on A; the male figure at right holds one on B. A libation is transferred on A; a lyre is transferred on B.[11] The text joins several common sympotic implements, wreath, ivy branch, libation, and musical instrument, and places male and female actors in the identical relationship to them. From this perspective, the female figure, presumably a *hetaira*, is depicted as equivalent to the male.

Each of the four examples just considered is a drinking vessel dating between 560 and 540 B.C. with multiple decorated fields. The topics explore a particular character, specific in the case of Athena and generic in the case of male and female elites and a *hetaira*, as understood through particular kinds of experience. In each instance, individual fields spotlight one typical experience for the subject. Repetitions among the various fields link the discrete segments and together they create a multifaceted view of divinity, of elite courtship, both homosexual and heterosexual, and of *symposion*. Although one can build a story from the images, narrative is not apparently the primary interest of the artist. Instead, to represent a collection of traits clearly integrated with one another is the result.

At about the same time, in the Group E workshop, there is a cluster of examples that explore perceptual (visual) point of view: a single subject appears not identically but very similarly, exposing different perspectives on each side of a vessel. An example

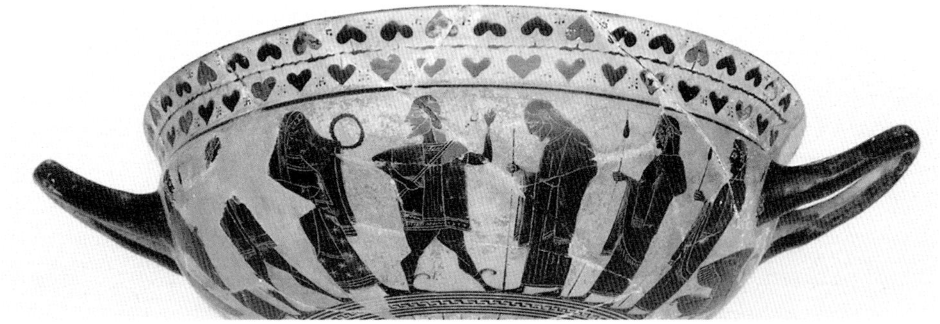

8.4. Black-figure cup by the Heidelberg Painter, ca. 565–555 B.C. Side A. Cambridge, Fitzwilliam Museum GR 4-1930. (Reproduction by permission of the Syndics of the Fitzwilliam Museum, Cambridge.)

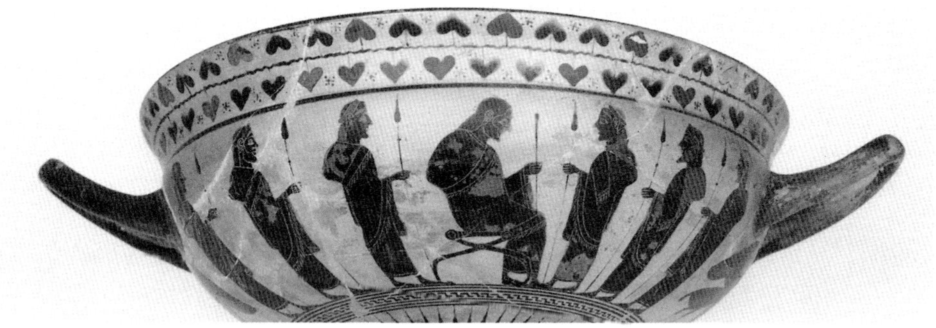

8.5. Black-figure cup by the Heidelberg Painter, ca. 565–555 B.C. Side B. Cambridge, Fitzwilliam Museum GR 4-1930. (Reproduction by permission of the Syndics of the Fitzwilliam Museum, Cambridge.)

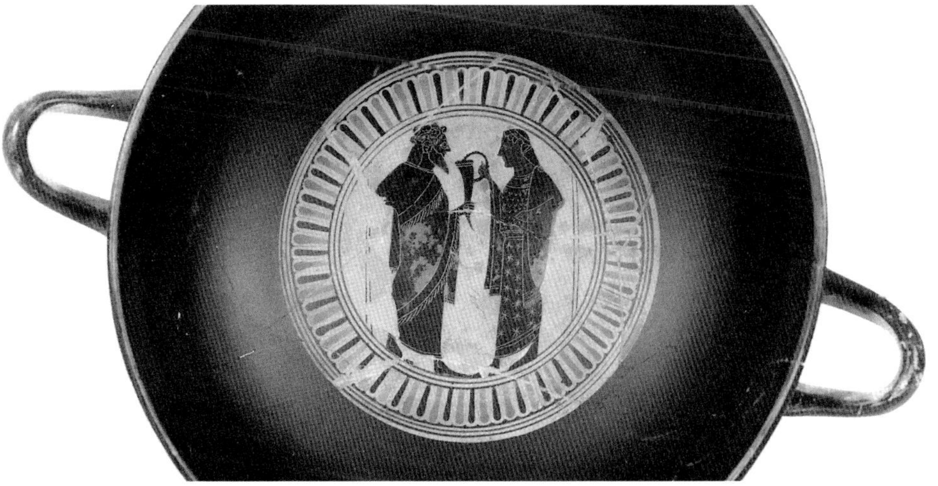

8.6. Black-figure cup by the Heidelberg Painter, ca. 565–555 B.C. Interior. Cambridge, Fitzwilliam Museum GR 4 1930. (Reproduction by permission of the Syndics of the Fitzwilliam Museum, Cambridge.)

in Würzburg depicts two versions of warriors setting out.[12] On A, four foot soldiers are sent off by two unarmed draped men [Figure 8.9]. The warrior's shields, blazons out, are prominent, held at their sides on the left shoulders. One shield is white and therefore especially distinctive. On B, warriors, with whom the departing figures on A share helmet-style, greaves, and spears, are depicted between two mounted riders, striding with shields held out in front, in profile at right angles to those on A, with a white shield again prominent [Figure 8.10]. The combination of the two scenes pairs a departure from home (A) with a departure for a campaign (B); the difference in setting and time is emphasized by the difference in perspective – frontal shields on A versus profile shields on B, held as if ready for battle. The difference in point of view distinguishes armor at rest from armor in use.

Pots and cups from the second quarter of the sixth century include several examples that pair slightly different scenes with horses.[13] A large group of at least six pots attributed to painters in Group E combine scenes with profile and frontal views of horses, often hitched to chariots, linking military chariot topics with such nonmilitary chariot topics as weddings and athletes. The group of vases appears to demonstrate that painters had a sustained interest in exploring the representation of different visual perspectives; the topics they focus on are two important status-indicators for elite Athenians, horses and chariots.[14] We pointed out at the beginning of this chapter that Exekias, who is associated with Group E, reflects this interest in combining perspectives on the Boston amphora: side A shows the pole horses in profile, whereas side B shows one trace horse in profile and one frontally[15] [Figures 2.3, 2.4]

Eye cups have come up several times as a series of very similar vessels that share characteristics of a Type as defined in Chapter 3. There is a very obvious linking syntax that holds together a single theme despite the separation of images in several subfields. Epiktetos' eye-cup in London exploits this potential to combine different perceptual points of view along with two facets of satyr-status. An ithyphallic satyr runs on each side between the eyes[16] [Figures 3.7, 3.8]. The facial features, hair, wreath, and *pelta* in each case are identical. The figure is completely in profile on B, whereas on A he runs to the left and twists at the waist, looking back over his shoulder to right, presenting a rear view of the torso. Attributes differ as well: the figure blows a *salpinx* on one side only and carries his *pelta* and an oinochoe; on the other, he carries a *pelta* and drinking horn. The repetitions and the syntax encourage the viewer to combine the images, to consider the two satyrs together; the differences in pose and attribute remind the viewer that the satyrs will appear differently to different viewers, and any one individual satyr does not necessarily possess all possible satyr-traits. The links forged by means of the repetitions in the images on the two sides are strengthened by the division of the painter's signature, with the name appearing on one side and the verb on the other, providing further impetus for the viewer to put the two sides together.

Another eye-cup by Epiktetos in the Louvre reflects two facets of experience for an elite youth, *sympotic* life and weapons training, and all three fields are linked by the

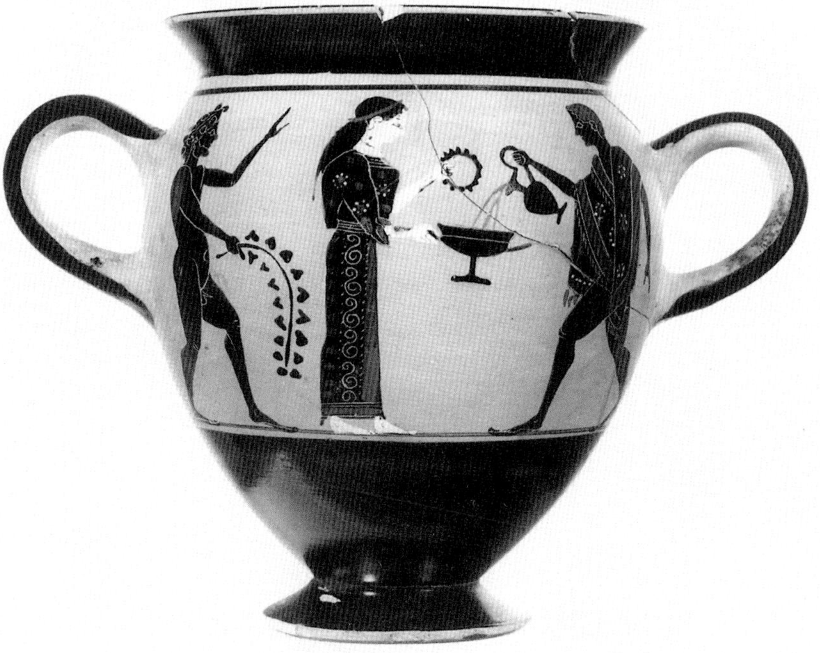

8.7. Black-figure mastoid cup by the Amasis Painter, ca. 550–530 B.C. Side A. Paris, Musée du Louvre F 70 (MNB 1686). (Photograph © Musée du Louvre, Dist. RMN / © Les frères Chuzeville.)

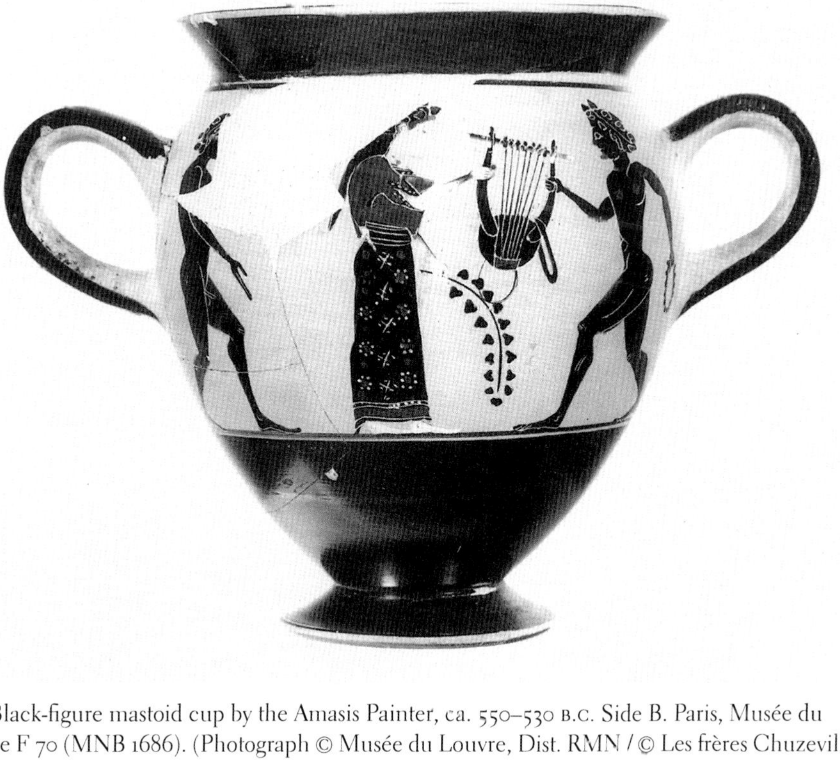

8.8. Black-figure mastoid cup by the Amasis Painter, ca. 550–530 B.C. Side B. Paris, Musée du Louvre F 70 (MNB 1686). (Photograph © Musée du Louvre, Dist. RMN / © Les frères Chuzeville.)

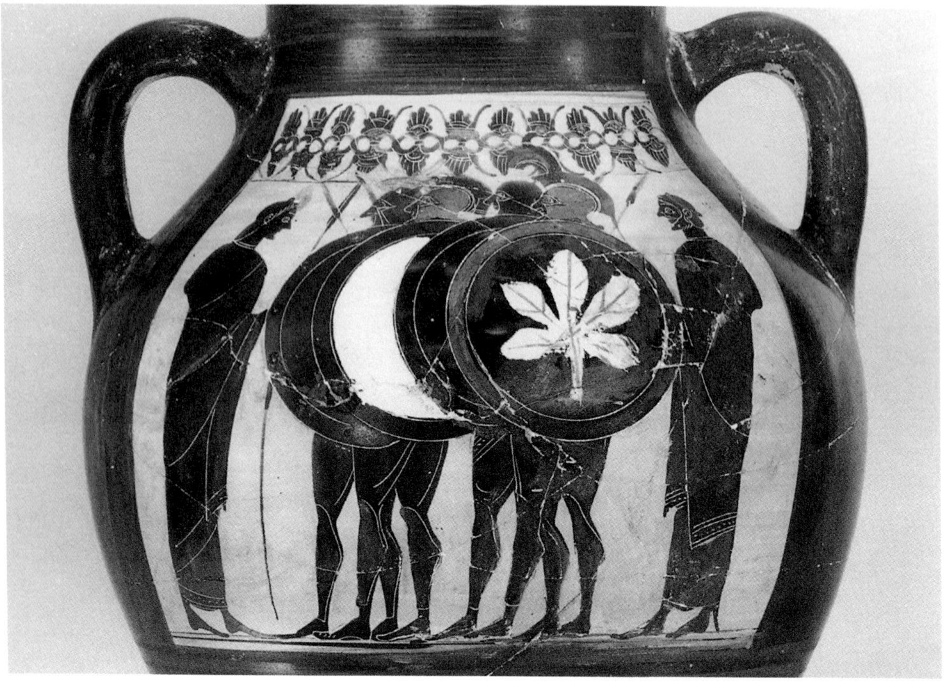

8.9. Black-figure amphora by Group E, ca. 560–540 B.C. Side A. Würzburg University, Martin von Wagner Museum 251. (Photograph © Martin von Wagner Museum der Universität Würzburg. Photo: K. Oehrlein.)

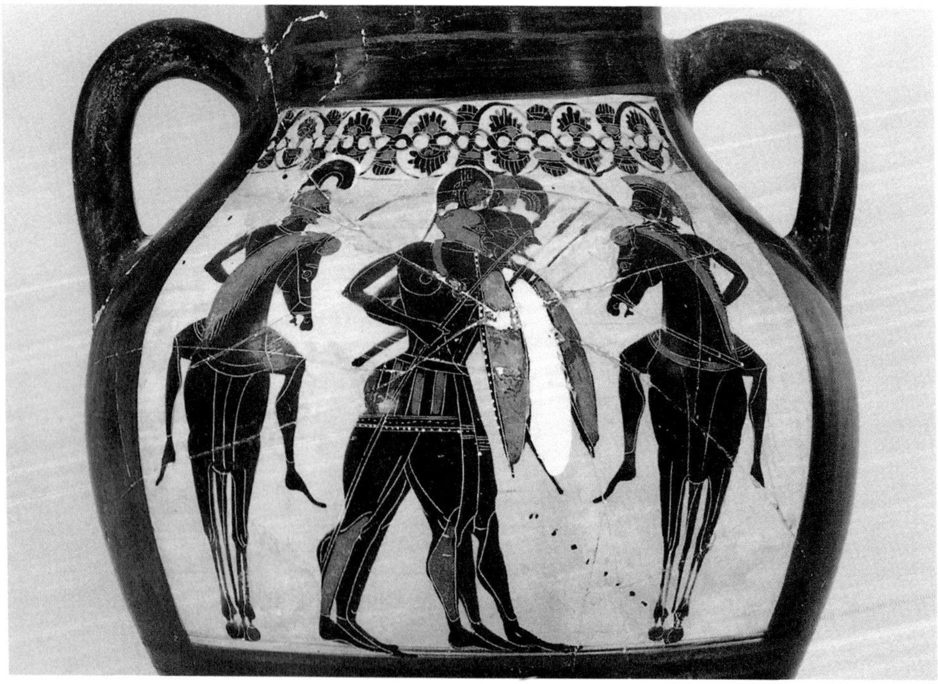

8.10. Black-figure amphora by Group E, ca. 560–540 B.C. Side B. Würzburg University, Martin von Wagner Museum 251. (Photograph © Martin von Wagner Museum der Universität Würzburg. Photo: K. Oehrlein.)

repetition of a youth adopting a consistent crouching position.[17] On B, a nude youth pulls an arrow from his quiver while extending his bow in his left hand [Figure 8.12]. On A the youth wears a helmet and carries a round shield; he picks up a spear [Figure 8.11]. (Note that his shield device is a satyr, an index of *symposion* and especially *komos*.) In combination we see two different types of fighting, by a hoplite and by an archer. Interconnectedness is also conveyed by means of inscriptions: the two most similar activities, public and military, on the exterior are linked by the presence of the painter's name on A and the verb on B. In the interior we see a nude youth crouched almost exactly like his colleagues on the exterior; however, his activity is very different. He holds an oinochoe between his legs so that he can urinate into it [Figure 8.13]. The tondo image is a surprise and a humorous reference to *symposion*. The potter's inscription (an important facet of authorship but obviously distinct from the painter's) accompanies the elite youth in the tondo. The visual perspective in the three images is identical and serves to link two facets of elite youth experience, *symposion* and military activity.

The Naples cup (to which Epiktetos contributed the tondo) presents a very careful visual account of *symposia* from two points of view.[18] The exterior scenes appear to be the reverse of one another, except for small details that create slight differences. On side A we see a reclining figure at right in a combination persective with chest displayed frontally, holding out a kylix in his right hand and a skyphos at his chest in his left. A small youth approaches from the left, and we see the right profile of his lower body. The B side of the cup depicts a reclining figure at left, and it shows his back to us; his outstretched right arm holds a skyphos or lekanis. A small youth approaches from the right; we see the left profile of his legs. The divided inscription is already discussed in Chapter 5. The two parts appear, in tandem, to create a statement: to the greeting ΠΡΟΣΑΓ ΟΡΕΥΟ on A is attached the subject of the verb, ΠΑΙΔΙΚΟΣ, on B.[19] The inscriptions are two correlating parts of a statement, "I, Paidikos, greet you!" as the images represent correlating, nearly identical scenes from the different perspectives of two different viewers.[20]

The combination of hoplite and Scythian on Psiax' alabastron in Odessa probably references a Trojan story, but here there is no event or action to develop the narrative.[21] Both hoplite and Scythian figures walk right, and this reiteration connects them.[22] The archer looks back toward the hoplite, and the hoplite gestures toward the archer, further uniting the two figures. The divided inscriptions identifying the artists create a unifying link and appear one on each side: the potter's signature is incised horizontally below the feet of the hoplite, and the painter's signature appears vertically to the right of the archer. The signatures of painter and potter in combination highlight these two crucial facets of the creation of the vessel, potting and painting, whereas their separation breaks down the creative process into maker and painter. Likewise, the images of hoplite and Scythian in combination create a single text about a second pair who often work

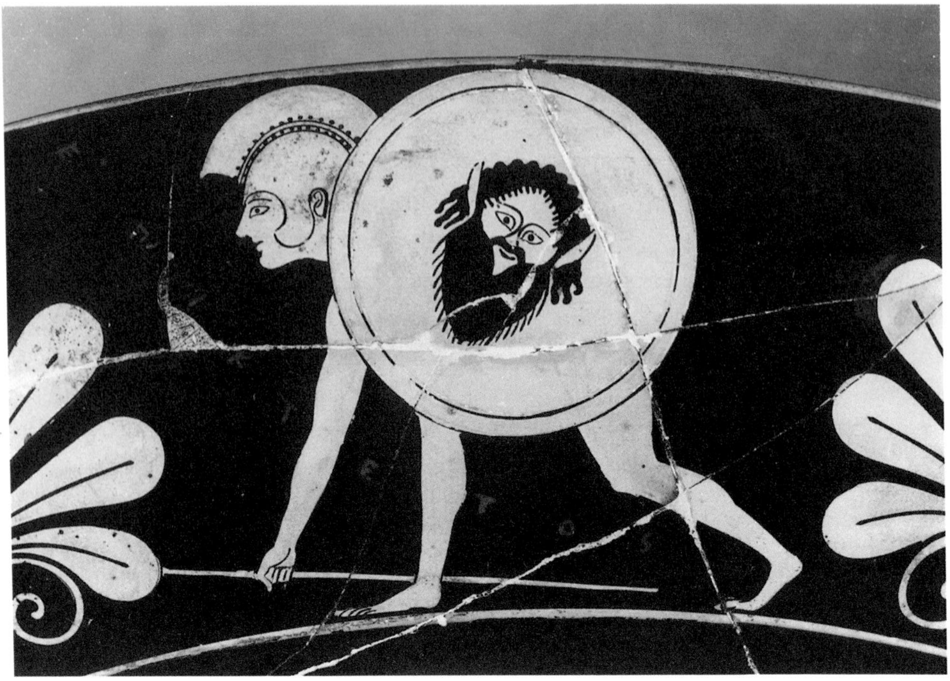

8.11. Red-figure eye-cup by Epiktetos, ca. 520–490 B.C. Side A. Paris, Musée du Louvre G 5. (Photograph © Musée du Louvre, Dist. RMN / © Les frères Chuzeville.)

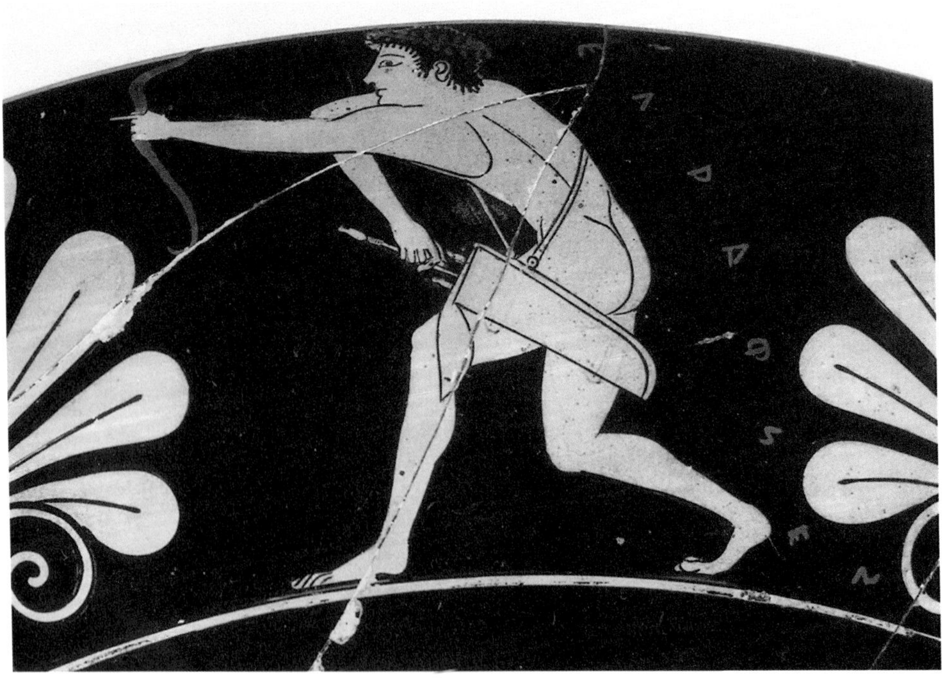

8.12. Red-figure eye-cup by Epiktetos, ca. 520–490 B.C. Side B. Paris, Musée du Louvre G 5. (Photograph © Musée du Louvre, Dist. RMN / © Les frères Chuzeville.)

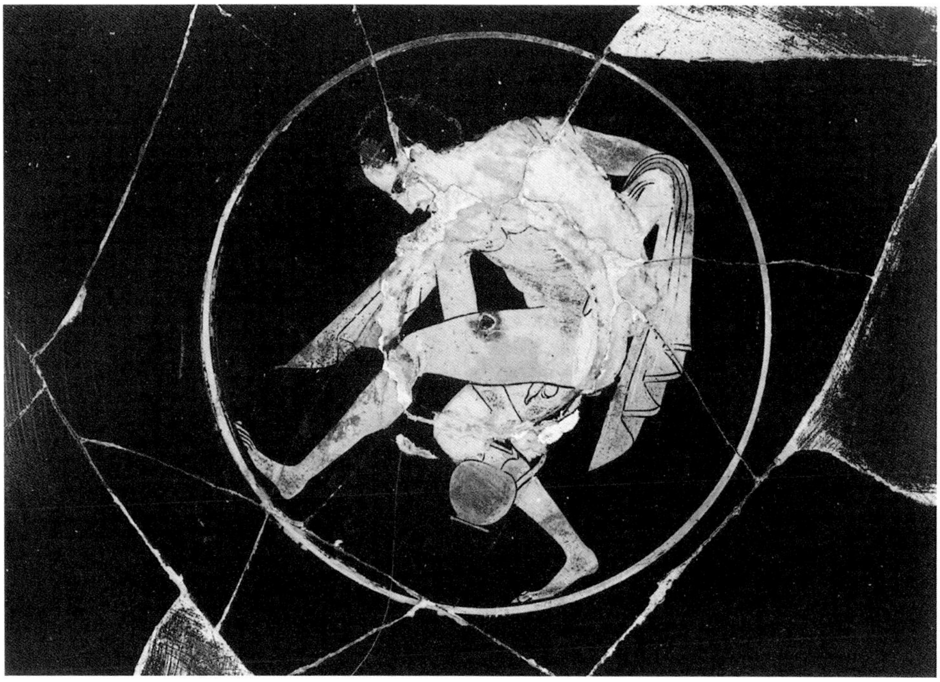

8.13. Red-figure eye-cup by Epiktetos, ca. 520–490 B.C. Interior. Paris, Musée du Louvre G 5. (Photograph © Musée du Louvre, Dist. RMN / © Les frères Chuzeville.)

together. The repetitions, together with the physical separations, pull apart for analysis two sets of collaborators – the painter/potter and the hoplite/Scythian.

Euphronios' Louvre neck-amphora includes a verbal record of a point of view in its inscription. The vase is very fragmentary, and much about it remains a puzzle.[23] Herakles on side A moves to attack an Amazon who is on side B [Figures 8.14, 8.15]. In this case, there are just a few visual repetitions between the two figures: each moves, striding towards the other with arms stretched out in front. We see the right side of Herakles and the left side of the Amazon. The artist places the name of each character in the same position on each side of the vase, vertically and behind the figure: the fragmentary.... ΚΛΕΕΣ on A, the last syllable of Herakles' name, and ΒΑΡΚΙΔΑ ("Barkida"), the Amazon on B. The artist reiterates elements to be connected – the figures who move toward one another – by means of the common placement of the inscriptions. There is a striking difference, though, between the two figures: Herakles appears to be a statue, striding on a base, inscribed with an enigmatic statement, ΔΟΚΕΙ⁝ ΣΜΙΚ⟨Ρ⟩ΟΙ⁝ ΙΝΑΙ (Immerwahr: ΕΝΑΙ): "It seems to be (thus) to Smikros." The inscription directly engages the viewer in contemplating perception – how something "seems" to another, so it makes the reader aware of Smikros' point of view. However, the inscription is confounding in two ways. We do not know if the subject is perceptual or ideological point of view, and the reader has no idea *what* "seems to be (thus)

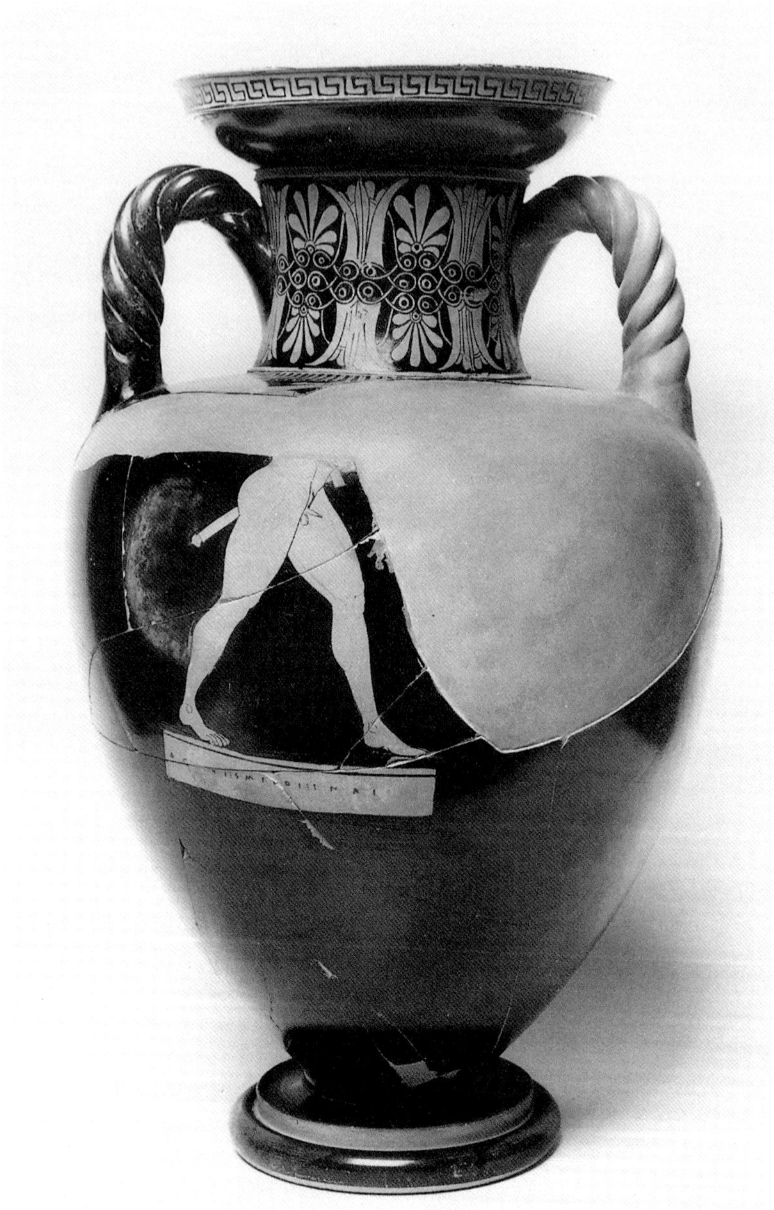

8.14. Red-figure amphora by Euphronios, ca. 520–505 B.C. Side A. Paris, Musée du Louvre G 107. (Photograph © Musée du Louvre, Dist. RMN / © C. Gaspari.)

to Smikros." The compositions and the labels on each side are otherwise so similar that the inscription on the statue base is not only striking but surely significant. The depicted inscription is an image of an inscription in a public space, probably a formal inscription, as the interpuncts would suggest, rather than *graffiti*, where the grammar

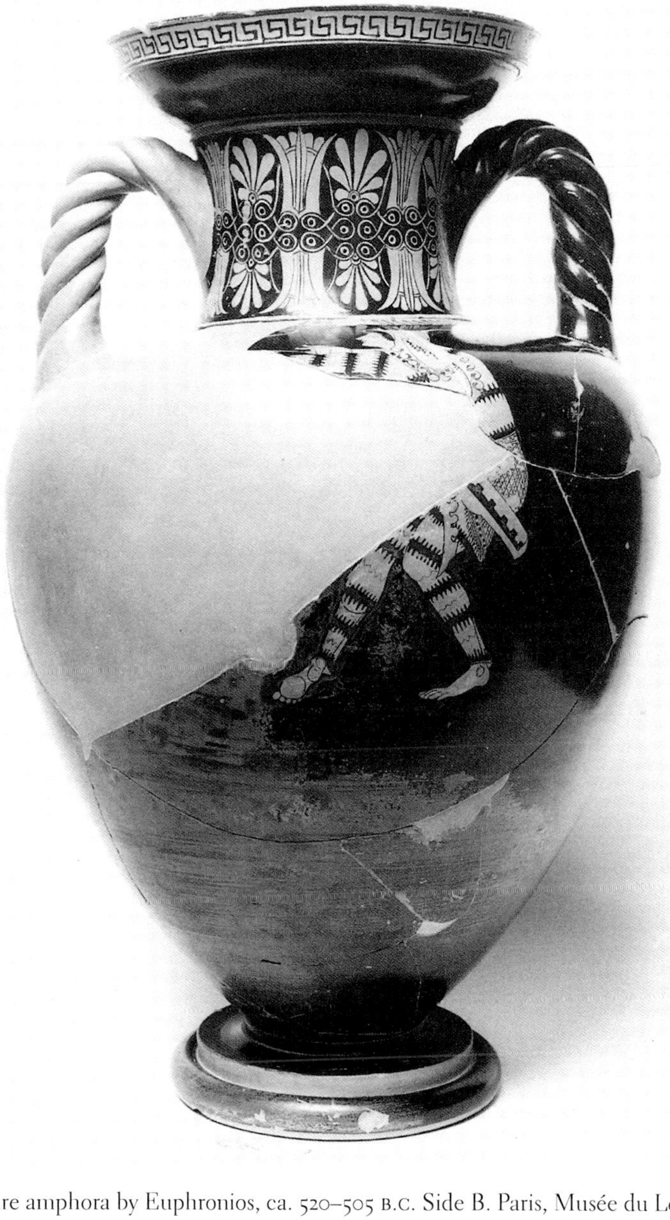

8.15. Red-figure amphora by Euphronios, ca. 520–505 B.C. Side B. Paris, Musée du Louvre G 107. (Photograph © Musée du Louvre, Dist. RMN / © C. Gaspari.)

and syntax have more parallels.[24] The formality in the style of writing is appropriate for a statue base even if the content is not.[25]

The actual language of the inscription brings point of view to the forefront: "it seems to Smikros." The viewer must think about the character of Herakles for himself, sorting out the "real" adversary of the Amazon, known to us in myth, from the plastic, sculptural representation of the hero. Because of the addition of the inscription, Euphronios' exploration of the character "Herakles" is far more subtle than the sixth-century parallel discussed above, where representations of the goddess Athena and a statue of her are linked through repetition on a Siana cup. Those images force the viewer to look at the difference between the "real" goddess and her image clearly depicted in two separate fields of a vessel[26] [Figures 8.2, 8.3]. Euphronios, on the other hand, shows only one image of Herakles. Through text, however, he prompts the reader to an intellectual leap resulting in the same type of recognition: there is a "real" Herakles who fights Amazons and lions and there is a statue-Herakles.[27]

Another neck-amphora by Euphronios in the Louvre displays images clearly connected by means of visual and verbal repetitions. The setting is *symposion* and the atmosphere created is erotic[28] [Figures 8.16–8.17]. Each side of the neck depicts an identical youth covered to the waist by a cloak and wearing a wreath in his hair, reclining against striped pillows. The artist displays facets of sympotic activity: the figure on A plays *kottabos*, with his knees spread apart and his torso frontal, while the figure on B plays the lyre, with knees raised and together and his torso in profile. An inscription on B conveys the text of a Sapphic song about desire sung by the reclining figure.[29]

Other inscriptions – one on each side – name Leagros as *kalos*, "handsome." Each of the *kalos* inscriptions is located above the reclining figure. The one on A is divided by the figure's head, with "Leagros" to the left and "*kalos*" to the right of it. On B the inscription is retrograde, with "*pais kalos*" or "the youth is handsome" beneath the name "Leagros." The location of "Leagros" at the top of each scene, with one of them inverted, establishes the two inscriptions as opposite iterations of one comment.[30] This verbal repetition, an inversion, underscores the explication of dual perspectives and *sympotic* activity, games and music, already apparent in the figures.

Two other examples display a figure-type from front and back in the context of linking two different elite experiences. Euphronios' Berlin krater preserves repeated images and repeated inscriptions,[31] both to create a continuous topic and to reveal various facets of grooming and preparation for *palaestra*-activity.[32] Youths in the *palaestra* appear on each side of the vase. Each figure provides us with a different (or slightly different) point of view from that of the nude youth who occupies the same slot on the opposite side of the vase. Frontal and back, standing and crouching, profile and three-quarters, profile and frontal are all opposite one another on the vessel. The array is an encyclopedic collection of different visual perspectives. The inscriptions naming the youths include two declaring "Leagros is handsome"; on A, the sentence, ΛΕΑΓΡΟΣ [Κ]ΑΛΟ̄Σ matches the same inscription on B. Based on the location of the inscription, we might conclude that Leagros may be present on A, in the person of the youth pouring oil out of a vessel; he is not depicted on B.

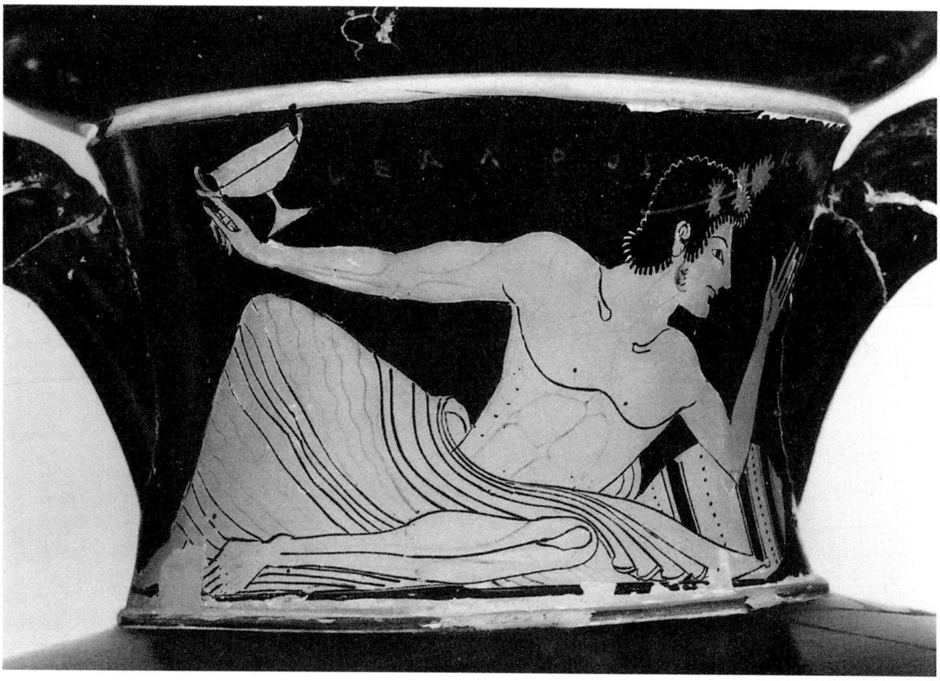

8.16. Red-figure neck-amphora by Euphronios, ca. 520–505 B.C. Side A, neck. Paris, Musée du Louvre G 30. (Photograph © Musée du Louvre, Dist. RMN / © Les frères Chuzeville.)

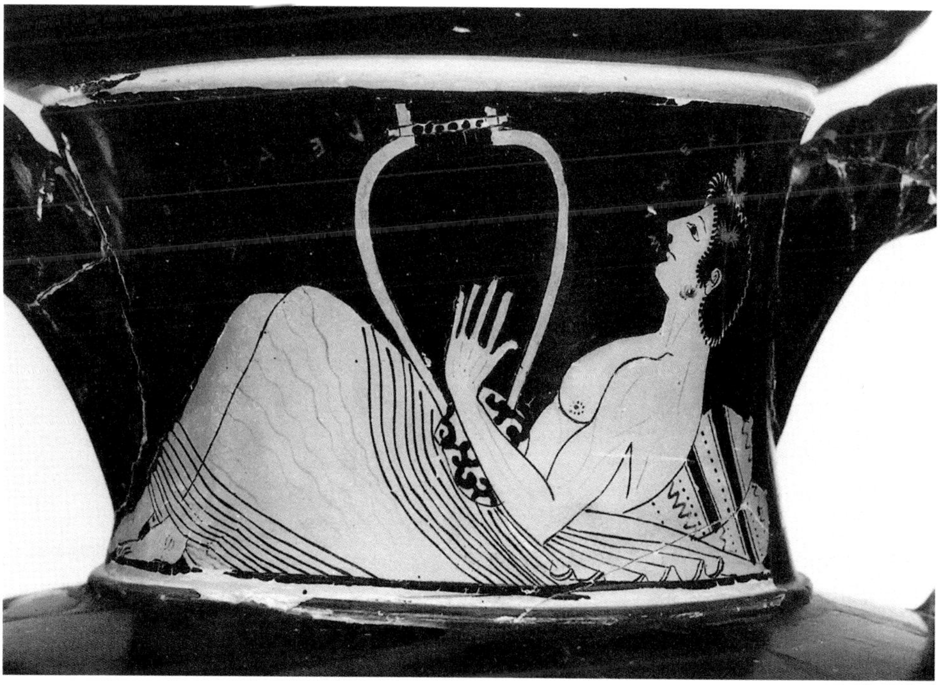

8.17. Red-figure neck-amphora by Euphronios, ca. 520–505 B.C. Side B, neck. Paris, Musée du Louvre G 30. (Photograph © Musée du Louvre, Dist. RMN / © Les frères Chuzeville.)

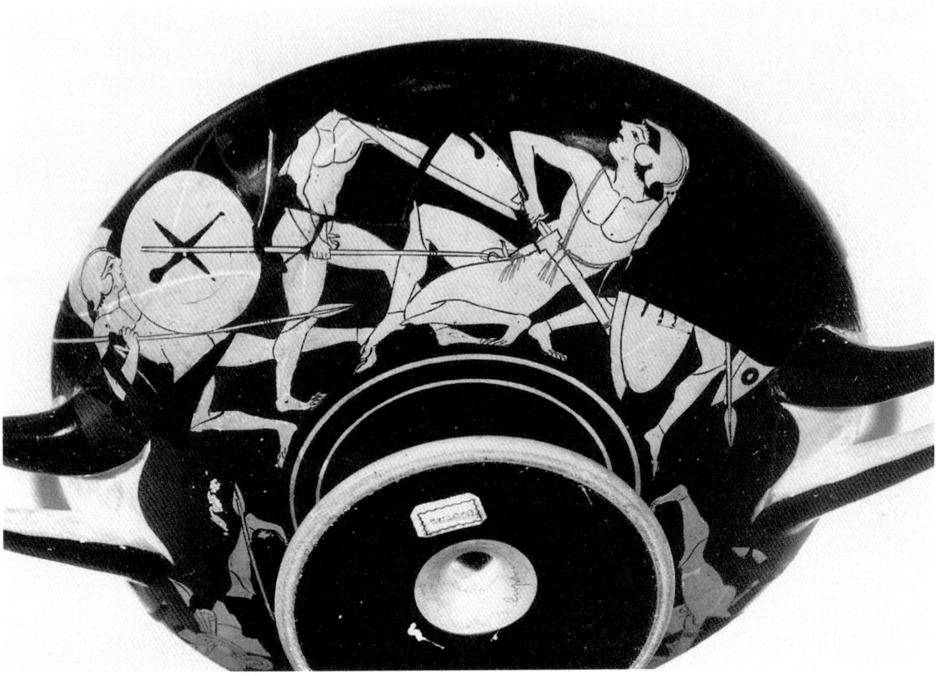

8.18. Red-figure cup by Onesimos, ca. 510–490 B.C. Side A. Boston, Museum of Fine Arts 01.8021. (*Battle Scene*. Findspot: Italy, Umbria, near Orvieto. Place of Manufacture: Greece, Attica, Athens. Height: 8.8 cm (3 7/16 in.); diameter: 23 cm (9 1/16 in.) Henry Lillie Pierce Fund. Photograph © 2000. Museum of Fine Arts, Boston.)

A similar treatment, this time of military activity, is provided by Onesimos. On the cup in Boston, a fight is the subject of both sides A and B; the poses of the figures on one side echo those of the other, but the figures are displayed from different perspectives.[33] There are additional distinguishing elements such as hair length and shield devices [Figures 8.18, 8.19]. Although the cup is fragmentary, the figures appear to be otherwise quite uniform: all are youths, wear greaves, hold spears, and have round shields. At the center of each composition is a falling combatant in a very similar pose. On one side we see a back view, a wound from a sword, and the interior of his round shield; his mate on the other side displays a front view, the exterior of his round shield, and draws his sword from his scabbard. The figures who frame the scenes adopt similar poses but move in opposite directions. As discussed in Chapter 5, the inscriptions invite the viewer to take in both sides as well: on the side where we see the rear view of the central figure, *h*O ΠΑΙΣ, "the youth," is written above the figure; above his matching figure on the reverse is written ΚΑΛΟΣ "is [understood] handsome." Onesimos' kylix, therefore, presents a catalog of military combat embedded in an analysis of perceptual point of view.

Smikros' Berlin amphora combines two views of satyrs in an apparent analysis of music and dance.[34] An ithyphallic satyr appears on each side [Figures 8.20, 8.21].

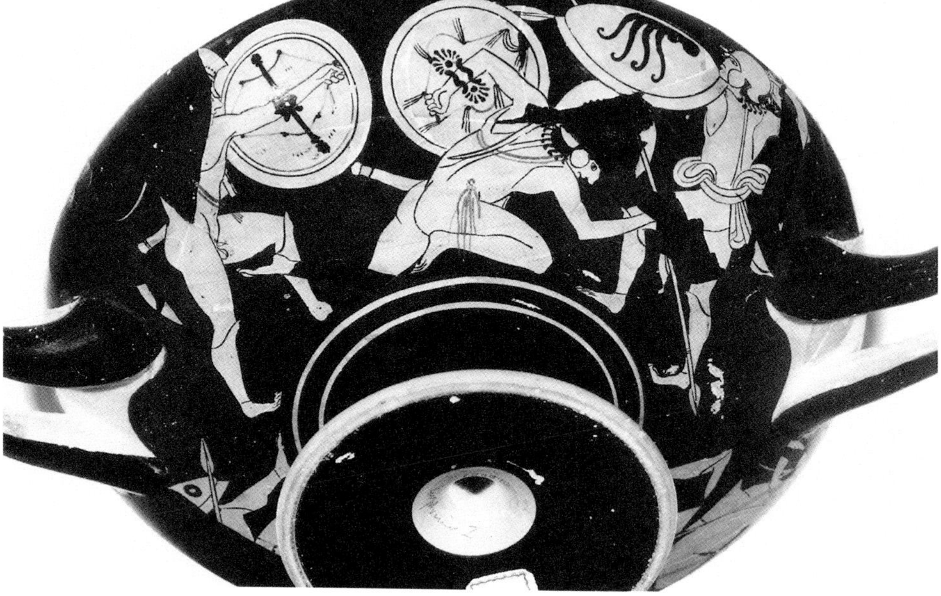

8.19. Red-figure cup by Onesimos, ca. 510–490 B.C. Side B. Boston, Museum of Fine Arts 01.8021. (*Battle Scene*. Findspot: Italy, Umbria, near Orvieto. Place of Manufacture: Greece, Attica, Athens. Height: 8.8 cm (3 7/16 in.); diameter: 23 cm (9 1/16 in.) Henry Lillie Pierce Fund. Photograph © 2000. Museum of Fine Arts, Boston.)

One pipes while the other dances, yet much is identical: each head is tipped back, and each figure is in profile from the waist on down. There are different perspectives revealed, as well as different props and different body types. On side A, the dancing figure carries spear and *pelta*. His name is written in a half-circle above his head: ΣΤΥΣΙ[.....]Σ, "Sty..... sis." The name is almost certainly obscene, as its root is στύω/στύομαι, "the standard improper word for getting an erection."[35] However the name is fully restored, it in some way describes the satyr, underscoring the fact that he has an erection. In a diagonal from the tip of his penis to his toes is the artist's signature: ΣΜΙΚΡΟΣΕΓΡΑΦΣΕΝ, "Smikros painted it," placed to look as if the satyr discharges the sentence from his erect penis. The satyr's name on B is also descriptive. He identified as ΤΕΡΠΑΥΛΟΣ, "Terpaulos," or "Takes-Pleasure-in-Flute," by means of an inscription at exactly the same place as the satyr's name on A, in an arc above his head. Physically, the two satyrs share tipped-back head, hair, beard, tail, and erect penis, but they are distinguishable because the *aulos*-player stands completely in profile, rather than dancing with a twist at the waist, and his belly is round and protruding, not well-muscled and flat, as is the dancing satyr's. The musician has a bit more hair as well, a tuft of bangs. The satyr on A turns his torso so that it is frontal. From the tip of the *aulos* on B and extending in a diagonal toward the figure's thigh comes an onomatopoeic

(?) inscription, NETENAPENEΓ(?)ENETO "Ne-te-na-re-ne-g(?)en-e-to" that appears to reproduce the sounds of the instrument.[36] Overall, the pairing of the two satyrs, one of whom accompanies the other's dance, is enhanced by the similar *positions* of the inscriptions that name them.[37] The combination of the two figures separates musician and dancer, allowing analysis of their commonalities and differences.

A kylix by Douris in Berlin depicting school scenes on each side links them by means of repeated figures, attributes, and inscriptions[38] [Figures 8.22, 8.23]. The different figures display many facets of elite school-boy experience, providing in sum a catalog of school activities. Striking at the center of each composition is a seated male figure draped in *himation* with chest exposed, with a standing boy facing him at right. There are more seated figures at the right and left of each scene. At left, the figures on A and B are very similarly posed, with one playing pipes and the other a *barbiton*. Their pupils differ: the student on B stands to watch his teacher play the pipes, whereas his counterpart on A is seated playing his *barbiton*. At right a seated adult is frontal on A, in three-quarters pose on B. There are many slight variations in position between analogous figures from side to side, as is fitting, in order to stress the different kinds of lessons in progress: *barbiton*, flute, writing with stylus, and reading. Across the top of each scene is a roster of school and sympotic implements, with only the *barbiton* repeated. In sum, the exterior images present an explication of "lessons" or "school." Across the top of each scene, further linking the two, is a carefully placed *h*IΠOΔAMAΣKAΛOΣ (A)/ *h*IΠOΔAMAΣ[KA]ΛOΣ (B) "Hip(p)odamos is handsome," appropriate owing to the presence of youth and adult men together, but not directly related to the school scene.[39] The artist's signature follows the curve of the tondo around an image of a bathing youth who shares hairstyle and headband with some of those on the exterior.

The most unusual feature of the cup, the scroll and its text held out frontally to the viewer by the master on side A, is set off by its contrast to the equivalent reading figure on B who writes on a tablet, shown in profile, with a stylus. The text, written in hexameter, reads, MOIΣAMOI / A⟨N⟩ΦIΣKAMANTPO /EYP⟨P⟩ΩNAPXOMAI/ AEI{N}ΔEN, translated by Immerwahr as two different ideas, beginning with "Muse, to me," and moving to "I begin to sing of wide-flowing Scamander."[40] The artist also maximizes the impact of this most unusual aspect of the cup, the way the written text is shown to the viewer. Douris' scripting of performance here is imaginative, close in spirit to, but at one remove from, Euphronios' vase on which he shows a lyre-playing symposiast singing Sappho[41] [Figures 8.17]. Douris depicts *school*, where skills are *learned*, but they will be *used* at the *symposion*; a reader who might repeat the lines in the vessel's use-context will be at *symposion* and not at school. As he reads, he undergoes a transition in point of view, from observer to performer. The artist also alludes to two temporal phases, one conveyed by the school-setting imagery and another, projected by both the *kalos* and poetic inscriptions, conveyed by the inscription as it plays out in

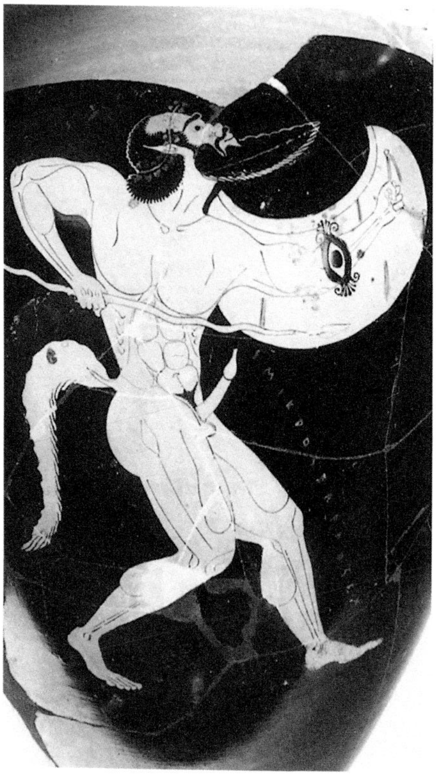

8.20. Red-figure amphora by Smikros, ca. 510–500 B.C. Side A. Berlin, Staatliche Museen 1966.19. (Photograph © Staatliche Museen zu Berlin, Antikensammlung [Inv.-Nr. 1966.19]. Photo: Johannes Laurentius.)

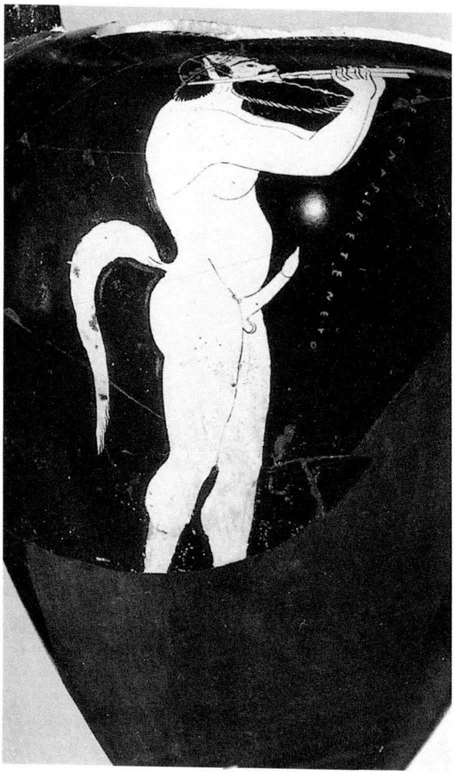

8.21. Red-figure amphora by Smikros, ca. 510–500 B.C. Side B. Berlin, Staatliche Museen 1966.19. (Photograph © Staatliche Museen zu Berlin, Antikensammlung [Inv.-Nr. 1966.19]. Photo: Johannes Laurentius.)

the use-context of the vessel. In addition to the many explications already described, the artist creates a union of locations where learning is exhibited, at school for the master and at *symposion* for company.[42]

CONCLUSIONS

Vases with more than one decorative field are ideal vehicles for exploring aspects of characters and social roles as well as for examining facets of activities such as school, battle, gymnasium or palaastra, and symposion; several examples, each comprising one aspect or facet, can be collected in a single text and these can be linked by repetition. The three-dimensionality of vases, providing two equivalent sides, a front and a back, invites an analysis of perceptual point of view as well. That some features remain the same in a character even when he is posed differently, regarded from differing

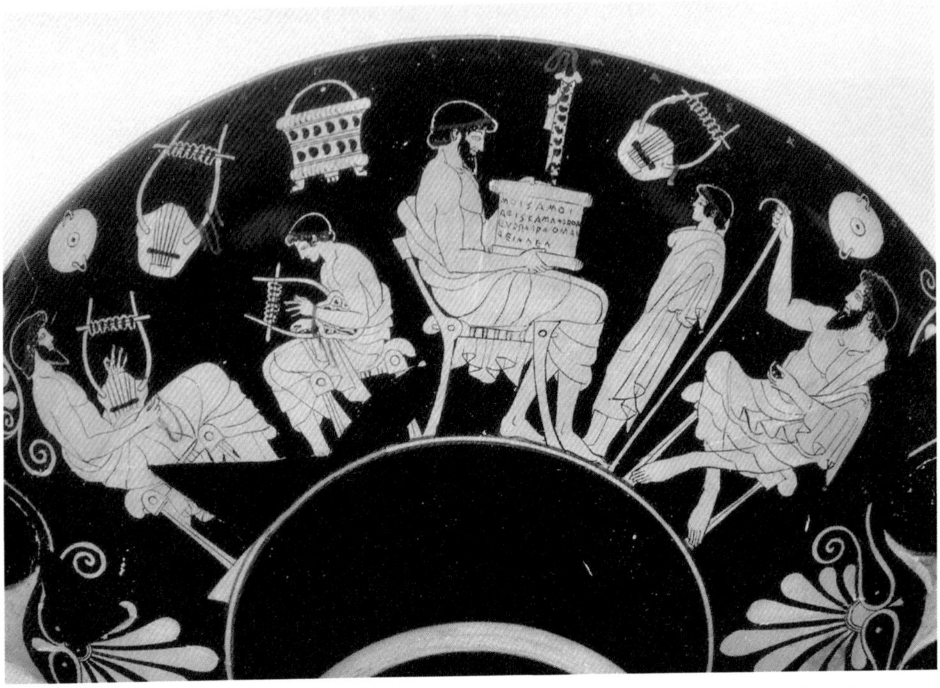

8.22. Red-figure cup by Douris, ca. 480–470 B.C. Side A. Berlin, Antikensammlung, Staatliche Museen zu Berlin 2285. (Photograph © Bildarchiv Preussischer Kulturbesitz / Art Resource, NY.)

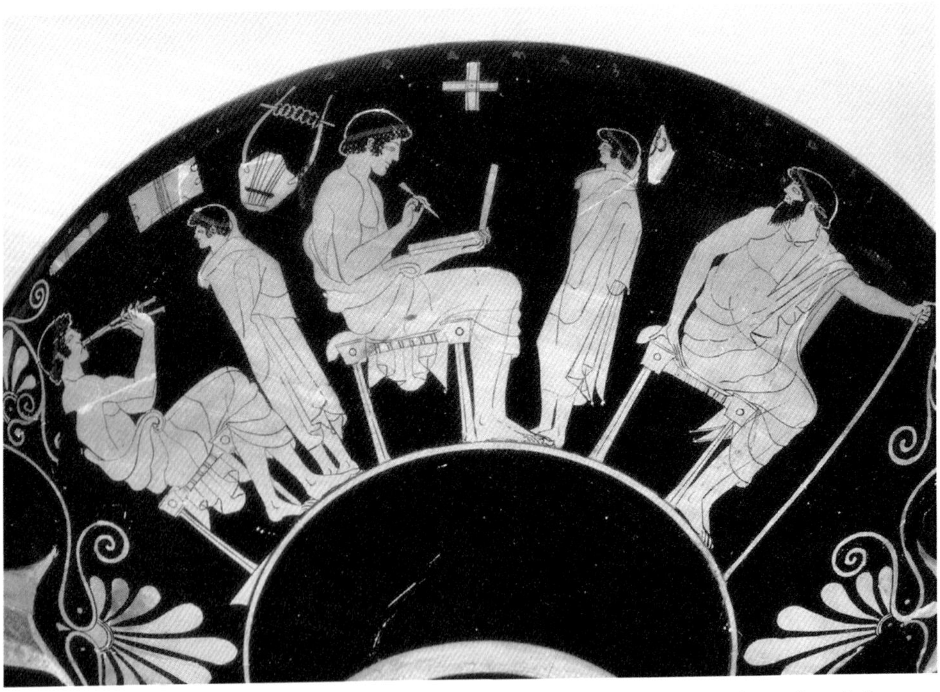

8.23. Red-figure cup by Douris ca. 480–470 B.C. Side B. Berlin, Antikensammlung, Staatliche Museen zu Berlin 2285. (Photograph © Bildarchiv Preussischer Kulturbesitz / Art Resource, NY.)

viewpoints, or engaged in distinct activities can be established effectively by means of repeated features.

Chapter 6 demonstrated how repetition is useful in depicting narrative, and substantial evidence exists to confirm that story-telling becomes a serious activity for many vase-painters, beginning in the middle of the first quarter of the sixth century.[43] The evidence discussed here suggests that artists' interest in depicting narrative is accompanied by separate exploration of some of its components. These building blocks include point of view, both perceptual and conceptual or ideological, as well as complex characters. The significant amount of evidence covered in this chapter, dating from the second quarter of the sixth century until its end, demonstrates that painters often explored these building blocks outside of a narrative context.

NINE

REPETITION AND PARODY

A nonsense inscription, ENEOINOIOIEN, on a cup by Exekias, discussed in Chapter 2 and again in Chapter 4, is paired syntactically with *epoiesen*, the verb in the signature of the potter meaning "so-and-so made it"[1] [Figures 2.1, 2.2]. The verb and the nonsense are located in the identical spot on opposite sides of the vase, and at the same time the nonsense parodies the sounds of both the verb in the signature and of a word not present, *oinos*, "wine" which will fill the cup. Several other vases preserving repetition, both verbal and visual, discussed throughout the previous chapters appeared to pair a straightforward representation or inscription with a parody of it.[2] From these verbal examples, we concluded that repetition of images likely created parodic results as well. The purpose of this chapter is to explore the theoretical justification for understanding parody as a product of repetition and to consider additional examples of its appearance on Athenian vases. We begin by reviewing briefly the role of repetition in parody from a theoretical perspective and then turn to look at a series of examples.

DEFINING PARODY

A recent modern treatment of parody defines it simply as "repetition with difference."[3] Goldhill points out that recognizing parody requires comparison of an original to a variation of it: "Reading parody . . . constitutes a particular example of the always complex process of recognizing similarity and difference."[4] Although these statements are very general, they affirm that parody relies on repetition, and therefore it is important for us to consider its relevance to a study of verbal and visual repetition on Athenian vases.

To refine the definition of parody, it helps to separate it from the related category of satire with which it is often confused. In Hutcheon's words, "just calling parody satire seems a little too simple as an instant way to give parody a social function."[5] Both satire and parody rely on irony, a statement where what is stated is not what is *really* intended; there is a second, implied meaning in ironic speech. Satire can rely on and incorporate parody, but satire is pejorative and has a mission to reform that is lacking in parody. Satire aims to fix something in society by pointing out that it is wrong. This discussion focuses on parodic results of repetition but not any that can be identified with confidence as satiric.

PARODY IN ATHENIAN COMIC PRODUCTIONS

Scholars have discussed parody thoroughly in relation to its presence in Athenian satyr-play and comedy, and to some extent it is possible to extrapolate from their observations in order to identify and assess the nature and purpose of parody as created by repetition on earlier Archaic Athenian vases. Satyr-performance based on myth seems to have begun at least as early as the late sixth century and, as convincingly argued by Hedreen, even the early sixth century.[6] Its roots are therefore contemporary with the evidence we are considering here. By the very beginning of the fifth century, satyr-play was part of tragic performance in Athens. These satyr-plays were written by the tragic poets in conjunction with their trilogy of tragedies, whose performance they immediately followed. There is evidence that the plots of satyr-play reworked the content of tragedies, and the poetic form of satyr-play intentionally parodied the meter and diction of tragic speech; it is clear that the genre relied explicitly on repetition to achieve its comic effect. Although the *overall* effect and intention of satyr-play is the topic of engaged, ongoing, scholarly debate, one certain result of the parodies it constructs is to ridicule and thereby diminish the status of the heroes who form its subject.[7] There are Archaic vases discussed here where heroes are parodied in a similar way.

Comedies are distinct from satyr-plays, written by comic poets as stand-alone performances and with characters and plots loosely if improbably focused on the present. Contemporary individuals and institutions are the subjects of parody. Components of what would become Athenian Old Comedy were present in the Archaic period, although very few of the extant fragments of comic plays, which surely have parodic elements, date much earlier than the mid-fifth century.[8] Just as is the case with satyr-plays, it is therefore appropriate to look at characteristics of parody in Old Comedy to gain insight into parody on sixth-century vases. Goldhill summarizes the ways that a Bahktinian understanding of the Athenian comic festival as carnival has led to one view of the social function of parody in Classical Athens as essentially rebellious, a critique of society.[9] Satyr-play, in its ridicule of important paradigmatic cultural heroes, especially Herakles, makes fun of social norms in its own way and likewise has its own unique but complementary effect.

Because both Old Comedy and satyr-play are regularly scheduled public events, they can be described as institutionalized "negotiated transgressions" as opposed to manifestations of spontaneous social upheaval or revolution.[10] From this point of view, the parodies in both comedy and satyr-play may serve then to eradicate social boundaries temporarily but predictably and thereby reaffirm them while creating *communitas* as defined by Turner.[11] Although *symposion*, the likely use-context for most parodic vases, is not regularly scheduled on the civic calendar on the same way as tragic and comic festivals, it can serve a similar purpose at the private, elite level: boundaries can be challenged, demolished, and then reconstituted, with the total experience creating a bond among the participants.

Recent scholarship analyzing the nature of parody in Old Comedy can illuminate our understanding of verbal parodies, particularly those created by inscriptions, that are products of repetition on vases. Looking beyond identification of the mockery and distortion created at the macro levels of comic plot, character, and their social effect, these new directions take into account the interplay between comedy and its poetic sibling tragedy as a central component of the parodic effect. Called "paratragedy" or "comic contrafact," the phenomenon describes a process where a comic situation relies in a systematic way on another specific genre, tragedy.[12] The effect is comic because it references in a humorous way components of tragic idiom, including "language, character, situation, spectacle, theme. . . ."[13] Parody created through repetition on vases does not reference tragedy, but instead references a parallel text usually elsewhere on the vase. Such parodies thereby employ the nuanced technique of comic contrafact likewise relying on a subtle reworking at the level of language. For example, on Exekias' cup in Athens [Figures 2.1, 2.2], the signature and its nonsense parody exist in a comically contrafactual relationship. Comic cause-and-effect are complete in the moment of the reading of the inscriptions. They are carefully choreographed by the author and do not require calling to mind an absent target other than the word for wine.

IDENTIFYING PARODY AND ITS PURPOSE

Imagistic parody, like verbal parody that does not rely on repetition of a model close at hand, can be hard to recognize and to interpret. Goldhill cites an anecdote that is relevant as a beginning to our discussion. Aelian (*Varia Historia* ii.13), writing in the second century A.D., describes the performance of Aristophanes' *Clouds* where a group of foreigners in the audience apparently asked "who is this Socrates?" and in response, Socrates stood up. As Goldhill points out, what is striking in this example is that the object of the parody and the parodic representation itself are side by side.[14] Ordinarily, comprehending parody as the author intends it to be understood requires the audience to have prior knowledge of a model that is not present but is known to the audience. This feature of parody is precisely what makes it an in-house, clubby activity.

On some vases there is a very similar situation to "Socrates parodied on stage/Socrates in audience"; the model and its parody are present together on the same vessel, and it is these vases on which we concentrate here. Assembling a corpus of examples is not easy, for to be certain that a repetition yields parody is difficult, and once parody is identified, it remains very difficult to know how and why an iteration ridicules. To get at the how and why, we need to try to recover the relationships among author, patron, performance venue, and audience.[15] For staged comedy, the situation is fairly straightforward. We can easily accept that Aristophanes created parodies of Socrates or Euripides and mocked civic and political activity. We know enough about the social and intellectual status of the tragic and comic poets and of the public festivals where their work was performed to allow us to see the entire phenomenon as an authorized transgression of accepted norms. The transgression takes place in a public space at a public festival creating a public experience. We have no parallel information on the creation and consumption of parody on vases, although we know the audience and venue were undoubtedly smaller, more private, and more spontaneous than those for publicly performed parody.[16] The authors of parody were craftsmen and not members of an educated elite. The parodies on vases must have been appealing to patrons and must have supported the social goals for their users and use-context. We have made the case in Chapter 4 that the craftsman himself is not to be perceived personally as the ridiculing agent. Rather, he is the scribe who orchestrates new versions of conventional content, one who has mastered the idiom of his constructed author-artist to suit the goals of the patron and the social situations where this idiom obtains. A survey of examples where repetition appears to yield parody will help to reveal more about the nature of the parodic aspects of this idiom as well as its social purpose.

PARODY ON ATHENIAN VASES

In Chapter 4, the evidence for reading vase-inscriptions aloud was considered in detail. The starting point here is the conclusion reached there: it is reasonable to assume that if anyone ever actually read vase-inscriptions, they were likely to have read them aloud on some occasions. The full argument for seeing the "ideal" or "intended" use context of Athenian figural pottery as the Athenian *symposion* is set out in the final chapter, and *symposion* will serve as the setting for the discussion of the parodic effect of repetition here.

When vase-inscriptions are read aloud, the vase becomes the script for a loosely performed sympotic skit for a private audience in a private setting.[17] A decorous elite symposiast reads a comprehensible, literate inscription; his colleague who reads the contrasting parody unwittingly takes on the role of the immoderate buffoon. By performing the lines, guests act out the model and its exaggerated parody. One individual is therefore cast in the role of an ideal symposiast, whereas the other is cast in the opposite role and is mocked. Although parody does not require a visible original, a Socrates or sober declaration present for comparison, when the model is present, the result is more certain and has the potential to reverberate identically multiple times. Overt visual and verbal repetition help to ensure the parodic result, and the result is repeatable: A single vase can prompt skits on many different occasions with different players.

Early Verbal Parodies

Little Master cups often feature parodic inscriptions, as their lengthy treatment in Chapter 5 demonstrates.[18] The cup by Epitimos, a member of the Lydan circle and discussed in Chapter 5 [Figures 5.5, 5.6],displays an artist's signature, ΕΠΙΤΙ ΜΟΣΕΠΟΙΕΣΕ[Ν] "Epitimos made (it)," opposite a statement, an invitation to drink, ΧΑΙΡΕΚΑΙΠΙΕΙΣ[Υ], "Welcome and drink!"[19] The opposed sentence is a *non sequitur* whose last three syllables repeat but distort the sounds of the verb in the signature on A. The verbal play is neither pun nor riddle, but akin to both, as it relies on clever and unexpected conjunctions of similar sounds, as in a pun, but requires a working out of the "why" of the conjunction, as in a riddle. Other examples preserve related plays on the word *epoiesen* that are not embedded in repetition, but they still suggest that parodies of the words used to attribute the creation of the vase to the potter exist well after the onset of red figure around 530. A cup in Malibu by Epiktetos, dating to about 510 B.C., depicts a bald man, wreathed, reclining and singing.[20] What comes out of his mouth is probably nonsense, read either as ΕΝΟΙΕΟΣΕΣ, "en-oi-e-o-ses," or ΕΥΟΙΕΟΣΕΝ, "eu-oi-e-o-sen."[21] This is a parody of the word *epoiesen*, which often appears in the tondo but is absent here. The sound of the nonsense evokes, though much less directly, the word *oinos*, "wine," as well.[22]

Epiktetos seems to play around with the affinity between *epoiesen* and *oinos* in another example.[23] In the tondo of a cup in Tarquinia, a satyr holds a huge wineskin in a position that suggests a phallos. Between his feet is a skyphos, possibly the vessel that he intends to fill. Around the border of the tondo, just where we would expect a potter's signature, ΕΠΟΙΕΣΕΝΟΧ,"***ep-oi-es***-en-och" is inscribed: the verb "made (it)" plus a nonsense syllable. On the wineskin itself we have not a label of contents, which would be ΟΙΝΟΣ, "wine," but ΕΠΟΙΕΣ, "***ep-oi-es***," a nonsense parodic combination, referencing both *epoiesen* and, again, possibly *oinos* as well. Although the connection with the word *oinos* is more remote because only one sound, the diphthong *oi*, is repeated, the fact that the nonsense labels a wineskin calls the word to mind. The artist plays with the conventional signature of his potter-colleagues, injecting a parody of the verb ordinarily used to name the potter in an image context where the "meaning" of the nonsense cannot be mistaken.

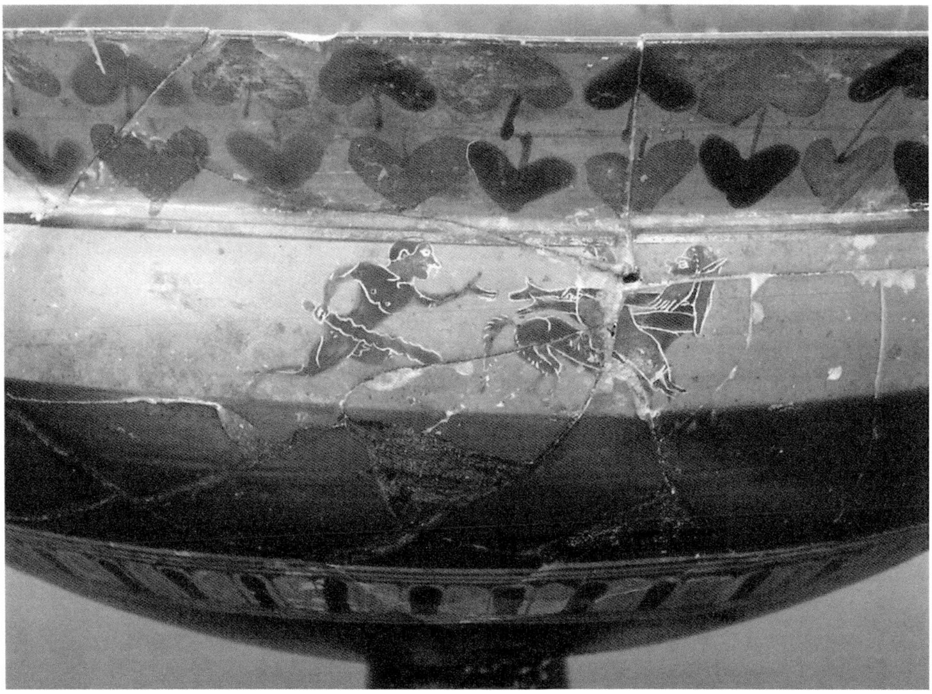

9.1. Black-figure cup by the Painter of the Burgon Sianas, ca. 565–555 B.C. Side A. Birmingham University cat. no. X 698. (Photograph © The Institute of Archaeology and Antiquity, University of Birmingham, UK.)

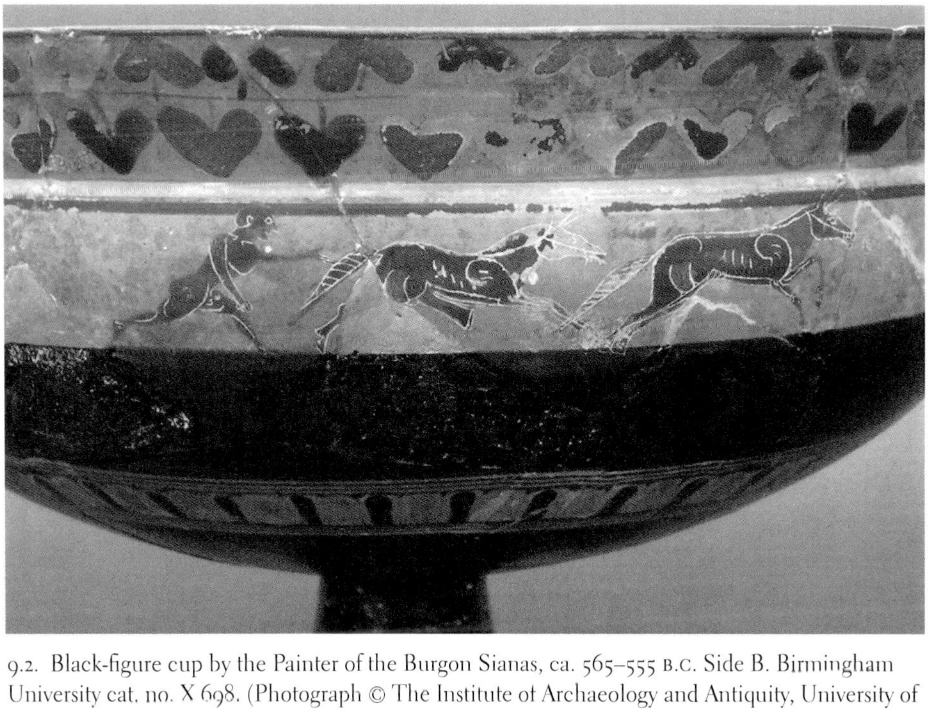

9.2. Black-figure cup by the Painter of the Burgon Sianas, ca. 565–555 B.C. Side B. Birmingham University cat. no. X 698. (Photograph © The Institute of Archaeology and Antiquity, University of Birmingham, UK.)

Early Parodies of Heroes

These examples of verbal parodies set the stage for identification of parody achieved visually. In Chapter 6, the work of the Painter of the Burgon Sianas provided an example of a sequence of ritual events, focused on two elements related to Demeter cult[24] [Figures 6.22, 6.23]. On the same painter's cup in Birmingham, a nude youth holding a knobby club pursues a centaur who runs off with a woman[25] [Figure 9.1]. Brijder titles this "Herakles pursuing Nessos with Deianeira." The "Herakles" figure is beardless. His pose, nudity, beardlessness, and general appearance are strikingly similar to those of the nude youth on the reverse who chases another amorous male trying to overcome a reluctant female, in this case an ithyphallic mule chasing a hinny [Figure 9.2]. There is a sufficient amount of repetition with difference to invite close scrutiny to figure out its purpose. The youth who chases the randy mule to protect the hinny is made analogous to Herakles, and the hinny is by association parallel to Deianeira. Herakles' challenger, the centaur, is like a randy mule who lusts after a she-mule. Ellipsis plays a role in making the two images analogous: beard and lion skin, ordinarily crucial parts of Herakles' iconography, are missing and their absence creates closer synonymy with the mule-chaser on B. The result of the repetition with difference is this: the heroic tale is parodied by an analogy drawn from the world of farm animals: the hero is brought down low. This cup is significant in part because of its date, around 550 B.C.; it is an early example showing how repetition of images alone can be used to achieve parody.

While we were considering repetition used to create paradigm in Chapter 7, the Lydan Judgment of Paris scenes on a lekanis lid in Palermo stood out because of the numerous repetitions connecting several separate scenes, each depicting a part of the story.[26] Among the many versions is one where the bridegroom, Paris, or the Paris-equivalent, runs off, gesticulating, and another where this bridegroom-to-be figure stands in a more composed and decorous manner. Raab has commented on the susceptibility of this myth topic to parodic visual representation, and in the Palermo lid we have the straight version and its parody coupled.[27] The effect of a figural scheme that is both paradigmatic and parodic is potent; its social purpose is to identify cultural standards and test them through mockery.

Later Visual/Verbal Parodies

Beginning with Epiktetos, there are many examples where repeated writing and images combine to create a parodic result. Epiktetos' London cup, discussed in Chapter 7 as an example of paradigm, shows youths being "like" Theseus.[28] Side A shows Theseus and the Minotaur, observed by two agitated female figures [Figure 9.3]. An inscription, the verb ΕΓΡΑΦΣΕΝ, "painted," corresponds to the artist's full signature on Side B,

ΕΠΙΚΤΕΤΟΣ ΕΓΡΑ [. .] EN, "Epiktetos painted (it)." The repeated verb is one of many features uniting the two scenes. On side B, a group of carousing youths play games, dancing while balancing a huge, apparently full, skyphos and cup at the borders of the scene, urinating into an oinochoe, and filling a cup from a huge krater at the center [Figure 9.4].The youths dancing at the borders of the scene appear ridiculous because their poses are identical to those of the distraught female equivalents on A.[29] The central figure on B, filling a skyphos from a krater, is equated with Theseus in his struggle with the Minotaur through his position in the repeated syntax. Although their hairstyles, smooth, hairless faces, and profiles make them very similar to the hero, the youths' activity is ridiculous in comparison to Theseus' intense struggle. The heroic struggle is actually diminished in turn by the comparison.

The youth-komast who urinates(?) into an oinochoe appears to sing, although with mouth closed: the artist's signature comes out of his mouth and curves around the central figure.[30] He presents a rowdy version of the tondo figure and text, where an adult male symposiast reclines, intently singing, as he plays the *barbiton*, and his song (?), "Hipparchos *kalos*" emanates throughout the field [Figure 9.5]. The unseemly posture of the urinating youth on B and the artist's self-promoting text of the "song" sung by him combine to create an absurdly ridiculous image. One parodies the other just as the youths on B are parodies of Theseus: the combined effect is that the signature of the artist could be the topic of a song analogous to the love song of the tondo singer. The location of the inscription on B plays with the fact that anything written on a vessel will, if read aloud, share auditory space with songs. Thus *kalos* observations by the participants and signatures of artists gain a kind of equivalance.

At the time of the Pioneers, c. 510, several examples suggest a parodic purpose behind repetitions, and these usually contain as well the potential for playing jokes on the reader of the mocking inscription. Euthymides' amphora in Warsaw, as discussed in Chapters 5 and 7, with a youth and a satyr paired, one on each side of the vase, includes the word for wine, *oinos*: ⱵΝΧΕ (=ΕΓΧΕΙ) *h*ΕΔ⟨ΥΝ⟩ ΟΙΝΟΝ, or "he pours sweet wine"[31] [Figures 5.10, 5.11]. A word modifying the name of the satyr Βρίκων on B, ΟΙΦΟΝ, not only is obscene (οἴφειν is "to mount"), but it is also a parody of the "ΟΙΝΟΝ" in the inscription on A, substituting a thick-tongued, vulgar approximation, of the type too much *oinos* will induce, for the correct articulation of the word for wine.[32] The satyr is a parody of the youth and his elite sympotic behavior.

In Chapter 8, discussion suggested that Smikros may create a parody of sympotic music on his Berlin amphora depicting two satyrs, one playing and one dancing[33] [Figures 8.20, 8.21]. On side A the artist's signature emerges from the satyr's penis as though he discharges it, ΣΜΙΚΡΟΣΕΓΡΑΦΣΕΝ, "Smikros painted (it)." The onomatopoeic (?) inscription, ΝΕΤΕΝΑΡΕΝΕΓ(?)ΕΝΕΤΟ, "ne-te-na-re-ne(g?)-en-e-to," emanating from the tip of the aulos on B sets up the reader to parody the flute's music, to

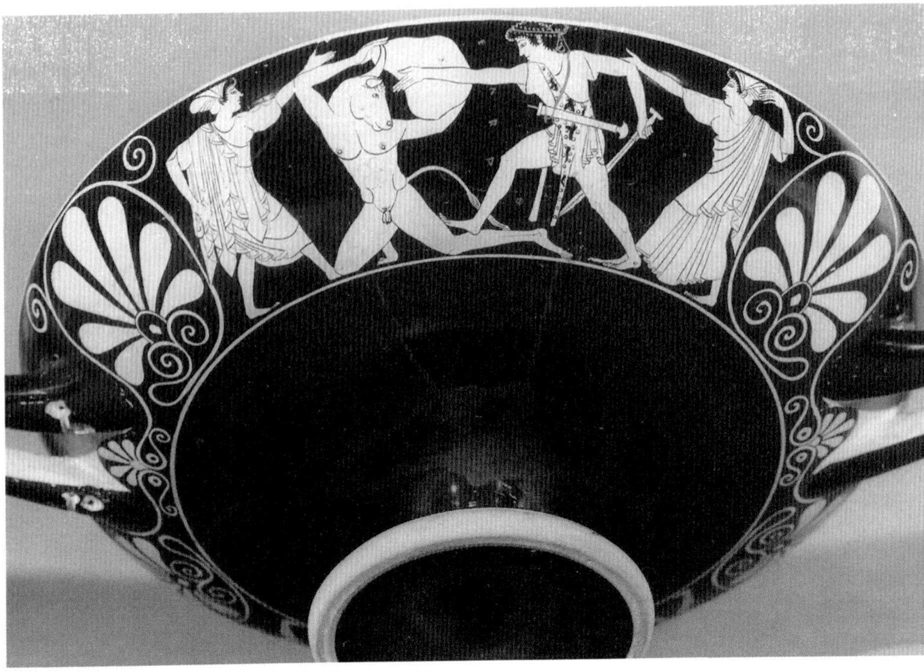

9.3. Red-figure cup by Epiktetos, ca. 520–490 B.C. Side A. London, British Museum E 37. (Photograph © Copyright The Trustees of The British Museum.)

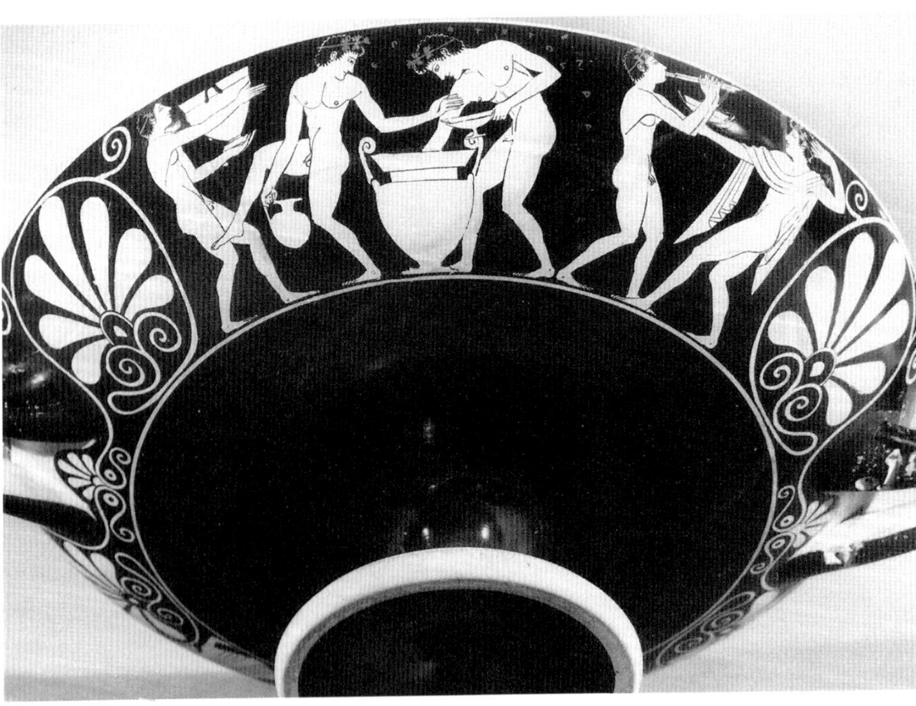

9.4. Red-figure cup by Epiktetos, ca. 520–490 B.C. Side B. London, British Museum E 37. (Photograph © Copyright The Trustees of The British Museum.)

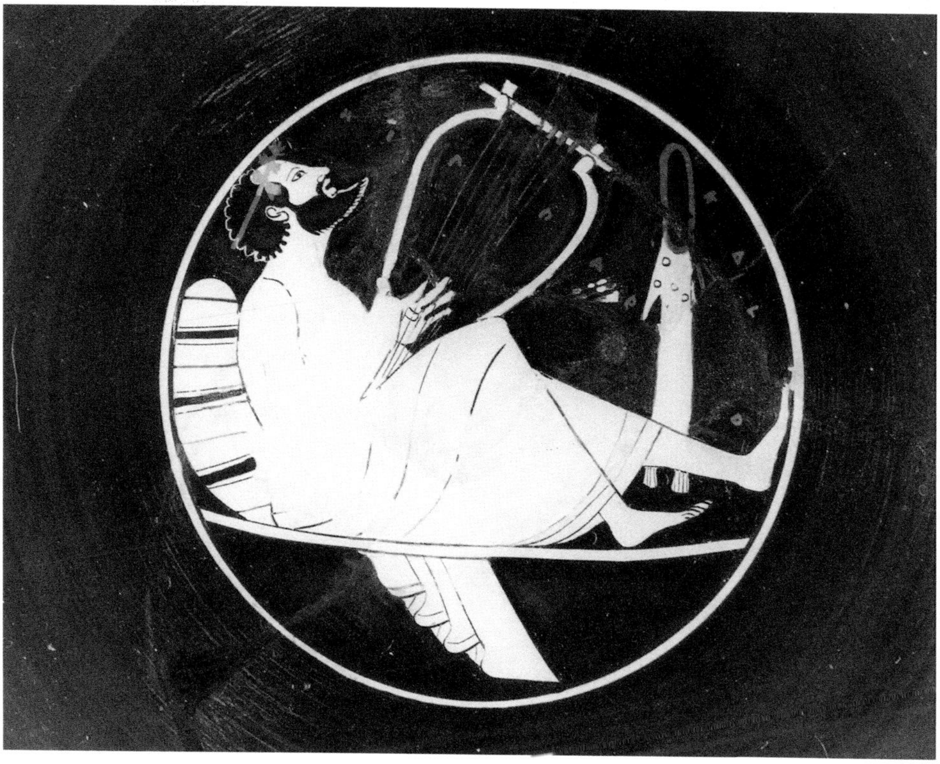

9.5. Red-figure cup by Epiktetos, ca. 520–490 B.C. Interior. London, British Museum E 37. (Photograph © Copyright The Trustees of The British Museum.)

speak when he ought to sing, or at the very least, to utter some nonsense syllables instead of poetry he has mastered or learned to improvise through his education; to speak music or nonsense makes him the object of a joke just as when he will appear to babble if reading a thick-tongued version of "OINOΣ."[34] But does the real author poke fun at himself, with the crude placement of his signature that suggests a stream of semen? Self-ridicule appears to be an expected component of the constructed author-artist's *persona*.

Nonsense is paired with sense in at least three other examples, creating diverse kinds of parody. An amphora in London by the Dikaios Painter repeats image-types and inscription-position to create parody solely on the level of text. The paired scenes are Apollo and Herakles fighting over the Delphic tripod on A and a departure scene on B[35] [Figures 9.6, 9.7]. On A, two goddesses watch on either side of the protagonists. The five inscriptions are placed very consistently: ATHENAIA, "Athena," is located vertically in front of Athena's face, and in a similar position is APTEMIΣ "Artemis" at left. AΠ[OΛ]ΛON, "Apollo" is also vertical, between Apollo's legs. The two remaining inscriptions, located between Herakles' legs, in front of Athena's legs and parallel to AΠ[OΛ]ΛON, are more enigmatic; in Immerwahr's words, "there has been much

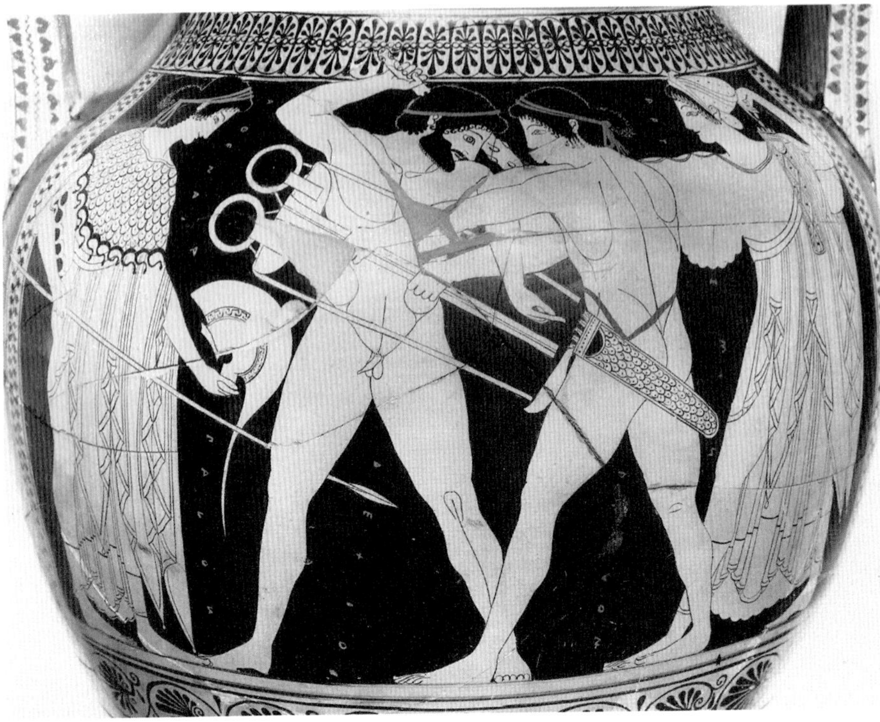

9.6. Red-figure amphora by the Dikaios Painter, ca. 510–500 B.C. Side A. London, British Museum E 255. (Photograph © Copyright The Trustees of The British Museum.)

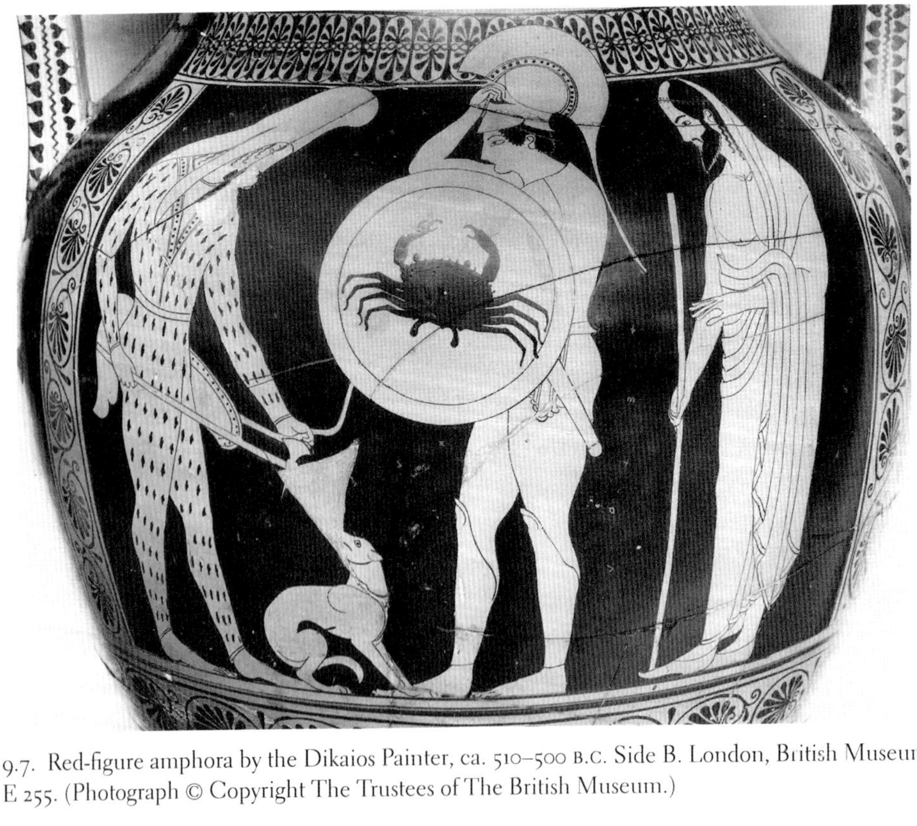

9.7. Red-figure amphora by the Dikaios Painter, ca. 510–500 B.C. Side B. London, British Museum E 255. (Photograph © Copyright The Trustees of The British Museum.)

discussion of ΔΕΧΙΟΙ, "Dekhioi," and ΠΑΛΟΣ, "Palos," usually combined in this order."[36] Immerwahr, following Beazley, concludes that the latter two inscriptions are nonsense, mock inscriptions creating syllables that approximate actual words.[37] If we imagine a reader pronouncing "Palos" aloud after reading "Athena," as would be expected if he continues vertically from top to bottom, the similarity to both *Pallas*, an epithet of the goddess, and *kalos*, "handsome," is clear.[38] Yet the word is neither – the reader will sound inaccurate and ridiculous, calling the goddess (almost) "handsome." We have then a particular kind of nonsense, similar to those examples based on *oinos*, a close parody of a "correct" word. Likewise, the inscription between Herakles' legs takes the position of a proper name, but it is apparently nonsense as well. The reader, by analogy to his reading of the names of Artemis, Apollo, and Athena, might expect to be pronouncing the hero's name, but finds another meaningless word instead.[39]

On B, the majority of the inscription-positions mirror those on A, and the composition itself is quite similar to that on A as well: there is one single central figure (instead of two as on A), the departing warrior, flanked by another figure on each side, a father-figure at right and a Scythian archer at left. Note especially the similarities between the figure of Athena on A and the Scythian archer on B. These reiterations of pose appear to feminize the archer and to create a link between the two sides that produces an effect only when combined with what is written.[40] The four inscriptions are placed vertically, similarly to their placement in front of Artemis and Athena on A. But here the inscriptions are all nonsense, and for two of them the harsh sounds that will result when they are read aloud evoke throat clearing or retching: ΓΕΧΓΟΥΧ, "gech-goukh," and ΧΕΧΓΙΟΧΕΧΟΓΕ, "Khekh-gee-okh-ehkh-o-ge." Does the constructed artist/author fool the reader into a parody of plain speech that suggests the foreign accents of the Scythian and, at the same time, casts doubt on the reader's status and his moderation?

This use of the nonsense with the image of the Scythian is similar to Euthymides' use of nonsense, ΧΥΧΟΣΠΙ, "Khu-khos-pi," in close proximity to a Scythian archer on Munich 2308[41] [Figures 9.8, 9.9]. As mentioned in Chapter 7, Euthymides appears to link the athlete Phayllos, identified by inscription, to a youth in the process of arming himself, creating a paradigmatic relationship between athlete and youth. A simple three-figure composition appears on each side of the vase and includes a youth at center: Phayllos' corollary on A, the youth Thorykion, dons a cuirass. The figures at the outsides of each scene adopt poses, including arm positions similar to those of their direct opposites on the reverse side of the vase. The purely visual repetitions serve to unite two activities of elite youths by linking them – athletics and the military – and thereby illustrating two facets of that social role. Vertical, similarly placed inscriptions identify all the figures on each side, and all figures are apparently mortals. At least four of the figures seem to have descriptive names: On B are ΠΕΝΤΑΘΛ[Ο]Σ, "Pentathlos," the athlete to the right of Phayllos,[42] and ΟΡΣΙΜΕΝΕΣ, "Orsimenes," the adult trainer at left. On A, ΘΟΡΥΚΙΟΝ, "Thorykion," is at center, and he is flanked by a Scythian

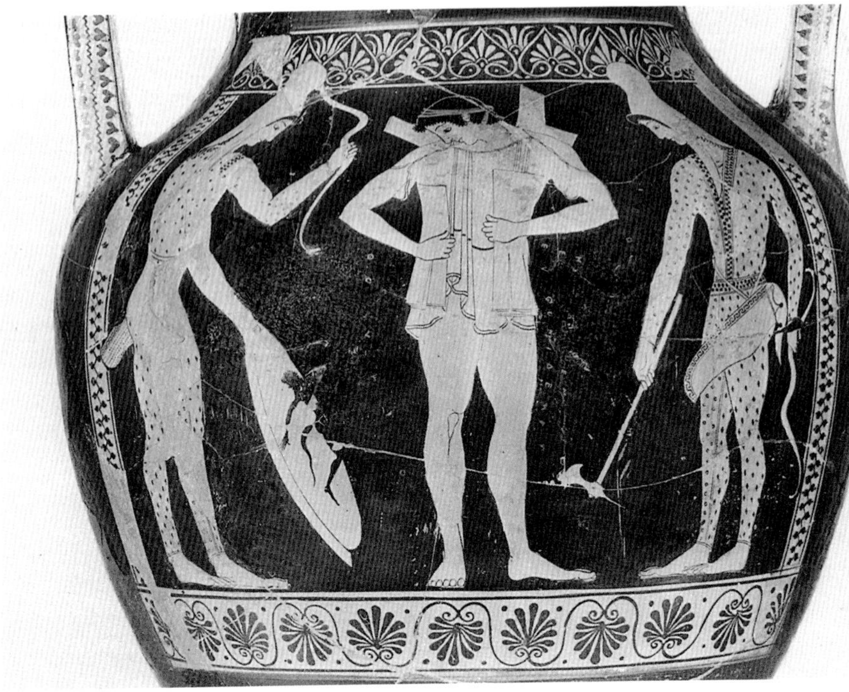

9.8. Red-figure amphora by Euthymides, ca. 510–500 B.C. Side A. Munich, Staatliche Antikensammlungen und Glyptothek 2308. (Photograph © Staatliche Antikensammlungen und Glyptothek München.)

archer on each side. The archer to his left is apparently named in a fragmentary inscription under his left elbow, but only one syllable is preserved: [1–2]MAE[...]Γ[.]. At right is a second archer ΕΥΘΥΒΟ[Λ]ΟΣ, "Euthybolos," "Straight-shooter." The Scythian at the far left has a second inscription, ΧΥΧΟΣΠΙ, "Khu-chos-pi," located in a vertical line in front of his left leg; it is placed in the identical location to the name "Pentathlos" on B. In the context of so much sense, the antonymous nonsense appears to be a trick played on the reader and an insult to the archer, a parody of foreign speech, with harsh "ch" sounds, much as in the Dikaios Painter's London amphora just discussed. The approximate positions of the corresponding athlete and trainer adopted by both Scythians suggests a parody of masculine postures as well, because they serve as feminized servants to the arming youth.[43] The foreigners are made distinct from elites through the parody.[44]

Phintias' Munich hydria has inspired a lot of discussion about its many apparent reversals, placing *hetairai* in *symposion* and an artist at school[45] [Figures 9.10, 9.11]. Considering it in light of its repetitive aspects and the tradition to which these belong allows us to make a few points to add to the discussion. It is primarily the inscriptions that link the shoulder and belly of the hydria – and these links are provocative, yielding results that are apparently parodic on several levels.[46] A statement(s) on the shoulder, ΚΑΛΟΙ(Σ)ΟΙΤΕΝΔΙ | ΕΥΘΥΜΙ(Δ)ΕΙ, where two *hetairai* in sympotic postures appear,

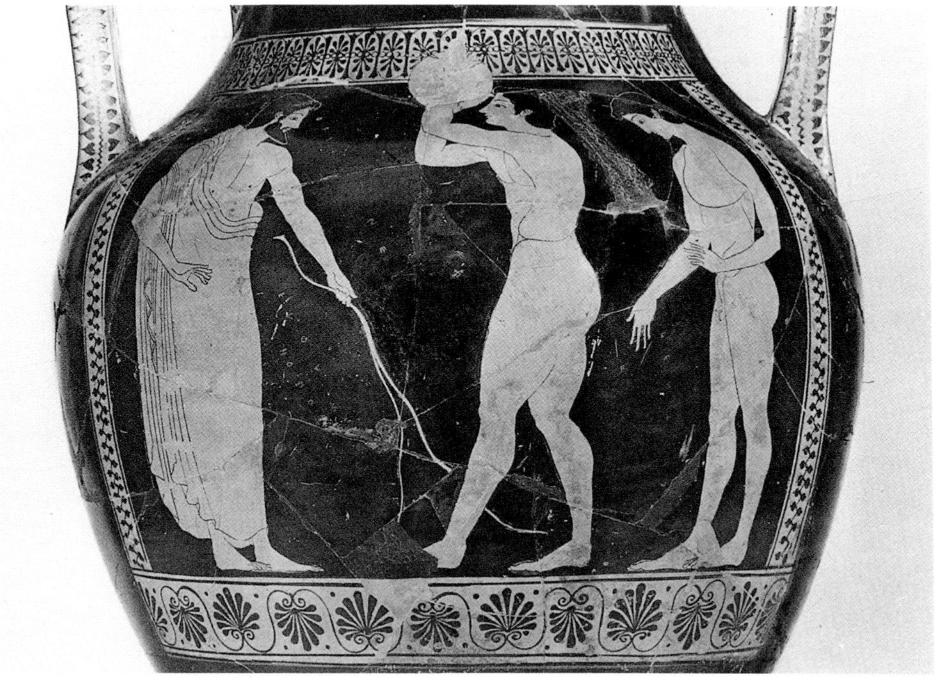

9.9. Red-figure amphora by Euthymides, ca. 510–500 B.C. Side B. Munich, Staatliche Antikensammlungen und Glyptothek 2308. (Photograph © Staatliche Antikensammlungen und Glyptothek München.)

can be read in at least two different ways: "For you, beautiful Euthymides, [I cast] this,"[47] or as a conversation between the two reclining female figures: "For whom [shall I toss] this?" "For beautiful Euthymides."[48] An unusual affirmative, NAIZON (Furtwangler NAI ZON), on the belly answers or comments on the shoulder-text; Immerwahr calls the word nonsense, while Neer, following Furtwangler, translates it as (an otherwise unparalleled statement in vase-painting), "Yes, he lives," which might mean something like,"he's a live one!"? Either reading has very general parallels in other examples. Statements in one field coupled with responses, sensible or nonsensical, in another, are on Little Master cups discussed in Chapter 5; and a *kalos* statement coupled with a response is paralleled on the Pioneer Boston pelike that initiated this study. A connection between the two inscriptions can be amply paralleled for either reading. If the inscription in the main field is a disconnected comment, "Yes, he's alive!" it is identical to that type attributed here to an absent spectator, a narratee or intended reader, and discussed first in Chapter 5 and several times thereafter.[49] The inscriptions identifying Euthymides, notably without verbatim orthographic repetition, ΕΥΘΥΜΙ(Δ)ΕΙ on the neck and ΕΥΤΥΜΙΔΕΣ on the belly, create an entirely different link: they make Euthymides both the central figure in the main scene and the person nominated in the exclamation on the shoulder. Indeed the instruction he receives in the school scene, lyre-playing, would *theoretically* contribute to his future success at *symposion* – the context where he is the potential love-object, identified as *kalos* in addition! – of the *hetairai* on the shoulder.[50] The placement of the inscriptions, particularly those located vertically at the outer edges of each scene, helps to unify the two fields visually as well.

The surprising appearance of the repeated painter's name here requires some additional comment. The two contexts – the school and the *symposion* – are not expected ones in which the craftsman's name "ought" to appear as the topic of conversation or as a label. A second look at the *symposion* reveals its peculiarities: we see *hetairai* holding their own *symposion* in a kind of parody or reversal of the ordinary male version, a fact that has engendered discussion in recent scholarship.[51] Csapo and Miller, in their analysis of the meaning of the *kottabos*-toast, have established that the person cited in the toast ought to be the prize for the successful dreg-flinger.[52] This would then compound the joke: *hetairai* who are usually the object of the game play it; likewise inverted, a male figure who ought to be competing for the prize is its object. The scene is a parody of an elite pederastic party-game. Indeed, it is very like a closely related scene on a psykter by Euphronios where a *symposion* of kottabos-flinging *hetairai* is accompanied by a similar inscription: ΤΙΝ ΤΑΝΔΕ ΛΑΤΑΣΣΟ/ΛΕΑΓΡΕ, "I throw this for you, Leagros!"[53] Here the inscription adds another dimension to the female parody of the male *symposion* – they nominate Leagros as their object of desire just as would the elite males whom they impersonate. The *kottabos*-toast is thus at odds with the imagery and the disjunction is humorous. Finally, an elite symposiast, both real reader and intended reader, who reads the inscription both merges identity with the women and yet speaks a line that is appropriate for him in expressing erotic attraction for Leagros. On the Munich hydria, the reader is insulted if forced by the inscription to state a desire for a craftsman, Euthymides.

The *hetairai* playing *kottabos* on the shoulder of the Munich hydria have only a few visual affinities with the men and youths in the school scene below, but they are startling ones: the *hetaira* at far right has her upper body exposed and her lower body wrapped in a *himation*, very much like the figure of the teacher Smikythos below her. Neer has pointed out how the musculature of the *hetairai* mimics the masculine forms below.[54] Neer interprets the vase as a subversive effort on the part of the painter Phintias to interject his colleague Euthymides into the elite world of the *symposion* as a hypothetical participant, part of a wider "egalitarian fiction" developed at the end of the sixth and beginning of the fifth centuries as a response to emerging democracy.[55] Neer appears to understand the artist as a real author speaking directly to his audience rather than through the guise of a constructed author-artist as that phenomenon is defined here in Chapter 4. The notion of this constructed author–artist makes an explicit case to the contrary, that the artist does not speak directly, but by means of a code that he manipulates exceptionally well, the inscription is not then an expression of his own voice. There is ample evidence beginning by the middle of the sixth century

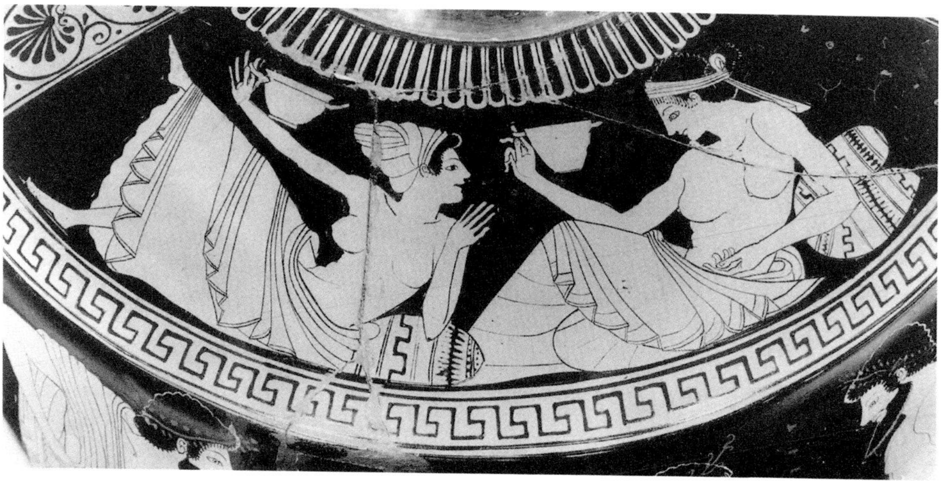

9.10. Red-figure hydria by Phintias, ca. 525–510 B.C. Shoulder detail. Munich, Staatliche Antikensammlungen und Glyptothek 2421. (Photograph © Staatliche Antikensammlungen und Glyptothek München.)

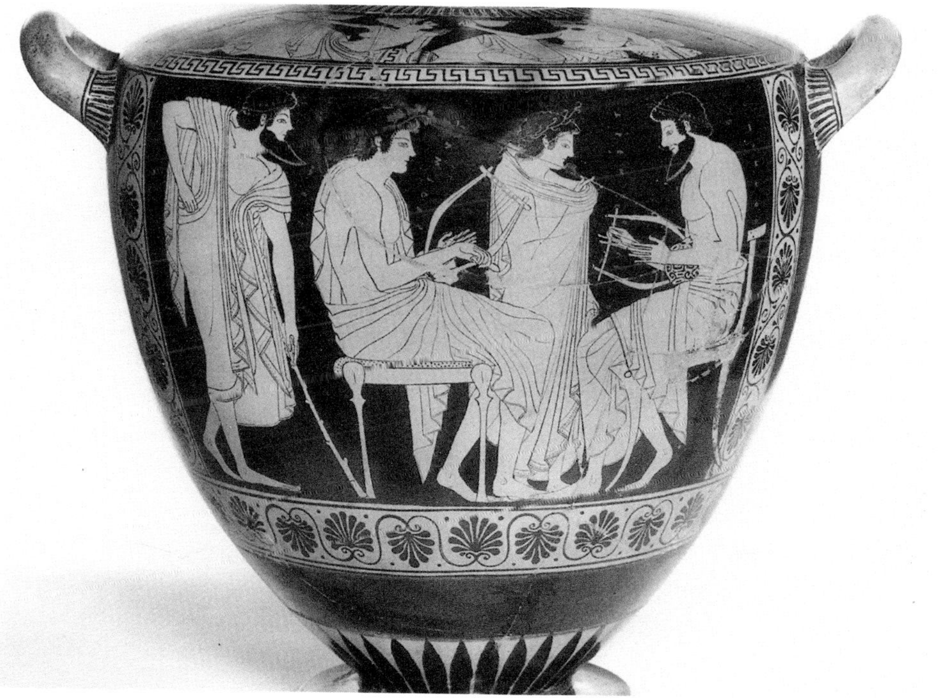

9.11. Red-figure hydria by Phintias, ca. 525–510 B.C. Main panel. Munich, Staatliche Antikensammlungen und Glyptothek 2421. (Photograph © Staatliche Antikensammlungen und Glyptothek München.)

for potter and painter names and signatures being interjected into scenes in ways that are "wrong." Their names appear in sympotic greetings and in song-texts and are often parodied; several such examples are treated earlier in this chapter as well as in Chapter 5.[56] If the inscriptions on the Munich hydria are read aloud in the context of *symposion* some excellent jokes are created. As mentioned above, an elite male reader would be in the position of speaking lines that belong to a woman in the image. In addition, a reading aloud of her speech would make him appear to seek the craftsman as his erotic prize.

The repetition of Euthymides' name in the main image suggests that it is a parody of the typical school scene: it ought to show elite education, but the name of a craftsman who has no need for elite enculturation is interjected and thereby confuses and amuses. The repetition of the name "Euthymides" in two fields actually reiterates and extends the parody. Unfortunately, the class associations of the other student named in the school scene are not clear. Tlempolemos, a name with a Homeric pedigree, is cited twice in *kalos* inscriptions on vases, once coupled with Hipparchos,[57] but the name is also that of a black-figure potter.[58] Figures with names very similar to Smikythos' appear on examples by Euthymides and Oltos, and in each case the figure is a musician, but a flute-player rather than a *barbiton*-teacher as here.[59] [Δ]ΕΜΕΤΡΙΟ(Σ), "Demetrios," is the only figure for whom we have no external evidence for his status.

As a whole, the vase parodies two facets of elite enculturation through a set of reversals. An individual of the "craftsman" class and not an elite youth is the love object for a sympotic game (itself reversed through the female actors who replace adult male elites) and learns an instrument for performance at *symposia*. It is important to note that in this example, both repeated sound, the artist's name, and repeated image combine to make the joke: inserting the illogical participants into the elite context brings the low up to the level of the high. In Chapter 11, the topic of how the ridiculing of social inferiors helps to reinforce class boundaries is treated more fully.

A return to Euphronios' very fragmentary Louvre neck-amphora depicting a statue of Herakles fighting an Amazon discussed in Chapter 8 provides a final example[60] [Figures 8.14, 8.15]. Herakles strides on a base as a statue, the base inscribed with the anomalous ΔΟΚΕΙ⁝ ΣΜΙΚ⟨Ρ⟩ΟΙ⁝ ΙΝΑΙ (Immerwahr: ΕΝΑΙ), "(Thus) it seems to be to Smikros." The content, "it seems to so-and-so" is often seen elsewhere as *graffiti* and is here conveyed with mock formality.[61] Because the compositions and the inscriptions on the two sides are otherwise so similar, this detail is not only striking but surely significant. The inscription, once read, proves to be contrary to the expectation of the real reader, which is demonstrated by the fact that their grammar and syntax find most of their parallels in *graffiti*.[62] Such *graffiti* statements usually succeed a comment, sometimes "so-and-so is *kalos*;" but just as frequently they come after a very insulting and usually abusive name-calling statement, typically a *graffito* rather than a painted inscription. Euphronios has blurred boundaries to make a joke, the point of which is not easy to understand fully: he uses a verbal formula at home in a *graffito*, but because he uses excruciatingly careful lettering, a common ground line, and even interpuncts, he seems to depict it as a formal inscription.[63] So it is "off" in terms of both its usual public form and its usual form on pottery, in both cases typically scrawled *graffiti*. Like Phintias' Munich hydria, here a painter's name is out of place, and we recognize the unexpected context for a painter's name to be a well-established trope and part of the constructed author-artist's code.

CONCLUSIONS

The examples surveyed in this chapter provide an overview of results of parody achieved through repetition. Objects of fun include paradigmatic heroes and social groups such as women, foreigners, and craftsmen. Formality itself is mocked. No group is safe from ridicule. Many examples create opportunities for one elite male, a patron or host, to get the better of another elite male, the user of a vessel, by providing an inscription that prompts *almost* correct but incoherent speech, suggesting the reader is preoccupied by wine and has consumed too much of it.

Looking at parody as a result of repetition on vases confirms that it is present as early as the second quarter of the sixth century, so it is at least as old as the forerunners of Old Comedy and satyr-play. Although the results are broadly the same, i.e., the transgression of norms through ridicule and, concomitantly, the ultimate reaffirmation of those norms, the venue for dissemination of parody on vases is private and elite. Chapter 11 delves further into discovering the broader social purpose of verbal and visual parody on Athenian vases.

TEN

READING EVERYTHING: SIX CASE STUDIES

Each of Chapters 3 through 9 focuses on a single result that repetition achieves. At times, the discussion has visited particular examples more than once – the Boston pelike [Figures 1.1, 1.2] is an obvious example, and Euthymides' Warsaw amphora [Figures 5.10, 5.11] is another – but has never considered the full impact that the redundant system of any one vase has on the viewer.[1] Now that the groundwork exploring many different types of results is completed, it is instructive to see how a single vase can exhibit multiple ways for repetition to create meaning. This chapter treats six examples fully as case studies; several of these case studies focus on well-known vases in order to highlight the kinds of new information looking at the results of repetition can generate and how often understanding that repetition creates meaning can confirm existing interpretations.

Psiax: Black-Figure Neck-Amphora Copenhagen 112

The painter Psiax, c. 530–510 B.C., shares with his colleague Epiktetos the habit of identifying the painter on one side, the potter on the other; often, though not always, the separated parts of the signature will occupy the same syntactical space, for example, along the top of the scene, just below the rim of a cup. He provides, therefore, a firm basis to reassure us that he intends viewers to take into consideration all fields of the vases he decorates.[2]

Keeping the signature-evidence in mind, we turn to Psiax' neck-amphora in Copenhagen, where repeated imagery is accompanied by inscriptions[3] [Figures 10.1, 10.2]. The poorly preserved scenes are very similar, two figures in a turning chariot in three-quarters perspective and a third, female, figure to the left of the chariot. In repeating an image, the painter places himself squarely in the tradition of exact repetitions, recalling Types, such as Horse-head amphoras, Komast-dancer cups, and *Glaux*-skyphoi, discussed in Chapter 3. Because this example is rare and possibly even unique, it aligns most closely with Exekias' Munich amphora with two depictions of Ajax with the body of Achilles [Figures 2.9, 2.10] and the bilingual examples by the Andokides/Lysippides Painters such as Herakles driving a bull to sacrifice.[4] In addition, the Group E pairings that present differing perspectives of warriors and horses and chariots, discussed in Chapter 8, are very close in spirit to the images on this neck-amphora [Figures 8.9, 8.10].

Important details suggest that the two depictions on the Copenhagen neck-amphora represent two distinct groups of people: the round shield held by the figure in the chariot in each case bears a different device, in one case a kantharos and in the other a left leg. In addition, the position of the woman differs. On A, she is depicted frontally, looking back over her shoulder to the left while holding out her skirt behind her and starting to walk away from the chariot. Her short mantle is open, exposing the full length of her form. Her long hair hangs loose. On B, the female figure faces the chariot in profile, hair neatly bound, wrapped in her mantle, holding her skirt out in front of her. Without the difference in shield devices, we might wonder if side A of the Copenhagen vase displayed a slightly later moment in time than side B; however, the difference in shield device suggests this is not the case. To corroborate this suspicion comes a narrator's voice, directing an interpretation in the form of inscriptions. The syntactical placement of the inscriptions is extremely similar; but in meaning, as far as the partial preservation permits us to judge, they appear to differ. On A, we can be certain of the inscription naming the female figure, ΕΡ[Ι]ΦΥΛΕ, "Eriphyle," so the subject is surely the departure of Amphiareus.[5] On B, the inscription is restored as [Α]ΔΡ[. . .]ΟΣ or "Adrastos." A second inscription, arranged vertically in front of the female figure, reads ΚΑΛΟΠΑ (misspelling of Kalliopa?) and probably refers to the woman rather than to one of the horses, although Kalliopa does not exist as one of the four names for the wife of Adrastos in literature.[6] These, then, are two extremely similar scenes, showing two men who departed from Argos to fight with the Seven against Thebes. One of them, Adrastos, survived, whereas the other, Amphiareus, whose wife Eriphyle betrayed him, does not. The placement of the two sets of individuals on different sides of the vessel works to extend discourse-time, creating in combination a powerful prolepsis. The scenes form a unified narration with simultaneous events taking place in two different locations. The inscriptions and the shield devices are two of the differences in the context of almost total similarity used by the artist to direct the viewer to see what is the same about two events that turned out so differently. The images reveal that from different points of view, the same action and the same character types can have opposite outcomes. Indeed Eriphyle, depicted exposed and unkempt on A, embodies a contrast to the paradigmatic well-wrapped loyal wife on the reverse.[7]

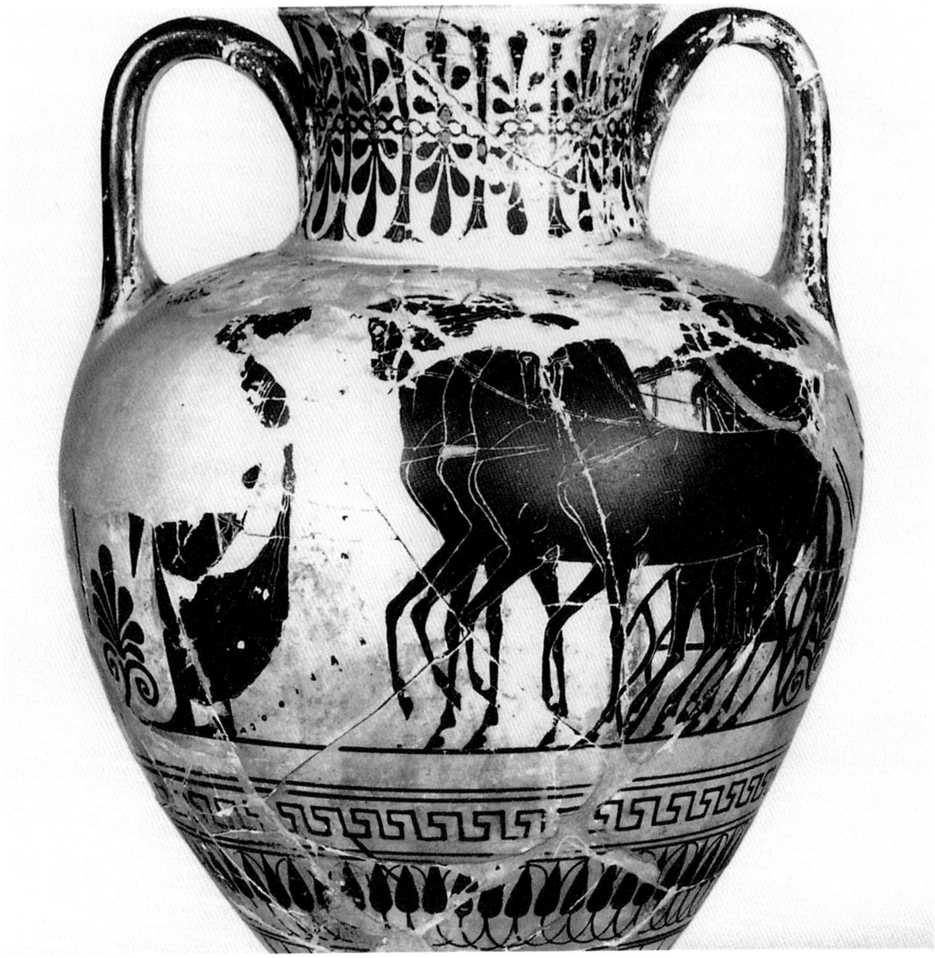

10.1. Black-figure neck-amphora by Psiax, ca. 530–515 B.C. Side A. Copenhagen, National Museum of Denmark 112 (ChrVIII3). (Photograph © Department of Classical and Near Eastern Antiquities, National Museum, Copenhagen.)

The amphora pairs two nearly identical scenes to analyze elements of the tale of the Seven against Thebes. The character "wife" is analyzed through the differing representations. Perceptual point of view is explored through the different poses, profile and three-quarters, of the two women. The poses in addition convey characterization, loose and disheveled as opposed to chaste and composed. The similarities between two male characters are highlighted through the nearly identical representations of the chariot, whereas the contrast in the depictions of women prompts the viewer to consider their very different fates. Perception of the small distinctions that yield "like" and "unlike" is heightened. For Adrastos and Amphiaraos, events with a great deal in common have two very different endings. When the artist heightens his contrast by including all the similarities between two situations – woman, men, and chariot

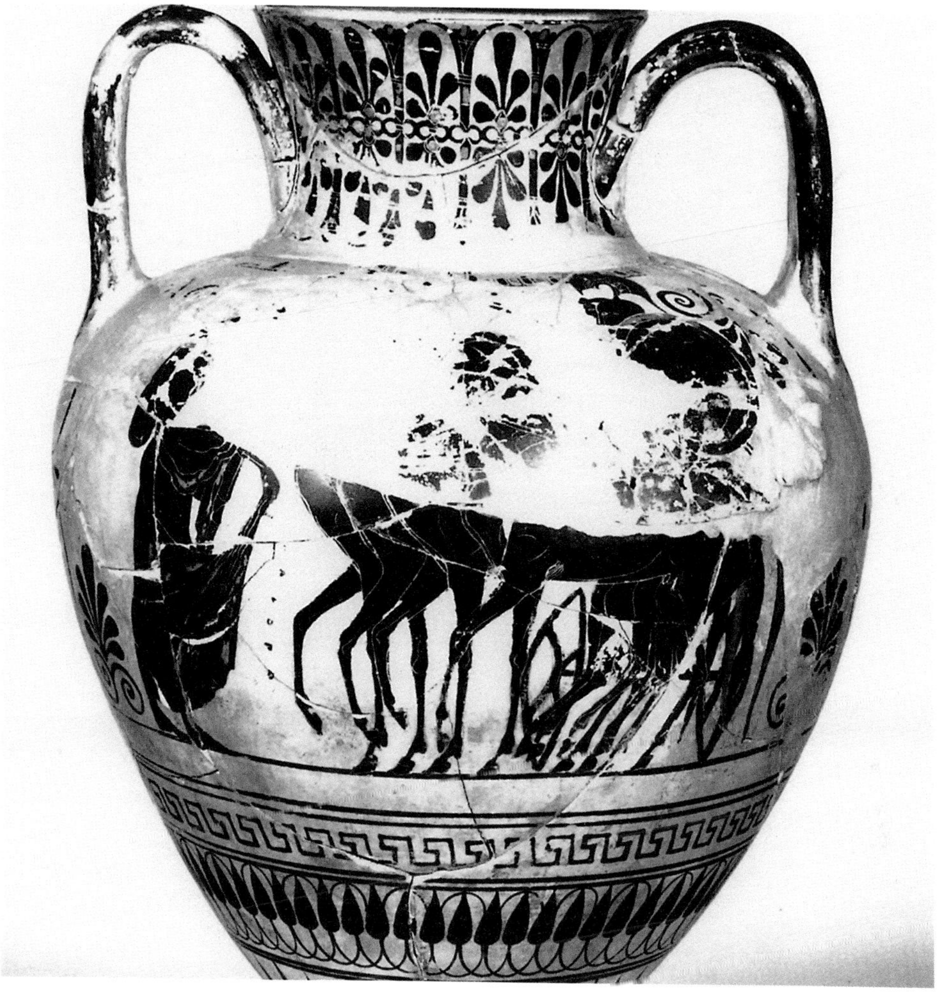

10.2. Black-figure neck-amphora by Psiax, ca. 530–515 B.C. Side B. Copenhagen, National Museum of Denmark 112 (ChrVIII3). (Photograph © Department of Classical and Near Eastern Antiquities, National Museum, Copenhagen.)

departing for war – he increases the poignancy of the difference in the outcomes of the two departures.

In spirit, Psiax' use of nearly verbatim visual repetition here is very much akin, as already remarked above, to that employed on black-figure works by Lydos and Exekias discussed in Chapter 2.[8] This vase is of the utmost importance because it confirms that nearly identical representation with very slight differences can represent different subjects. In light of the nuanced meanings created through repetition on the Copenhagen amphora, it is plausible that other examples preserving two nearly identical representations could in fact depict different characters and events as well.

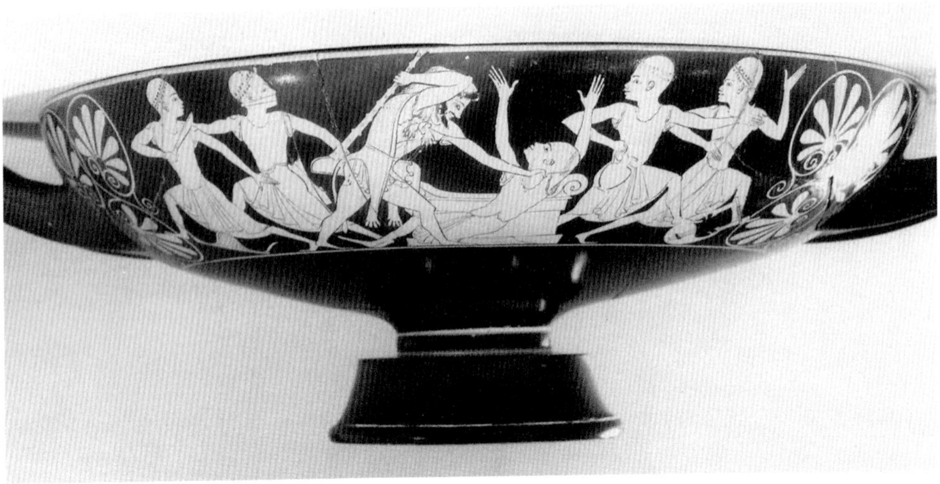

10.3. Red-figure cup by Epiktetos, ca. 520–490 B.C. Side A. London, British Museum E 38. (Photograph © Copyright The Trustees of The British Museum.)

Epiktetos: Red-Figure Cup London E 38

Consideration of many cups by Epiktetos offers assurance that the painter expected viewers to consider all fields when assessing a vase because he dispersed important information on the various fields, and the viewer is more fully informed when he puts it all together. For example, two cups by Epiktetos identify the painter on one exterior side and the potter in the interior tondo;[9] a variation on this scheme in other examples places the painter's name on one side, the verb on the other, and the potter's signature in the tondo.[10] On London E 38 (c. 510 B.C.), the syntactical role of the divided signature compels the viewer to connect the two sides of the cup, following a formula by now well-documented in the repertories of several painters beginning by the mid-sixth century with the Little Masters: each is written horizontally across the top of the scene, with potter signature on A and painter on B[11] [Figures 10.3–10.5]. This division supplies a directive, a metanarrative sign to connect the two sides. Here we see the use of paradigm as established in Chapter 7, particularly those examples connecting mortal and mythical *komoi* or *symposia*; likewise, this example combines a scene of a mortal *symposion* with one depicting the conflict of Herakles and Busiris, a mythical debacle in sympotic context. The combination identifies the mythical story as a negative paradigm for the elite party on B.

The differences between the A and B scenes are numerous, but are accompanied by several significant similarities: Side A depicts Herakles killing the Egyptian Busiris at an altar [Figure 10.3], whereas B preserves three reclining mortal symposiasts [Figure 10.4]. A fluteplayer and dancer occupy the tondo [Figure 10.5]. Side B presents, in one field, several facets of *symposion*. A variety of perceptual points of view are visible. The two symposiasts at left recline on couches in profile, and the viewer sees identical

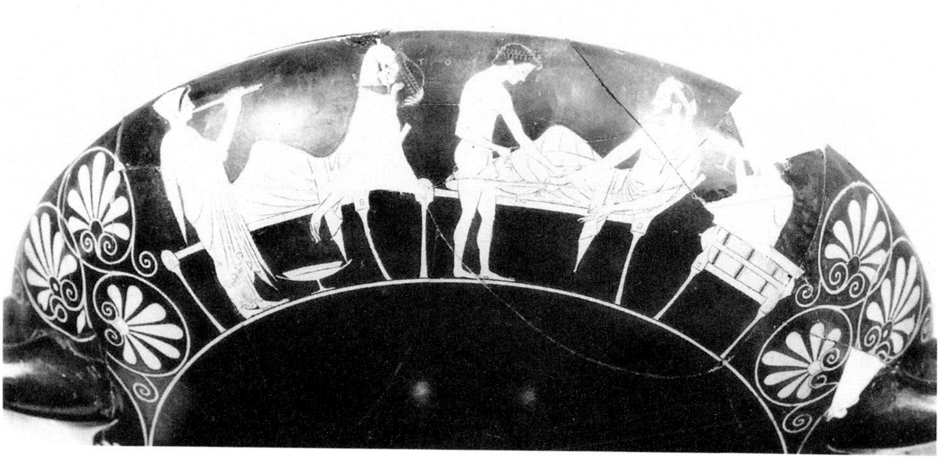

10.4. Red-figure cup by Epiktetos, ca. 520–490 B.C. Side B. London, British Museum E 38. (Photograph © Copyright The Trustees of The British Museum.)

profile views of their heads and lower bodies, combined with three-quarters and profile views of the torsos. By contrast, the couch at right appears frontally, from its head, and the back view of the symposiast on it is visible. The activities in which symposiasts are engaged display a range as well: the figure at left has *emptied* his cup and rests it on the floor, and he throws his head back with open mouth, presumably singing to the flute-playing performed by the female who stands at left. The middle figure *extends* his cup to be refilled from an oinochoe held by a youth. At right, the

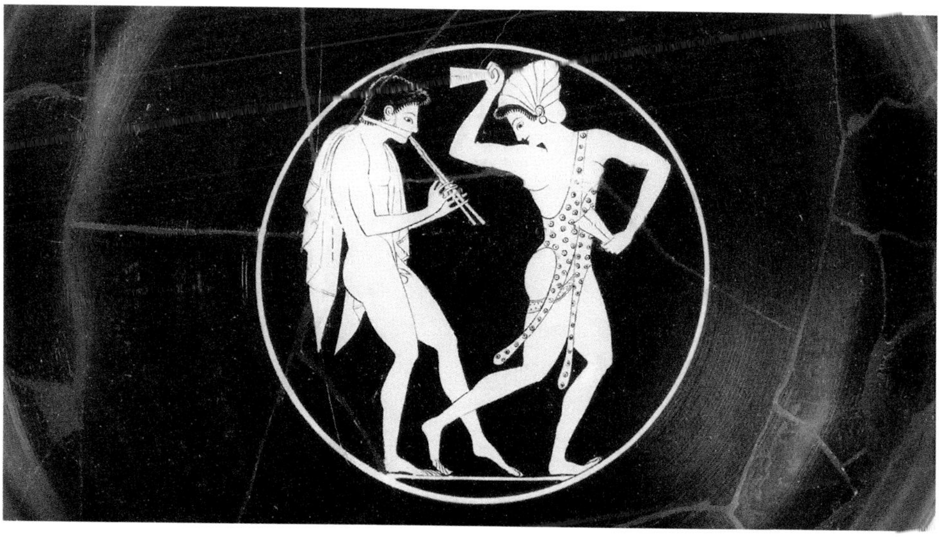

10.5. Red-figure cup by Epiktetos, ca. 520–490 B.C. Interior. London, British Museum E 38. (Photograph © Copyright The Trustees of The British Museum.)

figure is about to drink – he *lifts* his cup to his lips. Two types of attendant-roles are displayed here, the flute-playing female musician and the decorous wine-pouring youth. The tondo presents yet another facet of *symposion*: entertainment in the form of a castanet dance set to the pipes. The tondo entertainers are marked as like the B-side symposiasts through repetition of the wreath and pipes (youth) and *sakkos* (dancer).

The sacrifice on side A is not set in *symposion*, but by means of synoptic prolepsis, anticipates symposion through the inclusion of objects appropriate to both sacrifice and *symposion*. The attendants wear the same floral wreaths as the symposiasts on B and the musician-youth in the tondo. One, at left, wears a chinstrap like the tondo youth, but has lost his flutes. To the right of the altar a running figure holds an oinochoe, and his partner at far right has dropped his kithara. The musical instruments are useless, forgotten, and tossed aside in the chaotic pre–*symposion*; the flutes are in proper use in the correct versions on B and in the tondo. The artist conveys the difference through ellipsis: chin strap alone is present in A, flutes without chin strap in B, and both are pictured in the tondo. The images must be combined in order for the construction of the paradigm, the image of the positive available to serve as a contrast to the negative. The figures of the pouring attendants combine similarly. The Egyptian attendant on A holds the pitcher, but the cup into which it is poured is lost in the melee; the youth on B holds his oinochoe at the same angle as he pours into the cup; the ellipsis created on A emphasizes through the absence of the cup one indication of "wrong *symposion*." The all-out running postures of all the Egyptian attendants on A contrast to the controlled composure of the Greeks on B, and the Egyptians supply extreme exaggerations of the dancing posture of the tondo dancer. The negative paradigm highlights through exaggeration, omission, and displacement characteristics such as decorum, order, and grace that are essential to the proper conduct of the event.

Schefold has already interpreted the cup as follows: the tale of Herakles and Busiris is performed for entertainment at the event on B.[12] Lissarrague has pointed out how the two sides are thematically linked, and that such a story might well hold up a mirror to the "civilized" *symposion*: the mythical tale set in Egypt is a "dinner party" gone very wrong, the polar opposite or antonym of the civilized *symposion* on B, with its entertainment as depicted in the tondo.[13] The repetitions identified here help to make those interpretations convincing and expand the depth of the lesson: several facets of the ideal *symposion* are linked through repetition and the lesson explicating good versus bad is made redundant through the explicit presentation of its opposite.

There is a parodic result to the repetitions as well. The comparatively extreme running postures of Busiris' assistants, the very large size of the oinochoe on A, the props bouncing on the ground on A in contrast to their carefully placed corollaries on B and in the tondo are exaggerations suggesting caricature. The Egyptian scene not only is different from its companion on B, but it is also a compendium of misunderstood sympotic behaviors. The large pouring vessel suggests a lack of moderation; the ungainly running postures suggest burlesque rather than elegant dance; the lost pipes that

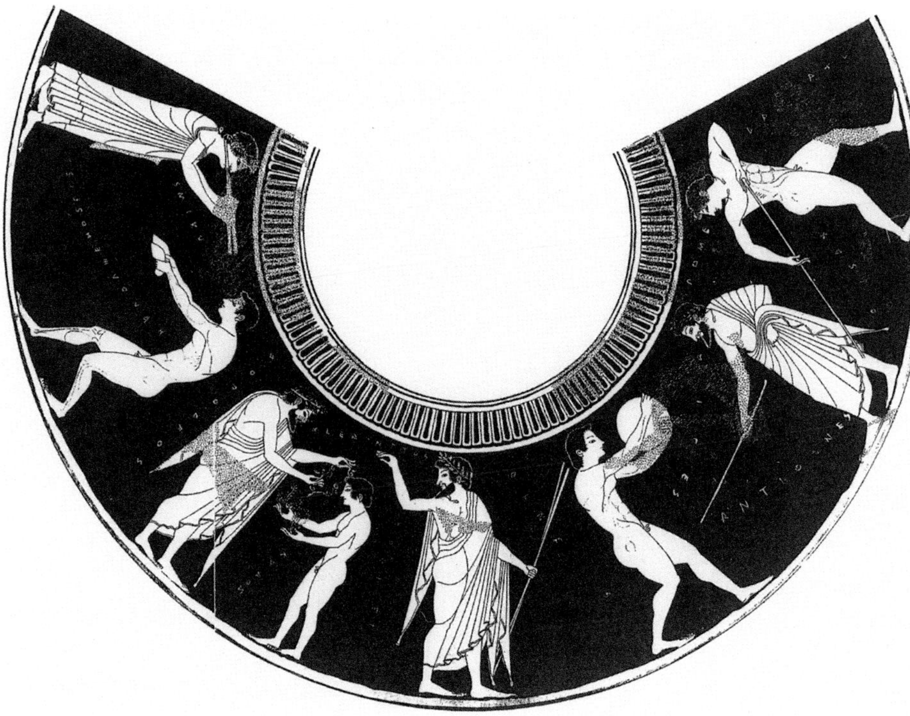

10.6. Red-figure psykter by Oltos, ca. 525–500 B.C. Drawing of entire field. New York, Metropolitan Museum of Art 10.210.18. (Photograph © The Metropolitan Museum of Art, Rogers Fund, 1910 [10.210.18]. All rights reserved, The Metropolitan Museum of Art.)

leave the strap hanging from the musician's chin make him appear ridiculous. The result of the parody is to confirm the status of the Athenian elites on B who carry out *symposion* the right way.

Oltos: Red-Figure Psykter New York M.M.A. 10.210.18

Oltos' psykter in New York, c. 510 B.C. depicts male figures in a combined context of athletics and pederasty[14] [Figure 10.6]. Overall, the painter lays out aspects of elite youth experience on the psykter, including athletes, trainers, and pederastic flirting with the exchange of love gifts in two groups of three and one of two. Like several of the painter's cups, this vase appears to display contemporaneous Athenian males, and here eight are named.[15] Figures of very similar types are directly opposite one another on the pot, effectively creating repetitions on two *sides,* if not exactly in two different fields; note in particular the youth jumping with *halteres*, ΔΟΡΟΘΕΟΣ, "Dorotheos," and the discus thrower, ΑΝΤΙΦΑΝΕΣ, "Antiphanes." There is ample visual impetus to pull the viewer into consideration of the entire field extending over both "sides" of the psykter. The tone of the imagery is pederastic; both inscriptions and imagery on this psykter not only present several facets of gymnasium activity combined with pederastic behavior, but the array of subjects also includes examples of two types, both "proper" and crude. The painter breaks down components of experience, and his intended reader comments on these experiences as well.

ΕΠΑΙΝΕΤΟΣ, "Epainetos," is garlanded by two adult males, ΚΛΕΑΙΝΕΤΟΣ, "Kleainetos," from the front, and from behind by ΑΛΚΕΤΕΣ, "Alketes"; Epainetos carries two handfuls of sprigs. ΚΑΛΟΣ, "handsome," between Kleainetos and Epainetos confirms the context as "properly" or at least typically pederastic.[16] The pair to the left of this threesome appear to be labeled ΔΟΡΟΘΕΟΣ "Dorotheos," about to jump and holding halteres, and ΣΜΙΚΥ[ΘΟΣ] "Smiky[thos]" who plays the double flute, and an unusual descriptive doubled future expresson, *h*ΑΛΟΥΜΕΝΟΣ ΕΙΣΙ, "(for the purpose of)jumping, he will go" appears between them. A third group of males, another threesome, at the far right of the scene includes a trainer, Α[ΝΤ] Ι[Μ] Ε[Ν] ΕΣ "Antimenes," between a discus thrower, ΑΝΤΙΦΑΝΕΣ "Antiphanes," and an acontist, ΒΑ[ΤΡ]ΑΧΟΣ, "Batrachos." In general outline the composition they form is very similar to that of the two adult males crowning Epainetos, but here, instead of *kalos*, there are two verbs between trainer and acontist that read ΠΟΜΕ and ΧΑΣΚΟ, translated as "drink me" and "I gape" or "I open my mouth wide" by Beazley and apparently accepted by Immerwahr.[17] Although Immerwahr sees these comments as referring to the function of the vessel, as if the vessel is speaking them, another interpretation is possible. Because the verb χάσκω is frequently used of the "gaping anus of passive homosexuals"[18] and we see it written next to the buttocks of Batrachos, perhaps it is dialogue, a crude invitation to Antimenes, spoken by Batrachos, playing on the idea that to be an athletic trainer is to have, and to want to have, access to beautiful youths in the hope of sexual encounters. The propositions are striking because they appear to come from the youth, rather than from the adult male. The second verb, reading "Drink me," sounds like another crude proposition, and it is located as if coming out of Batrachos' mouth.

The comment predicting that Dorotheos is about to jump cannot be attributed to a spectator; it is a disembodied observation of a absent narratee until the user of the vessel reads the inscription. The artist has omitted the spectator in the scene and replaced him with a script to be uttered, in an ideal world, by a living elite Athenian male. Although he is a living stand-in for a (missing) painted figure, his response is scripted: his reaction is not left to chance.

The role of repetition in creating these meanings is multilayered: (1) the repetition of individual figure-types and two- and three-person groups urges the viewer to connect and to compare the figures; (2) the repetition of similar three-person groups heightens the contrast between polite and impolite pederastic comments; (3) the repetition of names as "straight" descriptions makes the crude exclamations surprises, thwartings of expectation. There are important differences among the three verbal statements; the first, straight, statement is a third-person descriptive observation, whereas the second two are a first-person declaration and an imperative, and a real reader could utter them as such. Thus the psykter accomplishes more than depicting facets of athletic activity and their pederastic overtones. It creates both parody and set-ups for jokes.

Ridicule of pederastic behavior is achieved through contrast. Graceful adornment of a youth with garland and sprigs and a statement anticipating his colleague's performance contrast with the figures who make crude propositions to one another. In the cases where there are insulting propositions, both parties are named, possibly mocking particular individuals. Because a reader could articulate the inscriptions aloud, what is written also has the potential to make the reader a second object of the joke. Not only is the content itself funny, but the context also makes it unexpected: since the other inscriptions are either names or inoffensive descriptions, those that are off-color and insulting can surprise the reader when he comes to them. Moreover, the crude invitations come from a youth, suggesting a fantasy, an inversion of the usual adult-seeks-youth pederastic relationship. These jokes appear to buttress elite norms, where pederasty is, as characterized recently by Hubbard, "ours" and not "theirs."[19]

Kleophrades Painter: Red-Figure Stamnos, Philadelphia University Museum L 64.185

The Kleophrades Painter's stamnos in Philadelphia, c. 500–490 B.C., carefully sets up synonymy, a paradigmatic relationship between Theseus and Herakles, by means of both visual repetitions and inscriptions[20] [Figures 10.7, 10.8]. What is similar? Both heroes are nude; they are attacking animals, a lion and a bull respectively, whose front paws/hooves are flat on the ground and whose rear paws/hooves still "stand." A tree stands in each background, and unused weapons hang in the field. And in each case, ΚΑΛΟΣ ΕΙ, "You are handsome," appears in the field, embedding the heroic events in the discourse of pederasty and *symposion*. Along with the visual similarities, the repetition of the inscription links the two exploits, adding to the inventory of features that invite the viewer to compare the two scenes. Very loosely construed, the two scenes are sequential, with Herakles, the older hero, preceding Theseus. In the same way that paradigmatic heroes precede Athenian elites, Herakles comes before Theseus and serves as the younger hero's prototype.

Because, as we have seen, the *kalos* statement is identical to an assessment likely to be offered about each hero by a "real" member of the elite, the context created is essentially equivalence, much like a simile – the heroes are like one another because each is judged as *kalos*, and the generic *kalos* inscription, especially when vocalized, might well invite comparison with elite youths or men, conceivably assembled company in a sympotic context. To be sure, there are differences as well: Herakles is bearded and Theseus is not, and Herakles uses his bare hands to wrestle the lion, whereas Theseus is about to use his club and wears baldric and scabbard to fight the bull of Marathon Herakles is at left, Theseus at right. Even the repeated inscription appears in a slightly

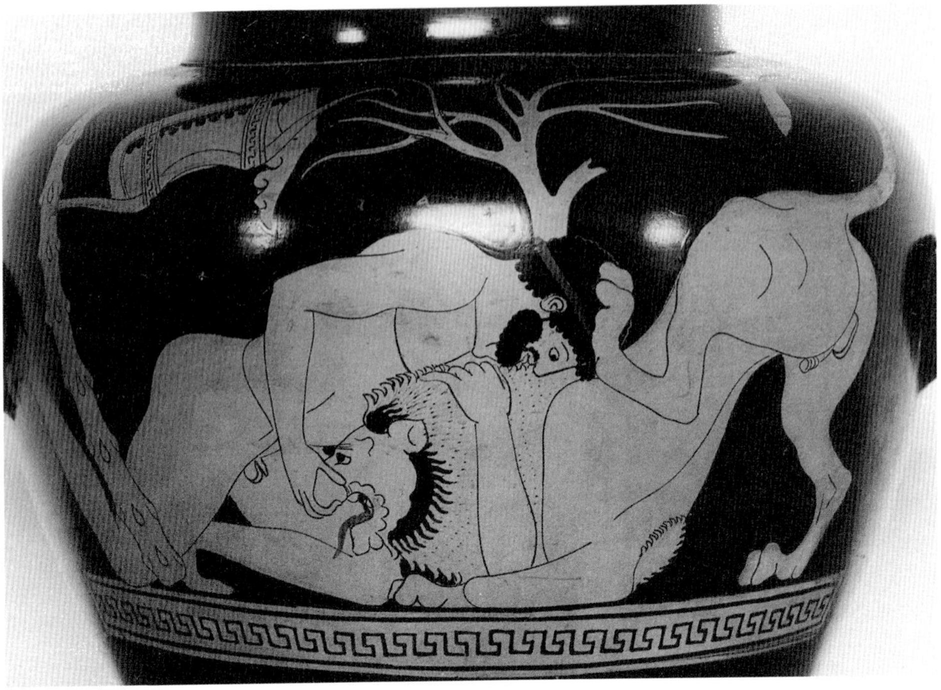

10.7. Red-figure stamnos by the Kleophrades Painter, ca. 505–475 B.C. Side A. Philadelphia, University of Pennsylvania Museum L64.185. (Photograph © University of Pennsylvania Museum [neg. #S8-2987].)

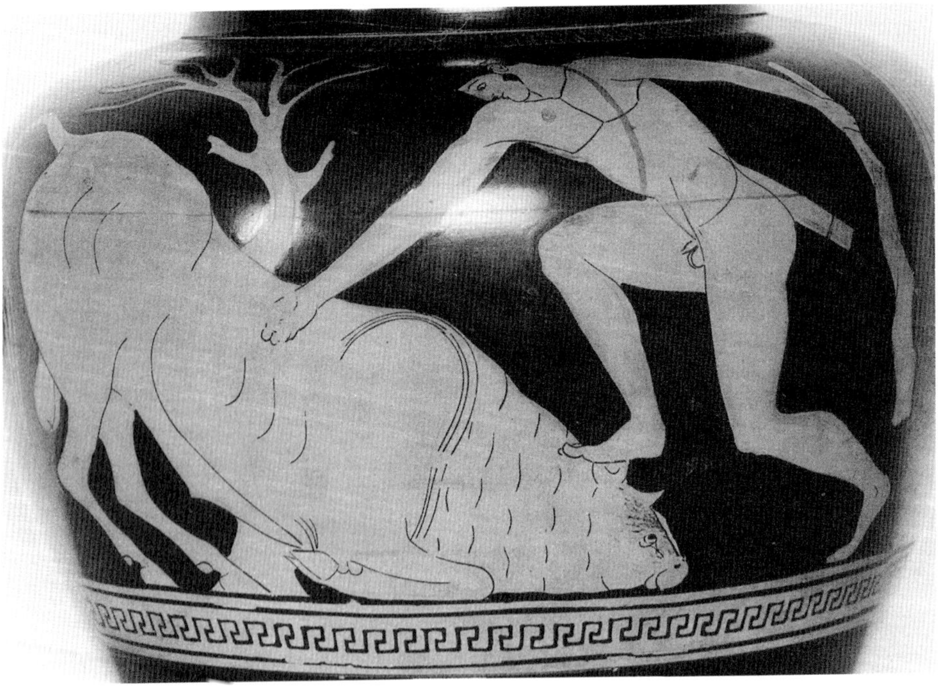

10.8. Red-figure stamnos by the Kleophrades Painter, ca. 505–475 B.C. Side B, detail. Philadelphia, University of Pennsylvania Museum L64.185. (Photograph © University of Pennsylvania Museum [neg. #S8-2990].)

different spot on each side: to the far left, between the club and chlamys of Theseus, on B, and over Herakles' back on A. This example offers us a vivid demonstration of the close relationship between synonymy and antonymy.

No spectators are present, but the evaluative ΚΑΛΟΣ ΕΙ, written on each side, is the same kind of endorsement spectators provide. Once again, the narratee (a spectator within the story), the intended reader (the ideal audience for whom the story is created), and, potentially, the real reader (an Athenian elite at *symposion*) merge in identity. The comments are metadiscursive directives as that concept is identified in Chapter 4, guiding the audience to one point of the conjunction of the images; the two in combination are to be linked to the discourse of fame and pederasty. This type of repetitive program, preserving the coupling of two similar exploits of two different heroes, has a long history, as this study has demonstrated. An example by Lydos couples Theseus and the Minotaur and Herakles and the Centaur as one of several examples of paradigms for courtship.[21] Examples by Group E combine Herakles and the lion with Theseus and the Minotaur.[22] In each of the earlier examples, anonymous and incongruous spectators frame the struggles, providing narratees, an audience within the narrative. This type of metadiscourse instructs about how to interpret the text, presenting an ideal way in the view of the author/artist that excludes other ways. Oltos' Copenhagen cup links Theseus and the Minotaur and Herakles and Kyknos with framing figures who look like anonymous/incongruous spectators but are labeled on one side with names. Although not recognizable as mythical, these names provide a specific designation and they may represent actual elites[23] [Figures 5.7, 5.8]. On the Philadelphia stamnos, the Kleophrades Painter completely *replaces* the bystanders with inscriptional comments. A real reader, an actual member of the elite, not his image-counterpart, will articulate a specific comment that ordains synonymy of the two heroic deeds. This reader will also connect the heroes to elites, who likewise call youths of their own social class "*kalos*." The artist provides for a living narratee, *outside* of the image, with a specific script.[24]

Euphronios: Red-Figure Krater Arezzo 1465

Euphronios' Arezzo krater offers a rich complexity of repetitions encompassing figures and inscriptions on four fields[25] [Figures 10.9, 10.10]. The body represents one subject, Herakles fighting the Amazons. On side A, Herakles and companions are in combat with Amazons, and on B, figures run to left. The groups are divided by palmettes placed under the handles; these serve as a syntactical barrier, but figural repetitions overcome them. The topic is narrative: the extension of the story over two sides of the vase, creating a unified narrative, increases discourse time in relation to story time.[26] The striped garments of the Amazons and their equipment are consistent and striking repetitions; repeated round shields and helmets offer more confirmation that the battle on A is the same as the battle on B. A kantharos shield device appears on each side,

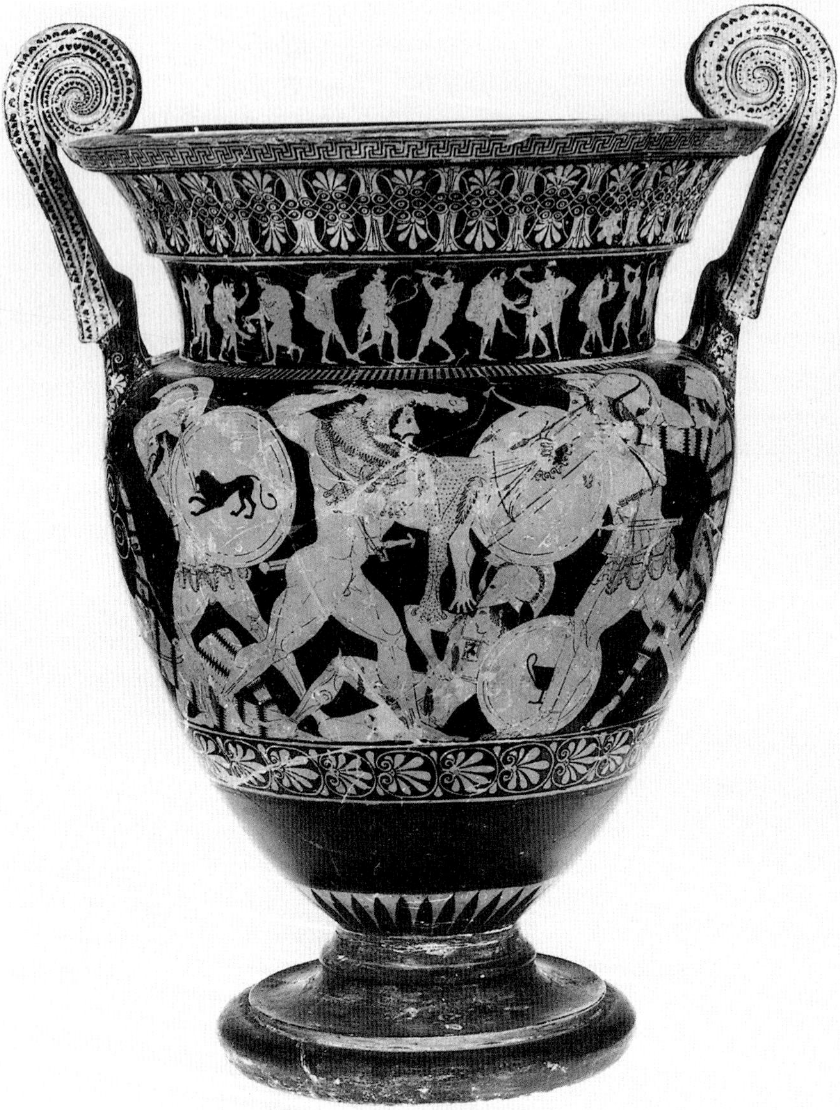

10.9. Red-figure krater by Euphronios, ca. 520–505 B.C. Side A. Arezzo, Museo Civico 1465. (Photograph © Soprintendenza Archeologica per la Toscana – Firenze.)

both examples on shields held by Amazons. Herakles, the major hero of the scenes, stands out on A as different, owing especially to his lionskin and club. The inscriptions name each of the seven figures on A, both Greeks and Amazons, and there are extras as well. One in particular is especially important for this discussion, near the left handle: a floating name, as restored and read by Immerwahr, reads [T]EI[Σ]IΣ, "Teisis." Side B apparently preserves no labels for the Amazons, but instead two *kalos* inscriptions, ΦIΛ{Λ}IAΔEΣKAΛOΣ, "Philiades is handsome," and XΣENO⟨N⟩KAΛOΣ, "Xenon is

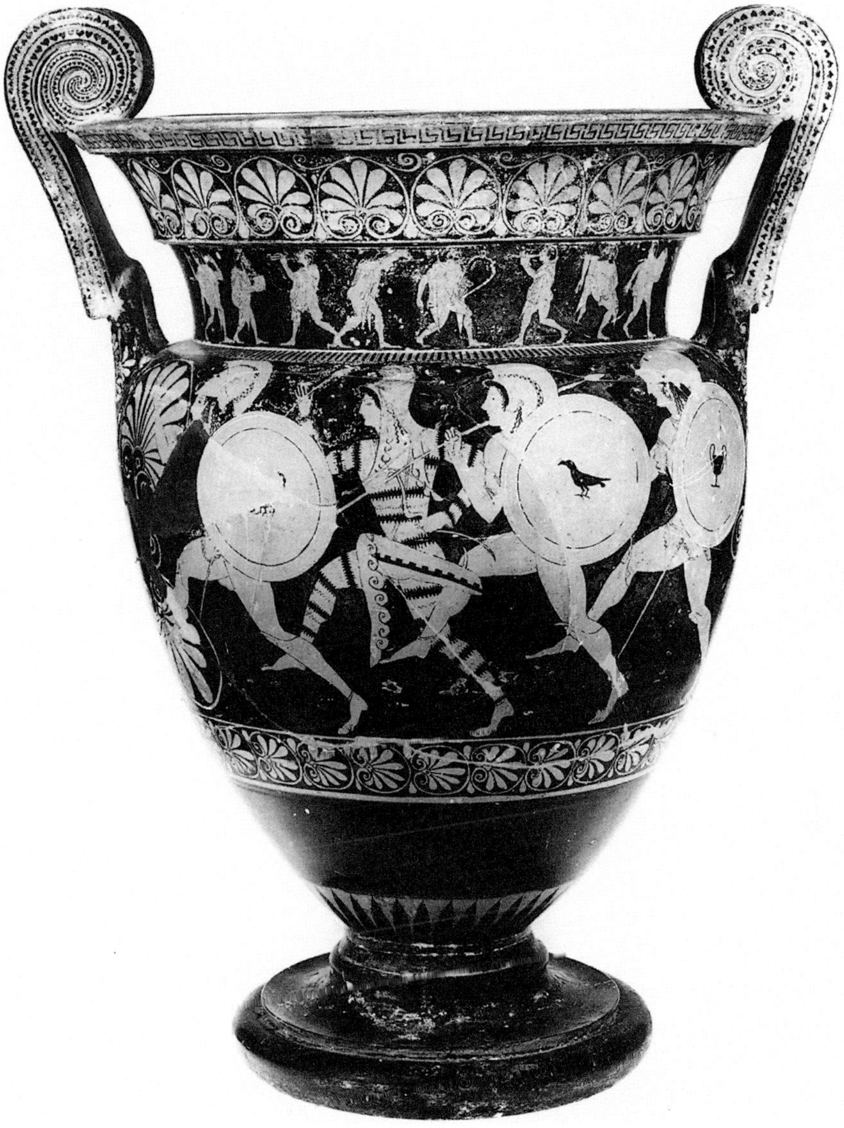

10.10. Red-figure krater by Euphronios, ca. 520–505 B.C. Side B. Arezzo, Museo Civico 1465. (Photograph (c) Soprintendenza Archeologica per la Toscana – Firenze.)

handsome," placing the vase in a sympotic context that is amplified by the topic on the neck.

The nineteen figures in the scenes of *komos* on both sides of the neck provide a thorough analysis of the character "komast." Those on A are all youths, whereas on B, three of the eight figures are adult men with beards. The figures on B provide a slightly more extreme and excessive set of poses and behaviors than those on A. The two sets of figures are linked by a number of figural repetitions joining the two parts of a *komos*: a confronting pair plays *barbiton* and double flutes near the center of each segment on A and B; a youth carrying an amphora while moving right and looking back toward the left appears both at the right hand terminus of B and at the left on A; and the fourth figure from left in both scenes dances in profile to right, both arms raised above his head, and wearing only a *himation*. These figures repeat the pose of the Amazon at far right on A, who is about to let loose an arrow from her bow; the komasts appear to parody the Amazon's pose. Like the *kalos* inscriptions on B, this repetition in pose creates a link between a subject of poetry, the Amazonomachy, and the world of elite conviviality.

The scenes on the neck of both A and B preserve inscriptions, most of which are placed vertically between figures. On A, the inscriptions are intelligible as proper names, sometimes with *kalos* added. One name probably describes the action of its (dancing) owner. Other names serving as labels include ΧΣΙΝΙΣ/ΤΕΙΣΙΣ/ΧΟΡΙΘΟΝ/ ΧΣΕΝΟΝΚΑΛ{.}ΟΣ/ΚΑΙΚΕΙΟΣΚΑΛΟΣ/ΛΥΣΙΣΚΑΛ{Λ}ΟΣ, "Xinis, Teisis, Khorithon, Xenon is handsome, and [that one] is handsome and Lysis is handsome." The "khor-" root of the name "Khorithon" appears to relate to the action of its owner, who is dancing. Two inscriptions, those identifying both Lysis and Xenon, appear to be both labels naming particular dancers as well as *kalos* evaluations of them; the third *kalos* floats, a general comment not attached to a specific individual ("and [that one] is handsome"). In contrast, on B, the wilder, apparently drunker version of the *komos*, there are inscribed letters arranged vertically between figures as on A, but they create nonsense. Immerwahr has pointed out that this is the only preserved example where Euphronios uses "meaningless" inscriptions.[27] In one case the reader of the inscriptions will find names, observations, and compliments, and in the other he will find nonsense except for one word, *kalos*, located between figures two and three at left. The remaining inscriptions, apparently at least five groups of one or more letters, include at least two that are very like endings of actual names or words: *-kos* and *-des*.[28] The reader will be almost comprehensible, but not quite.

The most obscenely posed komast appears on this same side, a man second from right who exposes himself as he steps wide and lifts a leg, providing a frontal view; he holds one hand near his penis, pointing. The written nonsense inscriptions add a verbal dimension that is an audible reflection of the *komos* experience depicted in the images, with coherent speech for the moderate participant on A in contrast to the incoherence, accompanied by obscenity and immoderation, on B.[29] Images and inscriptions are intertwined in a relationship that parses the *komos*, emphasizing and incorporating its closeness to dance as well as its dangerous proximity to movement that parodies trained, restrained performance.

The links created by repetitions between the neck and main scenes are interesting if few and subtle. The similarity in pose between two komasts and one Amazon, mentioned above, is one. There are two more: ΧΣΕΝΟΝ ΚΑΛΟΣ (a tag-*kalos*, "Xenon is handsome," referring to one of the *komasts*[30]) appears on the neck of A and the body of B; and Teisis is mentioned on side A on both neck (ΤΕΙΣΙΣ) and body ([Τ]ΕΙ[Σ]ΙΣ), where the name appears to float rather than to label. There is no chance that the mortal named as *kalos* fights with Herakles, as Sosias appears to do on the Morgantina krater by Euthymides [Figures 7.23, 7.24], but his name would be read together with those of the heroes.[31] The visual and verbal repetitions provide an encompassing frame, a powerful instruction in metadiscourse to consider the entire image-program as a whole, despite its division by field and topic. The Amazonomachy is a fitting subject for the *barbiton*-players' song on the neck, just as Herakles is a fitting paradigm for elite mortals in *komos*. The contrast between the two representations of the *komos* displays how easily paradigm can shift into parody.

Berlin Painter: Red-Figure Amphora Berlin 2160

On the name vase of the Berlin Painter, c, 490, repetition of inscriptions, characters, and attributes engages the viewer to combine images[32] [Figures 10.11, 10.12]. The decorative syntax is consistent on each side, with neck, handles, and ground line bearing identical patterns. A satyr appears on each side of the vessel, and each is wreathed and carries a *barbiton*. The artist displays the figures so as to present and explore two different visual perspectives. The lone satyr on B is in a perfect profile view, whereas on side A, the satyr is in a three-quarters view, looking back over his shoulder to his identical twin on B. The different physical points of view presented echo the analysis of this character, "satyr," that appears to be one purpose for the repetitions the two images share. As we can see in the case of the paired chariot-departures on Psiax' neck amphora in Copenhagen [Figures 10.1, 10.2], the satyr-depictions are so close that the viewer might think they were repetitions of a single satyr until reading the inscriptions: the figure on A is named ΟΡΕΙΜΑ{Χ}ΧΟΣ, "Oreimachos," and that on B is named ΟΡΟΧΑΡ{Τ?}ΕΣ, "Orochar{t}es."[33] The repetitions in the sound and meaning of their names, "Mountain-Fighter" and "Fond-of-Mountains," helps to convey that the two are close but not identical figures.

On side A, Hermes and a deer accompany the satyr. There is interweaving of the labels and attributes of the characters through the use of consistent syntax: the name of the satyr on B appears where Hermes' name is written on A, and Hermes on side A carries a kantharos, as does the satyr on B. Both satyrs carry a *barbiton*. Through these repeated directives, the Berlin Painter forces the viewer to consider several aspects of the figures depicted, including the satyr-aspects of Hermes as well as the Hermes-aspects of the two satyrs. Osborne has observed that the images seem to be integrated purposely, so that we have "a Dionysiac Hermes" on A, because he carries the kantharos, and "an Hermaic satyr," on B, who carries the *barbiton*.[34] The placement of Hermes' and Orochartes' names at the same spot on their respective sides of the vase supports this interpretation and further emphasizes the already engaging confusion about who is who on the A side of the vase. Osborn suggests the reason for creating this confusion is

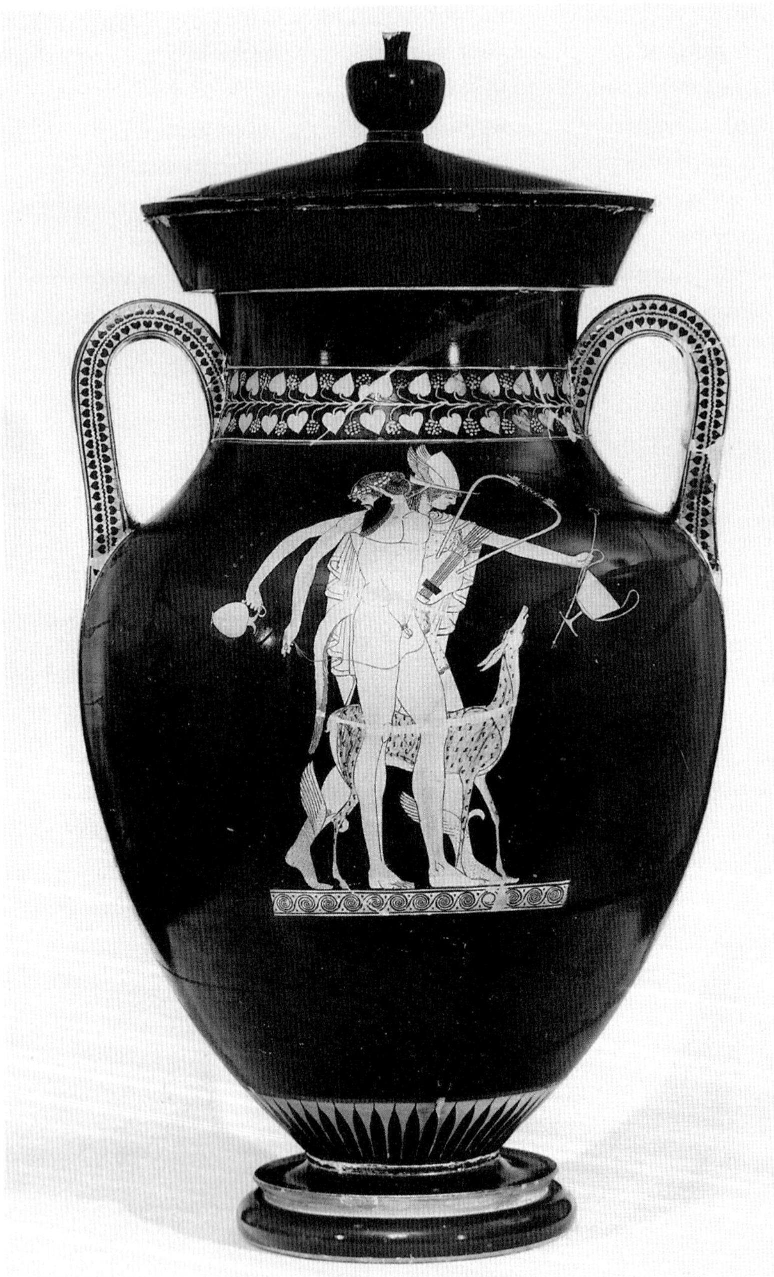

10.11. Red-figure amphora by the Berlin Painter, ca. 500–480 B.C. Side A. Berlin, Staatliche Museen 2160. (Photograph © Staatliche Museen zu Berlin, Antikensammlung [Inv.-Nr. F 2160]. Photo: Ingrid Geske.)

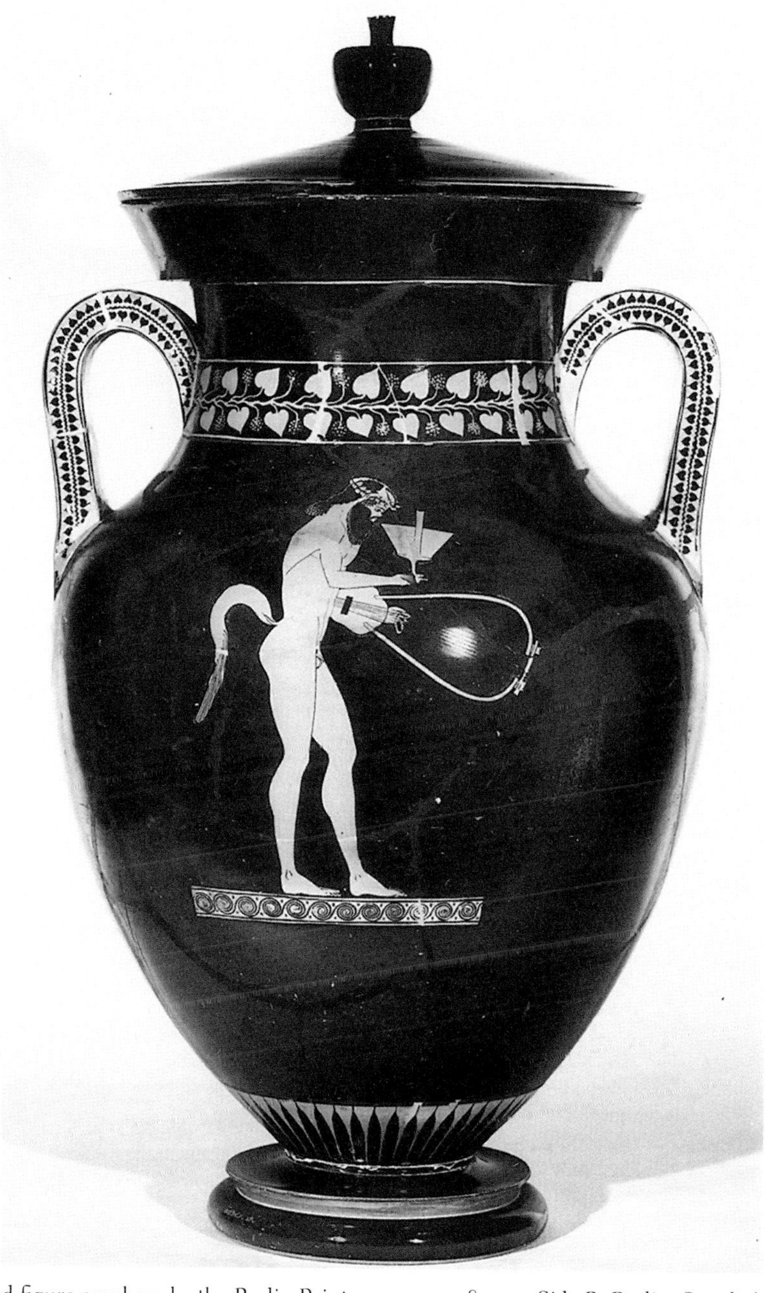

10.12. Red-figure amphora by the Berlin Painter, ca. 500–480 B.C. Side B. Berlin, Staatliche Museen 2160. (Photograph © Staatliche Museen zu Berlin, Antikensammlung [Inv.-Nr. F 2160]. Photo: Isolde Luckert.)

to press the viewer to analyze and to compare closely linked mythical figures, Dionysos and Hermes and their animal and satyr companions, in order to appreciate fully the story the artist presents to us. The presence of the spotted deer helps to convey this message: the hooves contrast with the very human feet of the satyr, but in their animal nature show affinity with the bird wings springing up from Hermes' ankles. Osborne's reading is in accord with the analysis here, that these repetitions bringing focus to different physical points of view. In addition, repetition invites comparison of aspects or facets of characters to yield a more complex interpretation of the figures depicted.

With these six case studies setting the stage, the next chapter explores more fully how the effects of repetition complement various aspects of society and culture in Archaic Athens, providing a redundant echo for some central themes.

ELEVEN

OVER AND OVER: READING GREEK VASES IN *SYMPOSION*

The previous chapters have revealed how vase-painters use repetition to tell stories, establish paradigms, explore characters and point of view, and create parody in a compact system complete in the vase itself. This chapter explores how the results of repetition on the vases are reiterated in the activities and setting in the environment where their owners used them. We begin with a discussion aimed at making the case that for the creators and users of Athenian figural pottery, *symposion* in Athens was both the intended use venue and the primary frame of reference for these vessels. Following this section, we turn to a detailed exploration of how the results of repetition set up echoes of both the activities and ethos of *symposion*. Athenian figural pottery reflects the physical space, the entertainment, and the social purposes of *symposion*; by repeating and echoing such elements, these vessels fit neatly into a mutually reinforcing redundant system that articulates central components of an elite Athenian world view. Finally, we will conclude with a discussion of how this world-view is rooted in specific historical conditions in Archaic and Classical Athens.

SYMPOSION AS THE INTENDED SETTING FOR ATHENIAN POTTERY

Background

A sympotic context for the use of Athenian vases cannot be taken for granted. There is considerable room for uncertainty about how Athenian painted pottery was used, and there is surmise behind every point of view. This situation is a result of both a lack of evidence and the character of the evidence we do have. A major problem is that most preserved Athenian pottery has been discovered in Italy, in Etruscan tombs, and relatively little has been recovered from definitively sympotic contexts in Greece. In addition, there are attested nonsympotic use-contexts for some shapes in the repertory of Athenian painted pottery, but there is not sufficient evidence for a full-blown, well-supported alternative to the *symposion* scenario. We have considerable textual evidence and some archaeological evidence that vessels used in elite *symposion* were made of precious metals, of gold and silver, yet very few of these vessels survive. Finally, there are many arguments for what vessels were used in *symposion* based on the iconography in images on the vases themselves. If we base our conclusions about what vases were used in *symposion* on this iconography, we are using the vases to define themselves. Clearly the evidence does not allow absolute certainty that Athenian painted pottery was intended for and used in *symposion*.

We turn now to a brief survey of the main scholarly views on the likelihood that Athenian *symposion* was the intended and actual primary locus for the use of figural pottery. A majority of scholars believe that this pottery was used in Athenian *symposia*, in elite masculine convivial events much like those depicted on vases. Many follow in general terms an argument developed by Webster in the 1970s, which amasses considerable evidence to support the hypothesis that figural pottery was actually commissioned by Athenian elites for specific celebratory *symposia*.[1]

The most widely held minority opinion is based on the fact that the majority of preserved Athenian figural pottery comes from documented archaeological contexts at Etruscan sites in Italy. Some scholars maintain, therefore, that Athenian painted pottery was made for the Etruscan market to suit Etruscan tastes, and its use as a document to interpret Athenian social history must take that into account.[2] A second view, espoused by Hoffman, hypothesizes that painted pots in shapes apparently designed for mixing, pouring, and consuming wine were not ever used in Athenian *symposia* but stood in as substitutes in funerary and votive situations for the valuable metal examples that were in fact used in *symposia*.[3] A third view, articulated by Vickers and Gill, maintains that Athenian elites most commonly used vessels in precious metal at *symposia*, and black- and red-figure vases were imitations of these vessels.[4] In their view, the main category of evidence for reconstructing elite *symposion*, metal vessels, is therefore lacking. Because they believe that red- and black-figure vases were direct copies of metal originals, Vickers and Gill would presumably support the use of painted vases in reconstructing aspects of *symposion*, but would see them as stand-ins for the lost evidence of metal vases. The implication of these minority viewpoints is that it is incorrect to try to understand vase-imagery and, specifically, the results of repetition in that imagery in terms of elite Athenian *symposion*. Consideration of archaeological evidence invites another view.

Archaeological Evidence for the Use of Pottery in Greek *Symposia*

A survey of the archaeological evidence in both Greece and Etrutria points to the conclusion that Athenians and other Greeks used painted pottery in *symposia*, and it suggests at the same time that Etruscans had a variety of uses to which they put it, none definitely sympotic. In Greece, evidence from at least five sites assures us that sympotic vessels, such as kraters, cups, and oinochoai, were used in settings of both public and private conviviality. In the Athenian Agora, debris from a magistrates' public dining place produced a very large number of red-figure kraters as well as pouring vessels and drinking cups.[5] Although this was a public dining place, there is substantial evidence that elite behavior and mores, anchored in the private sphere, dominated.[6] Elsewhere in the Athenian Agora is a deposit from a household well that preserves mixing bowls and drinking cups.[7] The Dema House, in the Attic countryside, preserved a room that may have been an *andron*, and among the pottery finds from the house are two red-figure kraters, two black-glaze amphoras, two black-glaze olpai, and at least twenty-eight black-glaze drinking vessels.[8] Elsewhere in Greece, at the northern sites of Torone and Olynthus, excavations have yielded substantial evidence for similar vessels along with architectural evidence for sympotic spaces.[9] The sympotic shapes found at Olynthus duplicate those from the Dema House.[10] "Sets" of red-figure and black-glaze pottery were found in various rooms in houses at Olynthus; Cahill identifies at least three such sets that included kraters along with other eating and serving vessels.[11] There is little doubt that some inhabitants of Olynthus used red-figure pottery in houses that included specially designed rooms for *symposion*, but the picture is not at all clear. Overall, evidence for figural sympotic shapes is rare enough so that scholars studying the material from the site have concluded they were indeed used in domestic contexts, but not commonly. There are only nine red-figure cups total from the site, and of these only six were found outside of graves. Only two of the forty-four kraters were recovered in an *andron* or its anteroom. The majority of kraters came from houses lacking an explicitly outfitted *andron*, a room specially outfitted for dining on couches and not easily serving a secondary purpose; the houses whose plans include luxuriously dedicated *andrones* were much less likely to produce pottery kraters (out of thirty-one total houses with *andrones*, five produced kraters together with an *andron*). Apparently, sympotic ware for the rich houses at Olynthus was most commonly made of precious metal and these vessels were removed by fleeing residents or looters after Philip's destruction of the site in 348 B.C. Despite its scarcity, nevertheless, figural pottery is attested in archeological contexts where *symposia* were celebrated. At a minimum, the evidence from Attica, Torone, and Olynthus informs us that any minority viewpoint holding that Athenian painted pottery was not used in elite *symposia* is too extreme.

Vase-Shapes and *Symposia*

It is also important to acknowledge that not all black- and red-figure vases were necessarily made with sympotic use in mind. Many "special use" Athenian shapes had very specific and dedicated functions that are not apparently or at least not exclusively sympotic. Oil-carrying shapes such as Panathenaic prize amphoras or white-ground lekythoi with funerary iconography are two good examples. Perhaps surprisingly, loutrophoroi and lebetes gamikoi appear to have held water for cleansing a corpse or for a prenuptial bath, yet both appear along with sympotic shapes at the Dema House and in the magistrates' dining-room debris in the Athenian Agora. At Olynthos, a lebes gamikos was found in an assemblage that included a krater. These funeral- and wedding-related shapes may have served as a backdrop for commensal events related to celebrations of marriage and death. Choes for the Anthesteria and krateriskoi for the cult of Artemis Brauronia are some other obvious examples of specifically Attic special-use vases; their cult-specific uses may have included communal drinking events, essentially or at least formally sympotic.[12] Other special use vessels overlap more closely with the sympotic repertory as well. For example, Karouzou has published a grave group from Athens that includes a red-figure skyphos and a pelike. In her discussion Karouzou cites two other pelikai that were likely to have been special-ordered for a funeral, because they are much larger than is typical to accommodate the human remains buried in them.[13] Her argument maintains that exaggerated forms of some sympotic shapes could have a dedicated purpose in the funerary realm.[14] Scheibler has made the well-argued proposal that the black-figure belly amphora acquired some of its unique properties of shape and decoration as the result of its central role, possibly as a prize vessel, in the Athenian Apaturia.[15] A final example is a group of eighteen fragmentary oinochoai, a good wine-pouring shape demonstrably present at symposia, almost all of which depict the chariot of Athena and were excavated in the Athenian Agora in the late 1930s.[16] Although the number of vessels is small, these oinochoai constitute a "Type" as defined in Chapter 3. Green hypothesized that these vessels may have been used in a cult to Athena Hippias, probably for pouring wine in the communal drinking elements of the ritual, in formal terms, essentially *symposia*.[17] In conclusion, several "special-use" pottery-groups, including large-sized pelikes, black-figure belly-amphoras, choes, oinochoai, and krateriskoi, are also connected with the storage or serving of wine despite the fact that they do not appear to have had a primary function in typical all-male drinking parties. We return to the subject of what vases shapes were used in *symposion* below, to deal with the unusual cases of red-figure belly amphoras and hydrias.

Was Attic Figural Pottery Made for the Etruscans?

Another important point of view places front and center the very large role played by Etruscans as buyers of Athenian pottery. This view draws support from the sheer quantity of evidence from Etruscan contexts and from a few cases where it is quite clear that Athenian craftsmen *did* tailor their products to the Etruscan market. Various quantitative studies, admittedly based on partial information, estimate that as much as 70% of extant Athenian pottery with known provenience went to Etruscan buyers.[18] Such a viewpoint also maintains that the craftsmen's knowledge of Etruscans as consumers brought about alterations in the imagery and shape of Attic pottery in ways that reduce its value as historical documents for Athens.[19] Certainly, some shapes and image-programs created by Athenian artists are wholly or partially intended to respond to Etruscan tastes.[20] Stissi, in an accessible and sober review of the evidence for Athenian pottery in Etruria, points out how small the number of documented adaptations of Athenian craft products for the Etruscan market really is.[21] Although it is possible to see how even a very Athenian pot can have some meaning, if not the primary intended meaning, in many Etruscan contexts, there is no need to believe that all imagery in all its nuances had to be understood by the Etruscans to be desirable to them; the intended readers could be members of the Athenian elite although the product remained appealing to an Etruscan farmer, an Athenian dweller in the Dema House, a member of the Etruscan elite, or an Athenian general.[22] A Panathenaic prize amphora is a good example of a vase created in very specifically Athenian terms that had meaning in Etruscan contexts.[23] A vessel that could only be won by an Athenian could apparently serve also as an appropriate Etruscan dedication.

Archaeological evidence confirms that in general Etruscans used typical Athenian black- and red-figure pottery in their own adaptive way without apparently *requiring* any particular changes in shapes or iconography. Overall, the Athenian pottery found in Etruria is very similar to what the Athenians produced for themselves. For example, the roster of painters and workshops whose wares appear in the excavations of the Athenian Agora has a great deal of overlap with the list of those Athenian craftsmen whose pottery has been excavated in Etruria; Reusser's recent comprehensive study of imported Attic red- and black-figure pottery in Etruria lists eighty-three Athenian painters and/or workshops, and of these, sixty-two are also represented in publications from the Athenian Agora alone.[24] There are no significant differences in shape or iconography between Agora products that remain in Greece and those that are exported.

Athenian pottery appears to have been used by a broad spectrum of social classes and in a wide diversity of Etruscan contexts, including tomb, sanctuary, and house, in both urban centers and the countryside.[25] Once Attic pottery reached the Etruscans, they did not always use it in the same ways as the Athenians, and within Etruria pottery played different roles in different Etruscan communities. The important Etruscan site of Veii has produced almost no Attic pottery, whereas Vulci alone has produced nearly 50% of the total.[26] Several recent studies of the distribution of Athenian pottery in Etruria suggest that the Athenian pottery used to furnish tombs appears to have filled gaps in the shape-repertory of locally produced pottery. Etruscans who have a particular shape, such a plate or oinochoe, available in their locally produced repertory of nonfigural fine-ware or in bucchero do not use imported Attic versions of that shape.[27] In tombs, at least some Etruscans used Attic pottery much differently than even elite Athenians at the Kerameikos cemetery in Athens. Whereas some recently excavated tombs at Vulci contain both Attic cups and amphoras in large numbers, a group of tombs of the same period from the Kerameikos in Athens have no pottery decorated in black and red figure except for black-figure lekythoi.[28] We do not know if Etruscans used Attic pottery in convivial events like *symposia*. Reusser believes that the Athenian or Athenian-like vessels represented in Etruscan tomb paintings were actually used in Etruscan banquets;[29] Small, however, believes that only metal vessels were used by the Etruscans and any figural pottery made of clay served only to enhance the setting of *symposion*. As evidence for this view, Small points out that in tomb paintings the figural pottery is not being used by the participants, but is always displayed on *kylikeia*, wooden shelves that furnish the banquet space.[30] Reusser makes the point that many of the most popular subjects of Athenian vase-imagery would have been easily understandable in Etruria – *symposion* and *komos*, Dionysiac scenes, fight scenes, departure of warriors, athletes, and scenes involving Herakles – even if the subtleties were lost on the Etruscan audience.[31] There is, in sum, no evidence to support the view that Attic figural pottery was significantly adapted to suit an Etruscan consumer.

The preceding review does not turn up any new evidence proving that the ideal use-context for much Athenian painted pottery is the Athenian *symposion*, but it does affirm that a convincing case can be made for such a claim. There is no support for an alternative to the position that these vases were intended for and actually used in Athenian *symposion* and, therefore, that in general imagery on vessels had an intended viewer other than an elite Athenian.[32] Archaeological evidence in Greece and in Athens in particular confirms that clay vessels were used in *symposia*. The imagery that appealed to Athenian elites worked well, or well enough, for a broad range of Greeks and Etruscans. Although recognizing that Athenian figural pottery may have had diverse use-contexts, this discussion will focus on the Athenian *symposion*-setting as the one in which the vases reverberate.[33] This discussion will make it clear that repetition on vases achieves effects perfectly suited to Athenian *symposion* as we know it from archaeological and literary testimony. These effects fit neatly into a complex of redundant cultural messages emanating specifically from *symposion*.

DEFINING *SYMPOSION* AS SETTING[34]

We can turn now to a brief review of what we know about *symposion* as an elite institution in Athens. Vetta provides a succinct description of Greek *symposion* that relies on textual and archaeological evidence:

> From its very first appearance, the *symposion* can be defined by certain constants to which other ingredients were sometimes added. It was a meeting of men that took place only following a meal. It had a ritual introduction with libations to the gods and the choral singing of the paean. It was not an everyday event but was linked to private or civic celebrations. The participants were

> related in various ways, rarely based on merely family ties, sharing the same life-style and behaving according to norms they regarded as specific to their ethnic group.
> Among its other ingredients, the most frequent and significant was poetry... Other important ingredients were games, courtship, the education of youths, and the continuation of the *symposion* in the form of the *komos* when the participants left the dining room as a group.[35]

Murray expands on this definition. He defines "*symposion*" in venues that include both public and private settings: the drinking that followed a meal and accompanied "public civic or sacrificial meal [as well as] (in) the activities of smaller exclusive groups (presumably in their houses)."[36] Evidence from the Athenian Agora supports his view: there is unequivocal evidence that painted pottery in shapes appropriate for *symposia* has been found in contexts that are both public, a magistrates' mess-hall or *syssition*, and private, houses near and distant from the civic space. The drinking ware found in the Agora is identical to that found in private houses.[37]

Lissarrague would agree with Murray that public and private *symposia* share essential characteristics. For example, he cites as a typical drinking space the dining rooms where the cult of Artemis was carried out at Brauron, and he mentions an offering in a public sanctuary at Sigeum;[38] yet much of the literary evidence he uses, including both Xenophon's and Plato's *Symposium*, refers to *symposia* that take place in private houses. From the understanding of *symposion* provided by Vetta, Murray, and Lissarrague, we have a basic understanding of the components of *symposion* and a sense of how thoroughly it is simultaneously a feature of private, civic, and religious life in ancient Athens.

Evidence for Vase-Shapes Used in *Symposia*

A distinctive feature of Lissarrague's assessment of *symposion* is its reliance on vase shapes and vase images depicting *symposion* to define the phenomenon. In essence, this study is using the same categories of evidence to understand further the relationship between setting and vessels to produce more information about *symposion* as a social phenomenon. Because we have established that there are Athenian vases, such as prize vessels and funerary lekythoi, with special use functions that do not appear to be directly sympotic, it is important to be as certain as possible that the shapes considered in the present discussion are in fact intended for sympotic use. Many of the vase shapes, primarily mixing bowls and pouring and drinking vessels, that appear in sympotic archaeological contexts appear also in the vase-imagery depicting *symposia*, and these have loomed large in the present discussion. However, scholars have noted the absence of hydrias and amphoras in painted scenes of *symposion* on

Athenian vases; this is a striking absence, because these shapes held water (hydrias) and, at least in some cases, wine (amphoras), the two ingredients mixed in the krater to produce the *sine qua non* of *symposion*.[39] Is it acceptable therefore for us to consider the results of repetition on hydrias and amphoras as providing information on a sympotic use-context?

A large part of the discussion here has relied on amphoras in particular. There are a few examples of amphoras in scenes related to *symposion*, but these are rare; for example, in a mid-sixth century Lydan krater in New York, we see a satyr pouring wine from a one-piece amphora, apparently without figural decoration but with broad red bands on the lower belly and the exterior of the rim, into a richly decorated black-figure volute-krater.[40] Such scenes, even mythical, are extremely rare; more utilitarian unpainted or black-glaze amphoras, used as storage containers for wine, are more common both in *symposion* scenes on vases and in archaeological contexts.[41] Moreover, scenes of *symposion*, so common on cups and kraters, are almost nonexistent in the image-repertory on amphoras. Despite this bleak picture, I believe there is substantial evidence that both hydrias and amphoras are enmeshed in sympotic discourse, evidence that overrides their almost total absence in images of *symposion*.

It is very clear that some belly-amphoras held wine, because images of belly amphoras *on* both belly-amphoras and other vessels so indicate. The Lydan example in New York just mentioned is one example. The images on vases attributed to the Amasis Painter also suggest that the shape was connected to wine and to Dionysos; not only is the divinity popular in the Amasis Painter's scenes on amphoras, but we also see him in contexts where wine is dipped out of belly-amphoras.[42] Although these are not scenes of mortal symposia, they show Dionysos, satyrs, and nymphs in their versions of wine consumption and *komos*, which are related on countless other red- and black-figure examples to mortal symposiasts and komasts.

Discussion throughout the previous chapters has shown that inscriptions on amphoras focus on an important aspect of sympotic activity, its pederastic component. In fact, in consulting Beazley's lists of *kalos*-inscriptions, a surprising statistic emerges: black-figure amphoras preserve more *kalos* inscriptions than any other black-figure shape, and, in red-figure, amphoras rank third to cups and lekythoi in the frequency of such inscriptions.[43] For these reasons – that amphoras are connected with the storage of wine and they carry *kalos*-inscriptions – they are included in this discussion, despite the fact that they are not commonly depicted in use in *symposia* on vases, and their presence is not apparently essential for *symposia*, from the evidence of archaeological assemblages of sympotic pottery. The results of repetition found on amphoras are more closely paralleled on cups, a shape demonstrably used in and central to *symposia* both in images and in the archaeological evidence, than on any other shape. If black-figure belly-amphoras were, as Scheibler suggests, prizes at festivals like the Apatouria, perhaps they were displayed at *symposia* that were tied to those special occasions whether or not they were holding the wine to be mixed with water consumed that evening.

Hydrias are also rare, if not totally absent, in images of *symposion*. Yet for hydrias, too, there is substantial evidence that decoration reflects sympotic mores. A scene of satyrs making wine on a black-figure amphora by the Amasis Painter shows a satyr pouring water from a hydria into a pithos.[44] Hydrias appear very frequently in the archaeological record with kraters and cups, and again black-figure examples preserve a very high percentage of the *kalos* inscriptions listed by Beazley: thirty-one on black-figure hydrias, second only to amphoras.[45] Figural scenes on hydrias include very prominently scenes of women at fountain-houses, and some scholars have hypothesized that this fact stands in the way of their being sympotic; recent discussion takes another point of view, that such women-only scenes, often depicting women dancing and otherwise uninhibited, are in fact erotic, a kind of soft-core pornography, and therefore very appropriate for *symposia*.[46] The high incidence of *kale* inscriptions on black-figure hydrias reinforces this hypothesis.[47] Some red-figure hydrias preserve scenes of male *symposia*.[48] In summary, there is substantial reason to include amphoras and hydrias, where repetition is everywhere prominent, with kraters, cups, and related shapes having more than one decorative field in a discussion of how messages on painted pottery sent by way of repetition are echoed and reinforced in the activities and setting of *symposion*.

Vases in Sympotic Space

A discussion of messages sent ought to address the setting of message reception. Who could see the vases and in what surroundings? It is important to establish the physical realities of that space and to assume that vase-painters were very aware of it.[49] The archaeological evidence for the space used for public – "ritual" and "civic" – and private dining is variable. Houses regularly have rectangular dining rooms, as do many public eating places, and both are often outfitted for couches, confirming that participants reclined.[50] The two standard configurations, seven- and eleven-couch dining rooms, are substantial in size: the smaller is 4.5 meters (14.76 feet) on a side with a diagonal of 6.4 meters (almost 21 feet) and the larger is 6.5 meters (21.265 feet) on a side with a diagonal of 9.2 meters (30.185 feet). "Conversation" was actually more akin to speechmaking. The substantial distance from corner to corner was probably not totally inhibiting for spoken activity, but it would preclude intimate conversation with anyone except the individual(s) at a neighboring couch or with whom one shared a couch.[51] A cup by Douris suggests that the painter had the setting of the *andron* very much in mind, since he represents accurately a very specific visual perspective that a reclining participant would have.[52] The images depict the point of view of a reclining symposiast along the long wall to the left of the doorway to an *andron* [Figure 11.1]. Each side of the cup shows three adult men on couches. Two couches and their occupants are displayed full-length as though seen by a viewer looking directly across the room. A third couch, the one to the right of the doorway to the room, is shown from behind its "head" as though the viewer is standing at its "pillow end," looking at the back view of the shoulders of the symposiast who reclines on it. The images portray accurately what one would see from a real position in the room. Again, this level of accuracy in the visual perspective represented suggests that artists were well aware of the space in which the vessels were used.

What were the opportunities for visual inspection of the vessels used for preparation and drinking of wine under such conditions?[53] Surely it would have been rather difficult to examine a full wine cup, but easy to do so with one that was empty. A drinker and his couch mate would be able to conduct a very close inspection. Vessels hanging on the wall, as depicted in Figure 11.1, would reveal part if not all of their decorative program. A krater placed in the center of the room would be harder to see, visible from the couches at a minimum distance of 10–15 feet. In both cases, an individual and his immediate neighbors could see easily both sides of a cup and occasional views of an oinochoe, but would have a fairly fixed view of one side of a krater. Prize vases, wedding-related vessels, and other shapes not actually used in *symposion* could be in the sympotic environment on display, either in the anteroom to the *andron* or in the room itself on *kylikeia*, open cupboards, although the latter are rarely if ever depicted on Athenian vases or documented in archaeological contexts.

We have established in Chapter 4 that there is a good case to be made for the view held by several scholars that inscriptions were at times read aloud in *symposion*. For N. Slater, an essential part of the sympotic discussion or performance is the reading out of inscriptions, and he believes this reading out might have prompted further conversation.[54] Slater follows a number of scholars who project close and careful analysis of pottery as part of how symposiasts interacted with these polyvalent implements.[55] Lissarrague, for example, postulates that drinkers "... who recognize the painted scenes and their own likenesses in the mirror of the vases" reacted expressly to the images.[56]

Classical literary accounts of *symposia*, to the extent that these can provide us with reliable evidence for the Archaic and Early Classical periods, do not confirm that participants took notice of imagery on vessels used, and comments about these vessels are actually minimal.[57] Indeed, remarks on visual images at all are quite rare in literary *symposia*.[58] In Plato's *Symposium*, participants do refer to images on monuments that are not present: Aristophanes to sculpted reliefs [193a] and Alcibiades to statues of Silenus [215b, 216d, 221e]; in Xenophon's *Symposium*. Critobolus refers to painted or sculpted portraits [IV.21]. Yet nonliterary clues do exist that vessels were coordinated to complement the actual setting, the content of sympotic discussion, and the ethos of *symposion* in a very direct way.

The vase-decoration itself includes many scenes that reflect an idealized version of an actual *symposion* taking place, and these scenes include some of the vessels used. Lissarrague discusses sympotic scenes that feature kraters on a number of different shapes including cup, pelike, krater, hydria, and oinochoe.[59] Ornament on vases repeats designs also integrated elsewhere in the setting. For example, at Olynthus in the late

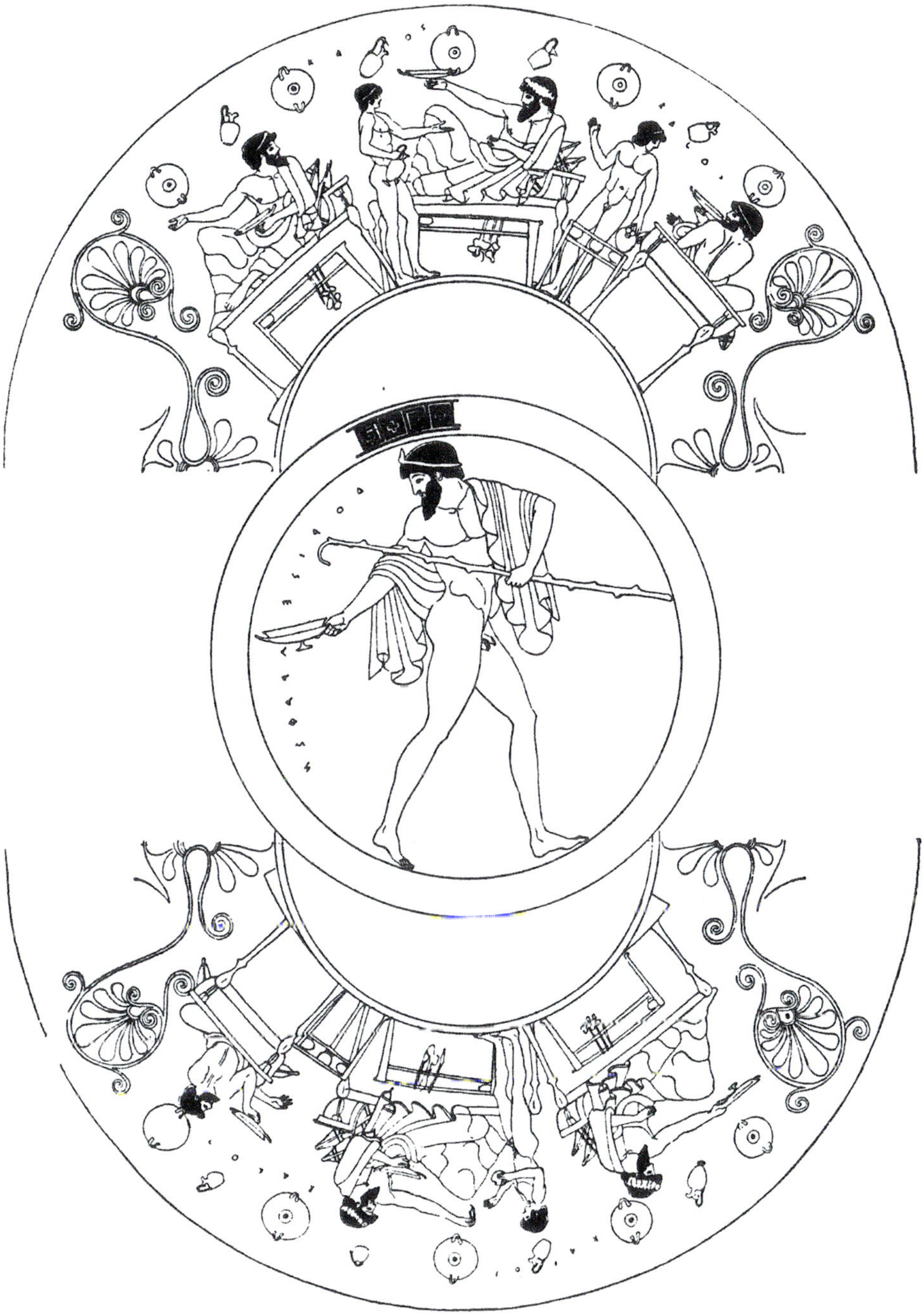

11.1. Red-figure cup by Douris, ca. 480–470 B.C. Side A, Side B, and Interior. London, British Museum E 49. Drawing, *Wiener Vorlegeblätter*, VI

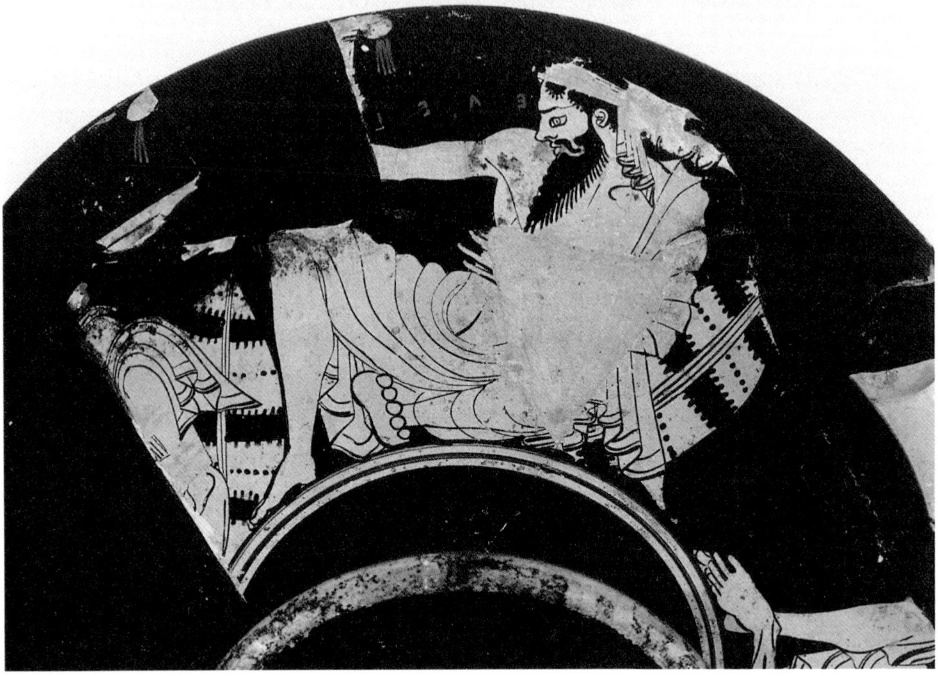

11.2. Red-figure cup by Onesimos, ca. 510–490 B.C. Side A. Munich, Staatliche Antikensammlungen und Glyptothek 2636. (Photograph © Staatliche Antikensammlungen und Glyptothek München [Neg.-Nr. S. 3230].)

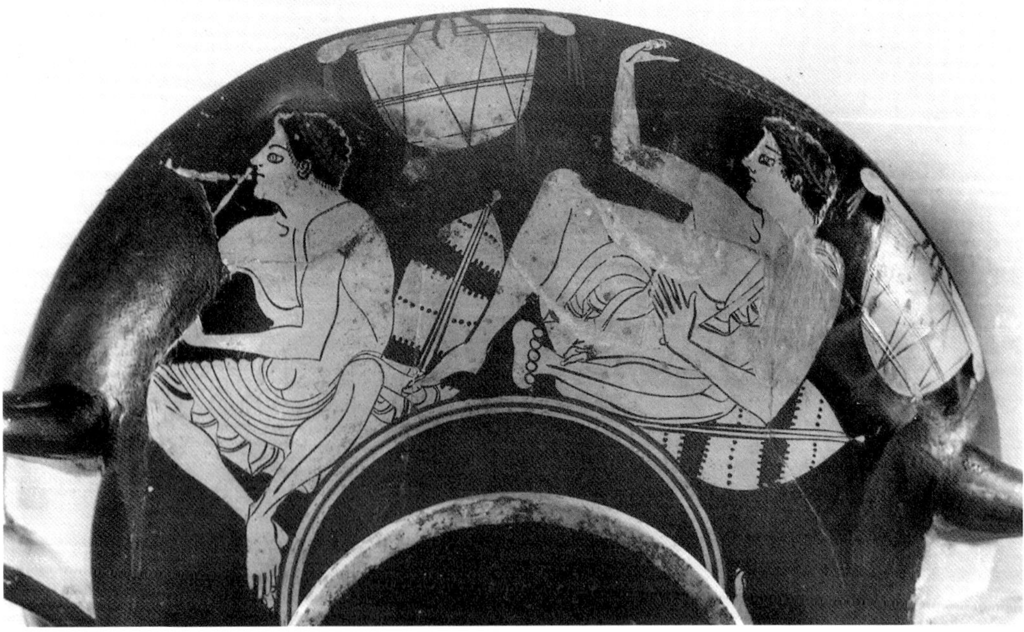

11.3. Red-figure cup by Onesimos, ca. 510–490 B.C. Side B. Munich, Staatliche Antikensammlungen und Glyptothek 2636. (Photograph © Staatliche Antikensammlungen und Glyptothek München.)

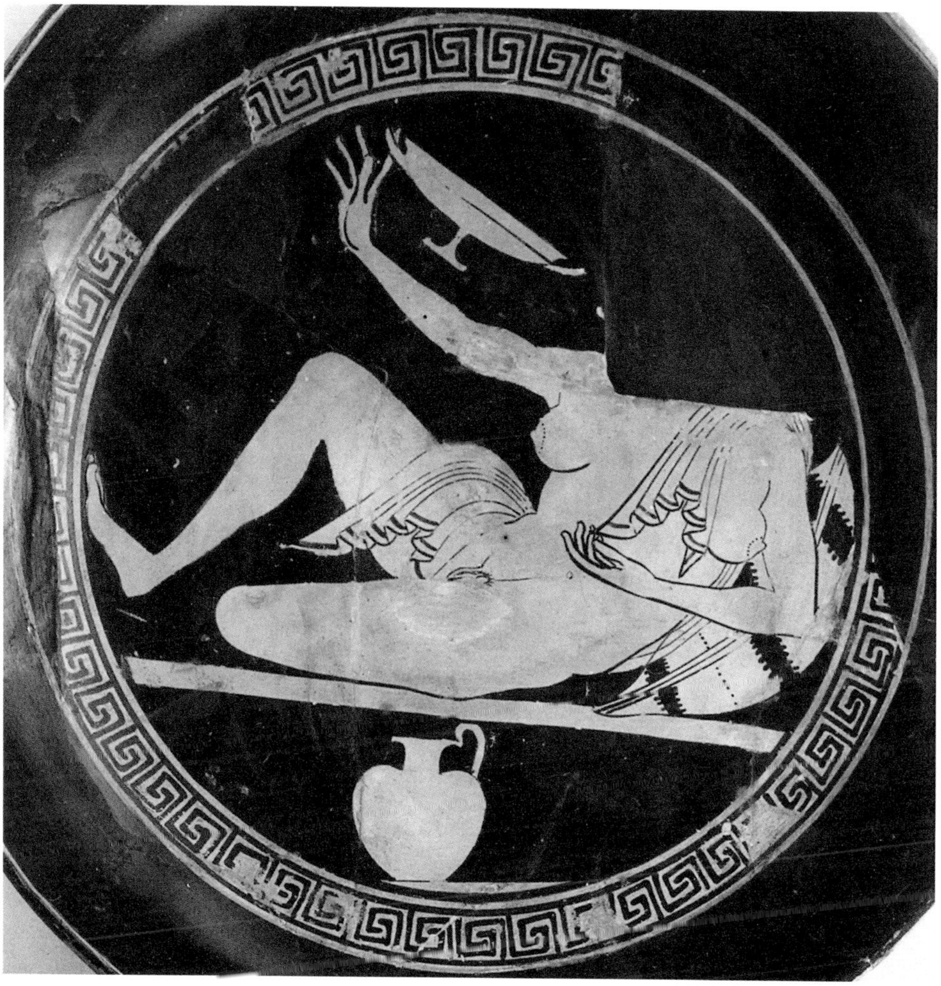

11.4. Red-figure cup by Onesimos, ca. 510–490. Interior. Munich, Staatliche Antikensammlungen und Glyptothek 2636. (Photograph © Staatliche Antikensammlungen und Glyptothek München [Neg.-Nr. S. 3229].)

fifth–early fourth century, mosaics in dining rooms repeat ornament seen on vases, further linking the vessels to the context in which they are used. The oblique palmette on the mosaic from the Villa of Good Fortune finds abundant parallels in earlier fifth-century examples such as a calyx crater by the Phiale Painter, dating to the second quarter of the fifth century.[60] These same motifs must also have appeared on tapestries hanging on walls or covering pillows and even on the participants' clothing.[61]

Here we turn to a brief analysis of three examples to illustrate the interconnections among images on vessels, the actual setting of *symposion* in the *andron*, and the events that constitute sympotic activity and entertainment. A cup by Onesimos depicts a painted idealized *symposion* and includes texts of poetic performance[62] [Figures 11.2–11.4]. An adult male on A extends a cup very like the one on which it appears, while apparently reciting a word from a line like Pindar's *O.* 9, 47, ΕΓΕΙ[ΡΕ],[63] "arouse..." or "awaken..."; his counterpart and visual analogue on B, a youth, holds the μυρρίνη, the myrtle branch, and declares Κ[ΑΛΟ]ΣΕΙ, "You are handsome." A third element of a typical *symposion* appears in the interior, where a nude female, posed very much like her fellow adult (A) and youthful (B) colleagues, utters the formulaic ΤΟΙΤΕΝ[ΔΕ] "For you," as she prepares to make a *kottabos*-fling. The cup she holds by one handle is again very like that which the scenes decorate. The youth and the *hetaira* may be parodies of "correct" behavior, because the youth ought to be called *kalos*, rather than naming another as such, and the *hetaira* is more correctly the object of a *kottabos* toast than its originator. Repeated cushions, cups, and poses connect three different types of participant – adult men, youths, and a *hetaira* – in one location, all using sympotic implements. Each type is then paired with typical speech or its parody: an amorous game for the *hetaira*, a *kalos*-declaration for the youth, and poetry for the adult man. In combination, the three scenes on the cup show different facets of the sympotic experience, as do many examples explored in the discussion of point-of-view and analysis of experience in Chapter 8, and the cups depicted in the scenes reproduce the shape of the drinking vessel the scenes decorate.

A second example, from a well-known class of "Anakreontic" vases, displaying male figures dressed in *sakkoi* and holding parasols, links two stages of a convivial evening, *symposion* and *komos*, via repetition of a lyre, a *sakkos*, and an ivy wreath worn by male participants.[64] The *symposion* scene includes two types of musicians, a flute player and a lyre player. The text on A, the *symposion*-scene, emanates from a singer's mouth. The text is reconstructed by Immerwahr as [Π]ΕΝΙΗΣ, and is connected by him to Theognis 1129:

> Ἐμπίομαι πενίης θυμοφθόρου οὐ μελεδαίνων
> I'll drink my fill, ignore soul-grinding poverty. (Translation West)[65]

Immerwahr suggests that the word [Π]ΕΝΙΗΣ serves as a title for the scene and is intended to relate the content of the poem to the scene depicted.[66] A second inscription on A, ΑΙΡΕ, is restored by Immerwahr as the greeting, *khaire*, and it appears, appropriately in a very self-referential way, on a cup held by one of the symposiasts. Additionally, the label ΑΝΑΚΡΕ[...] for "Anakreon," a poet whose verse is sung to lyre accompaniment, appears on one arm of the lyre held by a komast on B, together with ΙΟΟΟ, a "conventional rendering of the sounds of music."[67] Here greetings, poetry, and its musical accompaniment appear in combination with two phases of the "story" of a social event, an elaborate *symposion* followed by *komos*.

It is pertinent at this point to return briefly to an example considered in detail in Chapter 8, which serves as a good transition from this discussion of visual links between sympotic vessel and setting to a consideration of how pottery advances one of the overarching social functions of *symposion*, its role in enculturation. The cup in Berlin by Douris displays facets of school[68] [Figures 8.22, 8.23]. Students learn music and poetry, and wine cups hang on the wall of the school room. The wine cup views education exclusively through a lens of sympotic values and activity, bringing a scene of preparation for sympotic participation into the *symposion* itself.

The communicative function of these repetitions among setting, activities, and vessel is essentially metadiscursive and phatic. The repetitions open channels of communication and then inform the participant that there is a common message associating his own behavior with the setting and the implements for the consumption of wine. Setting and vessel mirror one another, and the images provide permanent visual and verbal records of what is said and done in *symposion*.

A SOCIAL PURPOSE FOR READING VASES IN ELITE *SYMPOSIA*

Paradigm and *Paideia*

In this section, we will investigate one specific category of messages produced by repetitions on vases, paradigms, and how they reverberate in *symposion*. The previous discussion has made clear how often vase-painters construct paradigms through repetition throughout the period considered here, from the early sixth century to the early fifth. Positive and negative paradigms, comparing elites to divinities, heroes, and other mortals, are created. Events involving heroes and divinities are cited as paradigmatic predecessors to important mortal rituals. Overall, paradigm-creation results in setting out the experiences of heroes as important guideposts to human values and behavior.

These ancestral models that appear as paradigms achieved through repetition on vases are also collectively the cornerstone of Greek education or *paideia*.[69] Scholars have amassed a great deal of both visual and written evidence showing that youths received this education not only at school and in the gymnasium but when they were present at *symposion*, observing the behaviors of their elders.[70] Literary works, including poetry performed at *symposion*, and the accounts of *symposia* written by Xenophon and Plato offer abundant testimony to this phenomenon. The cup by Douris, discussed above and in Chapter 8 and *used* at the *symposion*, is typical of a larger group that are more overt about the centrality of verse in education because they show youths at school learning what we know to be poetry of types also performed at *symposia*[71] [Figures 8.22–8.33]. The verse one youth learns from a scroll held by his teacher is Homeric or at least epic, including reference to the Scamander.[72] Such Homeric paradigms learned in school are later performed and heard again in *symposion*.[73] Although the setting of the scene appears to be wholly "classroom," there are proleptic props hanging from the walls, cups as well as musical instruments, that connect the scene with *symposion*. Education includes learning poetry for its paradigmatic value as well as for its performance.[74] The goal of the next section is to look carefully to see how the results of repetition on vases run parallel to the literary testimony on the content and process of *paideia* and how paradigm on vases plays out as a paideutic feature of *symposion*.

Symposion as Locus for *Paideia*

For ancient Athenians, paradigmatic ancestral models are usually conveyed in stories, and models are imparted through the action of the characters. Together with these paradigmatic actions is projected the distillation of experience through proverbs, maxims, and other gnomic expressions.[75] Not only were these paradigms and conventional wisdom material for coming generations to learn the parameters of their social roles, but they also served as a kind of continuing education, a set of rules of how to act, for adults. Such paradigms serve as analogies to provide guidance in daily settings and, almost assuredly, in legal disputes as well.[76]

Evidence on vases for the citation of ancestral models in *symposion* actually precedes the evidence considered in this study by well over a century, and the first examples are not figural. When the black-figure artists of the early sixth century create visual paradigms, they are therefore working in a very long tradition. Robb's observations on the oldest preserved example of a so-called "long" inscription in Greek writing, a hexameter inscription on a Geometric oinochoe, c. 750 B.C., reveal many similarities to the way visual mythic paradigms are expressed through repetition on Archaic vases.

The inscription on the so-called Dipylon oinochoe reads, *h*ΟΣΝΥΝΟΡΧΕΣΤΟ ΝΠΑΝΤΟΝΑΤΑΛΟΤΑΤΑΠΑΙΖΕΙ ΤΟΤΟΔΕΚΛ[.]MIN[. . .] or "Whoso now of all the dancers most playfully sports . . ."[77] Robb demonstrates that both meter and vocabulary are Homeric.[78] Further, he hypothesizes that the precise Homeric referent for the inscription is Alkinous' summons to young males to dance at the *symposion* after the feast in *Odyssey* VIII. 248–9. Confirming the Homeric precedent, Powell notes the structural similarity between the Dipylon inscription and *Odyssey* VIII.382.[79] Based on compelling parallels, Robb concludes that the Dipylon oinochoe was an improvised prize given at a private *symposion*.[80] Further, he hypothesizes that the words of the inscription record a proclamation actually delivered by the host. What is most striking about Robb's reconstruction is the degree to which the citation of the Homeric precedent is made explicit through the meter and vocabulary of the inscription.[81] In the making of this connection, a mythic paradigm is assimilated to the present, and it thereby becomes a tool of *paideia*. It taught the assembled company that there was a heroic prototype for their *symposion*.

Other early inscriptions, the "Nestor cup" from Pithekoussai and the "*xenos* oinochoe" from Ithaca, both sympotic shapes, have similar evocations of Homeric precedent and the possibility of similar paideutic applications.[82] Thomas suggests that the not-quite-metrical hexameter verse on the Nestor cup is essentially parodic as well, a light-hearted reference making fun of the reverence accorded to the esteemed symbol of wealth, age, and power that Homer bestows on the cup of Nestor in his text.[83] Instead, this inscription is making fun of the vaunted object by claiming for it aphrodisiac powers. After declaring in the first line, ΝΕΣΤΟΡΟΣ: Ε[ΙΜ]Ι: ΕΥΠΟΤ[ΟΝ]: ΠΟΤΕΡΙΟ[Ν] or "of Nestor, I am (or "I belong to Nestor) a delight to drink from," with its second line, "whoever drinks from this cup, straightway the desire of beautifully crowned Aphrodite shall seize," the author calls to mind the curse formula, "Whoever does/takes this. . . ."[84] As a result, there are two levels of parody. First, attaching Homer's epic reverence for a masterpiece in precious metal to a humble clay vessel is humorous. Second, the warning parodies the character of a curse, but its effect is hardly harmful. The appearance of parody as a result of repetition is well-established in this discussion, and its role in intra-elite competition in sympotic discourse is taken up again later here.

This look at the early inscriptions on vases confirms *symposion* is a locus where heroic sympotic predecessors are reproduced, creating an excellent forum for the dissemination of mythical paradigm and for its explicit connection to a present situation. The later figural examples of paradigm-creation considered here (Chapter 7) follow in this tradition. Robb's suggestion that the paradigmatic inscription on the Dipylon oinochoe was created in relation to a particular *symposion* inspires us to ask if *symposia* held in conjunction with specific occasions such as weddings or important civic rituals might have inspired the use of vases with myth-images appropriate to the instigating event to serve as exempla for it. Scheibler's study of the iconography of the black-figure belly amphora, which she sees as closely tied to the Apatouria, provides a good example.[85] If boys received belly amphoras to mark the successful rite of passage, the prize vessel would be displayed, decorated with appropriate paradigms, in the space of the *symposion*. The Judgment of Paris paradigms created in the workshop of Lydos would be appropriate jocular paradigmatic backdrops to a *symposion* held in connection with a wedding.[86]

Literary Evidence for Paradigm

Paradigmatic imagery echoes the connection between "then" and "now" made in the poetry performed at *symposion* and inscriptions on vases.[87] Evidence of poetry performed at *symposion* and literary accounts of *symposia* are full of examples where a mortal situation is connected to a prior mythical paradigm. Here we will review a few of these poetic examples to reconstruct the performance aspect of the sympotic context for paradigm as expressed on vases. The poetry collected in the *Theognidae*, deeply embued with a sympotic ethos, includes implied and overt mythical paradigms.[88] One example is Atalanta, who fled and ran but was ultimately caught from behind; she appears as paradigm for a reluctant *eromenos* (1283–94). Zeus and Ganymede are paradigmatic *erastes* and *eromenos* (1345–50). Theseus and Ajax son of Oileus are mythical examples of the power of Eros to bring victims to their knees (1231–34). Simonides directly connects the victory at Plataea with the victory at Troy.[89] Those who fought at Plataea are contemporary Greeks who are compared to heroic predecessors; at least two scholars reconstruct the occasion for recitation of the elegy to be private and convivial.[90] In literature, sympotic participants express an attitude revealing that Homeric heroes serve as positive role models. A simple example of this mentality is expressed by Niceratus, the pedantic Homer expert at the party described by Xenophon (IV.6):

> So if any of you wants to become an overseer or a politician or a general, or a hero like Achilles, Ajax, and Nestor, or Odysseus, he'd better cultivate my friendship. Because I know all about it.

Finally, many victory odes rely extensively on the construction of mythical paradigms, drawing the accomplishment of the victorious athlete into comparison with a mythical prototype. A case study of one such example follows.

Paradigm Performed in Pindar: A Case Study on Poetic Paradigm and Repetition

It is important to note that scholars do not agree that there is clear evidence for the performance of epinician poetry at *symposia*; indeed, the identification of the nature (choral or solo) and location (temple, sacred precinct, or private dwelling) for performance of victory odes is the subject of intense ongoing scholarly debate, and the evidence is indeed complicated and ambiguous.[91] However, references within the language of the victory odes themselves to performance of such odes in *komos*, understood as a public procession normally part of and usually succeeding a *symposion*, are numerous.[92] In addition, the language of epinician poetry also preserves evidence linking its mode of performance, sung while dancing to the accompaniment of lyre and *aulos*, to *symposion*.[93] Finally, there is evidence that regardless of the circumstances for the initial solo or choral performance, epinician poetry enjoyed reperformance in *symposion* for decades (if not longer) after the initial performance.[94] Therefore, a close look at how one epinician poet uses repetition to create paradigm provides a useful analogy to how artists do the same thing visually on sympotic vessels, because their context for dissemination is very likely overlapping.

Indeed, Pindar regularly compares mortals to heroes as a form of epinician praise.[95] A careful look at *Pythian* 6 suggests that in addition to the link between (the son of the) victor and heroes at the level of content in the poem, there are repetitions in sound and meter, redundancies, that help the listener connect mortal and heroic. Just as vases go beyond simply presenting mortal and hero in juxtaposed fields to repeat composition, pose, and elements of dress in order to make sure the viewer connects them, the poet provides several levels of repetition to ensure that listeners get his point.[96] In both poem and vase, the paradigm-creation is paralleled in written and visual material, and there is a mutual reliance on repetition to do so.

The last lines of *Pythian* 6 suggest a link between the youth praised in the poem and *symposion* because of a reference to the συμπόται or "fellow symposiasts" of the honorand, Thrasyboulos. The paideutic potential of the poem is clear from the content, but it is further uncovered through Kurke's demonstration of how it is fully informed by the conventions of Hesiodic *hypothekai*, a compendium of collective wisdom that includes directives in the form of gnomic wisdom.[97] Χείρωνος Ὑποθῆκαι or *The Advice of Cheiron* was well-known, apparently even outside of Athens, as a paideutic text for aristocratic youth.[98] This text is integrated into Pindar's ode when Cheiron is identified as having instructed Achilles both to honor Zeus and in addition to honor his own parents (l. 24–7). The poet then sets up the epic hero Antilochos and his filial piety as a paradigm for the youth Thrasyboulos, providing a model for how he might behave towards his father Xenocrates. There are thus two directives that rely on mythical paradigms: Cheiron's advice to Achilles to revere Zeus and to revere his parents as he reveres Zeus; and second, Pindar's own promotion of Antilochos as an exemplum of this kind of behavior, demonstrated when Antilochos laid down his life to save his father, Nestor. Antilochos' action in the story is paradigmatic for Thrasyboulos in its display of filial respect and of courage.

Lines 23–8, which contain the *hypothekai*, provide a formal model for the last lines of the poem, where the honorand is praised, lines 50–54. Thrasyboulos' high status is reiterated in several ways: he receives advice similar to that given to the hero Achilles, and his behavior is like that of another hero, Antilochos. Just as in the images, the simple citation of a paradigm is not enough. Repetitions of meter and sounds act to link as well. Kurke has pointed out that the location of the parallel lines is the same in each strophe.[99] To her observation, we can add that there are additional repetitions in meter and sound. The initial citation of the quoted advice from Cheiron concludes in a pattern of two long syllables followed by two shorts (l. 27). The same pattern concludes the Antilochos paradigm, and these exact repetitions appear in the last two feet of the line (l. 36). The poetic form allows for choices, so the repetition appears to be deliberate. The same metrical pattern also concludes the last line of the poem, the conclusion of the description of Thrasyboulos. Note also that there are repeated *sounds* – the ἀμεί root, a final word beginning with π, and the νον ending – as well as repeated rhythm:

ἀμείρειν γονέων βίον πεπρωμένον l. 27
μελισσᾶν ἀμείβεται τρητὸν πόνον l. 54

The overall effect of the poem rests then in several levels of repetition that we can now repeat and summarize: repetition of the actual words of another poem (the scholia indicate the *Cheiron Hypothekai*, attributed to Hesiod), thereby referencing another poetic genre, one that is aggressively and specifically aristocratic and paideutic, together with content linking mortal with heroic. There are then repetitions on several levels, including meter and sound, drawing the listener into the norms of the comparative act through redundancies of meaning and aural effect. A visual version of this paradigmatic relationship on a vase could be created in several of the ways we reviewed in Chapter 7. Repetition of figures, attributes, and even props would link a scene of Antilochos' brave act to one representing a mortal corollary. Pindar's ode apparently uses a very similar technique, although in his case verbal and metrical repetitions link the statement of the mythical prototype and its application to Thrasybolos. Poems like Pindar's *Pythian* 6 are verbal corollaries to those vessels where paradigm is created visually and rely on repeated lexical items and syntax to link the two comparable scenes.[100]

Narrative, Point of View, Character, and Parody in *Symposion*

Paradigm is not the only product of repetition on vases to have a discernible parallel in the poetry performed at and literary evidence for *symposion*. In the tangential references by the historians, parodies in comedy, descriptions in court speeches, and the literary *symposia* of Plato and Xenophon, there is tantalizing but partial corroboration for virtually all of the results of repetition discussed here. To illustrate this point, we will consider several literary sources that include references to the recounting of narratives, to key components of story-telling, such as point of view and character development, and to evidence of a jocular and parodic *symposion*-ethos. Each of these sections will in turn be complemented with a very brief review of the corresponding features on vases.

Although the literature preserving accounts of *symposia* does not contain many examples of lengthy narratives, there are frequent allusions to stories and story lines. Paradigms are often embedded in stories where behaviors to be emulated or avoided are displayed. The many vases discussed in Chapter 6 that use repetition to display narratives, whether a collection of a hero's adventures, a phased narration, or a series of causally linked events, permanently mirror this facet of ephemeral sympotic activity. Likewise, characteristic features of narrative, such as exploration of several aspects of character or multiple points of views so amply represented in the visual evidence, have parallels demonstrated in the literature performed at and describing sympotic entertainment.

Point of View and Character in Symposion: *Literary Evidence*

Collecting and comparing multiple points of view is the essence of sympotic conversation, as Plato and Xenophon convey it. Men reclining around the periphery of the room select a single topic, and each speaker gives his view of it. Just as each member of the group has a unique visual perspective on the *andron* and the assembled company, each individual will have a unique position on the topic at hand. Homeric epic, which formed the core text for the education necessary to prepare for sympotic participation, regularly explores both perceptual and ideological point of view, using repetition as the springboard for comparison. Integrated into elite mastery of Homer would be familiarity with the poet's methods of exploration of character and both perceptual and ideological point of view. A simple example from Homer is well-illustrated in *Iliad* Book 1. In the proem, the narrator provides an explanation for the plague in line 11: "because the son of Atreus had dishonored Chryses the priest" (Translation, Lattimore). Chalchas, when directly asked by Achilles for the cause of the plague, provides the same answer to the same question, but from his point of view, in line 94: "because of the priest whom Agamemnon dishonored" (translation, Lattimore):

οὕνεκα τὸν Χρύσην ἠτίμασεν ἀρητῆρα| Ἀτρεΐδης (I.11)
ἀλλ' ἕνεκ' ἀρητῆρος, ὃν ἠτίμησ' Ἀγαμέμνων (I.94)

Much of the vocabulary is repeated, although tense, case, and syntax are altered to reflect the changed perspective of the speaker. In one case it is the priest who is emphasized as the object of Apollo's concern, and in the other it is Agamemnon's dishonoring action itself that is the emphasized cause.

Another well-known example focuses on developing the character of Odysseus through his use of the scepter, appearing in *Iliad* Books II and III. In Book II, Odysseus is instrumental in reversing the mass retreat that comes as a consequence of the testing of the troops. His possession of Agamemnon's speaker's scepter is a significant element in the narrator's presentation of the events. First, Odysseus takes it from Agamemnon (II.186) as he moves among the troops, striking some (II.199) and calling them back to assembly. Then he uses it to strike Thersites (II.265), after which the narrator repeats that the scepter is still in his hand as he begins his final, effective speech to the troops (II.279). In these examples, the scepter works to establish Odysseus' power and blunt deployment of it. Later, in the *teichoskopeia* in Book III (161–244), Helen identifies Odysseus from the Trojan city wall, and Antenor, who is with Helen and Priam behind the city wall, offers a description of Odysseus as speaker from his own point of view. In recounting from memory Odysseus' speaking prowess, Antenor emphasizes his idiosyncratic use of a scepter:

> σκῆπτρον δ' οὔτ' ὀπὶσω οὔτε προπρηνὲς ἐνώμα
> ἀλλ' ἀστεμφὲς ἔχεσκεν ἀΐδρεϊ φωτὶ ἐοικώς·
>
> (III. 218–9)

> nor would he gesture with the scepter backward and forward, but hold it clutched hard in front of him, like any man who knows nothing. (Translation Lattimore)

Instead of a symbol of power wielded, the scepter here is an indication of a lack of proper rhetorical technique. The two different sources, narrator and fellow warrior, are linked by the repetition of a key element, the scepter, and an expansion of information about Odysseus' unorthodox use of it. We see a single topic presented twice, once from the point of view of the narrator and a second time from the point of view of another character. In sum, the two points of view contribute to a multifaceted portrait of the character Odysseus.

Epic also presents complex characters with a diversity of traits revealed in different situations. For example, the presentation of Athena's character as an actor in the *Iliad* begins in Book 1 when she appears to dissuade Achilles from fighting with Agamemnon (194–214); in Book VI (297–311), we see another aspect of the goddess, as cult statue. In Book VI.311 the poet masterfully unites the diverse traits of Athena as actor and Athena as image when he describes her rejection of the Trojan women's request by stating that Athena ἀνένευε, "raised her head" to say no. The cult statue cannot raise its head; only "real" Athena can do that. By merging the two, the poet brings both to mind.

Point of View and Character Analysis in Symposion: *Evidence on Vases*

Both of these phenomena, exploring point of view and character, are present in the repertory of images on Attic pottery. Many of the examples of vases discussed in Chapter 8 provide a visual counterpart to the presentation of the same topic or character from two different perceptual or ideological perspectives. Cups by painters such as Epiktetos [Figures 3.7, 3.8] and Euphronios [Figures 8.16, 8.17] offering different perceptual points of view of satyrs and symposiasts stand out. The bilingual vases of the Andokides and Lysippides Painters provide more subtle combinations exploring figurative point of view: two viewers can see the same actual view of a subject, but some difference in their "world-view" can cause them to see the two differently, [Figures 2.12–2.15]. A very direct parallel to the paired presentations of "real Athena" and "cult statue Athena" in the vase imagery is provided by examples where an "actual" divine character, Athena, in one scene is coupled with her statue in another [Figures 8.2–8.3]; the example by Euphronios [Figures 8.14, 8.15] where he playfully inserts a statue of Herakles in place of the hero himself and thereby calls to mind "hero himself" and "statue of hero" is another.

Jokes and Parody in Symposion: *Literary Evidence*

There is abundant evidence for joking and parody in the literary evidence for *symposion* and in the poetry performed there. Ridicule is an established trope, a fundamental part of the sympotic ethos. Even an heroic exemplum can be expressed as a joke with pederastic overtones.[101] For example, in Xenophon's *Symposium*, Socrates sets up a paradigm intended to deflate gently the self-importance expressed in Critoboulos' disquisition on his own good looks: "All right," said Socrates, "remember that we're going to have a beauty contest as soon as this discussion is over – and it won't be Priam's son Alexander who judges us, but these people who you think all want to kiss you" (IV.20).[102] Some of the sympotic participants, including Critoboulos, become the goddesses Hera, Aphrodite, and Athena, and others will become Paris and select the winner.

Lewis has suggested that a "riddling" or parodic ethos exists in Theognis (1029–1036), where the language evokes Odysseus as an unexpected but implied paradigm for the much-enduring *thumos* of the *erastes*.[103] The parody is produced by the repetition of formal and archaic Homeric vocabulary in an amatory context. Lewis adds that the result is a comment on the high political status of the speaker, who is like the hero and not like the *deiloi*. Levine discusses passages in the *Theognidae* that offer advice on being cunning and using deceit.[104] *Metis*, or "cunning intelligence," is cultivated through keeping on guard, and tricking one's *philoi* is a way to hone those important political and social skills.

There are in addition apparent verbal parodies of democratic process in the literary *symposia*. In Plato's *Symposium* (175e), Sokrates parodies a highly rhetorical mode of speech, appropriate for public venues, as he both takes up Agathon's invitation to join him on his couch and at the same time makes fun of him. The content of Sokrates' short speech, with its reference to the Thirty Thousand brings to mind the Assembly.[105] When party guests decide on the evening's program, their procedure is a light-hearted parody of democratic process: Sokrates says no one will vote against (Οὐδείς σοι ἐναντία ψηφιεῖται: 177d6) the proposal; his invocation, τύχῃ ἀγαθῇ ("with the blessing of fortune") (177e5) repeats what "sometimes heads the published decree passed by the Assembly."[106] In another exchange, later in the dialogue (219c5), Alcibiades is describing Sokrates' resistance to his sexual overtures, and he turns his fellow guests into a jury: he addresses them as "ὦ ἄνδρες δικασταί" ("members of the jury") and informs them "δικασταὶ γάρ ἐστε τῆς Σωκράτους ὑπερηφανίας" ("you are here to sit in judgment of Socrates' amazing arrogance and pride") as if he were prosecuting Sokrates for *hybris*.[107] Likewise, in Xenophon's *Symposium* (IV.2) Antisthenes stands up "ἐλεγκτικῶs" or "like a prosecutor." When the subject of the beauty contest comes up (V.2), the language used to interrogate Critobolus as to whether or not he will enter the contest mocks that of a *dike* or lawsuit. In this case, the mock trial even ends in a balloting with ψῆφοι or pebbles used in voting (V.8) that are cast κρύφα, secretly (V.9), and the decision-makers are οἱ κριταί, the judges. In sum, the literary *symposia* suggest that behaviors parodying some myths and some democratic processes were conventional at elite *symposia*.

Fehr, in a study attempting to identify the existence in the Archaic period of the *kolax* or *parasitos* character known to us from New Comedy, finds literary examples of social inferiors whom elites in sympotic settings ridicule.[108] These hangers-on, who in return for free meals oblige their superiors and tolerate abuse, include the disguised Odysseus and Iros in the *Odyssey* (18.8–107) and Philippos in Xenophon's *Symposium* (2.22). The boxing match into which the suitors force Odysseus and Iros is comic because it is a caricature of aristocratic agonistic activities, and, as a caricature, displays the beggars' physical and social inferiority. They scuffle, and the comic impact results from the contrast between this improvised scuffle and the formalized, highly competent events of aristocratic competitions. For our investigation, it is particularly important to note the role of repetition – the social inferior tries to repeat the moves of his superiors, but he does so poorly. Likewise, Philippos in Xenophon's *Symposium* (2.22) performs a caricature of an intricate dance performed by a young slave. Xenophon refers to Philippos as both ἄκλητος, "uncalled" or "unbidden," and γελωτοποιός, a "laugh-maker" or "buffoon." Xenophon tells us that his caricature is comical because the dance "made every part of his body look even more ridiculous than it was by nature." Once again, repetition is at the heart of the message: the uninvited guest does a poor imitation of the polished dance of the expert. This concept – needing someone inferior at whom to laugh – is so deep-rooted that it exists even on the divine level. In Book 1 of the *Iliad*, Hephaistos pours wine for the gods, and his physical deformity arouses their laughter. Fehr maintains that there is an implicit contrast with other divine wine-pourers, the beautiful Ganymede or even Hebe, whose movements Hephaistos imperfectly repeats.

Fehr suggests that these individuals clarify the social hierarchy, where the host and his guests have higher status than those whom they abuse. The paideutic goal is obvious: laughing at inferiors who cannot emulate elite behaviors perfectly teaches youths about skills exclusive to their social status, thereby educating as well as entertaining. It reminds adults of their superiority, and it shows part of what constitutes "best": physical beauty as well as know-how.

There are other literary examples of parody, where elites perform it themselves, either as a way of thumbing their noses at convention or as a form of one-upping their peers. The story of Hippokleides in Herodotus Book VI is one of our earliest literary testimonies for this sort of behavior. As Hippokleides repeated his right-side-up dance upside down, he parodied himself, thereby thumbing his nose at the suitor-testing process and requirements of proper behavior at *symposion*.[109] In this same vein, scholars bring up Alcibiades' alleged profaning of the Eleusinian Mysteries at a private *symposion*. The nature of his imitation and the extent to which it is appropriately called parody are topics of debate; but it is interesting to note two things: it is surely a repetition, an imitation of some aspect of the rite; and Thucydides' words used to describe it, ἐφ' ὕβρει, are clearly similar to those used by Plato's Agathon (Plato's *Symposium* (175e)) to Socrates after the latter has parodied highly rhetorical public speaking.[110]

Jokes and Parody in Symposion: *Evidence on Vases*

Chapter 9 established that parody is a common result of repetition. There are at least five sometimes overlapping categories of parodic effect on Athenian vases. One category consists simply of depictions of sympotic activity that is itself parodic and is not dependent on repetition of visual imagery or inscriptions to create parody. Fehr proposes that the dancers discussed in Chapter 3 appearing on the Types Komast-dancer cup and Komast-dancer skyphos are representations of social inferiors at *symposion*, like Xenophon's Philippos, in the midst of their ungainly dances.[111] A second category mocks elites' own heroic prototypes, their paradigms. Thus Herakles' struggle with Nessos, Theseus and the Minotaur, or the Judgment of Paris is exploited for its potential to be ridiculous [Figures 7.4, 9.1–9.4]. A third category provides setups for one user of a vase to make fun of another, enabling elite intra-competition. In these cases, an unsuspecting reader makes a fool of himself by reading an inscription aloud; he falls into a trap designed to make him look foolish. The root of the foolishness is usually that it suggests immoderation, either a drunken approximation of regular speech [Figures 2.1, 2.2],[112] speech that is vulgar or obscene [Figures 5.10, 5.11, 10.6], or merely silly [Figures 8.20, 8.21, 9.6]. In a few cases, the reader becomes foolish by taking on the identity of a nonelite. For example, uttering a mockery of the foreign accents of a *barbaros*, represented in the image of a Scythian, humiliates the elite reader by assigning him temporarily to a nonelite class [Figures 9.7, 9.8]. Likewise, the insinuation of a craftsman signature into a sympotic greeting or toast can require the elite reader to become his social inferior as he must identify himself as a nonelite: "I, Paidikos, greet you!" [Figures 5.3–5.6].[113]

A fourth category appears as self-parodies where the craftsman reveals social pretensions by ridiculing himself. When a painter's signature is integrated into a series of inscriptions labeling divinities and those declaring youths *kalos*, the writer displays a plucky refusal to acknowledge his real peer group. Likewise, a signature expressed in poetic meter suggests the craftsman is asserting his name as equivalent to the subject-matter of poetry.[114] In each of the latter, the parody is ridiculous because it combines semantic categories inappropriately. The vast difference between a painter's signature and the name of a *kalos* youth is articulated when a youth sings the signature while urinating [Figure 9.4] or the signature itself imitates a stream of semen [Figures 8.20]. Craftsmen not only ridicule themselves, they make fun of one another by placing their colleagues in situations that are preposterous because of their distance from reality – craftsman as elite student, as *kottabos*-goal, as the authority in a bungled formal public inscription [Figures 8.14, 8.15, 9.10]. A final, fifth category is related to the latter – parody makes fun of individuals or groups other than craftsmen who are "other." Women are ridiculed by their imitations of men [Figure 9.10], Scythians for their foreign accents and effeminate characteristics [Figure 9.7, 9.8], mythical Egyptians for their clumsy attempts at *symposion* [Figures 10.3–10.5].

Some specific examples from the literature of *symposion* parallel parodic results seen on vases. The Siana cup where a parody of Herakles and Nessos [Figures 9.1, 9.2] is created is reminiscent of Xenophon's characterization of the Athenian Niceratus, who believes he knows everything because he has memorized Homer and all the paradigms therein. Niceratus is clearly the object of fun because he has taken the importance of heroic paradigms to an extreme (Xenophon, *Symposion* IV.6). The Lydan examples that include a parody of the Judgment of Paris have an affinity to the jocular all-male beauty contest alluded to in Xenophon's *Symposion*.[115]

A vase not considered in earlier chapters may be a very close visual parallel to the kind of parody of democratic processes identified in both Xenophon and Plato. A cup in Dijon, dating to c. 470–460 B.C., preserves unusual depictions, scenes of *dikasts* casting their votes into a hydria.[116] The scene on side A is apparently "straight:" adults place *psephoi* into hydrias, observed by seated peers. Side B, however, repeating several elements including the chair types used by seated figures and the hydrias into which they throw their ballots, presents a very clearly linked aberration: youths, young men without beards, appear to be voting. Is side B, where youths play at being voting adults, a parody of A? The vessel is undoubtedly a drinking vessel, appropriate for *symposion*, and the figural program is one of a tiny number of extant examples where scenes of "democratic" activities appear. The illegal importation of youths into this adult-citizen activity provides a paideutic overtone conveyed through parody. In sum, there are many parallels in parodic imagery to assure us that it is very similar in nature to parody as presented in the literature of *symposion*.

AN ELITE WORLD-VIEW

The results of repetition on Athenian vases clearly reflect much of the experience of *symposion*, including the physical experience itself, entertainment, and the overall ethos of such events, as we can reconstruct it from archaeological evidence and from literary accounts of *symposia* and the extant poetry performed there. In addition, these vessels also convey something more fundamental, extending beyond the immediate situation of *symposion*, reflecting more generally the self-perception of social status and the world view of the elites who use them. Here we look at two ways the results of repetition yield evidence for exactly what that view was. Our first topic has to do with an apparent strongly felt community with heroes and divinities, and the second is a deeper delving into the purpose of parody as an affirmation of status.

Gods, Heroes, and Elites

In connection with the discussion of paradigm in Chapter 7, several examples came up where repetition links two scenes of mortals apparently *intermingling* with heroes, divinities, and mythical creatures, thereby implying an equivalence among these groups [Figures 7.29, 7.33–36]. Paradigm itself, as typically created through repetition on vases, suggests equivalence but with some distance; usually heroic and divine models appear in different fields from those compared to them. However, in Chapter 4 we discussed numerous examples by the Heidelberg Painter, Lydos, the Amasis Painter, and members of Group E where spectator-narratees observe and comment on gods and heroes at very close quarters. In other examples, inscriptions intersperse names of undepicted elite mortals with those of divinities and heroes, and if those inscriptions are read aloud in *symposion*, there is potential for the names of human and mythical figures to share equivalent acoustic space and thereby equivalent status. On Oltos' Vienna amphora inscriptions include a direct greeting to a divinity, "Welcome, Athena!"[117] There are many scenes where mortals appear in the physical trappings of the heroic age, such as chariots. If mortals, divinities, and heroes once intermingled, it is logical that elites see the accomplishments of heroes and gods as appropriate modals for themselves and their rituals.

There are several bits of literary evidence, not explicitly sympotic, that reveal a world view of an interconnected mythical-mortal society. This evidence serves to confirm the apparent picture we constructed from the evidence of images on some painted pottery. Lonsdale explores the mythical prototypes or paradigms for mortal ritual that includes dance, in this case as carried out on Delos. His analysis of the Homeric Hymn to Apollo posits not only that the chorus of the gods (ll. 146–76) is overtly paradigmatic for the Delians' ritual (ll. 182 – 206), but also that performing dance and music in the manner of the gods bestows upon the Delians agelessness and immortality (l.151).[118] Lonsdale quotes Plato's discussion of the dependence of mortals on divinities in worship and specifically in learning the combination of singing and dancing that is "chorus;" Plato refers to Apollo and the Muses as "fellow members or leaders" of the choruses in the compound *synkhoreutai*.[119] Yet describing the origin, a time in the past, requires the mortal to acknowledge a separation between then and now, thus necessitating the abundant reminders in imagery of that sublime prior moment when there was intermingling. The Delian hymn, by speaking of *aitia*, immediately acknowledges a starting point, an origin, that lies in the past. For mortal to reenact the role of the Delian maidens requires participants to conceptualize "then" vs "now" and to cope with a present separation while remembering a common past.

Similarly, the intermingling of divine and mortal is present in Bacchylides 17 (ll. 124–132), where the chorus of Theseus and the youths and maidens returning with him from Crete appears to be integrated with the chorus of mortal Ceans for whom the ode was written. Note the appeal to *aitia* for Apollo cult in the Theognid corpus: in lines 773–88, the poet suggests that mortals will dance around an altar on their citadel built by Apollo; in lines 11–14, the speaker prays to Artemis as did Agamemnon, founder of her cult at that spot.[120] Henrichs has examined choral self-referentiality, or comments the chorus make on their own performance as dancers, in Athenian tragedy. He mentions the passage in Sophocles' *Ajax* where the chorus invites first Pan (694–700) to come to act as their dancing-teacher and then Apollo (703) to join them.[121] In sum, these examples parallel many results of repetition on vases where similarity to heroes expressed through paradigm and interaction with divinities proclaims high status for elites. Once again, this attitude is a fundamental component of the world-view of elites that extends far beyond the context of *symposion*.

Why Parody?

Our second concluding topic, parody, helps to articulate another fundamental feature of elite status. We discussed in Chapter 9 the wider social role of satyr-play and Old Comedy in classical Athens, that they temporarily invert norms and hierarchies. These public parodies are "authorized transgressions" of social norms that result in an affirmation and solidification of the status quo. We have established that there are links between the nature of parody in Archaic *symposion* and in Athenian society at large. These links are demonstrated through fundamental affinities between satyr-play and Old Comedy and parody as produced through repetition on vases. Both the large-scale parodies, fun-making of public figures and heroes, for example, and the small-scale, more subtle and nuanced parodies at the level of language, are shared between public comedy and pottery-imagery.[122] Here we can expand on that discussion and apply the conclusions more broadly. There appear to be at least two roles for parody in *symposion*. First, elites make fun of each other as part of a general compulsion to compete, to challenge one another for "top spot" as practice for skills needed in public life. Elites then seek vases that permit one-upsmanship because they help to advance an important elite agenda. Prominence within their own group yields power. Second, those of high status mock persons and behaviors of low status in order to separate themselves from that level. Both effects are important to affirm the elite status of the adults and to enculturate the rising generation with this ethos.

A review of the evidence shows that parody as a result of repetition begins very early on vases and reaches a peak in terms of quantity and creativity in the repertories of the Pioneer painters, whose period of activity begins around 510 B.C. and ends at about 490 B.C. Little Master cups dating at or just before the middle of the sixth century [Figures 2.1, 2.2; 5.2–5.6] pair artist signatures with very similar inscriptions, either toasts or imitations of drunken babbling. Signatures are interspersed with heroic and divine labels and *kalos* declarations beginning with Exekias at around 540 B.C. Of the cups by the earliest red-figure cup-painters discussed in Chapter 5, at least one inscription on a cup dating to about 510 B.C. interjects the signature of a craftsman, Epiktetos, into a context that is elite and sympotic [Figure 9.4]. Among the Pioneers themselves, there are several examples, including statements identifying a craftsman as a love object and as a student [Figures 9.10, 9.11]. The parodic trope is evident from the mid-sixth century onward, and the intensity of interest in creating parodic examples coincides with the politically restive period in the last decade of the sixth century, culminating in the democratic reforms of Kleisthenes in 508 B.C.[123]

We have accepted throughout this discussion that the *symposion* is a custom generating from elites, deeply enmeshed in a paideutic, pederastic, and competitive ethos that defines their social class. In addition, we have reached conclusions several times that indicate members of other social classes are not excluded from *symposion* but in fact make very useful and necessary appearances there. For example, to include the name of an artist in writing on a vase creates the possibility the name will be spoken aloud, and permits a spotlighted appearance in *symposion*. Yet the craftsman artist is not likely to be a member of the elite. Is the artist himself claiming a space in the elite environment? Or does the appearance of his name serve some larger purpose in the elite agenda for self-definition? An explanation for presence of the craftsman is addressed to some extent in Chapter 4, where the cause for the apparent disjunction was identified by postulating a "constructed author artist." This constructed voice presents an elite world view and it permeates the author-artist persona. The voice is not necessarily a projection of the voice and attitudes of the actual craftsman, the real artist, who paints and writes on the vase. It is instead a voice that projects a position in line with the social goals of the elites. We are returning to this discussion here because some scholars have launched other explanations for the appearance of craftsman names and even images in sympotic contexts that deserve a fuller response, one that takes into account more broadly conclusions reached here in Chapters 4–9.[124]

There are several possible explanations for the appearance of both the names and even supposed portraits of craftsman in painted pottery. One is that, if the artists are well-known and their products are status symbols, to have a krater by Euphronios is an achievement. An announcement of that fact in *symposion* will enhance the reputation of the host. This explanation is pure supposition, because although it is logical and reasonable, we have no evidence to support or reject it. A second possibility is that the appearance of the craftsman's name creates a joke by mocking his pretensions when including him, incongruously, in a roster of images and /or names of heroes, divinities, and elites. Third, it may provide a more egalitarian sympotic discourse, one that includes fame-opportunities for artists who are not social and political elites, a discourse brought on by the emergence of a more democratic ethos around the time of the Kleisthenic reforms in 508 B.C.

We will explore the second and third possibilities further here, because many conclusions we have reached in this study appear to add information to the discussion. In a few cases, the potter's or painter's name written on a vase is not that of the artist who paints the images. Why would Euthymides write Smikros' name or Phintias write Euthymides', since it seems as though doing so would grant a competitor an advantage? The returns must have been great enough to supersede concern over the publicity granted as a result of advertising another craftsman's name. It is possible that the signature itself, the citation of the name of the artist, is perceived as a joke? Clearly when the signature is paired with nonsense, the nonsense statement makes fun of the artists's name. We have already cited the instance where a youth sings Epiktetos' signature as he urinates into an oinochoe [Figure 9.4]. When the craftsman's name is adjacent to a *kalos* inscription, is the juxtaposition incongruous and improbable and therefore humorous?

Nonsense inscriptions present another conundrum. We can understand easily that the purpose of a nonsense inscription is to provide a setup for one sympotic participant to trick another, to enable elite competitive games. Supporting such a view is Svenbro's understanding of the writer as "bugger," as part of a pederastic paradigm for writing, where the writer is perceived as the dominant *erastes*, the reader as penetrated, as the *eromenos*.[125] In this model, the writer forces himself onto the reader, and forces a spoken utterance as a demonstration of dominance. To force a reader to speak nonsense is an intensification of that dominance, since it adds ridicule to the violation. It is unlikely that craftsmen are in fact exerting dominance over elites. Instead, the craftsman participates in the creation of a constructed author-artist whose persona projects the tricky parody. Assessment of the evidence throughout this entire study suggests that jokes and setups are created for viewers and readers in the voice of these constructed author-artists who project the class mores prevailing at *symposion*: they are the equivalent of Xenophon's Philippos. Such evidence argues for a view where the constructed author-artist speaks not as a subversive craftsman who himself humiliates elites, but as one working in compliance with the elite, enabling them to accomplish their goals. Effective craftsmen know how to write inscriptions in the persona of the constructed author-artist to make unsuspecting guests appear ridiculous or to ridicule themselves, just as the *akletos* Philippos knows his own parallel but different parodic business, how to make himself ridiculous by dancing an ungainly dance.

Because this is a significant conclusion, it is worth restating. An increase in the creative ways artists' names and images are elevated in Pioneer productions is coextensive with political challenges to the power of the elite. These creations are the expression of an adept constructed author-artist who has inherited this characteristic trope, apparent since at least the middle of the sixth century, with his tradition. To create jokes relying on the ridiculous elevation of the status of craftsmen is desirable to elites because it achieves their paideutic goals for *symposion*, teaching youths about whom they are *not* like, while affirming their own distance from what they ridicule. When elites are in the process of losing power to nonelites, as they were at the end of the sixth century, an essential adaptation for elite enculturation would be to stress more firmly differences between elites and *demos*.[126] Joking and parody are well-established mechanisms for the expression of intraelite competition. To trick a friend into taking on the name of an artisan in a greeting,[127] to induce him to read a painter's signature as if it were poetry, to trick a reader into coarse sexual propositions [Figure 9.4], or to require a colleague to speak like an effeminate, barbaric Scythian are put-downs: what such inscriptions, all deriving added meaning through repetition, ridicule is what elites hope not to be. One measure of the success of a vase was its reception in its use-context; it is good business for craftsmen to create products that make fun of themselves, just as it is for Xenophon's Philippos. Philippos is present at the event, but his purpose is to demonstrate to elites what they are not. He, too, makes his living by being a willing player in this game. Whether or not elites got the point of Euphronios and Smikros making fun of one another is not really relevant, nor is the fact that one audience for this type of work was no doubt other painters as well, a kind of interworkshop banter. My contention is that the artists allow themselves to be, and in fact *make* themselves, pawns and butts of jokes in the context of intra-elite competition in response to the need for more intense class distinctions felt by elites.

Our review of the evidence supports the view that Pioneer artists take an existing predisposition towards verbal and visual parody to a new level in both quantity and quality. Neer sees this intensification as a new development with the Pioneers.[128] In an explanation that appears to merge the notions presented here of real author and constructed author-artist, Neer maintains that in images, painters appropriate the behaviors of elites, inserting themselves into an upper-class milieu as social challenges in order to call into question the validity of class boundaries. A depiction of Euthymides at school or as the object of a *kottabos* game [Figures 9.10, 9.11] then appeals to elites because they can regard the craftsman as an equal, a partner in the elite ethos of gift-exchange, rather than as an inferior commercial partner in a buy–sell arrangement. This is appealing to elites, according to Neer, because of a perceived necessity to eradicate class boundaries brought on by the political realities behind the Kleisthenic reforms. While acknowledging that the political tensions in Athens at the end of the sixth century do appear indirectly in the record of vase-painting in a variety of ways, I suggest that instead of going in a new direction, the artists remained behind the mask of constructed author-artist and took a long tradition of verbal and visual parody to a new level. This intensification, when viewed through the lens of the effects of repetition, is simply a new stage in the creation of "setups," offering opportunities for ridicule and gamesmanship among elites, creating competitive games for them to play with each other, and articulating distance between themselves and nonelites. Understanding the role of repetition in the creation of several of these Pioneer iterations allows us to see the Pioneer trend more squarely in the tradition of jokes and parodies and as about the *reinforcement* rather than eradication of class distinctions. Just as inscriptions can create parodies based on the affinities among the verb for the potter's signature, *epoiesen*, the word for wine, *oinos*, and even the word for poet and creating poetry, *poieo*, images of a craftsman participating in *symposion* and the educational preparation for sympotic performance can be parodic. These parodies indirectly articulate distance between social groups rather than breaking down class barriers. Donlan has made an effective case outlining a cause for this kind of negotiation between elites and other groups, what he calls "defensive alterations in the images of superiority which [elites] projected."[129] At a moment when elite political clout is seriously challenged, elites will respond to sympotic props that increase the distance between themselves and craftsmen through the use of jokes and parody. The craftsmen, in a move that demonstrates their sensitivity to the social needs of their clientele, collude and adapt their presentation of a constructed author-artist to reflect it. It is another kind of negotiated transgression, where the craftsmen work to give the appearance of challenging the social hierarchy but in fact do so with the implicit permission of the elite.

This concludes our final discussion of the ways some results of repetition on Athenian vases reflect more than the sympotic ambiance of their primary use-context. They provide information on the broader world-view of elite Athenians, a world-view where they are closely connected to divinities and heroes and at some distance from lower social classes. These components of world-view and self-concept are particularly important for elite Athenians to articulate and solidify in *symposion* because of the institution's role in *paideia*. It is a measure of the centrality of *symposion* in Archaic Athenian society that vase imagery and inscriptions on drinking ware reflect such fundamental aspects of elite identity.

CONCLUSIONS

What has this study of the effect of repetition achieved? We have seen that there are many and varied results of repetition in words and images on vases. The vase is a visual and verbal redundant text that interplays with the *andron* and the *symposion*. Words written on a vessel are just one element in a larger system of communication. Everything that appears on a vase repeats something of the sympotic environment: the images reflect participants and many dimensions of their self-perception, including the poetry and the subjects of the poetry they sing. The inscriptions repeat their discourse;

the ornamental patterns repeat the pattern on mosaic floors and tapestry, upholstery, and clothing. The *symposion* as a dynamic locus of Athenian culture reflected its reality and its evolution, so painted pottery likewise reflects social, political, religious, and civic realities and changes.

To what extent are the goals of this project set out in Chapter 1 achieved? Clearly apparent are the many types of repetition in the visual code that artists could implement to achieve results both aesthetic and communicative. Any doubt about the artists' expectation that viewers would look closely at all fields of a vase to consider and compare is allayed after considering those repeated inscriptions that respond to one another, repeating content as well as placement on the vase. The repetitions make clear the unity of the vase as a single text, thus created by repetition itself. Further, the many and diverse results of repetition themselves reflect the enculturating atmosphere of *symposion*, a primary locus for the dissemination of elite cultural norms.

The basics of the repetitive component of the code are established early on. They evolve and get put to new uses, but they remain constant. It is not possible to recover intent, but it is clear that different artists use repetition in idiosyncratic ways while creating within a common code. Application of "rules of repetition" might well have been largely unconscious, because such rules are as deeply embedded into the code as themes and formulas are into epic verse. The history presented here follows only one select strand of Archaic craftsmen, but the same uses of repetition are amply exhibited on many other vases. For example, although such vases have not played a central role in our discussions beyond Chapter 3, genres or Types of vases relying on consistent exact repetition on a particular shape continue to be produced until the early fourth century and even later.

Throughout this study, the integral role of repetition in storytelling is paramount. We have confirmed the basic outlines of the variety and evolution of narrative depictions in Archaic art, with a few surprises, where, for example, there is an early appearance of causally linked events. What is really new here is the vivid illustration of the role repetition can play in expressing narrative of all sorts, whether cyclical, unified, or phased. Repeated elements that convey connected events include repeated characters, repeated settings, or repeated objects. Moreover, various aspects of narrative, such as development of complex characters with several aspects, point of view, simile, compression, and expansion, are conveyed through repetition on vases even when they are not apparently depicted as integrated into a narrative. Looking at repetition has increased understanding of the role of spectator or narratee, both in images and via inscriptions. Finally, this study has brought to the fore the centrality of parody in this medium throughout its history.

Anthropologists tell us that repetition is crucial for the dissemination of the most important lessons a culture must teach. Information theorists tell us that so much noise is attendant upon communication that we cannot get a message through without a great deal of redundancy. Narratologists tell us that repetition is crucial not only for the creation and expression of narrative, but for the author to identify to the audience what is crucially important. It comes as no surprise that the vessels for the storing, mixing, serving, and drinking of wine, those used in *symposion*, a cultural institution where aristocratic concerns and values were expressed by Athenian men and taught to their sons, are superbly redundant, replete with repetition, and thereby loaded with meaning.

NOTES

CHAPTER 1: READING BEYOND AESTHETICS

1. Boston, M.F.A. 1973.88, *Addenda*[2] 396; Robertson (1977) figs. 10–13; Robertson (1981) 64.
2. Robertson (1981) 64, "Perhaps a youthful work of Euthymides. . . ." and "stands close to Euphronios but is hardly his . . .". Simon (1978) 68 agrees with the attribution to Euthymides.
3. Immerwahr (1990) 70, No. 416 is the source for the inscriptions.
4. Two studies, each intended as an introduction to how to look at Greek vases, serve as examples. Bron and Lissarrague (1989), in their introductory chapter to *City of Images*, make a series of assertions: "There is very often no direct link, other than proximity, between the different images decorating a vase, and at times one of them seems simpler and more ordinary, thus giving a front and a back to the vase. Sometimes, however, the painter aims for a complementary or contrasting effect, arranging the various images in a sequence on the vase." They conclude, "The study of iconography must take these effects into account" (Bron and Lissarrague [1989] 21), but without direct instruction on *when* to take such effects into account or *how* to do it. In another work, Robertson does not mention the question of whether or not to interpret the image in one field of a vase in light of other images in other fields; his co-editor, Beard, takes it for granted that the interpretation of each scene will take such combinations into account (Robertson [1991] 1–12; Beard [1991] 28–35. Several scholars make it clear in their analyses that they consider all fields of a single vase as a unified "text": Osborne (1987) 110–11; Lissarrague (1994); Cairns (1996) 156; Henderson (1999), esp. 22–8. In sum, virtually any discussion of iconography faces the issue of how to interpret juxtaposed images.
5. Morgan (1988) 64.
6. Morgan (1988) 65.
7. Morgan (1988) 47–8.
8. Morgan (1988) 163.
9. Marinatos (1993) 74.

10. Marinatos (1993) 75.
11. Palermo, from Chiusi, Beazley, *ABV* 114, 2, Manner of Lydos.
12. Once London Market (Sotheby's) ex Peek, A, Athena and (Herakles?) in chariot; B, warriors leading women off, Beazley, *ABV* 298,12; *Para* 129.
13. Athens, Akr. 2420, Beazley, *ABV* 130; 686; *Para* 53; *Addenda*^{2} 35; Near the Ready Painter. Beazley is quoting himself (*ABV* 115).
14. Froning (1988).
15. Geneva MF 154, *ABV* 299, 18; *Para* 130; *Addenda*^{2} 78; Steiner (1993) fig. 4.
16. Froning (1988) 199.
17. See Chapter 6 for a systematic discussion of these terms, coined by narratologists.
18. Vatican 343, Froning(1988) 190–91, abb. 17–18. See also the discussion here of Psiax' amphora in Chapter 10: Copenhagen 112, *ABV* 292,5; *Addenda* ^{2} 76; Immerwahr (1990) 59.
19. Pairings such as this can be described as "cohesive conjunction" for the purpose of signifying likeness/synonym or difference/antonym. Markoe (1989), like Marinatos (1993), makes use of the idea of the "pictorial simile." Throughout the discussion, he takes it for granted that juxtaposition of scenes invites comparison: "the artist's intention is clear from the juxtaposition of these two paneled scenes" (90). He does not discuss repetition *per se*. The creation of paradigms through repetition is explored fully here in Chapter 7.
20. "Kernels" are major events of the plot, "branching points which force a movement into one of two (or more) possible paths." Chatman (1978) 53. See also Barthes (1977) 93–5 and Hedreen (1996) 183.
21. Carpenter (1986) 40. See also Stansbury-O'Donnell (2006).
22. Carpenter (1986) 37–54.
23. Makay (1996) presents a provocative analysis, comparing the evolution of typical scenes in Homeric epic and typical scenes in black-figure iconography. This analysis is only tangentially related to the present discussion, but because Makay is discussing repetition from vase to vase and the power of elliptical images, those slightly altered from an expected repetition, that tangential relationship is significant.
24. Lowenstam (1993) 2.
25. Lowenstam (1993) 2.
26. As expressed by Hainsworth in Heubeck et al. (1988) commentary on *Odyssey* VI. 232–5.
27. Lowenstam (1993) 26 ff. In his discussion of this phenomenon, Lowenstam tackles two famously difficult examples: the "queenly mother" of the beggar Iros and the "stout hand" of Penelope.
28. Lowenstam (1993) xiii.
29. Kahane (1994). The authors of these two works do not refer to one another. Not only do they share a methodology, but both Lowenstam and Kahane also make comparisons between repetitions in the poetry of Homer and in music. (Lowenstam[1993] 11 and Kahane [1994] 43, 143 and *passim*.)
30. Kahane (1994) 5.
31. Kahane (1994) 143.
32. Kahane (1994) 2–3.
33. Kahane(1994) 135–8.
34. A typical example is the well-known amphora by Exekias, London British Museum B 210, *ABV* 144, 7; 672.2; 686; *Para* 60; *Addenda*^{2} 39, where Achilles fights Penthesileia, and Achilles is depicted at left. Boardman (1974) fig. 98.

35. See, for example, the interior of a red-figure cup by the Penthesileia Painter (Munich, Antikensammlung 2688, *ARV*[2] 879, 1: 1673; *Para* 428: *Addenda* [2] 300), Pollitt (1972) 23, where Penthesileia appears on the left and Achilles, the ostensible victor, on the right.
36. Campbell (1982) 17.
37. Campbell (1982) 58.
38. I have relied on this example in previous discussions (A. Steiner [1993] 197; [2003] 39).
39. Leach (1974) 63–4.
40. Gombrich (1960) and (1984); Barthes (1977).
41. Lissarrague and Schnapp (1981).
42. This term is an adaptation of the "Implied Reader" and both are discussed in Chapter 4. Most Athenian vases were recovered from Etruscan contexts in Italy, and there is a rich discussion of how to assess the impact of the Etruscan market on the shapes and images created by Athenian workshops. (See for example Reusser [2002] and Arafat and Morgan [1994].) The large quantity of Attic pottery exported to Etruria in relation to the amount excavated in Greece causes some scholars to wonder if the imagery is not Athenian-directed but modified for export. This important topic is addressed in Chapter 11.
43. Bérard et al. (1989).
44. Halliday and Hasan (1975; 1989 reprint) is a concise presentation of the various ways in which different kinds of repetition create cohesion. Bowditch (1976) 19–37 is a narratological application of some of these principles. Bowditch, relying on the categories of Halliday and Hasan, discusses the goals that writers want to achieve through various kinds of repetition.
45. Bowditch (1976) 19.
46. Bérard (1983) esp. 7, ff. "unites (iconiques) formelles minimales"; Morgan (1985) 10. See also Ferrari (2002) 21–5.
47. Stansbury-O'Donnell (1999) 79–82 discusses different types of syntax or compositions of narratives, called "narrative configuration," and the degree to which each encourages the viewer to associate a particular field with those that are adjacent. "Directional" compositions move from one side of the pictorial field to another. "Centrifugal" compositions show equal masses pivoting around a focal point. "Static" compositions display "no internal movement at all" and are usually symmetrical. "Containment," another aspect of composition, describes the extent to which action is complete within the field of view or extends beyond it. He ranks these in terms of how each type leads the viewer to other images. He points out that a closed, centrifugal, or static composition will be very contained and will "tend to evoke a greater sense of narrative closure to the viewer, that each episode or action is distinct and complete." Closed compositions are indeed contained, but I believe that repetition of syntax or figures from field to field will serve as a linking device and will overcome some of the inherent containment.
48. As W. Steiner points out, the definition of narrative varies widely among art historians of different periods; what one group calls "narrative" another may not. (W. Steiner [1988] 8–9.) For a general overview of narratology, see Prince (1990).
49. Prince (1987) *s.v.* "Narrative"; Prince (1982) 4; Barthes (1977); Chatman (1978). Much analysis of narrative depiction on Athenian vases cites Prince's basic definition, "Narrative is the representation of *at least two* real or fictive events or situations in a time sequence, neither of which presupposes or entails the other." So "Achilles left the battle and the Greeks began to lose" is a (short) narrative because neither Achilles' exit nor the Greeks' losing is a crucial, necessary condition for the other event to take place.

50. For example, W. Steiner (1982; 1988); Bal (1991b).
51. Prince (1987) *s.v.* “Narrative.”
52. Hedreen (2001).
53. See note 51.
54. Images depicting narrative can be classified according to how artists compose them. Four important relatively recent discussions of types of narrative are those of Snodgrass (1982), Froning (1988), Csapo and Miller (1998), and Stansbury-O’Donnell (1999). Hedreen (1996 and 2001) focuses on the role of setting elements and props in narration on Athenian vases. Stansbury- O’Donnell (1999) 18–53, “The Narrative Micro-Structure,” discusses the history of the analysis of narrative and offers a structure for further analysis. Chapter 6 of this volume is wholly devoted to a discussion of repetition and narrative.
55. This tendency of scholars is discussed by Ferrari (2002) 17–21.
56. Stansbury-O’Donnell (1999) 31–5; *contra* Ferrari (2003) 43–4.
57. Narratologists have identified a list of characteristics of verbal narratives, not all of which need to be in evidence for a text to qualify as a narrative; narratives can then be located on a continuum, where “weaker” and “stronger” examples exist in relation to the number and types of these identifying characteristics they possess. Following W. Steiner (1988) 9, I see this as a more productive model for creating a taxonomy of stories told in vase-paintings than trying to develop a simple up-or-down test that will establish whether a particular image does or does not represent narrative.
58. Less common perhaps is homonymy. In language it is identical *sound* but dissimilar *meaning*; in visual terms that would translate into identical visual elements representing dissimilar things, but linked to create an opposition (see Bowditch [1976] 20). A female figure who spins may appear with men who bring her gifts in one example and with other female figures who work wool in another (Ferrari [2002] 26).

CHAPTER 2: THE MEANING(S) OF REPETITION: A PRIMER

1. This chapter is largely based on an earlier article, A. Steiner (1997).
2. A discussion of the painter’s narrative interests is Moore (1987) 29.
3. Beazley (1951) 70; Boardman (1978) 24.
4. See Immerwahr (1990) 31–2: Paris, Seillière, attributed to Group E (*ABV* 133,9); Louvre F 53, signed by Exekias as potter, *ABV* 136, 49; 686; *Para* 55; *Addenda*^{2} 36; Toledo 1980.1022, *Addenda*^{2} 391, 400, signed by Exekias as potter. See also N. Slater (1999) 145 n. 4.
5. Athens, NM 1104 (CC.692), *ABV* 147, 5; Immerwahr (1990) 35, No. 146.
6. Immerwahr (1990) 35; 44, which also includes a discussion of the possible meanings of nonsense inscriptions. A second discussion, 27, focuses on inscriptions where sense and nonsense are mixed in a single field, as on the aryballos by Nearchos, New York, M.M.A. 26.49, *ABV* 83, 4; 682; *Para* 30; *Addenda*^{2} 23.
7. A discussion of the conventions for artists’ signatures on Little Masters cups is taken up more fully in Chapter 5.
8. Boston M.F.A 89.273 (r. 315), *ABV* 144,4: *Para* 59; *Addenda*^{2} 39. Cahn (1962) 79, pl. 3 has proposed that the fragments of another neck-amphora (Basle, Cahn 300, *Para* 60, 1 *bis*) preserve exactly the same subject and arrangement; he is supported by Moore (1968) 362.
9. This phenomenon of “visual dissonance” or “visual incongruence,” that is, images that depart from an expected norm, is also identified by Peirce. In her view, the observer creates

meaning through the resolution of the dissonance (Peirce [1998] 62; 78–9). Makay (1996) 53–4 describes this same sort of double-take, a recognition of what is missing from a usual and expected visual formula on Exekias' Vatican amphora, Vatican 344, *ABV* 145, 13; 686; *Para* 60; *Addenda*^{2} 40.

10. Chatman (1978) 71.
11. Halliday and Hasan (1975, 1989 reprint) 142–6.
12. Froning (1988) 188. See the discussion of Froning's work in Chapter 1, 7–8.
13. New York M.M.A. 17.230.14, *ABV* 144,3; 686; *Para* 59; *Addenda*^{2} 39. Beazley refers to the subject as "A, man and woman in chariot; B, the like." Moore and Bothmer (1976) 15 posit with a query that side A is a wedding procession, and they call B "procession in a chariot." Sinos and Oakley (1993) do not discuss this vase in their recent work on weddings, and the scenes seem to lack several crucial features of a typical wedding scene: the woman wears no mantle and she holds the reins of the chariot. Sutton (1981) does not discuss it in his work on chariot scenes, and he tells me (oral communication, July 14, 1994) that he knows of only one other example where a woman who is not obviously divine holds the reins in a chariot. The only female figure who is regularly shown holding reins in a chariot is Athena.
14. Another possibility, discussed at greater length below, is that the similarities between the two sides are meant to yield a comparison. Although it is not the intention here to discuss subject-matter *per se*, side A seems to have some direct parallels to the Eleusinian procession by the Antimenes Painter: Würzburg 308, *ABV* 267,19; *Addenda*^{2} 69. Perhaps the vase depicts a ritual on B and its mythical analogue and/or aition on A, as in several examples discussed in Chapter 7.
15. Chatman (1978) 63–79.
16. Philadelphia 3442, *ABV* 145,14; *Para* 60; *Addenda*^{2} 40; Beazley (1951) pl. 30. Ann Brownlee, *per ep*. March, 1997, informs me that she has looked carefully at additional fragments of this vase, not included in the published drawings of the fragments. One fragment confirms that the forward figure on Side B carries a *pelta*, securing his identification as an Ethiopian.
17. A discussion of story time versus real time is in Chatman (1978) 67–8 and is taken up again here in Chapter 6 on narrative. See also Ferrari Pinney (1983) for an interesting discussion of the temporal issues raised by a consideration of story time and ellipsis in these two scenes.
18. For narratological discussions of synonymy, see Halliday and Hasan (1975, 1989 reprinting) 278–9; Bowditch (1976) 20.
19. Beazley struggled with this fact (1951) 68–9. Beazley thinks the Antilochos episode, which decorates side B, extends over to side A, because he believes that the followers of Memnon would not have remained on the battlefield after the death of Memnon until the death of Achilles (because Achilles killed Memnon, if Achilles is dead, then Memnon must be dead and his followers dispersed). So "Menelaos is not driving them away from the body of Achilles, but from the body of Antilochos [on side B] while their master is still alive" (69).
20. In the words of Beazley, "Two episodes of one day, not simultaneous. . . ." Beazley (1951) 69.
21. Hedreen (2001) 172–3 points this out clearly when he cites Proklus' summary of the *Aithiopis*, M. Davies (1988) 47, lines 15–21, and Kullman (1960) 308–14.
22. Munich 2044 (J. 339), *ABV* 146, 21; 686; *Para* 60; *Addenda*^{2} 41, Schefold (1992) 252, 305, and 306.
23. Beazley (1951) 67–8.

24. Beazley (1951) 68; Schefold (1992) 252. Moore (1980) 422 thinks that both figures represent Patroklos. A complication of seeing both as Greeks is that each warrior seems to have fallen from the right-hand group of warriors, which ought to be the defeated group. However, on the Philadelphia amphora discussed above, Achilles has fallen from the left and Antilochos has fallen from the right, and both are Greeks.
25. For a discussion of polyscenic, causally linked narration as a subtype of continuous phased narration, see Csapo and Miller (1998) 107.
26. In another example, overt visual repetitions are lacking, but there may be temporal sequencing. On the neck-amphora London B 209 (*ABV* 144, 8; 686; *Para* 60; *Addenda*² 39) are Achilles and Penthesilea and Memnon and his squires. According to the *Aithiopis* (quoted by Beazley[1951] 68), first Penthesileia came to help the Trojans; then she was slain by Achilles. Then Memnon came and killed Antilochos and Achilles slew Memnon. The two images are excerpts of a more complex narrative sequence, one preceding the other, but the events are not causally linked. In view of the unity observed in Boston M.F.A. 89.273 (R. 315) [Figures 23, 24] and New York M.M.A. 17.230.14, it is reasonable to see here a single temporal and topographical setting, with Memnon ready and waiting in the wings to take the place of Penthesileia. Other interpretations can emerge as a result of the comparison of the two sides, a coupling of anomalies, from a Greek perspective: the woman who fights as a man; the Ethiopian who fights as a Greek does.
27. Orvieto 2745 (ex Faina 187), Beazley, *ABV* 145, 11; 686; *Para* 60, *Addenda*² 40; Wojcik (1989) 72–75.
28. I thank Elizabeth McGowan for this suggestion.
29. *ABV* 145, 11.
30. Boardman has made an argument for the possibility that chariots had some role in sixth century military affairs: Boardman (1983) 28–9. Sinos (1993) 73–91, esp. 75–6, rejects Boardman's suggestion.
31. Another example may combine two types of Exekian syntax already considered, both using repetition: the extension of a scene onto two fields and the repetition of a protagonist or composition to create temporal sequence. The result, though, is unclear: crowded scenes of figures departing in chariots with horses already harnessed, in strongly directional, open compositions, decorate each side of a belly amphora, Orvieto 2747 (ex Faina 77), *ABV* 144, 10; *Para* 60; Wojcik (1989) 69–70. Certainly repeated are a white horse, an old man wearing striped *himation*, and a woman wearing a garment decorated with a circle in a square. Obvious differences include the disposition and character of the participants. The possible interpretations are numerous: procession of departing chariots; single chariot at two distinct moments; two different individuals departing from two distinct locations. Similarities in image and syntax create a vivid format for comparison.
32. Halliday and Hasan (1975, 1989 reprint) 278–9; Bowditch (1976) 20.
33. Berlin 1718, *ABV* 144,5; *Addenda*² 39.
34. The scholarship on the Boeotian shield is integrated with that on the Diplyon shield, its putative forerunner in art. A complete discussion is Hurwit (1985a), which summarizes the important discussions of Lorimer, Webster, Snodgrass, and Boardman. Of these, Boardman alone believes that the Boeotian shield really existed in the Archaic period (Boardman [1983] 29–33), and he cites physical evidence in the form of shield bands to support his case. Hurwit expressly rejects Boardman's case, stating that if the shields were held with "scallops" at top and bottom, as they appear in art, they would expose the neck and genitals of the warrior and prove "fatally inefficient." To this observation I would answer that what

might be vase-painters' "errors" in the way they depict warriors holding shields do not constitute proof of how an article was used (Hurwit [1985a] 125, n. 16). It is surely safe to assert that although certain – but by no means all – heroes carry Boeotian shields, the inclusion of a Boeotian shield does not unequivocally mean that a scene is exclusively heroic.

35. Compare Woodford and Loudon (1980) 27 n. 11, who also see a link between the two sides of the vase: "Is it possible that considerations of Achilles within the context of his family were in Exekias' mind as he painted the other side of the vase, for there he showed the departure of a warrior in the presence of an old man and two female figures? Could he have intended this scene not merely as a generic representation but rather as a specific portrayal of Achilles taking leave of Peleus and Thetis and his bride Deidameia?" They also cite other vases where similar images are paired by other painters. Berlin 1720, the amphora identified as Exekias' earliest by Beazley (*ABV* 143, 1; 686; *Para* 59; *Addenda*^{2} 39), preserves links between the armor of Akamas and Demophoon on B and that of Athena in A: both heroes and goddess hold round shields held in profile and have similar crests on helmets.
36. Philadelphia 4873, *ABV* 145, 16; *Para* 60; *Addenda*^{2} 40; Beazley (1951), pl. 31.
37. Ferrari Pinney (1983) 131.
38. Munich 1470 (J. 1295), *ABV* 144,6; *Addenda*^{2} 39; Moore (1980) pl. 51, figs. 8, 9.
39. Moore (1980) 424–6.
40. There is no clear solution to the question of whether either artist or audience expected individuals in images to have a single, consistent shield device. Snodgrass (1989) 55 states that the original object of blazons was to identify the wearer. His evidence is from vase-painting, and he says that on early vases, each hoplite seems to have his individual badge, most commonly in the form of an animal or bird. Yet an example that appears to contradict this assertion is a Siana cup once in the London market, dated c. 570 B.C., where three figures all have lion's head blazons: Brijder (1982) No. 47, 240. Later, with the development of democracy (presumably after 508 B.C., and hence after Exekias and the bilingual painters), it was a more frequent practice, Snodgrass maintains, for hoplites to carry the uniform device of the city. In a fifth-century example from tragic poetry, the seven attackers at the gates of Thebes are described by the messenger (Aeschylus, *Seven Against Thebes*, 375 ff) as each having a unique shield device that reflects something of his character. (Thanks to Penny Small for reminding me of this passage.) There is apparently no evidence, other than from the images themselves, for how shield devices relate to or identify individuals. Whether a single individual could or would change devices from shield to shield or whether or not particular cities had a sort of "approved list" is unknown. Plutarch (*Alcibiades* 16.1–2) describes the gold shield Alcibiades had made for himself – an object that displayed his contemptuousness – as having no ἐπίσημον τῶν πατρίων or "ancestral device": it lacked one of the traditional devices of the Athenians. This passage suggests there may have been a single civic identifier or a set of civic or familial identifiers by the end of the fifth century; the evidence remains murky for the sixth century. Exekias does not seem to use a consistent shield device from vase to vase to identify particular heroes; that is, Achilles does not have the same shield device each time Exekias paints him.
41. Note that inscriptions help to distinguish the two nearly identical sides in an amphora by Psiax discussed in Chapter 10: Copenhagen 112, *ABV* 292, 5; *Addenda*^{2} 76; Immerwahr (1990) 59. The amphora Toledo 1980.1022, *Addenda*^{2} 391; 400, potted by Exekias, pairs

almost identical scenes and names one figure on side B and two horses on side A. It is not clear-cut that two different sets of people and horses are depicted.

42. The *Glaux*-skyphos (mainly Type B skyphoi, *ARV*[2] 982–84) and other clusters of vases called here "genres" or "Types" are the subject of Chapter 3.
43. Bal (1985) 77; Bal (1991b) 187–8. See also Prince (1987) *s.v.* "Narrative": "the 'same' story can have a different worth in different situations: A wants to know what happened, but B does not; A understands an account in one way and B in another."
44. Orvieto, Faina 2748 (ex Faina 78), *ABV* 144,9; *Para* 60; *Addenda*[2] 39; Wojcik (1989) 65–8.
45. One exception is that the dress pattern on the female figure at left on side A and the female figure at far right on B is repeated.
46. See the comments of Shapiro (1983b) 94: "Of all Herakles' Labors, the capture of Kerberos, with the hero's *nekuia*, most clearly prefigures his eventual apotheosis, the triumph over death. Surely Exekias had this in mind when he paired the Kerberos episode on the Orvieto amphora with the scene of Herakles among the Olympians." Shapiro maintains that the Kerberos episode may allude to an association between Herakles and the ancestors of Peisistratus; by pairing the Kerberos episode with the apotheosis, the artist aggrandizes the reputation of the tyrant.
47. For a discussion of this type of arrangement expressing narrative sequence, see Froning (1988) esp. 188 ff. Csapo and Miller (1998) 107 identify it as a subgroup of polyscenic narration, causally linked phased continuous narration, unusual for a sequence of a hero's labors, that is usually classified as cyclical.
48. Froning (1988) 177–8 would disagree with labeling the combination of any two deeds or labors, of a hero as continuous rather than cyclical. The terms "cyclical" and "phased" to describe narrative are defined fully in Chapter 6.
49. Another example where Exekias appears to avoid repetitions in two representations related in content is his neck-amphora London B 209, ABV 144,8; 686; *Para* 60; *Addenda*[2] 39. This piece couples Achilles and Penthesileia (uninscribed), A, and Memnon and his two squires (names of squires inscribed), B. The compositions differ: A is open, with the crouching Amazon fleeing to right and Achilles chasing her, whereas B uses a "parentheses" composition, where the outside figures enclose the central figure. In addition, there are the following contrasts: B side has names inscribed, A does not; negroes on B have black skin whereas the Amazon has white; round shield with *pelta* on A, round shield with figure-eight on A; Memnon wears a white cuirass, Achilles' is black. The pervasive avoidance of repetition may be a statement about difference – two distinct types of non-Greek adversaries of Achilles, the Ethiopian king who helped Priam at Troy and the Amazon queen.
50. For example, Boardman has suggested a thematic connection between the two sides of the amphora Leipzig T 355 and T 391 and Vatican 344, the gaming scenes and the return of the Dioskouroi (Boardman [1978] 24), and the discussion above hypothesizes a link between the two sides of London B 209. The point here is to make clear that there are also links in meaning between separate fields on other vases by Exekias that are not expressed or buttressed through repeated figures.
51. Boardman (1974) 105 has stated that "it is generally agreed that the Andokides' Painter was Exekias' pupil," and Robertson (1975) 217 follows him with: "In either case – one man or a partnership – the derivation is from Exekias." Cohen (1978) 2 and *passim* would disagree that the Andokides Painter was the pupil of Exekias. I do not complicate this discussion with a digression that rehearses the question of one painter or two, because the scholars

mentioned in this note do that adequately; here I regard the black-figure examples as by the Lysippides Painter, the red-figure examples as by the Andokides Painter and the painters of both as pupils of Exekias.

52. Cohen (1978) 16.
53. *ABV* 254–7.
54. London B 426, *ABV* 256, 20; 691; *Para* 114; *Addenda*² 67.
55. Munich 2080, *ABV* 256, 22; *Para* 114; *Addenda*² 67.
56. Weitzmann (1947) 21–3; Csapo and Miller (1998) 107; Froning (1988) 178–80.
57. *ARV*² 3–5.
58. Louvre F 203, *ARV*2, 4,13; *Addenda*² 150; Bothmer (1963) 154; and accepted by Schefold (1992) 116–17, figs. 135, 136.
59. Bothmer (1963) 154 describes it as bearing "a greater resemblance to an oriental cap with the flap turned under the fillet than to an ordinary *sakkos*."
60. Cohen (1978) 191–3.
61. Neer (2002) 35–6 also sees the appearance of bilingual vases as related to interest in the effects of repetition.
62. Palermo V 650, *ARV*² 5, 14; 37, 1; 1617; *ABV* 256, 21; *Para* 114; 321; *Addenda*² 150; Boardman (1974) 115, 160, 1–2.
63. Ferrari Pinney (1983) 133–9 establishes that Scythians as depicted on Attic vases belong entirely to epic legends.
64. Neer (2002) 38–41 interprets the cup in much the same way; he understands the complexity of similarities and differences as reflecting a sympotic ambiance of riddling or *griphos* ("riddle-net").
65. Boston M.F.A. 01.8037, *ARV*² 4, 7;1617; *ABV* 254,2; *Para* 113, 320; *Addenda*² 149; Boardman (1974) 19, 2.1–2.
66. Vatican 344, *ABV* 145,13; 686; *Para* 60; *Addenda*² 40; Boardman (1974) fig. 100.
67. For another suggestion on a different example of paired scenes of dice-players, see Froning (1988) 190 n. 80, where she suggests that two distinct pairs are shown: Achilles and Ajax and Palamedes and Protesilaos (for the latter suggestion she quotes Mommsen [1978] 142, 147, n. 26, pl. 34, 1–3). Neils (1992) 152 suggests that the artist shows the goddess Athena in two different moments of a sequence on Mississippi 1977.3.115 (ex Stroganoff and Robinson) *ARV*² 221, 6.
68. Munich 2301 (J.388), ARV2 4,9; 1617; *ABV* 255, 4; *Para* 113; 320; *Addenda*² 149, Schefold (1992) 44–5, 46 7; for a more recent discussion of this vase, see Wolf (1993) 18–19.
69. Carpenter (1986) 98 concludes that both figures are Herakles, but he believes it to be possible that the red-figure image represents Dionysos, because the Andokides Painter has other idiosyncratic representations of Dionysos. Hedreen (1992) 23 n. 88 agrees. However, Schefold (1992) 46 has interpreted these differences in the following way: in the black-figure example, the narrative, the scene as part of the story of Herakles' trip to Olympus, is more prominent and in the red-figure example it plays a secondary role. I interpret his remarks to mean that A is about the story, whereas B is about the characters and perhaps even their relationship.
70. Boston M.F.A. 99.538, Beazley, *ARV*²4, 12; *ABV* 255, 6; *Para* 113, 321; *Addenda*² 150.
71. The two sides are so close that Schefold is able to describe the differences only in the most subjective terms: the black figure side shows more "atmosphere," the red-figure side more "monumentality." Schefold (1992) 111.
72. Bal (1985) 77 ff.

CHAPTER 3: REPETITION AND TYPES

1. Munich 1470 (J.1295), *ABV* 144,6; Boston 01.8037, *ARV*² 4, 7; Munich 2301 (J.388) *ARV*² 4, 9; Boston 99.538, *ARV*² 4, 12.
2. Munich 2044 (J. 339), *ABV* 146,21; Palermo V650, *ARV* ² 5, 14.
3. For example, in the Group of Walters 48.42, *ABV* 205–7 (18); in cups by the Durand Painter, *ABV* 207–8 (4), by the Painter of Munich 2100, *ABV* 208 (3); by the Group of Vatican G. 66, *ABV* 209(2); by the Painter of Rhodes 12230. *ABV* 209 (2); by the Painter of Vatican G. 69, *ABV* 210–11 (12); by various painters in the Nikosthenic workshop, *ABV* 230–31 (5); and numerous other examples, some listed on *ABV* 211. On bilingual eye cups see Cohen (1978) 240–305; Boardman (1974) 107–8; Williams (1988) for a late archaic group of eye-cups; Jordan (1988) and Steinhart (1995) are important recent studies on eye-cups.
4. *ABV* x.
5. See Connor (1981) for a discussion of the hypothetical role of copy books in the creation of replicas in the work of the Painter of Louvre F6 and others.
6. Desborough (1952) 180–93; Boardman (1998) 15; *Lefkandi*, Popham (1980) 299–302; Catling and Lemos (1990) 22–3.
7. See, for example, New York M.M.A. 26.60.45.
8. See Boardman (1974) 18; Birchall (1972) carries out a study of the group. She lists the essential characteristics as Attic panel amphora of Type B; horse head in either (both) panel(s); horse head in profile to right; horse wears a simple halter. The differences among the examples are most commonly differences in style rather than iconography.
9. Boston M.F.A. 88.1078, *ABV* 25,11, lid fr. by KX Painter from Naucratis. There are two noteworthy exceptions to the repeated-subject rule on amphoras: One pairs a female head with a horse head: Munich 1360, *ABV* 16, 2. A second example pairs an adult male head with a horse head, and both are turned to the left: Louvre E 822, *ABV* 17.
10. Contemporaneous with the Gorgon Painter and the Horse-head amphoras, several painters such as the Androsiren Painter (*ABV* 18), the Panther Painter (*ABV* 18), the Ceramicus Painter (*ABV* 18), and their associates, including those in the Group of the Dresden Lekanis (*ABV* 21), often show *continuous* zones of animals on a variety of shapes, including lekanides, oinochoai, and skyphos-kraters. The figures sometimes line up so that the same type of animal is displayed at center on each side of the vessel. Isolating such animals or protomes individually in a panel may have inspired the single-head/single-panel scheme. Also analogous is an example by the Painter of Eleusis 767 depicting two women on each side of the neck of an amphora: Eleusis 767 from Eleusis, *ABV* 21,1; *Para* 13. See Scheibler (1961).
11. *ABV* 15: Beazley stresses the similarities in style between the Gorgon Painter's horses on Louvre E 874, *ABV* 8,1 and typical examples of the Horse-head amphoras. In addition, the Gorgon Painter's amphora in Avallon (Yonne) Musée Municipal depicts a lion on each side: *ABV* 9; *Para* 7, 9 *bis*.
12. Athens, NM 221 (CC. 652) *Para* 6; Karouzou (1963) 127 and pl. 93,1; Lullies (1964) pl. 29, 1. The siren is depicted full height in both cases, walking with wings held back on A, but has wings outstretched and held up on B.
13. Beazley (1956) 37–8; Karouzou (1963). The forerunners to this particular shape are not decorated with figures.
14. The term "Komast cup" is conventionally used to describe a shape. A very large subgroup of this shape is decorated with Komast dancers. Here the term "Komast-dancer cup" distinguishes this Type and "Komast cup" identifies the shape alone.

15. Not all cups of the *shape* under discussion manifest the characteristics of the Type, which must preserve Komast-dancers on each side to qualify: Brijder (1982) 31 and 223–30 lists 104 Komast-dancer cups or fragments of them.
16. A few examples include other elements, such as cocks and sirens, in addition to the dancers. Athens NM 533 (cc 648), Brijder (1982) No. K 203; *ABV* 68,2; *CVA* Greece 3 (Athens, National Museum 3) pl. 4–5. Painter of Athens 533.
17. Brijder (1982) 51.
18. They do appear on kraters, once paired with a military scene and another time paired with animals (military scene: London 88.6–1.599+ Oxford G. 128.18, *ABV* 33,4; animals: Athens, *ABV* 31, 3), and on a krater showing a boar hunt (Louvre C 1249, *ABV* 31,4), komasts appear under the handles.
19. Havana Lagunillas (Olmos Romera [1990] 31; no. 9, *Para* 16, 17 *ter*; Joslyn Art Museum, 1951.885, *ABV* 36, 4; *Para* 16; *Addenda*^{2} 9; [Figures 3.3, 3.4].
20. Vienna 3667, *ABV* 32, 12, 2; Brijder (1982) 225, no. K21.
21. Similar repetition also exists on at least one kantharos, but one example does not create a Type: Athens, British School, *ABV* 28. Boeotian imitators repeat komasts on kantharoi regularly. See *ABV* 30, 6–11.
22. Athens, NM 528 (CC. 634), *ABV* 26,22; *Addenda*^{2} 7; *CVA* Greece 3 (Athens, National Museum 4) pl. 1. A small number depart from the komast–only formula to include other elements of the *symposion*-setting: a skyphos in Athens shows a man holding a lyre with youths who hold a variety of drinking vessels on A, whereas on B similar youths move in a procession with an even greater variety of drinking vessels: Athens, NM 640 (CC. 631), *ABV* 26,21, *Addenda*^{2}; 7; *CVA* Greece 3(Athens, National Museum 4), pll. 3–4. Another example shows komast-dancers moving enthusiastically on one side and a stationary komast playing the double pipes with a companion who holds a kantharos on the other side: Athens, NM 940 (CC. 633), *ABV* 26,25; *CVA* Greece 3 (Athens, National Museum 4) pl. 2, 1–2.
23. Rhodes 5008, *ABV* 24, 1, by the KX Painter, *AM* 62, pll. 46–7.
24. Louvre, *ABV* 31, 4, by the KY Painter.
25. Some of the tripod-pyxides created by the Boeotian imitators of the KX Painter subjects continued, extending from leg to leg: *ABV* 29–30, 1–5.
26. See Moore (1997) 64 for a description of the Type, examples from the Athenian Agora, and full bibliography.
27. Johnson (1955) 119; 123.
28. Johnson (1951) and (1955) with earlier bibliography; *ARV*^{2} 982–4. A typical example is Cleveland, Collection of Jenifer Neils [Figures 3.5, 3.6].
29. Johnson (1951) 96.
30. An amphora of the same shape as Horse-head amphoras with an owl in each panel dating to about 500 B.C. is Munich 9406. The inscription ΔΕΜΟΣΙΟΣ identifies it as public property, possibly a standard measure. It is tempting to suggest that *Glaux*-skyphoi are likewise a standard measure, but there is no example known to me with an inscription identifying it as public property. See Kaeser (1987).
31. Athens Acr. 75, *ARV*^{2} 80, 1, "Bears some resemblance to Epiktetos." Graef and Langlotz (1925–33), pl. 5. Johnson (1955) 119 calls this "the ancestor of many owls on skyphoi."
32. Munich 9406. See Kaeser (1987) *passim*. See n. 30 *supra*.
33. See the discussion of exact repetition in conjunction with Figures 2.12–2.15 in Chapter 2.
34. There are several more examples akin to Types, both well-known and abundant, such as Panathanaic prize amphoras or choes (see Hamilton [1992]), and less common and less

well-known, such as an apparent group of special oinochoai from the Athenian Agora, all decorated with Athena and a chariot (Moore [1997] 43–4). Such examples repeat iconography and shape from example to example, but do not rely on repetition of images for their Type-identity. The oinochoai are discussed in Chapter 11.

35. Scheibler (1987a) 73. Scheibler suggests that the Type "Horse-head amphora" might have been developed in connection with Solon's agrarian reforms, possibly to monitor amounts of produce on the part of tenant-farmers. She points out further that the two functions – economic and ritual-festal – are not mutually exclusive.
36. London E 3, *ARV*[2] 70, 3; 45.102; 1623; *Para* 328; *Addenda*[2] 166; Cohen (1978) 424, B 93.

CHAPTER 4: "READ ME": REPETITION AS METADISCOURSE

1. Prince (1987) 51. See the important recent study by Stansbury-O'Donnell (2006).
2. Prince (1982) 125–6.
3. Brijder (1991) 372. Some examples preserving repeated spectators are Vienna 1672, *ABV* 63,8; Brijder (1991) No. 440, pl. 142, and Malibu 86.AE.155 (ex Bareiss), Brijder (1991), No. 428, pl. 141, both representing fights; Boston M.F.A. 1970.68 (once Newcastle-upon-Tyne), *Para* 27, 58 *ter*; *Addenda*[2] 18; Brijder (1991) No. 422, pl. 136 a–b.
4. Brijder (1991) provides a succinct tally of subjects used by the Heidelberg Painter in the charts that appear on pp. 384–5.
5. Shapiro (1990) 114–48; Brijder (1991) 336.
6. See, for example, Boston M.F.A. 03.852, *ABV* 51,2; *Addenda*[2] 13; Brijder (1991), No. 13, pl. 10b, fight between onlookers; Alpine, New Jersey, coll. of Stuart Tray, *Para* 24, 32 *ter*; *Addenda*[2] 14; Brijder (1991) No. 44, pl. 13, meeting of woman and youth, between onlookers.
7. The only earlier parallel is one recorded in the repertory of the Komast Group, where very different "lexical items" are embedded in a similar type of syntax: there is repetition of framing elements, sphinxes, but contrasting central figures, a floral ornament in one case and a figural scene in the other (Rhodes 5008, *ABV* 24, 1; *Para* 14; *Addenda*[2] 7). This example is discussed in Chapter 3, p. 46. In addition, note that one cup by the C-painter does preserve very similar judges and spectators to a wrestling match on each side of Bari 6233 (*ABV* 53,47; 681; *Addenda*[2] 14. Brijder (1982), attributes the cup to the Taras Painter, No. 169, pl. 32), but they are arranged in opposing order on each side.
8. Brijder observes that repetition is especially central to the Heidelberg Painter's decorative schemes in his early and middle periods, when 18 of 24 cups that have both sides preserved have the same subject on both sides, and 6 of 18 in the painter's late period: Brijder (1991) 337.
9. These terms are defined *supra*, pp. 16, 51.
10. Taranto 110339, *Para* 27.13*bis*; Brijder (1991) No. 366, pl. 120.
11. Brijder (1991) 337–40, provides us with a careful accounting and description of what he calls "onlookers and stock figures."
12. Brijder(1991) 337. Brijder also quotes Scheibler (1987b) 547–57; she agrees
13. Ferrari (2003) presents an interesting case study on fountain house scenes on Athenian pottery. She suggests that despite the "everyday" quality of the scenes, they may reflect a moment in the mythical past of the *polis*.

14. For sculptural examples, see the *kore*, Akr. 671, Boardman (1991) fig. 111; the calf-bearer, Akr. 624, Boardman (1991) fig. 112; grave *stelai*: Athens NM 36, seated woman and a girl: the woman wears *chiton*, *himation*, and a bracelet, Boardman (1991), fig. 238; the youths on Athens National Museum 3476, the "ball-player base" wear *himatia* and have elaborately coiffed hair, Boardman (1991) fig. 242.
15. See W. Steiner (1988) 11.
16. Labov (1972) 366.
17. Alberti (1976/1435–6) 78.
18. The role of the patron, who may have ordered the vessel and thereby had a role in its character, is taken up in Chapter 5, in the context of written inscriptions.
19. Chatman (1978) 146–51.
20. Wollheim (1987) 129.
21. Brijder (1991) 337.
22. Bal (1991a) 242.
23. Willcock (1978) 208 commentary on *Iliad* IX.502 .
24. Mackie (2003) 40–54 discusses verbal tags for the introduction of paradigmatic material from the past brought to bear on the present situation.
25. Prince (1987) 51.
26. Prince (1987) 71. Prince's example is, "Reader, are you still following me, or are you overwhelmed by the details I'm providing?" Malinowski discussed this type of speech first, and he emphasized that phatic language such as "how do you do?" binds hearer to speaker by a "tie of some social sentiment or other" (Malinowski [1953] 315). Jakobson elaborates that a phatic message, among other things, attracts the attention of the interlocutor or confirms his continued attention, "Are you listening?" Jakobson (1960) 350–77, esp. 355. I am grateful to Guy Hedreen for suggesting that I explore the possibility that the bystanders' function is partially phatic.
27. Some examples by Lydos are Basle, Kambli, *ABV* 109,25; *Para* 44; *Addenda*² 30; Tiverios (1976) No. 39, pl. 24, 25a,b. Scheibler (1987a) 91–2; Taranto 4359, *ABV* 109,26; *Para* 44; *Addenda*² 30; Tiverios (1976) No. 36, pl. 28.
28. Paris, Cab. Méd. 206, *ABV* 109, 27; *Addenda*² 30; Tiverios (1976) No. 35, pl. 26B, 27.
29. See A. Steiner (1983) 261.
30. Athens, Kerameikos Museum, *Para* 45; Tiverios (1976) No. 25, pl. 30; Göttingen, University and Paris, Cab. Méd., *ABV* 109, 19; *Addenda*² 30; Tiverios (1976) No. 28, pl. 31; Oxford, Ashmolean, 1966.768, *ABV* 113,80; *Para* 45; Tiverios (1976) No. 89, pl. 47; Karlsruhe, Bad. Landesmuseum, 69/61, Tiverios (1976) No. 93, pl. 65; Basle (Cahn), 925, *ABV* 113,78; *Para* 45; *Addenda*² 32; Tiverios (1976) No. 85, pl. 78. a.
31. London, British Museum, 1948.10–15.1, *ABV* 108,8; Tiverios (1976), No. 5, pl. 8.
32. Taranto I. G. 4363, *ABV* 113, 71, Tiverios (1976), pl. 35 (no number in Tiverios [1976]; Göttingen, University and Paris, Cab. Méd., *ABV* 109, 19; Tiverios (1976) No. 28, pl. 31; Taranto 20274, *Para* 46; Tiverios (1976) pl. 36; Copenhagen 6585, *ABV* 115; *Para* 46; Tiverios (1976) pl. 39; Oxford, Ashmolean, 1966.768, *ABV* 113,80; Tiverios (1976) No. 89, pl. 47.
33. New York, M.M.A. 1989.281.62, Norbert Schimmel collection, *Para* 67; *Addenda*² 46; Bothmer (1985) No. 60, 217.
34. One cup, a variant on type A, preserves no obvious repetitions: Boston M.F.A. 10 651, *ABV* 157,86; *Addenda*² 46; Bothmer (1985) No. 61, 221.
35. Richmond 60.23, *Para* 56,48 *ter*; *Addenda*² 36.
36. Munich 1471 (J. 476), *ABV* 137,60; *Para* 55; *Addenda*² 37.

37. On some vessels, inscriptions appear together with pattern work and with no accompanying figures. See the oinochoe decorated with palmettes and inscriptions: Munich 2447, *ABV* 425; Dover (1978) 118.
38. Prince (1982) 125.
39. Prince (1982) 125–6.
40. Jakobson(1960) 355.
41. Kilmer (2001); see also Karouzou (1937).
42. Dover (1978) 119.
43. Dover (1978) 117; see also Lissarrague (1999) 365.
44. Dover (1978) 119.
45. Dover (1978) 119.
46. Dover (1978) 121.
47. Chatman (1978) 147–51 uses the term "Implied Author" as distinct from the "Real Author." Booth (1961) 67–86 discusses the "intricate relationship of the so-called real author with his various official versions of himself," the "second self" or "official scribe" (p. 71).
48. Booth (1961) 74.
49. Chatman (1978) 149.
50. Immerwahr (1990) 72–3.
51. Beardsley (1958) 241–2 calls the intended audience the "implicit receiver."
52. Chatman (1978) 150.
53. Chatman (1978) 150.
54. Dover (1978) 117–18. Svenbro (1985; 1993) has written a recent work on reading in archaic and classical Greece, and he tackles written inscriptions in stone and on vases rather than literary texts. He uses as a point of departure a pederastic model, where writer "buggers" reader because the reader is the passive implement to convey the dominant writer's message. If Svenbro's model is accurate, it seems more likely that the vase-painter was not therefore the real author of what was written, but merely a component of the constructed author-artist. Chapters 5 and 11 treat Svenbro's theory more fully.
55. Agora P 5157, small lekanis, Lang (1976) P 13, No. C 18.
56. Athenaeus, *Deipnosophistae* XI, 465–7.
57. Fragment of Achaeus' *Omphale*, Nauck (1926) No. 33 (754) and Kannicht (1991) Achaeus I, No. 33, 87–9, quoted by Athenaeus *Deipnosophistae* XI, 498 E and 466 F. Achaeus was active from the mid-440s until the end of the century.
58. Svenbro (1993) 177. See also Krumeich et al. (1999) F 33, 539–42.
59. Balogh (1927); Knox (1968); Gavrilov (1997); Burnyeat (1997). See also Hendrickson (1929).
60. Thomas (1992).
61. Svenbro (1985; 1993) 166–7. See also Thomas (1992) 4: "Even where a written text existed, it was read aloud" and 61–5 and *passim*. Thomas does reserve some archaic inscriptions – *graffiti* including *abecedaria*, single letters, personal names, labels, and lists – as exploring unspoken statements, different possibilities of the written word in comparison to the large extent that most archaic Greek writing seems to be "at the service of speech" (65). Vase-inscriptions do not fall into her list of exceptions.
62. Gavrilov (1997) 59.
63. Thomas (1992) 92–3.
64. The metaphor begins with ὀφείλων "owe" in 1. 3 and continues in language referring to debt, interest, and repayment in 6–11. See Race (1997) 163. D. Steiner (1994) 27 identifies

the specific language of accounting and in n. 53 points out that the verb is commonly used for reading decrees (aloud) in the assembly and in lawcourts.

65. Gavrilov (1997) 70.
66. Schenkeveld (1992) 139.
67. Svenbro (1993) 48 and 51.
68. Knox (1968) 433; *Hippolytus* 856 ff. and *Knights* 115 ff.
69. See comment of Gavrilov (1997) 70; see Schenkeveld (1992) 130.
70. Thomas (1992) 64–5.
71. Boardman (2003) 110.
72. London E 37, *ARV*² 72, 17; *Para* 328; *Addenda*² 167.
73. Lissarrague (1994).
74. Svenbro (1993) 164.
75. Snodgrass (2000) 27–8.
76. Slater (1999) 158.
77. Svenbro (1993) 41–3. Thomas (1992) 64, when discussing the reading-aloud of inscriptions in stone written in the first person: "it is probably over-literal to object that the reader would then be forced to say aloud 'I am . . .' when he was not the 'I' in question, for surely the reader could make the imaginative jump of attributing their own spoken 'I' to the object."
78. Lissarrague (1990a) 57–9.
79. The black-figure neck-amphora by Exekias, Berlin 1720, *ABV* 143, 1;686; *Para* 59; *Addenda*² 39; Vatican 433, *ABV* 145, 13; 686; *Para* 60; *Addenda*² 40, black-figure amphora also by Exekias.
80. A parallel from another context is the late–sixth-century black-figure phormiskos where the vessel function is clearly in funerary ritual and the inscriptions are utterances from that context: Kerameikos 691, *ABV* 678; Immerwhar (1990) 74, No. 436, and Figs. 98, 99 a–b.
81. Berlin 1720, *ABV* 143,1; 686; *Para* 59; *Addenda*² 39; Immerwahr (1990) 32.

CHAPTER 5: READING WRITING

1. This discussion of inscriptions is limited mainly to the examples included in Immerwahr (1990), in order to ensure consistency in the reading of inscriptions. In a few instances transcriptions (and sometimes reconstructions) of inscriptions by Hoppin (1919 and 1924), Beazley (*ABV*, *ARV*²), and others are used.
2. Boston M.F.A. 1973.88. Robertson (1977), figs. 10–13.
3. Athens, NM 1104 (CC. 692), *ABV* 147, 5; Immerwahr (1990) 35, No. 146. Parody is one of many possible results of repetition-with-difference and is explored fully in Chapter 9.
4. For example, as discussed in Chapter 4, the cup by Epiktetos: London E 37, *ARV*² 72, 17; 1623; *Para* 328; *Addenda*² 167.
5. Athens, NM 1104 (CC.692), *ABV* 147, 5; Immerwahr (1990) 35, No. 146.
6. Immerwahr (1990) 35; 44. See Chapter 2, n. 6.
7. An example where repeated images create parody is Birmingham University X 698, Brijder (1982) No. 291, pls. 58, c-d, by the Painter of the Burgon Sianas, discussed in Chapter 9.
8. There is some additional evidence that artists who immediately followed Exekias paid attention to the *meaning* of inscriptions. Chapter 2 established that the bilingual painters

who appear to have been workshop colleagues of Exekias adopted his usage of repetition to varying degrees; they apparently also understood how he used inscriptions, and, to some extent, what they said. The black-figure amphora London B 211 (London 1851.8–6.15 (B 211), *ABV* 256, 14; 670; *ARV*² 1617; *Para* 113; *Addenda*² 66) by Exekias depicts Ajax and Achilles gaming. Exekias, in his typical practice, places the *kalos* inscription and the labels in very neat verticals, evenly spaced in the scene. The numbers revealing each hero's score are written out. On Boston M.F.A. 01.8037 (*ARV*² 4, 7; 1617; *ABV* 254,2; *Para* 113, 320; *Addenda*² 149), the Andokides Painter depicts a scene very similar to Exekias' formula for Ajax and Achilles as heroic game-players, but without inscriptions, in turn according to Andokidean habit. (Cohen [1978] 5–7 reviews scholarly opinion as to why early red-figure vases have so few inscriptions in general.) Instead, the right-hand figure, presumably Ajax, holds out two fingers and a thumb, the gestural equivalent of the score "three" actually written out on the amphora by Exekias (Cohen [1978] 8 quoting Caskey and Beazley [1931] iii, 5). Is it possible that the Andokides Painter read Exekias' inscriptions and, unable to reproduce them, translated them into imagery?

9. See Lissarrague (1990a) 62–7 for a discussion of inscriptions on Little Master cups.
10. Berlin inv. 4604, *ABV* 78,13, *Addenda*² 22; Immerwahr (1990) 46, No. 217; London 1948.8–15.1 and 2, 88.6–1.215, 424 (B601.4.1 and 2) and 427 (B 601.5) and Cambridge N 206, *ABV* 78, 14.
11. Philadelphia 3442, *ABV* 145,14; *Para* 60; *Addenda*² 40; Beazley (1951) pl. 30.
12. Harnessing, discussed in Chapter 2, Boston 89.273, *ABV* 144,4; *Para* 59; *Addenda*² 39 by Exekias.
13. Berlin 1756, *ABV* 162,3, Immerwahr (1990) 50, No. 241; London B 417, *ABV* 162,2; *Para* 68; *Addenda*² 46; Immerwahr (1990) 50, No. 240.
14. Psiax: alabastra: Odessa 26602, *ARV*² 7, 5; *ABV* 292; *Addenda*² 150 and Karlsruhe 242 (B120) *ARV*² 7, 4; *Para* 321; *Addenda*² 150; Epiktetos: calyx crater: Villa Giulia *ARV*² 77, 90; *Addenda*² 169; skyphos: London E 139, *ARV*² 77, 86; *Para* 328; *Addenda*² 168; cup: London E 38, ARV² 72, 16; 1623; *Para* 328; *Addenda*² 167; bilingual eye-cup, Würzburg 468, *ARV*² 71, 8 and 45, 105; *Addenda*² 167.
15. Cup: St. Petersburg, Hermitage B 2102 (Leningrad 645), *ARV*² 71, 4; 45.103; 1623; *Para* 509; *Addenda*² 167; cup: Basle, AntMus, BS 436 (once Arlesheim, Schweizer), *ARV*² 7105, 71 *bis*; 1705; *Addenda*² 167.
16. All by Epiktetos: bilingual eye-cup: London E 3, *ARV*² 70, 3; 45,102; *Addenda*² 166; cup: Berlin 2262, *ARV*² 72, 15; 1623; cup: Paris, Louvre G 5, *ARV*² 71, 14; 49, 175; *Addenda*² 167.
17. Oltos: amphora: London E 258, *ARV*² 54, 4; 1622; *Addenda*² 163; Epiktetos: cup: Louvre G 6, *ARV*² 72, 21.
18. Munich 2620, *ARV*²16, 17; 1619; *Para* 322; *Addenda*² 153.
19. Munich 2243, *ABV* 163,2; 160,2; *Para* 67, 68; *Addenda*² 46, 47; Immerwahr (1990) 49, No. 233. See Hoppin (1924) 60 for texts of inscriptions.
20. London 1867.5–8.962 (B 424), *ABV* 168, 169,3; *Para* 70; *Addenda*² 48; Immerwahr (1990) 48, No. 228.
21. Vienna University 631a, *ARV*² 54, 3; *Para* 326; *Addenda*² 163; Immerwahr (1990) 61, No. 339. The amphora is fragmentary. A depicts Apollo and Herakles fighting over the deer, whereas the fragmentary B side depicts Ares and Aphrodite.
22. Naples 81238 (2609) *ARV*² 73, 29.
23. London E 767, *ARV*² 31, 6; *Para* 324; *Addenda*² 157; Immerwahr (1990) 70. No. 413.

24. Note, however, that Hoppin (1919) reads the inscriptions on side B together: "Certainly, Dikaios!" (a figure labeled on B). On A, ΚΥΔΙΑΣ is labeled and on B, in addition to ΔΙΚΑΙΟΣ, is the fragmentary inscription [–?]ΧΑΡΧΟΝ.
25. Copenhagen, National Museum 13966, *Para* 48; *Addenda*^{2} 33; Tiverios (1976) No. 92 pl. 62–4.
26. Naples 81238 (2609), *ARV*^{2} 73, 29.
27. Berkeley 8/358, Immerwahr (1990) 54, No. 283. Bologna, Museo Civico, lip cup, Immerwahr (1990) 54, No. 284 is similar.
28. Vatican 344, *ABV* 145,13; 686; *Para* 60; *Addenda*^{2} 40; Immerwahr (1990) 33, No. 136.
29. London E 18, *ARV*^{2} 62, 86; 1700; *Para* 327; *Addenda*^{2} 165; London E 19, *ARV*^{2} 63, 95; 1600. Louvre G 18 (*ARV*^{2} 61, 68; *Addenda*^{2} 165) by Oltos follows this formula but much more loosely, because the positions of the inscriptions do not always correspond to one another.
30. Copenhagen inv. 3877, *ARV*^{2} 63, 87; 1600 by Oltos.
31. London E 17, *ARV*^{2} 62, 80, cup by Oltos.
32. Florence 3923, *ARV*^{2} 61, 72; 1599, a cup by Oltos, preserves *kalos Memnon* in three fields. London E 16, *ARV*^{2} 61, 75; 1599; *Addenda*^{2} 165, cup by Oltos, where tondo and side A are linked by repetition of *Memnon kalos*; and Louvre G 17, *ARV*^{2} 62, 83; 1599; *Para* 327; *Addenda*^{2} 165, where *Memnon kalos* links the tondo and side B.
33. Athens Agora P 24113, *ARV*^{2} 213, 242; 1634; *Para* 344; *Addenda*^{2}196.
34. Boston 01.8021, *ARV*^{2} 320, 14; 1567; *Addenda*^{2} 215, Epiktetos; Munich 2620 (J.337), *ARV*^{2} 16, 17; 1591; 1619; *Para* 322; *Addenda*^{2}153, Euphronios; Berlin 2180, *ARV*^{2} 13, 1; 1584; 1596; 1619; *Para* 321; *Addenda*^{2} 152; London E 438, *ARV*^{2} 20, 3; 1606; 1620; *Para* 322; *Addenda*^{2} 154, Smikros; Malibu 83.AE.285, Smikros; Philadelphia L 64.185, *ARV*^{2} 187, 62; 1632; *Addenda*^{2} 188, Kleophrades Painter; Berlin 2285, *ARV*^{2} 431, 48; 426; 1653; *Para* 374; *Addenda*^{2} 237, Douris; Vienna 3695, *ARV*^{2} 429, 26; 425; 1653; *Para* 374; *Addenda*^{2} 236, Douris.
35. Louvre G 30, *ARV*^{2} 15, 9; 1591; 1619; *Para* 322, *Addenda*^{2} 152, Euphronios.
36. New York M.M.A. 1972.11.10, *Addenda*^{2} 404–5, Euphronios.
37. Boston M.F.A. 1973.88, Euthymides under Euphronios' influence (attributed by Robertson (1977); Immerwahr (1990) 70 No. 416 [Figures 1.1, 1.2].
38. Louvre G138, *ARV*^{2} 365, 61; 1580; 1596; 1606; 1648; *Addenda*^{2} 223, Triptolemos Painter.
39. These concepts are explored fully in Chapter 4.
40. Copenhagen inv. 3877, *ARV*^{2} 63, 87; 1600; *Para* 327.
41. Johansen (1928) pl. 137 suggests that ΧΙΟΝ, "Khion," names Herakles' opponent (Beazley disagrees, *ARV*^{2} 63, 87), who is obscured owing to damage to the cup, and that *kalos* floats independently.
42. Transcriptions from CVA Denmark 3 (Copenhagen 3) pl. 137.
43. Warsaw 142332, *ARV*^{2} 27, 8; *Para* 324; *Addenda*^{2} 156; Immerwahr (1990) 65, No. 374.
44. Henderson (1991) 157 no. 238; Dover (1978) 114, 123.
45. Chatman (1978) 257.
46. Florence 3985, *ARV*^{2} 204, 110; *Addenda*^{2} 193; Immerwahr (1990) 82, No. 491.
47. London E 468, *ARV*^{2} 206, 132; 1633; *Para* 343; *Addenda*^{2} 194, Berlin Painter.
48. Louvre G 104 and Florence PD 321, *ARV*^{2} 318, 1; 1645; *Para* 358; *Addenda*^{2} 214, Onesimos.
49. Munich 2309 (J.410), *ARV*^{2} 27, 4; 1620; *Para* 323; *Addenda*^{2} 156, Euthymides. The subject extends over both sides of the vase: Theseus abducts Korone/Helen.
50. Villa Giulia 20846, *ARV*^{2} 494, 2; *Addenda*^{2} 250; Villa Giulia 20847, *ARV*^{2} 494, 3; *Addenda*^{2} 250.
51. Louvre G 138, *ARV*^{2} 365, 61; 1580; 1596; 1606; 1648; *Addenda*^{2} 223, Triptolemos Painter.

52. Morgantina (Serra Orlando) 58.2382, *ARV*[2] 28, 10; 1620; *Addenda*[2] 156, Euthymides.
53. Munich 2421, *ARV*[2] 23, 7; 1620; *Para* 323; *Addenda*[2] 155. Note that on Euphronios' krater, New York, M.M.A. 1972.11.10 (*Addenda*[2] 404–5), the *hipp* ("horse") root of a name appears on each side of the vase. Other evidence for interconnecting the two sides is discussed below in Chapter 7.
54. Arezzo 1465, *ARV*[2] 15, 6; 316; 1619; *Para* 322; *Addenda*[2] 152.

CHAPTER 6: REPETITION AND NARRATION

1. Philadelphia 3442, *ABV* 145,14; *Para* 60; *Addenda*[2] 40; and Orvieto, Faina 2748 and 3048 (ex Faina 78), *ABV* 144,9; *Para* 60; *Addenda*[2] 39.
2. There are several recent summaries of scholarly discussion on the visual representation of narrative, for example, those by Shapiro (1994), Csapo and Miller (1998), and Stansbury-O'Donnell (1999).
3. For example, Stansbury-O'Donnell (1999) 7, Table 1, lists continuous narration as having two or more pictures, yet its fundamental definition (see, for example, Shapiro [1994] 9, or Froning [1988] 177 ff, both going back to Wickhoff) requires that there be no frame-boundaries between episodes. Stansbury-O'Donnell, in an attempt to bring much-needed clarity to the discussion by the use of a graphic illustration, omits this detail in presenting the concept and may create confusion for some readers.
4. Robert (1881/1975) 14–15; 44 and *passim*; Weitzmann (1947) 14–17; 34; Snodgrass (1982) 4; Csapo and Miller (1998) 105, n. 30.
5. Robert (1881/1975) 14–20, *kompletive Vehrfahren*; Weitzmann (1947) 12–36 "simultaneous"; Snodgrass (1982) 4.
6. Wickhoff (1900) 35. Froning adds an important qualification to Wickhoff's definition: unbroken placement of scenes, involving the repetition of at least one character, in frieze form (with no interruptions by frame), *set out in several episodes that temporally follow one after another* (Froning [1988] 180).
7. Robert (1881/1975) 46 *Bildcyklen* and *Chroniken-Stil*. Froning (1988) offers the very best contemporary analysis of cyclic narration and its relationship to continuous narrative; in her discussion she points out that Weitzmann (1947, 35 ff.) confused the taxonomy by including Wickhoff's term "continuous" ("continuirende Darstellungsweise") when there are in fact crucial differences between the two (Froning [1988] 80; see also Stansbury-O'Donnell [1999] 7, Table 1, and Csapo and Miller [1998] 106 and 105 fig. 1).
8. One example already considered here of a hero's labors is the amphora by Exekias, where he combines Herakles fetching Kerberos and the hero's apotheosis; it is almost but not quite a simple cyclic narration, because the scene in Olympus is not itself a subsequent labor but the result of the successful completion of the tasks: Orvieto, Faina 2748 and 3048 (ex Faina 78), *ABV* 144,9; *Para* 60; *Addenda*[2] 39; Wojcik (1989) 65–8.
9. *Serial*, defined by Hurwit (1985a) 173: at least two fields involving no repeated characters, comprising more than one moment in time and more than one space. *Episodic*, defined by Connelly (1993) 89, is essentially identical to serial. *Progressive* is defined by Harrison (1983) 237–8 as a depiction in a single field, with no repeated characters over multiple moments in time of multiple spaces. The field displaying the narration may be very large, such as a frieze or a large wall-painting. *Unified*, defined by Shapiro (1992) 37–8 as two

or more separate scenes with no repeated characters, depicting one moment in time but multiple spaces.

10. Csapo and Miller (1998) 106–9.
11. Philadelphia 3442, *ABV* 145,14; *Para* 60; *Addenda*[2] 40; Beazley (1951) pl. 30.
12. Csapo and Miller correctly identify this type of narrative strategy as related to but clearly distinct from canonical continuous narration. With phased narration, each phase is depicted in a separate frame, whereas in continuous narration, the scenes are not in discrete frames but unfold as continuous units in a frieze. Csapo and Miller (1998) 109.
13. After Prince (1982) on "Narrativity," 145–51; Stansbury-O'Donnell (1999) 31–53.
14. Because some narratological vocabulary, particularly that developed by Chatman, is extremely helpful in clarifying this analysis of visual narratives, terms are identified and defined where appropriate and necessary. Chatman (1978) 23–6 defines the terms "story" and "discourse"; see also 63 ff for a discussion of story-time versus discourse-time.
15. In addition to Athens, NM 16389, *ABV* 2,1; *Addenda*[2] 1; see Athens NM 16391, *ABV* 2,2; *Addenda*[2] 1, also by the Bellerophon Painter and depicting the same story.
16. Chatman (1978) 31–4 and *passim*.
17. See the discussion in Chapter 3 of the predecessors of the Horse-head Type by the Gorgon and Nettos Painters, pp. 43–44.
18. Copenhagen, National Museum 13966, *Para* 48; *Addenda*[2] 33; Tiverios (1976) No. 92, pl. 62–4. Below on one side is a pair of warriors meeting on foot, and on the other, a pair meeting on horseback. The heads of the divinities are reminiscent of the type that appear on some exceptional Horse-head amphoras, where a female head is paired with a horse-head: Munich 1360, *ABV* 16,2; 679; *Para* 9; *Addenda*[2] 4. A second amphora pairs a man's head with a horse head, with both facing left: Louvre E 822, *ABV* 17; *Addenda*[2] 5; the Painter of Louvre F6 repeats one male head on each side of an amphora formerly on the Basle market: *ABV* 123.
19. Another important aspect of the repetitive context here, the inscriptions that are placed similarly between flanking figures, is discussed in Chapter 5, pp. 81–2.
20. Chatman (1978) 6379, esp. 67–78, where Chatman summarizes Genette's (see Genette [1970]) study of duration. See Shapiro (1992) 38, discussing later examples by Euphronios, who "turn[s] the architecture of the vase from a hindrance to an advantage."
21. Chatman (1978) 72. Chatman, quoting Gennette, defines this type of relationship between story and discourse as "scene," where story and discourse are of relatively equal length.
22. New York, M.M.A. 31.11.11, *ABV* 108,5; 684; *Para* 43; *Addenda*[2] 29; Tiverios (1976), pll. 53, 54, 55.
23. New York, Lois (ex Basle Market, MM) *Para* 57, 58 *ter*; *Addenda*[2] 37.
24. There are several interesting vases dating to the late sixth–early fifth century with this strategy for depicting narrative; many come up numerous times elsewhere in this discussion, but their use of unified narration is not considered individually here:

> Arezzo 1465, *ARV*[2] 15, 6; 316; 1619; *Para* 322; *Addenda*[2] 152; Immerwahr (1990) 63, No. 359, Euphronios; Munich 2309, *ARV*[2], 27, 4; 1620; *Para* 323; *Addenda*[2] 156, Euthymides; Berlin 2180, *ARV*[2] 13, 1; 1584; 1596; 1619; *Para* 321; *Addenda*[2] 152, Euphronios; Berlin 2278, *ARV*[2] 21, 1; 1620; *Para* 323; *Addenda*[2] 154, Euthymides (here the repetitions in imagery appear to have contributed to an error in labeling; Louvre G 43, *ARV*[2] 20, 2; 1619; *Addenda*[2] 154, Smikros; London E 767, *ARV*[2] 31,

6; *Para* 324; *Addenda*² 157, Dikaios Painter; Vienna 3725, *ARV*² 204, 109; 1633: *Para* 342, Berlin Painter.

25. Munich 2620 (J. 337) *ARV*² 16, 17; 1619; *Para* 322; *Addenda*² 153, Immerwahr (1990) No. 362.
26. New York, Lois (ex Basle Market, MM) *Para* 57, 58 *ter*; *Addenda*² 37.
27. Shapiro (1992) 37; Shapiro (1994) 77. See also Goemann et al. (eds.) (1991) No. 41, 199–204.
28. Shapiro (1994) 77.
29. Compare Vienna 3729, *ARV*², 288, 1; 1642; *Addenda*² 209; Simon (1985) 275–6, where different trees signify different locations in the myth of Io.
30. Schwerin 708, *ARV*² 862, 30; 1672; *Para* 425; *Addenda*² 298; Immerwahr (1990) 104, No. 718.
31. London E 41, *ARV*² 58, 51; 1622; *Addenda*² 164; Immerwahr (1990) 61, No. 337. Beazley attributed the cup to Oltos; for the reattribution to Euphronios, see Ohly-Dumm (1974 and 1984) and Williams (1992) No. 36, 190.
32. For the identification of B as the abduction of Helen and for the female figure in the tondo as Ariadne, see Neils (1981) 40–41; figs. 1, 3, 4.
33. Note the polyvalence of the figures on horseback: they are not named. If the scene is in fact the rape of Helen, the viewer might well name the figures as the Dioskouroi (see Neils [1981] 179). The latter make sense, because ancient kidnappings often involve horses to make a quick getaway. Without labels or specific attributes, the figures on horseback have much in common with elite Athenians.
34. For a scene of a *symposion* where participants greet one another with XAIPE, "Welcome!," see Morgantina (Serra Orlando), Museo Archeologico 58.2382, *ARV*² 28, 10; 1620; *Addenda*² 156, by Euthymides [Figures 7.23, 7.24].
35. Louvre G 104 and Florence PD321, *ARV*² 318, 1; 1645; *Para* 358; *Addenda*² 214. Goemann et al. (eds.) (1991) No. 55, 299–303.
36. Neer (2002) 155–9 also notes how distinctive the tondo is in comparison to the exterior scenes.
37. London E 41, *ARV*² 58, 51; 1622; *Addenda*² 164.
38. Note, for example, how different Onesimos' use of the tree as scene divider and/or setting element is here from the way it is used by the Kleophrades Painter in his stamnos, Philadelphia L 64.185, *ARV*² 187, 62; 1632; *Addenda*² 188 [Figures 10.7, 10.8]. Here the different trees are backdrop, distinguishing one location from another, contrasting to the identical trees here that serve as scene dividers.
39. Florence 3985 (E12), *ARV*² 204, 110; *Addenda*² 193; Immerwahr (1990) 82, No. 491. Compare the example where Phintias combines two episodes with Herakles: Munich 2590, *ARV*² 24, 12; *Para* 323; *Addenda*² 155; and London E 41, *ARV*² 58, 51; 1622; *Addenda*² 164 [Figure 6.5], which apparently links three.
40. For definitions of these types of narration, see pp. 95–6 *supra*. Berlin 1685, *ABV* 109, 24; 685; *Addenda*² 30; Tiverios (1976) No. 31, pl. 46, 47a. Stansbury-O'Donnell (1999) 166–7 discusses side B of this vase as representing a complex narrative, one with "both reversal and discovery."
41. *LIMC* I, s.v. *Achilleus* 290, 81. Other scholars suggest that the figure is Hekabe.
42. Hedreen (2001) 157, esp. n. 118, agrees that we do have a causal relationship between the ambush and the two events that take place after the fall of Troy. He lists other scholars who agree. See also Chapter 4, *passim*.
43. Shapiro (1994) 164, describes the relationship between sides A and B as a "subtle thematic link... surprising at this early date."

44. The combination of different perspectives in the poses and gestures of the two female figures, right profile in one case and left profile in the other are a type of link also used to join the repeated figures of youths on a band cup by the Painter of the Burgon Sianas, discussed below: London 1906.12–15.1, *ABV* 90,7; *Addenda*² 24.
45. Hedreen (2001) 154–5.
46. Philadelphia 3442, *ABV* 145,14; *Para* 60; *Addenda*² 40 [Figures 2.5, 2.6].
47. Shapiro (1994) 163 calls the scene on B one of the earliest and most successful merging of several episodes into a coherent composition and Henle (1973) 18 is more explicit: "two places have been drawn into one. The two events could not come at the same place in Troy, at least not in the same place at the same moment." Contrast Hedreen (2001) 48. See also Castriota (1992) 97; 169 and Stansbury-O'Donnell (1999).
48. The two events appear only very rarely in single scenes together on other vases. Princeton, Art Museum 1990–20a–b and y1990–54 by Makron (see Hedreen [2001] fig. 18). Hedreen states the case for the recovery of Helen and the death of Priam being at the same altar, thus linking the two events in a single place.
49. Kassel (T 674) *Para*, 56, 31 *bis*, *Addenda*² 36; see Lullies (1964).
50. These compositions and these repetitions anticipate those found on Exekias' masterpiece in Philadelphia, discussed here in Chapter 2, which couples the deaths of Achilles and Antilochos, events causally linked according to at least one tradition: Philadelphia 3442, *ABV* 145,14; *Para* 60; *Addenda*² 40; Beazley (1951) pl. 30 [Figures 2.5, 2.6].
51. Berlin 1685, *ABV* 109, 24; 685; *Addenda*² 30; Tiverios (1976) No. 31, pl. 46, 47a.
52. New York M.M.A 1989.281.62 Norbert Schimmel Collection 24; *Para* 67, *Addenda*² 46; Bothmer (1985) No. 60, 217.
53. Milne's interpretation, as expressed on a museum label in 1965, is quoted and affirmed by Bothmer (1985) 219.
54. Simon (1976) 84.
55. Bothmer (1985) 219 mentions the linking function of the figures under the handles.
56. Note that the iconography creates a paradigm as well: the spectators who help to alert the viewer to the fact that the two scenes are connected are visual testimony to the best-case narratees of this story: idealized men and youths who themselves would do well to remember the exhortation of Poseidon in battle, and for whom a close relationship with heroes and divinities is an expected norm. Such paradigm-creation is addressed here at length in Chapter 7.
57. Berlin 2264, *ARV*² 60, 64; *Para* 326; *Addenda*² 164
58. Berlin 1685, *ABV* 109, 24; 685; *Addenda*² 30; Tiverios (1976) No. 31, pll. 46, 47a.
59. New York M.M.A. 1972.11.10, *Addenda*² 396; 404; Immerwahr (1990), p. 64, No. 364.
60. The locations of the inscriptions are similar, too; but, as Boardman has pointed out, Euphronios is quite consistent in the way he relates names to figures, so the visual similarities in the placement of the inscriptions may not be especially significant here: Boardman (1992) 45.
61. For a different view, see Kilmer (1993) 183.
62. Bothmer (1976) 494 ff. and in Goemann et al. (eds.) 1991, No. 4, 93–105, suggested that the scene on B depicts Athenians rather than Trojans, protesters against Hippias' disarming of Athenian citizens after Hipparchos' murder. His evidence for this assertion is both the date of the vase and the fact that two of the names, Medon (read by Immerwahr as Megon) and Akastos, have a significant history for Athenian aristocrats, because they were the first two Athenian archons (Bothmer [1976] 494–5). Boardman asserts that the figures on the

B side are Trojans and Lycians (Boardman [1992] 47) and shows that several of the names on B are demonstrably associated with those groups. The use of visual repetition supports Boardman's view, but a Trojan name-connection is not necessarily negative for Archaic Athenian elites. See Kurke (1992) for a thorough discussion of the eastern orientation of elites in the Archaic period; *contra* see Miller (1999) 234–7.

63. Boardman (1992) 47 seems to support this view. A parallel example discussed in Chapter 5 would be the death of Patroklos coupled with Achilles' entrance into battle, Berlin 2264, *ARV*[2] 60, 64; *Para* 326; *Addenda*[2] 164, by Oltos. Stansbury-O'Donnell (1999) 105–7 interprets the two scenes in a paradigmatic rather than a temporal relationship: he suggests that "the heroic sacrifice of Sarpedon becomes a model for their actions"(106).
64. London E 468, *ARV*[2] 206, 132; 1633; *Para* 343; *Addenda*[2] 194; Immerwahr (1990) No. 82.
65. Copenhagen NM 112 *ABV* 292.5; *Addenda*[2] 76. Two epic fights are paired on Smikros' London E 438, *ARV*[2] 20, 3; 1620; *Para* 322; *Addenda*[2] 154. That on A is clearly Aias fighting Hector; on B one figure is identified as Eurymachos, but the only other label is too poorly preserved to read. These fights may be sequential, preserving a phased narration linked by several visual repetitions and by a repeated *kalos* inscription, but we cannot be certain.
66. Vienna 3695, *ARV*[2] 429, 26; 425; 1653; *Para* 374; *Addenda*[2] 236; note an example by the Brygos Painter (Malibu 86.AE.286 [once, Bareiss 346], *Para* 367, 1 *bis*, *Addenda*[2] 224; CVA Malibu 8 pll 418–20) shows the same story, also in three different fields, without the visual repetitions. Weitzmann (1947) 16 cites the Vienna kylix as an example where three "monoscenic" units are joined.
67. Lydos: Berlin 1685, *ABV* 109, 24; 685; *Addenda*[2] 30; Exekias: Philadelphia 3442, *ABV* 145,14; *Para* 60; *Addenda*[2] 40; Oltos: Berlin 2264, *ARV*[2] 60, 64; *Para* 326; *Addenda*[2] 164.
68. Csapo and Miller (1998) 109. Although Odysseus does appear in each scene, his reappearance is not the exclusive link among them.
69. Despite the fact that Hephaistos made both helmets, their repetition is homonymous – the form is repeated, but not with the same meaning, in much the same way as the repeated reclining figure – once a symposiast and once an Amazon, on Euthymides' Morgantina krater: Morgantina (Serra Orlando), Museo Archeologico 58.2382, *ARV*[2] 28, 10; 1620; *Addenda*[2] 156 discussed in Chapter 7. Thus, the repetition serves as a visual hook without an apparent link in meaning.
70. See Lissarrague (1994) 25 for a discussion of a possible mate for this cup, Vienna 3694, *ARV*[2] 427, 3; 425; 1652; *Para* 374; *Addenda*[2] 235, where the potter's signature also appears on the exterior of the foot, but is retrograde.
71. Würzburg University, Martin von Wagner Museum, L265, *ABV* 151,22; 687; *Para* 63; *Addenda*[2] 43; Bothmer (1985) No. 19, 113.
72. Athens NM 531 (CC. 641) *ABV* 55,92; *Addenda*[2] 15; CVA Greece 3(Athens 3) pll. 8–9. Other Siana cups where there is almost exact repetition are Toronto 929.22.9 (632), *ABV* 54,54; *Addenda*[2] 14 (two groups of standing figures and riders and two men conversing at right); Cambridge GR 20.1929 (29.20), *ABV* 54,55; *Addenda*[2] 14 (horseman and men); Berkeley 8.1, *ABV* 54,71; *Addenda*[2] 15 (figures in procession); Taranto 110338, *ABV* 56,99*ter*; *Para* 25; *Addenda*[2] 15 (Gorgon between horsemen).
73. Berlin 4516 *ABV* 52, 27; *Addenda*[2] 13; Brijder (1982) No. 54, pll 16,d and 17a. Similar is Tübingen 4351 (D33), *ABV* 59,6; *Addenda*[2] 16, by Brijder's (1982) Malibu Painter, No. 246. Each side shows figures – differing combinations of youths and men – reclining on couches at the ends of the scenes; on one side there are three figures, male and female, in between

the couches and on the other there are four. A cup in Helgoland (coll. Kropatscheck), Brijder (1982) No. 246, pl. 43, c. and d.) shows figures on couches at the edges of the scenes and komast-dancers near a column-krater in the center; on the other side the dancers are replaced by standing male figures who are clearly not dancers.

74. Hamburg 1908.255, *ABV* 56,102; *Para* 23; *Addenda*[2] 15, C-Painter, Brijder (1982) Vintage Painter, No. 256, pl. 49. Copenhagen 959 (62), *ABV* 56, 103; *Addenda*[2] 15; C-Painter, Brijder (1982) Vintage Painter, No. 258, pl. 49.
75. Shapiro (1992) 37–8.
76. Chatman (1978) 53.
77. Christchurch, Univ. of Canterbury 39/57, CVA Christchurch 1 pl. 25; Brijder (1982) No. 148, Taras Painter.
78. Florence, *ABV* 110,33; *Addenda*[2] 30; Tiverios (1976) pl. 67, No. 45.
79. Prince states that "a dramatic performance representing (many fascinating) events does not constitute a narrative either, since these events rather than being recounted, occur directly on stage." (Prince 1987 *s.v.* "Narrative.")
80. London 1906.12–15.1, *ABV* 90,7; *Addenda*[2] 24; Brijder (1982) No. 290, Painter of the Burgon Sianas, pl. 58, a-b. See Simon (1983) 20–21. Steinhart (2004) 85 is not convinced the two sides of the cup refer to one ritual event.
81. Ashmole (1946) 10.
82. I have made the argument elsewhere for seeing the depicted ritual as the *Proersia* (Steiner, *forthcoming*).
83. Louvre G 105, *ARV*[2] 324, 60; 1645; *Para* 359; *Addenda*[2] 215; Immerwahr (1990) 85, No. 507.
84. Cahn (1972) esp.18, figs. 12–13; Cahn (1986). Bugh (1988) 19 believes that at least two Athenian vase-paintings show the *dokimasia*, but (17 n. 3) those examples such as Louvre F 105 that do not show an official with tablet in hand cannot be certainly identified as representing the *dokimasia*. Spence (1993) 11–14 does not discuss this vase in particular, but he accepts that those images that preserve a scrutinizing official do show a *dokimasia*. See also Lissarragne (1990b) 226–9.
85. Onesimos, Louvre G 104, see n. 35; Philadelphia L 64.185, *ARV*[2] 187, 62; 1632; *Addenda*[2] 188.
86. Note that Cahn (1972) sees the tondo figure as ready for the parade, presumably before the assessor(s).
87. *ARV*[2] 1595–6.
88. Eaverly (1995) 114–15 discusses the relationship between vase-paintings of horses and particular horse-sculptures. She is doubtful about linking specific equestrian sculptures and paintings.
89. Raubitschek (1949) 264–5; for the grave stelai; for the votive relief, Moore (1975). Moore suggests that the votive relief may have been dedicated by the victor in a horse race.
90. Eaverly (1995), Nos. 5 and 11, suggests that the nonfunerary statues may have depicted heroes and dedicated by Athenians youths in thanks for equestrian victory or after a successful *dokimasia* (66–7).
91. Lissarrague (1999) 359–61 has collected and discussed such instances.
92. Lissarrague (1999) 361.
93. Shear (1984) 14–15.
94. In Chapter 8, Euphronios' Louvre neck-amphora (Louvre G 107, *ARV*[2] 18, 1; 1619; *Addenda*[2] 153; Immerwahr [1990] 69 No. 401) provides another example of a link between two types of public discourse – formal inscriptions and *graffiti*.

CHAPTER 7: REPETITION AND PARADIGM

1. This literature is cited extensively in Chapter 11.
2. Stansbury-O'Donnell (1999) 124–36.
3. Stansbury-O'Donnell (1999) 124.
4. Stansbury-O'Donnell (1999) 130.
5. Webster (1972).
6. Webster (1972) 250–51.
7. Webster (1972) 260.
8. Webster (1972) 62.
9. Webster (1972) 243.
10. Webster (1972) 269.
11. Scheibler (1987a) 95–7.
12. Scheibler's identification of this type of figure, a "typical" Athenian youth, extends to other types in the *polis* as well: maidens, as well as mature men and women. Her notion of the "typical" or "ideal" appears to have a great deal in common with that defined by Stewart (1990) 79 in his discussion of these phenomena as they relate to *mimesis* in Greek sculpture in particular: "the ideal is to be understood as a concrete presentation of notions as to what constitutes the 'typical,' 'general,' and so 'exemplary' human form, an 'everyman' free of individual peculiarities and quirks." In accepting Scheibler's interpretation, I agree with Carpenter (1986) 40 in his characterization of these figures as representing types of upper-class Greeks, but I am explicitly rejecting his conclusion that in some cases these "stock figures" are compositional fillers without semantic value in the image as a whole (37–54).
13. See Chapter 2 and 11; Sinos (1993) esp. 75–6.
14. As discussed in Chapter 2, Boardman has made an argument for the possibility that chariots had some role in sixth-century military affairs: Boardman (1983) 28–9. Sinos rejects Boardman's suggestion, with her hypothesis that the chariot connects the hoplite soldier to the heroes of epic, exalting his activity by comparison to theirs. See also Van Wees (2004).
15. Knittlmeyer (1997) conducts a general study of Trojan War themes as relevant to Athenian elites and values and their changing status in the period of the democracy, and so indirectly addresses paradigm. Ferrari (2003) 40 discusses pitfalls in oversimplifying paradigmatic relationships.
16. Discussions taking the existence of visual paradigm for granted are numerous. See Osborne (1987) 110–11.
17. Halliday and Hasan (1975; 1989 reprinting) 278–9; Bowditch (1976) 20.
18. Paris, Louvre E 817, *ABV* 9,7.
19. See Cairns (1996) 157 and discussion below for an analysis of a negative paradigm created by interconnected repetitions.
20. The discussion relies on Beazley's lists of attributions to the painter as well as new attributions by Bakir (1981).
21. Paris, Louvre E 819, *ABV* 38, 5; *Addenda*[2] 10; Bakir (1981) No. A9, Tafel 12, abb.22; Tafel 13, abb. 24–5. A panel amphora links two sphinxes distinguished only by a difference in position: on one side a sphinx faces right; on the other side the sphinx faces left with right paw raised: Havana, Lagunillas, Olmos Romera (1990) 22–3, No. 7. Attribution by Mommsen.

22. Close to both of these examples is Jena, inv. nr. 178 (*ABV* 39,7; *Para* 18; *Addenda*[2] 10; Bakir (1981) No. A8, Tafel 11–12, Abb. 21–2), where confronting lions and sirens are in panels and surrounded by rosettes, so syntax is repeated but figures are not.
23. Copenhagen NM 3259, *ABV* 61, 11; *Addenda*[2] 17; related to the C-Painter ([Brijder (1982)] No. 216, the Mailbu Painter, Fig. 52, pll. 38, a-b, 41a). A similar example, Basle Market (MuM), Brijder (1982) No. 29, pll. 11f and 12c, shows a running female, carrying spear and shield but without helmet, in the tondo, and warriors who stand on one side of the exterior, wearing helmet and carrying round shields and spears. In this case, there is less visual similarity between the "Athena" figure and the warriors. Paris, CA 6113, Brijder (1982) No. 20, pll. 10h-11d, depicts a running armed figure in the tondo who is an exact parallel in reverse for the Achilles-figure on the exterior and is paralleled again by the duelling warriors on the reverse of the cup (Brijder [1982] 238, for description). Malibu 77.AE.46 (Brijder [1982] No. 247, Malibu Painter, pll. 44a–b, 46f) preserves a warrior, wearing low-crested helmet, with spear and Boeotian shield in all three fields of the cup: alone, squatting in the tondo; in a phalanx on A; and with a horseman on B.
24. See Cole (1995) on citizen identification with patron divinities.
25. Taranto I. G. 4342, *ABV* 66,55; *Para* 27; Brijder(1991) No. 384, pl. 128, a–e.
26. Note that in this example there is no corollary composition on the other side of the cup – the comparison here is not between the two sides, but between the tondo and one side.
27. Brijder (1991) 336–7 and 376–7. The relationship of the scene on side A to the two lion fights is not clear, but the absence of precise repetitive links suggests that side A is not part of the (sub)text created by the tondo and side B. A male figure sneaks out from an Aeolic column toward an olive tree and two women who stand on either side of a date-palm tree and in front of a fountain-house. Brijder(1991) 377 quotes Sourvinou-Inwood (1985, 1987) as suggesting that we see here a scene of sexual pursuit, with the male figure the erotic predator of the marriageable *parthenoi*. If the male figure is Herakles, as suggested by Brijder (1991) 376, he is in disguise and differs markedly in clothing and attributes from the figure who fights the lion in the tondo. Note, however, that the women in the fountain-house scene wear clothing similar to that of the women who watch the lion-fighters on B, although their poses and gestures differ. This may provide a clue to the identity of the female spectators on side B and in general: *parthenoi* are destined for Athenian elite males who confirm their status through heroic behavior.
28. Several scholars have suggested that these figures represent Athenian elites. Brijder (1991) 337.
29. Berlin 3402, *ABV* 67, *Addenda*[2] 18; Manner of Heidelberg Painter, Brijder (1991) No. 470, pls 146, g-l.
30. Several additional examples of Siana cups show fighting heroes as paradigms for adult males. Bellerophon fighting the Chimaira: Basle Market, MuM, Brijder(1991) No. 356, Pls. 116a–b, 117a; Herakles and the lion: Minneapolis, Brijder (1991) No. 331, pl. 107 a–c. Louvre A 478, *ABV* 66,54; *Para* 26; *Addenda*[2] 18; Brijder (1991) No. 357, pl. 116 preserves an interesting interconnection between bystanders to Bellerophon battling the Chimaira on side B and the figure of Pandareos(?) on side A: the bystanders on B are identical (possibly even down to the headgear) to Pandareos except for the spears held by the figures on side B.
31. Taranto I. G. 4363, *ABV* 113,71; *Para* 45. As such, it is a "straight" version of the example by the Painter of the Burgon Sianas, an associate of the C-Painter, involving Herakles chasing Nessos to rescue Deineira, discussed in Chapter 9 and interpreted there as parodic: Birmingham Univ. Brijder (1982) No. 291, pls 58 c–d [Figures 9.1, 9.2].

32. Taranto 4359; *ABV* 109, 26; *Para* 44; *Addenda*² 30; Tiverios (1976) No. 36, pl. 28.
33. Florence 70995, *ABV* 110, 32, *Para* 44; *Addenda*² 30; Tiverios (1976), pll. 22–3; Raab (1972) Type A II, no. 11, p. 164.
34. London, British Museum 1948.10–15.1, *ABV* 108, 8; *Para* 44; *Addenda*² 29; Tiverios (1976) pl. 8,9; Raab (1972) Type A II, no. 10, p. 164.
35. Polygiros, Archaeological Museum, 235. Shapiro (1989a) 25–6 fig. 15.
36. Palermo, from Chiusi, Beazley, *ABV* 114,2, Manner of Lydos; Raab (1972) Type A I, no. 8, p. 161.
37. Raab (1972) p. 21.
38. Florence 70995, *ABV* 110, 32, *Para* 44; *Addenda*² 30; Tiverios (1976), pll. 22–3.
39. Shapiro (1989a) 29. In *LIMC* VII, s.v. *Paridis Iudicum* (A. Kossatz-Deissman) 176–88, two examples are listed with extra figures:. One by the C-Painter (Paris, Louvre CA 616 from Thebes, *ABV* 58,122; *Para* 23; *Addenda*² 16; *LIMC* VII, s.v. *Paridis Iudicum*, No. 6) shows a female figure confronting Paris and holding a wreath. She is identified as Eris, Iris, or Nymphe and interacts with Paris much more aggressively than the extra female figures in the scenes by Lydos. The other example includes Dionysos, clearly identified with ivy wreath and grape vines in his hand: Berlin 1894 from Vulci *ABV* 277, 14; 692; *Para* 122; *Addenda*² 72; Circle of the Antimenes Painter, *LIMC* VII, s.v. *Paridis Iudicum* no. 33. Other examples with extras are much later red-figure examples: *LIMC* VII. s.v. *Paridis Iudicum* 179.
40. London, British Museum 1948.10–15.1, *ABV*108, 8; *Para* 44; *Addenda*² 29 Beazley (1986) 41.
41. Polygiros, Archaeological Museum, 235. Shapiro (1989a) 25–6 fig. 15.
42. Palermo, from Chiusi, Beazley, *ABV* 114,2, Manner of Lydos. Although Raab (1972) lists this example under her Type A I, it does not appear in the list in *LIMC* VII, s.v. *Paridis Iudicum* (A. Kossatz-Deissman) 176–88, nor does it appear in *LIMC* 1 s.v. *Alexandros, B. Parisurteil(Auswahl)* (R. Hampe) 498–500. Beazley also observed a related image on a plate fragment in Athens, "A youth leading three women to a youth . . . 'the Judgement of Paris deheroized.'"Akr. 2420, Beazley, *ABV* 130; 686; *Addenda*² 35, Near the Ready Painter, also a companion of Lydos.
43. Beazley, *ABV* 115.
44. Just as on the lekanis lid, in another example the myths themselves, here Herakles and the lion and Herakles and centaurs, are nowhere exactly spelled out, yet they are everywhere behind the images, informing them. The neck-amphora Oxford 1965.135 (*ABV* 137, 59; *Para* 55; *Addenda*² 37) devotes four fields to two mythlike narratives; all involve individuals who share attributes and activities with heroic lion and centaur fighters. The message articulated by means of repetition is that an elite youth shares status with a "heroic" youth, one who participates in centaur fights, and with adult males who share characteristics with lion-fighters. The context is one of synonymy where elites "engage in" heroic activities.
45. Beazley, *ABV* 115.
46. New York M.M.A. 56.171.18, *ABV* 137, 61; *Para* 55; *Addenda*² 37, a neck-amphora by Group E, reveals paradigmatic compression into a single scenes like that on the Judgment of Paris examples. On the main scene on side A, a similar youth watches two incidents of a warrior leading a woman, a "recovery of Helen" and what appears to be its anonymous counterpart (?); shoulders are linked by the repetition of three figures on horseback flanked by youths wearing *chlamydes*. On B these equestrian groups are accompanied by two youths in *himatia* at the far left. Visual links between the shoulder and the spectators on both panel and shoulder on side A weave together three subjects: youths who ride horses, armed

men who recover women, and the men and youths on B, who dance to an *aulos*-player, either in chorus or *komos*.

47. Scheibler (1987a) 91–2 observes that scenes joined on Lydos' amphora in Basle (Basle, Kambli, *ABV* 109,25; *Para* 44; *Addenda*² 30; Tiverios (1976) No. 39, pl. 24, 25a,b) connect youths departing on B and Theseus who fights the Minotaur on A. The present discussion substantiates Scheibler's hypothesis by pointing to visual links that create a concrete foundation for comparison: the spectators at the left of each scene are very similar, with the youth at the far left on side A and the youth at the right on side B being nearly identical, both wearing spotted *himatia* with embroidery at the hemline. Here the youths themselves repeat the hero's iconography and appear in the scene with the hero, but they are not displayed participating in lion-fight, centaur-fight, or beauty contest ajudication.
48. Würzburg 247, *ABV* 134,17; *Addenda*² 36; Simon (1975.).
49. Exceptions to the nude Iolaos exist on Würzburg 248, *ABV* 134,18; Richmond 60.23, *Para* 56, 48 *ter*, *Addenda*² 36; and Kassel T 384, *ABV* 137,57; *Para* 55; *Addenda*² 37, where he wears helmet, cuirass, scabbard, and greaves.
50. Simon (quoted in *LIMC* 1 s.v. *Alexandros, L. Alexandros in Troja, mit Helena oder Priamos*, No. 69 [R. Hampe] 498–500) has, relying on *Iliad* 22.294, speculated that B shows Trojan warriors departing for battle, and names the figures: Priam, Andromache, Astyanax, Deiphobos, Helen, and Paris. Clearly they share many features with the figures on A, but the absence of labels creates uncertainty.
51. Munich 1397 (J.1079), *ABV* 134, 20; *Addenda*² 36. (The amphora once on the London Market [Hewett], *Para* 56, 20 *bis* is almost identical.) New York M.M.A. 41.162.143, *ABV* 134, 25; *Para* 55; *Addenda*² 36 links a Minotaur fight with a scene of Ajax and Cassandra. Nude figures at the edges of the panel run away from the scene at the Athena statue, and nude youths watch Theseus fight the Minotaur. In each of these cases, the nude figures are slightly different – long-haired youths versus short-haired youth and adult – and come close to being anonymous *participants* rather than observers.
52. Kassel T 384, *ABV* 137,57; *Para* 55; *Addenda*² 37, is another example with a similar point. An identical youth watches Herakles and the lion (A) and an adult greaving (B). The latter will be, once armed, identical to Iolaos on A. There is a double paradigm: the arming figure is like Iolaos and both are exempla for the anonymous elite youth. On the amphora Munich 1382, *ABV* 135, 47; *Addenda*² 36, the adult male spectator at the right of Herakles and the lion may parallel the figure at the far left of the birth of Athena on A, but the vase is too fragmentary for one to be sure.
53. Copenhagen 109, *ABV* 135,33; *Addenda*² 36.
54. Louvre F53, *ABV* 136,49; 686; *Para* 55; *Addenda*² 36; Immerwahr (1990) 32, No. 128.
55. On the amphora Harvard 1972. 42 (once New Haven, Watkins), *ABV* 133,8; *Addenda*² 35, there is a similar link: the figure arming on B puts on greaves and will don a high-crested Corinthian helmet like those worn by Geryon on A.
56. Closely associated with this group are two amphoras combining chariots on one side with hoplite and mounted cavalry on the other. An example in Würzburg (Würzburg 244, *ABV* 135, 36) depicts a chariot wheeling on B; the charioteer is accompanied by a warrior with prominent helmet-crest. On A, three hoplites wearing helmets identical to that of the warrior on B stand between two mounted men, one of whom also wears the same helmet. If it is correct to see heroic overtones in depictions of men fighting from chariots, we may see here a relationship of synonymy set up between contemporary hoplites and "heroes." The narrative is not specific or "strong," but the repetitions set up a powerful link.

57. See Beazley (1950) 311–15, No. 5, for transcription and commentary on inscriptions, which are very poorly preserved.
58. Turin 4123, *ARV*² 28, 11; 1620; *Addenda*² 156, Immerwahr (1990) 66, No. 377.
59. After Immerwahr, rather than ΚΛΥΤΟΣ (Beazley). Immerwahr argues, correctly I believe, that the inscription is too long for simply a two-syllable name.
60. Neer (2002) 159 agrees that the conjunction of A and B is paradigmatic.
61. Louvre G42, *ARV*² 23, 1; 1620; *Para* 323; *Addenda*² 154, Immerwahr (1990) 66–7, No. 385.
62. The name "Sosias" also appears twice on Euthymides' Morgantina krater (Morgantina [Serra Orlando] Museo Archeologico 58.2382, *ARV*² 28, 10; 1620; *Addenda*² 156, Immerwahr [1990] 66, No. 376). Phintias' Sosias, as depicted, appears to be among elites [Figures 7.23, 7.24].
63. Osborne (1987) 111 fig. 37.
64. Cairns (1996) 157.
65. Immerwahr (1990) 67.
66. Cairns (1996) 157.
67. Munich 2308, *ARV*² 26, 2; 1620; *Addenda*² 156; Immerwahr (1990) 65, No. 370. See discussion of Turin 4123, *ARV*² 28, 11; 1620; *Addenda*² 156 above.
68. Although this could be a description of Phayllos, the label appears to belong to the figure at left.
69. The figure to the left on A, an archer in Scythian dress, is named, but only one syllable is preserved. A nonsense inscription with sounds often used in close relation to images of Scythians, (ΧΥΧΟΣΠΙ)"Khu-khos-pi," appears in a vertical line in front of his left leg. A parodic interpretation for images and syllables is investigated further in Chapter 9.
70. Exekias: Louvre F 53, *ABV* 136,49; 686; *Para* 55; *Addenda*² 36. Phintias: Louvre G 42, *ARV*² 23, 1; 1620; *Para* 323; *Addenda*² 154.
71. Oltos: Copenhagen NM inv. 3877, *ARV*² 63, 87.
72. Epiktetos: London E 37, *ARV*² 72, 17; 1623; *Para* 328; *Addenda*² 167.
73. See the discussion of Lissarrague (1990a) 123–39.
74. Morgantina (Serra Orlando) Museo Archeologico 58.2382, *ARV*² 28, 10; 1620; *Addenda*² 156, Immerwahr (1990) 66, No. 376.
75. Here is an example of a visual "hook" without apparent intrinsic meaning that serves to draw the viewer into the process of comparison, much like the white horse on Exekias' Orvieto amphora discussed in Chapter 2: Orvieto 2747 (ex Faina 77), *ABV* 144, 10; *Para* 60; Wojcik (1989) 69–71.
76. Note that Immerwahr also believes the individual named in these inscriptions is the artist Sosias. However, Sosias appears commonly as a name for apparently elite Athenians and as a label for mortals as on Phintias' amphora, Louvre G 42. See J. Davies (1971) Sosias, 13179, 13180. See also Neils (1995) 439 for a discussion of Sosias' identity.
77. Immerwahr (1990) 66 cites another *khaire* in conjunction with the fourth symposiast on B, but it does not appear in the drawing in Neils (1995) 430, fig. 3b, nor is it discussed by either Neils or Stilwell (1959) 172.
78. Neer (2002) 108–11 believes that the lyre player is a portrait of the potter Sosias, and Immerwahr (1990) 72 believes that the potter's name is in the vocative and linked to the preceeding ΧΑΙΡΕ in a greeting; see n. 76 *supra*.
79. Komasts and heroic behavior are certainly associated if not synonymous on this krater. Immerwahr also suggests there may have been a now-lost "*kalos*" with Teisis; the name of

each of these two individuals, Sosias and Teisis, is embedded and articulated both in the context of the heroic exploit and in the "coherent" version of the elite *komos*. This topic is treated more fully in Chapter 10.

80. Euphronios: London E 41 [Figure 6.7], where deeds of Theseus on the exterior are linked with a "sympotic" Theseus on the interior, and London E 18 (*ARV*² 62,86; 1600; 1700; *Para* 327, *Addenda*² 165), where Anakreon is combined with Herakles and the Amazons. Epiktetos: London E 38 [Figures 10.3–10.5], where symposiasts in two fields are linked with Herakles and Busiris.
81. Mills (1993) 25 points out how in the late archaic period "a national hero such as Theseus is useful as an embodiment of the best qualities of the 'nation' in its own eyes."
82. New York, Cooper-Hewitt 1921.1.1 (Cooper Union), *ABV* 63, 5; *Para* 26; *Addenda*² 17, Brijder (1991) No. 423, 458, pl. 136–7.
83. On another cup in Paris, two figures in the tondo wear ivy wreaths and carry drinking horns, and both cannot be Dionysos: Louvre CA 576, *ABV* 63,3; *Addenda*² 17, Brijder(1991) No. 367, pl. 121. An identical figure stands in a divine procession, apparently on Mount Olympus, on a third example in Istanbul: Istanbul 9332, Manner of Heidelberg Painter, Brijder (1991) No. 446, pl. 144. The distinction between Dionysos and Dionysiac votaries is often hard to draw. Brijder (1991) does not discuss this issue.
84. Basel, Antikenmuseum und Sammlung Ludwig, Kä 420, *Para* 65; *Addenda*² 43; Bothmer (1985) 43, fig. 32; 47, fig. 40 a, b.
85. Note the closely related amphora Würzburg L265, *ABV* 151,22; 687; *Para* 63, *Addenda*² 43 where satyrs make wine on one side and they serve it to Dionysos on the other, discussed as an example of narrative sequence in Chapter 6.
86. Florence 81601, *ARV*² 64, 96, *Addenda*² 166, not in Immerwahr (1990). The cup Brussels R 253 + Naples, Astarita 306, *ARV*² 64, 104 is similar, but apparently exclusively mythical: it depicts nymphs (plus others) in all three fields and at least A and I share *kalos*(I)/*kale*(A).
87. Chilon is the name of the Spartan ephor in the mid-sixth century who ousted the last tyrant (a member of the family of Cleisthenes) in Sicyon (Hdt. I.59.2). Owing to the time difference, it is unlikely that Epiktetos' Chilon is the same Chilon who is mentioned by Herodotus; but the *kalos* Chilon could be a later member of an Athenian elite family who were also enemies of the family of Cleisthenes. The name without *kalos* also appears on the cup London E 19 by Oltos, *ARV*² 63, 95 with a roster of names apparently identifying revelers. In this case, the name Solon is also written, so the revelers may be early figures in Greek history; both are listed with the Seven Sages.
88. Villa Giulia, *ARV*² 77, 90; *Addenda*² 169; Cohen (1978) 400, No. C 48.
89. Warsaw 142332, *ARV*² 27, 8; *Para* 324; *Addenda*² 156, Immerwahr (1990) 65, No. 374. See Wegner (1979) pll. 8–9. Other examples that explore visual (perceptual) point of view by combining two perspectives in this way are discussed in Chapter 8.
90. Immerwahr does not record this inscription, but it is visible in the photographs of the vase in the Beazley Archive. The inscriptions are also discussed in Chapter 5.
91. The parodic implications are discussed again in Chapter 9.
92. An example by Phintias would also suggest that mythical protypes and mortal renactment are intermingled. A cup in Karlsruhe (Karlsruhe 63.104, *ARV*² 1700; *Para* 323,12 *ter*, *Addenda*² 155; Immerwahr [1990] 68 No. 395) depicts a running satyr on A and a running *hetaira* on B, both nude, and in poses that duplicate one another precisely. The semireclining, balding ithyphallic satyr on B parallels the reclining youth playing the *barbiton* on A. The similarities create a blending of mythical and "real" symposia.

The centaur in the tondo shares horse ears, shaggy beard, and shaggy hair with the satyr on the exterior and may form the subject of the youth's song. The exterior interconnections are emphasized by the duplication of the artist's signature extending horizontally across the top of each scene. Mortal and mythical time zones are equated, intermingled rather than separated.

93. Louvre G138, ARV^2 365,61; 1580; 1596; 1606; 1648; *Addenda*^{2} 223. See discussion in Chapter 5 *supra*. Ghiron-Bestagne (1976) 265–7 discusses the imagery as depicting a dithyrambic chorus making a turn around the *thymele* at the center of the orchestra of a theatre. The pair at center are identified as Dionysos and Oinopion in *LIMC* III s.v. "Dionysos" No. 786. Knauer (1976) 213 suggests it may have been a special commission for members of a (chorus)"class."
94. Istanbul 9332, Brijder (1991) No. 446, pl. 144. Another example is Palermo 1856, *ABV* 65,45; *Addenda*^{2} 17; Brijder(1991) No. 419, pl. 134. A "penguin-woman" watches Achilles being delivered to Cheiron, and other "penguin-women" both confront and watch meetings between men and women and youths and women on the other side. Thus the "penguin-women" are both participants in the upbringing of a baby hero and also interact with elite youths and adult males.
95. Bothmer (1985) 46. See a related discussion in Ferrari (2003) 37–44 on the issues that arise in trying to separate wholly mythical scenes from (apparently) wholly mortal scenes.
96. Berlin 1688, *ABV* 150,9; 687; *Para* 63, Bothmer (1985), No. 9,90.
97. A final example certainly includes repetitions, a pointed cap in one figure and two youths at right of each scene, but the subjects are not clear enough for me to discuss here. However, there is certainly a syntax of comparison: Paris, Louvre F 26, *ABV* 150,5; *Para* 63; *Addenda*^{2} 42, Bothmer (1985) No. 11, 94.
98. Basel Sammlung Ludwig Lu 19, *Para* 65; *Addenda*^{2} 43; Bothmer (1985) No. 6, 83. This tendency for the Amasis Painter to depict figures who are "almost but not quite" divine was remarked upon by Beazley in discussing an amphora in Paris (Paris, Louvre F 25 [MNB 1688], *ABV* 150,4; 687; *Para* 62; *Addenda*^{2} 42, Bothmer [1985] No. 12, 97): "It seems like the Paris picture is primarily a 'warrior' leaving home: soldier, father, or counselor, mother or wife. But the painter has spiced it with a trident and, if the purchaser calls the figures Ares, Poseidon, and Aphrodite, will not complain." Beazley (1931b) 259.
99. Munich 1383 (J.75) *ABV* 150,7.
100. Compare this amphora to the cup in Paris by the Triptolemos Painter discussed above where the figures in the tondo can be identified, via attributes, as Dionysos and Oinopoion: Louvre G 138, ARV^2 365,61; 1580; 1596; 1606; 1648; *Addenda*^{2} 223 [Figures 7.30–7.32].
101. Bloomington, Indiana University Art Museum 71.82 (once Switzerland, private), *Para* 65; *Addenda*^{2} 43, Bothmer (1985) No. 2, 74.
102. New York, Cooper Hewitt 1921.1.1; ABV 63, 5; *Para* 26; Addenda^2 17.
103. Scheibler (1987a) 107–8.
104. Side A of an amphora in Geneva (Musée d'Art et D'Histoire, I 4, Gosse Collection, *ABV* 150, 8; 687; *Para* 63; *Addenda*^{2} 42; Bothmer 1985 No. 15) is very similar. Youths surround Dionysos and carry attributes that link them to the god on side A: all of them hold ivy leaves, as does the god. Another youth, identical except he trades an ivy branch for a spear, bounds a departure scene on the other side of the amphora. In combination, the two sides linked visually by the repetition of the observer/participant refer to two important experiences for youths in Athenian society: to become initiated into religious activities of the *polis* and to learn the behaviors necessary for its defense. This tendency to explore facets of experience or social role is discussed fully in Chapter 8.

CHAPTER 8: REPETITION, CHARACTER, AND PERSPECTIVE

1. Chatman (1978) 107–38 (character) and 151–8 (point of view).
2. Chatman (1978) 151–2.
3. Chatman (1978) 107–31.
4. Aristotle's definition also states (*Poetics* VI (1449b–1450b) that "... the action is conducted by agents who should have certain qualities in 'both character and thought' (τὸ ἦθος καὶ τὴν διάνοιαν) (as it is these factors which allow us to ascribe qualities to their actions, too, and it is in their actions that all men find success or failure)" (trans. Halliwell).
5. Aristotle, *Poetics* XV.
6. Modern critics, such as Propp and his successors Tomachevski and Bremond, also see plot as the locus of character-creation. See Propp (1968) 20 and Tomachevski (1925) 293–8. Bremond (1973) 11–47 observes that character is determined by the specific set of plot motifs consistently bound up with a character and that the plot motifs can be rearranged to show character development. For Chatman, character does exist apart from plot. Character is a "paradigm of traits," where "trait" refers to a relatively stable or abiding personal quality that may or may not be made manifest in one activity (one plot event) or another. The individual traits may manifest themselves early and then disappear and be replaced by others, but they are indeed revealed. The psychological and moral changes a character undergoes are important to such a definition. Chatman (1978) 126.
7. London B 379, *ABV* 60,20; *Para* 26; *Addenda*² 16; Brijder (1982) Cassandra Painter, pl. 24, No. 121.
8. Athens "418", *ABV* 59,12 (manner of the C Painter); *Para* 25; *Addenda*² 16; Brijder's Painter of Athens "418" (Brijder [1982] No. 254, p. 259) *CVA* Greece 3 (Athens 3) pl. 11.
9. Cambridge FitzMus GR 4,1930 (30.4) *ABV* 63, 4; *Addenda*² 17; Brijder (1991) No. 369, pl. 122.
10. Louvre F 70, *ABV* 156,76; *Addenda*² 46; Bothmer (1985) No. 53, 199.
11. Bothmer appears to accept Pottier's suggestion that the scenes reflect a sequence of episodes, first preparations for a musical event as the lyre is handed over, followed by libations to celebrate the victory. Bothmer (1985) 198.
12. Würzburg 251, *ABV* 135,35.
13. Amasis Painter: Band cup, Berlin F 1795, *ABV* 156, 83; *Addenda*² 46; and Bonn University Akademisches Kunstmuseum 504, *ABV* 151,20; 687; *Para* 63; *Addenda*² 43. The fragmentary Lydan example where two apparently frontal chariots are coupled (Tarquinia 618, *ABV* 125.33) is surely a descendant of the Horse-head Type and may be connected to the Group E examples cited here in n. 14.
14. Neck amphora Tarquinia RC 1061, *Para* 56, 58 *bis*: wedded pair in chariot (profile) and partially hitched frontal quadriga; Type B amphora, Vatican G. 35, *ABV* 135,37: frontal chariot on B and chariot turning on A. A near replica of this piece is Frankfurt A/M Mkt (ex Bareiss 262), *Para* 56, 37*bis*. On a Type B amphora, Munich 1396 (J.1114), *ABV* 135,39; *Addenda*² 46, a frontal chariot is paired with one in profile; clearly the scene on A is military, a departure scene, and that on B is athletic: the lone charioteer is not armed, but he carries a long goad. A Type B amphora in Tarquinia 617, *Para* 56, 36 *bis*; *Addenda*² 36 shows a frontal chariot (athletic) paired with foot soldiers framed by mounted men. The horses on A and B are very similar. The hydria Louvre C 10659, *ABV* 138,69; *Para* 55 shows on the shoulder a chariot in profile in a departure scene. On the body there is a chariot wheeling with differences in armor between shoulder and body. On the fragments of

Athens, Akr 821; *ABV* 136, 51 there is a chariot on each side, but the vase is too fragmentary for analysis.

15. Boston 89.273, *ABV* 144,4; *Para* 59; *Addenda*² 39.
16. London E 3, *ARV*² 70,3; 45.102; 1623; *Para* 328; *Addenda*² 166; Cohen (1978) 424, B 93.
17. Paris, Louvre G 5, *ARV*² 71,14; 49.175; *Addenda*² 167.
18. Naples 81238 (2609), *ARV*² 73, 29; 97,2; 102,4.
19. This is apparently a kind of combination of greeting and signature (for a list of the vases signed by Paidikos as potter and those where his name appears but without verb, see *ARV*² 102).
20. The very fragmentary cup in Providence depicts dancing satyrs and nymphs with *thyrsoi* and wineskins in all three fields and may show the same type of event from two perspectives as well: Providence 25.077, *ARV*², 73, 34; *Addenda*² 168; Immerwahr (1990) 62, No. 347. The inscriptions are apparently repeated in all three fields as well: at least *kalos*, and possibly *ho pais kalos*, appears in each field.
21. Odessa 26602, *ARV*² 7,5; 292; *Addenda*² 150; Cohen (1978) 206,C11.
22. Ferrari Pinney (1983).
23. Louvre G 107, *ARV*² 18, 1, Manner of Euphronios; 1619; *Addenda*² 153; Immerwahr (1990) 69, No. 401. Now reattributed to Euphronios. See Neer (2002) 134.
24. Immerwahr reconstructs the inscription with interpuncts (Immerwahr [1990] 68–9). Denoyelle (1992b) shows examples suggesting that interpuncts in vase-inscriptions do not always indicate that the painter intends to represent an inscription in stone. Surely they do represent a level of formality, however.
25. The interweaving of the visual appearance and language of both formal, public inscriptions and *graffiti* inscriptions that appears in both public and private is seen also on Oneisimos' Louvre cup discussed in Chapter 6 [Figures 6.24–6.26]. Louvre G 105, *ARV* ² 324, 60; 1645; *Para* 359.
26. London B 379, *ABV* 60,20; *Para* 26; Brijder (1982) Cassandra Painter, Pl. 24, No. 121.
27. A discussion of how Euphronios' images and script on the vase are also parodic is taken up in Chapter 9.
28. Louvre G 30, *ARV*² 15, 9; 1619; *Para* 322; *Addenda*² 152; Immerwahr (1990) 63, No. 360; Goemann et al. (eds.) (1991) 154–6, No. 20.
29. Immerwahr, 63, identifies the song as a badly garbled approximation of a fragment by Sappho: Frag. 36: Page (1962) 34, No. 36. The fragment, of which only one line is preserved, goes as follows: καὶ ποθήω καὶ μάομαι . . . , "I both long for and seek after . . . " It is therefore a text about desire, appropriate for the image-context, which is *sympotic*, and in concert with the *kalos* inscriptions. This inscription is listed as No. 2 in a list complied by Csapo and Miller (1991) 381. See also Lissarrague (1990a) 133, who notes that the placement of the verse fragment makes the singer appear to be "caught in his own song." Note the similarity here to Epiktetos' London E 37, *ARV*² 72, 17; 1623; *Para* 328; *Addenda*² 167, where "Hipparchos *kalos*" is written as if it is a song coming out of the singer's mouth [Figure 9.5]
30. Another amphora in the Louvre, in the manner of Euphronios, is too fragmentary for complete assessment of the interaction among repeated imagery and repeated inscriptions, but such interaction surely existed on the complete vessel: Louvre G 106, *ARV*² 18, 3; *Para* 322; *Addenda*² 153. Immerwahr (1990) where Amazons, possibly named, appear on each side of the vessel.

31. Berlin 2180, *ARV*[2] 13, 1; 1584; 1596; 1619; *Para* 321; *Addenda*[2] 152; Immerwahr (1990) 63, No. 356. See Goemann et al. (eds.) (1991), No. 1, 61–9.
32. This krater carries further the analyses of athletic activities observed earlier in the repertory of the Amasis Painter and Oltos: London 1839.10–25.13 (B 191) *ABV* 152,24; 687; *Para* 63; *Addenda*[2] 43; Bothmer (1985) No. 22, 122. Oltos' analysis of pederastic activity in the gymnasium/palaestra on his New York psykter M.M.A. 10.210.18 (*ARV*[2] 54, 7; *Para* 326; *Addenda*[2] 163) is treated in detail in Chapter 10.
33. Boston 01.8021, *ARV*[2] 320, 14; *Addenda*[2] 215; Immerwahr (1990) 84, No. 505.
34. Berlin 1966.19, *Para* 323, 3 *bis*; *Addenda*[2] 154; Immerwahr (1990) 69, No. 404.
35. Henderson (1991) 112. Kossatz-Deissman (1991) 173 suggests the name, when restored as "Stysippos," may imply that the satyr is aroused by a horse. Although earlier scholars suggested the inscription ought to be restored as a *kalos* inscription, *Stysippos kalos*, Immerwahr (1990) 127 has rejected that view. An obscene name with an – *ippos* ending would be a parody of an aristocratic Athenian name.
36. Immerwahr (1990) 69; see also Lissarrague (1990a) 127. The inscription is possibly connected with νήτη, the highest note of the scale.
37. The placement of the signature on A may have parodic overtones as explored in Chapter 9.
38. Berlin 2285, *ARV*[2] 431, 48; 426; 1653; *Para* 374; *Addenda*[2] 237; Immerwahr (1990) 87, No. 533. Compare this discussion to that on Phintias' hydria Munich 2421 in Chapter 9 [Figures 9.10–9.11].
39. Immerwahr (1964) 23 mentions the vaguely pederastic characteristic of all school scenes, and Svenbro (1985; 1993) 187–98 develops a "pederastic model" for the activity of reading.
40. Immerwahr (1964) 18–19 and n. 3, attributed as Steisichorus fr. 26 (Diehl).
41. Louvre G 30, *ARV*[2] 15, 9; 1619; *Para* 322; *Addenda*[2] 152.
42. Lissarrague (1990a) 137–9 discusses this cup in much the same way, and he suggests that "by including the two cups the painter clearly indicates the ultimate goal of music and song."
43. Brijder (1991); Shapiro (1990).

CHAPTER 9: REPETITION AND PARODY

1. Athens, NM 1104 (CC 692) *ABV* 147, 5; Immerwahr (1990) 35, No. 146.
2. It is not necessary for there to be repeated imagery or words to create parody; scholars have identified vase imagery that appears to be parodic, but repeats, in altered form, imagery paralleled on other vessels entirely or examples of imagery that seems to derive its inspiration from parodic performance. See for example Brownlee (1989), where the author makes a case for an amphora in Boston (M.F.A. 1979.618) representing a parodic version of the Ransom of Hector. The Boston vase inscriptions appear to mock words, as they create real syllables without apparent meaning. Keuls (1988) discusses caricature and satiric intent on red-figure pottery.
3. Hutcheon (2000) 101. Hutcheon's work is focused on establishing a definition and description of parody in the twentieth century.
4. Goldhill (1991) 208.
5. Hutcheon (2000) 42.
6. Hedreen (1992) 155–61. See, more recently, Steinhart (2004) 101–27, for a discussion of Archaic representations of satiric performance.

7. An excellent summary of current views on the overall social purpose of satyr-play is Gibert (2001), where the auther reviews three recent monograph-length studies as well as several influential articles on the genre. See also Sutton (1980).
8. *OCD*³ s.v. "Comedy, Greek, origins of" (Davies). The earliest poet whose fragments survive in any significant number is Cratinus, whose career began in the mid-fifth century and ended at 423. B.C.
9. Goldhill (1991) 176. Bakhtin's discussion of the nature of parody includes frequent reference to ancient Greek examples, including epic parodies, satyr-play, and comedy: Bakhtin (1981) 51–68; Bakhtin (1984) 127ff.; 193 ff. Other recent studies of Athenian comedy analyze in detail the nature of the parodic relationship between Old Comedy and tragedy (Dobrov [2001] and Silk [2000]).
10. Goldhill (1991) 207.
11. Turner (1969/1995) 96.
12. Dobrov (2001) and Silk (2000).
13. Dobrov (2001) 16.
14. Goldhill (1991) 208.
15. Hutcheon (2000) Chapter 5: "Encoding and Decoding: The Shared Codes of Parody" (84–99). She identifies the danger of constructing a false hypothesis as to what the author intended: "the subject position of the producer of parody is that of a controlling agent whose actions account for the textual evidence; in a sense it is a hypothetical hermeneutical construct, inferred . . . by the reader from the text's inscription."
16. Keuls (1988), esp. 307–8, suggests that artists such as the Pioneers lampoon each others' social pretensions rather than ridiculing elites. Neer (2002) Chapter 3 sees the Pioneers' intraworkshop parodies as a fiction agreeable to both painters and elites and as a genuine attempt to insert the painters into an upper class milieu at a moment when class boundaries were most in flux – at the moment of the Kleisthenic democratic reforms. In Chapter 11 we return to these positions. See also Frel (1983).
17. The vase becomes a prop for an event such as Philippos' parodic dance in Xenophon's symposion, as discussed in Chapter 11. See Fehr (1990).
18. These examples provide the immediate history and context for the cup by Exekias discussed at the beginning of this chapter [Figures 2.1, 2.2], Athens, NM 1104 (CC.692), *ABV* 147, 5; Immerwahr (1990) 35, No. 146.
19. Copenhagen, National Museum 13966, *Para* 48, *Addenda*² 33; Tiverios (1976) No. 92 pl. 62–4.
20. Malibu 86. AE 279 (once Munich, Bareiss 142), *Para* 329, 83 *ter*; *Addenda*² 168.
21. Anderson (2005) 269 provides the second reading, with Immerwahr's support. Anderson sees the inscription as a fragment of poetry and the earliest attested appearance of the shout εὐοῖ made typically by the followers of Dionysos. He does not believe that the inscription is also deliberate nonsense, a parody of a potter's signature, but the rich set of comparable examples suggests even if his interpretation is correct, there is indeed a parodic level to the inscription as well.
22. CVA USA 33 (Malibu 8) p. 13.
23. Tarquinia RC 1091, *ARV*² 76, 65; Immerwahr (1990) 62, No. 345.
24. London 1906.12–15.1, *ABV* 90,7; *Addenda*², 24. Brijder (1982) No. 290, Painter of the Burgon Sianas, pl. 58, a–b.
25. Birmingham Univ. X698, Brijder (1982) No. 291, pls 58 c-d.

26. Palermo, from Chiusi, *ABV* 114,2, Manner of Lydos.
27. Raab (1972) 19.
28. London E 37, *ARV*² 72, 17; 1623; *Para* 328; *Addenda*² 167.
29. Like Philippos in Xenophon's *Symposion* 2.22, the youth performs an ungainly imitation. See Fehr (1990) and discussion in Chapter 11.
30. Compare this to Louvre G 5, *ARV* ² 71,14; 49,175; *Addenda*² 167.
31. Warsaw 142332 *ARV* ² 27, 8; *Para* 324; *Addenda*² 156; Immerwahr (1990) 65, No. 374.
32. Kossatz-Deissmann (1991) 164.
33. Berlin 1966.19, *Para* 323, 20.3*bis*; *Addenda*² 154; Immerwahr (1990) 69, No. 404.
34. Immerwahr (1990) 69; see also Lissarrague (1990a) 127 and Goemann et al. (eds.) (1991) 154.
35. London E 255, red-figure amphora *ARV*² 31, 2; *Para* 324; *Addenda*² 157; Immerwahr (1990) 69, No. 409.
36. Immerwahr (1990) 69 n. 33.
37. Beazley (1929) 364.
38. Both "pallas" and "palos" sound similar to "phallus" as well, and bringing this word to mind may be behind the nonsense as well.
39. The very fragmentary amphora by Oltos in Vienna discussed in Chapter 5, 80–81 (Vienna University 631a, *ARV*² 54.3; *Para* 326; *Addenda*² 163) also preserves the tripod struggle on side A, and the inscriptions are placed in a way that is similar to this London example, either vertically, in front of the figure, or between the legs. XAIPE is written in addition to the names. There is no obvious nonsense or parody here.
40. Lissarrague (1990b) 49 points out the feminine aspects of the Scythians.
41. Munich 2308 (J. 374), *ARV*² 26,2; 1620; *Addenda*² 156; Immerwahr (1990) 65, No. 370.
42. Although this could be a description of Phayllos, the label appears to belong to the figure at left.
43. Lissarague (1990b) 48–9 has pointed out how the Scythians play a feminine role in this scene because they help the hoplite arm as women often do; and Smith (1999) 138 discusses this vase in the context of another feminized depiction of a Scythian, on the well-known Eurymedon vase, Hamburg 1981.173, Dover (1978) R 1155, attributed by Schauenburg (1975) 175 to the Triptolemos Painter.
44. The poor *Greek* spoken by Scythians and other foreigners appears in fifth century comedy as a well-known trope. Austin and Olson (2004) present the characteristics of the poor Greek spoken by the Scythian character in *Thesmophorizeusae* (ll. 1001–1225) and cite its appearance in other Aristophanic comedy, 308–9. In the vase-inscriptions cited here, the native language of the speaker, rather than his poor Greek, is parodied.
45. Munich 2421(J.6), *ARV*² 23,7; 162; *Para* 323; *Addenda*² 155; Immerwahr (1990) 67, No. 389. See in particular Keuls (1988) 304–5; Neer (2002) 102–8. Neer's reading is in many ways identical to mine. One significant difference is that here the imagery and especially the texts are seen as part of a broader tradition, established earlier, whereas Neer sees them as products of a particular historical moment and part of a peculiarly Pioneer mind-set. See the discussion of Neer's view in Chapter 11.
46. See Lissarrague (1990a) 83–4.
47. See Immerwahr (1990) 67 and Kurke (1997) 136 and n. 90.
48. Csapo and Miller (1991) 373–9. For this discussion, to decide between the two is not important. See also the discussion of this vase in Kurke (1997) 135–6.

49. Neer (2002) suggests that the comment is from the painter himself (121). I would say instead that a measure of the painter's expertise in constructing an author-artist is that he has supplied an appropriate reaction for an undepicted narratee; the painter has replaced an image of a narratee with his comment.
50. Compare this school scene to that in the "straight" scene on Douris' cup (Berlin 2285) discussed in Chapter 8 [Figures 8.22–8.23].
51. Peschel (1987); Reinsburg (1989); Hoesch (1990); Pfsitterer-Hass(1990); Csapo and Miller (1991); Kurke (1997).
52. Csapo and Miller (1991) 379.
53. St. Petersburg, Hermitage 644, *ARV* [2] 16,15; 1619; *Para* 509; *Addenda*[2] 153; Immerwahr (1990) 63–4, No. 361; Csapo and Miller (1991) 373 No. 1.
54. Neer (2002) 106.
55. Neer (2002) 102–7; 131. Neer (2002) 118 and 134 (Nos. I 5, I 6, I 7) mentions other examples that support his view by artists of the Pioneer group.
56. For example, London 1867.5–8.962 (B 424), *ABV* 168; 169, 3; *Para* 70; *Addenda*[2] 48; Naples 81238 (2609) *ARV* [2] 73,29, both discussed in Chapter 5.
57. Cup, Kurashiki, Ninagawa (ex Lucerne market), *ARV*[2] 1611; 1625; *Para* 330, 91, 52 *bis*; *Addenda*[2] 171 by the Euergides Painter, where the *kalos* inscription is paired with "Hipparchos kalos." A second *kalos* inscription naming Tlempolemos occurs on the tondo of a cup in Orvieto, *ARV*[2] 1699.
58. *ABV* 178.
59. See Shapiro (1980).
60. Louvre G 107, *ARV*[2] 18,1; 1619; *Addenda*[2] 153; Immerwahr (1990) 69, No. 401. Formerly attributed as "Manner of Euphronios" by Beazley, then to Smikros, and now to Euphronios (Ohly-Dumm in Goemann et al. [eds.] [1991] No. 19, 152 [as quoted by Denoyelle]).
61. Several examples appear as *graffiti* on fragmentary pottery from the Agora: Lang (1976) C3 (P 23693) c. 550 B.C. ΑΝΘΕΜΕ ΚΑΛΕ [ΔΟ]ΚΕΙ ΑΙΣΧ["Antheme is beautiful, it seems to Aisch . . . ": C10 (P 14710) early fifth century; ΛΥΚΟΜΑΧ[ΟΣ ΚΑΛΟΣ]/[Δ]ΟΚΕΙ ΙΑΝΘΙΔ["Lykomach[os] is handsome/ it seems to Ianthid . . . " C19 (P 5160) c. B.C. 475–450 B.C. : ΑΛ⟨Λ⟩ΚΑΙΟΣ ΚΑΛΟΣ ΤΟ ΔΟΚΕΙ ΜΕΛΙΤΙ,"Al⟨l⟩kaios is handsome, it seems to Melis." There are other examples of mock inscriptions in vase-paintings that seem to be casual or vernacular in content but are displayed as formal inscriptions: On the tondo of a cup by the Antiphon Painter, there is a *kalos* inscription written in carefully spaced vertical lines on a boundary stone: Berlin 2314 and Rome, Villa Giulia, *ARV*[2] 336, 14; 1646; *Addenda*[2] 218; Lissarrague (1999) 369–70 fig. 9.
62. As mentioned in Chapter 8, n. 24, Immerwahr reconstructs the inscription with interpuncts (see transcriptions in Immerwahr [1990] 68–9), and Denoyelle (in Goemann et al. [eds.] [1991] 153) points out, citing additional examples, that interpuncts in vase-inscriptions do not always indicate that the painter intends to represent an inscription in stone. Neer (2002) 120–21 understands the statement to indicate that Smikros believes (or rather, mistakes) the statue to be a living thing; I would stress that a wealth of parodic associations derives from the contrast on the vase to the usual form and location of such inscriptions. As Lissarrague notes (Lissarrague [1999] 360–61, n. 10), there are a few painted inscriptions on vases that use the verb δοκεῖ: he lists six black figure examples and two in red figure.
63. Immerwahr (1990) 68–9.

CHAPTER 10: READING EVERYTHING: SIX CASE STUDIES

1. Boston M.F.A. 1973.88 [Figures 1.1, 1.2] in Chapters 1, 4, 5, and 8; Warsaw 142332, *ARV*^{2} 27,8; *Para* 324; *Addenda*^{2} 156 [Figures 5.10, 5.11] in Chapters 5 and 9.
2. Psiax: alabastra: Odessa 26602, *ARV*^{2} 7, 5; *ABV* 292; *Addenda*^{2} 150; and Karlsruhe 242 (B120) *ARV*^{2} 7, 4; *Para* 321; *Addenda*^{2} 150; Epiktetos: calyx crater: Villa Giulia, *ARV*^{2} 77,90; *Addenda*^{2} 169; skyphos: London E 139, *ARV*^{2} 77, 86; *Para* 328; *Addenda*^{2} 168; cup: London E 38, ARV^2 72, 16; 1623; *Para* 328; *Addenda*^{2} 167; bilingual eye-cup, Würzburg 468, *ARV*^{2} 71,8; 45,105; *Addenda*^{2} 167.
3. Copenhagen 112, *ABV* 292,5; *Addenda*^{2} 76; Immerwahr (1990) 59.
4. Munich 1470 (J. 1295), *ABV* 144, 6; *Addenda*^{2} 39; Boston 99.538; *ARV*^{2} 4, 12; *ABV* 255,6; *Para* 113; 321; *Addenda*^{2} 150.
5. Of another inscription apparently naming either a horse or one of the people in the chariot, nothing remained after cleaning. See Beazley (1950) 315, No. 6.
6. Beazley (1950) 315, No. 6.
7. See Ferrari (2002) 71–86 and *passim* for a discussion of the tightly wrapped mantle as signifying *aidos*.
8. Lydos: Naples 81292 (2770), *ABV* 109, 23; *Para* 44; *Addenda*^{2} 30, where the figure of a horseman with a squire appears twice and Exekias: Munich 1470 (J. 1295), *ABV* 144, 6; *Addenda*^{2} 39, [Figures 2.9, 2.10] where we see two images, nearly identical, of one soldier carrying his dead comrade off the battlefield. Another similar example is the amphora Toledo 1980.1022; *Addenda*^{2} 400, 391 signed by Exekias as potter. Here a turning chariot is repeated almost exactly Inscriptions cover three topics: two of the horses are named on A; one figure in the chariot is named on B. The labels on A are accompanied by the potter's signature and a *kalos* inscription, so we do not learn through them whether or not we see the same or different scenes. There are minute differences in the images, but it is unclear whether each side depicts different or identical individuals.
9. St. Petersburg, Hermitage B 2102 (645), *ARV*^{2} 71, 4; 45,103; 1623; *Para* 509; *Addenda*^{2} 167; Arlesheim, Schweizer, *ARV*^{2} 1705, 71, 6 *bis*; *Addenda*^{2} 167.
10. All by Epiktetos: bilingual eye-cup: London E 3, *ARV*^{2} 70, 3; 45,102; 1623; *Para* 328, *Addenda*^{2} 166; cup: Berlin 2262, *ARV*^{2} 72, 15; 1623, *Para* 328, *Addenda*^{2} 167; cup: Paris, Louvre G 5, *ARV*^{2} 71, 14; 49, 175; *Addenda*^{2} 167.
11. London E 38, *ARV*^{2} 72,16; 1623; *Para* 328; *Addenda*^{2} 167.
12. Schefold (1992) 143.
13. Lissarrague (1994), esp. 18–19, also suggests that all three fields of the cup are thematically linked, and he cites the repeated musical instruments as the binding mechanism. If Schefold and Lissarrague and the present analysis are right, this cup preserves results of repetition similar to those seen on the cup by Oltos where he links Anakreon with Herakles and the Amazons, London E 18 (*ARV*^{2} 62, 86; 1600; 1700; *Para* 327; *Addenda*^{2} 165).
14. New York M.M.A. 10.210.18, *ARV* ^{2} 54, 7; *Para* 326; *Addenda*^{2} 163; Immerwahr (1990) 61, No. 342.
15. London E 18 (*ARV*^{2} 62, 86; 1600; 1700; *Para* 327; *Addenda*^{2} 165), Anakreon, etc.; Florence 81601 (*ARV* ^{2} 64, 96; *Addenda*^{2} 166), Chilon; London E 19 (*ARV*^{2} 63, 95), Chilon. The transcriptions here are as in Richter and Hall (1936) 17–19; Immerwahr (1990) does not repeat them.

16. Richter and Hall (1936) 18 read the inscription as *Epainetos kalos*, but Beazley does not list it as a *kalos* inscription, and the figure of the youth does separate the two words. Note that the fluteplayer, ΣMIKY[ΘΟΣ], "Smiky[thos]" has a very similar name to the figure on the pelike in Boston (1973.88) [Figures 1.1, 1.2] attributed to Euthymides by Robertson, discussed throughout this monograph, and on Phintias' hydria, Munich 2421 [Figures 9.10, 9.11].
17. Immerwahr (1990) 61 n. 15–16.
18. Hubbard (1998) 57.
19. Hubbard (1998).
20. Philadelphia L 64.185, *ARV*[2] 187, 62; 1632; *Addenda*[2] 188; Immerwahr (1990) 82, No. 486.
21. Discussed in Chapter 7: Taranto 4359, *ABV* 109, 26; *Para* 44; *Addenda*[2] 30; Tiverios (1976) No. 36, pl. 28.
22. Würzburg 248, *ABV* 134, 18; Berlin 1699, *ABV* 136,53; *Para* 55; *Addenda*[2] 37; Munich 1397 (J.1079), *ABV* 134,20; *Addenda*[2] 36.
23. Copenhagen inv. 3877, *ARV*[2] 63, 87; *Para* 327 is discussed in Chapter 5.
24. Note the possible tag-*kalos* on Munich 2620 (J. 337), *ARV*[2] 16, 17; 1619; *Addenda*[2] 153; *Para* 322; Euphronios, where the phrase *h*ΟΠΑΙΣΚΑΛΟΣ, "the youth is handsome," appears above one of the youths on B. This comment may also be perceived as a replacement for a figural spectator.
25. Arezzo, Museo Civico 1465; *ARV*[2] 15, 6; 316; 1619; *Para* 322; *Addenda*[2] 152; Goemann et al. (eds.) (1991) No. 13, 128–36; Cygielman (1992). Immerwahr (1990) 63, No. 359. See Neer's discussion (Neer [2002] 55–6) for his careful analysis of "naturalism" on the vase.
26. Shapiro (1992) 37 discusses this vase as an example of unified narration.
27. Immerwahr (1992) 51.
28. Immerwahr (1992) 51 n. 33 is very cautious in his interpretation because the letters are not all visible and the only source for them is the drawing in Furtwangler and Reichhold (1905) ii, Atlas I, pl. 62.
29. This is the same kind of parodic contrast embedded in verbal repetition discussed in Chapter 9.
30. Immerwahr (1990) 63.
31. Discussed in Chapter 7: Morgantina (Serra Orlando), Museo Archeologico 58.2382, *ARV*[2] 28, 10; 1620; *Addenda*[2] 156.
32. Berlin 2160, *ARV*[2] 196,1; 1623; *Para* 342; *Addenda*[2] 190; Immerwahr (1990) 82, No. 490. Neer (2002) 68–70 discusses the vase in the context of an exploration of the social meaning of artistic style.
33. Kossatz-Deissmann (1991) 165.
34. Osborne (1998) 25–8.

CHAPTER 11: OVER AND OVER: READING GREEK VASES IN *SYMPOSION*

1. Webster (1972).
2. Spivey (1991) 139–42; S. Lewis (2002).
3. Hoffman (1994) esp. 29–31 maintains that clay vessels were created as substitutes, to be offered at sanctuaries or placed in the grave, for expensive metal vessels actually used in *symposia*. Nevertheless, he does acknowledge that Athenians might well have purchased

figural pottery for funeral banquets or *perideipna*, held in their homes in classical times (31). This does mean, then, that he sees them as used in a commensal setting in private. See also Hoffman (1997).

4. Vickers and Gill (1994) identify red- and black-figure ware as direct imitations of metal vessels, and they hypothesize that only Greeks who were not "elite" used pottery rather than metal in their private *symposia* in houses. Clearly, these two scholars also acknowledge use, although limited, for painted pottery in a commensal setting but by classes lower than elite.
5. Rotroff and Oakley (1992) 11–14.
6. A. Steiner (2002).
7. Agora deposit N 7:3, a deposit of household pottery, contained the following examples of red-figured pottery: 2 kraters, 25 drinking cups, 2 amphoras, 2 oinochoai among others. The original publication is Boulter (1953), and Moore (1997) provides a full discussion in the context of all red-figure pottery from the Agora. The deposit is listed on p. 365.
8. Jones et al. (1962) 87–100; Nevett (1999) 85 points out that the *andron* lacks several typical features of that room-type, but states "evidence for the existence of an *andron* is not conclusive, but it is possible that such a facility was provided."
9. For Torone the pottery is fifth and primarily fourth century: see Cambitoglou and Papadopoulos (2001). Of 198 fragments presented in the catalog of red-figure pottery, 113 come from kraters and most are Attic; skyphoi are the next most popular shape (McPhee [2001] 355–6). The find contexts are generally not clearly domestic, but construction fills.
10. Cahill (2002) 186–7 (pl. 1). Nine red-figure kraters have recorded find-spots, and only one was found in an *andron*. Cahill compares the minimal number of kraters found at Olynthus to the very large and very anomalous number found among the debris from the public dining room in the Athenian Agora. As Rotroff and Oakley point out, however, this large number is extremely unusual and presents a contrast to what is found in household contexts (Rotroff and Oakley [1992] 43–4). They compare the evidence from the magistrates' dining complex to that in another, possibly domestic, Agora deposit N 7:3. The pertinent finds from Olynthus are very similar in quantity and character to the evidence from the Dema House.
11. Cahill (2002) 181–2. Cahill states that the assemblage of pottery from the magistrates' dining room at the Agora preserved 10 times more drinking cups than kraters. This is correct, but the vast majority of the Agora cups are black-glaze and not figural.
12. Hamilton (1992).
13. Karouzou (1971) 138–45. She also cites examples of two pelikai that were used for burials: Athens, NM 14498, *ARV*[2] 1172, 11; *Addenda*[2] 339 which contained the ashes of the deceased and Athens, NM 14501, *ARV*[2] 1124, 2 which contained the bones of a very young person.
14. Shapiro (1997), in an interesting preliminary study of the black-figure pelike, notes that the iconography on these shapes reveals a concentration of "banausic" scenes that may well either reveal something about the clientele who purchased them or suggest a special use context.
15. Scheibler (1987a) 57–118.
16. Beazley named the group the Class of Agora P 15840: *ARV*[2] 1697.
17. Green (1962).
18. Scheffer (1988) 543–4; Hannestad (1999) 306.
19. Spivey (1991) 134; S. Lewis: (2002).

20. Nikosthenic neck-amphoras, kyathoi, Tyrrhenian amphoras, Perizoma class: see Spivey (1991) 138–42. Arafat and Morgan (1994) 109 cite two examples produced by Attic craftsmen, Sotades and the Kleophon Painter, that appear to be tailored for use by the Achaemenid empire. See also Osborne (2001) 278.
21. Stissi (1999) 98, and esp. n. 81; Arafat and Morgan (1994), in a critique of the core/periphery model, conclude that the vast majority of pottery imported by the Etruscans was decorated by Athenians for home use, and there is no evidence to support the idea that Athenians themselves were involved in trade to Etruria (108–110). See also Small (1995).
22. Spivey (1991) 144: "... it is clear that the images produced for the aristocratic fraternities of Athens more or less matched the expectations of Etruscans in search of ostentatious burials ... much of the imagery is consonant with their own art." See also Osborne (2001 and 2005).
23. Spivey (1991) 143.
24. Reusser (2002); Moore (1986b); Moore (1997). See also Hannestad (1999).
25. Hannestad (1988); Hannestad (1999); Reusser (2002) II. 270.
26. Veii: Small (1994) 54–5.
27. Hannestad (1999) 304–5 discusses the local and imported shapes in tomb groups at Vulci. She points out that shapes such as plates, readily available in local wares, do not appear in the repertory of imported Attic shapes.
28. See in particular Hannestad (1988) 226–9 and (1999) 304–6.
29. Reusser (2002) I.191–202.
30. Small (1994) 37–8; 41–4. Small believes much imported Attic pottery was purchased specifically to furnish tombs: 45–53.
31. Reusser (2002) I. 151.
32. The productions clearly geared for the Etruscan market, such as Tyrhennian and Nikosthenic amphoras and the Perizoma Group, are of course notable exceptions and not numerous. Spivey (1991) 138–44.
33. Lissarrague (1990a).
34. One reviewer of several works on *symposion* leveled the following criticism: "Unfortunately, what the works do not provide is any basic introduction to the defining characteristics of the *symposion* or any general hypotheses about the function, significance, persistence, and transformation of this institution." (Habinek [1993].) Fifteen years later, this situation is only marginally improved.
35. Vetta (1999) 97.
36. *OCD*[3] *s.v.* "Symposium" (O. Murray).
37. Rotroff and Oakley (1992); A. Steiner (2002); Lynch (1999).
38. Lissarrague (1990a) 19–20.
39. Gericke (1970) Tables 3–5; Boardman (2003).
40. New York M.M.A. 1997.388a–ee; 1996.56.a; 1997.493.
41. Note the red-figure amphoras from the Athenian magistrates' dining complex (Rotroff and Oakley [1992], Nos. 110–13).
42. Munich inv. 8763, *Para* 65; *Addenda*[2] 43; Scheibler (1987a) 70, fig. 6.
43. Based on Beazley's lists of *kalos*-inscriptions on black-figure vessels (Beazley *ABV* 664–78), more *kalos*-inscriptions appear on amphoras than on any other shape: 39 are on belly or neck-amphoras; 31 on hydrias; 17 on cups; 12 on lekythoi; and 10 on oinochoai. Only 1 black-figure krater is listed as carrying a *kalos*-inscription. In red-figure, the numbers are much larger, and cups become the most common vehicle for *kalos* inscriptions – over 400

of Beazley's examples (Beazley *ARV*² 1557–1616) appear on cups, with amphoras ranking third with just over 90. Interestingly, oil-containing vessels, both funerary and not, preserve over 130 *kalos* inscriptions; some at least may have been love-gifts. Among the red-figure examples, nearly 50 appear on mixing bowls.

44. Wüzburg Martin von Wagner Museum L 265 + L 282, *ABV* 151, 22; 687; *Para* 63; *Addenda*² 43; Bothmer (1985) No. 19, 113.
45. On red-figure hydrias, there are only six with *kalos* names listed by Beazley and three additional with *kale* and a female name.
46. Shapiro (2003); A. Steiner (2004) 457.
47. In Beazley's lists, fifteen *kale* inscriptions are preserved on black-figure hydrias; these are in addition to the thirty-one *kalos* inscriptions with masculine names.
48. London E 159, *ARV*², 24, 9; 1620; *Addenda*² 155, which also preserves "Megakles *kalos*;" London 1843.11–3.86 (E 161) *ARV*² 262, 41; *Addenda*² 205.
49. Lissarague (1990a) 20–23; Stansbury-O'Donnell (1999) 70–79 also discusses a variety of "viewing contexts" for Greek art and includes an assessment of the experience of viewing vases in use in symposion.
50. Bergquist (1990).
51. I rely here on evidence from Xenophon's and Plato's *Symposium*, to be discussed in more detail below. We have evidence for dining in round spaces in public buildings: Cooper and Morris (1990) survey evidence for round dining rooms. These range in interior diameter from 2.5 m at Nemea to 16.90 at the Athenian Agora, so they can be both more and distinctly less intimate than their rectangular counterparts. Because the testimony we have suggests that drinking wares and styles at these round buildings were not typically sympotic, we will not include round spaces in this discussion.
52. London E 49 and Villa Giulia, *ARV*² 432, 52; *Addenda*² 237. The imagery also includes a display of various moments in the use of the drinking-cup. All of the adult men hold cups. On A, a figure holds his partly full cup by its foot as he gestures to his companion who in turn extends his cup to be filled from a standing youth's oinochoe. The figure at far right holds his cup at his lips to drink from it. Each figure on Side B has a cup held in a position slightly different from those on A, completing a spectrum of "cup in use," from being filled, to full, to being drunk from; the tondo figure appears to stride in *komos* with his cup held out behind, probably empty. Both cups and oinochoai hang in the field on each side. ΚΑΛΟΣ, "handsome," appears twice across the top of each scene.
53. Several scholars have reconstructed viewing scenarios based on an assumption that viewers looked carefully at vases and the imagery and writing on them: Lissarague (1994) 12; Stansbury-O'Donnell (1999) 144–5; N. Slater (1999); Snodgrass (2000) 27–8.
54. N. Slater (1999) 143–61, esp. 155. *Contra* see Boardman (2003). The primary discussion here of reading inscriptions on vases is in Chapter 4.
55. See, for example, the comments of Osborne (1987) 109–12, where he walks the reader through a close scrutiny of figural pottery in the manner of a hypothetical symposiast looking at Louvre G 42 (*ARV*² 23, 1; 1620; *Para* 323; *Addenda*² 154; Immerwahr [1990] 66–67, No. 385). Cairns (1996) 152–8 carries Osborne's analysis further, anchoring the (repeated) inscriptions, both *khaire* and Artemis' name miswritten as *aidos* (a highly ranked value among elites who participate in *symposia*) on the same vase in sympotic discourse, identifying the scenes as interconnected, and ultimately identifying Tityos as he rapes Leto as a negative paradigm for elites. This example is discussed here in Chapter 7.

56. Lissarrague (1990a) 103. Lissarrague (1994) 14–21 carries out a very specific analysis of how a symposiast would analyze the cup London E 38, by Epiktetos, where all three fields are interconnected as discussed here in Chapter 10.
57. Plato's *Symposium*: 214a *psykter*; 223c *phiale*.
58. D. Steiner (2001) discusses the passages both from Plato (132; 200–201) and from Xenophon (194).
59. Lissarrague (1990a) figs. 81–77.
60. White ground calyx-krater by the Phiale Painter, Vatican 16586, ARV^2 1017, 54; 1678; *Para* 440; *Addenda*^{2} 315.
61. At a *symposion* in *Wasps* 1214–25, Bdelykleon tells Philokleon to admire (wall) hangings and the ceiling, presumably decorated.
62. Munich 2636, ARV^2 317, 16; *Addenda*^{2} 214.
63. See Immerwahr (1990) 84 and ARV^2 318.
64. Copenhagen inv. 13365, ARV^2 185, 32; *Para* 340; *Addenda*^{2} 187; Immerwahr (1990) 82.
65. West (1993) 149.
66. Immerwahr (1965) 153.
67. Immerwahr (1965) 152. Note that although Immerwahr follows Beazley in assuming that the name "Anakreon" labels the lyre-player, other scholars commenting subsequently believe that because there are no parallels for the name of a person being inscribed on an object he carries, the inscription is instead "an indication of the instrument's function by reference to Anakreon's poetry; this is the quintessentially sympotic barbiton." Miller (1999) 236 and n. 42.
68. Berlin 2285, ARV^2 431, 48; 426; 1653; *Para* 374; *Addenda*^{2} 237; Immerwahr (1990) 87, No. 533.
69. Robb (1994) 33: "an unconscious, willing acceptance of ancestral models, even as a *pais*, a boy, models himself on his male elders, his father and his older brothers, and his most admired peers, normally the group's best warriors or best athletes." The literature on *paideia* is vast; Robb's treatment is a recent one that includes the major bibliography pertaining to earlier work. The foundational study is of course Jaeger (1939–45). Other important contributions to the discussion include Havelock (1952) 95–109; esp. 100; Roesler (1980) 244; Levine (1985): Bremmer (1990) 135–48; Kurke (1991), esp. 252; Roesler (1995).
70. Xenophon's *Symposium* indictates that boys were indeed present at *symposia*, for it takes place in honor of a youth who is present throughout the event. Images also depict youths performing at *symposion*: New York M.M.A. 07.286.47, ARV^2 175; 1631; *Para* 339; *Addenda*^{2} 184, a cup by the Hegesiboulos Painter, shows a seated youth playing the lyre in a rather sedate *symposion* setting on A and again on B in a wild komastic context. Bremmer (1990) 138 n. 18 cites additional examples. The *symposion* from its inception and through most of the classical period "fostered both the composition and performance of sung poetry, much of it instructional and cautionary in tone" (Robb [1994] 35). There is a substantial amount of current bibliography exploring the role of *paideia* in *symposion*. An extremely useful collection of essays addressing various aspects of this topic is Murray (1990). Examples of *sympotic*, didactic poetry meant to enculturate boys are cited by Bremmer (1990) 137 n. 13–17, and his list includes works by Semonides of Amorgos, Alcaeus, and Theognis.
71. Berlin 2285, ARV^2 431, 48; 426; 1653; *Para* 374; *Addenda*^{2} 237. Immerwahr (1990) 87, no. 533. The important work carried out by Immerwahr (1964 and 1973) and Webster (1972) 57–60 is indispensable to our understanding of the relationship between school and *paideia* at symposia.

72. Robb (1994) 186–7, fig. 7.1, cites a fragment of a cup by the Akestorides Painter now in the J. Paul Getty Museum, Malibu 86.AE.324 (once Munich, Bareiss 63), *ARV*[2] 1670; *Para* 417, 4 *bis*; *Addenda*[2] 288, where a youth himself holds a scroll with a text, apparently about Herakles, together with a list of names. Robb reiterates that the education of youths was for their moral development and for performance both in competitions and at *symposia*. Robb (1994) 184.
73. Some literary sources make it clear that boys memorized poets and especially Homer for their moral instruction; this, for example, is clearly set out in Plato's *Protagoras*: 326a: "In the works of good poets, the (young boys) meet with many admonitions, and many descriptions and encomia of the great men of times long ago, so that the boy (*pais*) desiring to imitate (*memetai*) seeks to become like them . . . Moreover, when they have learned to play the kithara, they are taught the works of a whole other set of good poets . . . "
74. See Bourdieu and Passeron (1977) for a fundamental discussion of the interplay of education and class.
75. Robb (1994) 41 n. 25.
76. Robb (1994) 78–84.
77. Athens NM 192, Robb (1994) 24; 25 n. 8 presents the evidence for alternative readings of the end of the line. Immerwahr (1990) 7 presents one alternate reading: *h*ΟΣΝΥΝΟΡΧΕΣΤΟΝ-ΠΑΝΤΟΝΑΤΑΛΟΤΑΤΑΠΑΙΖΕΙΤΟΤΟΔ̣ΕΚΑ̣Ν̣ΜΙΝ̣(?).
78. Robb (1994) 27–8.
79. Powell (1991) 160.
80. Robb (1994) 32.
81. Robb (1994) 32.
82. Pithekoussai (Ischia)," The Nestor Cup:"

    ΝΕΣΤΟΡΟΣ: Ε[ΙΜ]Ι: ΕΥΠΟΤ[ΟΝ]: ΠΟΤΕΡΙΟ[Ν]
    *h*ΟΣ ΔΑ⟨Ν⟩ΤΟΔΕ Π[ΙΕ]ΣΙ: ΠΟΤΕΡΟ[Ο]: ΑΥΤΙΚΑ ΚΕΝΟΝ
    *h*ΙΜΕΡ[ΟΣ *h*ΑΙΡ]ΕΣΕΙ: ΚΑΛΛΙΣΤΕ[ΦΑ]ΝΟ: ΑΦΡΟΔΙΤΕΣ
    Of Nestor I am the cup, a delight to drink from.
    He who drinks of *this* cup straightway him
    Desire shall grip even of the fair garlanded Aphrodite (translation Robb [1994] 46).

    Robb cites *Iliad* XI (601–805 as the Homeric referent for the inscription on the cup of Nestor.
    The "*xenos* oinochoe" Ithaka may have originally preserved six hexameters, only one of which can be restored:

    [–Χ]ΕΝΟΣ ΤΕ ΦΙΛΟΣ [ΚΑΙ ΠΙΣΤΟ]Σ ΕΤΑΙΡΟ[—]
    Guest-friend dear and trusted comrade (translation Robb [1994] 49).

    The inscription on the *xenos* oinochoe, probably a guest-friend gift, has several possible Homeric references. Robb (1994) 49–52.
83. *Iliad* XI .631–7.
84. Thomas (1992) 58–9.
85. Scheibler (1987a).
86. See the discussion of these examples above in Chapter 7, 139–46.
87. Examples cited by Bremmer(1990) 137 n. 13–17 include works by Semonides of Amorgos, Alcaeus, and Theognis.

88. The *Theognidae* is dated 640–479 and was of particular interest to fifth century Athenians: Cobb-Stevens and Figueira (1985) 1. Levine (1985) explicitly makes the case for the poetry as sympotic, political, and paideutic. See also Calame (1999) 93–101.
89. Rutherford (1996; 2001). In what is apparently a poem about the Persian Wars (POxy 3965,West² [1992] Simonides 10w²–18w²), the Trojan War is compared to Plataea, and the fifth-century Greek warriors to Trojan War heroes (see Boedeker and Sider [2001] 4). Several scholars make suggestions as to where the elegy was first performed: Aloni (2001) 101–2 suggests that the occasion for the elegy was the construction of the tumuli, the construction of the altar to Zeus Eleutherios, and the establishment of the quadrennial games, the Eleutheria, for a contest in honor of those who died in battle; Boedeker (2001) 120, n. 2 determines that a Panhellenic setting, the Isthmian Games, was the most likely venue; Rutherford (2001) 41, n. 38 suggests another Panhellenic setting, Delphi, at the dedication of the serpent column.
90. Mace (2001) 202, n. 87 and 203; West (1993b) 5.
91. Heath and Lefkowitz (1991) make the case for solo performance by the poet; Carey (1989) and Kurke (1991) believe the performance was choral; and Morgan (1993) believes the initial performance was choral and subsequent reperformance was solo. Race points out the vocabulary that suggests that the intended performance for *Pythian* VI was processional (Race [1997] 15 and 312–13).
92. For support of this view, see Heath and Lefkowitz (1991) 175–6. Contra Carey (1991) 547–9.
93. Heath and Lefkowitz (1991) 180–1.
94. Morgan (1993) 11–13.
95. Kurke (1990) 96 notes that to a modern reader, many Pindaric paradigms seem overinflated.
96. This discussion is indebted to the analysis of Kurke (1990).
97. Kurke (1990) references the earlier work of Friedlander in describing this type of poetry. The hypothekic genre is "characterized by a proem, an address to a specific addressee, sometimes by mythical material, but mainly by a collection of injunctions and traditional wisdom, loosely strung together with gnomic material" (90).
98. Kurke (1990) 94.
99. Kurke (1990) 100.
100. There are several sources where the instructive paradigm appears in sympotic poetry, and the formal repetitions seen in the Pindaric and Homeric examples (cited earlier by Robb and Powell) are lacking, but evidence of instructive paradigm is still preserved. The poetry of Theognis is a "storehouse of advice to a *pais* on erotic, *sympotic*, and civil matters" disseminated at *symposion*. See Ford (1995) 89, and Levine (1985) 178–9 on Theognis 27–38. In Antiphanes fr. 85 K, Bremmer (1990) 138 assumes that the speaker is a boy who is complaining about having to listen to paradigms in the form of an "old-fashioned" song about heroes.
101. A recent commentary on Xenophon's *Symposion* (Huss 1999) identifies *paidia*, playfulness, or jest as one of two continuous themes throughout the work (34–7).
102. Trans. Larson (1980).
103. Lewis (1985) 201–2. Indeed, Neer (2002) 13–14 has identified the *griphos* or "riddle-net" as used by Theognis as a defining ethos of *symposion*.
104. Levine (1985) 186–90.
105. Nehamas and Woodruff (1989) 6. That Sokrates' remarks are parodic is affirmed by the response of Agathon: " Ὑβριστὴς εἶ " loosely translated as "Now you've gone *too* far,

Socrates." The use of "ὕβρις" (*hybris*) to describe the parody is very interesting when one is considering the similarities between the parodies of democratic procedures discussed here and Alcibiades' alleged profaning of the Eleusinian mysteries. Thucydides says the sacrilege was done "ἐφ' ὕβρει" which many scholars interpret as suggesting it was as a parody. (For a discussion and a conclusion that what Alcibiades did was not parody but simply reperformance, see Murray [1990b] 155–6.)

106. Dover (1980) 85; 89.
107. Dover (1980) 172.
108. Fehr (1990).
109. Herodotus VI. 126–9.
110. See n. 105 *supra*.
111. Fehr (1990) 188–91.
112. See also Berkeley 8/358, Immerwahr (1990) 54, No. 283.
113. Naples 81238 (2609) *ARV²* 73, 29.
114. Vatican 344, *ABV* 145, 13; 686; *Para* 60; *Addenda²*, 40; Immerwahr (1990) 33, No. 138.
115. See Chapter 7 and the discussion related to Figures 7.4, 7.12.
116. Dijon 1301 (ex Campana), *ARV²* 829, 37; *Para* 422; *Addenda²* 294; Neer (2002) 138–40.
117. Vienna Univ 631a, *ARV²* 54, 3 and 6; *Para* 326; *Addenda²* 163; Immerwahr (1990) 61, No. 339. Immerwhar understands the greetings to be in praise of the divinities.
118. Lonsdale (1995) 29.
119. Plato, *Laws* 665a; Lonsdale (1995) 33.
120. West (1993a) 140 and 64.
121. Henrichs (1995) 74.
122. Silk (2000) 351–2; Dobrov (2001) 14–16.
123. Ober (1989); Neer (2002).
124. See in particular Neer (2002) 91 n. 10, where he cites earlier explanations for craftsmen apparently being depicted as elites.
125. Svenbro (1985; 1993) 187–216.
126. See Donlan (1980) and below.
127. Naples 81238 (2609) *ARV²* 73, 29. The cup created c. 530 by Epiktetos, Paidikos, and an artist painting in the manner of the Euergides Painter is discussed in Chapters 4 and 8. The verb ΠΡΟΣΑΓΟΡΕΥΟ, "I greet you," is paired with ΠΑΙΔΙΚΟΣ on B for a total meaning of "I, Paidikos, greet you!"
128. Neer (2002) 122–3. See also Frel (1983) on the social ambitions of the Pioneers.
129. Donlan (1980) 178.

BIBLIOGRAPHY

ABBREVIATIONS

ABV	Beazley (1956)
Addenda^2	Carpenter, et al. (1989)
ARV^2	Beazley (1963)
CVA	*Corpus Vasorum Antiquorum*
Para	(Beazley) (1972)

Other abbreviations for books, series, and journals are those used by the *American Journal of Archaeology*.

Alberti, L. (1976/1435–6). *On Painting*. (J. R. Spencer, trans.). (New Haven, CT).

Aloni, A. (2001). "The Proem of Simonides' Plataea Elegy." In Boedeker and Sider (2001): 86–105.

Anderson, P. (2005). "A Verse Scrap on a *kylix* by Epiktetos." *TAPA* 135: 267–75.

Arafat, K. and C. Morgan. (1994). "Athens, Etruria and the Heueneburg: Mutual Misconceptions in the Study of Greek-Barbarian Relations," in I. Morris (1994): 108–34.

Ashmole, B. (1946). "*Kalligeneia* and *Hieros Arotos*." *JHS* 66: 8–10.

Austin, C. and S. D. Olson. (2004). *Aristophanes. Thesmophoriazeusae*. (Oxford).

Bakhtin, M. (1981). *The Dialogic Imagination*. (Austin, Texas).

(1984). *Problems of Dostoevsky's Poetics*. (Minneapolis, MN).

Bakir, G. (1981). *Sophilos, ein Beitrage zu einem Stil*. (Mainz).

Bal, M. (1985). *Narratology: Introduction to the Theory of Narrative*. (Toronto).

(1991a). *On Story-Telling: Essays in Narratology*. (Sonoma, CA).

(1991b). *Reading Rembrandt*. (Cambridge).

Balogh, J. (1927). "Voces Paginarum." *Philologus* 82: 202–40.

Barthes, R. (1977). *Image, Music, Text*. (New York).

(1977). "Introduction to the Structural Analysis of Narratives," in Barthes (1977): 79–124.

Beard, M. (1991). "Adopting an Approach II." In Rasmussen and Spivey (1991): 28–35.

Beardsley, M. (1958). *Aesthetics: Problems in the Philosophy of Criticism*. (New York).

Beazley, J. D. (1929). "Some Inscriptions on Attic Vases: II." *AJA* 33: 361–7.
(1931)."Amasea." *JHS* 51: 256–90.
(1950) "Some Inscriptions on Vases: V." *AJA* 54: 310–22.
(1951). *The Development of Attic Black-Figure.* (Berkeley, CA).
(1956). *Attic Black-Figure Vase-Painters.* (Oxford).
(1963). *Attic Red-Figure Vase-Painters.*[2] (Oxford).
(1972). *Paralipomena.* (Oxford).
(1986). *The Development of Attic Black-Figure* (reprint). (Berkeley, CA).
Bérard, C. (1983). "Iconographie-Iconologie-Iconologique," *Études de Lettres* (4): 5–27.
Bérard, C. et al. (1989). *City of Images* (D. Lyons, trans.). (Princeton, NJ).
Bergquist, B. (1990). "Sympotic Space: A Functional Aspect of Greek Dining Rooms." In Murray (ed.) (1990a): 37–65.
Birchall, A. (1972). "Attic Horse-Head Amphorae." *JHS* 92: 46–63.
Boardman, J. (1974). *Athenian Black-Figure Vases.* (New York).
(1975a). *Athenian Red-Figure Vases: The Archaic Period.* (New York).
(1975b). *CVA* Great Britain 14 (Oxford 3) (Oxford).
(1978). "Exekias." *AJA* 82: 11–25.
(1983). "Symbol and Story in Geometric Art." In Moon (ed.) (1993): 15–36.
(1991). *Greek Sculpture: The Archaic Period.* (New York).
(1992). "*Kaloi* and Other Names on Euphronios' Vases." In M. Cygielman et al. (ed.): 45–50.
(1998). *Early Greek Vase-Painting.* (London).
(2003). "'Reading' Greek Vases?" *Oxford Journal of Archaeology* 22 (1): 109–14.
Boedeker, D. (2001). "Historic Historiography." In Boedeker and Sider (2001): 120–34.
Boedeker, D. and K. Raaflaub (1998). *Democracy, Empire, and the Arts in Fifth-Century Athens.* (Cambridge, MA).
Boedeker, D. and D. Sider (2001). *The New Simonides.* (Oxford).
Bohr, E. and W. Martini (eds.) (1986). *Studien zur Mythologie und Vasenmalerei. Festschrift fur K. Schauenberg.* (Mainz).
Booth, W. (1961). *The Rhetoric of Fiction.* (Chicago).
Bothmer, D. von. (1963). *Amazons in Greek Art.* (Oxford).
(1976). "Der Euphronioskrater in New York." *AA* 91: 485–512.
(1985). *The Amasis Painter and His World.* (New York).
Boulter, C. (1953). "Pottery of the Mid-fifth Century from a Well in the Athenian Agora." *Hesperia* 22: 59–115.
Bourdieu, P. and J. Passeron. (1977). *Reproduction in Education, Society, and Culture.* (R. Nice, trans.). (London).
Bowditch, L. P. (1976). "The Role of Redundancy in Cohesion and Evaluative Functioning in Narrative: A Grab for the Referential Hierarchy." *Rackham Literary Studies* 7 (Winter): 19–37.
Bremmer, J. (1990). "Adolescents, *Symposion*, and Pederasty," in Murray (1990a): 135–48.
Bremond, C. (1973). "Le Message narratif." In C. Bremond, *Logique du récit* (Paris): pp. 11–47.
Brijder, H. A. G. (1982). *Siana Cups I and Komast Cups.* (Amsterdam).
(ed.) (1984). *Ancient Greek and Related Pottery: Proceedings of the International Vase Symposium in Amsterdam. 12–15 April 1984.* (Amsterdam).
(1991). *Siana Cups II: The Heidelberg Painter.* (Amsterdam).
Bron, C. and F. Lissarrague. (1989). "Looking at the Vase." in Bérard et al. (1989): 11–21.

Brownlee, A. (1989). "A Black-Figure Parody of the Ransom of Hector." *RA* 34: 3–21.
Bugh, G. (1988). *The Horsemen of Athens.* (Princeton, NJ).
Burnyeat, M. (1997). "Postscript on Silent Reading." *CQ* 47: 74–6.
Cahill, N. (2002). *Household and City Organization at Olynthus.* (New Haven, CT).
Cahn, H. (1962). "Exekias fragmente." *AK* 5: 77–80.
(1972). "Dokimasia." *RA* 17: 3–22.
(1986). "Dokimasia II." In Bohr and Martini (1986): 91–3.
Cahn, H. and E. Simon. (1978/1980). *Tainia: Festschrift fur Roland Hampe zum 70. Geburtstag.* (Mainz).
Cairns, D. (1996). "Veiling, *aidos*, and a Red-Figure Amphora by Phintias." *JHS* 66: 152–8.
Calame, C. (1999). *The Poetics of Eros in Ancient Greece.* (Princeton, NJ).
Cambitoglou, A. et al. (2001). *Torone* I. i–iii. (Athens).
Cambitoglou, A. and J. Papadopoulos. (2001). "The Excavations of 1975, 1976, 1978." In Cambitoglou et al. (2001): 89–272.
Campbell, J. (1982). *Grammatical Man: Information, Entropy, Language, and Life.* (New York).
Carey, C. (1989). "The Performance of the Victory Ode." *American Journal of Philology* 110: 545–65.
Carpenter, T. (1986). *Dionysian Imagery in Archaic Greek Art.* (Oxford).
(1989). with T. Mannack and M. Mendoça. *Beazley Addenda.* (Oxford).
Cartledge, P. et al. (1998). *Kosmos.* (Cambridge).
Caskey, L. D. and J. D. Beazley (1931). *Attic Vase-Paintings in the Museum of Fine Arts, Boston.* (Oxford).
Castriota, D. (1992). *Myth, Ethos, and Actuality.* (Madison, WI).
Catling, H. and I. Lemos. (1990). *Lefkandi* II. (Oxford).
Chatman, Seymour (1978). *Story and Discourse.* (Ithaca, NY).
Christiansen, J. and T. Melander (eds.) (1988).*Proceedings of the 3rd Symposium on Ancient Greek and Related Pottery, August 31 September 4, 1987.* (Copenhagen).
Cobb-Stevens, V. and T. Figueira. (1995). "Introduction." In Figueira and Nagy (1995): 1–8.
Cohen, B. (1978). *Attic Bilingual Vases.* (New York).
Cole, S. (1995). "Civic Cult and Civic Identity." In Hansen (ed.) (1995): 292–325.
Connelly, J. (1993). "Narrative and Image in Attic Vase-Painting. Ajax and Cassandra at the Trojan Palladion." In Holliday (1993): 88–129.
Connor, P. (1981). "Replicas in Greek Vase-Painting: The Work of the Painter of Louvre F 6." *BAbesch* 56: 37–42.
Cooper, F. and S. Morris. (1990). "Dining in Round Building." In O. Murray (ed.) (1990a): 185–95.
Crieland, J., V. Stissi, and G. van Wijngaarden. (1999). *The Complex Past of Pottery.* (Amsterdam).
Csapo, E. and M. Miller. (1991). "The '*kottabos*-Toast' and an Inscribed Red-Figure Cup." *Hesperia* 60: 367–82.
(1998). "Democracy, Empire, and Art: Toward a Politics of Time and Narrative." In Boedeker and Raaflaub (1998): 87–125.
Cygielman, M. (1992). *Euphronios: Atti del Seminario Internazionale di Studi.* (Florence).
Davies, J. (1971). *Athenian Propertied Families.* (Oxford).
Davies, M. (ed.) (1988). *Epicorum Graecorum Fragmenta.* (Göttingen).
Darcque, P. and J. Poursat (eds.). (1985). *L'iconographie Minoenne. BCH* supplement XI. (Paris).

Denoyelle, M. (ed.) (1992a). *Euphronios Peintre. Actes de la journée d'etude organisée par l'Ecole de Louvre et le département des Antiquitées grecques, étrusques, et romains du musée du Louvre 10 Octobre 1990.* (Paris).

(1992b). "Autour de cratère en calice Louvre G 110, signée par Euphronios." In Denoyelle (ed.) (1992a): 47–60.

Desborough, V. (1952). *Protogeometric Pottery.* (Oxford).

Diehl, E. (1949–52). *Anthologia Lyrica Graeca.*[3] (Leipzig).

Dobrov, G. (2001). *Figures of Play: Greek Drama and Metafictional Poetics.* (Oxford).

Donlan, W. 1980. *The Aristocratic Ideal in Ancient Greece.* (Lawrence, KS).

Donohue, A. and C. Mattusch (eds.). (forthcoming). *The Proceedings of the XVIth International Congress of Classical Archaeology, Boston 2003.* (Oxbow).

Dougherty, C. and L. Kurke (eds.). (1993). *Cultural Poetics in Archaic Greece: Cult, Performance, Politics.* (Cambridge).

Dover, K. (1978). *Greek Homosexuality.* (Cambridge, MA).

(1980). *Plato. Symposium.* (Cambridge).

Eaverly, M. (1995). *Archaic Greek Equestrian Sculpture.* (Ann Arbor).

Fehr. B. (1990). "Entertainers at the *Symposium*: The *Akletoi* in the Archaic Period." In Murray (ed.) (1990a): 185–95.

Ferrari Pinney, G. (1983). "Achilles Lord of Scythia." In Moon (ed.): 127–46.

Ferrari, G. (2002). *Figures of Speech: Men and Maidens in Ancient Greece.* (Chicago).

(2003). "Myth and Genre on Athenian Vases." *CA* 22: 37–54.

Figueira, T. and G. Nagy (eds.). (1985) *Theognis of Megara: Poetry and the Polis.* (Baltimore).

Ford, A. (1995). "The Seal of Theognis: The Politics of Authorship in Archaic Greece." In Figueira and Nagy (1995): 82–95.

Froning, H. (1988). "Anfange der Kontinuierenden Bilderzahlung in der griechischen kunst," *JdI* 103: 169–99.

Frel, J. (1983). "Euphronios and His Fellows." In Moon (ed.) (1983): 147–58.

Furtwangler, A. and K. Reichhold. (1905). *Griechische Vasenmalerei* II. Serie, Lieferung I. Munich.

Gavrilov, A. (1997). "Techniques of Reading on Classical Antiquity." *CQ* 47: 56–73.

Genette, G. (1970). "Time and Narrative in *À la recherché du temps perdu.*" In Miller (ed.) (1970): 93–118.

Gericke, H. (1970). *Gefassdarstellungen auf griechischen Vasen.* (Berlin).

Ghiron-Bestagne, P. (1976). *Recherches sur les Actuers dan la Grece Antique.* (Paris).

Gibert, J. (2001). "Recent Work on Greek Satyr Play." *Classical Journal* 98.1: 79–88.

Goemann, E. et al. (ed.). (1991). *Euphronios der Maler.* (Milan).

Goldhill, S. (1991). *The Poet's Voice.* (Cambridge).

Goldhill, S. and R. Osborne. (1994). *Art and Text in Ancient Greek Culture.* (Cambridge).

(1999). *Performance Culture and Athenian Democracy.* (Cambridge).

Gombrich, E. H. (1960). *Art and Illusion: A Study in the Psychology of Pictorial Representation.* (New York).

(1984). *The Sense of Order: A Study in the Psychology of Decorative* Art. (Oxford).

Graef, B. and E. Langlotz. (1925–33). *Die Antiken Vasen von der Akropolis zu Athen.* (Berlin).

Green, J. (1962). "A New Oinochoe Series from the Akropolis North Slope." *Hesperia* 31: 82–94.

Habinek, T. (1993). Review of O. Murray (ed.) (1990) *Sympotika: A Symposium on the Symposium*; W. Slater (ed.) (1991) *Dining in a Classical Context*; F. Lissarrague (1990a) *The Aesthetics of the Greek Banquet:Images of Wine and Ritual.* AJA 97: 177–8.

Halliday, M. A. K. and R. Hasan. (1975; 1989 reprint). *Cohesion in English*. (London).
Hamilton, R. (1992). *Choes and Athesteria*. (Ann Arbor, MI).
Hannestad, L. (1988). "The Athenian Potter and the Home Market." In Christiansen and Melander (ed.) 1988: 222–30.
(1999). "The Reception of Attic Pottery by the Indigenous Peoples of Italy: The Evidence from Funerary Contexts." In Crieland et al. (1999): 308–18.
Hansen, M. (1995). *Sources for the Ancient Greek City-State: Symposium August 24–27 1994*. (Copenhagen).
Hardee, A. and F. Henry. (1990). *Narratology and Narrative*. (Columbia, SC).
Harrison, E. (1983). "Direction and Time in Monumental Narrative of the Fifth Century B.C." *AJA* 87: 237–8.
Havelock, E. (1952). "Why Was Socrates Tried?" In White (1952): 95–109.
Heath, M. and M. Lefkowitz. (1991). "Epinician Performance." *Classical Philology* 86: 173–91.
Hedreen, G. (1992). *Silens in Attic Black-figure Vase-Painting*. (Ann Arbor, MI).
(1996). "Image, Text, and Story in the Recovery of Helen." *Classical Antiquity* 15: 152–84.
(2001). *Capturing Troy*. (Ann Arbor, MI).
Henderson, C. (1966). *Classical, Medieval, and Renaissance Studies Presented to B. L. Ullman*. (Rome).
Henderson, Jeffery. (1991). *The Maculate Muse*². (Oxford).
Henderson, John. (1999). "Smashing Bodies: The Corinthian Tydeus and Ismene Amphora (Louvre E 640)." In Porter (ed.) (1999): 19–49.
Hendrickson, G. (1929). "Ancient Reading." *CJ* 25: 182–96.
Henle, J. (1973). *Greek Myths: A Vase-Painters Notebook*. (Bloomington, IN).
Henrichs, A. (1995). "'Why Should I Dance?': Choral Self-Referentiality in Greek Tragedy." *Arion* 3:1: 56–111.
Heubeck, M., M. West, and J. Hainsworth. (1988). *A Commentary on Homer's Odyssey*. (Oxford).
Hoesch, N. (1990). "Hetaeren." In Vierneisel and Kaeser (eds.)(1990): 231–2.
Hoffman, H. (1994). "*Dulce et decorum est pro patria mori*: The Imagery of Heroic Immortality on Athenian Vases." In S. Goldhill and R. Osborne (eds.) (1994): 28–51.
(1997). *Sotades: Symbols of Immortality on Greek Vases*. (Oxford).
Holliday, P. (ed.) (1993). *Narrative and Event in Ancient Art*. (Cambridge)
Hoppin, E. (1919). *A Handbook of Attic Red-Figure Vases* (Cambridge, MA).
(1924). *A Handbook of Greek Black-Figured Vases*. (Paris).
Hubbard, T. (1998). "Popular Perceptions of Elite Homosexuality in Classical Athens." *Arion*: 48–78.
Hurwit, J. (1985a). "The Dipylon Shield Once More." *CA* 4: 121–6.
(1985b). *The Art and Culture of Early Greece, 1100–480 B.C.* (Ithaca).
Huss, B. (1999). *Xenophons Symposium: Ein Commentar*. (Stuttgart and Leipzig).
Hutcheon, L. (2000). *A Theory of Parody*. (Urbana, IL, and Chicago).
Immerwahr, H. (1964). "Book Rolls on Attic Vases." In Henderson (ed.) (1964): 17–48.
(1965). "Inscriptions on the Anakreon Krater in Copenhagen." *AJA* 69: 152–4.
(1973). "More Book Rolls on Attic Vases." *Antike Kunst* 16: 143–7.
(1990). *Attic Script: A Survey*. (Oxford).
(1992). "The Lettering of Euphronios." In Wehgartner (ed.) (1992): 49–56.
Jaeger, W. (1939). *Paideia: The Ideals of Greek Culture* (G. Highet, trans.). (Oxford).

Jakobson, R. (1960). "Closing Statement: Linguistics and Poetics." In Sebeok (ed.) (1960): 350–77.
Johansen, K. (1928). *CVA* Copenhagen 3 (Denmark 3) (Copenhagen).
Johnson, F. (1951). "An Owl Skyphos." In Mylonas (ed.) (1951): Volume II: 96–105.
(1955). "A Note on Owl Skyphoi." *AJA* 59, pp. 119–24.
Jones, J., L. Sackett, and A. Graham. (1962). "The Dema House in Attica." *BSA* 57: 75–114.
Jordan, Jeanne. (1988) *Attic Black-Figured Eye-Cups* (Diss. NYU) University Microfilms no. 8812638.
Kaeser, B. (1987). "Attische Massamphora." *Münchner Jahrbuch der Bildenden Kunst* 38: 228–31.
Kahane, A. (1994). *Interpretation of Order: A Study in the Poetics of Homeric Repetition.* (Oxford).
Kannicht, R. (ed.). (1991). *Musa Tragica* (Göttingen).
Karouzou, S. (1937). "Sophilos" *AM* 62: 111–35.
(1963). *Angeia tou Anagyrountos.* (Athens).
(1971). "Une Tombe de Tanagra." *BCH* 95: 138–45.
Keay, S. and S. Moser (eds.) (2005). *Greek Art in View: Essays in Honour of Brian Sparkes.* (Oxford).
Keuls. E. (1988). "The Social Position of Attic Vase-Painters and the Birth of Caricature." In Christiansen and Melander (eds.) (1988): 310–13.
Kilmer, M. (1993). "The Wild *Kalos* Name," *Classical Views* 37 (n.s. 12): 173–94.
(2001). "Sophilos' Vase Inscriptions and Cultural Literacy in Archaic Athens." *Phoenix* 55: 1–2: 9–43.
Knauer, E. (1976). "Fragments of a Cup by the Triptolemos Painter." *GRBS* 17: 209–16.
Knittlmeyer, B. (1997). *Die Attische Aristokratie und ihre Helden: Untersuchungen zu Darstellungen des trojanische Sagenkreises im 6. und fruehen 5. Jahrhundert v. Chr.* (Heidelberg).
Knox, B. (1968). "Silent Reading in Antiquity." *HSCP* 9: 421–35.
Kossatz-Deissmann, A. (1991). "Satyr- und Maenadennamen auf Vasenbildern des Getty-Museums mit Addenda zu Ch. Fraenkel, *Satyr-und Bakchennamen auf Vasenbildern* (1912)." *Greek Vases in the J. Paul Getty Museum* 5: 131–99.
Krumeich, R., N. Pechstein, and B. Seidensticker. (1999). *Das Griechische Satyrspiel.* (Darmstadt).
Kullman, W. (1960). *Die Quellen der Ilias (Troischer Sagenkreis). Hermes Einzelschriften* 14. (Weisbaden).
Kurke, L. (1990). "Pindar's Sixth *Pythian.*" *TAPA* 120: 85–107.
Kurke, L. (1991). *The Traffic in Praise: Pindar and the Poetics of Social Economy.*
(1992). "The Politics of *habrosyne* in Archaic Greece." *CA* 11: 91–120.
(1997). "Inventing the Hetaira: Sex, Politics, and Discursive Conflict in Archaic Greece." *CA* 16: 106–50.
Labov, W. (1972). *Language in the Inner City.* (Philadelphia).
Lang, M. (1976). *Graffiti and Dipinti. The Athenian Agora* 21 (Princeton).
Larson, R. (trans.)(1980). *The Apology and Crito of Plato and the Apology and Symposium of Xenophon.* (Lawrence, KS).
Leach, E. (1974). *Claude Lévi-Strauss.* (New York).
Levine, D. (1985). "Symposium and the Polis." In Figuiera and Nagy (1985): 176–96.
Lewis, J. "*Eros* and the *polis* in Theognis Book II." In Figuiera and Nagy (1985) 197–222.
Lewis, S. (2002). *The Athenian Woman: An Iconographic Handbook.* (London).

Lissarrague, F. (1990a). *The Aesthetics of the Greek Banquets: Images of Wine and Ritual.* (Princeton, NJ).

(1990b). *L'Autre Guerrier. Archers, Peltastes, Cavaliers dans l'imagerie Attique.* (Paris).

(1994). "*Epiktetos egrapsen*: The Writing on the Cup." In Goldhill and Osborne (1994) 12–27.

(1999). "Publicity and Performance: *kalos* Inscriptions in Attic Vase-Painting." In Goldhill and Osborne (1999) 359–73.

Lissarrague, F. and A. Schnapp (1981). "Imagerie des Grecs ou Grece des imagiers," *La temps de la reflexion* 2: 275–97.

Lobel, D. and D. Page (1963). *Poetarum Lesbiorum Fragmenta.* (Oxford).

Lonsdale, S. (1995). "*Homeric Hymn to Apollo*: Prototype and Paradigm of Choral Performance." *Arion* 3:1: 25–40.

Lowenstam, S. (1993). *The Scepter and the Spear: Studies on Forms of Repetition in the Homeric Poems.* (Lanham, MD).

Lullies, R. (1964). "Eine Amphora aus dem Kreis des Exekias." *Antike Kunst* 4: 82–90.

Lynch, K. (1999). "Black-Figure, Red-Figure and Communal Drinking in a Late Archaic Athenian Home" (abstract). *AJA* (103): 298.

Mace, S. (2001). "Utopian and Erotic Fusion in a New Elegy by Simonides." In Boedeker and Sider (2001): 185–207.

Mackie, H. (2003). *Graceful Errors: Pindar and the Performance of Praise.* (Ann Arbor, MD).

Makay, E. A. (1996). "Time and Timelessness in the Traditions of Early Greek Oral Poetry and Archaic Vase-Painting." In Worthington: (1996): 43–58.

(ed.) (1999a). *Signs of Orality: The Oral Tradition and its Influence in the Greek and Roman World.* (Leiden).

Makay, E. A. et al. (1999b). "The Bystander at the Ringside. Ring-Composition in Early Greek Poetry and Vase-Painting." In Makay (1999a): 115–41.

Malinowski, B. (1953). "The Problem of Meaning in Primitive Languages." In Ogden and Richards (1953): 296–336.

Marinatos, N. (1993). "Some Reflections on the Rhetoric of Aegean and Egyptian Art." In Holliday (1993): 74–87.

Markoe, G. (1989) "The 'Lion-Attack' in Archaic Greek Art," *Classical Antiquity* 8: 85–115.

McPhee, Ian. (2001). "The Red-Figured Pottery." In Cambitoglou et al. (2001): 353–90.

Miller, J. (ed.) (1970). *Aspects of Narrative.* (New York).

Miller, M. (1999). "Reexamining Transvestism in Archaic and Classical Athens." *AJA* 103: 223–53.

Mills, S. (1993). *Theseus, Tragedy, and the Athenian Empire.* (Oxford).

Mommsen, H. (1978): "Achill und Aias pflichtvergessen?" In Cahn and Simon (1978) 139 ff.

Moon, W. (ed.) (1983). *Ancient Greek Art and Iconography.* (Madison, WI).

Moore, M. (1968). "Horses by Exekias." *AJA* 72: 357–68.

(1975). "The Cottenham Relief." *J. Paul Getty Journal* 2: 37–50.

(1980). "Exekias and Telemonian Ajax." *AJA* 84: 417–34.

(1986a). "Athena and Herakles on Exekias' Calyx-Krater." *AJA* 90: 35–9.

(1986b). *Attic Black-Figured Pottery. The Athenian Agora* 23 (Princeton, NJ).

(1987). "The Amasis Painter and Exekias: Approaches to Narrative." In True (1987): 153–67.

(1997). *Attic Red-Figured and White Ground Pottery. The Athenian Agora* 30. (Princeton, NJ).

Moore, M. and D. von Bothmer. (1976). *Corpus Vasorum Antiquorum: The Metropolitan Museum of Art* 4 (USA 16) (New York).

Morgan, K. (1993). "Pindar the Professional and the Rhetoric of the *komos*." *Classical Philology* 88: 1–15.
Morgan, L. (1985). "Idea, Idiom, and Iconography." In Darcque and Poursat (eds.) (1985): 5–19.
(1988). *The Miniature Wall-Paintings of Thera*. (Cambridge).
Morris, Ian (ed.) (1994). *Classical Greece: Ancient Histories and Modern Archaeologies*. (Cambridge).
Murray, O. (ed.) (1990a). *Sympotika: A Symposium on the Symposium*. (Oxford).
(1990b). "The Affair of the Mysteries." In Murray (ed.) (1990a): 149–61.
Murray, O. and M. Tecusan (eds.) (1994). *In Vino Veritas*. (Rome).
Mylonas, G. (ed.) (1951). *Studies Presented to David Moore Robinson*. (Saint Louis).
Nauck, A. (1926). *Tragicorum Graecorum Fragmenta*. (Leipzig).
Neer, R. (2002). *Style and Politics in Athenian Vase-Painting*. (Cambridge).
Nehamas, A. and Woodruff, P. (trans.) (1989). *Plato's Symposium*. (Indiana).
Neils, J. (1981). "The Loves of Theseus: An Early Cup by Oltos," *AJA* 85: 40–41.
(1992). *Goddess and Polis*. (Princeton, NJ).
(1995). "The Euthymides Krater from Morgantina." *AJA* 99: 427–44.
Nevett, L. (1999). *House and Society in the Ancient Greek World*. (Cambridge).
Oakley, J., W. Coulson, and O. Palagia. (1997). *Athenian Potters and Painters*. (London).
Ober, J. (1989). *Mass and Elite in Democratic Athens*. (Princeton, NJ).
Ogden, C. K. and I. A. Richards. (1953). *The Meaning of Meaning*. (London).
Ohly-Dumm, M. (1974). "Euphroniosschale und Smikrosscherbe." *MuJb* 25: 7–26.
(1984). "Sosias und Euthymides." In Brijder (ed.) (1984): 165–72.
Olmos Romera, R. (1990). *Vasos Griegos: Coleccion Condes de Lagunillas*. (Zurich).
Osborne, R. (1987). *Classical Landscape with Figures*. (London).
(1998). "Inter-personal relations on Athenian Pots." In Cartledge et al. (1998): 11–36.
(2001). "Why did Athenian Pots Appeal to the Etruscans?" *World Archaeology* 33(2): 277–95.
(2005). "Workshops and the Iconography and Distribution of Athenian Red-Figured Pottery: A Case Study." In Keay and Moser (2005): 78–94.
Page, D. (1962). *Poetae Melici Graeci*. (Oxford).
Peirce, S. (1998). "Visual Language and Concepts of Cult on the 'Lenaia Vases.'" *Classical Antiquity* 17: 59–95.
Peschel, I. (1987). *Die Hetaere bei Symposion und Komos*. (Frankfurt).
Pfsitterer-Hass, S. (1990). "Ehrbare Frauen und der Wein." In Vierneisel and Kaeser (1990): 313–15.
Pollitt, J. J. (1972). *Art and Experience in Classical Greece*. (Cambridge).
Popham, M. et al. (1979 and 1980). *Lefkandi* I, i and ii. (Oxford).
Porter, J. (ed.) (1999). *Constructions of the Classical Body*. (Ann Arbor, MI).
Powell, B. (1991). *Homer and the Origin of the Greek Alphabet*. (Cambridge).
Prince, G. (1982). *Narratology: The Form and Functioning of Narrative*. (Berlin).
(1987). *Dictionary of Narratology*. (Lincoln, NE).
Prince, G. (1990). "On Narratology (Past, Present, Future)." In Hardee and Henry (1990): 1–14.
Propp, V. (1968). *Morphology of the Folktale*[2] (trans. L. Scott.) (Austin, TX).
Raab, I. (1972). *Zu den Darstellungen des Parisurteils in der griechischen Kunst*. Archaeologische Studien, vol. 1. (Frankfurt).
Race, W. (1997). *Pindar. Olympian Odes. Pythian Odes*. Loeb Classical Library: Volume 56. (Cambridge, MA).
Rasmussen, T. and N. Spivey (eds.). (1991). *Looking at Greek Vases*. (Cambridge).

Raubitschek, A. (1949). *Dedications from the Athenian Akropolis.* (Cambridge, MA).
Reinsburg, C. (1989). *Ehe Hetaerentum und Knabenliebe im antiken Griechenland.* (Munich).
Reusser, Christopher. (2002). *Vasen für Etrurien.* (Zurich).
Richter, G. and L. Hall (1936). *Red-Figure Athenian Vases in the Metropolitan Museum of Art.* (New Haven, CT).
Robb, K. (1994). *Literacy and Paideia in Ancient Greece.* (Oxford).
Robert, C. (1881/1975). *Bild und Lied.* (New York).
Robertson, M. (1981). *A Shorter History of Greek Art.* (Cambridge).
(1977). "Jumpers." *Burlington Magazine* 119: 78–86.
(1991) "Adopting an Approach I." In Rasmussen and Spivey (1991): 1–12.
Roesler, W. (1980). *Dichter und Gruppe.* (Munich).
(1995). "Wine and Truth in the Greek *Symposion.*" In Murray and Tecusan (1995): 106–12.
Rotroff, S. and J. Oakley. (1992). *Debris from A Public Dining Place in the Athenian Agora.* (Princeton, NJ).
Rutherford, I. (1996). "The New Simonides: Towards a Commentary." *Arethusa* 29: 167–92.
(2001). "The New Simonides: Towards a Commentary." In Boedecker and Sider (2001): 33–54.
Rutter, N. and B. Sparkes. (2000). *Word and Image in Ancient Greece.* (Edinburgh).
Schaeffer, A. (1997). *Unterhaltung beim griechischen Symposion.* (Mainz).
Schauenburg, K. (1975). "Εὐρυμέδων εἰμί." *AM* 90: 97–121.
Scheffer, C. (1988). "Workshop and Trade Patterns in Athenian Black Figure." In Christiansen and Melander (eds.) (1988): 536–57.
Schefold, K. (1992). *Gods and Heroes in Late Archaic Greek Art.* (Cambridge).
Scheibler, I. (1961). "Olpen und Amphoren des Gorgomalers."*JdI* 76: 1–47.
(1987a). "Bild und Gefass." *JdI* (1987): 57–118.
(1987b). "Die Kouroi des Amasis-Malers." In Christiansen and Melander (1987): Copenhagen: 547–57.
Schenkeveld, D. (1992). "Prose Usages of AKOYEIN 'To Read.'" *CQ* 42: 129–41.
Schmaltz, B. and M. Soldne (eds.) (2003). *Griechische Keramik im kulturellen Kontext.* (Muenster).
Sebeok, T. (1960). *Style in Language.* (Cambridge).
Shapiro, H. A. (1980). "Hippokrates Son of Anaxileos." *Hesperia* (49): 289–93.
(1983a) "Two Black-Figure Neck-Amphorae in the J. Paul Getty Museum: Problems of Workshop and Iconography." *Greek Vases in the J. Paul Getty Museum* 4: 11–32.
(1983b). "Painting Politics, and Geneaology: Peisistratus and the Neleids." In Moon (1983): 87–96.
(1989a). "Two Black-Figure Neck-Amphorae in the J. Paul Getty Museum: Problems of Workshop and Iconography." In *Greek Vases in the J. Paul Getty Museum* 4: 11–32.
(1989b). *Art and Cult under the Tyrants.* (Mainz).
(1990). "Old and New Heroes: Narrative, Composition, and Subject in Attic Black-Figure." *Classical Antiquity* 9: 114–48.
(1992). "Narrative Strategies in Euphronios." In M. Cygielman (1992): 37–41.
(1994). *Myth Into Art.* (London).
(1997). "Correlating Shape and Subject: The Case of the Archaic Pelike." In Oakley et al. (1997): 63–70.
(2003). *Brief Encounters: Women and Men at the Fountain House.* In Schmaltz and Soeldner (2003): 96–8.

Shear, T. L. Jr. (1984). "The Athenian Agora: Excavations of 1980–82." *Hesperia* 53: 1–57.
Silk, A. (2000). *Aristophanes and the Definition of Comedy*. (Oxford).
Simon, E. et al. (1975). *Führer durch die Antikenabteilung des Martin von Wagner Museums der Universität Würzburg*. (Mainz).
(1976). *Die Griechischen Vasen* (Munich).
(1978). "Zwei Springtänzer." *Antike Kunst* 21: 66–9.
(1983). *Festivals of Attica*. (Madison, WI).
(1985). "Zeus und Io auf einer Kalpis des Eucharidesmalers," *Archaeologischer Anzeiger* 100. II: 265–80.
Sinos, R. (1993). "Divine Selection: Epiphany and Politics in Archaic Greece." In Dougherty and Kurke (1993): 73–91.
Sinos, R. and J. Oakley. (1993). *The Wedding in Ancient Athens*. (Madison, WI).
Slater, N. (1999). "The Vase as Ventriloquist: *kalos*-Inscriptions and the Culture of Fame." In Makay (1999a): 143–61.
Slater, W. ed. (1991). *Dining in a Classical Context*. (Ann Arbor, MI).
Small, J. (1994). "Scholars, Etruscans, and Attic Painted Vases." *JRA* 7: 34–58.
(1995). "New Views on Greek Artifacts Found in Etruria." *JRA* 8: 317–19.
Smith, A. (1999). "Eurymedon and the Evolution of Political Personifications in the Early Classical Period." *JHS* 119: 128–43.
Snodgrass, A. (1982). *Narration and Illusion in Archaic Greek Art*, Eleventh J. L. Myres Memorial Lecture. (Oxford).
(1989). *Arms and Armour of the Greeks*. (Baltimore).
(2000). "The Uses of Writing on Early Greek Painted Pottery." In Rutter and Sparkes (2000): 22–34.
Sonnenfeld, A. (1999). *Food: A Culinary History from Antiquity to the Present*. (New York).
Sontag, S. (ed.) (1982). *A Barthes Reader*. (New York).
Souvinou-Inwood, C. (1985). "Altars with Palm-Trees and Parthenoi." *BICS* 32: 125–46.
(1987). "A Series of Erotic Pursuits: Images and Meanings." *JHS* 107 (1987). 131–53.
Sparkes, B. and L. Talcott. (1970). *Black and Plain Pottery. The Athenian Agora* XII. (Princeton, NJ).
Spence, I. G. (1993). *The Cavalry of Classical Greece*. (Oxford).
Spivey, N. (1991). "Greek Vases in Etruria." In Rasmussen, T. and Spivey, N. (1991): 131–50.
Stansbury-O'Donnell, M. (1999). *Pictorial Narrative in Ancient Greek Art*. (Cambridge).
(2006). *Vase Painting, Gender, and Social Identity in Archaic Athens* (Cambridge).
Stein-Holkeskamp, E. (1989). *Adelskultur und Polisgesellschaft*. (Stuttgart).
Steiner, A. (1983). "Gesture in Greek Vase-Painting: Lydos and *apgoreuein*" (abstract). *AJA* 87: 261.
(1993). "The Meaning of Repetition: Visual Redundancy on Athenian Vases." *JdI* (108): 197–219.
(1997). "Illustrious Repetitions: Visual Redundancy in Exekias and His Followers." In Oakley et al. (1997): 157–69.
(2002). "Public and Private: *Syssition* and *Symposion* in Fifth Century Athens." *Classical Antiquity* 21: 347–79.
(2003). "New Approaches to Greek Vases: Repetition, Aesthetics, and Meaning." In Warden (2003): 35–45.
(2004). "The Alkmene Hydrias and Vase-Painting in Late-Sixth-Century Athens." *Hesperia* 73: 427–63.

(Forthcoming). "Children in Athenian Cult: The Case of Demeter's Boy." In A. Donohue and C. Mattusch (eds.) (forthcoming).
Steiner, D. (1994). *The Tyrant's Writ: Myths and Images of Writing in Ancient Greece.* (Princeton, NJ).
(2001). *Images in Mind: Statues in Archaic and Classical Greek Literature and Thought.* (Princeton, NJ).
Steiner, W. (1982). *The Colors of Rhetoric.* (Chicago).
(1988). *Pictures of Romance.* (Chicago).
Steinhart, M. (1995). *Das Motiv des Auges in Der Griechischen Bildkunst.* (Mainz).
(2004). *Die Kunst Der Nachahmung.* (Mainz).
Stewart. A. (1990). *Greek Sculpture: An Explanation.* (New Haven, CT).
Stillwell, R. (1959). "Excavations at Sierra Orlando 1958. Preliminary Report III." *AJA* 63: 167–73.
Stissi. V. (1999). "Production, Circulation and Consumption of Archaic Greek Pottery." In Crieland et al. (1999): 83–113.
Sutton, D. (1980). *The Greek Satyr Play.* (Meisenheim am Glan).
Sutton, R. (1981). *The Interaction Between Men and Women Portrayed on Attic Red-Figure Pottery.* (diss. University of North Carolina, Chapel Hill).
Svenbro, J. (1985; 1993: translation). *Phrasikleia: An Anthropologie of Reading in Ancient Greece.* (Ithaca, NJ).
Thomas, R. (1992). *Literacy and Orality in Ancient Greece.* (Cambridge).
Thompson, H. and R. Wycherly. (1972). *The Agora of Athens. The Athenian Agora* XIV. (Princeton, NJ).
Tiverios, M. (1976). *Lydos kai to Ergo sou.* (Athens).
Todorov, T. (1965). *Théorie de la Litterature.* (Paris).
Tomachevski, B. (1925). "Thématique." In Todorov (1965) 263–307.
True, M. (ed.) (1987). *Papers on the Amasis Painter and His World.* (Malibu).
Turner, V. (1969/1995). *The Ritual Process.* (New York).
Van Wees, H. (2004). *Greek Warfare: Myths and Realities.* (London).
Vetta, M. (1999). "The Culture of the Symposion." In Sonnenfeld (1999): 96–105.
Vickers, M. and D. Gill. (1994). *Artful Crafts.* (Oxford).
Vierneisel, K. and B. Kaeser. (1990). *Kunst des Schale, Kultur des Trinkens.* (Munich).
Webster, T. B. L. (1972). *Potter and Patron in Classical Athens.* (London).
Wegner, M. (1979). *Euthymides und Euphronios.* (Munich).
Wehgartner, I. (ed.) (1992). *Euphronios und Seine Zeit.* (Berlin).
Weitzmann, K. (1947). *Illustrations in Roll and Codex. A Study in the Origin and Method of Text Illustration.* (Princeton, NJ).
West, M. L. (1989). *Iambi et Elegi*². Volume I (Oxford).
(1992). *Iambi et Elegi*². Volume II (Oxford).
(1993a). *Greek Lyric Poetry.* (Oxford).
(1993b). "Simonides Redivivus." *ZPE* 98: 1–14.
White, M. (1952). *Studies in Honor of Gilbert Norwood.* (Toronto).
Wickhoff, F. (1900). *Roman Art: Some of Its Principles and their Application to Early Christian Painting* (translation: E. Strong). (New York).
Willcock, M. (1978). *Homer: Iliad I–XII.* (London).
Williams, D. (1988). "The Late Archaic Class of Eye Cups." In Christiansen and Melander (1988): 674–83.

Williams, D. (1992). "Euphronios' Contemporary Companions and Followers." In Denoyelle (ed.) (1992a): 79–95.
Wojcik, M. (1989). *Museo Claudio Faina di Orvieto*. (Milan).
Wolf, S. (1993). *Herakles Beim Gelage*. (Cologne).
Wollheim, R. (1987). *Painting as an Art*. (Princeton, NJ).
Woodford, S. and M. Loudon. (1980). "Two Trojan Themes: The Iconography of Ajax Carrying the Body of Achilles and of Aeneas Carrying Anchises in Black-Figure Vase-painting." *AJA* 84: 25–40.
Worthington, I. (ed.). (1996). *Voice into Text: Orality and Literacy in Ancient Greece*. (Leiden).

INDEX OF VASES CITED IN TEXT

SUBJECT INDEX